Economic Crisis and
Rule Reconstruction

Economic Crisis and Rule Reconstruction

Chen Deming
Former Chinese Minister of Commerce, China

World Scientific

NEW JERSEY · LONDON · SINGAPORE · BEIJING · SHANGHAI · HONG KONG · TAIPEI · CHENNAI · TOKYO

Published by

World Scientific Publishing Co. Pte. Ltd.

5 Toh Tuck Link, Singapore 596224

USA office: 27 Warren Street, Suite 401-402, Hackensack, NJ 07601

UK office: 57 Shelton Street, Covent Garden, London WC2H 9HE

Library of Congress Cataloging-in-Publication Data

Names: Chen, Deming, 1949–   author.

Title: Economic crisis and rule reconstruction / by Deming Chen,
      Former Chinese Minister of Commerce, China.

Other titles: Jing ji wei ji yu gui ze chong gou. English

Description: New Jersey : World Scientific, [2016] | "Originally published in
    Chinese by The Commercial Press."

Identifiers: LCCN 2016008381| ISBN 9789814740937 | ISBN 9789814740944 (pbk)

Subjects: LCSH: International trade. | Trade regulation. | Global Financial Crisis, 2008–2009. |
      Finance--China. | China--Foreign economic relations. | China--Commercial policy.

Classification: LCC HF1379 .C3897513 2016 | DDC 382--dc23

LC record available at http://lccn.loc.gov/2016008381

British Library Cataloguing-in-Publication Data

A catalogue record for this book is available from the British Library.

《经济危机与规则重构》

Originally published in Chinese by The Commercial Press, Ltd.

Copyright © 2014 The Commercial Press, Ltd.

Translators: Phoebe Liaw Peiru, Timothy Ho Shen Teng, Lum Pui Yee,
          Sharon Khoo and Cao Youfang

Desk Editor: Dong Lixi

Printed in Singapore

Foreword

by Robert Azevedo
Director-General of the WTO

We are living through a period of profound change. Recent years have seen new economies emerge and old certainties vanish, challenging us all to look at the world afresh. By analyzing the evolution of international economic and trade rules in the context of the financial crisis, this book helps us to navigate this new landscape — and Chen Deming is the ideal guide.

Mr Chen has tremendous experience to bring to bear on these issues — both as a Minister during the crisis and as a trade negotiator at the World Trade Organization (WTO) where I had the privilege of working alongside him. He saw first-hand the process which led to the paralysis of the multilateral trading system in 2008 and the early steps towards resolving it, which led eventually to the successful Ministerial meeting in Bali in December 2013. That success has sparked a debate about the future of the WTO, the restructuring of trade rules and the conclusion of the Doha round — a debate to which this book is an important and timely contribution.

Within these pages you will find analysis that will shed light on how to address the match and mismatch between existing international economic rules and the shifting realities of the global economy. It highlights the importance of the rules-based multilateral trading system — much revived by the success in Bali — and the value of the WTO's dispute settlement mechanism.

There is also valuable insight here into China's perspective, with thoughts on many important issues, from regional trade initiatives to intellectual property, concluding with a prescription for further economic opening and engagement.

Any attempt to predict or prescribe actions on future trade-related initiatives will have to be soundly anchored on a proper assessment of the transformative events of recent years. With this book Minister Chen has made an early, important and insightful contribution to the debate. Certainly any conversation on rules restructuring within the WTO will benefit from his thoughts and analysis.

Foreword

by Pascal Lamy
Former Director-General of the WTO

As evidenced in this book, Chen Deming who is known as a seasoned trade negotiator in the world when he was the Trade Minister of China, is also an expert, an intellectual, and a reformist. I must add, in the interest of transparency, that he is a friend of mine.

The various facets of his talent appear throughout the chapters.

His analysis of the financial crisis which erupted in the US in 2007–2008 is spot on: it originated in the poor global regulation of the most global industry: finance. And the consequences were terrible worldwide. Not least because of the huge number of job losses. Looking at the past crises, and considering how fast globalization (or "re-globalization" as Chen puts it) has grown since, should have led to preventive action. Because of the absence of international consensus, this unfortunately did not happen. The G20 is now fixing the failure in global governance, the birth of which was midwifed by the crisis. However, it is being fixed too slowly in my view.

But finance is not the only weak spot in global economic governance. As described in various chapters, trade, investment, environment also need stronger international disciplines for globalization to be properly harnessed, and the author's suggestions cover much of this ground, including services trade, government procurement, trade remedies, intellectual property, and e-commerce. Chen's reforming credentials also appear in dealing with issues that are critical, as well as sensitive for China, such as state owned enterprises, or competitive neutrality.

Where I believe Chen deploys his formidable pedagogic qualities is in his description of the new patterns of international trade: global value chains, the real world we live in as opposed to the conventional world of trade most trade experts still have in mind. The increasing import content of exports is slowly making the traditional mercantilist approach irrelevant. The growing importance of non-tariff measures is questioning the old wisdom of reciprocity and special and differential treatment. In the past, most obstacles to trade were aimed at protecting domestic producers. In the future, obstacles to trade will lie more and more in measures the purpose of which is to protect the consumers. Or, to be more precise, in differences in managing consumer related risks through standards, norms or certification procedures. In short, opening trade is evolving from tariff reduction to regulatory harmonization.

To achieve this new stage in global trade regulation, Chen basically makes the case for an orderly coexistence of regional and multilateral approaches. This is one of the rare topics on which I beg to differ from him. I believe the necessary multilateral convergence which is needed to level the playing field, especially to the benefit of developing countries, will not happen without WTO members agreeing to restate the primacy of multilateralism over regionalism which lies in GATT/WTO article XXIV, and which needs, in my view, to be redrafted in order to avoid "regulatory discrimination". This is particularly true in the field of investment rules which I have advocated many times, to replace the spaghetti bowl of bilateral investment agreements by a multilateral regime. Needless to say, Chen's vision of China's new responsibilities in strengthening the rules based trading system has my full support. China's weight in the world economy is now such that its interests and policies cannot diverge from the rest of the world, nor can the rest of the world frame a new set of rules without China on board. This is fully in line with what I expect to happen: a new wave of trade opening in China, starting with services in order to improve China's productivity in this sector.

Finally, I must pay tribute to the deep thinking Chen devotes throughout his book to the inherent tensions within global market capitalism, as is stands today, whichever shape it takes. *Homo economicus* is both a worker and a consumer. As a consumer, he is fond of competition which brings innovation, better and cheaper goods and services. As a worker, he resents constant pressure on productivity, qualifications, mobility and looks for more human cooperation. How much competition? How much cooperation? Chen's answer to this question, which he raises many times, albeit often implicitly, remains tentative.

What I can say, as an old friend of China, is that a large part of the solution to this fundamental problem lies in the transformations of China. We all have a huge stake in China getting it right. Chen Deming's visions, explanations, suggestions, are as much about the construction of China as about the reconstruction of a better world order. They now go hand in hand and cannot be separated. For the better, I believe, like him.

Foreword

by Li Yining
Honorary Dean of Guanghua School of Management
Peking University

Since the outbreak of the US financial crisis in 2008, problems with rule reconstruction have been brewing in the international economy. Not only does this guide countries towards comprehending the basis of activities in the future, and learning how to make profits while avoiding losses, it will also affect the changes and realization of each country's economic strategic objectives. As a socialist country with increasingly great international influence, China must also deepen her understanding of international economic rule reconstruction. Comprehension is essential, yet we must also seize favorable opportunities, and set appropriate strategic objectives so that reform can be executed smoothly. Hence, under these new circumstances, how can we better understand the origin of these changes and what important adjustments we should make? Here, I sincerely recommend the book *Economic Crisis and Rule Reconstruction* written by Chen Deming and the relevant task groups under his leadership. I believe this is the best primer reading to help readers get a quick grasp of this research field, and at the same time, it is a necessary reference book that will aid readers in delving more in-depth into the topic and build upon their existing knowledge.

Contents

Preface

by Chen Deming

Former Chinese Minister of Commerce

*E*conomic Crisis and Rule Reconstruction (English Edition)* has finally been released thanks to the joint efforts of World Scientific Publishing Co. Pte. Ltd. in Singapore and The Commercial Press in China, as well as the hard work of the editors and translators. This is a book about global economic governance told by my young colleagues and me. When I was Commerce Minister of China, I personally witnessed the devastating effects of the international financial crisis in 2008, and attended numerous bilateral and multilateral meetings with presidents, prime ministers, ministers and senior economic officials. It is fair to say that we are still in the fitful recovery process of this crisis. Wei Zheng, a well-known prime minister in China's Tang Dynasty (618–907), once said that "whoever hears from both sides is enlightened, whoever believes one side of the story is benighted." This book provides a window to observe the perspective of emerging market economies, which may help us understand global economic governance in this transitional period, and China's position as a responsible power.

More than two years have passed since *Economic Crisis and Rule Reconstruction (Chinese Edition)* was published in early 2014. There have been many ups and downs in the global political and economic landscape in these two years. Some regions have suffered complex and volatile ethnic or religious tensions, frequent conflicts, and the surge of populism, resulting in economic globalization and trade liberalization becoming a scapegoat for the rich-poor gap. Extremism and terrorism have also spilled over into more places. The upcoming US presidential election, Brexit and the attempted coup in Turkey exposed deeper tensions and challenges. These events will have a profound geopolitical impact and add complexity to global economic governance.

There are new trends and changes in the global economic landscape. Distribution of power has become more balanced. Some emerging market economies, which once enjoyed robust growth, now suffer slowdowns, while growth in some developed economies has begun to rebound after sluggish recovery in the past few years. Divergence in economic growth has happened not only among major developed economies, but also among emerging market economies. The world economy is entering the new normal of low-speed growth. Global trade grew slower than the world economy for four consecutive years from 2012 to 2015. According to the World Trade Organization (WTO), the total value of global trade declined by as much as 13% in US dollar terms to $16.5 trillion dollars. In investment, global cross-border direct investment reached $2.27 trillion dollars in 2007, a year before the financial crisis, but plunged to $1.6 trillion dollars in 2014, and only recovered to $1.8 trillion dollars in 2015. The international debate on "deglobalization" has intensified. These new arguments, based on different positions, will affect the evolution of global governance. *The State of the International Order* by The Brookings Institution argued that, while the global economic order survived the crisis, fault-lines remain. This has made it more urgent and onerous to reform and improve global economic governance.

Changes happened at different levels of global economic governance in the past year. The G20 has become the premium forum for international economic governance, and the international community is looking forward to the G20 Summit in Hangzhou in September 2016. With the theme of "Toward an Innovative, Invigorated, Interconnected and Inclusive World Economy", the Hangzhou Summit is committed to facilitate G20's transition from a crisis-response mechanism to one focusing on long-term governance. The G20 Trade Ministers Meeting has just concluded in Shanghai in July. As the first meeting after G20 trade ministers were asked by leaders in the Antalya Summit to meet on a regular basis, the Shanghai meeting generated a series of fruitful results such as building trade and investment institutions. In the multilateral trading system, the Bali Package reached at the end of 2013 delivered a boost of confidence in the WTO. It went through many twists and turns before it was finally adopted by the WTO General Council on November 27, 2014. Thus, the Trade Facilitation Agreement became part of the multilateral trade agreements and the post-Bali work of the Doha Round came back on track. At the end of 2015, the 10th Minister Conference of the WTO concluded the Information Technology Agreement (ITA) expansion talks and reached consensus on export competition of agriculture and issues of the Least Developed Countries (LDCs). However, hindered by various factors, the Doha Round still drags on.

On a regional level, after the negotiation was concluded in 2015, the Trans-Pacific Partnership (TPP) requires that all parties go through domestic approval procedures. Therefore, the prospects of TPP remain to be seen. Meanwhile, the US and the EU are conducting intensive negotiations on the Transatlantic Trade and Investment Partnership (TTIP). China is stepping up negotiations on free trade areas as well. In 2015, China signed and implemented two high-level and comprehensive free trade agreements (FTA) with the Republic of Korea and Australia. Meanwhile, China signed the Protocol to Amend the Framework Agreement on Comprehensive Economic Cooperation between China and ASEAN, advanced FTA negotiations with the Gulf Cooperation Council (GCC), and Regional Comprehensive Economic Partnership (RCEP) negotiations. In general, as a "testing ground" of new issues and new rules, FTAs are becoming increasingly important in leading and promoting rules-making. It can be expected that FTA negotiation processes and outcomes between major economic regions will have a profound impact on the evolution of international trade rules.

Some positive changes occurred in the international financial order, but there is still a long way to go in reshaping international financial order. On November 30, 2015, the International Monetary Fund (IMF) announced the inclusion of the RMB in the Special Drawing Rights (SDRs) basket, and the new basket, of which the RMB makes up 10.92%, came into effect on January 1, 2016. The momentum of economic recovery has become more divergent in different parts of the world, leading to greater policy competition. After the adoption of quantitative easing in developed economies, more countries are following suit and devaluing their currencies. With total debt in major economies far outweighing their economic aggregate, the world economy may slide into a financial crisis again. People are now questioning whether monetary policy is still an effective macro-economic tool after the Jamaica Agreement. Against this background, the Asian Infrastructure Investment Bank (AIIB) came into being as a new approach to North-South financial cooperation and an equal, inclusive multilateral financial institution that takes into account the needs of emerging economies. The international community hopes this new financial institution will serve as a useful supplement to the existing international financial system.

The economic and trade rules discussed in this book have evolved to various extents over the last two years. Take the closely watched investment rules for example. China and the US, having concluded the bilateral investment treaty (BIT) negotiations, have gone through multiple rounds of discussions on their negative list offers. China-EU BIT talks are also moving forward. The future progress of these negotiations, I believe, will contribute to the establishment of global investment rules. When it comes to Global Value Chains (GVCs), the international community is increasingly aware that advancing cooperation on GVCs and building GVCs that foster inclusive growth is an important pathway to a new round of global economic and trade growth. In the meantime, as the new generation of GVCs-related economic and trade policies have received high recognition at national and international levels, more and more studies are dedicated to GVCs-related investment, innovation, labor skills, environmental protection and other behind-the-border policies. In the 2014 Leaders' Declaration adopted in Beijing, the economic leaders of the Asia-Pacific Economic Cooperation (APEC) endorsed the APEC Strategic Blueprint for Promoting Global Value Chains Development and Cooperation, the first guideline document on GVCs policies around the world. In the recent G20 Trade Ministers Meeting, consensus was reached in five areas, including promoting inclusive and coordinated GVCs. In the field of international development cooperation, the United Nations (UN) Sustainable Development Summit held on September 25, 2015 officially adopted the post-2015 development agenda, which includes 17 Sustainable Development Goals and 169 targets, covering many areas including poverty and hunger eradication, health, education, gender equality, water and sanitation, energy and climate change. The Agenda has charted the course for developing countries as well as international development cooperation for the next 15 years. It is worth noting that the Belt and Road Initiative, a major cooperation initiative put forward by China, has achieved good progress over the past two years. The principles of wide consultation, joint contribution and shared benefits in this initiative are hailed as a worthy endeavor for the global economic governance system. At the same time, discussions and consultations are continuing in areas such as trade remedy, trade in services, government procurement, IPR protection, competitive neutrality, and trade and sustainable development.

Looking ahead, the process to reshape global economic and trade rules will continue to be full of twists and turns. Geographical, institutional and even ideological differences will give rise to uncertainties. Nonetheless, the human race is fully confident about the globalization process and the progress in global governance, because productivity decides the progress of human society. Productivity, in turn, benefits from the advancement of science and technology. From steam engines to electric motors to computers, and from telegraph to radio to information network, every major progress in science and technology will expand the radius of global production and consumption and, consequently, push forward the economic globalization process. Now in this emerging new era of artificial intelligence, internet of big data and intelligent hardware make human beings almost omnipotent, capable of unveiling the mystery of life sciences, finding answer to riddles in materials science, and even exploiting the universe and searching for earth-like planets which will no longer be sheer fantasy. The power of any single country will bear no comparison with these great endeavors. Any economy that isolates itself from global cooperation will be marginalized or even abandoned. Do we have any alternative to globalization? Can we not improve rules in such deep-going globalization? Challenges and threats, be it economic inequality, regional development imbalance, terrorism, killings or even war, will persist, but I'm afraid they are not the most threatening. It is the shared challenge of climate change and survival crisis that is closer to the hearts of everyone in the global village. As a Chinese saying goes, a just cause enjoys abundant support while an unjust one finds little support. Anyone who goes against the law will not be able to play the bully forever. The world will see earth-shaking changes as the new age comes.

Having suffered centuries of self-imposed isolation in the Ming and Qing Dynasties and nearly 100 years of foreign aggressions and civil wars, China, with its population of over 1.3 billion, is committed to embracing globalization and peaceful development through reform and opening up. Please cast away any suspicion or fear, and seize the opportunity of common development. If you don't believe it, wait and see.

About the Author

Chen Deming holds a Doctorate in Management and Master's in Quantitative Economics from the International School of Business, Nanjing University, China. Since 1997, he has served as Mayor and CPC Committee Secretary of Suzhou City, Governor of Shaanxi Province, and Deputy Director of the National Development and Reform Commission (Ministerial level) successively. He was appointed as the Minister of Commerce from December 2007 to March 2013. In those five years, he participated in formulating the strategies for China's opening up and trade policies. As a seasoned trade negotiator in the world, he took part in a series of major international trade negotiations. He has also served as President of the Association for Relations Across the Taiwan Straits since April 2013.

Amidst his busy work schedule, the author is actively involved in academic research and puts theories into practice. His main research areas are management of national economy, economic globalization and opening trade *etc*. He has published the book *A Study on the Competitiveness of SMEs* (in Chinese) and essays "The Impact of Financing Modes on Corporate Governance Structure", "The Development of Foreign Direct Investment Location Theory and Its Inspiration for China", and "An International Comparative Study on China's Competitiveness in Attracting Foreign Investment".

Introduction

The fire of economic crisis caused by the financial sector collapse that swept across the world has lasted for five years after Lehman Brothers went bankrupt in 2008. The impact of the crisis is still lingering and spreading negative energy, affecting the future of society. When we look back, memory of the falling dominoes of the financial sector five years ago is so fresh yet so unbearable to recall. Today, people are vigilant of a revival of the crisis and struggle to get away from recession. Yet, few people talk about the cause of the fire and the liability of the arsonists. However, history shall not be forgotten.

This disaster — a rare occurrence over the last 80 years — inflicted heavier losses than any economic crisis ever recorded. According to the International Monetary Fund (IMF), the World Trade Organization (WTO) and the United Nations Conference on Trade and Development (UNCTAD), if the average nominal growth rate had been maintained, USD17.6 trillion worth of world GDP, USD10.2 trillion worth of trade and USD8.2 trillion of cross-border investment evaporated between 2008 and 2012. Worldwide cross-border investment in 2012 was merely 72% of that in 2008. Confidence is not yet returning. We continue to turn a blind eye to slumps in the property market and national income, the loss of jobs caused by the crisis, the decline of aid offered by rich countries for poor countries and greenhouse gas management while focused on austerity measures. Nevertheless, who shall pay for the excessive investment, overcapacity and capital bubble driven by the bogus boom before the crisis and for the spillover effect of quantitative easing policy and lingering inflation hence incurred? People cannot but ask whether or not the instigators have ever anticipated all these consequences.

Finding the right answer is much more difficult than solving a real arson, because the financial crisis and the subsequent global economic crisis are caused by institutional and rule-related reasons rather than by an individual. As early as in 1944 before World War II ended, the United States, as a major winner in the war and the owner of 75% of the gold in the world, held a Bretton Woods Conference in New Hampshire with its Western allies in a bid to end the global recession and the currency competition among countries, so as to establish a stable international economic order. The Conference ended with the victory of the White Plan over the Keynes Plan, the establishment of the gold exchange standard, the endorsement of principles of foreign exchange, capital and trade liberalization, the setting up of multilateral economic institutions, and the founding of governance platforms such as the IMF, the World Bank Group (WBG) and the WTO. Rules of these organizations were set and literally controlled by western developed countries like the US. Dollar crises broke out from time to time due to deteriorating fiscal deficit and worsening international balance of payments of the US, which led to the collapse of the Bretton Woods System 28 years after the IMF was founded. Despite this, the Bretton Woods Conference and the system and rules it set were, after all, the prototype of global economic governance and important safeguard for rapid recovery of world economy and revival of capitalism after the war.

The first sign of economic globalization in modern times was seen in the early days of capitalism. It became an economic model countries aspired toward despite all the ups and downs; the history of capitalism can largely be seen in four stages. The first stage is between the late 19th century and 1914, and is the golden age of globalization when the share of international trade in GDP increased quickly from 9% to 16% because of colonial expansion and trade promotion. The second stage is between 1914 and de-globalization at the end of World War II when the great depression triggered isolationism, nationalism and militarism, and protectionism prevailed. As a result, share of international trade in global GDP dropped to 5.5% when World War II broke out. The third stage is the re-globalization after World War II. During this period, international trade regained a strong momentum thanks to worldwide removal of trade barriers, advances in technology and lower transportation costs, and by the late 1970s it had returned to the level before World War I. The fourth stage is about the new globalization starting from the mid-to-late 1990s. With the end of the Cold War, global trade started to grow at a much faster pace than GDP. In 2012, global merchandise trade accounted for 25.5% of global GDP in terms of transaction value and services trade accounted for 6.1%.

Evolution of post-World War II globalization shows both a match and mismatch between existing international economic organizations/rules and global governance. Economic crises, imbalances between regions and countries and geopolitical changes caused by the imbalances make clear to all that rules must be improved in order to keep with the times. "Rule Reconstruction" highlighted in this book refers to the amendment and supplementation to existing international economic rules. We need to learn from the crisis and improve governance regime to boost economic growth. We also need to balance all the pros and cons and observe the principle of consultation for consensus. It is neither fogyism nor total negation. The reason is that the external environment for China remains an international community in which capitalist institutions dominate. Despite all the difficulties and conflicts, capitalist society has an extremely strong capability of self-healing thanks to strong productivity, along with scientific and technological power. In order to continue reform and opening up when faced with such an external environment, China must learn from the outside world and take advantage of the external environment to realize its own development agenda.

I had long hoped to dedicate more time to research on the evolution of economic globalization and rule construction relating to global governance and crisis control after I retire from the administration. I hope to record down the various experiences I have gained in the battle of rules governance between conservative powers and emerging powers over the past five years. Another important motivation is that of penning down my reflections and understanding of the world situation as our motherland and fellow citizens march forward towards our century-old dream. In the past 10 months, over 10 colleagues of mine and I worked together on the outline and chapters of the book. We consulted many Chinese and foreign experts. After rounds of revision, the book is finally completed. However, I do not feel relief. On the contrary, writing this book makes it even clearer to me how complicated and difficult the international environment will be in the future. In arenas of multilateral order and regional cooperation, at summits, forums or in senior officials' consultations, China is always encouraged by established and emerging economies to open wider, comply with more stringent international rules and thus generate greater benefits for the rest of the world through its own rise. Nevertheless, a look at domestic situation in China will show that entrenched problems are fermenting while marginal dividends of opening up and reform are diminishing. Despite rapid growth of aggregate economy, its structure and efficiency need to improve and proper mechanisms for competition and innovation remain absent. Perhaps China has come to a point of no return where the only way forward is to promote reform, development and innovation through greater opening up drive and as a trade-off the international community will open wider to China. Then China will win decades of peace to develop and improve an open economic system.

The book is composed of 15 chapters. The first five chapters discuss rules of global governance, reflect on the crisis rarely seen in the past century, and raise the proposition of rule reconstruction. Focus of this part is on multilateral trading system, regional economic cooperation and related international financial rules. Although it is not a platform for constructing rules, the Group of Twenty (G20) Summit was created under circumstances which called for its creation. Based on the G8+5, the G20 Summit plays an important role in highlighting changes in global architecture and guiding the process of global rule setting. In this book, the G20 is regarded as a bellwether for tackling crisis and reconstructing rules. It should be noted that analysis on the cause of the crisis focuses on specific elements rather than inherent characteristics of capitalist institutions. In fact, the irreconcilable conflict between private possession of means of production and socialized mass production inevitably leads to economic crisis. This causal link gets clearer and becomes the common reason for each and every crisis as productivity grows and globalization evolves. Since this book aims to discuss post-crisis rule reconstruction, analysis on the cause of the crisis stresses more on individuality. Of course it can be concluded that although the process of rule reconstruction provides temporary solutions only and cannot save capitalism, it does prompt us to think about the links between institutions and crisis and offer reference for China's development agenda.

Chapters 6 to 14 make detailed deliberations on trade remedy rules, global value chains (GVCs) and trade in value added (TiVA), services trade rules, government procurement rules, intellectual property rules, investment rules, state-owned enterprises and competitive neutrality, rules of international development cooperation, and trade and sustainability, *etc*. These issues are either the essence of international rules, or closely related to China's reform and opening up. Some of them might become key rules in the future. On top of the analysis on these rules or quasi-rules, the last chapter of the book provides an outlook on the path, direction and key issues of international economic rule reconstruction, and offers recommendations about China's engagement. These analysis, outlook and recommendations are merely my opinion and hopefully can attract more valuable ideas.

Consisting of 160 members, the WTO — a permanent international organization — is like a United Nations of the world economy. The WTO, together with the IMF and the WBG, constitute three pillars of the global economy. Unlike most international organizations, the WTO is equipped with its own legal framework and dispute settlement mechanism, and exercises its authority in supervision and enforcement. It is indeed an organization "armed to the teeth". The WTO also allows members, under certain circumstances, to restrict international trade through trade remedies like anti-dumping, coun-tervailing and safeguard measures in order to protect domestic industries of an import country from injury. During the crisis, different types of trade remedies were employed consecutively or excessively in some cases. There were over 1,000 anti-dumping and countervailing investigations in five years, and about one third of them were targeted on China. However, through the WTO's Appellate Body and bilateral consultations, China resolved over half of the cases successfully. The principles of reciprocity, transparency and non-discrimination were not subverted, but defied.

Committed to common development and counter-terrorism cooperation, the WTO launched the Doha Development Agenda (DDA) in the capital of Qatar two months after the 9/11 attack. Having lasted for 12 years, the Doha Round covers many important trade issues like agriculture, non-agriculture market access, services, intellectual property and rules, and also aims to resolve major issues like dispute settlement, environment and development. It once fell into a protracted hibernation. When people were about to lose confidence in the multilateral trading system, good news came from the 9th Ministerial Conference of the WTO held in Bali, Indonesia in December 2013. The Conference endorsed the "Bali Ministerial Declaration" and passed the "Early Harvest package" including 10 documents regarding agriculture, trade facili-tation and development. A commitment was made at the Conference to set clear work programs in the next 12 months to resolve outstanding issues and to conclude the Doha Round. This is the very first agreement that has real "teeth" since the WTO was established nearly 20 years ago and the Doha Round launched 12 years ago. Despite major divergences between parties, the outcomes of the Conference and the positive gestures of all parties revived the world's confidence in the multilateral trading system. At the same time, pluri-lateral negotiations between some members on the Trade in Services Agreement (TISA), expansion of the Information Technology Agreement (ITA) and engagement of emerging members in the Agreement on Government Procurement (GPA) are ongoing while discussions on environmental goods have started. Though only part of the WTO membership is now engaged, implication of these plurilateral processes for the future of the multilateral trading system cannot be underestimated. History shows that plurilateral negotiations as predictors are often accepted by the multilateral process. Seven of the nine plurilateral agreements during the Tokyo Round[1] are already

---

[1] The Tokyo Round refers to the seventh round of General Agreement on Tariffs and Trade (GATT) multilateral trade negotiations. It was started in Tokyo in September 1973 and held later in

multilateralized. As for the future, we still have to wait and see whether or not the multilateral trading system will truly revive and take the lead again in world trade and investment liberalization.

In sharp contrast to DDA's protracted standstill, regional economic cooperation has been on the rise since the crisis. According to WTO statistics, a total of 220 free trade agreements (FTAs) has been notified and took effect as of June 2013, accounting for 88% of regional trade arrangements. 52% of these agreements, or 114 agreements, were notified and took effect after 2008, marking a robust momentum. This upsurge of regional cooperation since the 1990s features an open-ended and cross-regional process in which actors in the region establish organizations for regional cooperation and rules of these regional cooperation organizations have started to converge with multilateral rules of the WTO. The European Union (EU) and the Association of Southeast Asian Nations (ASEAN) are typical examples of new regionalism. They appear in the international community as a "regional actor" and become important forces that other parties count on for support. Unlike traditional regional cooperation which is clearly exclusive, new regionalism adopts a flexible attitude toward cooperation with non-members. It employs multilateral disciplines as norms for trade arrangements and extends from border rules to behind-the-border regulation, protection of intellectual property, competition policy and so on. It is indeed an "experimental zone" for setting new trade rules. Ongoing processes like the Trans-Pacific Partnership (TPP), the Regional Comprehensive Economic Partnership (RCEP) and the Transatlantic Trade and Investment Partnership (TTIP) are all jumbos of regional cooperation and possible cornerstones for the multilateral trading system in the future. People often compare multilateral trading systems and regional economic cooperation as the two wheels of economic globalization. The first wheel aims to improve the rule of unanimous consent through reform and accelerate multilateral process. The latter wheel targets the points where the interests of established countries and of emerging countries can meet and creates conditions to drive forward the multilateral process. Given the overall

---

Geneva, Switzerland. Ninety-nine countries (including 29 non-contracting parties) participated in negotiations and the Round was concluded in April 1979. Agenda of the Tokyo Round included important issues such as agricultural trade, trade liberalization for tropical products, quantitative restriction and other non-tariff measures, tariff, arrangement of multilateral trade negotiation agreement, structural adjustment and trade policy, counterfeit trade, export of domestically banned products, export of capital goods, textile and apparel, trade of certain natural resource products, exchange rate volatility and its impact on trade, double pricing, and rules of origin.

advantage of established countries in rule reconstruction, a big test for emerging countries is how to take initiative in participating in plurilateral negotiations and regional economic cooperation. Having said that, this book includes a preliminary study on China's FTA strategy.

A prominent characteristic of globalization is the global expansion of production networks and supply chains of multinational corporations and, on top of that, the formation of GVC.[2] As more developing countries take part in labor division under the GVC, traditional statistical methodology of international trade is facing serious challenge. In 2012 for instance, total value of world exports was over USD20 trillion, nearly 60% of which was from trade in intermediate goods and services, and a large portion was "double counted". Therefore the TiVA methodology is introduced. TiVA measures import value added (IVA) and domestic value added (DVA) in export trade of a country. It avoids double counting, prevents exaggeration of trade imbalance, and helps assess precisely the true trade flow between countries. IVA reflects dependence of a country's export on imported contents, or analyzes positions taken by various economies in vertical specialization of the GVC. But in context of GVC, IVA may include DVA of the previous round of trade flow. Similarly, DVA may include IVA of the previous round of trade flow as well. So one of the topics discussed in this book is how to set up a mass database for precise calculation of TiVA. In economic terms, only DVA in export means contribution to GDP and employment, and it is decided by a country's level of skills of labor force, production cost, degree of openness, and its position in the GVC. Analysis indicates a major influence by multinational corporations (MNCs) in construction of the GVC because export from their global production networks accounts for 80% of the world total export and their export of manufactured goods are accompanied with export of large amount of services. Engagement in the GVC means a lot for developing countries in their efforts to create jobs, increase income, obtain new technology and realize economic catch-up. There will certainly be risks and challenges for developing countries such as lock-in in low value-added activities, vulnerability against international economic fluctuation, small contribution to domestic economy, and high pollution and

---

[2] Global Value Chain used to be known as value chain, commodity chain, production network, enterprise network, value network and input-output analysis and so on. It is best defined by United Nations Industrial Development Organization (UNIDO) as a global, cross-enterprise network that connects production, sales and recycling for the purpose of realizing the value of goods or services. It covers the whole process from procurement and transportation of raw materials, manufacturing and distribution of semi-finished and finished goods, to consumption and recycling.

emission. Hence, emerging economies have been encouraging their companies to go global in order to push ahead with construction of regional value chain and sharpen their competitive edge in the international market.

In general, international investment institutions and rules are still in a chaotic state. Relevant agreements get increasingly decentralized and complicated and exist at more layers. According to the UNCTAD, there had been 3,196 international investment treaties by the end of 2012, and 2,857 treaties were signed bilaterally. China signed 145 investment treaties among which 128 are bilateral ones. Along with stronger regional cooperation amidst globalization, regionalization of investment treaties is accelerating.

By the end of the first half of 2013, at least 110 countries had taken part in 22 regional negotiations involving investment clauses, a process that crosses multiple regions and focuses on investment liberalization. It is fair to say that regionalization conduces to the integration and unification of international investment rules, and paves the way for the multilateralization of international investment treaties. Over the decades, extensive discussions were made on a multilateral investment treaty. Developed countries like the US and the EU led several attempts, but no substantive results have ever been made. After five painful years of crisis, the international community once again puts this issue on agenda. China is rising as a major country of capital inflow and outflow and a large number of Chinese companies are going to the international market and take a role in the GVC. Therefore, China needs a multilateral investment treaty that offers protection more than ever. In light of that, the Chinese government announced after over five years of exploration to choose pre-establishment national treatment[3] and a negative list[4] at the 5th US-China Strategic and Economic Development Dialogue (S&ED) held in July 2013.

---

[3] Under international investment law, national treatment refers to the fact that treatment provided for foreign investors and investments is no inferior to treatment for domestic investors and investments under similar circumstances. In control schemes of traditional investment treaties national treatment applies to post-establishment phases. However, pre-establishment national treatment extends national treatment to pre-investment and pre-establishment phases.
[4] Negative list is an important international system of investment entry. Equivalent to the "blacklist" in investment field, negative list specifies sectors and industries in which foreign investment is not allowed. The academia believes all measures targeting foreign investment and incompliant with national treatment and most-favored nation treatment or restrictive measures related to performance requirement and senior executives shall be identified in the form of list. More than 70 countries adopt the scheme of "pre-establishment national treatment and a negative list".

This not only lays the foundation for the negotiations on investment treaty between China and the US, but also will greatly promote the early start of negotiations on a multilateral investment treaty. In some senses, this choice also offers China an institutional dividend in terms of transitioning national economy and encouraging capital to go to the real economy, innovative businesses, and small and micro businesses. If agreed upon, the China-US bilateral investment treaty will become another exemplary case of reform and development through opening up, and its importance is comparable to that of China's WTO accession.

Trade in services, government procurement and protection of intellectual property are the three key issues in the reconstruction of international rules. Competitive neutrality, development cooperation and sustainability are the so-called "21st-century new issues". These issues are discussed in this book because they are relevant to new international rules, and more importantly because coping with these new challenges is an arduous task for China given the existing Chinese laws and regulations as well as policy consideration. As a Chinese saying goes: "If you know your enemy and know yourself, you will win every war". Knowing the evolutionary path of economic rules in a globalization context will help readers of this book understand more profoundly the path of socialism with Chinese characteristics and the objectives of deepening reform in an all-around manner.

Agreed upon 20 years ago, the General Agreement on Trade in Services (GATS) sets the framework of worldwide liberalization and regulation of services trade. Since it is the very first multilateral agreement on services trade with a relatively short history, there are few judicial interpretations and practices and some enabling clauses need to be clarified. Therefore, adequate discussions have been made in the DDA negotiations on trade in services about domestic regulation and emergency safeguard measures. Developed members believe that the draft text for discussion has too low level of ambition and request to transform most "soft disciplines" into binding "hard disciplines" while developing members are more concerned about qualification requirements and procedures relating to movement of natural persons and special and differentiated treatment. Despite some substantial progress, discussions on this topic were stuck in standstill due to the deadlock of the overall DDA process. The US has evident advantages in services trade as its services sectors contributed 80% of its GDP and employment and its services trade had a surplus worth USD208 billion in 2012. The US and the EU are the major forces driving negotiations on liberalization of services trade. They and some developed, open economies formed the Real Good Friends of Services or the RGF[5] and launched the plurilateral negotiations on TISA in March 2013 when no results had been yielded in the DDA negotiations on trade in services. To date, 23 members including Chinese Hong Kong and Chinese Taipei have joined the RGF. Total value of services trade of RGF members accounts for about two thirds of the world's total even when intra-trade within the EU is deducted. The Chinese government announced to join in the TISA negotiations on September 30, 2013, which is a strategic decision. On the one hand, the export of services from China is far smaller than that of the US. The Chinese figure in 2012 is less than one third of the US figure, and even less than one fifth if income made by overseas subsidiaries from services export is included. On the other hand, China is in great need of economic transition given the constant rise of labor cost, value of its currency and prices of energy and raw materials; in great need of job creation given the new working population and labor force migrating from the countryside to cities; and in great need of more, higher-quality services given the rise of people's living standard and companies' competitiveness. Therefore, development of services industry should be a fundamental state policy of China, and the liberalization of services trade as well as segmentation and development of service sectors through trade seems to be the route China must take. For a country like China that has a large population, limited resources and a fragile ecological environment, it may after all be accepted as a long-term strategic choice to seek a freer international market through opening up its domestic market, and to win the global services market through opening up domestic services sectors.

The Agreement on Government Procurement (GPA) is a plurilateral agreement in the WTO package. Jurisdiction of the WTO covers trade in goods and trade in services, requiring all members to offer each other most-favored nation treatment and national treatment which are collectively referred to as "non-discriminatory treatment". But "procurement of goods and services for governmental purposes" is excluded from non-discriminatory treatment, which means priority can be given to domestic products and it is unnecessary to grant

---

[5] As the two most important exporters of services trade, the US and the EU are main drivers behind international negotiations on services trade liberalization. They have partnered developed economies like Canada, Australia, Japan, Switzerland and Chinese Hong Kong, open economies like Korea, Mexico and Chile, and a few developing economies with which free trade agreements have been signed such as Turkey, Columbia and Panama, to promote services trade liberalization and lower entry barriers to services trade. These economies declare themselves as "Real Good Friends of Services".

national treatment to imported products. Government procurement is also called public procurement and can constitute 10%–15% of a country's gross national product. In order to enhance mutual opening in this field, the US, the EU, Japan and Canada, among others, reached consensus on GPA according to which they opened government procurement markets to each other. Since it took effect in 1981, the GPA has expanded to 43 members. After rounds of revision, the 2012 revised text came into being and is ready to take effect after members ratify it. The US Congress passed the Buy American Act in 2008 when the crisis broke out, but at the same time required enforcement of the Act to comply with US obligations under international treaties. This literally targeted restriction on non-GPA members like China since GPA members were not subject to the restriction. China committed upon accession, to the WTO, that it would start as early as possible the process of joining GPA, and at the end of 2007 the Chinese government submitted its application for joining the GPA and a preliminary offer. The offer, although revised and improved four times, is far from meeting demands of GPA members. As a result, China is still kept out of the GPA. Apart from participants' stringent demands, another reason is that there are clashes between China's existing government procurement system and GPA rules. GPA members, represented by the US, requested procurement by Chinese sub-national governments and state-owned enterprises be covered by the Agreement. This is obviously too harsh a request as GPA members themselves are not able to meet it. China's Government Procurement Law provides a narrow definition of government procurement, and only procurement by governmental authorities, public institutions and public organizations under given conditions and funded by fiscal funds is regarded as government procurement. However, the GPA stipulates that all procurement for governmental purposes shall be defined as government procurement, including public tendering for projects supervised by government (referred to as construction services in the GPA). Therefore, it remains difficult for China to join the GPA right now.

As the civilized institutions, the intellectual property rights (IPRs) have gone through several stages of development from domestic regulation, the Paris Convention, the Berne Convention, the World Intellectual Property Organization (WIPO) rules to the WTO Rules. The institutions are now offering protection in other countries for intellectual creation of a country. Its purpose is to strike a balance between encouraging creation and facilitating shared utilization. IPR protection and prohibition of rights abuse are two sides of the same coin. Intellectual property rights are a private right and grow from capitalist soil. It incentivizes innovation, but conflicts to a certain degree with the protection of public interest. Therefore, boundaries and terms of IPR protection have been a key topic of debate. The WTO Agreement on Trade-Related Aspects of Intellectual Property Rights (TRIPS) provides for the minimum international obligations of global IPR protection. It is an international rule originating from the multi-lateralization of related contents in North American Free Trade Agreement (NAFTA) as insisted by the US. China naturally became a TRIPS member upon its entry in the WTO. Despite the changes in economic weighting between established and emerging countries during the crisis, the western countries maintain strong advantages in education, science and technology. Protection of IPRs is protection of their institutions in international context. Plurilateral negotiations on Anti-Counterfeiting Trade Agreement (ACTA) driven by the US and Japan were concluded in Japan in 2010. The ACTA provides clear stipulations on civil enforcement, border measures, criminal enforcement and protection in digital environment. Though whether or not the Agreement can be endorsed remains uncertain, it is evident that developed countries have high expectations on IPR protection. In the meantime, the US plans to add in TPP clauses regarding dispute settlement procedures for handling IPR cases, which is like implanting "teeth" for high-level protection. In the arena of international IPR protection, China is a latecomer but it is rapidly catching up; it has set up bilateral working mechanisms with the US, the EU, Japan and Russia. Remarkable progress is also made in domestic protection and widely acknowledged by the international community. However, China still has a long way to go. Problems like counterfeiting, infringement and piracy are criticized by the international community. China has to assess carefully and learn from the rules of countries that offer strong IPR protection. It is probably the right moment for China to enforce higher international rules and promote innovation through opening up.

21st century new issues in international economic rules include e-commerce, environment, labor, *etc.* Some of them are not "new" issues at all, but become new hot topics because of changes in international relations. One such issue is competitive neutrality. The original Organisation for Economic Co-operation and Development (OECD) definition of competitive neutrality is fair competition between business operators in marketplace. But today it is more about government and state-owned enterprises, and therefore is the debate between model of economic growth and model of corporate governance. Believing in an open market and private investment as the key to economic growth, the West is not in favor of improving competitiveness through government's support for state-owned enterprises (SOEs) because this model lacks long-term stability, resources are allocated in an inefficient way, small and medium-sized enterprises

(SMEs) lose competitiveness, and innovation, growth and employment are negatively affected. Of course the US also claims that it does not intend to judge whether or not state ownership is good, and competitive neutrality does not necessarily mean privatization. Rather, the US is concerned about whether SOEs compete with American private companies on a level playing field. However, the Chinese people should keep aware that subjects of ownership in most countries are different from that of China and therefore these countries are more likely to support the competitive neutrality rule advocated by the West and emphasize "disciplines of SOEs". This is actually also an issue very interesting to Chinese private companies. With this said, as guided by the decisions of the third Plenary Session of the 18th Central Committee of the Communist Party of China (CPC), China has to commit to its own path and cope with changes in major international trend at the same time when it comes to the issue of SOE reform and government functions. China must take all these factors into consideration and adopt corresponding strategies.

Rules regarding "international development cooperation" and "sustainability" are relatively easier. The former focuses on effectiveness of development cooperation, different natures and responsibilities of South-South cooperation and South-North cooperation, and the UN Millennium Development Goals and new rules guiding international development cooperation, and therefore helps ensure stronger planning on China's aid to foreign countries, higher degree of engagement by aid recipient countries, better results of aid projects, and closer coordination with other donor countries. The latter focuses on regional rules related to trade and environment. Models of NAFTA and the EU will be copied in the TPP and the TTIP, and dispute settlement mechanism will have a stronger binding power. Frequent extreme climate events make the issues related to greenhouse gas emission reduction heat up again and topics such as carbon tax, labor standards and human rights also become new trends in regional FTA discussions. China identifies development of ecological culture as a strategic objective and feels acutely the hazards of environmental pollution and extreme climate events. The paradigm of labor standard discussion is provided by FTA agreements with western countries like Switzerland. In general, the socialist system with Chinese characteristics makes sure that China will do a greater job in this field.

The international financial system and its rules were set up long ago and have been improved much over the years. Both headquartered in Washington DC, the IMF and the WBG are two international organizations that are deeply influenced by the US. Particularly in the IMF where the US has veto power, no attempts to modify US monetary policy would possibly succeed. Those who genuinely impact or intervene in the international financial order are US Federal Reserve and Treasury Department. To tackle the crisis, the Federal Reserve initiated the unconventional Quantitative Easing (QE)[6] policy when low interest rates failed to boost the domestic economy. It increased money supply through bond purchase and injected liquidity to the capital market. The massive amount of low-cost hot money generated by the QE policy forced many emerging economies to depend on high liquidity for their national economies. As a result, credit expanded, capital bubbles ballooned, corporate debt surged, public finance worsened, and economic fundamentals weakened or even deteriorated. Although QE policy generated some benefits for the US economy and the US housing market in particular, its marginal utility diminished, capital bubbles were inflated by excessive liquidity, and quality of investment declined inevitably. In fact, the QE policy cures the symptoms but not the disease. It accelerates economic recovery on the one hand, but stores up trouble of a new crisis on the other. Therefore, the US will have to retreat from QE sooner or later.

Due to the failure of the interest rate transmission mechanism, the EU's recovery is slower than that of the US. It practices its QE policy in a relatively prudent manner and will not retreat immediately. In Japan, the Abeconomics and its QE policies prevail, just like quenching a thirst with poison, and therefore it is still too early for Japan to retreat from QE. Judging from its overall interest, the US will gradually withdraw from QE policy as the economy recovers. However, a tentative signal sent by the US Federal Reserve in June 2013 triggered an overreaction of the entire capital market. Stock markets of emerging economies stumbled at once, currency value dropped, capital flowed out quickly, and social problems were magnified. People were worried if the Asian Financial Crisis originating from capital flight in Thailand in 1997 would repeat. Is it inevitable that emerging economies, victims of the economic crisis, will have to shed blood for QE retreat after paying for the QE? History does not repeat itself although it rhymes — a fall in the pit, a gain in the wit. Many emerging economies have started moderate monetary tightening and tried to protect their national economies through tools like floating exchange rate, reserving foreign exchange, balancing current account, reducing external debt,

---

[6] A Quantitative Easing refers to intervention by Central Bank after zero or near-zero interest rate is applied in the form of large liquidity injection through repurchasing medium and long-term bonds such as T-bond and increasing supply of monetary base. Quantitative easing is aimed at stimulating spending and borrowing, and therefore also described as printing more money indirectly.

speeding up bank reform and increasing operational transparency. Certainly these tools are a "double-edged sword", powerless in front of the strong Dollar Empire, and hurt emerging countries themselves. Just like what the then US Secretary of Treasury John Connally said about dollar spill over when the Bretton Woods System collapsed, "the dollar is our currency but your problem". Due to the QE policy, there are indeed capital bubbles in emerging economies that have to be crushed, and this is a risky and painful process. Issues relating to strengthening or improving global financial issues have been discussed for many years, yet there are few resolutions reached and even fewer implemented. There is all talk and no cider. Given the existing economic and financial system, particularly when the US dollar remains the single international reserve currency, new crises will be bred one after another when measures to tackle a crisis set the stage for the next crisis. The world has been learning from the crisis, but crisis has been transforming. How can we end the war between virtue and vice once and for all? Perhaps it is the time to produce new rules and new institutions.

The G20 is indeed a new platform for global governance that was created during the crisis for discussing new rules. In the early days of the crisis, international financial market fluctuated drastically every day and the whole world was in panic. The G8 Summit led by western countries was no longer able to handle the situation, and the "G8+5" model did not work because of the asymmetry in its form. The US, the perpetrator, wanted to enhance the uniformity of collective intervention in the form of conference. But France and the UK challenged the US by proposing a new Bretton Woods System. Emerging countries marginalized in global governance hope to take this opportunity to have a bigger say. Therefore the G20 Summit turned out to be the mainstay of global governance in the following years. For the first time, G20 Summits made emerging countries important participants in decision-making in global governance, and allowed them to vote on key economic policies and issues related to the international institutional system. Non-binding assessment and liability mechanisms were set up, and commitments were made not to practice further protectionism in investment and trade. As the crisis spread, however, G20 members saw divergence in macro-policy orientation. They had evident differences on issues like current account surplus percentage, trade protectionist measures, and solutions to the European debt crisis. As a result, its momentum of cooperation weakened and its legitimacy and efficacy was challenged. Several major countries failed to honor their commitments to cut deficit, implement "Basel III," modifying contribution percentage in the IMF and the WBG, or driving forward the DDA. The cost then was the decline of their credibility. It remains a concern where the G20 is heading toward.

The emergence of new rules and new institutions relies to a large extent on advance of science and technology and innovation of business models. These opportunities are rising. Worldwide networks that generate and analyze big data, display technology that enables super fine resolution, and on top of that, nanotechnology, new materials, gene deciphering and bio-engineering. All these will converge and the world will usher in a new, innovative and smart age. How to ensure effective global governance and crisis prevention and control in the new age will be a brand new topic.

This book tries to discuss above-mentioned issues from the angle of post-crisis rule reconstruction when we can neither change the fundamental institutional elements that caused the crisis nor afford to do nothing but watch with a pessimistic mood. Economic globalization will move on after all, no matter how long and difficult the journey will be. Peaceful development of China breaks the old balance of the world economy and helps achieving a new balance at the same time. China is absolutely able to seek more points where its interests can merge with others through greater opening up, and to revise and improve international trade, investment and finance rules. China is certainly able to exchange the opening up of other countries to China with its own opening and explore broader international markets.

Based on China's national strategy of deepening reform in an all-around manner and in view of the evolutionary trend of the international situation, this book provides some immature propositions and recommendations on improving an open economic system. Nevertheless, this is an attempt by my team and me. At least, our readers can learn more about the world they are in from this book, the realistic contradictions in international economy, and the valuable historic opportunities and challenges for China to engage in post-crisis reconstruction of international rules. I also hope this book will inspire colleagues and peers, the academia and laypeople to pay more attention to issues discussed in this book. I hope this book will accomplish its goal.

Chen Deming
Former Chinese Minister of Commerce

Chapter 1

Economic Crisis in the Era of Globalization

On September 15, 2008, America's fourth-largest investment bank, the 158-year-old Lehman Brothers announced it would file for bankruptcy protection with the US Bankruptcy Court for the Southern District of New York according to Chapter 11 of the American Bankruptcy Act. The global financial giant with a total of USD693 billion worth of assets and USD613 billion of debt had survived the turmoil of the 19th century railroad company closure, the Great Depression of the 1930s, the collapse of the capital management market at the turn of the century, and numerous other trials, yet came tumbling down in this sudden crisis, becoming the largest case of financial bankruptcy in the US history. This triggered another wave of economic trouble in the US subprime mortgage market with the fall of Bear Stearns in the summer of 2007. Following this, America's third-largest investment bank Merrill Lynch, was acquired by the Bank of America, the world's largest insurance company, and American International Group was brought to the brink of bankruptcy. This series of events raised the curtain on the new century's global economic crisis.

In comparison with several other economic crises in history, this meltdown was unique in its background, epicenter, degree of impact, evolution, and other aspects. The depth and breadth of its impact continues to exceed everyone's expectations. What is particularly noteworthy is that the crisis not only triggered intense philosophical and ideological debates, it also exposed the long-standing abuse of institutional structures and operational collaborations, and their respective regulations in the post-World War II global economic governance system, sparking off the search for new global governance platforms and reconstruction of trade rules. As globalization has developed in the past five years, many major changes have occurred in its dominant forces, manifestations, promotion platforms, trade patterns and other aspects. Some trends have begun to emerge as various old and new, multilateral, bilateral and regional platforms, as well as the economic powers supporting them, debate, negotiate and strategize vigorously to revise, adjust and improve upon existing global rules governing finance, trade, investment, intellectual property rights, development assistance as well as environment, labor, competitive neutrality and some new areas of economic and trade-related fields.

1 Outbreak of the Crisis

The 2008 economic crisis will be noted as one of the major historical events in the 21st century. Taking place just a few months after the US subprime mortgage crisis, it quickly evolved from a financial crisis into a global economic catastrophe and triggered a new round of European sovereign debt crisis with the rippling effect, and emerging economies also facing new challenges. Since the outbreak, the world's economy has plummeted, global rescue measures have shown unprecedented strength, and all parties have placed high hopes in new governance platforms. Yet, just as the global economy is showing signs of recovery, there appears to be policy differences and awkward coordination among the major economies and the progress of recovery has become uncertain. The disparate and perplexing economic phenomena reveals some of the unique characteristics of this crisis.

1.1 *Onset of the crisis*

Figures show that before the outbreak of the crisis in 2007, the world economy seemed to still be in the most robust period of growth since the 1970s. According to statistics from international agencies, the annual growth rate of the global economy from 2003 to 2007 was 4.9%; during that time, the growth rate of world trade volume was much higher than this, reaching an average of 7.9% per annum; transnational investment also increased from USD557.87 billion in 2003 to USD1.83 trillion in 2007, an average annual growth rate of 34.5%.[1]

Behind the "prosperous" figures, the US financial and real estate markets had already been showing symptoms of turmoil since 2007. On February 13 2007,

---

[1] Figures calculated based on data from the relevant IMF, WTO, UNCTAD databases.

the second-largest subprime mortgage[2] company in America, New Century Financial Corporation, announced a profit warning for the fourth quarter of 2006. Eventually on April 2, the company filed for bankruptcy, retrenched 54% of its staff, and became the biggest mortgage lender in the US to go bust in the real estate downturn. Following that, as enterprises and investment institutions successively reported their earnings, more problems in the subprime mortgage market came to light. Two credit rating agencies, Standard & Poor's and Moody's Investors Service reduced the credit ratings of hundreds of mortgage bonds respectively and the risk gradually began to spread. On August 3, Standard and Poor's lowered the debt ratings of the famous investment bank Bear Stearns. On August 8, Bear Stearns, America's fifth-largest investment bank, announced the closing of two of its funds and subsequently, several subprime-related financial institutions went bankrupt. From then on, the downturn of the real estate market and the collapse of the subprime mortgage market triggered a comprehensive credit crisis that hit and shook the entire global financial system.

To cope with the volatility and liquidity issues brought about by the financial markets, the US Federal Reserve and European Central Bank began joint "rescue" efforts. In early 2008, the major financial institutions in America reported severe losses, the real economy showed significant signs of decline, so the Federal Reserve continued and intensified its efforts to reduce interest rates. Despite their efforts, the ripple effect quickly spread. From the beginning of March 2008, subprime loan and debt losses extended to derivative securities, superior debt, credit cards and other areas, further triggering a credit crunch, short-term corporate financing difficulties, the plunging of loans and bond prices, and a large number of commercial banks were also struck by the "domino" effect. In July 2008, "Fannie Mae" and "Freddie Mac" faced severe financial difficulties due to heavy losses, forcing the Federal Reserve and Treasury to intervene and bail them out. From the onset of the subprime decline through its spread across the entire financial

---

[2] Subprime mortgage loans refer to lending institutions extending loans to borrowers with poor credit and low-income. This is because in the US mortgage market, lenders offer differential credit conditions to borrowers, according to their level of credit, thereby forming a two-tiered market with prime and subprime levels to service homeowners. Those with low credit are not eligible for prime loans and can only seek loans in the subprime market but the interest rates are typically 2%–3% higher than prime mortgages. The subprime mortgage market developed rapidly in the few years pre-crisis when the property market was booming. However, with substantial cooling of the property market and increasing interest rates, many subprime borrowers were unable to repay their loans, causing some lending institutions to suffer heavy losses or even go bankrupt.

chain to this point, a systemic crisis had, in fact, developed in the US financial system.

1.2 *Development of the crisis*

Before September 14, 2008, the global impact of the subprime mortgage crisis was essentially limited to direct losses associated with the subprime market. However, when Lehman Brothers filed for bankruptcy, Merrill Lynch was acquired by the Bank of America and another relevant series of events took place, the myth that financial giants were "too big to fail" was busted and investor confidence was greatly hit. This was the last straw for global stock and property markets, and the world was suddenly confronted with the huge risk of financial crisis.

In the financial sector, as global financial markets are closely linked and intertwined, financial institutions in Europe, Asia and other continents quickly felt the impact. British and Swiss financial institutions suffered heavy losses; the banking and financial industries of India, the Republic of Korea (hereinafter referred to as Korea) and others in Asia were also seriously affected. From September 15 to September 17, 2008, after the Lehman Brothers' bankruptcy, the three major stock indexes in the US experienced the greatest plummet since September 11, impelling sharp dives in the European and Asia-Pacific stock markets. In 2008, the global stock market incurred losses of up to USD17 trillion.[3] The already sluggish global housing market worsened and further declined. The combination of all these factors dragged more countries into the crisis. The monetary and financial markets of many emerging economies such as Russia, Korea, India, Brazil became increasingly volatile. Some countries such as Iceland even faced the risk of national bankruptcy.

The crisis also spread rapidly in the real economy. In December 2008, JP Morgan's global Purchasing Managers' Index (PMI) indicated that manufacturing had dropped to its lowest point since the beginning of the investigation 11 years ago. At the same time, almost all commodity prices saw dramatic plunges and further triggered the decline of the shipping and other production and services industries. The Baltic Dry Index (BDI) plummeted sharply from its highest recorded 11,793 points on May 20, 2008 to less than 1,000 points at the end of 2008. Indicators such as containers, port traffic, freight rates and others were broadly low. As these factors interplayed and continued brewing,

---

[3] Abstract from "Lehman Brothers' Bankruptcy Triggers Yet Another Subprime Mortgage Crisis" dated September 26, 2008 on Xinhuanet. Retrieved from http://news.xinhuanet.com/world/2008-09/26/content_10108799.htm. Accessed on August 6, 2013.

the steady continual growth of national economies was disrupted, business confidence was severely set back, international demand fell significantly, global product networks were affected, trade financing deteriorated and protectionism began to rise. By then, the crisis had rapidly spread from the financial sector to the real economy, and moved from developed economies to developing economies, turning into a rare and dire international economic crisis with wide-ranging effects and implications.

1.3 *Extension of the crisis — triggering the European debt crisis*

After the crisis broke out, the international community launched large-scale rescue measures rarely seen in history so as to curb panic in the market and stabilize confidence. However, in the latter half of 2009, just as all thought the worst part of the crisis was over, a new "storm center" emerged in the world economy — Greece was the representative case of the European sovereign debt crisis.[4]

Actually, as early as in October 2008, during the initial stage of the Wall Street financial turmoil, Northern European Iceland's sovereign debt issues had already surfaced before the debt crisis broke out in Central and Eastern Europe. However, as these were generally small national economies and there was prompt international aid, many problems were not fully exposed, thus larger global financial turbulence did not occur. It was only once the new Greek government came to power in 2009 when the fiscal deficit was significantly increased from the expected 6% to 12.7%, way higher than the 3% ceiling provisioned in the "Stability and Growth Pact",[5] and major credit rating agencies quickly downgraded Greece's sovereign debt ratings that the "tinderbox" was re-ignited. Due to the serious sovereign debt problems prevalent among the member of the Eurozone, the market began questioning Ireland, Spain,

---

[4] There were deeper reasons leading to the European debt crisis and there is no definite correlation between this and the US subprime mortgage crisis. Nonetheless, this article only focuses on painting the evolution and context of the global crisis. Therefore, this brief chronological review is given.

[5] The "Stability and Growth Pact" was enacted to ensure the stability of the Euro and prevent inflation in the Eurozone. The "Stability and Growth Pact" passed at the Summit in Amsterdam on June 17, 1997, stipulated that fiscal deficits of Eurozone governments should not exceed 3% of the gross domestic product (GDP) in the same year, and public debt should not exceed 60% of GDP. According to the pact, if a country's deficit exceeds 3% of its GDP for three consecutive years, the country is liable to be fined up to the equivalent of 0.5% of its GDP.

Portugal, Italy and other heavily indebted countries, bringing about the rapid spread of the debt crisis and global financial upheaval was set off once again.

As the debt crisis heated up, various short-term and long-term relief measures were subsequently launched. On May 2, 2010, the Eurozone kick-started the Greek rescue mechanism. Together with the IMF, the European Union (EU) and other Eurozone countries established a European Financial Stability Facility (EFSF) of up to 750 billion euros, to help those Eurozone member states in danger of falling into the debt crisis and prevent the spread of the Greek sovereign debt crisis. To further stabilize market confidence and strengthen fiscal discipline, after much deliberation, the EU also set up permanent mechanisms in response to the European sovereign debt crisis. They are mainly the European Stability Mechanism (ESM) and the Outright Monetary Transactions (OMT). Deterred by these measures and under pressure from the international community, EU members began to weigh up their "incentives" and "constraints". Most of the countries with excessive fiscal deficits rolled out clear deficit reduction plans and the European sovereign debt crisis was finally alleviated.

1.4 *Impact of the crisis and rescue measures*

The impact of the global financial crisis which broke out in 2008 was the greatest the world had seen in 100 years. First was the severe recession of the global financial industry. In late 2008, global stock market capitalization had fallen to almost half that of its peak, the notional value of financial derivatives had shrunk by nearly USD25 trillion.[6] Secondly, world trade and investment was severely hit. Global trade declined by 12.2% in 2009, with the decline of developed countries being particularly significant. In the same year, US exports fell by 17.9% while imports decreased 25.9%.[7] The UNCTAD's report also showed that cancellations of global M&A transactions increased year-on-year by 50% and transaction volume decreased by nearly a third in 2008, among which BHP Billiton gave up its USD147 billion acquisition of Rio Tinto, becoming the largest transaction revocation case in history; global Foreign Direct Investment (FDI) dropped from USD18.3 trillion in 2007 to USD12 trillion in 2009.[8] The economic slowdown of various countries seemed to synchronize especially in 2009. That year, world economic growth fell from

---

[6]Zhu Min, "Ten Major Changes in Global Financial Structure after the Crisis", China Finance 40 Forum, retrieved from http://www.cf40.com.

[7]According to WTO statistics.

[8]According to UNCTAD statistics.

1.3% in 2008 to −2.6% wherein developed economies dropped from zero growth to −4% and developing economies declined from 5.6% to 2.2%.[9]

The international community quickly launched a series of relief measures in response to the chain of negative effects brought on by the crisis. In the early onset of the crisis, the main response of the various countries was to inject liquidity into the market through measures such as bailing out the banks on the brink of bankruptcy to stabilize the financial markets and purchasing distressed debts to contain the negative impact. However, as the crisis broke out, the various assistance policies also shifted from the initial emergency and palliative measures targeting financial markets, to recovery and growth-oriented incentive measures to prevent further economic decline. Countries began to implement macroeconomic policies such as reduction of interest rates, Quantitative Easing, tax cuts, and increased government investment so as to stimulate economic development. In addition to the US government's massive USD700 billion financial rescue scheme, the Chinese government also introduced 10 measures in November 2008 to further expand domestic demand and promote stable and rapid economic growth. Other countries also committed to addressing their economic difficulties and outstanding issues by introducing crisis intervention packages. On the whole, the aid during this period of time was mainly provided independently by various nations.

Globalization brought about deepening interdependence amongst nations and the crisis this time occurred amid such a context. This is why a single country or region's rescue efforts are unable to affect a complete turnaround of the global recession and bring wide-ranged relief more rapidly. The developed economies at the center of the crisis took the lead in launching large-scale currency swaps among the central banks as a main form of financial cooperation. In April 2009, the US Federal Reserve signed bilateral currency swap agreements worth 30 billion pounds, 80 billion euros, 10 trillion yen and 40 billion Swiss francs with the Bank of England, the European Central Bank, the Bank of Japan, and the Swiss National Bank respectively.[10] Multilateral mechanisms such as the IMF, also provided loan assistance to some countries.[11] The G20 has also become an important platform for the international community to respond to the challenges of the crisis. The G20 held several leadership summits

---

[9] According to WBG statistics.

[10] "A Comparative Study on the International Financial Crisis and the Asian Financial Crisis", retrieved from http://gjs.mof.gov.cn/pindaoliebiao/diaochayanjiu/201108/t20110818_587338.html, accessed on August 27, 2013.

[11] For example, the relief aid given to Iceland.

where a number of political consensus and concrete initiatives in response to the crisis were successfully achieved.[12] For example, to tackle the broken chain in trade financing caused by the crisis and other global challenges, the WTO, Asian Development Bank (ADB) and the G20 London Summit have all introduced relevant proposals and measures to help enterprises, especially small and medium businesses which resist the exacerbated decline in exports due to commercial bank lending difficulties.

The implementation of these coordination efforts, assistance and support programs positively helped the world economy to go through the worst period of the crisis and restore market confidence. However, it should be noted that the main relief measures during the crisis were "symptomatic treatment" methods such as raising currency issuance, increasing government spending *etc*. Although they helped to prevent the "disease" from deteriorating, "every drug is toxic to a certain extent" and these measures also brought new risks to the world economy. At the same time, these emergency responses only helped to avert some deeper institutional, structural and regulatory problems temporarily, and had little effect on fundamentally fixing accumulated malpractices in the world economy.

2 Reflections on the Crisis

It has been more than five years since the crisis broke out in 2008. The initial shock has gradually waned and the world economy is back on the tortuous and slow path of recovery, but the impact of the crisis is still widespread. In particular, the exploration of the causes of the crisis is inevitably linked to the past 30 years of accelerated globalization and leads us to reflect upon many inherent theories, policies and practices.

2.1 *Root causes of crises from the economic cycle perspective*

Mankind has gone through several major economic crises since the 18th century. According to incomplete statistics, in the 212 years from 1788 to 2000, there have been 22 large-scale economic crises worldwide; the average cycle lasts about 10 years (see Table 1.1). The deep-seated reasons behind crises can be broadly classified into the following categories: surplus from relevant industries such as textile production, rapid investment development from

---

[12] The specific achievements and roles of the G20 Summits will be elaborated upon in subsequent chapters.

Table 1.1 Overview of major economic crises worldwide in the past 200 years.

No.	Year	Range of spread	Overview of causes and characteristics	Driving factors that helped economies overcome the crisis
1	1788	Britain	Rapid growth of cotton textile production led to oversupply, but limited to textile industry; small scale.	New markets (focusing on canals and waterways: Britain invested heavily in building new canals and inland waterways).
2	1793	Britain	Production capacity of the textile industry exceeded social spending power; 100 out of 400 local banks stopped issuing payments along with the onset of the banking crisis.	New markets (Britain exported textiles to America, destruction of war).
3	1797	Britain	Outflow of gold due to trade deficit, causing deflation and led to contraction in domestic demand.	New technology (textile machinery and technological progress, reduced costs, growing demand).
4	1810–1841	Britain	Lowered agricultural production led to decreased domestic demand, bursting the "false demand" bubble bolstered by credit.	Post-war recovery, once the wars in the US and Continental Europe were over, British exports to these two areas surged.
5	1816	Britain, the US, France, Germany	Caused by market saturation in Europe and the US; first overproduction of ferrous metallurgy and coal industries.	Public investment (first attempt of Keynesian theory in economic history, governments funded the construction of roads, bridges, ports and other infrastructure; monetary factors (purchase of foreign bonds, increasing their purchasing power for British goods).

(Continued)

Table 1.1 *(Continued)*

No.	Year	Range of spread	Overview of causes and characteristics	Driving factors that helped economies overcome the crisis
6	1819–1822	Britain, the US, France, Germany	Poor grain harvests, prices of raw materials from colonies increased, outflow of gold, contraction of domestic and international markets' demand again.	Monetary factors (providing loans to South America and increasing their purchasing power for British goods).
7	1825	Britain, the US, France, Germany	Growth in exports, promotion of investment and stimulate the price of raw materials; the previous plan to provide loans to South America so as to boost their import of British goods failed; machinery industry was seriously hit for the first time; Britain suffered a net loss of more than 10 million pounds in external debts.	New technologies (rise of the railway industry stimulated the upstream and downstream industries); monetary factors (export of capital to the US, boosting the US import of British goods). High grain yield (increased domestic demand).
8	1837–1843	Britain, the US, France, Germany	Excessive speculation in railway construction, sharp increase of construction costs, gains became losses; Bank of England controlled gold outflow, US credit tightened, British exports to the US fell by 2/3 from 1836 to 1837. The US also suffered heavy losses.	New technologies (reduction of railway construction and operating costs, rousing the new boom of railway construction; advancements in textile machinery and manufacturing technologies, reducing costs and expanding demand); new markets (opening up of Asian and African markets); monetary factors (providing loans to the US, Germany, increasing their exports to the UK).

9	1847–1850	Britain, the US, France, Germany	Saturation of external demand (for the UK), rise of bubbles in American railroad investment; French revolution broke out in Paris in February 1848, revolution also broke out in Berlin, Germany, in March 1848; In the US, other than metallurgy, the other areas began to grow independent of Britain.	New technologies (specialization of textile industry, improvement of steam engine technologies for the marine, telegraph and manufacturing industries); new markets (colonization, free trade opened up the developed markets); monetary factors (Californian and Australian gold mines).
10	1857–1858	Britain, the US, France, Germany, Russia	Burst of the speculative bubble, slow growth of workers' wages and income resulted in consumption and production imbalance. The prosperous period of 1854–1857 before the financial crisis was dependent on financial speculation.	New markets (expansion of China and India markets by military means); new technologies, new products (emergence of oil industry in the US; advancements in metallurgy and machinery manufacturing technologies, cost reduction, promotion of American railroad industry; British shipbuilding industry); monetary factors (discovery of Colorado gold mine and Nebraska silver mine).
11	1867–1868	Britain, the US, France, Germany, Russia	Prosperity led to excessive speculation and investment, oversupply of pig iron, spending power lower than production capacity. The financial crisis was the precursor.	New markets (end of Civil War, growth of US railroad demand); monetary factors (UK financing of US railroads boosted demand for British products).

(Continued)

Table 1.1 (*Continued*)

No.	Year	Range of spread	Overview of causes and characteristics	Driving factors that helped economies overcome the crisis
12	1873–1879	Britain, the US, France, Germany, Russia	Prosperity led to excessive speculation and investment, serious surplus in heavy industries, spending power less than production capacity; the financial crisis was the precursor, the Vienna Stock Exchange crisis set it off; cartels, trusts, syndicates and other monopolistic forms of organization developed during this period; since the 1873 crisis, the beginning and ending of crises in the US have steered the rise and fall of the world economy; prevalence of trade protection (the US, Germany).	New markets (US trade protection led to the relative increase of the domestic market; railways).
13	1882–1883	Britain, the US, France, Germany	Prosperity led to excessive speculation and investment, US railway construction ebbed, spending power lower than production capacity; the financial crisis was the precursor; large-scale development of US trusts throughout the railway, petroleum, sugar, meat, coal, wine and other industries; France also engaged in trade protection.	New technologies (revolution of US electrical industry, lights, telephone, trams, motors); new markets (rise of railroads again).

14	1890–1893	Britain, the US, France, Germany	Excessive investment, with the financial crisis as precursor.	New technologies (continued advancement of refining technology led to reduced cost and expanded scope of use of steel).
15	1900–1903	Britain, the US, France, Germany, Belgium	Triggered by the burst bubble of various states' investments in Russia.	New technologies (such as electricity, automobile, chemical); new markets (railroads).
16	1907–1908	Britain, the US, France, Germany	Financial speculation leading to unrealistically high commodity prices and accelerating the onset of the crisis.	Destruction of war (making armaments for World War I).
17	1929–1933	The entire capitalist world	Main cause being the imbalance between countries' investment and savings; imbalanced domestic investment and spending.	Destruction of war (World War II).
18	1957–1958	Britain, the US, Canada, Japan and various Western European countries	Under the Bretton Woods System, cost advantage of product trading was low due to high labor costs in the US, resulting in trade deficits and excess capacity.	Destruction of war (US preparation for Vietnam war); new markets (corporate equipment upgrades due to loan repayment; public investment (development of infrastructure).
19	1973–1975	The US, Britain, Canada, Japan and Western European countries	Surge in oil prices caused the sudden intensification of demand contraction, and overproduction occurred.	Public works (US expansionary fiscal policy).

(Continued)

Table 1.1 (*Continued*)

No.	Year	Range of spread	Overview of causes and characteristics	Driving factors that helped economies overcome the crisis
20	1980–1982	The US, Britain, Canada, Japan and Western European countries	The second oil crisis	War, political reform (cost reduction).
21	1990–1991	The US, Britain, Canada, Japan and Western European countries	Developed manufacturing industry shifted to developing countries, reduced welfare and wage cuts of workers in developed countries, relatively lowered global consumption and purchasing power, growing imbalance in consumption and production; Japan fell into a long-term recession henceforth.	Monetary factors (US supply and consumption modes).
22	2000	The US, Britain, Canada, Japan and Western European countries	Burst of the Internet technology bubble.	Monetary factors (US easing of monetary policies stimulated growth in consumption).

Source: Han Deqiang (2001), sorted by Gongdao Institute for Strategic Studies, retrieved from http://www.dajunzk.com/gongdao.pdf.

railway construction and other areas, accumulation of speculative bubbles from financial sectors *etc*. A crisis breaks out when these underlying structural risks are triggered by some specific factors (for example, reduced food production resulting from major natural disasters, huge fluctuations in oil prices set off by unexpected factors *etc.*).

Some Western economists conducted in-depth research from a technical point of view on these crises arising from the capitalist countries, and accordingly, proposed the "economic cycle theory" — including the 2–4 year Kitchin cycle, 9–10 year Juglar cycle, 15–20 year Kuznets cycle, 40–60 year Kondratieff cycle *etc*. Coherently incorporating previous views, Schumpeter further summarized with the long wave theory. He explained the occurrence of long-term economic fluctuations with the cycle impact of the emergence of major technological innovation clusters and the depletion of its technological revolutionary potential, and following Kondratieff's arguments, further divided the capitalist economic development before the 1950s into three "long waves".

According to the "long wave" theory, this global financial crisis marked the onset of the decline of the world economic development wave, and is a largely inevitable result of the adjustments in the long and mid-to-long economic cycles. The wave's climb period began in the 1980s, brought about by the scientific and technological revolution represented by IT and the Internet, and formed a new wave of global economic growth with an average annual growth of 6.3%,[13] higher than that of the mid-20th century. However, by the late 20th century, the steep upward trend of the economy began to show signs of declining. Particularly after the year 2000 with the diminishing effects of the information technology revolution and globalization dividends, the momentum of growth in the Western countries' real economy weakened and corporate profitability declined — these were in fact, the "prelude" to the crisis. After that, due to the implementation of the low interest policies, the "false prosperity" phenomenon brought by the virtual economy prolonged the spread but eventually, the burst of the financial asset bubble triggered by the subprime mortgage crisis completely destroyed the dream. Therefore, some foreign scholars point out that this crisis was just a delayed recession that occurred when the financial turmoil struck.[14] From this perspective, economic crises

---

[13] The average world economic growth from 1980–2007. *Source*: World Economic Outlook database, April 2013, IMF.

[14] Wessen, "The Current World Economic Recession according to Schumpeter's Theory of Business Cycles". Retrieved from http://www.aisixiang.com/data/32937.html, accessed on July 6, 2013.

seem to be "fated", with the only differences being the interval lengths, the degree of impact and the factors that led to their manifestation.

Furthermore, should mankind's economic and social development history be analyzed at a systemic level, crises seem to have already become an important part of the capitalist economic system. In his book *Das Kapital* Volume One, Marx said:

> Because of the irreconcilable contradiction between the social character of production and private appropriation, economic crises will inevitably occur periodically… The crises are always but momentary and forcible solutions of the existing contradictions. They are violent eruptions which for a time restore the disturbed equilibrium.

It is through this recurrent "boom-crisis-recession-depression-recovery" cyclical mode of operation that man, during crises, can forcefully get rid of the bubbles accumulated over the rapid development periods and achieves the necessary adjustments of the economy. Based on this theory, we are better able to reflect upon the many deep-seated structural problems accumulated over the new round of economic prosperity after the 1980s, including the detachment of the real economy and the virtual economy, absence of financial supervision, expansion of global imbalances, defects in governance structures *etc.* This has also become a different theoretical basis from which to analyze the specific reasons for the crises. If it is hard to resolve these deep-seated contradictions at a systemic level, then footholds have been left for the occurrence of the next crises.

2.2 Causes of the crisis from the perspective of lack of financial supervision

This crisis began from the US subprime mortgage market and the financial sector bore the brunt of the blame. For a long period of time after the crisis broke out, criticism of loose monetary policies, enquiries into derivative financial products and accusations of financial supervision oversight rolled out unendingly. For a while, "Wall Street" became synonymous with "the culprit" behind the crisis. Five years later, the initial radical rhetoric has gradually returned to rational thought. We have had to face the difficult question of "original sin" regarding finance — how should we look at the double-edged sword of finance? Exactly how should the balance between *laissez-faire* and supervision be struck?

Needless to say, since neoliberal economic theory took over Keynesian theory as the mainstream concept for decision-making in the mid-20th century, a direct consequence is expanding of the positive financial effects and the corresponding general relaxation of regulations. The US Federal Reserve has always believed that "minimal supervision is the best".[15] In the late 20th century, the US Congress repealed or amended a series of bills with the objective of removing separate operation and other strict controls of the financial industry, and even permanently abolished the Commodity Futures Trading Commission's regulatory powers on financial derivatives.

Together with the relaxation of the system came great financial development brought about by technical factors and globalization. A wide variety of new financial products emerged that on the one hand, sped up the flow of funds worldwide, and promoted the allocation of resources, while on the other hand, accrued various high risks because of asset securitization, high leverage and the lengthening of financial transaction chains. During this time, to prevent recession after the "9–11" incident, the US implemented long-term expansionary monetary policies, fueling the disorderly development of the subprime mortgage business and the swelling of highly leveraged investments such as subprime mortgage derivative products.[16] Relevant data showed that in 2000, the total value of global financial derivatives was USD100 trillion and by early 2007, it had jumped to USD516 trillion of which the US accounted for USD340 trillion while its real loans associated with the real economy were less than USD20 trillion.[17] Data from the Bank for International Settlements (BIS) showed that in the fourth quarter of 2007, the global financial derivatives market was worth up to USD600 trillion, 11 times the global GDP at that time, revealing the serious discrepancy between the virtual economy and the real economy.

The above-mentioned "absence of financial regulation" and "unruly financial innovation" coexisted for a long period of time, eventually turning the trading of financial derivatives into a "wild stallion" and led the global economy

---

[15] Cao Fengqi, "The Financial Crisis and Financial Regulatory System Reforms", retrieved from http://caofengqi.blog.caixin.com/archives/43777, accessed on August 12, 2013.

[16] From January 2001 to June 2003, the US Federal Reserve consecutively cut funds rate 13 times, causing interest rates to fall from 6.5% to a historical low of 1%.

[17] Li Xingshan, "Lessons from the US Financial Crisis, and Following the Path of Scientific Development Unswervingly", originally published in *Journal of China Executive Leadership Academy in Pudong*, retrieved from http://www.npopss-cn.gov.cn/n/2012/1127/c352530-19713042-2.html.

into a crisis after the bubble burst. Taking the direct cause of the crisis — subprime mortgages as an example, neither the US Federal Reserve Board nor the United States Securities and Exchange Commission were clear about which regulatory organization was to be held accountable. As such, there were jurisdiction overlaps and regulatory blind spots.[18] In the absence of regulation, financial derivatives became more and more complex in design, the real value of products, risks and other items became less transparent and the development of subprime loans and relevant derivative businesses went out of control. As the unruly financial derivatives market and the rapid expanding bubble in the US real estate market mutually and unrealistically boosted one another, a chain reaction was sparked when the bubble burst, leading to the meltdown and spread of the crisis.

The outbreak of the crisis led more people to reflect upon the relationship between financial innovation and financial regulation. The expansion of financial innovation undoubtedly puts forward higher requirements for financial regulation both domestically and internationally, but financial regulation is also not originally designed to impede or limit the expansion of financial innovation. Essentially, the question is how the relationship between virtual and real economies can be better handled. An important issue that affects the future direction of financial rules is how financial innovation and financial regulation can be better coordinated and developed unitedly in the dynamic game at play.

2.3 Crisis management and control from the perspective of global financial governance

In addition to the financial regulatory deficiencies mentioned previously, the crisis also revealed deep, structural problems in the international monetary system which can be traced back to the post-World War II Bretton Woods dollar-centric system. It should be acknowledged that the system was a major innovation in global finance and was effective in bringing stability and promoting economic recovery in the post-war financial environment. However, the smooth running of the system was dependent on strong US economic power with the stability of the US dollar, adequate gold and other reserves as prerequisites.

---

[18]Wang Zhijun and Hu Chunhua, "Observing the Development of Financial Innovation and Regulatory Coordination from the US Subprime Mortgage Crisis", *Hebei Finance*, Issue 9, 2012.

Eventually, due to the frequent incidence of oil crises and US economic crises as well as the inherent contradictions in this system, it collapsed in 1973. However, the disintegration of the Bretton Woods System did not resolve the fundamental problem of the global financial sector. The US dollar had lost its credibility and status, but as it was difficult to find a substitute, it remained as the main international reserve currency and was no longer subject to any institutional arrangements. In a system with such serious institutional flaws, the US dollar continued to be the essential tool to back the continual growth of the US economy. At the same time, because of its liquidity and stable value, the US dollar became the first choice currency for most developing countries in addressing balance of payments surpluses. As such, these developing countries had to become the "positive" force holding up the international monetary and financial system. Another aspect of this virtual economic cycle is reflected in the persistent accumulation of "global imbalances" in the real economy and the uneven distribution of benefits. On the surface, it seems that "global imbalances" are a "push factor" of the crisis, yet that is in fact, ignoring the real factors such as the anomalous and unreasonable international monetary system established after World War II. If no structural changes are made to this system, the deep-rooted issues in the global economy cycle will not be fundamentally resolved.

Other issues such as the improvement of global financial governance were also raised from there. Despite the rapid advancement of financial globalization over the past 30 years, global financial governance has developed at a much slower pace. Under the global financial governance structure set up after World War II, the IMF is responsible for international monetary affairs such as exchange rate arrangements and multilateral payments in respect of current transactions *etc*. The WBG on the other hand, is more focused on development aid as the main means of financial support, and the WTO multilateral trading system framework only promotes the openness and access of relevant members' financial markets. The risk regulation rules, standards and division of regulatory responsibilities after liberalization of the financial market are mainly drawn up by the Basel Committee and the International Organization of Securities Commissions (IOSCO) *etc.*, but when the rules are first introduced by these institutions, they are usually not legally sanctioned.[19] Although the IMF possesses a number of channel and technical advantages, it has been widely

---

[19] International Monetary Fund: Lessons of the Financial Crisis for Future Regulation of Financial Institutions and Markets and for Liquidity Management, February 2009.

criticized for its shortcomings such as harsh conditions and tardiness in responding to crises. The governance structure described above is unable to adapt to the needs of the times, and evidently in need of multilateral institutions and mechanisms dedicated to preventing and controlling international financial risks and crises.

Other financial governance and rule problems in practices were revealed after the crisis. For example, the relevant countries implemented "quantitative easing" policies several times in order to stimulate the economy, yet because of the strong position of their currencies, the implementation and pulling out of these policies both cause huge risks of fluctuations in the world economy. The resulting series of turmoil in the financial markets, inflation, international "currency wars" and their associated complications such as risk transfer, have already had or will soon have complex and profound influences on the world economy — and yet global financial governance is still lacking. This is undeniably a major flaw in the governance system and necessitates more attention and discussion.

The once-in-a-century economic crisis has caused many people to ponder its causes from different levels and angles. Apart from the three perspectives above, other deeper issues have become the focus of public thought and study. Is the current process of globalization sustainable? How much government interference is deemed reasonable in the market? Is the so-called liberal development model of capitalism facing new changes? Are people able to defuse crises with mutually beneficial collaborations, even radically reducing the incidence of crises and degree of harm through institutional frameworks? The exploration of these issues will continue to enrich our understanding of globalization and the world economy's development laws.

3 The Issues of Global Governance and Rule Reconstruction Proposed after the Crisis

Compared with previous economic crises in history, the outbreak of this crisis has two distinctive contextual characteristics: the rapid expansion of economic globalization, as well as the structural adjustment of global power represented by the collective rise of emerging economies. To some degree, these two characteristics were the product of the institutional framework and rules system established by post-World War II global governance. At the same time, the upheaval caused by both characteristics had also been quietly changing global governance itself such that the various rules that had constrained and controlled the global economy for a long time were faced with new challenges and demands.

The exacerbation of the crisis accelerated the urgency for such a change, and it became more imperative to deal with the issue of rules reconstruction.

3.1 *The development of globalization and global economic governance before the crisis*

Global economic governance follows the development of economic globalization to a large extent and gradually entered the history books. Economic historians usually regard the repeal of "Corn Laws" by Great Britain in 1846 as a symbolic event to mark the beginning of economic globalization. The old capitalist countries shifted from mercantilism to free trade policies, establishing the foundation of globalization on an ideological and theoretical level. From the second half of the 19th century to the early 20th century, the second industrial revolution was the driving force for Western developed countries to move into the heavy industries period represented by the iron and steel, petrochemicals, electronics, machinery and automobiles industries. Productivity received a new development boost. During this time, the tram, automobile, railroad, and steamship became new means of transport while the telephone, radio, and telegraph became the new modes of communication, greatly reducing the time and distance between people and laying the infrastructural foundation for the large-scale development of international trade. As Kevin H. O'Rourke *et al.* mentioned in the book *Globalization and History*, "By 1914, there was hardly a village or town anywhere on the globe whose prices were not influenced by distant foreign markets".[20] During this period, the economic relationships among the countries evolved from external contact in commodity trading to further integration of production and division of labor. The whole world began to embark on a process of global integration. But in general, whether in terms of concept or framework, global governance lags far behind in its practice of globalization and this is part of the reason for the outbreak of two successive world wars.

Before the middle of the 20th century, two world wars broke out in succession. These were setbacks for the development of economic globalization, but development did not stop progressing. After World War II, global governance structure was built up at all levels and gradually became more comprehensive so as to promote economic recovery and resolve the contradictions and frictions caused by increasingly close economic interactions among the countries. Especially in the field of economic governance, apart from some economic institutions under United Nations (UN), the international community

---

[20] Kevin H. O' Rourke and Teffrey G. Williamson, *Globlization and History: The Evolution of Nineteenth-Century Atlantic Economy.* (Cambridge: The MIT Press, 1999), :62.

strongly promoted the establishment of the IMF, the WBG and General Agreement on Tariffs and Trade (GATT)[21] and other institutions and mechanisms, forming the three pillars of the post-war global economic governance. In addition, the OECD, BIS and other institutions also bore some of the responsibilities. After entering the 1980s, a number of regional platforms such as Asia-Pacific Economic Cooperation (APEC) were launched one after another and they continued to explore new regional or global issues, putting forward their views. These different areas and levels of mechanisms formed the basic framework for the existing global economic governance.

The international economic coordination mechanism established after World War II mainly promoted a series of global rules which were conducive to economic recovery and growth. For example, GATT encouraged the trade integration process, the WBG worked diligently to facilitate regional development; UNCTAD contributed to relax global investment liberalization regulations, APEC pushed forward the integration process in the Asia-Pacific *etc*. These mechanisms and rules objectively created a stable and predictable environment for development, building the institutional foundation for the deepening of globalization and sustainable development of the world economy. Especially after the end of the Cold War, the neoliberal "Washington Consensus" was accepted widely by many developing countries. This further laid the policy theory and foundation for globalization. And the rapid development of scientific and technological revolution which relied mainly on computer and information technology, built up the technical reserves for globalization. Global trade and investment grew rapidly, catalyzed by such a series of system and technical factors and driven by the distribution of multinational companies worldwide. The world economy was closely-knitted as a body, and economic globalization has also entered a new period of expansion.

3.2 *New changes in global economic and trade pattern since the crisis*

As mentioned earlier, the post-World War II global governance system and trade rules were established based on the power struggle between the individual countries at that time, as well as international trade and investment development needs. But in the ever-expanding wave of globalization, profound changes were gradually underway especially with the increasing depth of the GVC, resulting in some new adjustment in the international trade and investment trends.

---

[21] Now known as WTO.

In global trade, the shares of developing countries in international trade showed accelerated growth. The percentage of goods export increased from 32% in 2002 to 44% in 2012 while the percentage of imports rose from 29% to 41%. The main reason behind this change in trading was the globalization of the manufacturing industry and value chain development, among which the East Asian region is a typical example. In addition, the emerging economies' increased investment in basic infrastructure, rise in per capita income and consumption structure were also factors of influence. In particular, with the sustained economic growth of emerging countries, the demand for most commodities such as resources, energy, some agricultural products and other large commodities continued to rise. Besides the increase in shares, many developing economies, including China, showed growing competitiveness in many of the mid- to low-end manufacturing industries, and even mid- to high-end manufacturing industries.

In the field of international investment, the role of developing economies in transnational investment also continued to rise. From the point of view of FDI inflow, the developing countries, including economies in transition, attracted more foreign capital than developed countries in 2010. Just the developing countries alone attracted more foreign investment than developed countries in 2012, changing the direct investment structure in which the developed countries were the main mutual investors before the crisis. The Asian developing countries and the Latin America and Caribbean regions especially thrived in the crisis and became the high points of attraction of foreign direct investment. Currently, they account for 28% and 14% of the global FDI inflows, respectively. In 2011, the FDI inflow of Southeast Asian countries grew by 26%, reaching USD117 billion. On FDI outflow, even though developed countries still accounted for 70% of global FDI outflow, the proportion of developing countries was still on the rise. One of the important factors was the increase in foreign investment from Brazil, Russia, India, China and South Africa or the BRICS countries. By the end of 2011, 42% of the foreign investment from BRICs countries was concentrated in developed countries and 43% went to their neighboring countries. Influenced by these changes, the major share of global service investment which had been dominated by developed economies for a long time, decreased by 10% in four years,[22] since the outbreak of the crisis while the primary sector and manufacturing investment supported by the emerging economies increased

---

[22] UNCTAD: World Investment Report 2012.

Table 1.2 International trade flow structure: unit %.

Exporting countries / Destination	Developed countries		Developing countries		Asian developing countries		American developing countries		African developing countries	
	2008	2011	2008	2011	2008	2011	2008	2011	2008	2011
Developed countries	72	68	47	43	42	38	63	59	65	56
Developing countries	24	28	51	55	56	59	35	39	34	43
Asian developing countries	16	19	41	45	49	52	11	17	20	28
American developing countries	5	6	6	6	3*	4	22	20	4	4
African developing countries	3	3	4	4	3	3	2	2	10	11

Source: UNCTAD.

Notes: (1) calculation based on UNCTAD data. For distribution of economies, refer to UNCTAD. (2) *denotes that 3% of the goods from Asian developing countries were exported to American developing countries in 2008, other data can also be interpreted similarly.

in proportion, they respectively rose from 8% and 41% before the crisis to 14% and 46% in 2011. Since the crisis, the scale of transnational mergers and acquisitions led by developed economies also began to shrink. In 2010, it recovered slightly but fell again by 41% to USD310 billion in 2012. In contrast, the proportion of transnational mergers and acquisitions by developing countries rose to 37% of the global figure, reaching a record high of USD115 billion. For the investing organizations, large multinationals were still significantly dominant, but the proportion of Sovereign Wealth Funds (SWFs) in FDI was evidently higher than that before the crisis. By the end of 2011, SWFs accumulated USD125 billion of foreign investment. This investment was still relatively very small in comparison to the USD5 trillion worth of assets, so there is still great potential for future development.

The above-mentioned change in international trade and investment pattern was attributed to the more salient point that the competitiveness of emerging economies in related fields was rising comprehensively, challenging the traditional developed economies on all fronts. Compared with the overall strength of different countries, the economic growth of emerging markets and developing economies was on average 5% higher than developed economies, increasing substantially from 39% to 45% of the world GDP from 2003 to 2008. After the crisis, there was significant differentiation in economic acceleration among different countries while the balance of power continued to narrow rapidly. In 2012, the GDPs of the world's major economies were: Europe 19.4%, US 18.9%, China 15%, India 5.7%, Japan 5.6%, Russia 3%, Brazil 2.9%.[23] Among them, those of Europe, US and Japan continued to decline. China, India, Russia and Brazil have increased and in 2012, India surpassed Japan for the first time, becoming fourth in the world. The continual development of the balance of power and trade structure also prepared the ground for global trade rules reconstruction (see Table 1.2).

3.3 *Problems with global economic governance and rules reconstruction arisen after the crisis*

There were many challenges to global governance and rules and the symptoms had begun to show before the crisis. However, the outbreak of the financial crisis in 2008 highlighted the issues of economic governance. Both developed and developing economies lobbied to consolidate and strengthen their competitive advantage. They fought over the modification and improvement of future

---

[23] If there is no special description, the data comes from IMF.

economic and trade rules. Overall, the current economic governance structures and rules are faced with the following three questions, to say the least.

First, the governance structure — how can changes in the power structure be reflected proactively?

The first challenge that the outbreak of 2008 financial crisis posed to the existing system of global governance was — how changes in the global economic landscape could be reflected in a more balanced manner.

Needless to say, there were some new signs in the global economic governance mechanism after the crisis. On the one hand, the G20 rose quickly from an unknown ministerial-level dialogue mechanism to the frontline of crisis coordination, and was elevated as a leadership summit. Moreover, it was considered to be broadly representative because it encompassed more than two thirds of the total global population and 85% of the world's total GDP. On the other hand, emerging economies sought more involvement in international affairs, especially in the global governance system, through strengthened cooperation. During the BRICS New Delhi Summit in 2012, the establishment of the "BRICS Development Bank" was proposed. The Durban Summit in 2013 discussed the establishment of the "Contingent Reserves Arrangement" (similar to the BRIC Fund) *etc*. These moves showed that emerging economies have begun to seek cooperation beyond the original system, to gain authority in rule-making, and influence that are aligned with and match their strength and power. At the same time, there were some adjustments in the traditional governance platform. For example, the IMF proposed to increase the share of 54 countries in its reform, placing Brazil, Russia, India and China among the top 10 shareholders, while increasing the decision-making rights of the low-income countries on the Executive Board *etc*. Although the US Congress opposed the change and the share distribution was not passed at the end, there were some signs of positive change.

On the whole, the authority and dominance of the developed economies on the existing global governance and rules system has not changed. No significant and substantial adjustment has been made even after the crisis. There are many deep-rooted factors that led to such a situation like the absolute gap between economic powers and poorer countries, as well as differences in soft power, such as deep-set institutional differences and intellectual reserves *etc*. Take for example, agenda-setting power, the topics of discussion at the G20 and APEC such as global economic imbalance, climate change, financing, liberalization of environmental goods and services *etc*., embody the interests of developed countries whereas developing countries are often stuck in the passive state of struggling to respond, highlighting the serious imbalance in soft power.

In the future, the global governance mechanism must find a new balance between the Western dominance and change in power structure, so that the governance structure can achieve new breakthroughs in fairness, transparency, accountability and so on. While participating in various areas of coordination and decision-making, the developing countries at large should seek to possess shares and rights that match their economic power, and strengthen their voice in decision-making in the international system. In terms of practical needs, improvement in global governance is inseparable from better cooperation between the traditional developed economies and emerging economies. Emerging economies also need to provide public goods aligned with their strength in the future global governance framework, to promote the building of a more efficient, fair and sound governance framework. There is no doubt that greater commitment, a willingness to compromise and innovative thinking is needed from all parties in order to properly deal with the above-mentioned challenges.

Second, the system of rules — how can the differing economic and trade interests and demands be balanced?

As previously mentioned, the many structural changes in global trade and investment caused significant differences between the interest demands of traditional developed economies and emerging economies. The former felt that the emerging economies are beneficiaries of the last round of globalization and rules system, so on the one hand they required the latter to assume greater international responsibility and introduce a wider range of open initiatives. On the other hand, they made use of the new rules to regulate and even "restrict" the development of the latter, in order to better maintain and strengthen their competitive advantage. For the latter, on the one hand they did not want to remain in a passive position, hoping to participate in the process of new rules adjustment with a more constructive attitude. Yet at the same time, they did not want to undertake the so-called "international responsibility" imposed by the developed economies and be obliged to bear "constraint conditions" higher than their development and competitive level.

These differences that stemmed from interest demands resulted in chaotic discussion about rule-making platforms and rules from the time of the crisis. Rule dominance, geopolitical and economic interests are all factors behind the stagnation of the multilateral trading system and faster regional integration process. In the recent years, on the rapidly growing regional economic integration platform, discussion topics have already gone beyond the traditional trade areas, into areas such as increasingly diverse investment, intellectual property, competition policy, environment, labor, state-owned enterprises, and other trade and "pan trade" areas, reflecting new ideas and demands of developed economies to different degrees. For example, with regard to investment rules, the US and Europe jointly developed "Shared Principles for International Investment" in 2012 and promised to implement the seven principles of open and non-discriminatory investment policies, including pre-establishment national treatment and a negative list, competitive neutrality, labor, environmental protection, safety review, settlement of investment disputes and other new issues. This indicated that the developed economies shared a common philosophy of having many rules, and gave them competitive advantage over others in the fields of intellectual property and service trade. Concerning this, developing economies need to draw lessons from reasonable rules so as to better facilitate their reform and development. On the other hand, there are also various explicit and implicit obstacles with regard to fully accepting the above-mentioned rules and being constrained by the systemic framework and stage of development; this will not take place overnight. It can be predicted that in the future, the discussions surrounding these rules will be intense and complexly competitive. The search for a rule system that is able to balance various interests demands, an efficient, fair and equal institutional framework which really promotes the development of all countries, will be a major issue that economic globalization has to face in the future in order to continue developing in depth.

Thirdly, innovation of ideas and agenda-setting and creation — how can the new and ever-changing demands of governance be met?

As more countries with different social systems, development levels and cultures are being incorporated into the global economic system, a variety of new contradictions and problems are successively arising, therefore the concept, object and subject of global governance philosophies are faced with new challenges. From the economic point of view, the post-World War II neoliberal theory had been in supportive stance for a long time. The essence of this theoretical foundation was to loosen the power of capital so that countries could reach a compromise in the capital battle, such that the power of capital enters self-regulation state of governance. However, it was precisely this over-confidence in the market that resulted in the excessively "loose" implementation which eventually led to the crisis.[24] This is why the economic

---

[24] Yao Lu and Liu Xuelian, "Development of New Trends in Global Governance during Post-crisis era", *Foreign Theoretical Trends*, Issue 8, 2013.

basis of the neoliberal concept was questioned after the crisis. Arising from this, there was also a dilemma between equality and efficiency in global economic governance. Although globalization has brought considerable benefits, whether internationally or domestically, the "profit" or "cost" of globalization in different industries, groups or regions is not equal. Pessimists even fear that globalization may become a process that is uncontrollable by any country or organization, resulting in global wealth polarization, and ultimately dragging the whole world into economic crisis.[25] The new concept of global governance needs to be reconstructed to respond to the basic questions mentioned above.

The issues that global governance and rule reconstruction dealt with were related to more and more new areas from traditional trade, investment, finance to macroeconomic coordination and trade-associated environment, ecology, resources, climate and other "pan trade" fields. With the expansion of GVCs as an example, the global spread of different enterprises engaged in design, product development, manufacturing, marketing, delivery, consumption, after-sales service, and finally recycling and other value-added activities greatly deepened the dependency of various national economies, bringing about enormous changes in the nature and trend of global trade, inspiring all sectors to call for adjustments to the international trade statistical system based on traditional production divisions and economic boundaries. New directions and trends on intellectual property, trade remedy and the environment *etc.* have also emerged as various countries move toward encouraging innovation and green development as the main direction to increase competitiveness. The ability of the global economy and trade, and the agenda-setting and institutional arrangements of its related fields, to deal with these increasingly prominent global challenges directly affect the vitality of the relevant rules. It is foreseeable that the discussions today may be transformed into a new consensus for tomorrow, forming more complete and conclusive new rules to impact the global development profoundly in a future era. Observing the voices from different platforms closely, especially the new changes in economic trade rules across a range of professional fields, and providing independent and forward-looking analysis and opinions, undoubtedly help us to have accurate insight into the future development trend of economic globalization. This is what we will explore in the following chapters.

---

[25] Hans Martin and Harald Schumann, *The Globalization Trap* [M] (Beijing: Central Compilation and Translation Press, 1998), pp. 153–161.

Chapter 2

G20 and New Developments of the Global Governance Platform

On the morning of November 15, 2008, the G20 Summit officially began in the National Building Museum in Washington DC, in the US. This was a time when the international financial market had been devastated and was unpredictable. People were hopeful for the success of the summit but they were not without doubts.

Ten days before the G20 Summit, the Democratic Party candidate, Barack Obama, was elected as the US president. The host of the conference, President George W. Bush, was about to step down. It was said that he was a "lame duck" host by then and there were people who joked that Bush did not even know what nations the G20 consisted of a few weeks before the summit. However, according to what Bush wrote later in his memoir *Decision Points*, it was revealed that the conference was held because he had proposed the idea over the phone to the French President at that time, Nicolas Sarkozy, but Sarkozy had only intended to hold a G8 Summit for leaders.

Naturally, the 20 member-countries participating in the summit were thinking of their own interests. The US, being the country where the crisis originated, and the one hardest hit by it, hoped to reach a consensus of collective interventions through the conference while President Sarkozy and British Prime Minister Gordon Brown jointly proposed the establishment of a new Bretton Woods System — an effort to push for the "abdication" of the American "boss". The most striking development was the emerging market countries that had just taken center stage. They had been hovering around the center of global governance for so many years, why then should they provide money to help alleviate the difficulties of the older developed countries?

But who would expect the seemingly makeshift G20 Summit to continue to become the main platform and discussion forum for global economic governance in subsequent years? Regardless of the positive or negative media comments, being named "tower of strength", "indecisive, good for nothing" *etc.*, its existence has already proven its necessity.

1 The Rise of G20 Cooperation

From the point of view of traditional western political science, the world is anarchic in its natural state. Each individual may be threatened. War is a norm. To get out of this state of endless troubles, mankind has not only established nations and their governance institutions, "government", based on tribal society, but also set up some kind of international governance system as production developed. The early age of empires is a kind of governance model in which one country rules with sovereign power. In modern times, especially after a number of major world wars, treaties are often signed to identify major global or regional systems or arrangements to form a power-distribution-based governance model. Such arrangements aim to prevent wars from recurring and/or winning parties from forming a strong position in governance. For example, after the Thirty Year War in Europe, the Westphalian system was established in 1648; in the early 1800s after the collapse of Napoleon's empire, the victors led by Britain, Russia, Austria, Prussia (Cyrus), established the Vienna system in the European continent through the Vienna Congress; after World War I, the Allies, also known as Entente Powers, established the Versailles system through the Treaty of Versailles. After World War II, the political and economic relations that major countries had with each other became more intertwined globally, and national interests increasingly clashed. Mankind reflected and sought solutions as the tragedies and consequences of war continued to unfold in modern history; the true meaning of global governance was hence, birthed in the process. Although the Yalta system marked the two camps of the East-West divide, the international community ultimately established the UN organization which has more authority than the sovereign states, forming relatively stable global governance. In the economic sphere, the Bretton Woods System is an important part of the global governance model. Since the birth of this system, it has faced constant challenges, reform and innovation. With further improvement in economic globalization and regional economic integration, the deficiencies of global economic governance have been exposed even more and the need for answers has become more urgent. Of course, contradictions may intensify and sudden changes may happen though the probability is still small at the moment.

1.1 *Post-war organizational system of global economic governance*

After World War II, the two camps of the US and the Soviet Union were formed. In response to the threat of the Marshall Plan, the Soviet Union created the Council for Mutual Economic Assistance (Comecon or CMEA). But it was unable to change the US' leadership position in the world. In July 1944, the US led the "United Nations Monetary and Financial Conference" in Bretton Woods in New Hampshire. The participants agreed to establish two major international financial institutions, the International Monetary Fund and the Word Bank Group, to manage the global financial and monetary system. In February 1945, during the Yalta meeting, the Allies led by the US, the Soviet Union, Britain, France and China agreed to initiate the establishment of the UN. On October 24, 1945, the UN was formally established with the five countries as the permanent members of the UN Security Council. On December 27, 1945, the IMF and the WBG were formally established. The former was responsible for giving short-term loans of funds to member states, with the purpose to protect the stability of the international monetary system; the latter provided long-term credit to promote economic recovery in the member states. The IMF and the WBG were specialized agencies under the UN but they had strong autonomy. On October 30, 1947, in Geneva, the US and 23 other countries signed the GATT which did not have international legal status. It was responsible for the coordination of multilateral trade matters. In 1995, GATT was changed to the internationally legislative WTO. The IMF, the WBG, the GATT/WTO constituted the three pillars of the global economic governance system. The three pillars played very important roles in promoting post-war economic recovery, maintaining the relative stability of international trade, monetary and financial systems, contributing to maintain the prosperity and stability of the post-war global economy as a whole, and keeping the peace and development of the world. For over 60 years, there were no major disruptive events affecting the three pillars. The biggest change in the international monetary system was that it moved from being US dollar-centric, when Bretton Woods which implemented the fixed exchange rate system collapsed, to the Jamaica system where the fixed exchange rate regime and floating exchange rate regime coexist. The Soviet Union system ultimately collapsed due to the failure to follow the market economy rules.

Besides international organizations, global economic governance had another important structure: international forums. These forums formed the consensus documents such as official reports, declarations *etc.* at the country leadership levels. They demonstrated the will of the great powers and had major influence and practical significance in the setting and revision of rules of international organizations. The Group of Seven (G7) formed by developed countries, which then evolved into the Group of Eight (G8), had played such a role for a long time and became an important tool for influencing the global economy and directing global trade rules for the past 30 over years. In addition, there are some regional forums that have an impact on global economic governance.

1.2 *The need for existing global economic governance mechanisms to improve*

Although the global economic governance formed by the UN and three economic pillars, the IMF, the WBG and the WTO, were relatively complete, deficiencies emerged continuously with the expansion of globalization, collective rise of the emerging market countries and greater difficulty in coordinating global economic policies.

The focus of the UN was on political, security and other issues. It had little influence in the economic field and was unable to take the lead in dealing with the new challenges in globalization. Especially with the international financial crisis in 2008, the UN and its related agencies failed to respond quickly and effectively.[1] UN Deputy Secretary-General, Sha Zukang believes that UN principles which treated sovereign states equally and were widely inclusive, delayed the decision-making process to some extent. In order to strengthen the role of the UN, it had to be reformed.[2] On the other hand, although the IMF, the WBG and other institutions were specialized agencies of the UN, the UN did not have much power in coordinating the organizations and there were even mutual constraints. The UN did not take the leadership role it should have taken.

Different circles questioned the role of the IMF as the core of the international financial and monetary system, especially in the time of international financial crisis which led to deep reflection on IMF functions. Firstly, it was based on the concept of a free market economy in Western countries ("Washington Consensus"). The IMF did not pay enough attention to or effectively supervise how the excessively financed and leveraged virtual economy was so seriously out

---

[1] Jin Biao, "New challenges facing the United Nations and Global Governance", *Journal of University of International Relations*, Issue 4, 2011, pp. 54–55.

[2] Sha Zukang, "Exercising the Role of the UN in Global Economic Governance", *Review of Economic Research*, No. 49, 2011, p. 13.

of sync with the real economy. The financial crisis was triggered by the exaggerated US financial innovations and highly leveraged bank operations. Secondly, there were different standards used on developing and developed countries. When receiving assistance from the IMF, developing countries were often forced to accept harsh and inflexible economic conditions, but loan conditions were relatively relaxed for some developed countries. Thirdly, the IMF, in general, maintained the US dollar as the international reserve currency and was limited in the establishment of a pluralistic and rational international monetary system, and creating super-sovereign currencies reserve. Fourthly, the IMF focused on economic risk of individual countries and did not sufficiently monitor and give early warnings with regard to global systemic risk. Fifthly, the governance structure and share allocation of the IMF did not fully reflect the share of emerging markets and developing countries in the world economy. The representation and actual economic strength of developing countries was not proportionate.

The WBG also received a lot of criticism, largely because developing countries lacked representation and influence in WBG. Many of the WBG's actions were influenced by the major developed countries so their policies often tended towards the interests of those countries. In general, the WTO played a positive role in maintaining the trade system and curbing protectionism. However, the negotiations in Doha could not progress, causing much pessimism about the prospects of a multilateral trading system.

On the global forum level, the G7 and G8 have always faced a problem of insufficient representation. With the rise of emerging market communities, the G8 which accounted for about 65% of the world economy in the mid-1990s of the 20th century, has gradually declined to less than 50% currently. It has already had difficulties directing global economic affairs. In order to expand its representation, the G8 Summit began to invite some emerging markets to participate beginning in 2003. In 2005, five countries, namely China, India, Brazil, Mexico and South Africa, were regularly invited to participate, forming the "G8+5" dialogue mechanism. But there was no equal participation in the "G8+5" dialogue as western nations hoped that the emerging countries could accept western rules and international responsibility through the dialogues. Emerging markets considered that this way of discussing global issues did not adequately reflect their status and influence. Faced with the sudden international financial crisis, the G8 had difficulties coming up with a holistic response plan. It was even harder for other regional international forums to coordinate effectively at the global level to overcome the crisis and propose remedies. A more influential and representative global governance platform was primed to emerge from this situation.

1.3 *The birth of the G20 summit mechanism in the international financial crisis*

In September 2008, the outbreak of the international financial crisis became the greatest economic turmoil since the Great Depression in the last century. Western countries recognized that it was difficult to pull themselves out of the world economic crisis on their own and it was necessary for the major emerging markets to come together to weather the financial crisis. At this time, the developing countries including the emerging markets had already more than four trillion US dollars in foreign exchange reserves and accounted for about 40% of global exports. They were a new force to stabilize the global financial situation and maintain economic growth. Meanwhile, Western countries also believed that the underlying cause leading to the international financial crisis was the global economic imbalance. Emerging markets have become the main countries with global payment surplus while the Western powers became countries with long-term deficits. Therefore, the Western powers pulled together the emerging markets to deal with the crisis payment and jointly negotiated the problem of structural imbalance. However, there were discrepancies in solving the global economic problem together.

With the above-mentioned as the backdrop, President Bush proposed to hold the G20 Summit with the existing G20 finance ministers and central bank governors to discuss the response to the international financial crisis and improve the reform of the relevant international organizations and other issues. As the original designer and leader of the global economic system, the US experienced first-hand the deficiencies of this system. It therefore recognized the need to build a new system with the participation of emerging markets in order to respond more effectively to new global challenges. In 2008, the US first advocated the G20 Summit after the global financial crisis, hoping "to inject new system philosophies into the old system", thereby maintaining the form and function of the major international institutions with the G20 giving political leadership and governance in these institutions, while including emerging markets in the range of governance.[3] The US also targeted European countries in some ways although the US and Europe are allies. In the areas of globalization of the financial industry, status of the dollar and euro in reserve currencies, macroeconomic policy formulation and other issues, the two sides disputed over obvious conflicts of interest. Of course, the US did not abandon

---

[3] Yang Jiemian, "The Transformation Options and Prospects of G20", *International Studies*, No. 6, 2011, p. 52.

the G8 but continued to discuss the core issues of political, security and development at the G8 Summit, which kept up the relationship between the allies of the US and Europe.

With regard to the US' proposal, each country and international organization had their own opinion.

The European countries had helped push for the reform of the G8 mechanism. It was at the G8 Summit that French President Nicolas Sarkozy proposed the convening of the G14 with the inclusion of some emerging market countries, but hoped that European countries could have greater agenda-setting authority. Therefore, the European countries were in a dilemma with regard to the G20. They recognized the development in emerging markets but were worried about the decline of their role and influence. Meanwhile, within the EU, other countries were in the same boat, having differing opinions, but the attitude of the EU headquarters was quite positive.

The global influence of Japan and Canada was relatively weak, but because they are members of the G8, they have been among the key decision-makers in global affairs. However, after the establishment of the G20 Summit, the status of the two countries has been overtaken by emerging markets which were mainly Brazil, Russia, India and China or the BRIC countries. Therefore, Japan and Canada were the major supporters of the "G8 revival".

High-income middle powers such as Australia and Korea were mostly allies of US but not members of the G8. After establishing the G20, these countries were accepted in the circle to participate in global economic governance. They have actively participated in various cooperation efforts in the G20 and promoted the institutionalization of the G20.

Representatives of emerging markets like Brazil, Russia, India, China, South Africa (BRICS countries) cherished the historic opportunity to join the global economic governance center so they generally advocated for the positive functioning of the G20. They called for greater representation and voice of the emerging markets and upheld the interests of emerging markets and developing countries in collaborations. At the same time, they were also concerned about taking on more responsibilities and being more restricted in the international regime.

More than 150 countries outside the G20 still feared that their fate would be directed by dominant powers; therefore they still questioned the legitimacy of the G20 and hoped the UN would play a greater role.

The G20 is a new system set up by the US under the guise of the old system. The IMF, the WBG, the Basel Committee, the Financial Stability Board (FSB) and other international agencies are the stakeholders or even beneficiaries of the G20 Summit mechanism. All of them have actively advocated the strengthening of this mechanism. The IMF got new resources, power and missions from the G20 Summit mechanism so it was able to continue and even expand its range of influence. The WBG also progressed in resources and organizational reforms. The WTO was also a beneficiary of the G20 and continued to sustain the Doha negotiations by holding on to the political commitment given by the G20 Summit leaders, and received the authority to oversee global protectionist measures too. The attitude of the UN towards the G20 was more complicated. The G20 Summit mechanism posed a challenge for the status and role of the UN. As the topics for G20 discussion grew, the functions of the UN were further narrowed. On several occasions, UN Secretary-General Ban Ki-moon proposed that the summit be held at UN Headquarters but there was no response from others. However, the UN recognized the progressiveness of the G20 mechanism on the whole, and hoped to use this new platform to promote its moral superiority and strengthen its position so that, the two would be mutually complementary through cooperation rather than have the UN be replaced by the G20.[4]

Although there were differing viewpoints from various parties, as the US actively advocated for it and in the face of the severe global financial crisis, the original ministerial mechanism where only finance ministers and central bank governors participated was upgraded to a national leaders' summit mechanism. The G20 members consisted of the G8 countries (US, Japan, Germany, France, Britain, Italy, Canada, and Russia) and 11 key emerging markets (China, Argentina, Australia, Brazil, India, Indonesia, Mexico, Saudi Arabia, South Africa, Korea and Turkey) as well as the EU. Under the G20 Summit mechanism, there were two main channels: Sherpa meetings, and finance minister and central bank governor meetings, as well as the growth framework working group, development working group and various other small groups. Depending on the issues, relevant ministerial meetings were organized by host countries selectively without fixed regularity. In fact, the G20 effectively integrated the two wheels of global governance because the G20 was the international forum with more participating countries than the G8, so there was more economic policy coordination across a wider range of countries, and at the same time, the political promises made had greater representation among relevant international bodies, hence it could promote substantive reform of the relevant international organizations more easily. Thus, global economic governance entered a new phase with "G8 + 5" dialogues becoming the G20 Summit.

---

[4] Yang Jiemian, "The Transformation Options and Prospects of G20", *International Studies*, No. 6, 2011, pp. 53–54.

2 Main Conditions of Previous G20 Summits

2.1 *Unity at the Washington Summit*

In November 2008, the G20 Summit was held for the first time in Washington. The members reached a consensus on the origin of the financial crisis, the strengthening of cooperation to oppose trade protectionism, the support of economic growth and other issues. The "Washington Declaration" proposed the universal principles of financial market reform where an agreement was reached on strengthening transparency and accountability, reinforcing prudent supervision, promoting integrity in the financial market, reforming international financial institutions and so on. The "Washington Declaration" also promised to avoid setting up new barriers to investment or trading of goods and services in the next 12 months. This was the first time that the international community made a collective commitment to oppose trade protectionism.

The focus of the Washington Summit was to explore the root cause of the financial crisis. The US and other developed countries had different views from the emerging markets. The main difference was whether the US financial regulatory issues or the imbalance between developed and emerging markets had led to the financial crisis. The developed countries were also arguing amongst themselves. German Chancellor Angela Merkel had bluntly criticized the "greed, speculation and mismanagement" of the US as the root cause of the crisis, for which Bush retorted, "But many European countries had much more extensive regulations, and still experienced problems identical to our own." To enable the emerging countries to work together with the developed countries to respond to the economic crisis, the US did not amplify the argument at the summit but admitted that the direct cause of this financial crisis was inadequate financial supervision. Therefore, the main outcome of the summit was a consensus to put in effort to increase demand in response to the crisis, strengthen financial regulations and reform the international financial system. On one hand, the summit reflected that the US was willing to compromise. On the other hand, the participating countries actively adopted expansionary monetary policies after the summit, which reflected the responsibility of the countries. The emerging markets especially began to proactively assume international responsibility.

2.2 *Mutual assistance at the London Summit*

In April 2009, the second G20 Summit was held in London. The "Global Plan for Recovery and Reform" was adopted by the G20 leaders at this summit.

The meeting proposed to take all necessary measures to restore confidence, economic growth and job opportunities, recovering the financial system to give loans again and strengthening financial regulations to rebuild trust. Increasing the capital of international financial institutions and reforming them went together, thus promoting global trade and investment, and opposing protectionism. The leaders agreed to provide funds totaling USD1.1 trillion for the IMF, the WBG and other multilateral financial institutions; the need for regulations of all financial institutions, products and markets with systematic implications was raised. For the first time, it was proposed that hedge funds be put under financial supervision.

There were two focuses at the London Summit. One was the issue of financing; the other was the issue of the continuation of expansionary policies. With regard to the issue of financing, the London Summit reached an unprecedented financing arrangement for international financial institutions. The available resources to the IMF was doubled and increased to USD750 billion. The member states provided USD250 billion for emergency financing then increased the capital to USD500 billion in the new loan arrangements. There was support to increase USD250 billion in Special Drawing Rights (SDRs) and help for multilateral development banks to give at least USD100 billion of additional loans. At the same time, to facilitate trade development and boost global economic recovery, the summit decided to provide USD250 billion in the next two years to support trade finance through export credit, investment agencies and the multilateral development banks. To fulfill this financing agreement, developed and emerging markets assumed their funding responsibilities. There were many rounds of intense discussion before the summit but all parties showed a collaborative spirit during the summit and the shirking of responsibilities was not as severe as originally expected.

The countries were doubtful if they should continue executing expansionary policies with the moderation of the international financial crisis. The countries that had discontinued expansionary policies earlier were particularly unsure because they might have benefitted from the outflow of increased demand from other countries' implementation of expansionary policies. The summit was successful in unifying the direction of policies, coordinating all parties to agree to continue using expansionary monetary policies, and promoting economic recovery and employment.

In addition, the countries agreed to establish a unified global regulatory framework with high standards to strengthen the financial regulations, and set up a functionally stronger FSB. They agreed to accept China and other emerging markets as members of the FSB, and allow emerging markets a greater voice in the international financial system.

2.3 *Institutional building at the Pittsburgh Summit*

In September 2009, the third G20 Summit was held in Pittsburgh. There were not many successes during the summit but the important decisions made had great long-term impact, achieving major breakthroughs in the institutionalization of the G20 Summit organization and governance structure reforms of international financial institutions.

In terms of rules and systems, the summit in Pittsburgh formally recognized the G20 as the main forum for international economic cooperation and the summit was systemized. On issue of separating the G20 and the G8, emerging markets insisted that the G20 Summit should not be held in the same country as the G8 Summit and that new rules on organizing the summit should be established. Some of the G8 countries were unsure about this idea but they still hoped that the two summits could be linked. Finally, the G20 Summit was formally separated from the G8 Summit, becoming the main mechanism for emerging market economies to participate in decision-making of global economic affairs.

With regard to the governance structure reform of international financial institutions, the summit clearly stated that the target of the IMF and the WBG was to transfer shares and voting rights to developing countries. The IMF should transfer 5% of the shares from countries with overvalued shares to countries with undervalued shares. The WBG should increase voting rights by at least 3% for developing countries.

The summit also formulated the "G20 Framework for Strong, Sustainable and Balanced Growth", clarifying that the G20 members have the responsibility to adopt policies to achieve strong, sustainable and balanced growth, building a resilient international financial system to become a main framework for promoting balanced global economic development and structural reforms.

2.4 *The target of debt and deficit reduction at the Toronto Summit*

In June 2010, the fourth G20 Summit was held in Toronto, Canada. This summit was the first meeting after the G20 was recognized as the main international economic forum during the summit in Pittsburgh. The meeting was held during a period of weak recovery of the world economy. There was more emphasis on stabilizing the economic situation due to the European debt crisis.

The focus of this summit was to develop the goals of financial consolidation. The summit requested advanced economies to commit to at least halving their deficits by 2013, stabilizing or reducing the proportion of government debt to GDP by 2016. The development of these quantified goals for European countries played a catalytic role in deficit reduction and set the foundation to prevent the European debt crisis from getting out of control. However, the effect of this indicator was not obvious for the US and Japan. In addition, the financial consolidation targets were mainly for developed countries, while developed countries felt that that there was no form of effective control in terms of balanced growth for emerging markets. This laid a foundation for trouble in external balance for emerging markets in the future.

The summit had a number of important achievements, including the implementation of reform in international financial institutions. The summit endorsed the important voice reforms agreed by shareholders at the World Bank. Developed countries transferred 3.13% of the total voting rights to developing countries, making their cumulative voting rights higher by 4.59% since 2008. With regard to trade issues, the commitment not to take on new trade protectionist measures was extended by three years.

At the same time, more contradictions and differences between the members were exposed at the summit, including those between America and Europe. During the summit, the EU and European countries pushed for the collection of financial tax, but the US wanted to maintain its bank competitiveness and resolutely opposed the idea. The summit failed to reach a final agreement on the financial tax issue.

2.5 *The upholding of a development agenda at the Seoul Summit*

In November 2010, the fifth G20 Summit was held in Seoul, Korea. The conference adopted the "G20 Seoul Summit Leaders' Declaration", "Seoul Summit Achievement Paper", "Seoul Development Consensus for Shared Growth" among other documents.

The important outcome of this summit was its focus on development issues. The summit adopted the "Seoul Development Consensus" and the multi-year action plan. This was the first time that the G20 Summit raised "development" as one of the topics for the meeting, and determined nine key areas — infrastructure, human resource development, trade, private sector investment and job creation, food security, resilient growth, financial inclusion, domestic resource mobilization and knowledge sharing in the multi-year action plan.

During the summit, the arguments on hot topics from different parties were even more outstanding. They were mainly reflected in issues like external balance and exchange rates. China was also involved in the heat of the debate. On currencies, the developed countries requested a clear "avoidance of undervalued exchange rates", referring to the Chinese Yuan. Eventually after much debate, this was classified as "avoidance of competitive devaluation". On balanced growth, the US proposed the quantification of the absolute value of current account balance as less than 4% of gross domestic product (GDP). China believed that the government and other factors such as market exchange rates are unable to influence some items listed among the profits and losses of the current account, such as overseas investment *etc*. To respond to the needs of the current crisis, one should pay more attention to the trade balance under the current account. At the same time, due to the conditions of the global value chain, emerging markets only account for a very small part in the growth of export through processing trade. The exchange rate factors cancelled each other out in the import and export of processed goods trading, hence the impact was minimal. The trade surplus or deficit was determined by the stage of a country's economic structure; the bilateral trade surplus or deficit was more subjected to the open trade policy in the country. Therefore, China did not agree with setting artificial restrictions and quantifying constraints. In order to show their willingness to cooperate and ensure the success of the Seoul Summit, China agreed to research and formulate the "Indicative Guideline" to give a proper assessment of continued significant imbalances.

Furthermore, the US and European countries differed greatly on the IMF quota reform. To seek the support of emerging markets, the US pushed for share transfer to the emerging markets, but ensured that its own share was not less than 15% and the main transfer of share came from European countries. After much deliberation by the US and Europe, it was ultimately proposed that 6% of the IMF shares be transferred to emerging markets, developing countries and countries with low share values.

2.6 *Clouded with European debt at the Cannes Summit*

In November 2011, the sixth G20 Summit was held in Cannes, France. The meeting published the "G20 Leaders Summit Communiqué", "Cannes Action

Plan for Growth and Jobs" and the declaration "Building our Common Future: Renewed Collective Action for the Benefit of All".

During the preparation of the summit, the focus of the debate was establishing the "Indicative Guideline" to achieve all-rounded and balanced growth. The process was full of obstacles. First, according to the views of China and other members, the guideline should not only reflect the external balance indicators such as the current account proposed by the US but also reveal the internal balance indicators such as the finance, public debt, and consumption and savings. Second, in determining external indicators, China opined that the trade balance, capital gain, transfer payment and other sub-items in the current account were of a different nature and system, and should not be balanced in an indiscriminate and simplified manner. Therefore, finance ministers and central bank governors should analyze the trade balance, capital gain balance, and transfer payments balance in the current account as three separate indicators. Lastly, in assessing imbalances, especially for balance indicators that the government cannot directly control, there should not be a quantified limit. The relevant assessment primarily serves as a comprehensive measure to see if there is a large-scale imbalance, and indicate the direction of the imbalance. The finance ministers reached a consensus on these issues and decided to refer to the established criteria in the reference guidelines to evaluate the relevant economic balance issue. But the various parties and the public were still worried about whether the summit would continue "quarreling" over the problems of equilibrium.

Just a few days before the summit, there were dramatic changes to the focus of the summit. Greek Prime Minister George Papandreou suddenly called for a referendum on October 31 regarding an assistance package proposed by the EU. The move was interpreted as an indicator that Greece might leave the EU, causing jitters in the financial markets and disrupting preparations for the upcoming G20 Summit. To "save" the summit, French President Nicolas Sarkozy, German Chancellor Angela Merkel and IMF Managing Director Christine Lagarde organized a "banquet" to have an emergency meeting with Greek Prime Minister George Papandreou. Merkel asked, "The referendum in essence is about nothing else but the question, does Greece want to stay in the euro zone, yes or no?" Although Greece cancelled the referendum on the day before the summit started on November 3, the debt crisis undoubtedly became the most important issue of discussion and this slight hiccup embarrassed the EU to some extent. In response to the crisis and to save face, the members of the Eurozone government pledged to take all necessary measures and actions to ensure the stability of the Eurozone.

Meanwhile, trade issues became another focal point of the summit. On opposing trade protectionism, Brazil was under pressure from domestic industries and wanted to withdraw from the abstinence of new protectionist measures, breaking the G20 commitment. Regarding the Doha Round negotiations, the US appeared to reject the results of past Doha Round negotiations and seemed inclined to reinventing the wheel. The BRICS countries including India, South Africa, Brazil and China adhered to safeguard the development authorization and complete negotiations based on past summit outcomes. The discussion of trade issues continued till the last minute of the summit. Finally, the parties showed high political flexibility, and agreed to continue rejecting protectionism. The parties also agreed to keep on looking for "new and reliable ways" to facilitate Doha Round negotiations based on the foundation of recognizing development authorization and past summit outcomes.

2.7 *Placing hopes on BRICS countries at the Los Cabos Summit*

In June 2012, the seventh G20 Summit was held in Los Cabos, Mexico. The summit adopted the "G20 Los Cabos: Leaders' Declaration" and "Los Cabos Growth and Jobs Action Plan". They played a positive role in responding to the severe downward trend of the world economy and strengthened the accountability of G20 in new ways.

The focus of the summit was once again the issue of capital increase. In order to increase the available resources and build a more effective financial safety net, the IMF hoped to raise more capital. However, the US had made clear that it would no longer provide additional capital. It was difficult to achieve the goal set by the IMF Managing Director Lagarde with the capital commitment of other countries. The parties placed high hopes on the BRICS countries, as they had not made any commitments until then. There were all kinds of speculation. Some even said that the key to the success of the summit was determined by whether the IMF could successfully increase capital. Finally, the BRICS countries showed mature political wisdom and committed USD93 billion to the fund, accounting for 21.6% of the total capital promised in the summit. They did not pledge beyond their capabilities but showed themselves to be responsible countries.

The G20 Summit also contributed to the establishment of accountability mechanisms. The summit in Los Cabos established the accountability assessment framework, formally setting up a process evaluation system for "strong, sustainable and balanced growth", advocating the implementation of various commitments pledged. Even if the commitment was not honored, an explanation was needed to ensure the credibility of the countries' commitment to the G20. This was an important progress in strengthening G20 cooperation.

2.8 *Divergence of voices at the St. Petersburg Summit*

On September 5, 2013, the eighth G20 Summit was held in St. Petersburg, Russia. The international situation was very complex at the time. In economic terms, developed countries showed slight improvements and the collective growth of emerging markets slowed down. The power of developed countries to "grant rights" in the area of global economic governance was weakened. In terms of political diplomacy, the relationship between the US and Russia was tense because of the civil war in Syria and Edward Snowden incident. German newspaper *Berliner Zeitung*, Thailand's *World News* and other publications described the event as "the most divisive G20 Summit".

The "Leaders' Declaration" issued at the end of the summit stated various countries' commitment to take actions to promote growth and increase employment, and highlighted the "St. Petersburg Development Outlook" in the field of international development. The results of this summit were ordinary on the whole and the only highlight was the common resolution to combat tax avoidance. Before the summit, Russia had proposed the drafting of the public debt disciplines. The emerging markets were also highly concerned about the US withdrawing from the quantitative easing policy. As the focus of conflicts was mainly against the US, it was difficult to reach a consensus and strong constraints were not successfully established. This showed that the G20 Summit was just an arena where all kinds of governance concepts were challenged but were mostly dialogues and it was arduous to make decisions on some complex issues.

The stark contrast between the G20 Summit and informal BRICS meeting held during the summit pointed out that the former was ordinary and the latter was outstanding. BRICS banks and contingency reserve arrangements reached a number of substantial consensuses because emerging powers displayed mature and active diplomacy.

3 The Influence of G20 on Global Governance and Rule Reconstruction

The emergence of the G20 significantly changed global economic governance. No longer did the concept of "neoliberalism" dominate the field of global governance; a "competition of philosophies" now arose. The outbreak of the international financial crisis indicated that the liberal "Washington Consensus" belief had been shaken. In particular, more countries recognized that a *laissez-faire* system creates great moral hazards and systemic risks in the financial and monetary fields. In response to the financial crisis, the US also greatly strengthened the role of the government, directly intervening in many ways including providing loans to major automotive manufacturers, recapitalizing banks even to the extent of nationalizing them, implementing major fiscal stimulus policies, and the "independent" Federal Reserve also issued debt securities to the federal government. At the same time, countries with emerging markets proposed a series of global governance philosophies such as "fair, balanced and inclusive international economic order", "common but differentiated responsibility", and "peaceful development, mutual benefit and win–win principles" *etc.* by developing practices and their own requests. Of course, the US is still striving to maintain liberalism. At the Washington Summit, President George W. Bush urged that the free market economy not be abandoned. He said,

> Government intervention is not a cure-all... History has shown that the great threat to economic prosperity is not too little government involvement in the market, it is too much government involvement in the market... free market principles offer the surest path to lasting prosperity...

This has led global governance mechanisms to stay in the state of "competition of philosophies".[5] Significant changes in global governance have taken place with the emergence of the G20, whether in terms of mechanisms or specific rules.

3.1 *G20's influence on global governance mechanisms*

Emerging markets have become participants in decision-making. As the world's political and economic structure moves from being "one super-dominant power" to "one superpower with several other strong contenders", especially with the development of emerging markets in recent years, the "rise of the east and decline of the west" trend has become clearer. The global economic and trade center is shifting from developed economies toward the emerging and developing economies. According to data from the IMF, from the 1990s to early 2010, the proportion of GDP of emerging and developing economies in the world economy rose from 20% to 34%. The BRICS countries in particular, climbed from 5.8% of the world economy to 18%. Therefore, emerging

---

[5] Huang Chao, "Changes in Global Governance Mechanisms in the Context of the Financial Crisis," *International Review*, No. 3, 2012, p. 28.

markets now have a greater voice in asking for distribution of power, and decision-making in global governance, and there is a more urgent need to establish new global governance principles and mechanisms that are better able to adapt to new challenges, reflect the changes in power and respond to multilateral requests. When the G20 Summit was formed, there were nine members from developed countries and 11 from emerging markets. Although the developed countries led by the US still possessed hegemony on many issues, the voice of emerging economies was significantly stronger. It became difficult for the developed countries to control major global issues and participation in global governance became diversified. This evolution in international power is conducive for the establishment of a fair, just, balanced and reasonable international economic order. The G20 Summit is also where decisions regarding the world's major economic policies and international system reforms are made, which not only eases the problem of the low decision-making efficiency of the UN, but to a certain extent, lessens the unfairness in the decision-making processes of international organizations such as the IMF and the WBG who mainly rely on voting. At the same time, the G20 boosts reforms of the WBG and the IMF, which is difficult to achieve if one is wholly dependent on the voting mechanism in place.

The G20 overcomes the lack of implementation mechanisms of international forums to some extent. During a crisis, the G20 Summit mobilizes various forces including developed countries, emerging markets, international bodies *etc.* to deal with the crisis together, so that each member will be better able to fulfill their specific roles in the international economic organizations. The executive functions of international organizations such as the IMF, the WBG and the WTO have been further enhanced by the G20, and in turn, mobilized the enthusiasm of international institutions, taking full advantage of the resources of the original system such that the consensus and decisions made by leaders at the G20 Summit are better implemented. The G20's role as a weather vane for policies has also enhanced member states' consciousness in carrying out the relevant decisions made by the G20.

The G20 established non-binding accountability mechanisms for evaluation purposes. In order to boost the compliance of the G20 commitments, non-binding evaluation and accountability mechanisms were established in the relevant areas. To grow the framework working group, following the "strong, sustainable, and balanced growth framework", the G20 set up a mutual evaluation system in accordance with the "Reference Manual", to assess if member states met the targets of strong, sustainable and balanced growth in their macroeconomic, fiscal, financial, monetary and other policy measures. At the

2012 Los Cabos Summit, the above assessment was officially put forth as the "Los Cabos Accountability Framework". In the field of trade and investment, with regard to the promise to not take new protectionist measures at the summit, the WTO, Organisation for Economic Co-operation and Development (OECD), and the United Nations Conference on Trade and Development (UNCTAD) jointly launched the "G20 Trade and Investment Measures" supervision mechanism whereby supervisory reports are released within six months. The system reflects the various trade and investment measures taken by each member during the supervised period. In the area of development, the development working group committed to conducting accountability assessments on the development of the G20 from the year 2013 onwards. The nine priority areas and the implementation of commitments for development made at the relevant summit were assessed at the Seoul Summit. Although the evaluation and accountability mechanisms established by the G20 are temporarily unable to fundamentally resolve some of the problems in implementation, enhanced accountability undoubtedly holds great significance for the improvement of the G20 mechanism construction. The lack of legal constraints and non-obligatory nature of commitments made at the summits are more or less compensated by moral constraints and "peer pressure". Because of this, it can be seen that a considerable part of the G20 commitments have been adequately met.

3.2 *The impact on related fields*

The G20 has strengthened international macroeconomic policy coordination and expanded the scope of national coordination. Leaders of major countries around the world come together to study and coordinate international macroeconomic policies — this is a major change in the rules of procedure among global economic governance mechanisms. The UN and the G8 are unable to strike a balance between representation and efficiency. The G8 economic policy coordination is not comprehensive and unfair to emerging markets. Included in the G20 are the world's major powers, and some developing countries, which also represent the voices of other developing countries. It is therefore significantly more representative and at the same time, it is also somewhat efficient. To date, the G20 has, on the whole, motivated the international community to take measures in response to the numerous ups and downs of the world economy brought about by the crisis, the European crisis and other issues. For example, after the crisis, the G20 mobilized the countries to collectively take on fiscal and monetary policies to stimulate the economy and prevent the world economy from sliding further. As the situation improved, the G20 discussed the orderly discontinuation of stimulation policies so as to avoid confusion in the market. With regard to the high deficits and debts of developed countries, the G20 proposed setting deficit reduction targets. In the meantime, the G20 also proposed the effective expansion of domestic demand and other issues for countries with trade surpluses.

In the financial sector, the issue at hand was to promote the reform of international financial institutions. The G20 toughened the role of relevant international financial institutions, reformed the governance mechanisms of relevant bodies, and enhanced the coordination and cooperation among the institutions. These developments led to international financial institutions becoming an integral part of global economic governance that have both independent decision-making capabilities as well as unified leadership and command. One of the important reform measures was the establishment of the Financial Stability Board (FSB), which began as the Financial Stability Forum (FSF), a cooperative organization established by the G7 to boost the stability of the financial system. As the impact of emerging markets on financial stability gradually grew, on April 2009, the London Summit decided to replace the FSF with the FSB extending the membership to include all the member states of the G20, including China, as well as Spain and the relevant international organizations. Compared to the FSF, the FSB possessed stronger organizational features, had a broader membership base, and bore more responsibilities as well as a larger mission to promote financial stability. The FSB was tasked with developing and implementing regulatory and other policies to enhance financial stability, resolve the problem of financial fragility, coordinate the work of various nations' financial departments and international institutions, develop and strengthen the implementation of effective regulatory, supervisory and other financial policies. The FSB also partnered the IMF to sound early warnings for risks of macroeconomic and financial crises, and strove to eliminate negative factors that affected the stability of the global financial system. In reality, the FSB became a platform for developing financial stability policies, and coordination mechanism for implementing financial regulatory standards such that the originally fragmented international regulations and rules became more focused and orderly. Another reform driven by the G20 was the reform of the IMF and the WBG's share/voting rights. Beginning with the London Summit, attention was paid to this item of reform at the successive summits. The Pittsburgh Summit, especially, set two goals: that the IMF share be shifted at least 5% from overvalued countries to undervalued countries, and that the WBG increase the voting rights of developing and transition countries by at least 3%. In June 2010, the Toronto Summit verified and approved the reform plan for the transference of 3.13% of voting rights to developing countries such that the overall voting rights of developing countries rose from 44.06% to 47.19%, among which China's voting rights grew from 2.77% to 4.42%. The Toronto Summit also approved the voice reform of the International Finance Corporation (IFC) where 6.07% of voting rights were transferred to developing countries. In March 2011, the IMF completed the 2008 reform program and the voting rights of developed countries decreased from 59.5% to 57.9%, and that of developing countries increased from 40.5% to 42.1%. At the November 2010 Summit in Seoul, it was proposed that the IMF continues transferring more than 6% of shares to emerging economies.

The G20 also pushed for new rules for global finance. This financial crisis revealed that financial regulation was a weakness in global governance, and the self-regulation of independent states was no longer adequate for the highly integrating international financial and monetary markets. Thus, since its formation, the G20 Summit has prioritized the strengthening of financial supervision and seen remarkable results. Firstly, they advocated international cooperation in financial supervision and standards compliance. The G20 actively encouraged the establishment of a new system for international financial regulatory standards. The Basel Committee on Banking Supervision carried out a major reform of existing international rules and issued the "Basel III" in 2009. "Basel III" took new complementary approaches to supervision — micro-prudential supervision and macro-prudential regulation, in accordance with overall requirements such as equal emphasis on capital regulation and liquidity regulation, simultaneous improvement of capital quantity and quality, as well as balanced capital adequacy and leverage ratios; all of which set new benchmarks for international banking supervision. The G20 proposed that all members effectuate the provisions of "Basel III" from 2013 to 2019. In January 2010, the FSB published the "Framework for Strengthening Adherence to International Standards", encouraging all member economies to receive financial sector stability assessments and peer reviews, and conduct relevant stability assessments on wage mechanisms, risk assessment, implementation of "Basel III" provisions, reform of over-the-counter (OTC) derivatives, hedge funds, and supervision by external rating agencies *etc*. Secondly, they strengthened the supervision of systemic risks in the financial sector. This crisis highlighted the importance of the assessment, monitoring and mitigation of systemic risks, the need to consider both the systemic and the individual financial institution's risks in general, and to break out of the traditional regulatory concept based on the balance sheets of individual financial institutions. The G20 initiated a new risk regulatory system and gave "risk" a richer definition. Not only did quantified regulatory standards such as capital and liquidity have to reflect systemic risk factors and improve the financial system's ability to respond to external shocks; the cross-border and cross-market influence of financial risks were weakened and probability of a systemic financial crisis was reduced by strengthening financial market infrastructure, building financial safety nets and enhancing cross-border financial regulatory cooperation. Thirdly, they pushed for the bridging of gaps in international supervision. In October 2010, the FSB published the "OTC Derivatives Market Reforms" report and made 21 recommendations covering the standardization of OTC derivatives, exchange/electronic trading platforms, centralized settlement of central counterparties, and reporting to the Trade Information Warehouse. In June 2009, the International Organization of Securities Commissions (IOSCO) published "Principles for Hedge Funds Regulation", a report that included mandatory registration requirements, continuous monitoring, providence of information on systemic risk and others. In addition, the IOSCO also revised the "Code of Conduct Fundamentals for Credit Rating Agencies", increased the transparency of rating agencies, took appropriate measures to ensure the credit rating quality, set up assessment mechanisms for new product ratings, and cautiously rated new, complex financial products or products with a weak data backing; In October 2010, the FSB released "Principles for Reducing Reliance on CRA Ratings". The G20 also required that the shadow banking system be subject to appropriate supervision, so as to better respond to the impact that banking-like risks outside of the ordinary banking system might inflict on financial stability.

The G20 actively curbed trade protectionism and safeguarded the multilateral trading system. The global multilateral trading system built with the WTO at the core had always been advanced by way of trade negotiations, binding commitments, legal treaty obligations and so on. This approach clearly defines rights and obligations and is highly effective in implementation. Once members fail to fulfill their obligations, there are also dispute-resolution mechanisms in place and appropriate sanctions are applied. However, this approach of negotiations put the countries in an exchange of interests with distinct boundaries and weakened these countries' attention to the common goals and shared values. Especially when their mutual interests cannot be reached through negotiations on certain details, this approach lacks the flexible and political means to enable the parties to seek for shared and balanced interests at a higher level and in a bigger picture. The G20 mainly conducts trade discussions from the angle of responding to financial crises together, and boosting growth and employment via trade, to encourage all parties to promote free trade, close the Doha Round as soon as possible and refrain from implementing new protectionist measures. Although the commitments made are non-mandatory and non-binding, better unified understanding among the parties is achieved so that common goals can be established and political signals given out. In the circumstance that Doha negotiations reach a standstill and prospects are bleak, G20 is undoubtedly important to boost confidence, forge consensus and energize multilateral trade negotiations, as these are beneficial to achieving a more inclusive and mutually beneficial outcome.

In the area of development, the G20 vigorously mobilizes international development resources and pushes for the resolution of development problems. Solving global development problems is a long-term concern for the world. To this end, the UN established relevant development agencies, and the WBG and other international multilateral development banks are also providing development funds. At the bilateral level, due to historical responsibilities, developed countries are obligated to provide official development assistance (ODA) to developing countries, and developing countries also support each other through the South-South cooperation framework. Despite the UN's unanimous agreement to coordinate the development of resources via the Millennium Development Goals (MDGs) by the UN, there is still obvious fragmentation of international development resources. The Development Consensus was determined at the G20 Seoul Summit as a complement to other channels of development, highlighting governance of international development, focusing on building comprehensive global development partnerships, mobilizing international organizations and the private sector to be more involved in the development consensus. The development working group drew up action plans according to the nine areas identified during the Seoul Summit and earnestly implemented these plans. The WBG, the UN Development Program (UNDP), the International Labor Organization (ILO), the Food and Agriculture Organization (FAO), and the OECD put forward proposals on improving development in various fields, improved the infrastructure lending practices by the WBG and the regional multilateral development institutions, and established a "policy toolbox" for developing countries in the relevant fields to strengthen knowledge sharing and capacity building. Thus, in the area of development, the G20 was a uniting force and it integrated resources, improved measures and enhanced governance, reflecting the international community's considerations and betterment of development systems and the efficiency of development measures.

4 G20's Future Direction

4.1 *Problems faced*

As mentioned at the beginning of the chapter, the evolution of global govern-ance system is an ongoing process of sublation. The establishment of any new system necessarily means a reformation and improvement of the old, and is bound to inherit some problems that the old system was temporarily unable to resolve. Therefore, the new global governance mechanism with the G20 as its main platform inevitably has its flaws, and faces inherent challenges. Currently, the more prominent issues are the following.

4.1.1 *How to maintain the strong collaborative momentum?*

As all the countries were facing enormous pressure from the crisis, the impor-tance of cooperation was widely recognized at the first few G20 Summits. There were more common interests, and all the countries demonstrated the spirit of solidarity and collaboration; there were relatively less differences and disputes, and more consensuses on strengthening macroeconomic coordina-tion, joint stimulation of the economy, increasing resources of international financial institutions, heightening financial regulation and reducing protec-tionism. Member countries however, began to clash during the recovery pro-cess and alleviation of the crisis. They frequently differed in fiscal policies, balanced growth, quantitative easing, bank taxes and other issues. The negative effects of some countries' national policies began to spill over and spread, mak-ing it more difficult for the G20 to coordinate macroeconomic policies. At the same time, various countries fought for favorable conditions for recovery, even set their eyes on strategic post-crisis considerations and began to squeeze in topics that limited the room for other countries' development into the summit. Since the Seoul Summit, the clashes have become even more intense. There were significant disagreements and disputes with regard to the proportion of current account surplus in GDP at the Seoul Summit, trade issues were the controversial topics at the Cannes Summit, finding solutions to debt problems was the cause for strife at the Los Cabos Summit and at the St. Petersburg Summit; countries conflicted over quantitative easing policy and the spillover effects of discontinuing. The G20 Summit is becoming weaker in its collabora-tive spirit and consolidating cooperation has become an important issue in strengthening the G20's role as the main platform for international economic cooperation.

4.1.2 *How to improve legitimacy?*

Although the economic output of the G20 member states makes up 90% of the world and it is much more representative than the G8 as its members include both developed and developing countries, legitimacy issues still exist. There are still more than 150 countries and regions apart from the G20 members, most of whom are UN members. Due to the democratization of international relations, it is becoming increasingly challenging for the G20 to play a policy-making role in global economic affairs. At the same time, the G20 does not have the power of conventions or charters; it has no internationally recognized legal power, nor a secretariat. It is currently still an international economic forum whose main issues and directions are largely guided by the host country. As such, another problem to resolve is how the G20 ought to relate and coordinate with the UN, relevant international organizations and the large number of non-member countries.

4.1.3 *How to overcome the lack of effectiveness?*

The G20 resolutions are characteristically non-binding and often, this results in "discussions without decisions, and decisions that are not implemented". For example, the G20 has already promised to carry out IMF quota reform, and although this reform does not affect America's share and right to veto, and the US supported it enthusiastically at first, the US has delayed the implementation of the reform time and again. Despite being submitted to Congress for consideration, it has failed to be passed and approved. This is the first time a reform has not been implemented due to a country's domestic procedures. The US Congress approved the IMF Reform Plan finally at the end of 2015. In another case, before the 2010 Seoul Summit, the US first requested that current account surplus or deficit of various countries be kept within 4% of GDP, but it later expressed that a trade balance to GDP ratio no higher than 4% was acceptable, and eventually the parties reached a compromise on this with the "Indicative Guideline". China has made great efforts to reduce its trade surplus to GDP ratio to 2.1% in 2011 but the US has not done its best to improve its external balance, and its trade deficit has grown to more than 4.8% of GDP. The country that set the trade balance target did not achieve its goal! Furthermore, in terms of deficit reduction and fiscal consolidation, the US did not honor its commitment to consolidate objectives for the Toronto 2016 Summit; the US and EU also proposed postponing the implementation of "Basel III"; the US' promotion of "purchase American products" is a grave violation of the commitment to reject trade protectionism while Brazil and other countries have also introduced several new trade protection measures. All of the above have lowered the credibility of the G20.

Encumbered by such difficulties and challenges, there may not be high expectations on the G20 for a period of time in the future. It is impossible for the G20 to resolve the numerous acute and complex problems arising from globalization in a short amount of time. There are several possibilities of development for the G20. From the current situation, a trend that we hope not to see is that the G20 Summits become useless, "idle talk sessions" that simply play a coordination role for certain fields. The worst case scenario is that the G20 Summit mechanism is abandoned, completely marginalized or dissolved. It is evidently somewhat alarmist to speak of such a risk at this point in time. From the perspective of emerging markets, what China and other members hope to see is that the G20 Summit continues to play a strong balancing role. This outcome depends on how willing emerging economies are to bear international responsibilities, as well as the attitude of US-led Western countries. If the US neglects its responsibilities or falters on important policies or agreed items, and allows the negative effects of their own policies to spill over to affect other countries in the world, they will inevitably incur the criticism of other members and the unity and spirit of cooperation among the G20 member states will be hurt, which would further weaken the G20's strength and progress.

4.2 Problems that have to be resolved to improve G20 governance mechanisms

Looking at how the G20 is developing, a balance between adapting to the new global economic landscape and coordinating the collective interests as well as national interests must be found in order to satisfy the diverse demands. Emerging economies consisting mainly of BRICS countries generally hope for the G20 to continue playing a major role in international economic governance so that they can carry on consolidating and strengthening their status as "decision-makers" and share power with the developed countries. The US will have its leading role in the G20 and as long as this mechanism continues to fulfill its strategic intent, the US should persist in supporting the G20. Therefore, in order to meet the expectations that most countries have of the G20, the following areas regarding how it can be improved must be explored.

4.2.1 *Find proper solutions for the building up of G20 mechanisms*

The G20 ought to move towards long-acting governance system by building up its mechanisms. Systemization is best done through "entities", that is, evolving from a forum-based summit to a system of entities, including establishing a Secretariat, determining relatively fixed topics for discussion and number of members, and improving constraining and assessment mechanisms.[6] The systemization of the summit also requires the support of strong mechanisms in specific areas. The meeting systems for financial and central bank governors, trade ministers and development ministers should be improved. Close and fixed channels of communications with business communities should be established. Although there is a G20 Business Forum at the moment, its organization is relatively relaxed, the expression of intent is not sufficiently clear, and dialogue and communication amongst leaders is not smooth.

4.2.2 *Improve coordination with relevant international organizations*

The G20 does not have specific executive functions and implementing agencies, its main achievements so far have been reliant on the major international institutions. Reforming the global governance system does not mean subverting the existing system of governance; rather, the existing order should be maintained if reasonable, while old, incomprehensive and unreasonable rules should be changed and new rules be developed. The key to the success of the G20 depends on its ability and processes for complementing and promoting the reform of existing international organizations, and it should not become a competitor or seek to replace existing international organizations.[7] Governance agreements can be reached by the summit in the relevant areas, and international organizations can appropriately turn these agreements into more strongly binding action plans, multilateral disciplines and even international treaties. Having legally approved international institutions implement the relevant decisions is helpful for strengthening the legitimacy of the G20 commitments.

---

[6] Yang Jiemian, "G20 Transformations and Development Prospects," *International Studies*, No. 6, 2011, pp. 55–56.

[7] John Kirton, "The G20 and Broader Multilateral Reform", quoted from Chen Suquan, "Role Analysis of G20 in Global Governance Structure", *Around Southeast Asia*, Issue 10, 2010, p. 91.

4.2.3 *Balancing rights and obligations*

Firstly, distribution of rights should be balanced. Currently, emerging markets make up more than half of the members of the G20 but the actual power and voice for agenda-setting are still mainly in the hands of developed countries, largely because the major international agencies are led by developed countries. As such, the G20 ought to continue promoting the reform of international institutions' governance structures and effectively enhance the voice and influence of emerging countries, including persisting in promoting the reform of shares and voting rights in the IMF and the WBG, and electing more candidates from developing countries as senior management and leaders of international organizations.

Secondly, developed countries should assume more responsibility for balance and maintaining the international monetary system. On the one hand, only if developed countries conscientiously push for domestic structural reforms, and release greater production potential, will there be reduced dependence on imported goods, and the huge trade deficits and budget deficits be reduced. On the other hand, only by carrying out structural reforms will monetary policies be effective, rather than freeing large amounts of money outside the real economy, causing a negative spillover effect.

Next, emerging economies must courageously take on more international responsibilities. The purpose of strengthening the voice of emerging market countries is not simply for obtaining "better bargains" in international cooperation, but emerging markets should actively shoulder appropriate responsibilities, safeguard effective international community rules and participate equitably in the formulation of new rules. The G20 Summit was formed when developed countries were unable to manage global economic governance on their own; it is generally favorable towards emerging market economies. Thus far, emerging market countries have demonstrated a strong spirit of responsibility with regard to the capital increase of international financial institutions and other issues. This is an important boost to help the G20 achieve results.

4.3 *The development of BRICS and G20*

Since the establishment of the G20, Brazil, Russia, India, China and South Africa have actively participated in the summit. While safeguarding their own interests and fighting for the rights and interests of emerging market economies, they have also made important contributions to the cooperation and development of the G20. At the same time, looking at the long-term development of the G20 mechanism, BRICS is an important and rising force as the representative of emerging markets. The stability and development of the G20 is dependent on the active participation and contribution of the BRICS countries.

4.3.1 *BRICS countries have contributed positively to G20 cooperation and demonstrated trustworthiness*

BRICS countries have actively carried out macroeconomic policies coordination alongside other G20 members, and have participated in collaborative efforts to overcome the financial and European debt crises. In 2009, the BRIC countries (at that time, they were four countries — Brazil, Russia, India and China) collectively joined the IMF's "New Arrangements to Borrow" (NAB), and together, pledged to provide more than USD80 billion worth of funds, among which China promised to purchase IMF bonds to inject USD50 billion to the NAB. In 2012, the IMF required another capital increase and BRICS countries pledged USD93 billion funds at the last moment, of which China pledged USD43 billion, to help the IMF achieve its target of USD430 billion.

BRICS has actively opposed trade protectionism and pushed for Doha Round negotiations at successive summits. Russia and China firmly support the summit in opposing trade protectionism and under enormous pressure, Brazil, in view of the overall situation, made clear commitments to go against protectionism at the previous summit. This is an advance in preventing the global spread of trade protectionism after the crisis. BRICS countries accept the development authorization of the Doha Rounds and defend the negotiation outcomes. They have also played an important role in preventing negotiations from going off the authorized track or revisiting topics unnecessarily. BRICS countries have been actively involved in the discussions on all areas including financial supervision, oil subsidies, stabilizing commodity prices, reference guidelines, and global development, and they have also put forward many constructive comments and suggestions.

4.3.2 *BRICS countries should play a greater constructive role in G20 development*

BRICS countries have become a notable force in the world economy. Objectively, they need to participate in global economic governance for their own development. At the same time, rising BRICS countries are also qualified to play a greater constructive role in international affairs, and shoulder responsibilities appropriate to their ability and stage of development.

BRICS countries should become a vital force in pushing for continuous reforms in global economic governance. BRICS countries ought to strengthen the voice and influence of developing countries to increase representation in global economic governance, and actively voice the opinions of developing countries at G20 Summits. At the fifth BRICS Summit, President Xi Jinping expressed,

> Regardless how the global governance system changes, we must actively participate and play a constructive role in promoting the development of a more just and equitable international order to provide institutional security for world peace and stability. We must continue to strengthen coordination and cooperation within the frameworks of the UN, G20, and other international economic and financial institutions, and safeguard common interests.

BRICS countries should therefore contribute to enrich global economic governance. At the G20 Summits, BRICS countries have shown the world the successful practices of various types of emerging powers, and provided new ideas for national development and the global economy, reflecting the ideals and requests of developing countries in global economic governance. Developing an open world economy, achieving comprehensive sustainable and equitable development of the world economy while addressing imbalances in global development and other proposals put forward by BRICS countries are beneficial to fostering diversity and inclusion in global economic governance.

BRICS countries also ought to courageously assume more international responsibility. BRICS countries have done well in increasing the capital of international financial institutions, but it is undeniable that some of the BRICS countries have their concerns about taking on international rules duties and responsibilities as they do not wish to limit their own development space with rules. The G20 is a forum for the world's rule-makers and development bodies. To promote the development of the G20, the BRICS countries must contribute to G20 cooperation; to gain more power in international rule-making, the BRICS countries must first bear greater responsibility in international rules duties.

Chapter 3

Difficulties and Prospects of the Multilateral Trading System

It was not a hot summer in Geneva in July 2008, yet the atmosphere at 154, Rue de Lausanne, the WTO headquaters was tense and almost suffocating. This was the final sprint in the Doha Round. Since July 20, trade ministers from the key WTO members had been doing their utmost to achieve compromise in negotiations day and night in the famous Green Room located on the second floor of the building. Over the past one week of negotiations, the faces of all the ministers were full of weariness and anxiety. US Trade Representative Susan Schwab was restless and in a frustrated mood; some of the ministers who were unable to participate in the Green Room negotiations and had to endure the long wait outside, returned to their home countries. On July 29, the negotiations finally collapsed due to irreconcilable disputes on the agricultural special safeguard mechanism between Schwab and the Indian Union Cabinet Minister of Commerce and Industry Kamal Nath.

At around the same time across the Atlantic Ocean on New York's Wall Street, the Lehman Brothers' empire was crumbling. This was the quiet beginning of the financial storm that would soon hit the world and sweep across the globe.

It was at this WTO meeting that China joined as one of the core G7 members in the negotiations and played a crucial and constructive role in the process. China's Minister of Commerce, Chen Deming, who was head of the Chinese delegation at that time summarized his view on the breakdown of talks: "This is a tragic failure. It is going to become a marker in the history of world trade and economy... This is also a serious setback. Particularly in the face of world economic downturn, serious inflation and imminent financial risks, the failure will have a major impact on the fragile multilateral trading system. To respond to this, we need to get ourselves fully prepared."

History has proven that it was indeed a serious setback. As the financial crisis intensified, WTO members differed even more evidently in their interests, taking up positions that were further apart, and the Doha Round seemed to have descended into a state of "intensive care," despite the fact that two-thirds of the Round had already been completed. It was only in December 2013 at the Bali Ministerial Conference that there was a gradual awakening.

1 The Ups and Downs in the Twelve-Year History of Doha Round

When one searches for a place named "Doha" through Google maps, you have to first focus the southwest corner of the Persian Gulf, and then increase the magnification to zoom in on a tiny city. This is the capital of Qatar, a harbor city with a mere population of 200,000 inhabitants. Although it is small in size, Doha is a heavyweight in the world economic and trade circle. It is not famous for its drip irrigation systems, beautiful coasts, or palm-tree-like islands, but for being the location where the global multilateral trading system launched the ninth round of WTO negotiations in 2001, henceforth the Doha Round negotiations. It was during that same year at that very meeting that China became the 143rd member of the WTO.

Twelve years have gone by. The all-powerful ministers in those days have disappeared and the diplomats in Geneva have been replaced time and again, yet the end of the Doha Round is still nowhere in sight. One wonders what is happening to the Doha Round and what will become of the multilateral trade system?

1.1 *History of the Doha Round talks*

1.1.1 *The "Development Agenda" after September 11*

Peace and development are closely related. They are reciprocal conditions bearing the dreams of several generations of politicians, and they are also issues that the international community is constantly troubled by. Along with the development of economic globalization at the turn of the century, the accumulation of problems over the long run within the international economic system, as well as global economic imbalances, has become diversely intertwined with the individual interests and demands of various countries. Conflicts between the North and South have intensified, and global hunger and violent incidents have occurred at increased frequency. At that time, the developed countries who make up 20% of the world's population accounted for 86% of the world's GDP and 82% of total exports, while the developing countries making up an overwhelming majority of the world's population accounted for only 14% and 18%, respectively.

At the turn of the century, the most vulnerable groups of people that form 20% of the world's population only accounted for 1.1% of global GDP.[1] Then UN Secretary-General Kofi Annan stressed, "National markets are held together by shared values. In the face of economic transition and insecurity, people know that if the worst comes to the worst, they can rely on the expectation that certain minimum standards will prevail. But in the global market, people do not yet have that confidence. Until they do have it, the global economy will be fragile and vulnerable — vulnerable to backlash from all the 'isms' of our post-cold-war world: protectionism; populism; nationalism; ethnic chauvinism; fanaticism; and terrorism… if we do not act, there may be a threat to the open global market, and especially to the multilateral trade regime."[2] The President of WBG at that time, James Wolfensohn, similarly warned, "That unless we can deal with the questions of development and the questions of poverty, there's no way that we're going to have a peaceful world for our children."[3]

There was no doubt that, development had become one of the compelling international issues of the time. In September 2000, the United Nations held the Millennium Summit where 189 countries signed the "United Nations Millennium Declaration" aimed at reducing poverty and promoting development as "Millennium Development Goals".[4] However, the belated consensus reached by the international community failed to stop the spread of terrorist forces. On September 11, 2001, the New York World Trade Center "Twin Towers" collapsed after two hijacked airliners crashed into them, leading to the highest death toll US had ever suffered since the Pearl Harbor attack during World War II. This devastating terrorist attack raised concerns all over the

---

[1] United Nations Development Program "Human Development Report 1999," Oxford University Press (New York, 1999), retrieved from http://hdr.undp.org/sites/default/files/reports/260/hdr_1999_en_nostats.pdf.

[2] Speech by Kofi Annan at the Davos World Economic Forum, January 31, 1999.

[3] Interview with James Wolfensohn published in *Les Echos*, France, June 5, 2000.

[4] At the UN Millennium Summit in September 2000, world leaders agreed on a set of time-bound goals and targets for eradicating poverty, hunger, disease, illiteracy, environmental degradation and discrimination against women. They were namely eradicating extreme poverty and hunger; achieving universal primary education; promoting gender equality and empowering women; reducing child mortality rates; improving maternal health; combatting HIV/AIDS, malaria and other diseases, ensuring environmental sustainability; and forming global partnerships for development. These objectives and targets were set as the core of the global agenda and were collectively known as the Millennium Development Goals.

world. On the one hand, the incident reflected the failure of America's unilateral Middle-Eastern policy, and the escalation of the conflict between Islamic and Western civilizations; on the other hand, more and more politicians were of the view that poverty was an important breeding ground for terrorism, and while fighting the "war on terror", global poverty and development issues had to be addressed.

With this as the backdrop of international politics, a new round of multilateral trade negotiations hurriedly commenced in Doha, Qatar, merely two months after the September 11 terrorist attack. This round was known as the "Doha Development Agenda" (DDA) and it acted as a reflection of the concern for developing countries' interests as well as a response to the UN Millennium Development Goals.

There are three general aspects to DDA negotiations: the first being development issues — almost all trade and development-related demands are covered; the second being market access issues such as the opening up of the agricultural, non-agricultural products (*i.e.* industrial products) and trade in services markets, the elimination of various tariff and non-tariff restrictions; and the third aspect concerned modifying and establishing rules such as improving anti-dumping policies, anti-subsidy disciplines and dispute settlement mechanisms rules, improving relevant rules related to regional trade agreements, and establishing rules with regard to the liberalization of environmental goods, and the possible launch of rules that dealt with "Singapore issues."[5] Compared to the previous eight rounds of multilateral trade negotiations, the Doha Round had the most extensive coverage and was the most intense, covering 96% of global trade. Its level of ambition and market openness was two to three times that of the Uruguay Round. The WBG estimated that if a comprehensive agreement can be reached, it will bring USD160 billion worth of economic benefits to the world. According to the schedule, all negotiations ought to be completed by January 1, 2005.

1.1.2 *Competition of interests under the "development" banner*

The core objective of the Doha Round is development, which is in line with the common aspirations of the majority of developing members. However, competition among members always exists around the drafting of specific agenda and expectations tend to differ greatly. Agricultural issues, especially

---

[5] The main "Singapore issues" include investment, competition policies, transparency in government procurement and trade facilitation. These are referred to as "Singapore issues" because the WTO first proposed them at the first Ministerial Conference held in Singapore earlier in 1996.

with regard to how agricultural domestic support should be cut, have become the focus of conflicts and disputes among main parties. WTO statistics show that 90% of global agricultural subsidies are concentrated in 23 developed members including the United States, the EU and Japan. In 2009, the annual subsidies in the EU the US and Japan were up to USD30.6 billion, USD120.8 billion and USD46.5 billion respectively.[6]

Cairns Group,[7] the major exporter of agricultural products, emphasized that agriculture was the gateway issue at this round of negotiations and if there was no progress with regard to the agricultural issues, there would not be any positive outcomes for other issues. They emphasized that the three pillars in agricultural negotiations (market access, export competition, and domestic support) had to meet high standards in order for a complete turnaround of existing international agricultural trade conditions that were severely biased, and to promote fair trade of international agricultural products.

India, Kenya, South Africa, Brazil, China and other developing members strongly requested for the correction to the imbalance of the existing WTO rules. They asked for benefits to be improved for developing members, particularly the least developed ones. They were also strongly critical of the US for obstructing the settlement of intellectual property rights and public health issues, dissatisfied with the huge agricultural subsidies in the EU, the US and other developed countries, and urged that these problems be resolved through negotiations.

As the prime motivators for multilateral trade negotiations across history, the US and EU have their own concerns. The EU is the main promoter of this round, and has placed great importance on the development of rules regarding environmental and "Singapore issues". They are determined to succeed in this round of negotiations. Other areas, particularly market access of non-agricultural products (*i.e.* industrial products) and trade in services, are also core issues the EU strongly pursues. The US is focused on market access of non-agricultural

---

[6]OECD-FAO "Agricultural Outlook 2008–2017", retrieved from http://www.oecd.org/tad/40715381.pdf.

[7]The group was established by 14 agriculture production and export countries in August 1986 in Cairns, Australia. Its members include most of the developing members exporting agricultural products who, due to low productivity and lack of funds, suffer because of the export subsidies in Europe and America and urge to redress the unfairness in agricultural trade. The Cairns Group initially comprised of 14 countries including Australia, Argentina, Brazil, Chile, Colombia, Hungary, Indonesia, Malaysia, the Philippines, New Zealand, Thailand, Uruguay, Fiji and Canada, and were later joined by Bolivia, Costa Rica, Guatemala, Paraguay and South Africa. There are currently 19 members who together make up a quarter of the world's agricultural exports.

products and services, and has stressed the need to achieve high level of ambition. Like the EU, the US has been criticized for their agricultural subsidies, and for not being active in rule-making, but it has expressed that if there are great improvements in market access, it will consider reforming its agricultural subsidies policy and play a more active role in rule-making. On the one hand, the US and EU try to pressure developing members to open up their markets, yet on the other hand, they restrict imports of agricultural products from developing members and hold on to the high subsidies given to the production and export of their national agricultural products. This double standard has caused great dissatisfaction among all developing members. Pressured, the US and EU proposed a compromise that promotes "reduction rather than elimination", and agreed to gradually reduce tariffs and relax the import of agricultural products from developing members, and phase out agricultural subsidies in stages and according to categories at the same time. All this is still a far cry from the developing members' requests.

1.1.3 *The "Lee Kyung-hae" incident and the Cancun setback*

Lee Kyung-hae, an otherwise unknown Korean farmer, became a figure that cannot be ignored in the history of Doha Round negotiations. In September 2003, the Fifth WTO Ministerial Conference (known as the "Cancun Ministerial") was held in the southeastern coastal town of Cancun, Mexico. The conference aimed to determine the negotiation modality of the Doha Round, and a decision was to be taken about initiating "Singapore issues" discussions. The scene during the conference looked like that of a warzone with 6,000 police on the streets, four warships coasting and helicopters armed with missiles patroling the sky 24 hours a day. The host country spent 50 million pesos on an all-rounded defense system to deter terrorist attacks but they failed to stop the protests of farmers. On the opening day on September 10, thousands of people gathered outside the venue and then WTO Director-General, Supachai Panitchpakdi, was twice interrupted by the sound of demonstrations during his opening remark. Just as ministers entered the heated discussions on agricultural issues and on whether to initiate "Singapore issues", a 56-year-old Korean, Lee Kyung-hae, bearing a sandwich board with slogan "The WTO kills farmers", climbed across the police line of defense, flashed a Swiss army knife and stabbed himself in the chest in front of several TV video cameras. This was Lee Kyung-hae's second suicide attempt after the first at WTO Geneva headquarters in 1993. He was announced dead at the scene. The "Lee Kyung-hae" incident made the dispute and confrontations between the developed and developing members even more difficult to reconcile. Negotiations ended in deadlock after five days of fierce altercation.

The failure of the Cancun Ministerial cast a dark shadow on the prospects of the Doha Round. The US and the EU blamed developing members for the setback, with the US even threatening to shift the attention from multilateral to bilateral and regional cooperation. Since then, developing members have expressed their willingness to resume negotiations and the US has been increasingly criticized by the world for their hardline stance. Under pressure in this context, the US and the EU gradually changed their attitude from a rigid stance and moved toward strategy adjustments by mediating to resume negotiations. In January 2004, US Trade Representative Robert Zoellick wrote to the various ministers proposing that 2004 not be a "lost year" and called on all parties to work together to push for DDA talks.

1.1.4 *The "July Framework Agreement" provides vision*

In late July 2004, the WTO General Council and a number of bilateral consultations were held in Geneva, Switzerland. This was the most important negotiation since the failure of the Cancun Ministerial. Its goals were to deal with the unresolved issues from the Cancun Ministerial and determine the framework of negotiations and essential elements required for the next step of DDA. After long and arduous rounds of negotiations, in the early morning of August 1, the parties finally reached a framework agreement on agriculture, non-agricultural market access, trade in services, trade facilitation and development issues, and determined the basic direction and path for the Doha negotiations. The relevant resolution was named the "July Framework Agreement" or "July Package".[8]

The "July Package" consists of five parts: trade in agricultural products, non-agricultural market access, development, trade in services, and trade facilitation. The "July Package" clearly stipulates that the US and the EU shall gradually phase out agricultural subsidies and reduce import tariffs in response to the requests of developing members. In return, the developing members agreed to lower the industrial market access threshold; allow some members in extreme poverty to continue to implement protectionist policies in certain key areas. At the same time, the "July Package" also granted more flexibility to the benefits given to least developed members and recently acceded members.

---

[8]"Doha Work Programme", also known as "Framework Agreement" or "July Package", retrieved from https://www.wto.org/english/tratop_e/dda_e/draft_text_gc_dg_31july04_e.htm.

Nevertheless, the vision provided by the "July Package" did not last long. Progress remained slow in subsequent negotiations. The deadline that negotiations ought to have been completed in 2005 had to be postponed repeatedly. In December 2005, the Sixth WTO Ministerial Conference was held in Hong Kong, China. With Director-General Pascal Lamy's mediating, the ministers held closed-door negotiations for 72 hours non-stop and reached a partial consensus. The "Hong Kong Ministerial Declaration" was then issued. The Hong Kong Ministerial Conference made some progress in pharmaceuticals and public health, export subsidies, DFQF (Duty-free and Quota-free) access for least developed countries and other issues. Ministers also agreed that agriculture and non-agricultural related issues should be put forward first, but the actual outcome was far from that. Before the ink had dried, the "Hong Kong Ministerial Declaration" came under fire. Since then, several WTO mini-ministerial meetings have been held in Geneva, Pakistan, Brazil, India, France and other places, but the conclusion of negotiations has been repeatedly delayed due to differences among the members on key issues.

1.1.5 *Hopes and disappointments before the financial crisis*

By the end of July 2008, the world economy was in doldrums, food prices were inflated, energy prices had soared, the financial markets were in turmoil, and the 35 WTO member representatives gathered once again in Geneva in efforts to conclude the Doha Round. This was the closest the Doha Round came to concluding. On the one hand, two thirds of the negotiation subjects formed the Chairman's text, key members were close to a consensus on most issues, and the US and the EU had also expressed satisfaction with the signifyings for services by China and other emerging economies. On the other hand, the term of US President George W. Bush, who had put forth lackluster domestic economic policies, was coming to an end, and it was widely believed that the Bush administration would leave a positive political legacy by successfully concluding the Doha Round.

This was the first meeting that China was invited to join the seven WTO members (the US, China, the EU, India, Brazil, Japan, and Australia, also known as "G7") in the mini-ministerial Green Room meeting, marking the formal acceptance of China as one of WTO's core negotiating members. In the continuous nine days of talks, China fully demonstrated a flexible and constructive attitude in dealing with issues by looking at the overall situation, putting in positive efforts and making necessary concessions. These issues included trade distorting domestic support by developed countries, sensitive products produced by developing members, special safeguard measures, and other policies. China's Minister of Commerce at that time, Chen Deming, played a constructive role at various critical moments during the talks, making clear that as long as it was acceptable to other developing members, China would not hinder the progress of any issue in discussion. Nonetheless, on the last day of talks, India still insisted that developing members be granted special safeguard measures, such as increasing tariffs, to protect domestic agriculture from import surge of over 40%. The US firmly opposed this stance, leading to the tragic fallout of the Doha talks. The headline "We have never been so close to an agreement" on the WTO official website that day expressed their regret for the breakdown of negotiations. Brazilian Foreign Minister Celso Amorim said, "Any outside observer would not believe that after the progress made here, we could not conclude." EU Trade Commissioner Peter Mendelson said "We should not preclude the possibility of returning to the table," although he added that he did not think that there was "any chance" of modalities being agreed either this year or in the foreseeable future.

At almost the same time as the abrupt end of talks in Geneva, Lehman Brothers announced their bankruptcy on Wall Street. An investment bank that had weathered 158 years of storms came crashing down, triggering intense turmoil in global financial markets. The fortuitous timing of the two significant events exacerbated the world's concerns about the prospects of the multilateral trading system and worsened the negotiations. The financial crisis led to high unemployment in developed countries, the continual brewing of other issues such as high debt levels and "industrial hollowing", among other issues. The willingness to continue talks fell dramatically. Influenced by domestic politics, the US launched a massive economic stimulus package and double American exports campaign; its trade policies were tweaked and showed an obvious focus on domestic issues; and "anti-globalization" voices among common folk grew louder and drifted further away from Doha negotiations. Once seen as a round of multilateral negotiations that gave much room for prospective vision and imagination, the DDA fell into a prolonged state of "hibernation".

1.1.6 *Turning points at the Bali Ministerial Conference*

At the close of 2011 during the Eighth WTO Ministerial Conference, intense wars of words between members ensued in a bid to restore credibility within the multilateral trading system to regain credibility. The majority of members agreed to give up the single undertaking approach[9] that they had held

---

[9] Negotiating parties either accept and resolve all problems as a package, or do not resolve anything at all. Parties are not allowed to selectively accept some programs while rejecting others.

onto for a long time and to try new ways to advance talks by achieving "Early Harvest" on certain less-disputed topics. The US stressed that the Doha mandate had changed with time and new emerging economies ought to make greater contributions. In early 2012, it chose to try plurilateral negotiations — beginning with the service sector, where they had advantage — but it was met with the collective boycott by emerging economies. Subsequent plurilateral talks on services gradually drifted away from the multilateral processes and were named "Trade in Services Agreement" (TISA), formed by more than 20 members at the outside of the WTO framework. Nevertheless, most members did not want to give up on the Doha Round; they wanted to determine a clear direction in concluding the Doha Round by continuing various technical talks. They also strived to achieve "Early Harvest" agreements on trade facilitation, some agricultural issues and development issues by the Ninth WTO Ministerial Conference held at the end of 2013. However, the negotiations in Geneva moved with great difficulty. India and the US clashed severely on the issue of food security while Cuba, Bolivia, and Venezuela were not interested in the "Early Harvest" agreements and held on strongly to their positions. On November 26, Director-General Azevedo had no choice but to halt the talks in Geneva and the remaining issues were referred to the Bali Ministerial Conference for further negotiation.

On December 3, 2013, the Ninth WTO Ministerial Conference was inaugurated in Bali, Indonesia as scheduled. All the parties generally opined that the outcome of the Bali meetings would have a profound impact on the future of WTO, regardless of which direction it went. The planned four-day conference began with India standing firm on its position, declaring that there was no room for negotiation with regard to India's stand on food security, and if these conditions were not met, it would be tough to reach a final agreement. Cuba and the other four Latin American countries also expressed that the agenda of the Bali conference was not to their interests and there was also a lack of procedural transparency, thus they could not accept outcome reached at any Bali. There were no breakthroughs in the discussions on December 6 the last day scheduled. Azevedo and Indonesian Trade Minister Gita Irawan Wirjawan decided to extend the talks by another 24 hours in a last-ditch attempt to try for the "Early Harvest".

By the early morning of December 7, the heads of delegations meeting was forced to adjourn due to obstruction from Cuba and the other four Latin American countries. Small-scale consultations were conducted instead. At the break of dawn, news broke out that India had finally accepted the olive branch from the US but Cuba was not loosening its stance. At this time, in his office in downtown Beijing, Minister Gao Hucheng was making a long-distance call to the Cuban minister, and expressed how "China understands and supports the reasonable concerns of Cuba... and hopes that Cuba is able to look at the overall picture of safeguarding the interests of the developing member states...." At 11:30am, after five days of round-the-clock consultations, Azevedo excitedly announced when the first agreement reached by all WTO members, "For the first time in our history: the WTO has truly delivered". The moment the world had been waiting for had finally arrived. The "Bali Ministerial Declaration" reached at the conference included 10 "Early Harvest" documents on agriculture, trade facilitation, development and other issues, and promised to develop clear work objectives for outstanding Doha issues within the next 12 months so as to ultimately conclude the Doha Round negotiations. This was the first time in 18 years since the WTO was established, and the first in the 12 years of the Doha Round talks that a meaningful partial agreement was reached.

1.2 *Why the Doha Round went through so many difficulties*

The long-standing deadlock in the Doha Round talks reflects the competition for globalized interests and international discourse of power in the international political, economic and trade fields. Several key factors hindering the negotiation process can be seen from this round of talks.

1.2.1 *Innate issues*

Against a changed international environment after September 11, the DDA was a stopgap set up by the international community to a certain extent, for focusing on development and working together against terrorism. Former US Trade Representative Carla A. Hill once clearly stated in an article published in the *New York Times*: "The Doha Round of multilateral trade negotiations was launched in 2001, two months after the 9/11 terrorist attacks in the United States. It sought to boost economic growth through trade liberalization for all nations, but particularly for developing members. The security dimension was real."[10]

---

[10] Carla A. Hil, "A Trans-Atlantic Trade Pact for the World," *New York Times,* April 24, 2013, retrieved from http://www.nytimes.com/2013/04/25/opinion/global/a-trans-atlantic-trade-pact-for-the-world.html?_r=0.

One of the objectives of the multilateral trading system is development, but the Doha Round that was launched in a hurry due to security issues failed to fully address the actual concerns and reality of economic globalization in its attempt to correct the deficiencies of the multilateral trading system. Some of its goals even clashed with the WTO's rules, which stood for basic concepts of fairness and freedom. The economic disequilibrium and interconnected social conflict among countries accumulated in the process of globalization set the current round of talks on a course of fierce confrontation among members in the fight for core economic interests.

1.2.2 *Institutional issues*

Unlike past rounds of multilateral trade negotiations which focused more on tariff reductions, this round of talks included a wider range of topics and had the most number of participants. There are currently up to 159 parties taking part in the Doha Round negotiations, with varying economies of scales, levels of development and participation capacities. Nearly 20 topics in eight fields such as agriculture, non-agricultural market access, services, intellectual property rights, rules, dispute settlements, trade and environment as well as trade and development were covered. Not only were traditional areas such as the opening up of markets included, new fields like fishery subsidies, trade facilitations, geographical indications, and biological diversity convention were also discussed. Some sensitive topics involving direct conflicts of interests between developed and developing members were touched on, impacting the core of various countries' economic management. Furthermore, as the Doha Round negotiations followed the principle of "consensus" and conduct in the mode of single undertaking, the premise for a possible conclusion to the negotiations was that participants would agree on all issues discussed. The Doha Round has to resolve many historical issues that it had inherited from the Uruguay Round. It also has to meet the realistic needs of 21st century economic globalization, and the "unlimited" scope and high expectations of the negotiations ultimately make it overburdened and it can be likened to that of an over-decorated Christmas tree.

1.2.3 *Leadership issues*

The US and the EU have long had decisive voices in negotiations due to their positions as major promoters of trade liberalization and also the founders and leaders of the multilateral trading system. Consistency of fundamental interests is the foundation that has been jointly pushed for by the US and EU in past rounds of multilateral trade negotiations. However, in the Doha Round, the US strongly focused on market access while the EU was more concerned about protecting its own interests. The two differed greatly on geographical indications, anti-dumping, agriculture and other issues. Particularly, the 2008 financial crisis and debt crisis made them vulnerable and their policy coordination had been much weakened. At the same time, the emerging economies collectively rose up and negotiation groups were formed by developing members, particularly because many developing members could not become "free riders" in this round of negotiations and were unwilling to follow the advice of the US and EU. Both entities became increasingly unable to lead the negotiations as the days went by. In addition, the US government's "trade promotion authority"[11] expired at the end of 2007 and this gravely limited the US Trade Representative's authority for negotiations and also caused other members to doubt America's negotiation bids.

On the other hand, multinational companies used to be the biggest beneficiaries of international trade liberalization. The success of the Uruguay Round was largely due to the active participation and vigorous boost from the business community. Nonetheless, some issues that were of greatest interests to American and European multinational companies such as investment, competition policies, and technical standards, were not included in the agenda for negotiations. Instead, the focus was on the interests of small farmers. Many enterprises, especially multinational companies, were not interested in this round of negotiations and turned to bilateral free trade agreements to obtain direct access to certain countries' markets.

1.2.4 *Impact of regionalism*

As an important exception to GATT Article XXIV and Article V of the General Agreement on Trade in Services (GATS), regional trade agreements (RTAs) have long been bounded by multilateral disciplines and are broadly consistent with the WTO rules, in terms of scope and transparency *etc*. In recent years, as

---

[11] Refers to a foreign trade bargaining power granted by the Congress of the United States to the President, known as Trade Promotion Authority (TPA). This authorization allows the US Congress to approve or reject US trade agreements with foreign parties, but not modify the contents of the agreements.

Doha Round has been at an impasse, WTO members have emphasized regional trade liberalization more than multilateral liberalization, directly boosting the development of regionalism vigorously. Not only are more countries involved, developed members are also a strong force in this.

Regional and bilateral free trade agreements not only provided relevant partners with new choices for market access, these choices were also relatively less competitive than those market opportunities gained from multilateral agreements. At the same time, in RTA negotiations, the parties involved set their own topics and agenda for discussion, thus the negotiation cycle is short and there are quick results. Consequently, many WTO members gradually lost interest and patience with the more complex, technical and time-consuming DDA, and shifted their resources and policies towards bilateral and regional trade negotiations.

1.2.5 *Complicated state of interests*

In the Doha Round, developing members pay more attention to group defense, their negotiating power and leverage are significantly strengthened but their wide differing interests make negotiations more complicated. For example, developing members such as Brazil and India formed the "G-20 Group of Developing Countries" (G20)[12] and requested that the US and the EU greatly reduce agricultural tariffs and subsidies which distorted international trade; other developing members, led by Indonesia, formed the "G-33 Group of

---

[12] The "G-20 Group of Developing Countries" or G20, refers to the coalition of 20 developing countries pressing for reforms on agriculture. In August 2003, on the eve of the WTO Ministerial Conference in Cancun, some developing members submitted a joint proposal on agricultural negotiations. Thereafter, the mechanism of these countries in strengthening collective consultation and coordinating their stand is known as G20. From the initial 16, it has increased to 20 participating developing members and was once a coalition of 23 countries including Argentina, Brazil, Bolivia, Chile, China, Egypt, Cuba, Guatemala, India, Indonesia, Mexico, Nigeria, Pakistan, Paraguay, the Philippines, South Africa, Tanzania, Thailand, Uruguay, Venezuela, and Zimbabwe. Brazil is the presiding nation over the coalition group while China, India, Argentina and South Africa are core members. In order to upkeep a stable external image, the G20 members agreed to stay with the name, G20, regardless of how many participating nations there are in the future. The Group discusses extensively agricultural issues and strives for the interests of developing members. During agricultural talks, the G20 requests that developed members greatly reduce domestic support, eliminate export subsidies, reduce tariff peaks *etc*. In particular, the G20 proposals on market access and tariff reduction have been widely recognized at the Doha Round.

Developing Countries" (G33)[13] and proposed that the "three rural issues" of developing countries be granted special and differential treatment; the African "Cotton-4"[14] joined hands in requesting that the US cut cotton subsidies; 11 developing members led by South Africa and Brazil, formed the Non-Agricultural Market Access-11, or "NAMA-11"[15] which advocated for and ensured the developing members' implementation of "non-reciprocity" in terms of tariffs; and China and other recently acceded WTO members formed the group of "Recently Accepted Members" (RAMs), which requested that their contributions and concessions made during the accession process be considered.[16]

---

[13] The "G-33 Group of Developing Countries" or G33 refers to the coalition of 33 countries focused on agriculture. Founded around the time of the 2003 WTO Ministerial Conference in Cancun, the number of participating countries in G33 changes frequently along with the negotiation process. Currently, there are about 40 members with the main members being Indonesia, the Philippines, Cuba, Korea, Peru, Turkey, India, Honduras *etc*. To maintain a stable external image, the G33 members agreed that the group be called G33 regardless of the number of participating countries. Indonesia is the presiding country of G33 and the members are mainly developing members, with China being one of G33's observers. In terms of policy, G33 requests that developing members be granted Special Products (SP) and Special Safeguard Mechanism (SSM) privileges. Developing members can select SPs according to food security, farmers' livelihood and rural development needs, as well as be exempted from tariff cuts and commitments to expand tariff quotas. Relative to the SSG, SSM can only be used by developing members, and only for protecting certain agricultural products from the impact of imports.

[14] Africa's major cotton-producing countries: Benin, Mali, Chad, and Burkina Faso.

[15] During the Hong Kong Ministerial Conference in 2005, 11 developing members including China, submitted a proposal of principles. Gradually, the group evolved into a coalition for some of the developing members to discuss issues invovling non-agricultural market access (NAMA). Because "NAMA-11" takes a more conservative stance in negotiating formulas and flexibility which is distinct from China's stance, China did not join this coalition group, but this group is still known as "NAMA-11".

[16] "Recently Acceded Members" (RAMs) is a concept proposed by China at the WTO Doha Round negotiations. The group seeks flexibility in four areas including no concessions on certain products and lesser concessions in other products, longer implementation periods and longer grace periods because members who have recently joined WTO have made extensive commitments and great contributions in the accession process but are still in a transitional period. As one of China's core issues of concern, this issue of treatment of new members has already been widely acknowledged by WTO members. Paragraph 12 of the July Framework adopted by the WTO General Council in 2004 requires members to discuss the issue of treatment of new members. Paragraph 58 of the "Hong Kong Ministerial Declaration" states that "we recognize the special situation of recently-acceded Members who have undertaken extensive market access commitments at the time of accession. The situation will be taken into account in the negotiations". But members still have considerably different opinions about new membership criteria, new membership, and treatment or privileges of new members.

In addition, the "Least Developed Countries" (LDCs), "African, Caribbean and Pacific Countries" (ACP),[17] "Small and Vulnerable Economies" (SVEs) also proposed motions to bid for their group interests. The diverse interest demands of various negotiating groups continually eroded the ambition of the Doha negotiations and turned the main contradiction from "the North-South conflict" of previous rounds to the "North-South conflict + South-South conflict".

2 Wrangling Over Rules-setting at the Doha Round

The Doha Round talks — along with global power dynamics — have undergone profound changes. The talks have become an important and intense battlefield for the rights to shape circumstances, set trade rules and lead discourse. The collective rise of emerging economies and developing members and their desire to change economic power into institutional power has become a notable force in promoting the reform and adjustment of international order. Developed members who have long dominated international trade rules will not let go of their power easily. Various parties are fighting for their own interpretations of rules and the introduction of new rules. As negotiations deepen, the debate becomes more intense and the impact on multilateral trading system becomes more far-reaching.

2.1 *The discords on introducing new rules*

The "Singapore issues" have been named as such because they were first brought up at the 1996 WTO Ministerial Conference in Singapore. They cover issues such as investment, competition policies, transparency in government procurement, and trade facilitation. The debate among developed and developing members, as to whether "Singapore issues" should be included into WTO rules, was the main focus of the 2001 Doha Ministerial Conference, the 2003 Ministerial Conference in Cancun, Mexico, as well as the 2004 mini-ministerial discussions in Geneva. The Cancun conference ended fruitlessly and the Doha Round experienced its first setback as a result of WTO members differing considerably on the mode of discussion for the four issues mentioned above, on top of disagreeing about cotton export subsidies and other issues.

---

[17] The international economic organization of African, Caribbean and Pacific developing countries.

The EU and other developed members were initiators of the "Singapore issues" talks but some developing members strongly opposed its inclusion into the Doha Round. Developing members were worried that the outcome would increase their obligations and not bring much tangible economic benefits. Some of the developing members led by Brazil and India expressed that if developed members could not make concessions on the reduction of agricultural subsidies, they would not agree to participate in negotiations on new issues. Other small economies and least developed members said that due to their limited resources and capabilities, they did not advocate the discussion of "Singapore issues".

After the failure of the Cancun conference and months of internal deliberation, the EU decided to be flexible on certain topics of discussion. Pascal Lamy, the EU Trade Commissioner at that time, said in December 2003 that the "Singapore issues" could be decoupled and not negotiated as a package; all parties could take a voluntary approach to the talks, and it was recommended that discussions should first begin on trade facilitation and transparency in government procurement. The results of the negotiations can also be selectively applied. Despite these concessions, there was still a wide gap between the flexibility that the EU showed on "Singapore issues" and the desires of the developing members (who only agreed to work on trade facilitation and not the other three issues).

In July 2004, "Singapore issues" once again became the focus at the mini-ministerial conference held in Geneva. To prevent the talks from entering a crunch again, US Trade Representative Robert Zoellick and EU Trade Commissioner Pascal Lamy ultimately compromised and conceded on the issues of investment, competition policy and transparency in government procurement, starting negotiations on trade facilitation instead. Eventually, the parties reached a consensus and drafted the "July Framework Agreement" at the Doha Round.

The fight for a stronger voice on "Singapore issues" also planted seeds of trouble for the Doha Round. In fact, the topics of investment, competition, government procurement and technical standards were precisely the issues of priority for US and European multinational companies who used to be the important driving forces of the multilateral trade negotiations. Service sector made up more than two thirds of the developed countries' economic activities and hence were in their interests. When the focus of talks shifted from the service sector to agricultural subsidies, the engine of international trade liberalization seemed to have quietly lost power.

Property rights and public health were also issues of contention. Since the "Agreement on Trade-Related Aspects of Intellectual Property Rights" (TRIPS) was developed at the Uruguay Round, there have been continual debates between developed and developing members on whether the scope of TRIPS and depth of patent protection should be expanded. Developed countries hoped for high level protection of intellectual property rights, while developing members wanted to consider public interests and appropriately loosen intellectual property protection. One of the focuses of debates was the compulsory licensing of pharmaceutical drugs in addressing public health crises.[18]

At the Doha Ministerial Conference in November 2001, South Africa, Kenya and other countries that were, and still are, facing public health problems caused by AIDS, tuberculosis, malaria and various epidemic diseases, requested ministers to grant authorization for negotiations on relaxing the compulsory licensing system for patent protection in the TRIPS Agreement. The Ministerial Conference passed the "Declaration on the TRIPS Agreement and Public Health", recognizing the rights of developing members to protect public health and access to medicines, and established rules of interpretation. It stressed the need for the TRIPS agreement to be amended accordingly as part of the international community's initiatives to address public health problems.

The parties continued battling and debating from the start until the end of negotiations. The developing members advocated the authoritative interpretation of Article 30 of the TRIPS agreement: enabling the compulsory licensing system to be included among the exceptions of exclusive patent rights, and rules regarding export rights be increased so that developing members had rights to produce, sell and export medication. Developed members including the EU and Switzerland, on the other hand, advocated for the amendment of Article 31 of the TRIPS agreement, which involved the reduction of existing stringent limitations placed on export rights, and increased supervision and restraints on the use of compulsory patent licensing. The US proposed the amendment of Article 31 to be delayed until an appropriate period and not activate the WTO dispute settlement mechanism, and only restoring it when public health problems eased.

After several consultations in 2002, the developing members agreed to resolve the issue by modifying Article 31. However, due to pressure from its domestic industries, the US insisted on narrowing the range of diseases covered by the amendment, causing negotiations to run aground. In 2003, due to political pressure from the SARS epidemic, the US made concessions on the scope of diseases but requested that the General Council refine provisions on preventing the abuse of power and avoid injuring patent protection by issuing

---

[18] Cheng Xiuqiang, "Controversial Values Affecting the Reform of the WTO Dispute Settlement Mechanism," in *Ten Years and Rising* (Shanghai People's Publishing House, 2011).

a presidential statement. This action finally led to some consensus being reached among developing members.

In using the TRIPS agreement to address the establishment of consensus on public health problems, the WTO members had made a breakthrough in the TRIPS patent protection system, legally defining developing member countries' rights and procedures to import drugs with compulsory licenses. It was one of the few achievements the Doha Round had been able to make and implement so far. As the first beneficiary of this outcome, Canada legally exported the first batch of generic copies of a patented AIDS drug to Rwanda in 2007. Nevertheless, at present, members continue to struggle to improve those TRIPS terms against various public health rights, obligations and monitoring mechanisms. To date, the "Amendment to those TRIPS Agreement" adopted by the WTO General Council in December 2005 has not been officially put into effect.

2.2 *Contention on existing rules*

Rule negotiation is one of the most important issues in the Doha Round. Paragraph 28 of "Doha Ministerial Declaration" explicitly authorizes rule negotiation: (Parties shall) agree to negotiations aimed at clarifying and improving disciplines under the Agreements on Implementation of Article VI of the GATT 1994 and on Subsidies and Countervailing Measures, while preserving the basic concepts, principles and effectiveness of these Agreements and their instruments and objectives, and taking into account the needs of developing and least developed members. As can be noted, interpretation, modifications and implementation of WTO rules could be made according to the needs of developing members, especially the least developed countries.

2.2.1 *Special and differential treatment*

Special and differential treatment refers to the principle that developing members are allowed to make lesser reduction commitments than developed countries. One of the core principles of multilateral trade rules is the most-favored nation treatment.[19] In the first 20 years after the signing of GATT, the

---

[19] Most-favored nation (MFN) treatment states that the benefit, favor, privilege or immunity given to a product's country of origin or destination country should immediately and unconditionally be granted to any other parties with the same product. In other words, the benefits, favors, privileges, or immunity that a country (or region) grants to another state (or region) according to treaty must not, regardless when, be lesser than the preferential treatment given to another third party (country or region).

contracting parties abided by the principle of *de jure* equality and multilateral rules regarded developed and developing members equally, but this form of equality did not lead to equitable economic and social effects. The Tokyo Round determined the right of developing members to enjoy special and differential treatment[20] in the multilateral trading system. The additional terms in GATT Articles XVIII, XXXVII, XVI and XXVIII provided space for developing members to implement policies flexibly. This was a giant step forward for the multilateral trading system and they have greatly enhanced the attractiveness and influence of the system.

According to statistics released by the WTO Development Committee in October 2000, WTO developing members accounting for more then 80% of the total, are entitled to as many as 145 special and differential treatment provisions among the many WTO agreements and decisions. Besides the commonly discussed issues such as non-reciprocal market access, technical assistance and capacity building, the "best endeavor" clause and special exceptions, the development dimension of the Doha Round is aimed at achieving the respective development goals of relevant members by way of special and differential treatment. These focuses of the Doha Round include the treatment of new members, the cotton issue, DFQF (duty-free and quota-free), tropical products, food security, weak countries, island countries, landlocked countries, compulsory licensing, erosion compensation, and capacity building. The negotiations are far more complex than we can imagine.

On the other hand, in order to receive special and differential treatment, several groups can be seen fighting for their own interests and even going against each other in the talks. For example, the G-20 Group of Developing Countries which emphasizes the interests of agricultural exports from developing countries and the the G-33 Group of Developing Countries which advocates the protection of interests of developing members' agricultural producers had fundamentally different opinions on the opening up of developing

---

[20] The content of special and differential treatment can be summarized as follows: To fulfil the purpose of WTO, taking into account the special circumstances and needs of developing members. Developing members may, under certain terms and conditions, depart from the general rights and obligations of WTO Agreements and enjoy more favorable treatment. The essence of special and differential treatment is to allow developing members to depart from the MFN principle and assume their obligations in a non-equal manner. It embodies the pursuit of substantive equality and the principles of fairness and mutual benefit in international economic law; it is a development of the traditional principle of equality and mutual benefit.

members' agricultural markets; the NAMA-11 not only disagreed with the developed nations on the opening up of industrial markets, its claims were also not accepted by Chile, Singapore, Costa Rica and other export-dependent small and medium developing members; countries within the ACP feared the reduction of tariffs by the US and Europe would affect its textile and apparel export industry and asked for compensation due to "preference erosion".

The battle of rules for special and differential treatment has not only become the focus of the Doha Round and the reason for the decline in level of ambition. It has also led to the intensification of competing interests and antagonism among members, making it even more challenging for the multilateral trading system. In July 2008, it was precisely because neither India nor the US would concede on the special safeguard mechanism provision for agricultural products that the Doha Round was near 80% completion reached an impasse. Even at the time of the ninth ministerial meeting in 2013 when parties strove to achieve the "Early Harvest" with low level of ambition, issues such as special and differential treatment in trade facilitation, and food security, among others, were still the most sensitive and difficult to resolve in the talks.

2.2.2 *The preference erosion and compensation*

The preference erosion and compensation was another issue of contention. The preference erosion refers to the compromising of unilateral tariff concessions made by the developed country. For historical reasons, some countries that enjoy tariff preference and exemption when exporting to European and American markets feared losing their current competitiveness in the markets because of multilateral NAMA tariff reductions. As such, they took a hardline stance in the Doha Round negotiations and expressed that whatever way reductions are made, the preference erosion must first be addressed and greater flexibility be granted.

Since GATT era, the principles of MFN and national treatment have always been at the core of multilateral trade rules, and have been respected and abided by all members. Only in very exceptional circumstances and with the consent of all parties can individual members temporarily depart from these principles. However, in the Doha Round negotiations, due to various existing preferential arrangements among members, multilateral trade liberalization inevitably has had an impact on the vested interests of certain members. For example, some ACP members enjoy duty-free treatment exports of textile and apparel to the US and the EU markets while China,

India and other countries without bilateral preferential arrangements were subjected to a 20% tariff. According to the Swiss formula, US has to cut its apparel tariffs by around 8%. Countries who enjoy duty-free treatment would either seek compensation for "preference erosion" or ask by the US and the EU to delay tariff cuts so as to keep their export competitiveness for a longer period of time.

Exclusive preferential trade agreements are in fact discriminatory to other exporting countries and go against the principle of MFN. Actually, the high tariffs and tariff peaks of developed members in textiles, clothing and footwear industries are precisely sensitive topics left behind by the Uruguay Round and what the Doha Round seeks to address; yet the preference erosion demands made by the "interest losers" during the negotiations provide a reasonable excuse for the US and the EU to maintain their high tariff rates. Another strange phenomenon in the Doha Round negotiations is the dissent among LDCs with regard to DFQF initiatives. African LDCs are apprehensive about the competitiveness of Asian LDCs and worry that their duty-free treatment would be eroded by the implementation of DFQF. Therefore, they are opposed to the full implementation of DFQF and this also provided the "legitimacy" for the US of no commitment on the DFQF. There is a very important systems issue at stake here — which, multilateral trade liberalization or bilateral trade arrangements, should be the main channels? If preferential trade arrangements supersede the principle of MFN, then the seriousness and binding power of the multilateral trading system are inevitably affected.

2.2.3 *Voluntary participation in sectoral concessions*

"Sectoral concessions" are a negotiation mode where some members commit to initiating trade liberalization on a particular class of products. The "Information Technology Agreement" (ITA) is considered one of the most successful outcomes of sectoral concessions negotiations since the establishment of the WTO.

Since the Doha Round started, the issue of sectoral concessions has always been a hot topic of contention in non-agricultural market access negotiations. Paragraph 16 of "The Doha Ministerial Declaration" as well as the "July Framework Agreement" clearly state that products of sectoral concessions should be of export interest for developing members; the "Hong Kong Ministerial Declaration" further clarifies the voluntary nature of sectoral concessions. Nevertheless, developed members and developing members were at loggerheads throughout the Doha Round with regard to "voluntary participation" and "selection of products of interest".

During the July 2008 mini-ministerial meeting, the developed members came to realize that there were limited market access opportunities according to the NAMA tariff reduction formula, and it was better to pressure China and other emerging economies into opening up their chemical, machinery, electronic and other sectors. Pressured by the developed members, WTO Director-General Pascal Lamy suggested, in a footnote of his one-page text that sectoral concessions be included in the next phase of negotiations. China and the other emerging economies, however, opposed.

In the second half of 2009, the US attempted to bypass the multilateral negotiations on sectoral concessions and submitted a direct bilateral request to China, India and Brazil on tariff-cut of products in chemical, mechanical, and electrical and electronic sectors to the same level as that of the US. These demands were once again rejected by the emerging economies. In October 2010, Japan and Canada proposed the idea of "Basket Approach", suggesting that different products be classified into different baskets and tariff cuts negotiated accordingly so as to increase flexibility for developing members and attract more of them to participate in sectoral concessions. The US insisted that the vast majority of products must be included in the zero-tariff basket. Brazil rejected their proposal.[21]

Thereafter, in multilateral and bilateral consultations, the US repeatedly stressed the critical mass of sectoral concessions and emphasized that the emerging economies would have to bear the responsibility for the failure of the Doha Round if they refused to participate. At the March 2011 Trade Negotiations Committee meeting, the US openly denounced the lack of sincerity in negotiations shown by the emerging economies and sent out a clear message that they would abandon the Doha Round.

The sectoral concessions dispute epitomizes the struggle of competing interests between developed and developing members. To achieve their goal of market access, developed members ignored the rightful "voluntary participation" nature of sectoral concessions and did not consider the provision of "products of export interest for developing members" at the Doha Round, shifting the blame to the emerging economies based on the "responsibility"

---

[21] Fu Kangrong, "Sectoral Concessions — The Great Hindrance of the Doha Round" in *Ten Years and Rising* (Shanghai People's Publishing House, 2011).

argument. This resulted in a rift of trust among the main members and the Doha Round, once again, fell into a state of crisis.

3 The Future of the Multilateral Trading System

History tells us that the world economy and trade system undergo a major reshuffle and huge adjustments after every crisis. In recent years, global economic governance has generally been characterized by the lack of power in the Doha negotiations, unusually active regional and sub-regional cooperation, the emergence of a wide range of international trade rules, and the development of the multilateral trading system is at a critical crossroad. Compared with previous financial crises, the dominance of "American governance" that had continued for 60 years after World War II has, to some extent, been broken. The turbulent consolidation period in the development of a multipolar global economic governance system may last for a longer period of time, and the multilateral trading system will also undergo a painful period of integration.

3.1 *The irreplaceable multilateral trading system*

The poor start to the Doha Round does not indicate that there are fundamental problems with the multilateral trading system. In fact, rule negotiations are a big part of the multilateral trading system. Looking back at the last 60 years, one will notice that economic globalization could not have taken place without the multilateral trading system.

In 1929, an unprecedented economic crisis broke out in the capitalist world. The major capitalist countries successively implemented strict trade protectionism policies and in the US, the Republican government passed the "Smoot-Hawley Tariff Act",[22] raising tariffs to record-high levels. However, such a beggar-thy-neighbor policy eventually led to the collapse of international trade, further exacerbating the crisis and worsened conflicts among countries. Since

---

[22] This bill raised the import duties on 890 kinds of goods. On average, import duties were increased to about 60% of the taxable commodity values. As a result, in 1931, the average tax rate on imported goods of the US was 41.5% higher than in 1914. The Tariff Act sparked a global tariff war. Thirty-three countries protested, and seven countries took retaliatory measures when the act was implemented. By the end of 1931, 25 countries had joined in the boycott. From late 1931 to early 1932, the US issued another decree imposing 10%–100% import duties on some industrial and agricultural products, causing scuffles in the tariff duties boycott movement, and the complete shake-up of the global free trade system.

then, few with insight have begun seeking the establishment of an effective new order and rule-based system for regulating international trade. After World War II, GATT was established and the multilateral trading system was set up.

Since its establishment, the multilateral trading system has not stopped improving itself. GATT has presided over eight rounds of multilateral trade negotiations, and each round of negotiations has opened up global trade further. After numerous and continuous amendments and additions, by providing a rules-based system, and practical and effective dispute settlement procedures, as well as long-term binding commitments made by contracting parties with regard to economic and trade policies, the multilateral trading system has fostered a transparent and non-discriminatory environment for international trade.

On January 1, 1995, the WTO was formally established, becoming the greatest reform of the multilateral trading system since World War II. The WTO is a legal international organization that promotes free trade, mainly responsible for the formulation of multilateral trade rules, promoting international trade liberalization and facilitation, and its main functions cover three aspects.

The first is the management and improvement of multilateral trade rules including trade in goods, trade in services, TRIPS and many other agreements, ministerial declarations and commitments, and managing the above rules by establishing relevant committees, boosting international trade liberalization for members and providing a negotiation platform for improving WTO rules. Trade in goods, trade in services, and intellectual property are all under WTO jurisdiction, thus the WTO has greater authority than GATT in mediating trade disputes among members. The second is the management of trade disputes. Trade disputes among members can be submitted to the WTO Dispute Settlement Body (DSB) for trial. The third aspect is the supervision of members' trade policies. The WTO conducts regular trade policy reviews on members to enhance transparency and assess the impact of their domestic policies. This international financial crisis once again demonstrated the irreplaceable role of multilateral trade rules. Since the financial crisis in 2008, the WTO has released 11 copies of supervisory reports related to key members' trade policies, and called upon all members to commit to not taking any new measures that are inconsistent with WTO rules, effectively suppressing the rise of trade protectionism.

In 1948 when GATT was newly established, there were only 23 parties who were mostly developed countries. Today, the WTO has grown to over 160 members, including almost all the countries around the world participating in international trade. Even when the Doha Round reached an impasse and members were worried about the future of the multilateral trading system, Russia and Moldova, countries that are vastly different in size and influence still decided to join the WTO, indicating that the international community recognized the value of the multilateral trading system.

For many years, the strongest intuition people have of the multilateral trading system is to encourage members to open up markets, but an important role of the multilateral trading system is to develop a set of rules of conduct, in particular, an effective trade dispute settlement mechanism[23] that is uniform, efficient and mandatory, to provide broad space and a platform for members to safeguard interests and participate in global governance. In the case of the Doha Round, such negotiations within a multilateral trading system have been hampered for many reasons. Besides a lack of leadership and differing opinions, poor agenda-setting and negotiating mechanisms are also evident. With the surge in regional trade agreements, people understandably became more suspicious and worried about the prospects of the multilateral trading system. Although the "Early Harvest" negotiations were successful, the contradictions inherent in the Doha Round were not fundamentally resolved.

The Doha Round negotiations on market access and rules will not see great results in the near future. The US and other major developed members will continue to pursue the plurilateral, regional and bilateral negotiations where their major interests lie. Therefore, the multilateral trading system will enter a slump period where its role in negotiation is weak and the dispute settlement mechanism lacks the capability to handle 21st century trade frictions. The US and the EU are likely to choose mega-FTA approach supplemented by multilateral agreements to promote trade liberalization, and gain advantages in rule-making. At the same time, we should also observe that both entities are still highly interested in the multilateral trading system and their determination to obtain more market access through multilateral agreements has not changed. In fact, whether the current Doha Round's "Early Harvest", ITA expansion, "Agreement on Government Procurement" (GPA) negotiations, or future non-agricultural "sectoral concessions", reduction of agricultural subsidies, or even implementation of TISA and APEC environmental goods lists, the multilateral trading system is still the best means to take. Thus, in the long run, as global value chains develop further, regional trade agreements will gradually move towards anchoring, integrating, and return to the non-discriminatory multilateral trading system. The time required for this regression is dependent upon the collective wisdom and efforts of the governments of WTO members.

---

[23] According to the WTO website, from its establishment in 1995 until the end of September 2013, the WTO had handled to 467 trade dispute cases among members. Retrieved from http://www.wto.org/english/tratop_e/dispu_e/dispu_status_e.htm.

In the Doha Round "Early Harvest" negotiations, all parties held out and eventually succeeded, proving that the multilateral trading system is still the most preferred trade policy for most WTO members. The confidence and expectations that people have towards the multilateral trading system, in particular, the WTO negotiation function, is able to alleviate the enthusiasm for regional trade agreements. At the same time, as the struggles among the different parties grow increasingly fierce and complex, it has become more difficult to reach consensus in multilateral negotiations. Whether by way of negotiating small packages such as the "Early Harvest" agreement, or through plurilateral approaches such as "Information Technology Agreement" or "Environmental Goods Agreement" to advance negotiations, the benefits will be enjoyed by all members following the MFN principle. This has become increasingly recognized by all members. However, the multilateralism of plurilateral negotiation outcomes allows other members to reap the profits of others' efforts and enjoy free riding — this phenomenon will erode the progress of global trade liberalization to varying degrees and ought to be closely watched. For example, the recently launched plurilateral negotiations on environmental products are focused solely on tariff elimination in the pursuit of market access, overlooking the social development and environmental protection concerns of the majority of developing members. The relevant authorities in China ought to pay attention to such a trend.

3.2 *Multilateral rules to undergo an awkward phase of fragmentation*

The WTO has designated "preferential trade agreements" and "non-tariff measures" as the main topics for the *World Trade Report* in 2011 and 2012 respectively, considering the two to be the biggest challenges faced by international trade rules currently. As of March 2013, the WTO members have notified 210 free trade agreements that are still in force. Undoubtedly, the number of regional trading agreements will continue to rise and will become an important part of international trade relations in the long run. There are several types of non-tariff measures, some were birthed out of public policy considerations such as health, safety and the environment, and others were aimed at influencing market competitiveness. While public policy and non-tariff measures can create trade flows, they may also produce policy substitution effects. The regulatory diversity of regional agreements results in the continual increase of international trade non-tariff barriers, causing a discriminatory effect on trade, and also creates challenges for WTO's focus and objectives, as well as affects the value that governments place on WTO's role in global trade relations.

Over the last few decades, the focus of regional trade agreements was on tariff reductions while the recent regional trade agreements focus more on rule reconstruction, especially those beyond the scope of the WTO rules. Research shows that more than one third of the regional trade agreements concluded since the start of the Doha Round contain rules that are beyond the scope of the Doha Round negotiations and are not covered by current WTO trade rules. Among these agreements, 47% of them refer to competition policies, 39% have to do with capital flows, 37% include items on intellectual property not covered under TRIPS, and 31% discuss investment. In addition, bilateral investment agreements are more related to rules regarding the core of global value chain, namely: trade, investment, services.

In current and future global competition, the domestic regulatory mechanisms in areas such as product standards, competition policies, investment policies, state-owned enterprises policies, government procurement policies as well as environmental and labor standards will play increasingly important roles and have significant impact on international competition. It is more flexible and easier to coordinate agreements through bilateral or regional trade agreements among a few countries than doing so through multilateral agreements. Henceforth, for a period of time, WTO members may prefer to carry out deeper and integrative cooperation under the FTA or RTA framework. The Trans-Pacific Partnership (TPP), Transatlantic Trade and Investment Partnership (TTIP), TISA and other partnerships led by the US, have proposed integrating relevant standards in automotive safety, environmental protection, food and drug safety, intellectual property protection and other fields among participating parties. These partnerships aim to fully unleash the potential, enhance the compatibility of bilateral and regional rules, and simplify relevant procedures by improving market access so as to ensure a more business-friendly environment.

As early as in 1995, Jagdish Bhagwati, Professor of Economics at Columbia University, in his paper on "US Trade Policy", used the term, "spaghetti bowl" phenomenon[24] which rapidly became a buzzword in international trade theory. The "spaghetti bowl" phenomenon refers to the different preferential treatment and rules of origin in various bilateral and regional trade agreements which are intertwined, inseparable, and chaotic, thereby complicating trade rules among

---

[24] Jagdish Bhagwati, "U.S. Trade Policy: The Infatuation with Free Trade Areas", in Claude Barfield (ed.) *The Dangerous Obsession with Free Trade Areas* (The AEI Press, 1995), pp. 1–18.

the different countries. "Most Favored Nation" treatment of the WTO eventually became the "Worst Favored Nation" treatment. Tariff rates based on the "MFN" principle actually became the worst tariff rates among WTO members. On the one hand, the boom in regional trade arrangements boosted the liberalization and facilitation of global trade investment but on the other hand, it also challenged the authority and binding strength of multilateral rules. Renato Ruggiero, the first WTO Director-General, pointed out that once Europe and the US joined hands, regardless of the degree of openness, there would objectively be a conflict with the multilateral trading system and it might even override it, undermining the functions and prestige of the multilateral trading system.[25]

3.3 *Intensified conflict between emerging powers and developed nations*

The financial crisis caused both the US and the EU to fall into the greatest post-WWII economic crisis, and profound changes took place in economic globalization. On the one hand, emerging developing members led by China seized the opportunity and rose rapidly while Western developed countries declined in strength. On the other hand, global economic governance became multipolar, and the competition of rules grew increasingly fierce. Developed countries reflected deeply about this new context, adjusted their globalization strategies promptly, and attempted to establish large-scale bilateral FTAs to regain rule control and build an "upgraded" version of economic globalization. The power battle between emerging economies and developed ones intensified.

Bilateral and regional cooperation is flexible and more efficient in negotiations. Not only can a greater range of topics be discussed as compared to WTO negotiations, countries can also have a stronger say in proposing rules. In recent years, the US and EU have made efforts to create rule templates through regional trade arrangements such as TPP, TTIP and TISA. As these regional agreements are massive, have high standards and cover a broad range of fields, once they are established, they will form a cross-regional FTA network with the US as the center, radiating out across the global economic map. This ensures that the US continues dominating and receiving maximum benefit from the new round of economic globalization. The US will then take the highest ground with regard to creating 21st century global trade and investment rules, introduce these rules into the WTO platform to promote their multilateralization,

---

[25] Liu Yueju, "The US and EU's FTA Idea Has Resurfaced (The Economic Perspective)," *People*, May 16, 2012, http://finance.people.com.cn/GB/17897344.html.

forcing the majority of developing members to accept the rules and thus, defend its profit mechanism in the international arena.

Undoubtedly, the financial crisis has also caused developed members to begin adjusting their attitudes and strategies to a certain extent, and this has provided opportunities for China and other emerging economies to participate comprehensively in global governance. It was precisely in the year the financial crisis occurred that China become a core member of G20 and the WTO Doha negotiations. On the other hand, developed countries turned their attention to regional and bilateral negotiations, objectively freeing up room for developing members, particularly emerging economies, to expand their influence on the multilateral trading system. In 2013, during the WTO Director-General elections, it was subtly noted that the US and the EU who had traditionally dominated multilateral trade issues, were unable to continue controlling the results of the Director-General elections. This has objectively formed the unwritten convention that developed and developing members, as well as different regions, will take turns to the role of Director-General. The voice and influence of developing members in the multilateral trading system had grown significantly stronger. Emerging economies ought to seize the chance, face the new challenges of economic globalization upfront, courageously take on responsibilities and duties, so as to gain a footing in the new round of contested rules.

3.4 *The imperative WTO reform*

Back in 1999, then EU Trade Commissioner, Pascal Lamy, complained that the WTO was operating at "medieval" efficiency and called for a reform. Since the establishment of WTO, relevant discussions regarding various WTO legislative, judicial and administrative functions, have not stopped. With the deadlock of the Doha Round, improving WTO legislative powers has become the focus of attention. In April 2013, the panel nominated by Lamy made specific recommendations including compliance with the principles of non-discrimination, transparency and inclusiveness, effective handling of the equality and flexibility of members' rights and obligations, simplifying and strengthening the decision-making mechanism, improving the professionalism, research capabilities and management standards of the WTO Secretariat, among others.[26]

As an intergovernmental organization, the "member-driven" and "consensus" principles of the WTO fully reflect the compliance with its value of

---

[26] Panel Report on Defining the Future of Trade, "The Future of Trade: The Challenges of Convergence", World Trade Organisation, April 24, 2013, https://www.wto.org/english/thewto_e/dg_e/dft_panel_e/future_of_trade_report_e.pdf.

non-discrimination. However, with the substantial increase in the number of members and the subjects of negotiations, the disadvantages of the "consensus" principle are becoming increasingly apparent. On the one hand, for many of the members with limited resources, absence from the meetings means acquiescence when a resolution is passed. On the other hand, the adoption of essential measures that have to be approved as a resolution may be hindered with the objection of a single member. Due to the protraction of the Doha Round, the "single undertaking" negotiation approach of the WTO has also been widely criticized, affecting the confidence of members participating in the negotiations and even becoming an important push factor for members to seek for plurilateral negotiations instead of multilateral negotiations.

The essence of multilateralism should be mutual respect for various parties' interests and rights. If the WTO maintains status quo, it would only be able to handle old trade issues at best and gradually become marginalized or fragmented. Only by going with the times can it continue and consolidate its viability. Over the years, various parties have actively explored WTO reform. Most countries are not opposed to the "consensus" principle in terms of decision-making, so the issue at hand is: How can its operations be improved? Some advocate "multispeed forward", that is, depending on the respective content and member obligations, to improve the efficiency of decision-making by way of consensus, critical mass, majority wins, reverse consensus *etc.*; some advocate allowing NGOs, stakeholders and the general public to participate directly in WTO affairs. In terms of negotiation approach, some advocate abandoning "single undertaking" for "variable geometrical agreements" such as plurilateral or critical mass modes; some advocate following the GATS schedule. With regard to management of content, some are for prompt adjustments to be made for prioritized issues so as to reflect the change of times; some have pushed for the enhancement of trade policy reviews and supervision, and strengthening of compliance with member policy notification; some have advocated improving the research functions of the WTO Secretariat and granting it the rights to submit, incorporate content of members' policies, and urge members to amend and confirm content.[27]

---

[27] Richard E. Baldwin, "Twenty-First Century Regionalism, Doha, and the Future of the WTO", German Marshal Fund, Policy Brief, April 11, 2011; Patrick Low, "WTO Decision-Making for the Future", WTO Staff Working Paper ERSD-2011-05, May 2, 2011, retrieved from https://www.wto.org/english/res_e/reser_e/ersd201105_e.pdf; Petersen, P. (2006) "The WTO Decision-Making Process and International Transparency", *World Trade Review*, Vol. 5, No. 1 Warwick Commission, "The Multilateral Trade Regime: Which Way Forward?" Warwick, University of Warwick, December 2007, retrieved from https://www2.warwick.ac.uk/research/warwickcommission/worldtrade/report/uw_warcomm_tradereport_07.pdf.

Whether it concerns managing content or making decisions, the WTO should be a multilateral institution that helps the majority of its members achieve their goals. WTO reform cannot be over compensative, neither should it meddle in others' affairs. It has to maintain the uniqueness and professionalism of the multilateral trading system and complement other organizations. Its fundamental tasks include harmonizing national trade policies, balancing international trade relations, settling trade dispute, restraining protectionism, and striving for world economic growth in a balanced, inclusive, sustainable, innovative and secure way. As a big family with 160 members, it is impossible for the WTO to please all members but it should seek to pursue fairness for all members, and avoid abusing the rights of minority countries. Therefore, regardless of how the reform takes place, non-discrimination and transparency must remain as WTO's core principles.

4 Practice and Thoughts on China's Participation in the Multilateral Trading System

In today's era of economic globalization, there are objective reasons for the continual emergence of regional trade agreements, yet history has shown that fair, transparent and non-discriminatory multilateral trading systems are eventually the preferred national trade policy. As a major beneficiary of the multilateral trading system, there is an urgent need for China to study how it can better adapt to the new trends of the international community, and actively and prudently play its role in the system.

4.1 *Make full use of the system*

The greatest benefit China received upon joining the WTO is the dividend system of being a member. The WTO membership was the most important milestone for China since it began its reformation period and opening up more than 30 years ago. Not only has joining WTO tremendously improved China's external environment and its conditions for participation in the international division of labor and trade, it has also provided strong external impetus for domestic reforms. During accession to the WTO, China underwent the largest, most comprehensive and thorough cleansing of laws, regulations and policy measures in history. The central government and its departments reviewed more than 2,300 laws, regulations and departmental rules; the local governments revised more than 190,000 legislative items, regulations and other policy measures. The long-term benefits brought forth from this far outweigh the benefits resulting from the opening up of the market. China actively uses the dispute settlement mechanism of the WTO to safeguard its own interests so as to avoid factors such as bilateral politics from interfering in foreign trade.

By participating fully in WTO activities, China's role and status in the multilateral trading system and global economic governance have undergone significant change. From being a new member that had to learn and familiarize itself with WTO's rules and regulations, it has gradually applied and mastered the rules and become a "mature member" who now participates in rule formulation. Such maturity is reflected in how China appropriately and professionally manages trade and economic relations with more than 150 WTO member nations in the multilateral trading system.

The international trade arena is the best playing field for China to participate in global governance and show that it has and can exert significant influence. Currently, there is a lack of leadership and driving force in multilateral cooperation. Objectively, the financial crisis has weakened the leadership of the US and the EU in the multilateral scene, making room for China to step in and take a greater leadership role in the WTO. At the same time, the absence of free trade agreements between China and the US, and China and the EU means that the convergence of interests between either two parties is still on the multilateral end. In the near future, the US and EU will still be largely reliant on the multilateral trade system in their exploration of the Chinese market. In the long run, the promotion of multilateral trade liberalization remains the basis of cooperation in global economic governance. China ought to leverage on the multilateral trading system to stabilize China-US and China-EU relations, and quickly tap on the "soft power" of participating in multilateral trade negotiations, including the opportunities to set agendas, draft proposals, resolve disputes and guide public opinion.

4.2 *Strong participation in rule-making*

Due to the long deadlock in the Doha negotiations, regionalism is likely to make up the mainstream of international trade. The trade creation effect and trade diversion effect generated in the process will definitely provide impetus for the reconstruction of regional trade relations and lay the foundation for the formation of new global trade patterns and international rules. Therefore, China should flow with the development trend of global value chains and move from a defensive stance to an offensive mode by initiating rule formation, taking on a leadership role and undertaking due obligations in multilateral negotiations. While participating in and formulating trade rules for future competition and protection of its own interests, it can push for a more equitable and reasonable international economic order.

In particular, China should be keenly involved in the discussion of international rules through the G20, APEC, China-US Strategic and Economic Dialogue (S&ED), China-US Joint Commission on Commerce and Trade (JCCT), China-EU high-level economic and trade dialogues and other important mechanisms, and hold a positive and open attitude towards climate change, international investment, resources, energy and food security, as well as the environment and labor standards. Candid dialogues, effective participation in international policy coordination are helpful for China to enhance its role in future exploration and agenda-setting in the construction of the multilateral trading system.

Based on the "Early Harvest" achieved in Bali, China should seize the opportunity to promote the development of the "post-Bali" work plan, enhance the implementation of Trade Facilitation Agreement, and strive for the Doha Round negotiations. Existing framework and progress in the Doha Round negotiations are conducive to China. Hence, China ought to strengthen its cooperation with the US and the EU to enhance mutual trust; strengthen coordination with emerging economies such as India and Brazil, caring for and resolving the concerns of the LDCs. China should also timely adjust its position in the negotiations on agricultural, non-agricultural and service sectors according to domestic industrial structural adjustments and development of enterprise competitiveness, and actively push for sectoral approach by focusing on its own interests, comprehensively building up the image of a major power that is honest, courageous and willing to bear responsibilities.

China should also vigorously promote regional trade liberalization and take ownership of future rule-making. China began participating in regional economic cooperation relatively later, and is thus less internationally oriented. In order to take the initiative in future global economic integration, China should boost its top-level-designed strategy, and actively and steadily participate in regional economic cooperation, coming up with a regional economic development strategy that gives full consideration to geopolitical and economic security factors, and is also in line with China's industrial structural adjustments and market diversification. Presently, the implementation of Regional Comprehensive Economic Partnership (RCEP), and China-Japan-Korea FTA negotiations should be expedited, China-Korea and China-Australia FTA negotiations ought to be concluded as soon as possible, and China should be ready to participate in TISA negotiations so as to have the initiative in the future development of international trade rules.

4.3 *Expand opening up and speed up reforms*

China gained institutional dividends of economic development when it joined the WTO, but the marginal effect of these dividends has been gradually decreasing, and the momentum for reform has begun to subside. At present, the irrational contradictions in China's economic structure are relatively prominent. The problems of imbalanced, uncoordinated and unsustainable development have grown increasingly apparent. In foreign trade, besides the gradual erosion of cost advantages, China also faces dilemmas between expanding exports and reshaping economic growth models and between transforming foreign trade development models and increasing employment. To resolve the above-mentioned dilemmas and problems, maintain the sustained, healthy development of economy, and avoid the "middle income trap", China must promote a new round of reform and opening up, and establish and improve the open economic system.

After 35 years of reform and opening up, China's economic output and industrial competitiveness have dramatically improved. China is now equipped with the conditions for opening up further and expansion of the international market in exchange for more external skills, resources, and capital. The Third Plenary Session of the 18th CPC Central Committee focused on deepening reform, emphasized the decisive role of the market in allocating resources, and outlined the main tasks and major implementing measures for more comprehensive reform. Promoting reform and development by way of opening up is still China's fundamental path towards future economic and social development. China has initiated a series of reforms in the administrative and investment systems, by setting up the China (Shanghai) Pilot Free Trade Zone, and starting a new round of opening up of markets through pre-establishment national treatment and a negative list. These reforms ultimately aim to promote the opening up of trade in services and inject new vitality into economic trade.

Currently, the developed members within the WTO strive to promote the construction of new rules in trade and investment via Mega-FTAs which are not only for their own interests but also reflects, to a certain extent, the objective requirements of deepening development of economic globalization. From the current state and stage of development, it is difficult for

China to fully accept these rules; yet from a long-term perspective, most of these rules favor the liberalization of international trade and investment and is useful for enhancing China's market competitiveness. Therefore, as a peacefully developing emerging power, China should participate actively in all kinds of multilateral and regional economic and trade cooperation for strategic and tactical purposes. It should actively participate in all negotiations that are beneficial for its reform and development, seeking confirmation by conducting local tests for items that are uncertain, and exemption or extension for those that temporarily cannot be fulfilled. In addition, China is also perfectly poised to push for progress in multilateral negotiations such as the Doha Round in the multilateral trading system, through reform and opening up, for example, by joining the WTO's "Agreement on Government Procurement", promoting the expansion of the "Information Technology Agreement", "Trade in Services Agreement", "Environmental Goods Agreement" and other plurilateral negotiations as well as through the multilateralization of the outcomes of the above-mentioned negotiations.

Chapter 4

The Rise of Regional Economic Cooperation and Global Rule Reconstruction

On November 20, 2012, the leaders of the 10 ASEAN countries and China, Japan, Korea, India, Australia and New Zealand officially launched Regional Comprehensive Economic Partnership (RCEP) negotiations at a series of meetings of East Asian leaders held in Phnom Penh, Cambodia. On June 17, 2013, the Group of Eight (G8) Summit, also known as the "rich men's club", was held in Northern Ireland, United Kingdom. On the same day, US President Barack Obama, President of the European Council Herman Van Rompuy, President of the European Commission Jose Manuel Barroso and British Prime Minister David Cameron announced the official launch of Transatlantic Trade and Investment Partnership (TTIP) negotiations. Earlier on March 15 in the same year, Japanese Prime Minister Shinzo Abe announced at a press conference that Japan would join the US-led Trans-Pacific Partnership (TPP) negotiations. On July 25, Japan sent a large delegation of about 100 people to participate in the 18th round of TPP negotiations held in Malaysia. Another heavyweight had joined the ranks of TPP. To date, the establishment of "three pillars" of global FTA — the RCEP, TTIP and TPP — is almost pattern shaped.

The three networks are all mega free trade areas that include major economies such as the US, Europe, Japan, China, and India. There are 16, 12 and 29 members respectively in the groups, accounting for 49%, 11% and 12% of total world population, 28%, 38%, and 47% of total economic output, and 35%, 32%, and 28% of total foreign trade volume respectively.[1] From the above data, RCEP is the FTA with the greatest population and foreign trade

---

[1] Intra-EU trade data is not included.

volume, TTIP is the FTA with the most economic output, and TPP is formed across North and South Americas, Asia and Oceania.

The world was perplexed with the establishment of the three global FTAs: some welcomed them, some were suspicious, and others were worried or cautious. Would RCEP become an important place of cooperation for emerging economies such as India and China? Would TPP and TTIP change the patterns of global trade and delay the "rise of the east and decline of the west"? Would they subvert WTO's role as the main channel for the promotion of trade and investment liberalization? Would the main voices of global rules be controlled by the US, Europe and Japan? Would they trigger a corresponding response in global economic and trade rules? And as an emerging power, what should China do?

1 The New Wave of Regional Economic Cooperation

Regional economic cooperation is neither new, nor did it suddenly occur. By the mid- to late 20th century from the 1960s to 1980s, there had been global waves of regional cooperation. The EU, the Andean Community (abbreviated as CAN in Spanish), the Southern Africa Custom Union[2] (SACU), the Gulf Cooperation Council (GCC), the Association of Southeast Asian Nations (ASEAN) and other important organizations of regional economic cooperation were successively established during that period of time. These organizations of regional economic cooperation still play pivotal roles in international and regional affairs but apart from the EU, ASEAN and other few, most of the regional organizations have failed to achieve the goal of tight integration of regional economies.

Since the 1990s, there has been another wave of regional economic cooperation on a global scale and its scope was wider, involving a greater number of issues, and the degree of integration deeper. During this period, the North American Free Trade Area (NAFTA), APEC and other regional organizations were established and developed rapidly, injecting new vitality to global regional economic cooperation. The new wave of global regional economic cooperation has persisted to this day. In particular, after the 2008 international financial crisis, the US, Europe and other developed economies accelerated the pace of

---

[2] Custom unions refer to a conclusion of agreements between two or more countries, unifying customs territories and eliminating tariffs or granting mutual concessions within the territories. They impose the same customs tariffs on goods imported from outside the territories, thereby forming a trade area. Customs unions are a high level of regional economic cooperation.

development of FTAs, driving the rise of large FTAs such as the TPP and TTIP, boosting and accelerating the evolution of global trade and trade rules; bringing this round of regional economic cooperation to a new peak period.

1.1 *Current development of regional economic cooperation*

Some scholars have compared the current development of regional economic cooperation and its characteristics with the so-called "old regional cooperation" under the backdrop of the Cold War, and proposed the concept of "new regionalism". This concept has the following features: comprehensive cooperation, which refers to cooperation extended from one dimension such as politics and security to economics; inter-regional cooperation refers to cooperation is no longer confined to a fixed geographical area, "inter-regional cooperation" and other collaborations have been formed across continents or oceans.[3] In fact, the new era of global regional economic cooperation exhibits characteristics distinct from past features or trends. There are, for example, more diverse forms of cooperation; participating bodies have become more extensive; cooperation has deepened; and the current idea of regional economic cooperation advocates a more open and inclusive nature of cooperation.

1.1.1 *Diverse modes of new regional economic cooperation*

In the last wave of regional economic cooperation, some countries carried out higher standards of cooperation such as Customs Union (CU) or Common Market[4] (CM), attempting to achieve political and economic integration as quickly as possible. However, as various conditions were not in place, more haste made less speed, or as a Chinese saying goes — "The thunder roars loudly, but little rain falls" — and the expected results were not achieved. In the current wave of regional economic cooperation, the participants have learned from previous experiences, cooperating forms are richer and more in line with the actual development of various countries. Some of the networks of cooperation are principle oriented, others are practice oriented, some are

---

[3] Zheng Xianwu, "The Core Characteristics of 'New Regionalism'," *International Review*, No. 5, 2007, pp. 23–28.

[4] The Common Market, also known as the single market, refers to a community with free movement of commodities, labor and capital, formed by two or more countries by way of treaty. It is more highly integrated than a customs union.

regional cooperation forums focused on policy dialogues,[5] others are sub-regional cooperation focused on project-based collaborations,[6] and there are also Regional Trade Arrangements[7] (RTA) characterized by institutional cooperation. These regional economic cooperation of different levels provide a wide range of options for countries at different stages of development to carry out regional economic cooperation.

RTAs are currently the form of regional economic cooperation with the broadest scope and greatest impact. According to WTO statistics, if agreements on goods, services and member expansion were calculated separately, there would be a total of 582 RTAs notified to the WTO, of which 376 are still in force,[8] by the end of 2013. If RTAs are graded with low to high points according to the degree of liberalization, the three most common types of agreements are Partial Scope Agreement (PSA) where a few product tariffs are reduced, FTA where most product tariffs are abolished, and CU where a unified tariff is implemented. As FTAs are relatively highly liberalized and at the same time do not require members to transfer a great amount of sovereignty, it has become the most mainstream RTA.[9]

However, if agreements on trade in goods and trade in services belonging to the same agreement were calculated together and not double-counted in the "member expansion notification" of various RTAs, the actual number of RTAs

---

[5] "Regional economic cooperation forums" are relatively "soft" form of cooperation. These forums focus on policy dialogues and enhancing mutual understanding and do not conduct substantive negotiations. Examples of such forums include the Asia–Europe Meeting, East Asia Summit and APEC.

[6] Sub-regional cooperation generally covers a part of bordering territories of member states, with interconnecting infrastructure and other cooperation projects as vehicles, their main cooperation bodies being the local governments. They are a "hard" or practical form of cooperation, and are characterized by quick results, flexibility and less risk. China's participation in the Greater Mekong sub-region is a classic example.

[7] Regional Trade Arrangements (RTAs) are international treaties signed by two or more countries or separate customs territories to eliminate all trade barriers and regulate trade cooperation among the participating members. RTAs are institutional arrangements between the parties and enforced by international law. They are also a relatively "hard" form of cooperation.

[8] According to WTO statistics, retrieved from http://www.wto.org/english/tratop_e/region_e/region_e.htm.

[9] It is worth noting that according to GATT provisions, it was originally intended that FTAs be referred to liberalization agreements in the field of trade in goods, and not trade in services and others. Yet in practice, FTAs are broadly understood to include both trade in goods as well as trade in services. This is the so-called "first-generation" FTA. With the continuous development of FTAs, "second-generation" FTAs are no longer limited to goods and services, they also involve new issues such as intellectual property, government procurement *etc.*

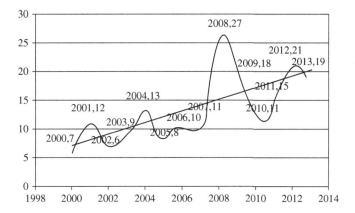

Figure 4.1 Number of FTAs the WTO was notified of, and remained in effect, after the year 2000.[10]

as of late 2013, still in force and made notified to the WTO stood at 247 — of which 14 were PSAs and 17 were CUs. Among these RTAs, 216 were FTAs, accounting for 88% of all RTAs. If we include the 41 FTA negotiations that the WTO had been "early notified" about, that is, those that were in the process of negotiation or had been signed but not yet in effect, then a total number of 257[11] FTAs were in effect across the world by the end of 2013.

As today's main vehicle for regional economic cooperation, large numbers of FTAs emerged after the year 2000. As shown in Figure 4.1, at the end of 2013, there were only 29 FTAs that the WTO was notified of and they were still in effect before 2000, but there were 187 after 2000. Before 2008, the number of FTA notifications was generally stable but there was a sharp increase after the outbreak of the financial crisis in 2008. There were a total of 111 FTAs created after 2008, accounting for 52% of the total FTAs already in effect. This suggests that after the financial crisis, countries paid more attention to developing regional economic cooperation through FTAs.

1.1.2 *FTAs promote and deepen regional cooperation*

In accordance with WTO requirements, an FTA requires the elimination of most product tariffs and non-tariff barriers by the parties involved so as to achieve a free flow of basic goods. Therefore, the implementation of FTAs can greatly enhance the proportion of internal trade in the area, promote a high

---

[10] According to WTO statistics.
[11] According to WTO statistics, retrieved from http://rtais.wto.org/UI/PublicMaintain RTAHome.aspx.

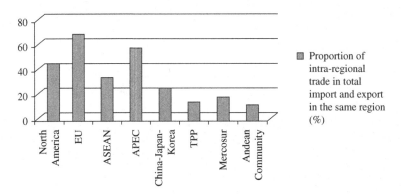

Figure 4.2 Proportion of internal trade of major global regional blocks.[12]

degree of economic integration and speed up the process of regional economic integration. As shown in Figure 4.2, among the world's eight major regional economic organizations and economic "blocks", since the development of FTAs, internal or intra-regional trade of the EU, North America and ASEAN have accounted for a large proportion of total foreign import and export from the regions, being 63%, 40% and 25% respectively. This reflects the high degree of regional economic integration in the areas. Although there has not yet been a singular "Asia-Pacific FTA" signed in the APEC region, there are up to 49 FTAs in effect or under negotiation at the moment. Each of the 21 APEC members negotiate two or more FTAs on average. Furthermore, given that the world's most important market (the US) and the world's leading exporter of manufactured goods (China) are both in the region, the APEC economic region is highly integrated, and the proportion of intra-regional trade is as high as 55.3%.

In general, the higher the proportion of intra-regional trade, the greater the opportunity for more in-depth regional cooperation; the more evident the momentum of regional economic groupings, the greater the voice members have when expressing their views to other regions.

Regional economic organizations have emerged successfully with the continual promotion of free trade construction among developed and developing countries. Competition between countries has also more shifted to competition between regional cooperative organizations. Some more mature

---

[12] According to 2012 WTO and GTA data.

regional cooperative organizations have also begun to march to the regional and global arenas as "regional actors". Thus, the world's political, geographical, and economic spheres have to face more adjustments. For decades, the EU has spared no effort in promoting integration, becoming an important party in world multipolarization. It is a successful example of regional cooperation among countries. ASEAN is a successful example of regional cooperation among developing countries. Although the total economic output of each of the 10 ASEAN member countries is small, ASEAN plays a more and more pivotal role in Asia-Pacific regional economic cooperation because of the organization's high level of integration, and has thus grown into an important force that the various member countries rely on.

1.1.3 *New regional cooperation advocates greater openness and inclusiveness*

As the exception to WTO's MFN principle, regional economic cooperation that is mainly in the form of an FTA is essentially discriminatory and exclusive. As such, many might hold the view that FTAs and other regional cooperation are "stumbling blocks" for the multilateralism that the WTO stands for. Objectively speaking, "old regionalism", which was not regulated, exhibited signs of introversion and external discrimination. To overcome those problems as much as possible, "new regionalism" emphasizes the compatibility of regionalism and multilateralism — despite being practiced inadequately — and it promotes open and inclusive regional economic cooperation, and drives the implementation of "open regionalism". This concept is mainly reflected in the following two aspects: Firstly, the WTO disciplines have a strong regulatory effect on FTAs. The WTO members are required to notify the organization if they negotiate or sign any FTAs and accept its reviews, and members will be challenged if FTAs are not sufficiently liberalized. The stipulation of GATT Article XXIV on "substantially all the trade" and GATS Article V on "substantial sectoral coverage" concern the degree of liberalization in all FTAs. In actual negotiations, most participants interpret Article XXIV as such: that the final zero-tariff products as agreed upon in FTAs should cover 90% or more of trade volume and tariff lines, and trade volume should be prioritized. While the above-mentioned provisions are not binding, it is widely recognized by WTO members that FTAs must be the WTO plus that the level of liberalization must exceed the WTO commitment level.

Secondly, new regional cooperation goes beyond geographical limitations, has a stronger emphasis on common ground, and is more inclusive. From a political point of view, "closed regionalism" generally requires members to be similar in ideology, political system, as well as cultural and historical background. From a geographical point of view, closed regional cooperation usually covers neighboring countries geographically close to one another. From the economic point of view, closed regional cooperation often requires members to transfer greater economic sovereignty. New regional cooperation, on the other hand, does not require the above-mentioned conditions of political similarity, geographical proximity and releasing of sovereignty as prerequisites. APEC is an example of a representative organization of open regionalism — with its members spread throughout the Pacific Rim covering four continents including Asia, Latin America, North America, and Oceania. Although the backgrounds of its members differ rather greatly in social systems, cultural values, economic scales, productivity *etc*, it can be argued that APEC would have been impossible to establish under a closed regionalism model.

On the whole, FTAs are only the second best option to the promotion of free trade but due to the temporary stalled multilateral trading system, the rapid development of regional cooperation such as FTAs reflects the real needs and rational choice of various countries in the world in pushing for the liberalization of trade and investment. In fact, if the new era of regional economic cooperation adheres to the principles of openness and inclusiveness, and also strives to be compatible with the disciplines of the multilateral trading system, it will be able to advance and drive the liberalization of global trade and investment. From this point of view, new regional economic cooperation is a stepping stone for the multilateral trading system and will work together with the multilateral trading system to promote global trade and investment liberalization. The two are expected to converge in the end.

1.2 *How major economies such as the US and Europe are promoting FTAs*

According to WTO statistics, at the end of 2013, among the 216 FTAs notified to the WTO that remain in effect, 151 FTAs including members from the world's top 12 largest economies, account for 69% of all FTAs (see Table 4.1).

Currently, the major powers and economies are forming regional and global connections through FTAs, building up communities of interest and promoting the formation of three major economic blocks — North American, European, and East Asia. FTAs have become an important part of US and European

Table 4.1 The development of free trade zones among the world's 12 largest economies.[13]

Number	Economy	No. of FTAs	No. of FTA partners	Proportion of trade with FTA partners in total import and export volume (%)	Proportion of import from FTA partners in total import volume (%)	Proportion of export to FTA partners in total export volume (%)
1	Mexico	13	43	81.16	71.03	91.30
2	Canada	7	12	68.14	59.39	77.03
3	Turkey	17	46	44.14	41.40	48.39
4	The US	14	20	39.45	34.66	46.43
5	Korea	8	45	34.76	32.07	37.31
6	The EU	34	66	27.47	24.91	30.19
7	Australia	7	14	26.68	35.16	18.42
8	China[14]	10	18	25.56	21.43	29.22
9	Japan	13	15	18.92	18.16	19.77
10	India	9	19	16.77	15.06	19.65
11	Brazil	5	11	14.25	12.44	15.91
12	Russia	12	13	9.13	7.52	10.04

[13] According to data consolidated from the WTO and the GTA in 2013, in descending order of the proportion of FTA coverage in total foreign trade volume.

[14] The number of FTAs signed by China does not include the "China-Switzerland FTA" or the "China-Iceland FTA". The two were signed in 2013 but only took effect in July 2014. Furthermore, if Chinese Taipei, Chinese Hong Kong and Chinese Macau are excluded, China has signed 7 FTAs with 15 FTA partners. The proportion of China's trade volume with its FTA partners in total import and export volume would therefore be 12.3%, the proportion of the total import volume from its FTA partners would be 13.2%, and the proportion of total export volume to FTA partners would be 11.5%.

foreign affairs and foreign policy strategies. The US, based on NAFTA, with the two Mega-FTAs (TTIP and TPP) as wings, has sought to strengthen economic integration with like-minded countries and formed a giant regional bloc extending from North America to Europe and even Korea and Japan in East Asia. Developing free trade area through these blocs are in line with the "Larger West" strategic objectives set by US strategist Zbigniew Brzezinski in 2012.[15] Meanwhile, the EU hopes through the TTIP to achieve deep economic integration with the US. It also hopes to build upon a foundation of closer strategic transatlantic relations to strengthen strategic collaboration with the US and consolidate the US's and Europe's leadership in the world.

1.2.1 *America's free trade area strategy*

The US is the world's sole superpower. Its moves in promoting and developing free trade areas are closely watched and emulated by other countries. The US's establishment of FTAs reflects its strategic vision. The number of the US FTA partners are not many but the influence of the FTAs is significant. In the past 20 years, every time the US vigorously promotes the establishment of free trade areas, the global economic and trade patterns, and even the political patterns, shift significantly. As early as the 1990s, the US established NAFTA together with Canada and Mexico to create the North American bloc, one of the world's three largest regional economic blocs. The existence of NAFTA helped the US to face the challenges brought about by the formation of the EU. Its high standards and wide-ranging negotiation modes become a model for other countries in developing free trade areas and this has not changed to date. In the 21st century, the US continues to increase inputs in the establishment of free trade areas, making greater moves all over the world. Its global free trade area network has taken shape.

In 2001, the Bush administration proposed the establishment of the Free Trade Area of Americas (FTAA) covering 34 countries in the American

---

[15] In 2012, Brzezinski published an article titled "Balancing the East, Upgrading the West:U.S. Grand Strategy in an Age of Upheaval" in the magazine, *Foreign Affairs*. He suggested that the central challenge of the US over the next several decades is to revitalize itself, while promoting a larger West and buttressing a complex balance in the East that can accommodate China's rising status. Brzezinski's "larger West" extends from North America and Europe through Eurasia (by eventually embracing Russia and Turkey), all the way to Japan and Korea.

continent. Due to strong opposition from Brazil, Venezuela and other countries, the proposal submitted by the US was frustrated at the Fourth Summit of the Americas held in 2005.[16] The US then turned to bilateral negotiations, establishing free trade relations with 10 countries on the American continent including Chile, Colombia, and Costa Rica.

In 2003, in line with its global counter-terrorism strategy and the "Greater Middle East Initiative", the US suggested the formation of a Middle East Free Trade Area (MEFTA) in an attempt to establish a free trade area with the Middle Eastern countries. The US aimed to promote economic liberalization in the Middle East and integrate the Arab world with the global economic system through this proposed free trade area. After several years, there have been a number of successes despite MEFTA never being formally established. Previously, the US had only signed an FTA with Israel in 1985. Currently, the US has signed FTAs with Bahrain, Jordan, Morocco and Oman and is negotiating FTAs with Egypt, the United Arab Emirates and other countries.[17]

In the Asia-Pacific region, in line with its "Asia-Pacific Rebalancing Strategy", the US joined the TPP initiated by Brunei, Chile, New Zealand, and Singapore, and attempted to build the TPP into the main platform for economic integration of the Asia-Pacific region. With vigorous boost and leadership from the US, the TPP has become a large regional economic project involving 12 countries such as Australia, Peru, Malaysia, Vietnam, Canada, Mexico, Japan among others. Its total economic output, foreign trade volume and population size account for 38%, 32% and 11% respectively of the world's total. TPP's economic size will be bigger than that of NAFTA or the EU and it will become the world's largest free trade area. Currently, Korea, Indonesia, Thailand, among others, have expressed interest in joining the TPP.[18] The Korean

---

[16] Chen Zhiyang, "New Trends in Latin American and Asia-Pacific Regional Economic Cooperation: An Analysis of the Establishment of the Pacific Alliance," *Journal of Latin American Studies*, No. 12, 2012. According to the article, the US excluded Cuba from the FTAA claiming that the Cuban government was not democratically elected.

[17] Li Yanli, "FTA Strategy and Oil Security of the United States," *Journal of International Economic Cooperation*, No. 12, 2012; and Zhu Ying, "Free Trade Agreements and America's Strategy with the Middle East," *West Asia and Africa*, No. 4, 2009.

[18] David Pilling and Shawn Donnan, "Trans-Pacific Partnership: Ocean's Twelve," *Financial Times*, September 22, 2013. Retrieved from http://www.ft.com/intl/cms/s/0/8c253c5c-2056-11e3-b8c6-00144feab7de.html#axzz2gGG5RAk8.

government officially announced that it would join TPP in September 2013 and was studying the schedule and impact of its possible accession.[19]

In June 2013, the US took another important step forward in building free trade areas that sent shockwaves around the world. This time, the US chose to form an FTA with the world's largest economic body, the EU. Together, they would promote the construction of TTIP. Presently, the US and European economies are worth a total of USD32.3 trillion, with total foreign trade amounting to USD8.3 trillion, attracted FDI stock being USD11.8 trillion and a total of 820 million in population, which account for 45%, 28%, 52% and 12% respectively of the world total.[20] As such, the TTIP is another world's largest regional economic integration project to date.

1.2.2 *The EU's development of free trade areas*

The EU is a pioneer in regional economic cooperation. After 50 years of development, the EU has developed from an industrial consortium of coal and steel into the economic region it is today where there is free flows of labors, capital and goods, becoming a successful model of regional economic integration for other countries. Others have learned from its valuable experience and are emulating the model. As the EU has been a staunch supporter of the multilateral trading system, it worries that FTAs could weaken the role of the WTO and has not made many moves in terms of establishing FTAs out of the region.[21] To date, there are 34 FTAs the EU has signed with external parties that remain in effect. Sixty-six countries and regions are involved in these FTAs but most of these partners are small economies. Therefore, the proportion of free trade of the EU covered by FTAs is relatively small at only about 28%.

In recent years, the EU has put more and more emphasis on cooperation of free trade areas. Presently, the EU is conducting FTA negotiations with the South American Common Market (Spanish abbreviation MERCOSUR, including five countries — Brazil, Argentina, Uruguay, Paraguay and Venezuela), the Gulf Cooperation Council (GCC, including six countries — the UAE, Oman, Bahrain, Qatar, Kuwait and Saudi Arabia), India, Ukraine,

---

[19] "Korea to Join Trans-Pacific Partnership," *Korean Daily News,* September 9, 2013. Retrieved from http://english.chosun.com/site/data/html_dir/2013/09/09/2013090901471.html.

[20] According to 2013 data retrieved from UNCTAD.

[21] The EU implemented a unified trade policy where individual members did not have the right to sign FTA with other countries.

Malaysia, Thailand, Vietnam, Georgia, Armenia, Moldova and others. In particular, since 2013, the EU has not only completed FTA negotiations with Canada, it has also launched FTA negotiations with Japan, and TTIP negotiations with the US. If these countries are all included, the EU's trade with FTA partners will account for 62% of its total foreign trade.

1.2.3 *Development of East Asian free trade areas*

As East Asia develops to become the engine of global economic growth, it is also becoming a hotspot and focus of the development of world free trade areas. Among the East Asian countries, Korea is the most active in developing free trade areas. It has already formed free trade relationships with the US and Europe, and the proportion of its trade with FTA partners accounts for up to 35% of its total foreign trade volume, ranking first amongst the East Asian countries. After Korea completes its free trade area negotiations with China, Japan and other countries, the share of trade with FTA partners will increase to 69%. Japan's current trade with FTA partners accounts for a mere 19% of its total foreign trade volume, but it is accelerating its pace in establishing free trade areas now and has already joined RCEP and TPP negotiations. It is also negotiating FTAs with the EU, Canada and other countries. Should FTAs be successfully established with these countries, Japan's trade with FTA partners will account for 78% of its total foreign trade.

Presently, the East Asian region is moving forward with negotiations on large FTAs such as China-Korea, China-Japan-Korea, and RCEP FTAs. Among them, RCEP negotiations are particularly noteworthy. ASEAN initiated the establishment of RCEP and 16 members are included which are ASEAN, China, Japan, Korea, Australia, New Zealand and India. Its total economic volume, foreign trade, and population account for 28.4%, 34.9% and 48.6% of the world's respective figures. Its total foreign trade volume and population size indicators exceed those of TPP and TTIP. It is the world's most populous and largest FTA in terms of population. Japan, Australia and other developed countries, as well as China, India, Korea, Indonesia, other emerging economies, and other least developed countries such as Myanmar and Laos, are all members of RCEP. The region is far more complex than others and it will be difficult to set up a completely liberalized trade and investment area. However, trade cooperation involving economies of different sizes at various levels of development reflects the reality of the diverse economic development in the Asia-Pacific region. As such, if successful, the RCEP will set a good example for a more inclusive form of Asia-Pacific economic cooperation.

On the whole, it is hopeful that the RCEP will, together with the TPP, become an pathway approach for Asia-Pacific regional economic integration.

1.3 *Economic reasons for the rapid development of regional economic cooperation*

The rapid development of regional economic cooperation, in particular, the rapid emergence of FTAs in recent years is a duel result of deep-set global geopolitical adjustment factors as well as the economic effects of trade creation and trade diversion of free trade areas. It follows the development trend of the regionalization of global production networks and is influenced by the slow progress of the WTO Doha Round.

1.3.1 *Static and dynamic effects*

The primary reason for the rapid development of regional economic cooperation is both positive and negative static effects, trade creation and trade diversion. In the 1950s, economist Jacob Viner identified the "trade creation" effect, citing customs unions as an example. He pointed out that the elimination of tariff and non-tariff barriers between participants led to the replacement of products with high costs of production in the importing country with low-cost products from free trade partners, which can create new trade. Importers can also reallocate the resources that were used for producing high-cost goods to the production of low-cost products, optimizing the allocation of resources and thus boost social benefits in general.

For example, should the EU complete negotiations and implement FTAs with the US, Canada, Japan, ASEAN and other countries, the total economic output of the EU could increase by 2%, equivalent to a total of 250 billion euros.[22] Among that, the completion of TTIP will increase exports from the US to the EU by 8%–17%, and increase exports from the EU to the US by 7%–18%, while total US and European economic output would increase by 0.99%–1.33% and 0.32%–0.47% respectively.[23]

---

[22] European Union, "Concluding Trade Deals Could Boost EU's GDP by 2 Percent," July 20, 2012. Retrieved from http://europa.eu/rapid/press-release_MEMO-12-587_en.htm.

[23] European Centre for International Political Economy (ECIPE), "A Transatlantic Zero Agreement: Estimating the Gains from Transatlantic Free Trade in Goods," October 1, 2010. Retrieved from http://www.ecipe.org/media/publication_pdfs/a-transatlantic-zero-agreement-estimating-the-gains-from-transatlantic-free-trade-in-goods.pdf.

At the same time, since FTAs came into effect, countries have conducted free internal trade with their partners thus reducing external imports as these are replaced by imports from FTA partners. Trade direction changes and this trade diversion effect results in non-FTA countries being "marginalized", with their trade interests being reduced and eroded. A situation where only those who participate in FTAs will benefit and those who are excluded will lose out is bound to arise. In a certain way, this forces all parties to participate actively in free trade cooperation.

Apart from the above static effects, regional economic cooperation that is mainly formed by FTAs also creates various dynamic effects promoting the economic integration of parties involved. Firstly, FTAs improve production efficiency through market competition. The EU experience revealed that a 1% increase in economic openness is matched by a corresponding 0.6% improvement in labor productivity.[24] Secondly, they help to gain economies of scale, reduce production costs and expand the market by promoting economic integration between participants. Thirdly, they help increase investment opportunities and promote a high degree of economic integration by eliminating access barriers to trade in services and investment.

1.3.2 *Conforming to the regionalization of production networks*

The rapid development of regional economic cooperation is closely related to the current regionalization of global production networks. Since the 1990s, with the intensification of economic globalization and trade liberalization as well as support from communications, logistics and other technological improvements, more and more countries are participating in the various segments or sections of production and supply activities of the production process of specific products. The production process of one single product can be transnational, forming cross-border production networks. Some experts name this phenomena as "vertical specialization", "fragmented production", or "division of the value chain". Such cross-border activities could be global or regional.

In East Asia, as the economies are heterogeneous and multinational companies have increased investment, regional production networks are relatively mature, and the share of trade within the East Asian region has continually risen. China has become a major importer of intermediate products while Japan

---

[24] EU, "Concluding Trade Deals Could Boost EU's GDP by 2 Percent," *ibid.* p. 126.

and Korea have become major suppliers of intermediate products.[25] At the same time, East Asian production networks are strongly export-oriented and rely greatly on the US market. To a certain extent, this has become a trend of East Asian production and US consumption. This is also an important reason why despite the lack of an FTA, intra-regional trade in the APEC region is much higher than those with single FTAs.

The accelerated regionalization of production networks is a natural result of trade and investment integration. There is a need to promote regional economic cooperation, eliminate the tariff, non-tariff barriers and other obstacles that affect regional production networks, and more effectively achieve the optimal allocation of various economic production factors in production networks and balanced development of industries. For example, many US and European product value chains are long, with a large amount of bilateral trade consisting of trade in intermediate products and internal trade among multinationals. For the US, 48% of its imports and 30% of its exports are intra-firm trade. As many products on both sides have to be imported and exported several times, tariffs are paid multiple times. Although the tariffs between Europe and the US are low, this results in a substantial increase in costs. Hence, there is an urgent need for US and Europe to establish a bilateral FTA to eliminate these trade barriers.[26]

1.3.3 *Slow progress of Doha negotiations*

The development of regional economic cooperation has accelerated in recent years, one of the direct causes being the slow progress of the WTO Doha negotiations. Regional cooperation thus became an important platform for promoting the liberalization of trade and investment, as well as rule negotiation. Since WTO Doha negotiation takes a package approach to cover multiple areas including goods, services, investment and others, its impact will be great there are a lot of potential benefits. Therefore, it is the best way to liberalize trade and investment. It is estimated that the completion of the Doha Round

---

[25] Lin Guijun, Tang Bi and Shen Qiujun, "Development of Regional Production Networks in East Asia and the Deepening of East Asian Regional Economic Cooperation," *Journal of International Trade*, No. 11, 2012.

[26] ECIPE, "A New Era for Transatlantic Trade Leadership," The German Marshall Fund of the United States, February 2012. Retrieved from http://ecipe.org/publications/new-era-transatlantic-trade-leadership/.

could stimulate the global economy by at least USD150 billion a year.[27] However, as many members are involved, there are many differences in economies of scale and levels of development, and members take different positions on issues, the costs of coordination are high, making negotiations extremely challenging and it has been difficult to arrive at an outcome that is satisfactory to all parties. Thus, after a decade of delays, the Doha Round is still inconclusive. Compared to the 160-member Doha negotiations, the FTA "trade creation effect" is smaller, and the benefits are relatively limited as well. This is but the second best option to promote free trade. On the other hand, in FTAs, one can select partners, the range is controllable and negotiation is faster, hence when multilateral negotiations hit an impasse, FTAs become an important policy option for many countries.

On December 7, 2013, the WTO Ninth Ministerial Meeting reached the "Early Harvest" agreement at the Doha Round. This was the first time there was a breakthrough after 12 years of stagnant WTO talks.[28] However, the agreement was reached regarding only a small part of the framework of the Doha Round, as there were significant differences between the developing and developed countries' demands on the multilateral trading system, and there was still a long way to go before the Doha Development Round could be completely concluded. Furthermore, WTO members would not give up on promoting free trade areas. In the future, FTAs will coexist with the multilateral trading system for a long time. The two will complement each other and serve to promote global trade and investment liberalization together.

2 The "Experimental Field" for New Rules of International Trade

With the in-depth development of economic globalization, the traditional international economic and trade rules constructed by the developed countries under the guidance of the WTO in the past are no longer able to reflect their interests and demands. This is because traditional international economic and trade rules focus on addressing trade measures at the borders, and emphasize the implementation of free trade of manufactured goods by reducing or

---

[27] G20 London Summit-Leaders' Statement, April 2009; retrieved from http://www.imf.org/external/np/sec/pr/2009/pdf/g20_040209.pdf.

[28] Information Office of the Ministry of Commerce, "Statement by Ministry of Commerce Spokesperson Shen Danyang on the 'Early Harvest' Package reached at the WTO Ninth Ministerial Meeting," December 7, 2013. Retrieved from http://www.mofcom.gov.cn/article/ae/ai/201312/20131200416131.shtml.

eliminating tariffs. Profound changes, however, are taking place with regard to the competitiveness of developed and developing countries in the manufacturing sector and such trends are difficult to reverse. In this new situation, current WTO trade rules favor developing countries' increased competitiveness and market expansion rather than reflect the developed countries' demands for trade liberalization in the service industry and other advantageous industries.

On the whole, as the global division of labor shifts from end products to factors of production based on industrial chains, developed countries have changed their competitive focus to that of globalization. Developed countries have also shifted their focus from traditional trade in goods to trade in services, from free trade to so-called fair trade, from end products to value chains, and from acquisition of resources to integration of elements. To adapt to this new situation, developed countries, especially the US, are bypassing the WTO and other multilateral institutions and implementing new international trade rules and standards at the level of regional economic cooperation. They are doing so through FTAs and other RTAs as the "experimental field" for new international trade rules, creating the "real model of 21st century trade agreements" and taking the reins of future development. The normative content of these new rules and standards extends from trade to industrial policies, and the regulations found in these new rules cover from border to behind-the-border that go far beyond the scope of traditional trade agreements.

2.1 *"Border measures" and other traditional market access issues*

The market access issues discussed among WTO members generally refer to the conditions laid out by a member for the entrance of goods, services, labor and capital from another member into its market. Among these, market access of trade in goods is also the core issue of border measures. Border measures refer to the restrictive measures taken by a country or an economy (including separate customs territories and customs unions) with regard to the incoming and outgoing of products from or into the country or its economic customs territory. Of these restrictive measures, the main ones are tariffs, quotas, quantitative restrictions, customs supervision and other measures. To a certain extent, border measures may also be referred to simply as tariff barriers. After years of efforts by multilateral trade organizations such as the WTO, members have made good progress in eliminating border measures. According to the agreement reached at the Uruguay Round, members committed to progressive reduction of tariffs after the establishment of the WTO. For example, developed members would reduce tariffs on industrial goods by 40% within five years after 1995, and average import tariffs on industrial products would be reduced from 6.3% to 3.8%. In addition, the trade volume of developed members' industrial products that enjoys zero tariffs should increase from 20% to 44%.[29] However, there was still a relatively high amount of tariff peaks in many economies, and the applied tariff rates and bound rates varied widely. In particular, some emerging economies had set relatively high market access barriers. Take for example, the BRIC countries. India MFN bound rates were 48.7%, applied tariff rates were 13%, among which applied agricultural rates were as high as 31.8%; Brazil bound rates were 31.4% with applied tariff rates being 13.7%; South Africa bound rates were 19%, applied tariff rates were 7.7%; Russia's applied rates were 9.5%.[30] In negotiations about tariff reduction in sensitive industries such as agricultural products, it was difficult for developed and developing members to reach an agreement, and this was an important factor for the "frozen period" of the Doha Round.

Under such circumstances, many economies, especially the developed members, turned to regional economic cooperation, free trade zones in particular, to promote high standards of market access, achieve a high level of liberalization in goods, services and investment. Therefore, strictly speaking, the market access issues dealt with in free trade areas did not go beyond the scope of the WTO, and did not involve creating new rules. Rather, they set a new standard that was higher than that which participants committed to with the WTO.

2.1.1 *Market access for trade in goods*

In the field of trade in goods, the level of liberalization in free trade areas is considerably higher than that which participants committed to with the WTO. As mentioned above, according to GATT Article XXIV, the establishment of FTAs requires the elimination of tariffs of substantially all the trade. Although the WTO has not given a clear binding explanation with regard to this standard at the moment, in actual bilateral trade negotiations, members generally ask for more than 90% of products in tariff lines and trade volumes to be ultimately granted zero tariffs. In FTA negotiations where developed

---

[29] WTO, "Tariffs: More Bindings and Closer to Zero," retrieved from http://www.wto.org/english/thewto_e/whatis_e/tif_e/agrm2_e.htm.

[30] Chen Zhiyang, "Analysis and Countermeasures for the Post-Doha Era 'Rise in FTAs' Phenomenon," *International Economic Cooperation*, No. 5, 2012.

members are involved, the standard of liberalization is even higher. For example, the US-Korea FTA states that nearly 95% of bilateral trade in consumer and industrial goods be granted zero tariffs within five years after implementation, and the EU-Korea FTA requires both parties to reduce more than 98% of their tariffs. The two large FTAs — TPP and TTIP — promoted by the US and Europe are of an even higher standard.

During TPP negotiations, the US called on all parties to reduce the tariff lines of up to 11,000 products. On principle, there were no exceptions.[31] Such a high standard of liberalization puts great pressure on participants and even developed members to open up markets. For example, Japan has a strategic need for joining the TPP, but because Japan firmly opposed the US' requests for it to abolish tariffs on agricultural products and fully liberalize its agricultural markets, the Japanese government has had to postpone its decision to join the TPP time and time again. It was only in February 2013 when Japanese Prime Minister Shinzo Abe visited the US that the biggest obstacle for Japan to join the TPP was removed: the two parties clarified that Japanese agricultural products were sensitive products in the negotiations and a certain amount of room was given to Japan to conduct negotiations.[32]

In TTIP negotiations, the US and Europe, being the world's largest and most developed economies, had high expectations on the liberalization of trade in goods. Both parties mentioned in a joint feasibility study report that tariffs should be abolished for all products at TTIP negotiations, with most products being granted zero tariffs with immediate effect from the date of enforcement of the agreement. With regard to more sensitive agricultural products, a certain transition period or the gradual increase of countries' quota could be considered in the implementation of tariff reduction but the ultimate goal would still be to completely eliminate tariffs from the above-mentioned products.[33] It was generally believed that because average tariffs in the Europe and the US had been reduced to 5.2% and 3.5% respectively, and average trade-weighted tariffs

---

[31] USTR, "Outlines of the Trans-Pacific Partnership Agreement", http://www.ustr.gov/about-us/press-office/fact-sheets/2011/november/outlines-trans-pacific-partnership-agreement.

[32] Zhang Jindong, "Abe Visit led to Major Progress in TPP Negotiations with Critical Support from the US," retrieved from http://international.caixun.com/zjd/20130224-CX03aihm.html.

[33] USTR, "Final Report of the US-EU High Level Working Group on Jobs and Growth", February 11, 2013, retireved from https://ustr.gov/about-us/policy-offices/press-office/reports-and-publications/2013/final-report-us-eu-hlwg.

had fallen below 1.5%, it would not be difficult for both parties to achieve zero tariffs on most products.[34]

2.1.2 *Market access for trade in services and investment*[35]

To ensure results of a high standard in negotiations on trade in services, the TPP framework requires all service sectors, including financial and telecommunications sectors to be covered under the agreement, and the FTA takes the negative list approach to negotiations. The so-called negative list approach means that other than the services sector, which clearly has to be protected, there will be no restrictions on market access and national treatment in the other service sectors that are committed to being opened up. This approach allows various parties to retain existing national protection measures to protect service sectors, which clearly require protection, yet prohibits the setting up of new protection measures. It also calls for a commitment to gradually release control after the agreement takes effect, ultimately achieving liberalization. Various members are also allowed to establish the necessary regulations and policies to protect and manage certain special service sectors according to their needs.

Both the US and Europe have tried to implement liberalization of trade in services and investment at the highest level, as can be seen from TTIP. According to the joint feasibility study report, TTIP takes the negative list approach to negotiations. Based on the commitments of both parties in other FTAs, (where the US is NAFTA while the EU is the FTA with the European Free Trade Association (EFTA), which includes Switzerland, Norway, Iceland, and Liechtenstein), both parties will be expected to grant the highest liberalized treatment that they are currently granting to third parties, to each other. From the contents of the two agreements mentioned above, both Europe and the US will grant each other comprehensive national treatment including pre-establishment national treatment, establish performance standards that are even more lenient than the WTO Agreement on Trade-Related Investment Measures (TRIMS), and allow the free remittance of investment-related funds as well as for investors to directly approach international arbitration bodies to arbitrate investment disputes.

---

[34] ECIPE, "A New Era for Transatlantic Trade Leadership," *ibid.* p. 128.
[35] Chapter 8 will discuss this in further detail. The topic will only be briefly introduced here.

2.1.3 *Government procurement*[36]

The TPP requires all members to open up the government procurement market to the greatest extent possible. There is currently a plurilateral Agreement on Government Procurement (GPA) under the WTO framework whose members are mainly developed members of the WTO. The basic rule for this agreement is national treatment. This rule states that in government procurement processes, the treatment of goods and services enjoyed by foreign suppliers must not be less than that received by domestic suppliers. In TPP negotiations, many developing members involved in the TPP are not members of the GPA, and the distribution of authority between the central government and local governments of TPP members complicates the situation.

In the TTIP framework, both Europe and the US are GPA members and they have a common basis for negotiations. Therefore, the level of ambition on both sides is correspondingly higher and they have agreed to include local government procurement in the negotiations. However, it is also not easy for negotiations to progress. For example, there are more than 10 states in the US that have not joined the GPA and are not bound by it. Moreover, the "Buy American Act" introduced by the US in response to the financial crisis is strongly trade protectionist, and it is highly challenging to make amendments to US domestic law. The EU is nominally more open but its member states differ greatly in practice, and there are still a lot of hidden barriers with regard to foreign products entering the EU market.

2.2 *Behind-the-border measures*

If what was raised in the FTA's dealing of traditional market access was the standard, then the new round of regional economic cooperation would have made a great leap forward in creating new rules when handling behind-the-border measures.

Although behind-the-border measures are related to trade, they traditionally belong to the context of affairs of a sovereign economy. To a certain extent, the purpose of behind-the-border measures is similar to that of the WTO's non-tariff barriers, but its connotation and extension are much broader than non-tariff barriers. For example, domestic regulation, technical barriers to

---

[36] Chapter 9 will discuss this in further detail. The topic will only be briefly introduced here.

trade, sanitary and phytosanitary measures, intellectual property, competition policy and so on, are all behind-the-border measures. There are many types of measures, and they are covert and difficult to predict, forming a major obstacle to the further freeing up of trade and investment. Due to limitations in economic development, management systems, knowledge and other factors, coupled with behind-the-border measures that might require transfers of sovereignty, developing countries are often reluctant to address these issues in regional cooperation. But with the GATT/WTO gradually and successfully reducing tariff barriers, the basic principles of tariff restrictions were established and developed countries began to focus instead on the impact of behind-the-border measures on trade and investment liberalization. Consequently, regulatory coherence, intellectual property protection, competition policy and other issues became focal points in discussions.

2.2.1 *Regulatory coherence*

Eliminating behind-the-border measures that were inconsistent with regulations was of important economic significance for the parties involved in regional economic cooperation. Using TTIP as example: according to the joint feasibility study report, the tariff barriers between the US and Europe were already very low. The regulatory inconsistencies on both sides had become the biggest obstacle to trade growth. Due to the differences in regulatory regimes and standards, many commodities from the US and Europe were subject to several verifications before entering each other's markets, hence increasing bilateral trade costs greatly, especially in the health and hygiene-related industries such as chemical, automotive, medicine and medical equipment. According to estimates, the inconsistent standards between the two sides in just the automotive industry alone had resulted in duplicate tests and certifications, and other non-tariff barriers that were equivalent to an increase of import duties by 10%–20%.[37]

Economists from the US and Europe also studied the economic effects of Non-Tariff Barriers (NTBs) based on elimination of regulations. The results showed that if both sides standardized food safety measures, drug regulatory certifications, patent applications and certifications, manufacturing technology and safety measures, regulations and certifications *etc.*, the EU economy would

---

[37] European Commission "Questions and Answers — About the TTIP." Retrieved from http://ec.europa.eu/trade/policy/in-focus/ttip/questions-and-answers/.

grow by 0.72% annually and exports to the US would increase by 2.1%, and the industries that would benefit most would be the automotive, chemical, pharmaceutical, food and electrical products. The US economy would grow by 0.28% annually, exports to the EU would increase by 6.1%, and the industries that would benefit most were the electrical, chemical, pharmaceutical, financial services and insurance industries.[38] Due to the huge potential economic benefits, the US and Europe have already reached a consensus to focus on the discussion of regulatory coherence during TTIP negotiations. However, due to distinct differences in regulatory philosophies, institutional and regulatory standards as well as giving up some national sovereignty, the most difficult issues at TTIP negotiations would be achieving regulatory coherence and mutual recognition of standards.

In TPP negotiations, the parties would deliberately use regulatory coherence to achieve seamless and efficient trade among members to create a friendlier business environment. The topics of discussion include reducing inconsistencies within the standards of the region, improving transparency, abolition of excessive testing and certification, and cooperation on specific regulatory issues. As there are many big countries that export agricultural products among TPP members, members agreed to commit more to research on food safety, animal and plant health and other issues building upon the various parties' WTO rights and obligations. Meanwhile, TPP members also recognized the complexity of the regulatory coherence issues and agreed on a "living agreement" approach to pragmatically resolve the problem.

2.2.2 *Protection of intellectual property*[39]

Intellectual property is another important issue in behind-the-border measures. TRIPS is an important part of the WTO legal framework, as well as one of the most important legal documents in the international intellectual property law system. However, some economists believe that the TRIPS agreement is detrimental. As mentioned by Jagdish Bhagwati in his book, *In Defense of Globalization*, TRIPS not only prevents drugs from entering developing countries, it also facilitates the transfer of wealth transferred from developing countries to the copyright and patent holders in developed coun-

---

[38] ECIPE, "A New Era for Transatlantic Trade Leadership," *ibid.*

[39] Chapter 10 discusses on this topic and it is only briefly introduced here.

tries.[40] In contrast, developed countries, believing that the current global system of intellectual property protection could not protect their interests, tried out other methods/systems beyond TRIPS. To this end, nearly 40 countries including the US and the EU signed the multilateral Anti-Counterfeiting Trade Agreement (ACTA) at the end of 2011. This served to strengthen the comprehensive protection of intellectual property in international trade.

Developed countries further enhanced intellectual property protection in free trade agreements. Take the EU negotiating for mandate in the TTIP process as an example: the European Parliament made it clear that intellectual property was the cornerstone for modern knowledge-based economy and the driving force for creativity. The Parliament also asked that TTIP negotiations should give clear definitions for intellectual property rights and provide strong protection for them. For now, the US and Europe will work through TTIP to maintain and promote a high level of intellectual property protection and law enforcement. Taking into consideration the effectiveness of both parties' intellectual property rights systems, bilateral negotiations will not be focused on the full integration of the two systems, but the resolution of problems and differences in individual systems.

During TPP negotiations, the parties committed to the negotiation of intellectual property issues according to their respective rights and obligations in TRIPS. According to relevant analysis, the TPP agreement would include a section on intellectual property covering trademarks, geographical indications, copyright and related rights, patents, trade secrets, genetic resources and traditional knowledge *etc*. Overall, the section requires that TPP members bear the responsibility for protecting intellectual property rights at a standard higher than that of TRIPS. For example, TPP recommendations on trademark restriction stipulate that the visibility of a trademark cannot be a prerequisite for registration, nor should a trademark decline registration as it features a sound or a smell. This is a stark difference from the premise in Article 15 of TRIPS where members may request visibility of a trademark as a prerequisite for registration. This has greatly expanded the scope of protection for intellectual property.[41]

---

[40] Jagdish Bhagwati, *In Defense of Globalization* (Oxford University Press, 2005).

[41] Jimmy H. Koo, "Trans-Pacific Partnership-Intellectual Property Rights Chapter Section by Section Analysis," Draft Paper, April 2011. Retrieved from http://infojustice.org/wp-content/uploads/2011/04/Koo-TPP-Section-by-Section-Analysis-April-2011.pdf.

2.2.3 *Competition policy*[42]

Competition policy is a typical behind-the-border measure. Multilateral or regional trade agreements can significantly improve the access conditions of the products and services markets for the involved parties. But if the import market fails to operate according to fair competition, the full economic effect of trade and investment liberalization will not be achieved with the trade agreements, then competition will become a problem for trade. In order to protect competition and promote genuine trade liberalization, there is a need for competition policy to prevent monopolies and other forms of unfair competitive behavior.

Currently, many of the WTO rules are directly or indirectly related to competition policy but they are scattered in GATT, GATS, TRIPS and other agreements. They are applied under strict conditions and unsystematic. More importantly, the rules of WTO competition regulate mainly government behavior although there are certain constraints on non-governmental organizations (NGOs) and other trade associations. Generally, it is difficult to regulate enterprises, guilds and other non-governmental bodies.[43] At present, the developed countries have shifted focus from improving competition rules to free trade agreement. During discussions regarding the TPP, the US explicitly expressed great concern on competition issues. Although TPP is a closed-door negotiation and the specific negotiation content of current competition policy was not disclosed, a proposal initiated and submitted by the American Chamber of Commerce revealed some of the demands of the US: Firstly, a section on competition issues was established in TPP, indicating the emphasis on competition issues; and secondly, the negotiation between the US and Korea was conducted based on the terms of competition in their free trade agreement (e.g., setting reasonable restrictions and ensuring fair competition for governments to participate in economic activities through state-owned enterprises).

The American Chamber of Commerce gave detailed recommendations to the TPP committee on how to regulate the market behavior of state-owned enterprises: Firstly, they recommended the removal of the clause in the WTO that mentions state-owned enterprises can "operate in accordance with commercial considerations" because the provision was ambiguous, giving

---

[42] Chapter 12 comments on the competition issue of state-owned enterprises and the issue is only briefly introduced here.

[43] Wang Heng, "Regulations of Competition under the WTO framework: Present and Future," *Social Science Research*, No. 5, 2006.

state-owned enterprises space for unfair competition. It should be replaced with "operate in accordance with their own commercial interests", clarifying that state-owned enterprises can only gain profit, cut spending and increase efficiency through normal commercial activities. Secondly, to distinguish between commercial and non-commercial activities of state-owned enterprises, and ensure fair competition among state-owned enterprises and other enterprises in the market, include the concept of "competitive neutrality" clearly in writing. Thirdly, state-owned enterprises should increase the transparency of procurement. They should conduct competitive bidding in the open market to procure vendors. Fourthly, TPP members should take initiative to announce government granted competitive advantages for state-owned enterprises and designated monopolies, even if other members did not request for it.[44] In general, these recommendations were ambitious and went far beyond the provisions of the US-Korea free trade agreement.

It is foreseeable that once other parties accept the recommendations put forth by the US, the dominance of state-owned enterprises of some TPP members will be undermined in the markets. The spillover effect of such a rule is that the state-owned enterprises in other countries may face greater developmental challenges.

2.3 *Noteworthy "21st century topics"*

Besides the border and behind-the-border measures, the regional economic cooperation in recent years has also covered some so-called "21st century topics" as defined by foreign scholars and governments from the US and Europe. Some of these topics are completely new, such as electronic commerce and climate change, while others are traditional topics. But in recent years, issues such as environmental protection, labor rights, and even human rights or anti-corruption issues have captured the attention of many countries. Overall, these so-called "21st century topics" largely reflect the new requirements and trends in the recent phase of international trade and investment liberalization. They are expected to become new hot spots for the rule construction process in international trade. However, as these issues are highly complex and sensitive, both developed and developing countries have very different stances and it is difficult to reach a consensus at the multilateral level. The US and Europe have therefore

---

[44] US Chamber of Commerce, "Priorities for TPP Competition Chapter." Retrieved from http://www.uschamber.com/sites/default/files/grc/TPP%20-%20Competition%20WG%20-%205-27-10.PDF.

turned to FTAs to promote their ideas and rules, and the TPP and TTIP have become the most recent platforms for these new issues.

2.3.1 *Electronic commerce*

With the rapid development of the Internet, the cross-border online transactions of digital products such as movies, music and software continue to grow every year. Thus, electronic commerce emerged in the digital era. The e-commerce in FTAs focuses on two issues. Firstly, whether digital products should be given the same treatment as physical products in the traditional form, for example, should they be granted the same benefits even though digital products are sold by electronic trading and are not bound by traditional customs territories? There is also the question as to whether tariffs should be set for digital goods in cross-border transactions. Secondly, how should countries handle the free flow of cross-border information on the Internet. The free flow of cross-border data is extremely important for business operations in the Internet age. However, there may be conflicts between various countries in terms of privacy protection laws and internet governance systems.

The US has been the leader in the Internet industry and has actively promoted the liberalization of global e-commerce. It first tried to build a trade framework for global digital products and it believes that the relevant provisions of GATT should apply to digital products, and digital products should be permanently exempted from tariffs by the WTO at the same time. Some EU members opposed the US' position. The EU proposed that the relevant provisions of GATS should be applied to e-commerce and put forward the principle of "cultural exception". Since it was not possible to reach an agreement within the WTO framework, the US tried to advocate the liberalization of e-commerce through FTAs.[45]

Among the FTAs that the US has signed to date, other than NAFTA and the FTA with Israel, which do not include e-commerce because they were signed at an earlier time, more recent FTAs were signed with e-commerce content, and separate provisions were set up to detail regulations. Take the signing of United States-Korea Free Trade Agreement in 2007 for example, the agreement clearly stipulates that the relevant provisions of the WTO should apply to e-commerce and tariffs ought not to be imposed on digital products. Both nations should provide national treatment and MFN

---

[45] He Qisheng, "Regulation of Digital Trade Products in American Free Trade Agreement," *Journal of Henan University of Economics and Law*, No. 5, 2012.

treatment to each other for digital products. However, the agreement also stipulates that the national treatment and MFN treatment of e-commerce do not apply to cross-border trade in services, investment and financial services where measures are inconsistent. To a certain extent, this weakens the trade liberalization of digital products. In addition, some of the FTA signed by the US and other countries include e-commerce sections like electronic authentication, online consumer protection, paperless trade management and transparency principles.

The US has also advocated in TPP negotiations that no tariffs should be imposed on these digital products whether transactions of these digital products are in virtual form or physical forms such as disks. At the request of US high-tech companies, the US government also advocated that TPP ban members from impeding cross-border flow of internet data, not making restrictions to data storage and server location. With regard to this, Australia and New Zealand felt that the claims of the US might conflict with its individual privacy protection laws in China. Even though related multinational companies formulated relevant privacy policies, there was still a gap between the level of protection and regulatory requirements, so the government should intervene appropriately with the flow of data. Due to censorship and other considerations, Vietnam and Malaysia need localized data storage.[46]

2.3.2 Environmental issues[47]

Issues related to environment and trade have been of concern to many countries long before the WTO was established. Developed countries believe that because developed and developing countries differ greatly in environmental standards — with developing countries being more relaxed — developed countries have greater incentive to relocate their industries. At the same time, the lower environmental standards in products exported from developing countries may also give them low-cost competitive advantage. This really affects similar products in developed countries and is a form of unfair competition, or what is called "green-dumping". Therefore, trade restriction measures should be taken acoordingly. While developing countries consider that the strategy of "green protectionism"

---

[46] Ian F. Fergusson, Mark A. McMinimy and Brock R. Williams, "The Trans-Pacific Partnership Negotiations and Issues for Congress," March 20, 2015. Retrieved from http://www.fas.org/sgp/crs/row/R42694.pdf.

[47] Chapter 14 will discuss the details of this issue. The issue is only introduced in brief here.

adopted by developed countries should be resolutely opposed. In addition, as climate change becomes a global concern, some developed countries suggest that the main reason behind the sharp rise in carbon emission is international trade. Carbon emissions are high in developing countries and the total volume of emission continues to increase. Furthermore, the developing countries do not bear the responsibility of obligatory emission reduction. "Carbon tariffs" should therefore be imposed on the products exported from these countries to developed countries so as to promote the reduction of emissions globally and offset the "unfair" competitive advantage that the developing countries enjoy. Due to the contrasting stands of developed and developing countries which affect their direction of development, future development potential and other interests, it is difficult to reach a consensus by all parties on trade and environmental issues at the multilateral level. They were thus unable to form binding trade and environmental rules.

The US has always fervently pursued its claim on environmental issues in regional economic cooperation. In the NAFTA signed back in the 1990s, the US made it clear that trade and environmental issues were related. The ancillary agreements that came with managing environmental issues constrained and limited the environmental policy for NAFTA members through public participation, deliberation and other measures. Mechanisms were also established to punish those who committed violations. An important element in the relevant provisions of NAFTA was that members could not lower environmental standards as a way to attract foreign investment and promote trade. The FTA signed by the US after that basically dealt with environmental issues in accordance with the NAFTA model. Currently in TPP negotiations, the US is leveraging its strong position to actively encourage the TPP members to accept the NAFTA model in which trade and environmental issues are related. In TTIP negotiations, the US and Europe have distinctly set rules which are related to trade and environmental issues so as to influence the multilateral rules.

It is worth mentioning that besides promoting the NAFTA model in dealing with environmental issues in free trade areas and the WTO, the US also promotes its stances through the regional economic cooperation forum like the Asia-Pacific Economic Cooperation (APEC). It promotes dialogue on policies to actively liberalize environmental goods and it has achieved positive results thus far. In September 2012, after intense negotiations among the parties, APEC members made a clear commitment to reduce tariffs substantially for 54 environmental goods with six-digit tariff code before 2015. This was to bring about the liberalization of environmental goods in other regional and multilateral organizations and set a good example for them.[48] In June 2013, Obama explicitly announced that the multilateral negotiation process of environmental goods and service liberalization in the WTO would be based on the APEC list of environmental goods.[49]

On January 24, 2014, 14 WTO members including the US, China and EU announced in Davos that the official launch of environmental goods negotiations would be based on the APEC list.[50] It can be said that the regional environmental regulations of APEC prompted and speed up the formation of the WTO environmental rules. However, as current negotiations on environmental goods are only plurilateral, how to ensure the multinationalization the negotiation outcomes and the prevention of "free rides" by non-participants are issues worthy of further thought and study.

2.3.3 *Labor issues*[51]

Labor issues are closely associated with human rights, freedom and other political rights. They are related to a country's economic management system, social system and ideology, and are more sensitive and controversial issues. Developed and developing countries have vastly different beliefs with regard to the inclusion of labor standards in trade agreements. Developed countries believe that low labor standards are the main reason why developing countries enjoy greater competitive advantage for labor-intensive products, creating a so-called "social dumping" problem and appropriate measures could hence be taken to limit trade. Developing countries, on the other hand, consider this move protectionist and resolutely oppose the idea.

Developed countries have been trying to negotiate labor standards and relevant issues in the WTO. In 1996, during the Singapore ministerial conference, the issue was almost successfully integrated into the WTO with the US, Europe and other developed countries being the driving forces. However, due to strong resistance from developing countries, labor issues ultimately remained

---

[48] Asia-Pacific Economic Cooperation (APEC), "Annex C-APEC List of Environmental Goods," September 8–9, 2012. Retrieved from http://www.apec.org/Meeting-Papers/Leaders-Declarations/2012/2012_aelm/2012_aelm_annexC.aspx.

[49] USTR, "President Obama Announces Actions to Address Climate Change," http://www.ustr.gov/about-us/press-office/blog/2013/june/obama_climate_change.

[50] EU, "Joint Statement Regarding Trade in Environmental Goods," January 14, 2014. Retrieved from http://trade.ec.europa.eu/doclib/docs/2014/january/tradoc_152095.pdf.

[51] Chapter 14 will discuss the details of this issue. The issue is only introduced in brief here.

out of the scope of WTO negotiations. Currently, it is still difficult for the WTO to handle labor standards. Therefore, as they did with environmental issues, the US has also been trying to advocate their ideas and policies of labor issues through FTAs.

First, the US explicitly linked trade and labor standards in NAFTA. The ancillary agreements that came with managing labor issues in a separate section constrained and limited the labor policies of NAFTA members through public participation, deliberation and other means. Mechanisms were also put in place to punish those who violated the regulations. In general, the relevant core regulations in NAFTA required member states to recognize the rights of workers in collective negotiations, the elimination of forced labor and other "core labor standards," preventing the lower labor standards in certain countries from granting them "unfair" competitive advantage. During the TPP negotiations, the US also actively encouraged TPP members to accept the NAFTA model of associating trade with labor standards. In TTIP negotiations, the US and Europe have also evidently set rules relevant to trade and labor issues so as to set an example for multilateral rules.

3 Rules Reconstruction in China and Regional Economic Cooperation

In recent years, the rapid development of regional economic cooperation — FTAs in particular — has become the new way for developed countries to create platforms for constructing new international trade rules. China has been trying to keep up with and participate actively in regional economic cooperation, especially in FTA cooperation. In fact, although China only started participating in FTAs much later, it has done much and its involvement in negotiations has had great impact. Since the China-ASEAN FTA negotiations started in 2002, China has been able to see some results in the construction of free trade areas. This is significant for China as it is able to utilize both international and domestic markets and resources effectively.

However, compared to developed countries and major developing countries, China's level of construction of free trade areas is not high, the scope of construction is not wide and there is still a lot of room for development. Especially in the areas related to new international trade rules and standards, the relevant industries in China are less competitive and there are still great differences in their operating systems and management levels, compared to its international peers. This has led to policy and systemic hindrances for China when it conducts its relevant in-depth negotiations; making it difficult for them to commit to participating in FTAs. But if China does not make a high level of commitment, it is tough for them to play a leading role in regional cooperation, and some developed countries even refuse to discuss FTAs with China for these reasons. Therefore, China is in a dilemma with regard to increasing its level of participation in FTAs. It can be said that this is an important reason why China is still hesitant to participate in the TPP and other negotiations.

In the long run, once countries accept the new standards and rules, which have been strongly recommended by the US and Europe in TPP and TTIP negotiations, multilaterally, the existing enterprise and management systems in China will be faced with new challenges. Development costs may rise and restructuring may be hindered. In order for international economic and trade rules to be constructed in favor of the development of China, China needs to deepen and broaden reform, participate more actively in the construction of free trade areas and play a more active role in the regional economic trade rule-making process.

3.1 *Overview of China's participation in regional economic cooperation*

In this round of regional economic cooperation, China participated fully and had major breakthroughs. Specifically, China was actively involved in RTAs, which mainly took the form of FTAs. In these RTAs, China further eased the market access of goods, services and other areas based on their level of commitment to the WTO. Secondly, it participated in APEC, ASEM and other various regional economic cooperation forums, which mainly carried out policy dialogues, trade promotions and information exchanges. Thirdly, it was involved in the Greater Mekong and other sub-regional economic cooperation. It carried out pragmatic cooperation projects that aimed at improving infrastructure and capacity building within the neighboring countries and regions. In regional cooperation, the establishment of free trade areas between China and relevant countries and regions was the most important.

In 2002, just one year after the accession of China to the WTO, the Chinese government was keenly aware of the new trends in the development of global free trade areas and took initiatives to adapt to the new situation in global regional economic integration. It began to participate actively in the construction of free trade areas and started FTA negotiations with 10 countries in ASEAN. In 2007, the report to the 17th National Congress of the Communist Party of China (CPC) clearly stated "the implementation of FTA Strategy", raising the establishment of FTA to the national strategic level. In 2012, the report to the 18th National Congress of the CPC once again made it clear "to accelerate the implementation of the FTA Strategy". After 10 years of development, China has successfully constructed some FTAs and achieved good results.

To date, China has signed and implemented 11 free trade agreements involving 19 countries. The free trade partners are in Asia, Latin America, Oceania, Europe and other regions. The trade with FTA partners accounts for about 28% of total foreign trade in China. These FTAs are the "ASEAN-China FTA", "China-Pakistan FTA", "China-Chile FTA", " New Zealand-China FTA", "China-Singapore FTA" "China-Peru FTA", "China-Costa Rica FTA", "China-Iceland FTA", "China-Switzerland FTA", "China-Korea FTA" and China-Autralia FTA.[52]

It is worth mentioning that as Chinese Hong Kong, Chinese Macao and Chinese Taipei (in the name of separate customs territory of Taiwan, Penghu, Kinmen and Matsu) are separate customs territory members of the WTO, so there are some calculations that the "Mainland and Hong Kong Closer Economic Partnership Arrangement", "Mainland and Macao Closer Economic Partnership Arrangement" (CEPA) and their supplementary agreements and Cross-Straits Economic Cooperation Framework Agreement (ECFA) are included in the scope of FTAs signed by China. If the above trade agreements are included, China has signed a total of 14 free trade agreements involving 22 countries and regions. In 2015, the trade volume between China and the 22 free trade partners, accounted for 38% of the total foreign trade in China.

In the aspect of implementation, the establishment of FTAs in China has had good economic effect and has driven China and bilateral FTA partners to develop faster and have a "bigger share of the cake" in bilateral trade. According to statistics, the bilateral trade between China and its 15 partner countries amounted to USD475.4 billion in 2012, an increase of 10.3%, which was higher than the global growth rate by 4.1%. It accounted for 12.3% of the total foreign trade in China, an increase of 0.5% over 2011.

At present, China is still in negotiations for eight FTAs involving 26 countries. The FTA negotiations are China-Japan-Korea, RCEP, China-GCC and China-Norway *etc.* In addition, China has also launched FTA joint feasibility studies with Colombia, Nepal and other countries, ending the RTA joint study with India.[53]

---

[52] FTA commerce department website, retrieved from http: //fta.mofcom.gov.cn/index.shtml.
[53] *Ibid.*

Although the establishment of FTAs in China has had some successes, the FTA partners of China are generally smaller in economic size and are relatively limited in influence as compared to developed countries and major emerging economies. Besides Korea, Australia, Switzerland and Indonesia, other FTA partners which have reached an agreement with China are ranked out of the top 20 world economies in total economic output. Overall, the development level of FTAs in China is low. It might lag far behind the developed countries, but among the major emerging economies, it ranks just above Russia.[54]

3.2 Difficulties of China participating in regional economic cooperation — the TPP as an example

In 2008, the United States joined the TPP and vigorously promoted the expansion of TPP members, seeking a way to integrate the Asia-Pacific regional economy. Since then, the hot topic within the Chinese academic community has been whether China should join the TPP. This has been especially pressing since July 2013 after Japan joined the TPP negotiations. In general, most scholars were of the view that China should take the initiative to join the TPP as soon as possible.[55] There were also some scholars who suggested that China study the situation carefully and there was no hurry to join. The decision could be made after observing for a few years.[56] There were still others who believed that it was imperative to speed up the implementation of China's own FTA strategy to offset the impact of TPP.[57]

Joining the TPP would significantly enhance economic trade cooperation between China and TPP members, and improve the process of Asia-Pacific regional economic integration. It could also press in towards some domestic reform. There was basically no objection to these points. Yet, the question if

---

[54] See Table 4.1 in the same chapter for the top 12 world economies in terms of FTA development.

[55] Wei Jianguo, "Taking the Initiative to Join TPP is More Favorable for China," *Global Times*, July 26, 2013. Retrieved from http://opinion.huanqiu.com/economy/2013-07/4173941.html.

[56] Xu Changwen, "TPP Development and How China Should Respond," *International Trade*, No. 3, 2011.

[57] Peng Zhiwei and Zhang Weibo, "The Economic Effect of TPP and Asia-Pacific Free Trade Area and China's Countermeasures", *Journal of International Trade*, No. 4, 2013.

China should join the TPP ought not to be just analyzed in terms of benefits and costs, but also with regard to the feasibility of both China's internal and external aspects. In other words, the first question was whether China met the conditions in the short term to join the TPP. The second was whether the US would sincerely welcome China in joining TPP so soon. The following analysis on difficulties comes mainly from the macro level.

3.2.1 *The domestic obstacles for China if it participates in TPP and other high-level FTA negotiations*

The lack of preparation was a direct obstacle for China's participation in the construction of new rules and in improving the standard of trade liberalization in economic trade development. This is both because of the country's insufficient knowledge as well as a lack of negotiating capacity. The new topics and regulations promoted by developed countries at TPP and other FTA negotiations extend beyond traditional trade fields to non-trade and even ideological areas, clashing with China's current systems, mechanisms, and relevant laws and regulations. It is hard to tell if accepting the above-mentioned new regulations and standards would bring more benefit than harm, or do more harm than good to China's foreign trade, national economy and society. Therefore, it is more important to strengthen basic research and assessment of impact at this stage.

The fundamental obstacle was the great difference between the rules and level of openness of relevant fields in China with the demands of other high-level free trade regions such as the TPP. The new rules and standards proposed by the TPP and other free trade regions often involved areas that China had always needed to protect in various trade negotiations. If China accepted them, it would likely impact its current industrial development model and affect existing domestic interests. Modifying and improving existing laws and regulations required substantial adjustments to existing domestic management mechanisms. Chinese Prime Minister Li Keqiang pointed out that "reform has entered a high level".[58]

The first obstacle that China would face is that the TPP requested that tariffs be eliminated for all products in terms of trade in goods. Some of the

---

[58] China News, "Li Keqiang: Reform has Reached High Levels, Be Courageous to Break the Benefits and Interests Trend," November 3, 2011. Retrieved from http: //finance.chinanews.com/cj/2013/11-03/5457345.shtml.

companies in domestic sectors with higher interests, tighter security requirements and stronger dominating power believed that further tariff concessions
would affect industrial competitiveness and it would be difficult to resist the
impact brought by foreign imports. In agricultural products, the further expansion of imports would complicate the tariff quota system of grain, cotton and
sugar, and this could affect agriculture and food security.[59] Until now, the "trade
adjustment assistance system" has not been established domestically to compensate for the impact of industries opening up. There were difficulties restructuring the relevant industries.[60]

The second obstacle for China lies in the area of trade in services. The TPP
committee requested for members' finance, telecommunications and other
sensitive sectors open up and called for negative list negotiations. OECD and
other international organizations believed that China had implemented more
stringent controls in the retail, energy, finance, telecommunications and other
service sectors so there were great difficulties in lowering the threshold for
market access.[61] China, however, is quite new to the negative list approach in
the FTA negotiations.

The third obstacle lies in the area of investment, where the TPP's core
request was to grant foreign capital full national treatment and the implementation of negative list management. Grant of full national treatment requires
that the Chinese government reform the current system of foreign investment
management. The transition from approval management to service management, and from the existing management of "certificate first, license second" to
the management of "license first, certificate second" would be a major institutional change. Negative list management refers to the management measures and performance requirements for foreign investment which are not
entitled to national and MFN treatment, should be set out in a list mode. This
management approach requires "no legal prohibition" if it is not stated in the

---

[59] Ni Hongxing, "The Six Major Errors of Choice on Agricultural Trade Policy Choice,"
Agricultural Trade Policy under Open Trade Conditions (China: China Agricultural Press, 2011).
[60] Chen Zhiyang, "The Four Major Difficulties to Accelerate the Establishment of FTA and the
Countermeasures," *Foreign Trade Practice*, No. 11, 2012.
[61] According to the Product Market Regulation Index (PMR) by the OECD Development,
China was ranked first place and much higher than other countries in the market regulation in
professional services, retail, energy, transport, telecommunications and the majority of service
sectors after an investigation in 37 countries (including developed countries and four emerging
economies Brazil, India, China, Russia). OECD, "Indicators of Product Market Regulation
(PMR)," retrieved from http://www.oecd.org/eco/growth/indicatorsofproductmarketregulation
homepage.htm.

list, so there are higher requirements for the management level in the foreign investment department of China.

The fourth difficulty lies with behind-the-border measures: the TPP rules are related to economic, social management system and other issues. On issues such as competition, the institutional system of anti-monopoly law in China was not complete. The functional segmentation agency in multi-sectoral enforcement made the situation even more complex. In particular, how state-owned enterprises could compete in neutrality, as well as the relationship between state-owned enterprises and the government in the market were yet to be further clarified. On the issue of intellectual property rights, China has greatly improved IPR protection and its standard, but it has been cautious in making international commitments beyond TRIPS.

The fifth obstacle China faces is in some areas where the rules of the TPP touch on 21st century issues such as those which concern political issues and ideology. For example, developed countries try to relate human rights, labor and other issues with trade. This is contrary to China's general stance that political issues should not be associated with foreign trade negotiations.

3.2.2 *The attitude of the US towards the accession of China to the TPP*

The TPP is a FTA negotiation led by the US. The attitude of the US towards the countries applying to join TPP is a determining factor. For China, the government officials from the US have publicly welcomed China to join the TPP on several occasions in the last two years, stressing that the TPP was not against China. This seemed to indicate that the US is open to the accession of China to the TPP,[62] but further observation and analysis is needed to determine if the US' stand is real or just diplomatic.

In recent years, the US and some developed countries have thought that although China, India and other emerging economies have risen up, they are still unable to assume the corresponding responsibilities of the opening up of their markets. It was believed by some developed countries that the low level of ambition in negotiations was an important reason for the stalled Doha Round negotiations. One of the important motivations of the US to develop a free trade area is to construct rules within a small circle of "like-minded"

---

[62]Chen Qin, "US Under Secretary of State: Welcoming China to TPP," September 9, 2012. Retrieved from http://international.caixin.com2012-09-09/100434763.html.

countries first, and then push for economic and trade cooperation using the above rules with other developing countries to play up its strong position. Finally, they would push for this on a multilateral level, forcing other developing countries, especially emerging economies, to accept the rules. There are many in the US who believe that if China was introduced to the TPP negotiations prematurely, China could become a "black sheep" who would reduce the level of ambition, and even cause TPP negotiations to stall. This is exactly what the US tried to avoid by going round the WTO and promoting TPP and TTIP.

But for the US, China is an important country to be involved in Asia-Pacific economic integration. Without the participation of China, its significance will be greatly reduced. For the US' sake, it is likely that the US will formally invite China to join TPP again after the conclusion of the TPP negotiations and ask China to accept what the parties have agreed upon. During the process of joining the TPP, the applicant countries need bilateral consultations with the existing members and the existing members have to agree to applicants' membership before the latter can formally join.[63] There are similar procedural requirements for accession to the WTO so the applicant countries in this process are in a passive position. The US can fully use its dominant position in the course of this process, making strong demands for applicant countries to achieve the goal of maximizing its economic, political and diplomatic interests. When Canada and Mexico applied to join the TPP, the US proposed that the two countries not make any changes to the agreement, which the TPP parties have agreed upon, and Canada and Mexico were to accept all of them. To successfully join TPP, the two countries were forced to accept the requests. Some in Canada, were of the belief that Canada was participating as a "second-class citizen" in the negotiation process.[64]

By analyzing TPP, we can see the challenges China faces internationally and domestically in speeding up the establishment of FTAs. To achieve a higher level of FTAs, there is a need to advocate deeper domestic reforms and make tougher choices based on interests. In addition, China has to make efforts to take initiative in the complex competition in the international and political economy.

---

[63] USTR, "Trans-Pacific Partnership Ministers Chart Path Forward on Key Issues and Confirm Next Steps on Japan's Entry," April 2013. Retrieved from http://www.ustr.gov/about-us/press-office/press-releases/2013/april/joint-statement-tpp-ministers.

[64] Scott Sinclair, "Canada's Humiliating Entry into TPP Trade Deal," June 26, 2012. Retrieved from http://thetyee.ca/Opinion/2012/06/26/TTP-Trade-Deal/.

3.3 *Thoughts on speeding up the implementation of China's FTA strategy*

3.3.1 *The necessity of China participating actively in the rules reconstruction in regional economic cooperation*

As global free trade development enters a new phase in history, China should adhere to strategy — "get the wheel of multilateral trading system and the wheel of regional trade arrangements moving at the same time"[65] whether in terms of international trends, the experience of power countries, or its own practice in promoting free trade areas, and accelerate the implementation of its FTA strategy. While adhering to the overall direction of trade liberalization, China should expand, deepen and broaden the scope of mutually beneficial cooperation to promote regional economic integration through flexible arrangements.[66]

FTA is an important part of China's strategies to open up, and an important platform for the implementation of a more proactive opening up strategy. It is also a crucial starting point for domestic reform. With China participating actively in the development of regional economic trade rules, it can obtain greater dividends for opening up while still achieving a more significant goal — to promote domestic reforms and institutional innovation to have a breakthrough in the system. It should be said that amidst TPP, TTIP and other high standard FTA negotiations, some new rules and standards on intellectual property rights, innovation policy, government procurement, investment rules, environmental protection, pre-establishment national treatment, and e-commerce among other areas reflect the new trend of the economic globalization. At the same time, these rules and standards are coherent with the China's socialist market economic development direction to some extent, and align well with China's transformation in economic development, and the inherent conditions of the comprehensive construction of a well-off society. This will be the focus of reform in China, and China has to face this situation sooner or later.

Participating actively in regional economic cooperation will also be beneficial for China to lead the development of international and regional economic

---

[65] Li Keqiang, "Work Hand-in-Hand to Create a New Future of China-Switzerland Pragmatic Cooperation — A speech at Luncheon with Swiss Economic and Financial Community on May 25, 2013". Retrieved from http://www.gov.cn/ldhd/2013-05/25/content_2411267.htm.
[66] Chen Zhiyang, "Strategies to Open Up and Build a Big Nation," *Chinese Social Sciences Today*, April 17, 2013, p. A06.

trade rules in its favor. As the emerging power with great influence in the Asia-Pacific region and globally, China must not be contented to follow or oppose global multilateral and regional trade rules, but to advocate and lead the way in rule reconstruction. In the new round of regional economic and trade rules remodeling, China must approach external negotiations with an open mind and not avoid sensitive issues, so that maximum consistency with relevant trade partners can be reached. At the same time, China should offer new ideas, initiatives and programs to enhance the international and regional influence so as to shape the new rules for international and regional trade, contributing as it should have done.

3.3.2 *Favorable conditions to accelerate the implementation of FTA strategy*

China has the economic base to further open up. After 30 years of reform and opening up, the overall national strength and international competitiveness of China have greatly increased. It has become the second largest economy in the world, the largest country on trade in goods and the country with the most foreign exchange reserves. China surpassed the US in 2010 to be the country with the largest manufacturing industry in the world, with its proportion of manufacturing output near to 20% in the world.[67] The market attractiveness, economic radiation and increasing industrial competitiveness of China, are better foundations for opening up as compared to the past. It possesses the conditions to develop FTAs more actively. Meanwhile, after joining the WTO, the domestic application of international trade rules and the ability to cope with risks have improved significantly.

The Chinese government has the political will to push towards further opening up. The reconstruction of FTA rules mentioned earlier involves border measures, behind-the-border measures and 21st century issues. There is a need to accelerate reform in related fields domestically. In order to participate at a deeper level and set high standards in international economic and trade rules, the foundation of domestic institution must be laid. As the relevant reforms involve the major problems of current reforms in the opening up process, the Chinese leaders are required to make political decisions. After the new government took office, China has a stronger will to accelerate reform and the pace of

---

[67] Wang Zheng, "Unswervingly Taking the Road of New Industrialization with Chinese Characteristics (A Restrospect after 10 years)," September 18, 2012. Retrieved from http://politics.people.com.cn/n/2012/0918/c1001-19033586.html.

reform became faster with more innovative approaches. All these have created more favorable conditions for China to participate in high standard FTA negotiations.

For example, the "top design" for reform is seen through the "Decisions made by CPC Central Committee on Comprehensive Deepening Reform and Major Issues" which was passed on November 12, 2013. It mentioned that "accelerating the establishment of free trade areas... accelerating the implementation of FTA strategy with neighboring countries as the foundation... reforming management system on market access, customs supervision, inspection and quarantine, and speeding up negotiations of new issues such as environmental protection, investment protection, government procurement, e-commerce and other new issues so as to form a global free trade area network of high standards."[68] This has injected a powerful political force into the China's establishment of free trade areas.

Another example of internal initiative to amend the law dates to August 30, 2013, when the Standing Committee of the National People's Congress decided on the revision of trademark law. For the first time, the regulation stated that a sound could be used for trademark registration. This took the Chinese intellectual property protection system an important step closer to gradual global integration.[69]

China also takes initiative to participate in negotiations of a high standard. In July 2013, at the fifth round of the China-US Strategic and Economic Dialogue, China agreed to enter into substantive negotiations on investment agreements with the US on the basis of pre-establishment national treatment and a negative list.[70] This gave China's investment system reform a huge impetus and formed the conditions for China to accept high standards in international investment rules in future FTA negotiations.

Another example was the pilot projects: In order to explore effective ways to build a new open economic system, the State Council officially approved the

---

[68] Xinhua News Agency, "Authorized Release: The CPC Central Committee's Decisions on Overall Reform Development and Major Issues," November 11, 2013. Retrieved from http://news.xinhuanet.com/politics/2013-11/15/c_118164235.htm.

[69] National People's Congress, "The Standing Committee of National People's Congress on the Decision of Amending [the] People's Republic of China Trademark Law," August 31, 2013. Retrieved from http://www.npc.gov.cn/npc/xinwen/2013-08/31/content_1805119.htm.

[70] Ministry of Commerce , "Ministry of Commerce Spokesman Shen Danyang's Remarks on Actively Promoting Investment in China-US Agreement Negotiations," July 12, 2013. Retrieved from http://www.mofcom.gov.cn/article/ae/ag/201307/20130700196677.shtml.

establishment of China (Shanghai) Pilot Free Trade Zone in August 2013. This was to explore specifically a new way and model for China to open up in the region including the accelerated transformation of government functions, active exploration of innovative management models of investment, expanding the opening up of services, deepening the opening up and innovation of the financial sector.[71] On September 29, 2013, China (Shanghai) Pilot Free Trade Zone was officially inaugurated. Minister of Commerce Gao Hucheng pointed out in an interview with reporters that the main significance of establishing Shanghai as Pilot Free Trade Zone was "to form the basic institutional framework through tests so as to connect with international trade rules, and become an important carrier to further integrate into the global economy".[72] On September 30, the "Special Administrative Measures (Negative List) on Foreign Investment Access to the China (Shanghai) Pilot Free Trade Zone (2013) (The "Negative List")" was published. The list only included 190 specific administrative measures involving 18 industry categories. Foreign investment projects in other fields apart from the negative list were changed from the approval system to the record system, consistent with the principles of foreign and domestic investment.[73] Some experts said that the initiative to stimulate domestic reform through the China (Shanghai) Pilot Free Trade Zone will promote the accession of China to TPP.[74]

3.3.3 *Possible ways to accelerate the implementation of FTA strategy*

In general, China could sped up the implementation of FTA strategy in two ways. One of them was the "easy things first" approach, when one can start negotiating with a small country and then move on to a big country; or start with a developing country and move to developed countries. The standards of

---

[71] Ministry of Commerce, "The State Council Approves the Establishment of China (Shanghai) Pilot Free Trade Zone," August 22, 2013. Retrieved from http://www.mofcom.gov.cn/article/ae/ai/201308/20130800262548.shtml.

[72] Ministry of Commerce, "Interview with Gao Hucheng on the Establishment of China (Shanghai) Pilot Free Trade Zone," http://www.mofcom.gov.cn/article/ae/ai/201309/20130900330136.shtml.

[73] "The 'Negative List' of Shanghai Free Trade Zone Announced", http://news.163.com/13/0930/01/ 9A02B9GM0001124J_all.html.

[74] "Experts Claimed that the Free Trade Zone Reform will Promote the Accession of China to TPP and Other International Arenas," August 30, 2013. Retrieved from http://ndfinance.oeeee.com/html/201308/30/189960.html.

FTA negotiations in major economies, especially developed countries, are high. Discussing FTAs with these countries and economies may result in large economic benefits, but it is very difficult to negotiate with them. This may also impact China's economy and institutions greatly. Therefore, China can consider first establishing free trade areas with smaller economies, countries and regions with high dependence on the Chinese market to gain experience, and gradually discuss FTAs with larger economies. China has mainly adopted this approach, as seen from the current negotiations of China in foreign trade areas. Among the 14 FTAs China has with 22 trade partners, besides Korea, Australia, Switzerland and Indonesia, the economies of scale of China's FTA partners are not within the world's top 20.

Another approach is to promote FTA negotiations with key economies directly. When the economic output and market capacity of the FTA members are larger, the effect of trade creation is greater. The active promotion of FTA negotiations with important economies will bring greater economic effect to China. In recent years, although there has been exploration into this approach, there was no major breakthrough. From China's experience in joining the WTO negotiations, the huge external impetus and pressure of the negotiations have successfully stimulated the reform of domestic institutions and expansion of opening up even more, thereby releasing huge dividends. If there are only negotiations with small countries and economies, these will not be sufficient to pressurize larger domestic interest groups or obligate and push for comprehensive and deep domestic reforms. Therefore, actively promoting FTA negotiations in China-Japan-Korea, RCEP and other major economies, and even creating conditions for the US and the European Union to carry out FTA negotiations can play an important role in pioneering and stimulating the establishment of FTAs. This will contribute to China playing a constructive role in the new round of rules reconstruction in trade, hastening the completion of the open economy system in the country.

Chapter 5

International Rules of Finance

On September 17, 2011, thousands of demonstrators gathered in Manhattan in an attempt to occupy Wall Street. Some even brought their tents and threatened to prolong the protest. Some of the demonstrators asserted, "We launched this protest because we feel that there is a need for the US to change. Many people have lost their jobs, and are homeless. The entire country is hurt and those who have caused this have gone scot-free and remain aloof about our plight." From then on, the "Occupy Wall Street" movement escalated rapidly, spreading across more than 120 cities in the US. Other cities, around the world, big and small, also got involved and participated. This series of protests reflected the citizens' resentment against those in the financial industry who only took care of themselves while others paid for their mistakes.

On the surface, this immense crisis seems to be the consequence of the US' excessively loose monetary policy and loss of regulatory control over financial innovation. In fact, many insiders recall that in 1971, when President Richard Nixon announced that the US could not convert the dollar to gold according to established parity, the Bretton Woods System collapsed due to the breach of contract by the largest economic power. When negotiating with the European diplomatic mission, a famous quote by the US Secretary of Treasury John Connally quickly spread throughout the world, "The dollar is our currency but your problem." The crisis spread rapidly across the world, once again re-affirming this finance official's "foresight", turning the eyes of the world towards the USD-dominated international monetary system. When the Bretton Woods System was set up early in 1944, then the US Secretary of Treasury, Henry Morgenthau Jr., ambitiously pushed for the White Plan, causing the medical condition of the famous British economist, John Maynard Keynes, to worsen. Keynes became physically and mentally exhausted, and passed away suddenly two years later. The international monetary system's concepts advocated by the US, emerged victorious: including exchange rate stability, deficit countries bore the responsibility for imbalance, no shortage of the US dollar, and no depreciation of the US dollar. Yet in less than 30 years, the rule-maker himself violated these rules and allowed the Bretton Woods System to collapse completely. Many inevitably raised the question: "Is the IMF, one of the three economic pillars of the international economy, or the US Treasury and US Federal Reserve more important in global financial governance?"

1 Summary of the Defects and Reconstruction of International Rules of Finance

The financial sector is the core of the modern economy and is often the source or center of contemporary economic crises. In the 20th century, the concept of capitalism evolved to that of financial capitalism; the rapid development of finance caused the 19th century economic crisis of overproduction to transform into another type of economic crisis of the 20th century, with the financial sector as the fuse. The Great Depression and the financial crisis this time round are very similar. On the surface, the outbreak of the financial crisis appears to have "three excesses": excessively loose monetary policy, excessive financial innovation and excessively relaxed financial supervision. At a deeper level, it reflects the flaws in the international monetary system: after the collapse of the Bretton Woods System in the 1970s, the Jamaica Agreement replaced it and a floating exchange rate system emerged. The hegemony of the US dollar was weakened but it remained the dominant reserve currency. The repeal of the gold clause led to increased volatility in the international financial markets and the international monetary system entered a state of "anarchy". Some academics also named the Jamaican System as "the post-Bretton Woods System". In this context, with the acceleration of economic globalization and the progress of financial liberalization, international financial crises occurred more frequently. The global financial crisis this time round further exposed the shortcomings in global financial rules with regard to the prevention of and response to future crises. The reform and adaptation of existing international financial rules to the new state of economic and financial globalization is the core issue for global financial governance in this post-crisis era. It is a major issue that policymakers have to face if they wish to ensure global financial stability.

1.1 *The crisis revealed the flaws in the international rules of finance*

The international rules of finance in the latter half of the 20th century, from the establishment of the international monetary system to rules of financial regulation, have played a positive role in the global economy. However, there are inherent flaws in this set of financial rules and these shortcomings were further exposed in the era of economic globalization.

1.1.1 *Imperfect regulatory rules of international finance*

Excessive financial innovation sowed the seeds of trouble leading to this crisis. The securitization of many subprime loans shifted the risk of default to capital markets, the consumers of subprime securities bore the risk of default and the highly leveraged operation of capital became the channel of risk diffusion. After the outbreak of the crisis, the value of financial assets held by investment banks and other financial institutions shrunk dramatically, resulting in the selling of risky assets, raising of capital and other measures to implement the deleveraging process. This ultimately provoked a liquidity squeeze in the entire market, causing systemic risk in credit markets. A major driving force for the crisis was the absence of US financial regulation. Under the influence of neoliberalism and its dominant policies, the United States made efforts to abolish the "Glass-Steagall Act" after 1991. Implemented during the Great Depression, this Act enacted sub-sector regulation and placed restrictions on banks' speculative investments. In 1999, the "Financial Services Modernization Act" officially replaced it.

Financial regulation in the US is a typical "two-level, multi-authority" regulatory model. "Two-level" indicates that both federal and state governments possessed regulatory rights while "multi-authorities" meant that the Federal Reserve, the Office of the Comptroller of the Currency (OCC), and the Federal Deposit Insurance Corporation (FDIC) are responsible for supervising commercial banks; the Securities and Exchange Commission, the Commodity Futures Trading Commission and the American investment protection companies are responsible for supervising the securities and futures markets; the Office of Thrift Supervision is responsible for supervising savings and loan associations; and the Federal Reserve is also responsible for supervising financial holding companies while state governments are responsible for supervising insurance agencies. The partition of the financial regulatory system easily causes blind spots in supervision, difficulties in coordination and the weakening of regulations, which leads to disorderly development of financial innovation. There was dislocation or a lack of regulation in mixed operation institutions' derivatives trading, and a lack of legal regulation of certain credit rating agencies. As such, overestimation of credit and underestimation of risk for the sake of individual interests were common. These credit rating agencies also easily become instruments for attacking other countries, for example, in fueling the European debt crisis.[1] Meanwhile, large investment banks created an endless stream of speculative instruments and became "too big to fail" because they had grown to be the political and economic core of American society.

From an international perspective, the IMF, as a major international financial organization, once again revealed its impotence in international financial regulation.[2] In the aftermath of the IMF's failed Asian and Latin American economic adjustment programs in the late 1990s, the IMF was virtually declared *persona non grata* in both of those regions. IMF fared even worse in terms of crisis warnings. It did not fulfill its due roles in the severe post-war financial crises. It failed to anticipate the 2008–2009 collapse of the US financial markets; neither did it forewarn about the European debt crisis, let alone monitor it.

1.1.2 *Inadequate internal governance by international financial institutions*

The global financial system is basically in a state of anarchy and it lacks effective public goods and authoritative middle-management agencies. The "Basel Accord" was a useful public good but it was not nearly enough to maintain

---

[1] Thomas L. Friedman author of the book *The World is Flat* commented in 1996, "There are two superpowers in the world today in my opinion. There's the United States and there's Moody's Bond Rating Service. The United States can destroy you by dropping bombs, and Moody's can destroy you by downgrading your bonds. And believe me, it's not clear sometimes who's more powerful." In today's world, who holds the reins of the global bond market and pricing in the capital markets? The answer is, the US has credit rating agencies with Moody and Standard and Poor as representatives. Faced with the severe consequences of poor credit ratings, the governments of Greece, Portugal and Spain condemned the credit rating agencies' behavior of "adding insult to injury". US rating companies never lowered the US' sovereign credit ratings. The US Treasury always remained at the top of credit ratings.

[2] Desmond Lachman, lifelong researcher at American Enterprise Institute and former IMF economist, puts forth this notion in this article, "A Crass Failure at the IMF," American Enterprise Institute, October 31, 2012, retrieved from https://www.aei.org/publication/a-crass-failure-at-the-imf/.

stable and efficient operation of the global financial system. Since the 1990s, international financial crises have occurred frequently, such as the Latin American debt crisis in the early 1980s, the British currency crisis and European Exchange Rate Mechanism crisis in 1991–1992, the Asian financial crisis in 1997–1998, the 1998 Russian financial crisis, and the global financial tsunami triggered by the US subprime mortgage crisis in 2008 *etc*. Of course, these problems could be attributed to the internal problems of individual countries but if there had been a strong and powerful external agency to instill mandatory discipline and timely assistance from the international community, the crises could have been avoided — or at least, the extent of their damage could have been greatly reduced.

Before World War I, there were no international financial institutions. As gold was the standard and there was an automatic adjustment mechanism, exchange rates were stable. In addition, there were surpluses in the balance of payments of the majority of major capitalist countries. Currency credit and international settlement systems had not yet been established. Therefore, in those circumstances, there were no grounds for setting up international financial institutions. To handle German reparations after World War I, the victors established the "Bank for International Settlements" (BIS) in Basel, Switzerland. This was the first international financial institution. After World War II, various countries in the world wanted to establish a stable international financial order to end the chaotic situation in international finance, thus, the IMF[3] was established. Its main task was to provide short-term funds to member states, resolve member states' temporary imbalances in international payments, and meet their foreign exchange needs, so as to promote currencies' stability and expansion of international trade. Over the past decades, the IMF has played a positive role in promoting global monetary cooperation and ensuring global financial stability, but since the date of its establishment it has its institutional drawbacks: (1) the organization is in fact controlled by the US and the EU; (2) the distribution of the Fund's shares and voting rights is unreasonable as the US has veto power on IMF's major decisions; (3) it maintains the US dollar as the main international reserve currency, yet the US does not bear the responsibility of the world's reserve currency and ignores its role as the super-sovereign reserve currency; (4) it is unable to adjust the Balance of International Payments, resulting in severely imbalanced global payments.

---

[3] When the IMF was first established, there were only 44 member states. There are currently 187. Its highest authority is the Council, while the Executive Board is the agency formed by 23 members responsible for handling IMF's daily operations.

Using the right to vote as an example, the IMF board system requires 85% of all votes before decisions are adopted. However, the US voting rights make up 16.77%. This mechanism basically ensures the US has veto rights and IMF resolutions often reflect the interests of developed countries led by the US. At the same time, there seems to be a tacit understanding that IMF presidents are Europeans, vice-presidents are Americans (the President of the World Bank Group is generally an American), and the headquarters are in the US. Under such circumstances, the IMF easily becomes a tool for major developed countries to control global financial markets. The mainstream views held by the US and Europe (such as the "Washington Consensus") have dominated the IMF and it is thus not surprising that at times, policies that do not favor developing countries are adopted.

Over the past four decades in particular, the emerging economies have grown rapidly, trade has expanded quickly, and there has been massive accumulation of foreign exchange reserves. Capital in US dollars has been exported to the US and other deficit countries instead, and emerging economies have become the world's creditor. A situation has formed where developing countries have become financiers to developed countries in global capital flow. However, in the IMF governance structure, the growing status of developing countries, especially emerging economies, has not been adequately reflected. Insufficient attention has been given to their ideas, aspirations and interests, and the IMF has become one of the most criticized international institutions.

1.1.3 *Inherent instability in the existing international monetary system*

The outbreak of this global financial crisis fully reflected the shortcomings of the international monetary system. Before the crisis, the unique position of the US dollar allowed the US to use global financing to make up for its huge trade and budget deficits, and this was the source of global imbalances. At the same time, the US, as issuer of the main reserve currency, is unwilling to assume the obligation of maintaining a stable dollar, and subsequently, its domestic policies have had huge spillover effects, becoming an important source of global inflation and blind global capital flows. It is the weather vane of the turmoil in the global financial market.

The establishment of the international monetary system has generally gone through the various stages of the gold standard (gold bullion standard system, gold exchange standard); currency groups (the sterling currency zone, the US dollar zone, the franc zone); the Bretton Woods System; and the Jamaican

Table 5.1 Comparison of the White Plan and Keynes Plan.

The US' White Plan	Britain's Keynes Plan
1. International Stabilization Fund Plan.	1. International Clearing Union Plan.
2. Principle of Deposit.	2. Principle of Overdraft.
3. Establish an international currency stabilization fund with a total capital of USD5 billion, paid for by member states using gold, their currencies and other means.	3. Establish a global central bank where various countries can use gold in exchange for Bancor, but not vice versa.
4. The share to be paid depends on the country's national GDP, gold and foreign currency reserves, as well as differences in international balance of payments. The amount paid determines the country's voting rights.	4. Share proportion depends on the average import and export volume for three years. There is no payment of gold or cash, only the opening of a current account is required. When there is a surplus, the surplus is deposited into the account, when there is a deficit, account holders can apply for funding. Total funding required is USD30 billion.
5. Issue an international currency, the Unita, as a computation unit consisting of 13,717 gold grains and equivalent to USD10.	5. Issue Bancor as a clearing unit, Bancor is equivalent to gold.
6. Stable exchange rate. Each country sets the parity of its own currency with the Unita which cannot be changed without approval from the Fund.	6. Surplus and deficit countries share the burden of adjusting international imbalances. Exchange rate flexibility is emphasized.

system. Its main function is to assist member states in addressing the imbalance of international payments and safeguard international monetary order. The current international monetary system was established towards the end of World War II as a vision the US had for international financial order. At the 1944 Bretton Woods Conference, Britain proposed the "Keynes Plan" (see Table 5.1), which stressed the shared responsibility of both surplus and deficit countries in adjusting the imbalance in international payments. A number of measures proposed in the plan were in favor of vulnerable economies, and monetary policy was suggested to be of much greater importance than trade policy.[4] The

---

[4] "If countries allow their currencies to float without agreement, tariff programs would be extremely difficult to implement… without any monetary agreement, discussing tariff matters is like a tree without roots." Quote taken from Zhang Zhenjiang's *From the Pound to the Dollar: the Transfer of International Economic Hegemony* (Beijing: People's Publishing House, 2007), p. 236.

US, on the other hand, put forward the "White Plan" and advocated that deficit countries be liable for international imbalances. They believed that the main task of the IMF was to maintain stability, and proposed the establishment of a gold-dollar-based, adjustable, floating exchange rate regime where national currencies were pegged to the dollar and one ounce of gold was worth USD35. This would in fact establish the hegemony of the dollar, reflecting the Treasury's ambition to lead the world economy. Since its inception, the IMF has set strict conditions and smaller amounts on the providence of loan assistance, and maintained interfering with the economic sovereignty of member states. This was fully shown during the Latin American and Asian financial crises which happened later.

There is an inherent contradiction in the Bretton Woods System, that is, the "Triffin Dilemma".[5] The US could continually issue dollars to make up for the deficits in balance of payments and budget, which meant that the US had the privilege of holding national levies of "seigniorage". By the 1960s, there was a flood of US dollars in the international market, and a "dollar disaster" took place. As such, in 1971, US President Richard Nixon announced the implementation of a "new economic policy" where US dollars were no longer exchanged for gold. The dollar depreciated and this was essentially the US defaulting on its debt. It was also the largest case of default in modern times, which resulted in the collapse of the Bretton Woods System. It was ironic that the year the US launched the White Plan, which was the cornerstone of the Bretton Woods System, a lot of pains were taken to prevent the dollar from running short, to stabilize the exchange rate and prevent the devaluation of currencies. *The New York Times* also criticized Keynes as "the enemy of exchange rate stability… and the head of currency devaluation and financial expansion". US officials accused the British of being "as cunning as the devil in international finance".

---

[5] In 1960, American economist Robert Triffin mentioned in his book, *Gold and the Dollar Crisis: The Future of Convertibility*, As the dollar was pegged to gold and other currencies were pegged to the dollar, the US dollar become the core international currency, yet to develop international trade, other countries had to use the US dollar as the settlement and reserve currency. This led to the continuous dollar glut abroad which would result in long-term deficit in the US; on the other hand, the premise for the US dollar becoming the core international currency was that the US dollar had to be stable and strong, this in turn requires the US be a country with long-term trade surplus. These two requirements are contradictory and paradoxical. This inherent contradiction is coined as the Triffin dilemma.

The establishment of the system marked the peaks of the careers of the Secretary of the US Treasury, Henry Morgenthau, Jr., as well as the designer of the White Plan. They firmly believed that the IMF and the World Bank were not only able to create a healthy global economy after the war, but also ensured the control of the US Treasury in international finance.[6] More than 40 years later, the US violated almost all the conditions that they had set when they first established the IMF, from a shortage of dollars to a dollar disaster; from a stable exchange rate to a floating exchange rate; and from a stable dollar to the sharp devaluation of it.

In 1976, after years of research and exploration, the IMF signed the "Jamaica Agreement" in Kingston, the capital of Jamaica. Subsequently, they also passed the "Second Amendment to the IMF Agreement" and formed a new international monetary system named the Jamaican System, also generally referred to as the post-Bretton Woods System. Its main contents include the introduction of a floating exchange rate system, the implementation of non-monetary gold, and enhancing the role of the SDR. The results were reserve currency diversification, long-term floating exchange rates, and the worsening problem of international payment.

The main drawbacks of this system are firstly, with diversified international reserves, the lack of a unified and stable monetary standard; countries issuing the reserve currency still enjoy privileges such as "seigniorage", and this easily leads to international financial instability. Secondly, the fluctuations with a floating exchange rate increases foreign currency risks and to a certain extent, inhibits international trade and investment, and has a particularly significant adverse impact on developing countries such as excessive accumulation of foreign exchange reserves in developing countries after the Asian financial crisis. Thirdly, the adjustment mechanism for international balance of payments is not comprehensive and exacerbates global imbalances. If the international financial crisis was primarily localized under the Bretton Woods System, it evolved into a regular, comprehensive, continual outbreak of small crises under the Jamaican System, and major crises have since occurred occasionally. Therefore, the international community generally considers that the existing international monetary system is transitional and imperfect, and there is a need for thorough reform. In the post-Bretton Woods era, although the dollar no longer "monopolizes" the market, the German mark, Japanese yen followed by the euro and renminbi *etc.* have gradually risen and floating exchanges rates

---

[6] Randell Bennett Woods, *A Changing of the Guard: Anglo-American Relations, 1941–1946* (Chapel Hill: University of North Carolina Press, 1990), p. 115.

have become global. While there has been extensive financial liberalization, the dominance of the US dollar has still not been shaken and the dollar is still effectively the *de facto* world currency. At the beginning of the 21st century, it still made up 65% of international reserve currencies, 50% of settlement currencies and more than 80% of foreign exchanges. Furthermore, the increased volatility of exchange rates aggravated economic risks and caused world reserves to soar. From 1948 to 1970, global international reserves grew by only 0.9 times but from 1971 to 2007, the growth was about 70-fold. After the Latin American and Asian financial crises, developing countries accelerated the accumulation of foreign exchange reserves to guard against financial risks and the share of global foreign exchange reserves rose from 1/3 to 2/3. These foreign exchange reserves then had to be invested in US bonds and thus flowed back to the US. A situation of "deficits in the US led to [the] outflow of dollars — trade surpluses and accumulated foreign exchange reserves in East Asia and oil exporting countries — and the US dollar flows back to the US by way of bonds" formed, and goods and the US dollar circulated around the world. This was what former US Secretary of the Treasury, Lawrence Summers, referred to as the global "balance of financial terror". In this way, the US absorbed 3/4 of the world's net savings and developing countries became net capital exporters instead, which outwardly appeared as surpluses on the US capital account and deficits from developing countries, thus the "imbalanced international capital flow". Developing countries faced a dilemma: on the one hand, to prevent risks, satisfy the needs of trade, and enhance international liquidity, they hoped to increase their holding of dollars, yet on the other hand, the more their US dollar holdings increase, the greater the impact of the dollar and the loss of wealth. Furthermore, an increase in foreign exchange reserves leads to oversized proportion of foreign exchange which affects domestic monetary policies. For example, China is troubling over the reduction of foreign exchange reserves (see Table 5.2).

Thus, after the disintegration of the Bretton Woods System, international crises occurred frequently. In particular, as this crisis originated from the US, a central country, and spread quickly to the world, it is undeniably associated closely to the US dollar. More specifically, the existing international monetary system contributed to global financial turmoil in the following four areas.

First of all, it exacerbated international economic imbalance. The international status of the US dollar allows it to receive financing from the world to meet the excessive domestic demands of consumption. The US only needs to print more dollars and issue bonds in order to purchase world goods and services while other countries need to provide labor, resources and commodities in order

Table 5.2   Foreign currency reserves of major economies: USD in billions.

Rank	Economy	Foreign currency reserve	Date
1	China	3,821.3	December 2013
2	Japan	1,275.4	November 2013
3	Euro zone	790.6	October 2013
4	Saudi Arabia	717.9	October 2013
5	Switzerland	531.5	October 2013
6	Russia	524.3	October 2013
7	Chinese Taipei	420.8	October 2013
8	Brazil	364.5	October 2013
9	Korea	343.2	October 2013
10	Chinese Hong Kong	309.6	October 2013
11	India	291.3	November 2013
12	Singapore	271.8	October 2013
13	Germany	210.7	October 2013
14	Algeria	191.6	December 2012
15	Mexico	177.2	October 2013
16	Thailand	167.5	November 2013
17	France	156.9	October 2013
18	Italy	155.2	October 2013
19	The United States of America	146.4	November 2013
20	Malaysia	137.1	October 2013
21	United Kingdom	136.2	October 2013
22	Turkey	134.2	October 2013
23	Libya	130.3	December 2012
24	Poland	105.5	October 2013
25	Indonesia	957	September 2013
26	Denmark	880	September 2013
27	The Philippines	836	October 2013
28	Israel	785	August 2013
29	Canada	715	October 2013
30	Iran	699	December 2012
31	Peru	668	October 2013

Source of Data: Various statistical websites and Google searches.

to earn dollars. A "double cycles" and "international circulation" of global goods and capital flow appeared. East Asian countries and petroleum exporting countries have high trade surplus while the US has high trade deficit. The "commodity flow" is from these countries to the US. The US will issue various bonds to attract the dollars back while the countries with high trade surplus will buy the US bonds to consume their foreign reserves, which forms the "capital flow". In this way, "the US produced US dollars and other countries produced goods and services, and the two parties traded", as such, the US trade deficit is also known as the "tearless deficit". Creditor nations such as China also had to worry about the devaluation of the US dollar and the shrinking of their wealth after purchasing excessive US bonds. As former US Secretary of the Treasury Conally said, "The dollar is our currency but your problem." There was an even more classic saying from Kissinger, "Control oil and you control nations; control food and you control the people; control money and you control the world." This is a true reflection of the strong position of the dollar.

Secondly, the US dollar depreciated over the long term. Figure 5.1 shows the trend of the US dollar index from 2001 to 2013. From the graph, it can be seen there was an overall trend of devaluation, apart from the crises when the US dollar was able to withstand the crunch and when it appeared to appreciate as the market favored the currency. From February 2002 to date, the dollar experienced two dips in value. One took place between February 2002 and July 2008 when the dollar depreciated by 26.4%; another occurred between March 2009 and July 2011 when the dollar depreciated by 14.9% as the US launched the

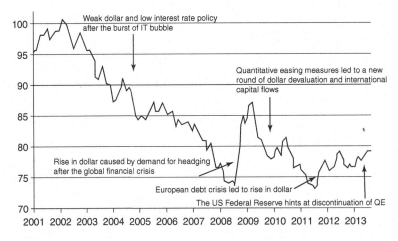

Figure 5.1   Long-term trends in the nominal dollar index (January 2002 = 100).
Source: Wind Database.

quantitative easing policy and the European debt crisis intensified. In early 2013, the US fiscal budget issues with the debt ceiling caused worries in the market over US debt unsustainability, and the US continued to pursue a low interest rate policy and introduced a new round of quantitative easing measures (QE4). All these factors led to short-term fluctuations in the dollar index.[7] The long-term depreciation of the US dollar caused countries with strong foreign exchange reserves, who mainly invested in the US, to suffer huge capital losses. This is the reason why American economist Paul Krugman wrote that the devaluation of the dollar was the "dollar trap" in *The New York Times*.[8]

Thirdly, the international currency issue became a problem of US finance. The Triffin dilemma persisted even after the disintegration of the Bretton Woods System. There was an inherent contradiction between the US trade deficit and the security of the US dollar as a reserve currency. Under the floating exchange rate system, the central banks of various countries purchased safe government bonds to consume foreign exchange reserves. This meant that the country providing the reserve currency needed to continually issue bonds. Despite the continual deficits the major reserve currency provider experienced, the US remained the main source of global reserve assets;[9] resulting in the issues of international reserve currencies and international economic imbalances ultimately becoming the US' fiscal problems. As such, a situation where the US "used currencies to pay for financial bailouts" appeared after the crisis. The monetization of fiscal deficit was equivalent to the Federal Reserve's direct financial injection. In this sense, the US' financial bailout capital was being borne and shared by US citizens and the countries who held dollar assets, which indirectly indicated that the US had imposed inflation tax on other countries and people.

Fourthly, the powers of the reserve currency issuing country did not correspond with its responsibilities. In the absence of international supervision and restraint, the domestic policies of the major reserve currency issuing country tend to have a strong spillover effect that is often negative. Since 2009,

---

[7] For further discussion on the trend of the dollar, refer to Gao Haihong and Chen Sichong, "Situation and Prospects of the International Financial Market 2013," in Wang Luolin and Zhang Yuyan (eds.) *2013 World Economic Situation and Forecast (2013)* (Beijing: Social Sciences Academic Press, 2012).

[8] Paul Krugman, "China's Dollar Trap", *New York Times*, April 2, 2009, retrieved from nytimes.com/2009/04/03/opinion/03krugman.html.

[9] Maurice Obstfeld, "The International Monetary System: Living with Asymmetry" Working Paper 17641, December 2011, retrieved from http://www.nber.org/papers/w17641.

developed countries have responded to crises with quantitative easing monetary policies. By the end of February 2014, the total amount of the Federal Reserve's four-round quantitative easing measures[10] had reached USD4.1 trillion, coupled with that of Japan, Europe and other regions, the total quantitative easing amount in the world was about USD10 trillion (see Table 5.3), and this amount is still increasing. This will lead to more floods in global liquidity and emerging economies will face two risks: first, the large amounts of capital inflows will cause inflationary pressure, asset bubbles will grow and accumulate faster, there will be risks of an overheated economy; secondly, there is the risk of QE exit policies. The large amounts of capital returning to the US will again bring devastating impact to the financial stability of emerging economies. For example, in India, Brazil, Indonesia and other countries, there have been signs of a deteriorating financial situation such as substantial devaluation of currency and decline in foreign exchange reserves in 2013. The international currency issuing countries ought to shoulder the corresponding international responsibilities and not just enjoy seigniorage. However, the US' monetary policy is mainly domestic and they are unwilling to take on the corresponding international responsibilities. In September 2013, Russian President Vladimir Putin criticized US President Barack Obama for the American "exceptionalism". In fact, the US does have "exceptionalism" in its role as an international currency issuing country; that it can enjoy the benefits that come with being an international currency reserve and yet, not bear the relevant international responsibilities.

1.2 *New changes in international rules of finance after the crisis*

As this crisis began from the financial sector, the improvement and strengthening of international financial governance naturally became the focus of attention after the crisis. Changes in international financial rules include areas such

---

[10] In the first round of QE measures, a total of USD1.725 trillion worth of long-term government bonds, mortgage-backed securities *etc.* was purchased, "the crisis was curbed, and market confidence stabilized"; from November 2010 to June 2011, long-term bonds worth a total of USD600 billion were purchased in the second round of QE measures run by the US; in September 2012, to stimulate the real estate market, the Federal Reserve rolled out the third round of QE measures: USD40 billion worth of mortgage-backed securities (MBS) were purchased monthly; on December 12, 2012, the Federal Reserve announced a fourth round of QE measures (QE4), purchasing an additional USD45 billion worth of long-term government bonds monthly from January 2013 onwards, on top of the original USD40 billion monthly purchase of mortgage-backed securities, amounting to a total of USD85 million per month.

Table 5.3 QE measures by the US, Japan and the EU since the crisis: USD in billions.

Economy	QE	Time period	Open market operations		
			Product	Amount	Total
The US	QE1	November 2008–March 2010	Purchased mortgage-backed securities (MBS)	1,250	1,725
			Purchased long-term government bonds	300	
			Purchased government-sponsored enterprises (GSE)	175	
	QE2	November 2010–June 2011	Purchased long-term government bonds	600	600
	Distorted operations	September 2011	Sold government bonds that would mature in 3 years or less; purchased government bonds with a maturity of 6 to 30 years	400	400
	QE3	September 2011–	Purchased mortgage-backed securities (MBS)	40/month	Total accumulated amount by end of 2013 was 1,125
	QE4	December 2012–	Purchased long-term government bonds	45/month	
	Total for the five QE		39,500 (including policies before QE measures were taken, increased liquidity was up to USD5 trillion		
The EU			The scale of EQ conducted by the European Central Bank was about USD2.2 trillion, the assets of the Bank of England were about USD650 billion, and assets of the Swiss National Bank were about USD630 billion		Approximately 3,500
Japan			As of November 2013, purchased Japanese government bonds, commercial papers and corporate bonds		2,551.6

Source: Balance sheets from the US Federal Reserve, European Central Bank and Bank of Japan. Should the US Federal Reserve gradually exit from QE in 2014, its asset purchases are expected to increase by another USD600–700 billion. Japanese QE will go on till April 2015 and it is expected that approximately another USD1 trillion in assets will be purchased.

as international financial regulation, reform of international financial institutions, initiatives for international monetary system reform, and global macro-financial policy coordination. In April 2009, the issues of international monetary system reform were brought up at the G20 Summit, covering financial regulation, reforms of capital increase and quota of international financial organizations. In the same year, the reforms mentioned above were further implemented at the G20 Summit in Pittsburgh in September. At the 2010 G20 Toronto Summit and Seoul Summit, the issues of selection of international financial executives, reform of IMF voting, financial regulation and other aspects were discussed. The "IMF quota reforms", "Basel III" as well as international norms of Systemically Important Financial Institutions (SIFI) and others were passed. In 2012, the French government pushed for deeper discussion on the reform of the international monetary system. High-level meetings were convened frequently and there was a call for the establishment of a more stable and more risk-resistant international monetary system, expansion of the IMF's SDR basket of currencies and strengthening of financial supervision.

1.2.1 *Building a global safety net through multi-level cooperation*

The focus of global banking regulation is on reconstructing the banking regulatory framework. In September 2010, the Basel Committee on Banking Supervision adopted a reform program for strengthening capital requirements of the banking system, known as the "Basel III" (hereinafter referred to as Agreement III). Agreement III is the largest reform in the field of banking supervision in recent decades. It plays an important role of encouraging banks to reduce high-risk businesses, preventing a repeat of the international credit crisis, and ensuring the smooth operation of the banking sector. The core content of Agreement III is to improve capital adequacy ratio, raising the minimum requirements for ordinary shares from the original 2% to 4.5%. The minimum requirements for capital adequacy ratio Tier 1 (including common stocks and other Tier 1 capital financial instruments) were raised from 4% to 6%. At the same time, Agreement III also specifically proposed a capital conservation buffer of 2.5% so as to better respond to economic and financial shocks. Once the banks' capital conservation buffer falls below standard requirements, bank regulators will restrict the auction, the repurchasing of shares and the distribution of dividends. This provision helps to prevent banks from the wrong practice of issuing huge bonuses and dividends even when the bank's capital conditions are worsening. It also helps increase the level of corporate bank governance correspondingly. In addition, Agreement III is founded on a broader macro-prudential goal — it requires the countries, according to their own country's circumstances, to implement counter-cyclical capital buffers with buffers accounting for 0%–2.5% of ordinary shares, to protect the banking system from reducing credit surges during times of economic expansion.

In regulating financial derivatives trading, the US, being the most active, prominent and innovative country in derivatives trading, introduced the "Over-the-Counter Derivatives Markets Act" (OTC derivatives Act) in 2009. Firstly, OTC derivatives trade was "standardized" while higher capital standards and other requirements were set for non-"standardized" derivatives. Secondly, standards for OTC derivatives product trading security deposits and the own capital of both trading parties were set to control leverage ratio of transactions and prevent excessive risk concentration. Thirdly, information disclosure for OTC derivatives transactions was strengthened, allowing any relevant federal financial regulatory agency, under the premise of confidentiality, to check on OTC derivatives trade, and the general public can also obtain overall information of the OTC derivatives market's trading positions and quantities. Fourthly, there is a clear division of the Commodity Futures Trading Commission (CFTC) and Securities and Exchange Commission's regulatory powers over OTC derivatives products. Fifth, requirements and standards for OTC derivatives trading qualified investors were strictly defined to protect small and medium investors from OTC derivatives abuse. In 2010, the US promulgated the "Dodd-Frank Act", and proposed a regulatory framework for investment banks and derivatives transactions. The main contents include a sound regulatory organization, limiting high-risk transaction, and the establishment of a new mechanism for bankruptcy liquidation. In 2012, the US Commodity Futures Trading Commission approved a series of new supervisory regulations aimed to strengthen supervision of so-called credit default swaps and other derivatives trade. The new regulations include the registration requirements for major swap market participants, new business standards for trading between banks and swap buyers, reporting and recording regulations, and new swap data storage mechanisms.

In the macro-financial regulatory system, systemic risk was included into the financial regulatory framework so as to establish a macro-prudential supervisory system. Proposed improvements include the establishment of a regulatory system that is linked to the macroeconomic financial environment and economic cycle, which would then weaken the positive feedback between the financial system and the real economy; strengthening supervision of systemically important financial institutions including implementing more stringent capital and liquidity regulatory standards, and improving regulatory strength and effectiveness; establishing a "self-help" mechanism, reducing the moral hazard of being "too big to fail"; and last but not least, for financial institutions that have significant impact on the global system: enhancing the sharing of information and collaboration between regulatory bodies, establishing cross-border crisis management arrangements, and reducing cross-border transference of risks.

In regulating capital flow, IMF has given an official "status" to capital controls earlier in 2010 by including capital controls in the policies toolbox. At the end of 2012, IMF also published a report titled, *The Liberalization and Management of Capital Flows: An Institutional View*. It highlights the orderly and gradual liberalization of capital accounts and advocates that various macro-management approaches can be taken to deal with abnormal capital flow. Whether capital outflows or inflows, attention should be paid to the negative spillover effects of capital flows so as to ensure prudent macroeconomic policies. Compared to the financial liberalization policy under the IMF's "Washington Consensus", this was great progress. There are two main lines of defense that emerging economies have set up in response to the large-scale capital inflow caused by excessively relaxed policies of the developed countries: the first is unilateral resistance. Many emerging economies have resorted to using capital control tools. Classic examples would be Brazil and Korea who emphasized the control of foreign exchange derivatives trade. Brazil exercised capital control mainly by controlling prices, through taxing foreign investors for investments in stocks, bonds and financial derivatives, it eased the domestic asset bubble, and increased the independence of the monetary policy; Korea exercised capital control using quantitative controls as its core, limiting the trading scale of foreign investors' bonds and derivative transactions, and successfully reduced the volatility of the Korean won. The second would be joint resistance, by stepping up on global or regional financial cooperation and taking joint, collective action. For example, many countries signed a currency swap agreement with China. Korea, India and others have clearly suggested the establishment of a global financial safety net to protect against the impact of capital inflows. Future cooperation, while respecting national policies, would strengthen multi-level financial cooperation, establish risk sharing and crisis relief mechanisms on a global, regional, bilateral and multi-level scale, to build a global financial safety net.

With regard to multilateral and regional regulatory cooperation, G20 recommended enhancing the financial industry regulatory standards, strengthening the capital adequacy and liquidity management framework of financial institutions, and setting up regulations for shadow banking supervision. This suggestion was highly regarded by various nations. The Bank for International Settlements put forth even more stringent requirements for banks' core capital and liquidity standards. IMF also committed to a secure and transparent financial system with "lesser leverage". The sovereign debt crisis was the second wave of the crisis. The European debt crisis was particularly staggering. In June 2012, the President of the European Union proposed the establishment of a banking union which would be a part of the monetary union so as to sever the relationship between the bank crisis and sovereign debt crisis.

1.2.2 *Reform of international financial institutions and the rising status of emerging economies*

At the G20 Summit held in London in 2009, the G20 leaders reached a consensus on the need for IMF reform. From 2009 to the present, the amount of funds the IMF has lent out has risen from USD250 billion to USD750 billion. It has greatly increased efforts to provide loan assistance. On the whole, the reform of the IMF reflected the importance of emerging economies and the new trends in the international financial crisis.

IMF reviewed their previous demanding and rigid modes of lending to maximize flexibility by adjusting loan conditions, loan periods, types of loans *etc.* according to the new characteristics of the crises. This improved the effectiveness and timeliness of loans to a certain extent, and was done so as to prevent the recurrence of substandard and inadequate remedies, such as calls for fiscal austerity during economic downtowns that were dished out during the Latin American and Asian financial crises.

An important change in supervisory functions is that the IMF chose to conduct a comprehensive research on individual countries' choice of policies in response to the impact of capital flow, changing the hardline stance it had held for a long time against the implementation of capital control by developing countries. For the first time, it recognized the rationality of capital controls given certain conditions. The change met the practical needs of developing countries with small domestic financial markets and fragile domestic financial sectors.

In governance structures, the issues of improving shares and voting rights of emerging economies including China became a focus among IMF reforms. In December 2012, the IMF Board of Directors approved a reform package which committed to making the largest adjustment of shares in history, increasing the voting rights of dynamic emerging economies and developing countries by 6%, in addition to doubling their total share. In that case, the four BRIC countries of China, Brazil, India and Russia, would be among the top 10 countries with the most voting rights. At the same time, to reflect the concerns of poor countries, IMF reserved shares and voting rights for low-income countries. However, these voting rights were transferred from Europe and did not affect the US' decisive status even a single bit. In spite of this, on March 11, 2013, the US Congress rejected President Obama's request to provide funding for IMF and as such, the IMF's capital increase and quota reform was delayed.[11]

After the financial crisis, the quota China provided to the IMF increased threefold. On November 6, 2010, the IMF Executive Board passed the reform program. China, as the world's second largest economy, had its proportion of shares raised from 3.66% to 6.39% and its voting rights increased from sixth place to third place, following the US with 17.4% and Japan with 6.46% (see Table 5.4). The voting rights of China in WBG also increased from 2.77% to

Table 5.4   Top ranking IMF members in terms of voting rights.

Country	After the reform was implemented in 2010		2008	
	Voting rights	Rank	Voting rights	Rank
The US	17.41%	1	16.77%	1
Japan	6.46%	2	6.02%	2
China	6.39%	3	3.66%	6
Germany	5.59%	4	5.88%	3
France	4.23%	5	4.86%	4
Britain	4.23%	5	4.86%	4
India	2.75%	7	1.89%	13

Source: IMF.

---

[11] The US Senate Appropriations Committee rejected President Obama's request for the Appropriations Committee to approve a permanent increase in US funding to the IMF. Some US lawmakers noted that the temporary government funding bill passed by the Congress previously did not allow the government to approve a permanent increase of USD65 billion to the IMF. Some experts believe that with the tight US budget, it was difficult for Congress to accede to the request. According to Reuters, hundreds of scholars had petitioned and urged the US Congress to pass the replenishment program as soon as possible so that the IMF could complete the quota reform in 2010. *The Financial Times* believed that the US should not delay IMF reform. The current governance structure no longer met the needs of the times and the cost of delays was continually rising.

4.42%, putting it in third place after the US and Japan. An important area in IMF governance structure is that of executive appointments. Christine Lagarde, the current President is from France and Zhu Min is the IMF's first Vice President from China, reflecting the IMF's concern and attention on emerging economies. However, there are still voices asking for the usual practice of European and American governance to be broken and a more reasonable reflection of the interests of emerging economies.

1.2.3 *Reserve currency diversification and reform of the international monetary system*

In the existing international monetary system, the international reserve currency is also the currency of the sovereign country that has contradictory domestic needs and international responsibilities. The US dollar is both a country's currency as well as a world currency. The US ought to have an independent monetary policy as the US dollar is its country's currency; yet as a world currency, it should be bound by global macroeconomics. The currency faces a dilemma because of its two functions. Several experts suggest there be hard constraints set for the reserve currency issuing country to ensure the stability of the currency and the sustainability of the country's finances should be the premise, meaning the ratio of its public sector debt to GDP should be within the designated range.

However, as the reserve currency issuing country, the US refuses to accept expert opinions. For example, they expressed that their exit from quantitative easing was due only to domestic economic situations.[12] To reduce the international monetary system's reliance on the dollar, people have come up with various ideas including the construction of a multiple reserve currency system with stable internal mechanisms. Experts have envisaged a variety of possibilities regarding changing the international monetary system: the dollar being still

---

[12] Former Chairman of the Federal Reserve, Ben Bernanke repeatedly stated that his considerations for whether to leave quantitative easing policies or not were solely domestic factors such as employment and inflation, and that he had not considered international influence and responsibilities. Dennis Lockhart, President of the Atlanta Federal Reserve Bank said, "...some emerging economies may face pressure when U.S. monetary accommodation is reduced. They may have to make policy and business adjustments". James Bullard, President of the Federal Reserve Bank of St. Louis also mentioned that the domestic economy is the primary objective for the policy, and the US Federal Reserve will not change its policies simply because of volatility in the emerging economies.

dominant; the dollar, euro and yuan becoming the three pillars; Special Drawing Rights (SDR) system — the SDR becoming a major global currency, a multiple reserve currency scenario. Among them, the formation of a multiple reserve currency structure was considered the most probable. SDR was created in 1969 to supplement dollar liquidity. In the past 40 years, its functions as a currency have been limited. The international reserve currency diversification has notably improved since the beginning of the 20th century. According to statistics from the IMF, from 2000 to 2012, the proportion of US dollars in the total foreign exchange reserves among member states fell from 55.8% to 34.0%; that of the euro increased from 13.9% to 15.6%. It is noteworthy that in the same period, the proportion of foreign exchange reserves with undetermined currency structures in total foreign exchange reserves rose from 21.5% to 44.5%. To some extent, this reflected the gradual growth of emerging economies' currencies, especially that of China (see Figure 5.2).

In addition to the reserve currency, the importance of emerging economies' currencies has also increased in international trade and capital transactions. According to the BIS' latest announcements, the US dollar was still the main trading currency in global foreign exchange market transactions in 2013; this was followed by currencies of developed countries such as the euro, Japanese yen, and English sterling pound. Among the top 20 currencies, those of emerging economies accounted for eight seats; in 1998, emerging economies only made up five

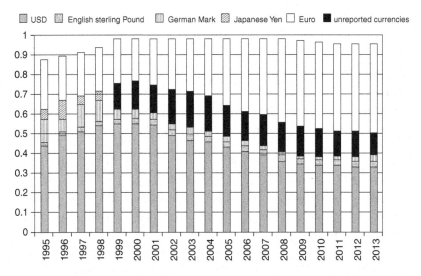

Figure 5.2 IMF members' reserve currencies structure: % of total reserves.

Source: IMF.

Table 5.5 Transaction volume of international foreign exchange market: %.

Currency	1998	2001	2004	2007	2010	2013
US Dollar	43.4	44.95	44	42.8	42.45	43.5
Euro	0	18.95	18.7	18.5	19.55	16.7
Japanese Yen	10.85	11.75	10.4	8.6	9.5	11.5
English Sterling Pound	5.5	6.5	8.25	7.45	6.45	5.9
Australian Dollar	1.5	2.15	3	3.3	3.8	4.3
Swiss Franc	3.55	3	3	3.4	3.15	2.6
Canadian dollar	1.75	2.25	2.1	2.15	2.65	2.3
Mexican Peso	0.25	0.4	0.55	0.65	0.65	1.25
Chinese Yuan/Renminbi	0	0	0.05	0.25	0.45	1.1
New Zealand Dollar	0.1	0.3	0.55	0.95	0.8	1
Swedish Krona	0.15	1.25	1.1	1.35	1.1	0.9
Russian Ruble	0.15	0.15	0.3	0.35	0.45	0.8
Hong Kong Dollar	0.5	1.1	0.9	1.35	1.2	0.7
Norwegian Krone	0.1	0.75	0.7	1.05	0.65	0.7
Singapore Dollar	0.55	0.55	0.45	0.6	0.7	0.7
Turkish Lira	0	0	0.05	0.1	0.35	0.65
Korean Won	0.1	0.4	0.55	0.6	0.75	0.6
South African Rand	0.2	0.45	0.35	0.45	0.35	0.55
Brazilian Real	0.1	0.25	0.15	0.2	0.35	0.55
Indian Rupee	0.05	0.1	0.15	0.35	0.5	0.5

Source: Bank for International Settlements.

of the top 20 (see Table 5.5). Apart from this, data from the Society for Worldwide Interbank Financial Telecommunication (SWIFT) showed that the RMB rose rapidly up the ranks of international currencies of payment, from 20th in January 2012 to 11th in January 2013. In the short span of two years, the RMB's global market share as currency of payment had more than doubled. As the RMB capital account convertibility program rolls out in the future, its significance as a global currency will become increasingly apparent.

However, the dollar's dominance is still unshakable in the short term. At the moment, there is no suitable alternative currency for the dollar. The decision-making efficiency of the sovereign country must be greater than that of the nation's independent states, the US dollar has higher credibility than the euro;

even if the euro could gradually replace the US dollar, it would also face the same issues as the US dollar. Promoting the role of the SDR requires consensus from IMF members, in particular, recognition from the US. Presently, only the US dollar, euro, sterling pound and Japanese yen are in the SDR basket of currencies. The Chinese RMB is still not in the basket.

In short, we should soberly note that the establishment of the current international monetary system and the hegemony of the dollar are results of the world's economic development and the contest of various countries' economic power. From a certain perspective, it is rational. Particularly before a world central bank and a super-sovereign currency like the "Bancor" are established, taking the lead from the currency of a world power is the second-best option. In the short term, it is not quite possible to find another currency or establish another "international currency" that can replace the US dollar. Even if the euro or RMB continues to rise, they will be but the enhanced version of a diversified international currency. The international monetary system will remain in a state of chaos and "anarchy".

1.3 *China and international financial rule reconstruction*

China's strategic response to adjustments in international monetary and financial rules must begin from its own needs for reform and opening up. It has to respond well to the uncertainty brought about as the international monetary system transits from the US dollar system to a multi-level system, and at the same time, receive various positive reform recommendations, including reasonable proposals for SDR reform, and actively participate in governance of international financial institutions, deepen international financial cooperation and guard against financial risks.

1.3.1 *Active participation in international finance rule-making*

China actively participated in G20 Summits, BRICS Summits and other important international forums and platforms, and played a significant role in improving international financial regulations.

Firstly, China participated actively in various cooperative mechanisms under the G20 framework, from discussions at the working group level to finance ministerial and central bank governors' meetings. At some informal occasions, it has also put forward views on a "super-sovereign currency", advocating the establishment of a super-sovereign international reserve currency that is decoupled from the sovereign state and is stable for the long term, thus expressing its strong concern regarding the non-sustainability of the current international monetary system, as well as its dissatisfaction with the irresponsibility of the country issuing the international reserve currency.

Secondly, as the world's second largest economy, China works closely with other BRICS and developing countries to participate in the development of international finance governance rules. In particular, the BRICS countries held a brief meeting before the G20 Summit as usual and formed pre-summit coordination mechanism to share a collective voice at the G20. This was helpful in strengthening the voice and influence of the emerging economies. For example, they urged developed countries to adopt responsible monetary policies to avoid liquidity flood, curb excessive volatility of cross-border capital flows at the source, and further improve management and other rules of international capital flows.

Thirdly, China cooperates with developed economies to explore solutions for long-term problems in the world economy, such as addressing international economic imbalances, improving international governance, international financial regulation, reform of the international monetary system and other mid to long-term problems.

Fourthly, China actively participates in the construction of precautionary measures for global crises. For example, it provides financial support to the IMF and other international financial organizations, participates in the construction of BRICS' emergency repository, and signs currency swap agreements with other countries.

Fifthly, it participates in and implements the BIS' banking supervision rules. China was adamant in implementing "Basel III", showing that it was not affected by Europe's delayed implementation, and put forth even more stringent regulatory standards. For example, in June 2012, it issued the trial version of a strategy titled "Capital Rules for Commercial Banks (Provisional)", setting the minimum Tier 1 capital adequacy ratio for (ordinary shares) at 5%, 0.5% higher than that stated in "Basel III"; the capital adequacy ratio for major banks was set at no less than 11.5%, wherein additional capital requirement was designated as 1%, while there was no such requirement mentioned in "Basel III".

1.3.2 *Active promotion of international financial cooperation*

Given that it is not possible to conduct a fundamental reform of the existing international monetary system in a short time, China has strengthened bilateral, pluri-lateral and regional financial cooperation to reduce dependence on the dollar, promote exchange rate, trade and economic stability.

First, China has signed currency swap agreements[13] with many countries. To respond to economic crisis, stabilize the exchange rate, prevent risks and promote the internationalization of the RMB, China signed its first currency swap agreement with Korea in December 2008. By November 2013, the People's Bank of China had already signed currency swap agreements with 24 central banks (monetary authorities) worth a total of 2.6 trillion yuan. For example, on October 9, 2013, the People's Bank of China signed the EU-China bilateral currency swap agreement worth 350 billion yuan (45 billion euros) with the European Central Bank, with the objective of providing support for future bilateral economic and trade exchanges, and maintaining financial stability.

Second, China promoted the establishment of the BRICS Development Bank. On March 27, 2013, a decision was reached at the fifth BRICS Summit on the establishment of the bank aimed at simplifying settlement and lending operations between BRICS countries so as to reduce reliance on the US dollar and euro, and safeguard financial flow and trade among members; at the same time, preparation were made to set up a BRICS countries' repository and establish the Business Council. The functions of the BRICS Development Bank cover the areas of common foreign reserves and contingency funds, regulating the bank's future investment direction, including loan and investment measures for mid- and long-term investment in infrastructure construction and industries of developing countries *etc.*

Third, China participated in regional financial cooperation in East Asia. China is the initiator and largest contributor to East Asia's multilateral "Chiang Mai Initiative". China contributes 32% of the total reserves of USD240 billion in the repository. The ultimate goal of the "Chiang Mai Initiative" is to establish an Asian version of the IMF, that is, the Asian Monetary Fund (AMF). In 2011, the Chiang Mai Initiative, a multilateral mechanism, began official operations and established the Office of Asian Macroeconomic Research with a Chinese representative serving as its first Director. At the same time, China, together with ASEAN Countries, and the Japan–Korea Finance Ministers Meeting, agreed to allow the Asian Development Bank to roll out credit guarantees and investment measures. China also actively considered the establishment of a regional clearing system, to discuss the construction of financial infrastructure such as regional bonds and credit rating agencies.

---

[13] Currency swaps refer to an exchange of two different debt capitals of different currencies worth the same amount, in the same period using the same interest rate calculation methods. At the same time, there is also a swap of currencies with different interest rates.

1.3.3 *Promote the internationalization of the RMB*

The internationalization of the RMB is a part of international reserve currency diversification. In 2004, mainland China allowed Hong Kong to make RMB deposits, opening up the offshore RMB market. From 2008 onwards, China signed currency swap agreements with more than 20 central banks (monetary authorities). In 2010, China fully liberalized RMB trade settlements and it developed rapidly. Subsequently, the convertibility of the RMB in capital accounts was also put on the agenda. With the internationalization of the RMB, its coordination with other policies became a point of attention. China's path to internationalizing the RMB has to be aligned and adjusted accordingly with the opening up of capital projects, reform of the exchange rate system, domestic financial reform and financial supervisory capacity.

1.3.4 *Strengthening financial supervisory capacity*

China has to strengthen financial supervision to ensure financial stability — be it learning lessons from the international financial crisis or dealing with the needs for expanding financial liberalization. The Third Plenary Session of the 18th CPC Central Committee proposed "the promotion of two-way opening up of capital markets, orderly improvement of cross-border capital and financial transactions convertibility, establishment of an external debt and capital flow management system under a comprehensive macro-prudential regulatory framework, acceler-ated implementation of RMB capital account convertibility" and other hard financial liberalization measures. To achieve these, China needs to further strengthen international financial regulatory cooperation, implement financial regulatory reform measures and robust standards, and clearly define central and local financial regulatory responsibilities and risk management duties, so as to ensure safe and efficient operation of financial markets and overall stability. Many scholars including former WBG Chief Economist Lin Yifu[14] have expressed their concerns about the opening up of capital projects.[15] Such concerns reflect, to a certain extent, the significance of financial regulation and risks of reform.

---

[14] Justin Yifu Lin, "Why I Do Not Support Capital Account Liberalization," *China Economic Journal*, Vol. 8, No. 1 (2015), pp. 86–93, retrieved from http://www.tandfonline.com/doi/pdf/10.1080/17538963.2015.1002178.

[15] Yu Yongding , "The Current RMB Exchange Rate Volatility and RMB Internationalization," *International Economic Review*, Vol. 1, No. 1 (2012), retrieved from http://en.cnki.com.cn/Article_en/CJFDTOTAL-GJPP201201003.html.

2 Trade and Exchange Rate Issues

Exchange rate refers to the ratio at which a country's currency is exchanged for another country's currency. This is determined by the supply and demand in the foreign exchange market, and measured according to the condition of the countries' international balance of payments. In other words, besides the US, other countries are not able to sustain long-term imbalances in international payments. Exchange rates also reflect a currency's domestic and foreign price relationship to a certain extent. Therefore, exchange rate volatility affects the international competitiveness of a country's goods and services. If a country manipulates its currency such that it is undervalued, it can drive down the foreign currency prices of its goods and services, thereby raising its international competitiveness and expand exports; or vice versa. However, this situation is not sustainable for the long-term as exchange rate is a double-edged sword that affects exports as well as overseas consumption such as imports, investment and tourism. In a way, the issue of exchange rates is also one of governments' preference for trade policies, whether intervening by the invisible hand of the market or visibly with administration. As such, the exchange rate issue often becomes a point of contention amongst countries in international trade. After the global financial crisis, the exchange rate and trade issues heated up again. In this section, we first examine voices from both sides of the debate: emerging economies are more concerned about the negative impact on trade and the economy brought about by the significant fluctuations in exchange rates due to developed countries' excessively loose monetary policies, while developed countries advocate that emerging economies have to implement more market-oriented exchange rates in order to regain global balance. It can be observed that exchange rate is not an issue a single country can resolve by itself. It relies on the wisdom of group decision-making and requires international organizations to play a more important role.

2.1 *Heated trade and exchange rate issues after the financial crisis*

Since the financial crisis, external demand declined sharply due to the slowdown in various countries' economic growth, international trade significantly decreased and various forms of trade protectionism arose. The exchange rate issue, closely linked to trade relations, which had been a hot topic before the crisis, heated up again.

2.1.1 *Brazil submitted proposals on exchange rate and trade to the WTO twice*

After the crisis, exchange rates were no longer a tool for the developed countries with deficits to blame emerging economies with surpluses. There were also disputes regarding exchange rates and trade arising among the emerging economies and Brazil was the representative country for this. In the first half of 2011, the Brazilian real saw increasing appreciation for a period of time as it was affected by the main international reserve currency country issuing a quantitative easing monetary policy. At the same time, Brazilian exports fell and there was high domestic inflation, which put enormous political pressure on the government. In order to maintain domestic economic stability, the Brazilian government promulgated a number of trade protection measures and sought a legal basis of international trade rules for its trade protection behavior. In April and September 2011, Brazil submitted proposals to the WTO's "Working Group for Trade, Debt and Finance" (WGTDF) twice, requesting for discussions on the relationship between exchange rates and trade issues, intending to link exchange rate issues with trade.

According to the proposal of April 2011, Brazil believed that the WGTDF's activities since 2008 had been focused on trade financing support and currently, market conditions for international trade finance have improved. Thus, Brazil proposed analyzing and discussing the relationship between exchange rates and international trade in 2011–2012 to come up with a final solution. This proposal was adopted by the WGTDF at the 22nd meeting on May 10, 2011. In its proposal in September the same year, Brazil recommended that the working group review trade subsidies and other matters to appropriately deal with the impact of currency fluctuations on "the delicate balance of commitments and concessions resulting from negotiations at the WTO" and reduce "damage to negotiations outcomes" caused by currency volatility.

In response to Brazil's proposal, WGTDF reviewed relevant literature on the relationship between exchange rates and trade, and on September 27, 2011, the WTO Secretariat announced the publication of the research report, "The Relationship between Exchange Rates and International Trade: An Economics Literature Review". The research report is based on 30 written papers provided by the WTO members, with a focus on literature after the 2008 international financial crisis. On the whole, the supposed "exchange rate and trade" issue can be divided into two portions: one being the impact exchange rate volatility or disorder has on international trade; another being whether the WTO ought to formulate appropriate trade regulations for this effect. The WTO's procedures for developing trade rules suggest that first, the "kind of impact exchange rate fluctuations and disorder has on international trade" has to be determined. If an agreement cannot be reached on this issue, then there is no basis for discussion of "trade rules". Thus, the "impact of exchange rate fluctuations or disorder has on international trade" has to be thoroughly researched and analyzed.

After reviewing relevant studies, the report's conclusion suggests that the relationship between exchange rates and trade is complex as the cause and effect between the two are hard to distinguish, and it is even tougher to quantify their relationship.

Firstly, the impact of exchange rate volatility on trade is uncertain. Research findings show that the impact of exchange rate fluctuations on trade is still somewhat uncertain, whether theoretically or empirically. Some institutions and scholars, using different approaches, have conducted research on various subjects and data to try to draw a conclusion on the negative impact of exchange rate volatility on international trade. However, some studies have found that exchange rate volatility does not have an adverse impact on trade, and even if the impact exists, it is insignificant.

Secondly, the relationship between exchange rate levels (disorder) and trade is extremely complex. Theoretical analysis suggests that if there is no distortion in the market, exchange rate fluctuations could affect international trade, particularly the import and export of some price-sensitive commodities. However, these short-term effects are not very direct and depend on factors such as which currency the production companies use for pricing, as well as whether the goods were produced in multiple countries. In the long-term, exchange rate volatility will not change prices correspondingly, as such, its impact on trade will be small, unless there are market distortions such as incorrect information or market failure *etc.* Empirical studies also show that the complexity of the relationship between exchange rate volatility and trade produces varying and confusing results.

Although Brazil's proposal was ultimately not passed,[16] the emerging economies' discussion on exchange rates and trade is noteworthy.

2.1.2 *The US pressures China for RMB appreciation*

After 2002, as China's current account surplus grew and exports to US increased, the US began exerting pressure on the RMB. In 2003, New York Democratic Senator Charles Schumer proposed the first compelling proposal on the RMB. The proposal suggested that the RMB was 15%–40% undervalued and if the

---

[16] Refer to the following analysis of the WTO for details.

RMB did not appreciate within six months, the US would impose punitive tariffs of 27.5% on all imports from China. Today, in the US Congress, Schumer has become the senator leading attacks on the RMB exchange rate. Today, the RMB exchange rate issue remains the top trade issue in Schumer's political capital, as noted on Schumer's official homepage. In fact, as early as the period from 2004 to 2008 and before the 2008 financial crisis, the US had been putting a lot of pressure on the RMB exchange rate.

After the crisis, there was a great change in the scale of trade between China and the US. Figure 5.3 shows the trends in China to US trade balance and RMB exchange rate. China's exports to the US after the crisis dropped significantly and its trade surplus shrank rapidly. From 2008 to 2009, distracted by the financial crisis, the US paid less attention to the RMB appreciation. From 2010, the US economy began to recover and China's trade surplus from China-US bilateral trade rose; the RMB issue thus became a hot topic once again. At that point of time, the pressure on the RMB manifested in two forms. One of which was through traditional channels, the "upgraded version" of the Schumer Bill being the best example. On September 29, 2010, the US House of Representatives passed the "Currency Reform for Fair Trade Act" proposed by Congressman Tim Ryan. The Act was aimed at recognizing countries with undervalued currencies as receiving export subsidies, thus imposing special countervailing duties. Since then, supporters of the Act have been seeking the support of the Senate, and Schumer and his supporters expect that after

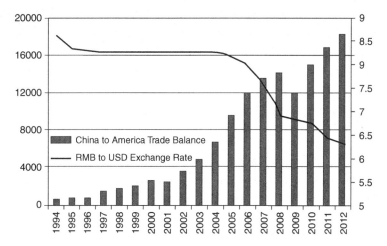

Figure 5.3 Ratio of China to US trade balance, and the exchange rate of the RMB against the USD.

Source: CEIC Database; trade balance in units of a million USD, and the exchange rate is determined by the direct quotation approach.

Thanksgiving in 2013, the Senate would put the Act up for voting. The US Treasury continued to publish the "Semiannual Report on International Economic and Exchange Rate Policies". In the nine published reports during Obama's tenure, China had not once been labeled a "currency manipulating country". Yet, the report still believed that the RMB or Chinese Yuan was significantly undervalued; it suggested that the RMB would further appreciate and that the US should still continue to pay attention to the appreciation of the RMB. Many American scholars have criticized the RMB exchange rate issue, for example, pioneer of the "China-US G2"[17] and former Director of the US Peterson Institute for International Economics, Fred Bergsten who still believes the RMB is 40% undervalued against the dollar five years after the RMB exchange rate reform in 2010; Professor Niall Ferguson, a history professor at Harvard University who coined the term "Chimerica",[18] also believes that the undervaluation of the RMB is the key problem behind global imbalances; Nobel laureate in Economics, Paul Krugman believes that the undervaluation of the RMB has caused a negative structural impact in the world. As can be seen, the US has been exerting pressure on the RMB exchange rate all the while, albeit light at times and strong at other times, but the pressure has never been lifted.

In addition to directly exerting pressure, the US also sought to pressurize the RMB indirectly by criticizing the grave undervaluation of the RMB at international organizations such as the IMF and the WTO, hoping that the international organizations would also put pressure on China. However, as China's trade surplus mainly came from bilateral trade with the US and Europe, there were a lot of differences in trade restrictions and statistics involved. In trading with most other regions, China was overall still slightly in deficit or general balance, thus the indirect pressure approach failed.

---

[17] The idea of the "G2" (Group of Two) was proposed by famous American economist Fred Bergsten, referring to China and the US forming a Group to replace the old G8, to work together to solve the world's economic problems. He believed that China is already a true economic superpower, and the US should work together with China such that China can become the legitimate architect and manager of the international economic order and take on its role as a global economic superpower. This approach obviously does not correspond with complex realities and ignores the huge differences between China and America. It also does not align with the multipolarization trend of the world, and is but a form of "flattery".

[18] "Chimerica" is another name for the American G2 approach. The term was jointly coined by Professor Niall Ferguson of Harvard University and Professor Moritz Schularick of the Free University of Berlin, emphasizing the close economic relationship between China and the US, and claiming that China and the US are entering the phase of symbiosis.

In 2010, at the G20 Summit in Seoul, the US proposed setting a quantitative limit of less than 4% of GDP on current account deficits, and criticized China for manipulating exchange rates and creating huge current account surpluses. More details can be found in Chapter 2 ("G20 and New Developments of the Global Governance Platform"). The following year, China kept well within the limits set by the US while the US, as the setter of the limit, went way beyond the limits, thus the matter was hushed.

2.1.3 Friction between trade and exchange rates have existed for a long time

Historically, Germany and Japan, which traded closely with the US, have had conflicts regarding exchange rates. US-Japanese trade friction began from the late 1950s to the late 1980s and continue to grow, eventually culminating in a trade war (see Figure 5.4). In 1971, on the grounds of reducing trade deficits and the undervaluation of the Japanese yen and other currencies, the US imposed a temporary 10% levy on all imports including Japanese products, and removed the levy a few months later when the yen appreciated. In the 1980s, the conflict between the US and Japan broke out. The conflict was not limited to a few particular products, it spanned across various fields including

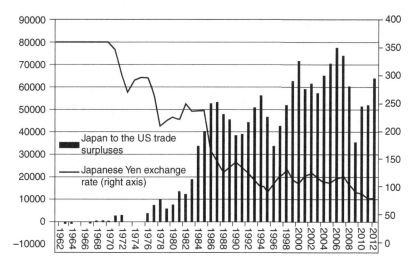

Figure 5.4 Ratio of Japan to the US trade surpluses, and the exchange rate of the Japanese yen against the USD.

Source: Data before 1980 retrieved from Japanese Statistics Bureau; data after 1980 retrieved from IMF (expressed in units of a million USD, Japanese yen exchange rate taken from CEIC).

cutting-edge technology and finance. Japan had long insisted that the yen had a stable exchange rate but was forced to appreciate sharply after signing the Plaza Accord in 1985. Before signing the Accord, Japan had taken various measures to control the yen's appreciation. From 1973 to 1985, the yen had only appreciated by 28%, but after the Accord, the yen rose from 230:1 to 140:1 against the dollar in February 1987. The cumulative appreciation was more than 200% in 1995.

The trade friction between the US and Germany was mainly concentrated in the 1970s but it was less tense than the conflict between the US and Japan. After World War II, Germany saw rapid economic development, its trade surpluses grew continually and caused US dissatisfaction (see Figure 5.5). However, as more of Germany's trade surpluses came from within Europe, and Germany also raised the German mark to USD exchange rate on its own accord in 1961 and 1969 respectively, the German-American trade friction was greatly eased. Nevertheless, in 1971, the temporary 10% import levies that the US imposed in 1971 also covered German products, forcing the appreciation of the German mark against the dollar. In 1971, when Germany adopted the floating exchange rate system, the German government took the initiative to gradually appreciate the German mark and by the time of the Plaza Accord, the German mark had already been

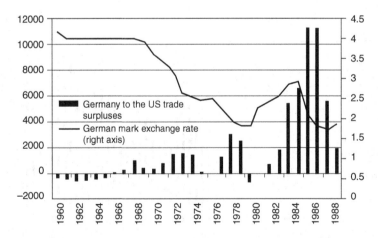

Figure 5.5 Ratio of Germany to the US trade surpluses, and the exchange rate of the German mark against the USD.

Source: Data before 1980 retrieved from "Palgrave World Historical Statistics: American Volume", data after 1980 retrieved from the IMF. German mark exchange rate taken from CEIC (expressed in units of a million USD).

appreciated by 50% against the US dollar. Although the German mark continued to appreciate against the USD after the agreement was signed, it was on a much smaller scale than the yen and by 1995, the German mark had appreciated against the dollar by 100%.

The examples of Japan and Germany show that the changes in the relationship between exchange rates trends and trade imbalances are unclear. The German mark had already undergone large-scale appreciation against the USD since the late 1960s and yet in that period, German to US trade moved from a deficit to a surplus. On the other hand, in the mid-1980s, the Japanese yen appreciated substantially and the impact on Japan-US trade surplus was relatively limited. Trade surplus only narrowed slightly and rapidly increased again after that. As such, it can be seen that as economic globalization developed today's global value chains formed by transnational corporations, and adjustments in exchange rates do not have a significant impact on trade balance, especially with bilateral trade imbalances. However, if the conflict with the top economic power is dealt with inappropriately, it could result in a serious negative effect for both parties. For example, the sharp appreciation of the Japanese yen and the inadequate adjustment of the country's macro policies are among the important reasons for Japan's 20 years of economic stagnation.

2.2 *International views on the relationship between trade and exchange rates*

After the collapse of the Bretton Woods System and the formation of the Jamaican System, the exchange rate system became more diversified as major countries entered an era of floating exchange rates. At the same time, the constraints between currencies were further eased, exchange rates became more volatile and many countries changed their exchange rate regime after going through numerous crises. For example, Southeast Asia, which had followed a fixed exchange rate that was pegged to the dollar, eventually abandoned the fixed exchange rate system after experiencing sharp currency devaluation in 1997. Imbalances in trade and international payments are significant factors in exchange rate volatility but the major international organizations are generally tolerant with regard to the relationship between exchange rates and trade, and have not specified which exchange rate regimes ought to be implemented or clarified how to handle the relationship between trade and exchange rates.

2.2.1 *IMF's views on exchange rate regimes and the relationship between trade and exchange rates*

Judging from international organizations' division of labor, before the current financial crisis happened, the IMF had a strong influence over the monitoring of member countries' exchange rates. The organization was originally established to deal with the international balance of payments crisis, and exchange rates are an important variable of adjustment in the balance of payments crisis — the latter has therefore became a focal point for the IMF in evaluating countries' economic policies. Nonetheless, the outbreak of the global financial crisis, to a large extent, was not an international balance of payments crisis, and the problems no longer occurred in traditional emerging economies. Thus, the IMF's heavy emphasis on exchange rates in the past has come into question.

To avoid being marginalized, the IMF also underwent a large-scale reform after the crisis. This reform was not only a reform of the member states' representativeness; it also reflected a reform of work mindsets. The IMF no longer emphasized the role of exchange rates as it did in the past. When in discussion and negotiation with the member states, it would conduct more comprehensive research, evaluation and recommendation for the overall macroeconomic situation and financial market. Nonetheless, the exchange rate issue was still an important point of concern for the IMF. Once the global economic recession was alleviated, trade resumed growth and global imbalances re-emerged, the exchange rate issue became the focus of the IMF's attention and research again.

The IMF's views on the exchange rate system have changed several times. Before the collapse of the Bretton Woods System, the fixed exchange rate system was widely used. The fixed exchange rate system's core was the "double peg", which means it was pegged to both the US dollar and gold. Other currencies were pegged to the dollar, and a floating exchange rate was strictly prohibited. Under the Jamaican System, exchange rate regimes began to diversify. Currently, there are many different exchange rate regimes among the member states. In the IMF's classification, a total of 10 different exchange rate systems are classified into four categories according to the degree of float.

The first category are the hard pegs, and there are two types of hard pegs, one of which is an exchange rate arrangement without a separate legal tender. These countries do not have their own currencies and adopt the currency of another country (usually USD or euro) as their country's official currency. There are currently 13 economies with such a system. The other is a currency board system where the monetary authorities of the country need to ensure that their national currency and the currency they are pegged to maintain a fixed exchange ratio, and the issuing of their national currency has to be strictly in accordance with the ratio. Every unit of the currency issued has to be backed with the equivalent amount of foreign exchange reserves as a payment guarantee. The Chinese Hong Kong belongs under this currency board system. There are currently 12 economies that have adopted this exchange rate system.

The second category is soft pegs, and there are five types in this category. The first is the conventional peg where pegged currencies generally fluctuate less than 1%. Currently, there are 43 economies who adopt the conventional peg. The second is a stabilized peg with bands where the exchange rate volatility is less than 2% within a six months' period. Currently there are 16 economies using a stabilized arrangement. The third type is the crawling peg where exchange rates are adjusted periodically according to a pre-announced range. Currently there are three economies adopting this system. The fourth type is the crawl-like arrangement. China belongs in this category.[19] Currently, there are 12 economies using the crawl-like arrangement. The fifth is the pegged exchange rate within horizontal bands. Only one economy adopts this system currently.

The third category is the unpegged system and there are two types in this category: one is the floating system where the market basically determines the exchange rate and there is no way to predict changes. Currently, 35 economies adopt this system. The other type is the free-floating system where there are very few interventions so the exchange rate is a fully floating one. There are currently 31 economies using this system.

The fourth category covers the rest of the uncategorized exchange rate arrangements. There are 24 such economies under this category at the moment.

Recent trends show that more and more member states are shifting from the fixed exchange rate regimes to floating ones. One of the reasons why the emerging economies did not undergo a major crisis during the recent financial crisis is mostly because they adopted a more flexible floating exchange rate.

---

[19] The IMF classification of exchange rate arrangements is *de facto*. A country's exchange rate regime is classified according to indicators such as the country's exchange rate volatility and the degree of intervention by the central bank in the foreign exchange market. This is not necessarily the same as what the country announces of its own exchange rate regime. For example, the People's Bank of China believes that China falls under the category of managed floating exchange rate arrangements.

After the crisis, the IMF redeveloped the External Balance Assessment,[20] which is aimed at helping countries achieve an equilibrium exchange rate[21] by assessing if a country's exchange rate is at a reasonable level. This approach was a significant improvement compared with the previous IMF analyses of equilibrium exchange rate. Before this, the IMF directly took the exchange rate estimated according to the model as the equilibrium exchange rate, and indiscriminately regarded the difference between the real exchange rate and the estimated exchange rate as deviations from the equilibrium exchange rate value, inherently implying that there was a need to adjust it completely. The improved External Balance Assessment breaks down the deviation of a country's exchange rate from the equilibrium value into cyclical and policy factors. Cyclical factors may change with external conditions and are not within the scope of exchange rate adjustments whereas policy factors are related to a country's economic structure and its current stage of development, and thus ought to be adjusted according to the overall situation. The implementation of the new approach allows the IMF to look at a country's exchange rate more pragmatically and the new approach's interpretation of the exchange rate formation mechanism has more policy implications and instructional significance.

Further discussion is needed regarding the IMF's approach and its conclusion of China. As the yuan is not yet freely convertible under the capital account, there are still certain restrictions in trade, thus the supply and demand of foreign exchange reflected currently is different from the supply and demand after opening up. Capital account convertibility should be realized first before RMB exchange rate is discussed (see Figure 5.6).

2.2.2 *WTO's views on the relationship between trade and exchange rates*

The WTO is not the regulatory body handling exchange rates, but over the past two years, it has organized wide-ranging discussions on the issue. An example

---

[20] External Balance Assessment (EBA) is presently the IMF's main approach for rebalancing the global economy and assessing exchange rates. It does so by conducting panel regression-based analyses to estimate a country's current account and exchange rate equation and from there, obtain a reasonable current account balance and exchange rate, comparing it with the country's real situation, so as to estimate the "policy gaps" and make relevant recommendations for the country's international payments and exchange rate adjustments.

[21] Here, the equilibrium exchange rate refers to the reasonable exchange rate of a country calculated based on the IMFEBA model.

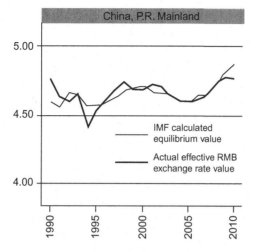

Figure 5.6 China's equilibrium exchange rate according to IMF's EBA algorithm.
Source: Author's own data.

is as mentioned previously, in 2011, Brazil brought up the topic of exchange rates and trade to WTO for comprehensive discussion. In the same year, Brazil, together with Argentina, advocated that the devaluation move by the developed countries ought to be recognized as "currency dumping" and be subjected to punitive tariffs. The WTO turned down this request. Then WTO Director-General Pascal Lamy explicitly denied the request in his speech in March 2013. He pointed out that the resolution of exchange rate fluctuations and currency manipulation issues depended heavily on the international monetary system. Countries still had a long way to go in terms of resolving these issues and the WTO could not solve the problem alone. He claimed that "trade issues should not be blamed for the flaws in the international monetary system." This essentially denied the speculation that the WTO could meddle in exchange rate and trade issues.

However, the successor for WTO Director-General Pascal Lamy in 2013 was precisely Brazil's ambassador to WTO at that time, Roberto Azevêdo. It cannot be guaranteed that exchange rate and trade issues will not be taken to the WTO in the future, considering the variability of liquidity of financial markets in the coming years, the frequent changes in emerging economies' exchange rates, and adverse changes that have also occurred in current accounts.

2.2.3 *G20's assessment of trade and exchange rate issues*

G20 has not set up a separate discussion for exchange rate issues but exchange rate issues are inevitably raised up at each summit. At the G20 Summit in Seoul, the ministers proposed and adopted setting the current account surplus or deficit as less than 4% of GDP and this was taken as the reference for exchange rate policies, although there is still a lack of evidence that this objective was established. In fact, after the last crisis, the current account balance of both China and the US rapidly shrunk. China's current account surplus to GDP dropped from 10.1% in 2007 to about 2% in 2012 and that of the US fell from 5.1% to 3.1% in the same period. As can be seen, China's adjustment was much larger than the US but both countries reached the target of less than 4% (see Figure 5.7). In 2013, at the G20 finance ministers and central bank governors' meeting, the G20's stand on the exchange rate issue was expressed: the G20 remained committed to promoting a market-oriented exchange rate system rapidly, raising exchange rate flexibility, to better reflect the fundamentals of the economy and avoid disorderly exchange rate fluctuations. Excessive capital volatility and unruly changes in exchange rates would have a negative impact on the real economy and financial stability.

The G20's views on the exchange rate and trade issues essentially reflect the different demands of developed and developing countries on exchange rate issues: on the one hand, the G20 still emphasizes a market-oriented exchange rate system, and raising of exchange rate flexibility, which basically reflects the developed countries' requests for developing countries to further reform their

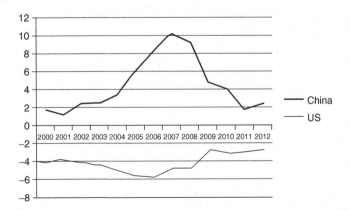

Figure 5.7   2000–2012 surplus or deficit in US, China trade/GDP: %.

Source: IMF.

exchange rate formation mechanisms; on the other hand, the G20 is also concerned about the negative impact that may be brought about by the excessive volatility of capital and exchange rates, which essentially reflected the developing countries' unhappiness with the excessively loose monetary policies of the major developed economies.

2.2.4 Unrecognized consensus: Exchange rates are but one of the factors affecting trade balance

Apart from exchange rates, there are several other important factors such as economic structure (relationship between savings and consumption), trade policies (export controls, other trade barriers), cross-border investment, industrial chain division, international status of currencies and statistical differences, affecting international trade revenue and expenditure, particularly bilateral trade balance. Take economic structure as an example, early in 1996, famous American textbook[22] pointed out that the determinant for the performance of current accounts (mainly trade revenue and expenditure) is the difference between savings and investment in a country. A country's domestic structural factors such as population structure, cultural differences, level of financial development *etc.* all directly affect the country's savings and investment decisions, thereby affecting the country's trade revenue and expenditure.

Previously, most criticisms of the RMB exchange rate originated from the massive trade surplus from China and the US bilateral trade. These criticisms from Western officials, academics or media opine that the yuan was being manipulated and such manipulation led to the massive China-US trade surplus. This view carries political overtones and lacks supporting economic evidence. On the one hand, there is no consistent, robust, quantifiable conclusion currently with regard to the relationship between exchange rates and trade surpluses. Many studies tend to conclude that the relationship between exchange rates and trade balances is not close, and in particular, the analysis of the impact of the RMB exchange rate on China-US trade surpluses concludes as such. In global value chains (Chapter 7 is devoted to this topic), China and

---

[22] Refer to the textbook *Foundations of International Macroeconomics* (Cambridge, Massachusetts: MIT Press, 1996), compiled by two famous international economists, Maurice Obstfeld and Kenneth Rogoff. The Chinese langugae edition was published in 2002 by China Financial Publishing House.

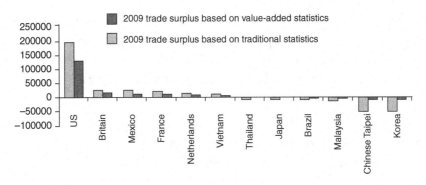

Figure 5.8 China-US bilateral trade surplus based on value-added statistics (2009).
Source: OECD-WTO Trade in Value-Added Database.

other emerging economies earn a small part of the profits through processing trade, and exchange rate factors even out in the import and export of processing trade, thus the impact is insignificant. On the contrary, the different national trade policies in bilateral trade have a great impact on trade surpluses and deficits. To date, the US still implements "Tiananmen Sanctions",[23] greatly limiting the amount of high-tech product exports to China. As a result, the fundamental conditions for convenient free bilateral trade are still not met till today. On the other hand, along with the improvements and updates in global value chain trade data, the phenomenon of large-scale trade surpluses in China-US trade will not last. Every year, the Ministries of Commerce from both countries form customs statistical teams consisting of professionals and experts to verify import and export trade data, announcing the figures on their official websites only after a consensus is reached. According to the statistics published by the US Department of Commerce, the trade deficit with China has, on average, been overvalued by 20% and more, yet academics and the media have never utilized the corrected and lowered figures. At the same time, the traditional way to measure trade flows does not accurately reflect the reality of China-US trade. According to estimates on trade in value-added released by WTO-OECD this year, based on value-added calculations, the China-US trade surplus rapidly shrunk to just two thirds of the original (see Figure 5.8).

---

[23] "Tiananmen Sanctions" refer mainly to a series of sanctions implemented by the US "Foreign Relations Authorization Act for Fiscal year 1990–1991" which restricts exports of weapons, satellites, and high-tech products to China.

2.3 *Thoughts on China's response to trade and exchange rate issues*

China can creatively learn from Germany's experience in strategically respond-ing to trade and currency agreements. On the one hand, focusing on itself, China can actively promote exchange rate reform, to construct a stable, market-oriented exchange rate formation mechanism. On the other hand, it can actively develop new markets, reduce trade dependence on developed coun-tries, defuse pressure from the US and promote a more balanced Chinese international balance of payments.

Firstly, China should strengthen international dialogue and trade consulta-tions on trade and exchange rate issues. Despite the lowered external pressures on China's trade and exchange rate issues recently, there will still be controver-sies with regard to trade and exchange rates in the future due to the inherent contradictions in the existing international monetary system. China ought to actively participate in discussions on exchange rate and trade issues conducted by international organizations, objectively and truthfully reflect on the rela-tionship between exchange rates and trade, and actively express its views and requests on international platforms such as the IMF, the WTO and G20; thereby preventing the promulgation of unfavorable policies and regulations. It could actively track the latest developments in global trade value chain research, interpret the relationship between the country's exchange rates and trade in the context of globalization and strive for a stronger voice in this field. At the same time, China must set its eyes on the entire international balance of payments problem. Presently, the exchange rate discussions overemphasize product trade balance, yet this proportion of product trade in current accounts is expected to drop in the future. The proportion of trade in services and invest-ment projects in current accounts is expected to rise. With the continual open-ing up of China's service industry, the deficit in trade in services will continue to grow; and as China's foreign investment grows in scale, income surplus will continue to increase as well. On the whole, the impact of exchange rates on current accounts will gradually weaken. With the realization of capital account convertibility, and opening up of individual overseas investments, the supply and demand in the foreign exchange market will become more balanced, the exchange rate mechanism will improve, and the disputes in relevant trade and exchange rate issues will also be alleviated.

Secondly, China should promote the reform of exchange rate formation mechanisms. China can choose exchange rate regimes based on its national conditions and in line with its economic development. China has to build a more sophisticated open economic system which requires an exchange rate system that is more flexible and mainly market-determined so as to reduce price distortions and truly allow the market to play a decisive role in resource allocation. The convertibility of the yuan should be accelerated. Only when every citizen can freely convert foreign exchange apart from forex trading between agencies at the Shanghai Foreign Exchange Trading Center, a mechanism where exchange rates are determined by market supply and demand really will be formed. Therefore, China should adhere to the established direction, continue to actively promote the reform of the RMB exchange rate formation mechanism, make exchange rates more responsive, more flexible, reflect the market's real supply and demand, and fulfill the basic role of exchange rates in domestic and foreign resource allocation. It is hard to predict how the exchange rate at that time will be, or whether it is currently higher or lower than the one formed at the Shanghai Foreign Exchange Trading Center; all these need to be tested by the market. However, it can be imagined that if there were more personal overseas investments, there would be reduced pressure on foreign exchange reserves, greater return flow and liquidity of the RMB, which would be generally favorable for the macroeconomy. We ought to have confidence in the transformation and structural adjustments of Chinese enterprises, and believe that they would gain greater competitiveness in the international market.

Thirdly, China should grasp the stability and flexibility of exchange rate policies in the international environment. The reform of the RMB exchange rate not only concerns the stability of the RMB and close attention should also be paid to the development of other currencies, international hot money flows and prevention; it requires coordination with other countries through various dialogue mechanisms. Although the world's major economies are actively implementing floating exchange rate regimes, there have been numerous occasions where governments have intervened, pressured or influenced the market since the crisis. Since then, major currencies, especially the Japanese yen, have depreciated against the USD. Governments have even initiated the process and the risk of competitive devaluation of national currencies has increased significantly. There is a need to guard against the adverse effects that active or passive devaluation of other currencies have on China. China should actively call for the strengthening of international coordination, and urge the various central banks not to implement monetary policies that promote currency devaluation to stimulate exports, so as to avoid competitive devaluations. There are presently still risks in world economic recovery, the path and scale of the US exit from quantitative easing is uncertain, the European Union and other developed countries have not completely recovered, and emerging economies are experiencing a slowdown in growth. In such an international environment, exchange rates act as the link between domestic and external economic environments, and should thus be treated with extra caution as it could go forward or backwards. In fact, contingency plans with a huge amount of hot money inflows and outflows ought to be made, and efforts should be put into maintaining the stability of the RMB exchange rate.

3 On Rules of Trade Finance

Since the economic crisis, the Obama administration has revitalized the manufacturing sector and implemented economic policies to double exports to quicken the boom of the US economy. To this end, the US, on the one hand, emphasized the promotion of exports by export credits, and further developed and expanded the role of the US Export-Import Bank; on the other hand, they hoped to restrict emerging economies' export and foreign investment with international export credit rules, and expand their international market space. At the same time, the US and Europe have sped up research in recent years and actively promoted competitive neutrality rules, requesting that governments adhere to the principle of neutrality in the areas of finance, taxation and law *etc.*, prohibiting state-owned enterprises from obtaining unfair competitive advantages. The export credit policy formed the major part of the US and Europe's competitive neutrality rules. Export credit problems are likely to become an important issue after exchange rate issues, which the US and Europe used to put pressure on emerging economies.

Due to the differences in stages of development and business needs, the developed countries and emerging economies differ in export credit policies and practices and these differences remain today. There is a lack of a set of global rules that covers both developed and developing countries in the field of export credit. Currently, only the "gentlemen's agreement", *i.e.* the "Agreement on Guidelines for Officially Supported Export Credits" which is a plurilateral arrangement of the OECD, is in place. Although the agreement only indicates a moral promise, the "gentlemen's agreement" has become an important reference document in international export credit due to the important status of OECD countries in the world. It has gradually become an important international convention that not only constrains OECD member states, but is also increasingly being emulated and referenced by official export credit agencies around the world. In particular, the WTO comprehensively learned from the outcomes of the "gentlemen's agreement" in the "Agreement on Subsidies and

Countervailing Measures", and recognized its effect, further enhancing the agreement's influence in the coordination of international export credit affairs.

3.1 Provisions of the WTO "Agreement on Subsidies and Countervailing Measures" on export credits

The use of officially supported export credits to support one's merchandise exports, obtain world markets and resources, and raise the international competitiveness of their country's commodities and enterprises, is a common practice around the world. However, the determination of interest rates and other factors have to be subject to the relevant WTO provisions, especially the "Agreement on Subsidies and Countervailing Measures".

The provision directly related to export credit interest rates in the "Agreement on Subsidies and Countervailing Measures" is clause k in "Annex 1 Illustrative List of Export Subsidies" among prohibited subsidies: "The grant by governments (or special institutions controlled by and/or acting under the authority of governments) of export credits at rates below those which they actually have to pay for the funds so employed (or would have to pay if they borrowed on international capital markets in order to obtain funds of the same maturity and other credit terms and denominated in the same currency as the export credit), or the payment by them of all or part of the costs incurred by exporters or financial institutions in obtaining credits, in so far as they are used to secure a material advantage in the field of export credit terms. Provided, however, that if a Member is a party to an international undertaking on official export credits to which at least 12 original Members to this Agreement are parties as of January 1, 1979 (or a successor undertaking which has been adopted by those original Members), or if in practice a Member applies the interest rates provisions of the relevant undertaking, an export credit practice which is in conformity with those provisions shall not be considered an export subsidy prohibited by this Agreement."

According to the above, the WTO determines if official export credits constitute export subsidies, and the key is whether export credit rates are lower than the cost of capital or comparable to market interest rates. The WTO also provides for exemption of subsidies, whether they are OECD member states or not, as long as they are loans granted according to the "gentlemen's agreement", they are not prohibited by the WTO. As can be seen, the WTO "Agreement" practically offered two choices to its member states with regard to export credit rates: either to comply with the provisions regarding prohibition of subsidies in the "Agreement" and ensure that export credit rates are no less than the cost of capital or market interest rates; or comply with the interest rate provisions given in the "gentlemen's agreement" and apply the OECD commercial interest reference rates (CIRR), thus not apply the provisions relating to prohibited subsidies in the "Agreement". Previously with WTO cases, the preferential export credits such as "advance payment refund guarantee" and "pre-shipment loans" provided by Export-Import Bank of Korea for ship export, as well as Brazil and Canada's "rate stabilization plan" established for regional aircraft export all did not meet the above conditions and were identified as export subsidies.

It is worth noting that the "gentlemen's agreement" does not cover export sellers' credits as it is only applicable to export buyers' credit provided for foreign buyers. That means that as export seller credits do not fall within the scope of the "gentlemen's agreement", therefore the second paragraph on "safe harbor" under the Annex 1 clause k in the WTO's "Agreement on Subsidies and Countervailing Measures" is also not applicable. Whether export subsidies constitute export sellers' credit has nothing to do with the "gentlemen's agreement", rather, there is a need to analyze if they fall under the category of WTO regulations on export subsidies.

3.2 *Main content of the "gentlemen's agreement"*

In February 1978, OECD developed a "gentlemen's agreement". It took effect on April 1, 1978, and since then, there have been constant revisions and adjustments made. The main purpose of the agreement is the orderly use of basic government-supported framework for export credits so as to eliminate relevant subsidies and trade-distorting measures, and to provide a fair, competitive environment. The parties involved in the agreement include Australia, Canada, the EU, Japan, Korea, New Zealand, Norway, Switzerland and the US. At the same time, the participants of these agreements may invite other members of the OECD and non-OECD members to join them.

The "gentlemen's agreement" established restrictions such as minimum interest rates, risk fees and maximum repayment period on the government-supported export credits, and made provisions for mixed loans. In addition, the agreement also clarified the relevant procedures, including advance notification, consultation, exchange of information, reviews on the bids of export credit that were exceptions to the rules *etc.*

The "gentlemen's agreement" was mainly applicable to goods and services export (including finance leases) by the government or on behalf of the government. The repayment period of two years or more was supported officially.

The official support can take three forms: (1) export credit guarantee or insurance (pure insurance); (2) official financial support (including direct financing and refinancing, or interest rate support); (3) a mixture of the previous two. Meanwhile, there were individual "Sector Understandings" in the "gentlemen's agreement" for shipping, nuclear power plants, civil aircraft, renewable energy and water projects, as a separate annex in the "gentlemen's agreement". Even if it was not included in the gentlemen's agreement, it could also be separately read for sector understanding. Besides, the "gentlemen's agreement" also applied to binding assistance loans and non-binding trade-related assistance loans. It is worth noting that the "gentlemen's agreement" did not apply to exports of military equipment and agricultural products. Meanwhile, the OECD export credit was limited to the loans for overseas buyers, so the "gentlemen's agreement" was only applicable to export credit provided for overseas buyers and did not include export credit for sellers.

3.2.1 *Export credit agreement under normal conditions*

(1) Concerning advance payment, maximum official support and local costs. Firstly, the buyer is required to give an advanced payment of not less than 15% of the export contract value for goods and services. The official support cannot exceed 85% of the export contract value. Secondly, it can provide support for local costs,[24] but it cannot be more than 30% of the export contract value. It cannot obtain more favorable official support conditions than other related export. If the official support for local costs exceeds 15% of the export contract value, acceding countries should give advanced notice to other acceding countries, and a detailed explanation on the situation should be given where the local costs are officially supported.

(2) Concerning the longest repayment terms. Using the World Bank estimates of per capita income in the country classification review as a benchmark, the borrowers are divided into two categories, high-income OECD countries and other countries. For high-income countries, the maximum repayment period is five years and after following the relevant procedures of pre-notification, the longest repayment period can be up to 8.5 years. For

---

[24] Fees for the purchase of goods or services in the importing country. These fees must be spent on the implementation of export contract or completion of project (the project constitutes part of the export contract). Local fees do not include the fees that exporters pay to agencies in the importing country.

other countries, the maximum repayment period is 10 years. For contracts involving more than one importing country, the acceding countries should seek to establish a common understanding in accordance with the relevant procedures and agree on a suitable repayment period. For non-nuclear power plant, the maximum repayment period can be up to 12 years.

(3) On principal repayments and interest payments. The principal export credits should be repaid in equal instalments. The principal should be repaid within six months with a one-time interest. The first principal repayment and interest payment are made no later than six months after the start date of the credit. For the export credits provided for leasing transactions, the payment of interest can be in equal instalments but it is not necessary to repay the principal in equal instalments.

(4) Minimum fixed interest rates. The fixed-rate loans provide official financing support for the acceding countries and CIRRs are adopted as minimum interest rates. CIRR is determined as the benchmark interest rate for each country plus 100 basis points, unless otherwise agreed by the acceding countries. The acceding countries have the following two options in the benchmark interest rate system for their national currency. One option is for credit to be issued with a repayment period not exceeding five years (inclusive) to use three years of government bond as yields; for credit with repayment period of over five years, but not more than eight and half years (inclusive), five years of government bond yields are applicable; while for credit with repayment period of more than eight and half years, seven years of government bond yields are applicable. The second option is for credits with different repayment periods and five-year government bond yields are applied for all.

3.2.2 *Industry-specific export credit agreement*

Annex 1 to 4 of the "gentlemen's agreement" are sector understandings whose role is to provide specialized guidelines for the official export credit in specific industries. The "gentlemen's agreement" now includes the understanding of the following industries: shipping, nuclear power plant, civil aircraft, renewable energy and water projects.

For the export of goods and services that are included in sector understanding, the acceding countries can provide official support in accordance with the provisions of sector understanding. If the sector understanding does not make corresponding provisions, the acceding country of the sector understanding may apply the provisions of the "gentlemen's agreement". As part of the "gentlemen's agreement", the sector understanding can also apply the "safe harbor" provision in clause k of Annex 1 in the "Agreement on Subsidies and Countervailing Measures". That is, if the official export credit of a specific industry in a country is in line with the rules of the relevant sector understanding, it will not be considered export subsidies. Sector understanding can be added individually. The acceding countries may be non-OECD members and non-participating parties of the "gentlemen's agreement".

3.2.3 Tied aid agreement

Tied aid is the foreign aid that must be spent in the country providing the aid (the donor country) or in a group of selected countries. A donor country will provide a bilateral loan or grant to a recipient country, but mandate that the money be spent on goods or services produced in the selected country. The aid provided by the donor country includes loans, grants and other financing packages with concessionary rate of above "0". Tied loan policies should provide external funds for countries, industries or projects that are basically unable or completely unable to get help from the finance market. While ensuring optimal use of funds, distortion from normal trade is minimized. The money is then used to promote development effectively.

Tied aid includes: (1) official development assistance loans; (2) official development assistance grants; (3) other official assistance, including grants and loans but excluding the export credit supported officially in the "gentlemen's agreement"; (4) any other relevant assistance (such as a mixture of assistance). The concessionary rates of the aid provided by the donor countries in principle should not be less than 35%. When the recipient country is a least developing country (LDC), the concessionary rates should not be less than 50% in principle.

3.3 International exchange and dialogue on export credits

In May 2011, the discussion of export credit issues was, for the first time, included in the third round of the China-US strategic and economic dialogue. Joint Fact Sheet on Strengthening U.S.-China Economic Relations released during Chinese President Xi Jinping's visit to US in February 2012 stated: "The United States and China decided to hold two bilateral seminars to promote transparency and mutual understanding of each other's export credit agency programs: the first meeting, in early February, brought together senior technical experts representing the U.S. Treasury Department and the U.S. Export-Import Bank on the U.S. side and the Ministry of Finance, China Ex-Im Bank, and Sinosure on the Chinese side; the second meeting is to take place prior to the next S&ED and is to include senior policy officials as well as technical experts. In addition, the United States and China are to establish an international working group of major providers of export financing to make concrete progress towards a set of international guidelines on the provision of official export financing that, taking into account varying national interests and situations, are consistent with international best practices, with the goal of concluding an agreement by 2014".

- In February and April 2012, the two countries held talks on export credit technology that senior technical experts from both countries attended.
- In September 2012, the international working group of export credit held its first meeting. In November 2012, the international working group of export credit held its first plenary meeting in Washington in the US. A total of 15 countries and regions, namely China, the US, the EU, Brazil, Australia, Canada, Israel, Japan, Malaysia, New Zealand, Norway, Korea, Russia, Switzerland and Turkey participated. The preliminary meeting agreed: Firstly, the "gentlemen's agreement" is not a blueprint for the new international rules. Secondly, specific industries like shipping will begin consultations. Thirdly, the international working group temporarily included a total of 18 countries: the nine member states in the "gentlemen's agreement" (the US, the EU, Japan, Korea, Australia, Canada, New Zealand, Norway, Switzerland), the five BRIC countries (Brazil, Russia, India, China, South Africa), Indonesia, Israel, Malaysia and Turkey. The export credit would be absorbed on a case by case basis so that poorer countries can join in the future. Fourthly, the international working group was to meet three times a year and the Member States would take turns to hold the meetings.
- In May 2013, the international working group of export credit held its second plenary session in Beijing, China. The initial plan was for the medical device industry to be the second consultation industry.

In addition, the China-German and China-European export credit agencies also made contact with regard to cooperation. In July 2010, according to the consensus reached by Chinese Premier Wen Jiabao and the German Chancellor Angela Merkel, the Chinese Ministry of Commerce signed a "Memorandum of Understanding in Export Credit Agency Cooperation" with Germany's Ministry of Economics and Technology, and decided to "strengthen the exchange of experiences among the export credit agencies". Under this framework, in June 2011 and March 2012, the two sides conducted two rounds of talks which were mainly technical exchanges. In August 2012, China and Germany held a second round of government consultations and the joint declaration stated that "the two sides will continue their dialogue on questions relating to export financing in the international framework". In February 2012, the 14th China-EU leaders meeting news report said that "leaders highlighted the importance of continued discussions on improving their respectives policies concerning export credit among relevant agencies". In September 2012, the press release of the 15th China-EU leaders meeting stated that summit leaders "recalled the conclusions of the 14th EU-China Summit on export credits and looked forward to continued discussions in the international working group of major providers of export finance."

3.4 *The export credit system and reform prospects of China*

3.4.1 *The current export credit system in China*

In 1980, the Bank of China opened the credit business for export sellers, providing loans for the export of Chinese electromechanical products. In 1988, China started to offer export credit insurance businesses run by Chinese insurance companies. Backed by the national credit reserve, foreign exchange guarantees, risk management and financing facilities were provided for the export of Chinese electromechanical products. In order to construct a socialist market economic system to adapt to the needs in 1994, an official export credit agency was established to achieve the objective of distinguishing policy finance from commercial finance. The China Export-Import Bank promoted Chinese economic and trade cooperation with other countries by providing loans and insurance for export enterprises. In 2001, in order to further deepen financial reform and improve policy financial institutions in China, the State Council approved the establishment of the China Export & Credit Insurance Corporation (Sinosure) which specializes in export credit insurance business.

Since joining the WTO, China has started forming commercial financial institutions led by two policy-oriented financial institutions, the Export-Import Bank of China and CITIC insurance company to complement the export financing system along with the establishment of the socialist market economy. The Export-Import Bank of China is mainly engaged in export credit and import credit businesses. It is also the specialized agency through which the

Chinese government provides preferential loans; Sinosure mainly engages in export credit insurance and guarantee businesses.

3.4.2 *Chinese export credit policy and international practice*

China is not a member of the OECD. China has already referred to the export credit arrangements of OECD as far as possible on major principles related to export credit. At the same time, as a developing country, the export credit arrangements of China have distinctive characteristics of the developing countries that are different from the OECD. The "gentlemen's agreement" of OECD aims to solve the problem of international competition among developed countries and does not fully reflect the development concept of developing countries. Till now, there is no precedent of developing countries joining the "gentlemen's agreement" in the international community. It can be said that China does not possess the conditions for joining the "gentlemen's agreement" at present.

All along, the Export-Import Bank and credit insurance company have done business in accordance with the "guaranteed profit" principle. On the whole, they determine loan conditions independently, but in accordance with commercial principles, and are able to achieve financial sustainability. The operation of Export-Import Bank credit refers to the relevant provisions of "Arrangement on Officially Supported Export Credit Guidelines" in OECD. Its loan interest rates refer to the commercial interest reference rates (CIRRs) announced by OECD which are fixed interest rates, or they are based on the London Interbank Offered Rate (LIBOR) which is a floating rate. Its interest rate policy is in line with the internationally accepted practices of export credit. There is fundamentally no difference between the export credit insurance arrangements of credit insurance companies and the export credit insurance arrangements of OECD in terms of down payment, the longest repayment period, country risk, premium and other technical problems.

But it should be noted that there are differences between China and developed countries in terms of export credit structures. The policy-oriented financial institutions in developed countries mainly engage in export credit insurance and guarantee business by adhering to a philosophy of how "small investments lead to immense profit", leveraging more credit funds of commercial banks. For example, the direct loans provided by the US Export-Import Bank account for only about 10% of its export credit business, the rest are guarantees and insurance. The official export credit agencies from Britain,

France, Germany, the Netherlands and other countries do not even provide direct credit funds. Currently, China still mainly provides export credits, with insurance and guarantee as supplements. In recent years, the mid- and long-term export credit insurance of credit insurance companies amount to only about USD$20 billion and does not represent a large proportion of all the export credit business in China.

3.4.3 *Outlook of export credit rules and international coordination*

There are still some differences between the export credit policies of emerging economies including China, and the "gentlemen's agreement", shown mainly in the more relaxed credit conditions and relatively high transparency. Currently, China is an important party in the international working group of export credit. With continual progress, the parties involved will come up with new international export credit rules together. This will help to establish a fair international dialogue mechanism, regulate global export credit order, and achieve impartial competition among the emerging economies, as well as that of emerging economies with developed economies. But in the short term, some of the emerging economies have already shown that they can be easily affected.

The preliminary prediction is that the new rules of the working group will be a compromise between the "gentlemen's agreement" and the current approach of emerging economies. While promoting the general rules, applicable exception clauses might be considered for special industries and even special countries (region). This is to achieve broad consensus and strive for the sustainable development of world economy and trade, creating a more equitable and suitable development for the actual credit environment. For emerging economies, including China, these are the options for the new rules.

First, with reference to the practice in Japan, Germany, Korea and other developed countries, there is initiative to speed up the adjustment of the position and direction of official export credit, gradually promoting the shift to overseas investment loans. There are no purchasing restrictions of loans for different countries, loans are not linked with our country's exports and emerging economies strive to avoid being restricted by new regulations.

Second, it is to further improve the market and introduce commercial financial institutions to be involved in the operations, adhering to the principles of commercial priorities. If all commercial credit can be provided or has been provided, the official export credit will not intervene so as to avoid vicious competition with the commercial credit.

Third, with reference to the development model of official export credit agency in developed countries, adjustments to the official export credit system have been accelerated to become bigger, export credit insurance and guarantee business have been strengthened and expanded to rely more on approaches that are more trusted, such as insurance and guarantees, to bolster the development of foreign trade.

Fourth, emerging economies can accept the new rules, and then research and improve upon the policy-based loan policies from time to time, drawing comprehensively from the experiences of Europe, the US, Japan and other countries. They can make necessary adjustments to improve the terms, direction of support, loan conditions, operating methods *etc.* of the official export credits, and gradually merge and assimilate with the new rules. At the same time, it is important to maintain the continuity and stability of the policy to ensure a smooth transition.

Meanwhile, taking into consideration that the official development assistance loans of some emerging economies have not fully met the 50% concession requirements for LDCs and heavily indebted poor countries as stated in the "gentlemen's agreement", the new international rules for export credit may require a higher concession and grant component. This is likely to promote the expansion of the scale of assistance to enhance the intensity of foreign assistance.

Chapter 6

Rules of Trade Remedies

Since the financial crisis, the topic of opposition towards trade protectionism has become a constant at G20 Summits and a variety of international trade conferences. Various leaders have reiterated their stance which clearly reflects that their countries have experienced the threat of trade protectionism. When it comes to trade protectionism, the first impression that people have may be more related to trade remedy measures. In recent years, the use of trade remedy measures has indeed been a cause for concern. According to statistics, WTO members have initiated 1,160 trade remedy investigations from 2008 to the end of 2012. Among them, 968 were anti-dumping cases, 101 were countervailing cases and 91 were cases on safeguard measures. Trade remedy measures are import restrictions that the WTO allows its members to legally apply. Their normal use does not constitute trade protectionist measures, only when they are overused or misused are they considered trade protectionist measures. The current WTO trade remedy rules system provides corresponding rule protection to protect the domestic industries of importing countries and maintain the export interests of exporting countries. Despite all this, there are still some issues of concern: there is still room for abuse of trade remedy measures; it is necessary to clarify and improve trade remedy rules and efforts have been made and subsequently, actions have been taken with regard to this. The rules negotiations that took place at the WTO Doha Round is one example of such effort. The main objectives for China's active participation in the negotiations are to clarify and push for stricter trade remedy rules, as well as stand against the abuse of trade remedy measures.

1 Trade Remedy Rules System

Trade remedies generally refer to anti-dumping, countervailing and safeguard measures. There is a long history in the regulation of trade remedy rules as there were great differences between the rules of countries and regions in the earlier days. After decades of development and improvement, the WTO has formed the "Anti-Dumping Agreement", "Agreement on Subsidies and Countervailing" and "Agreement on Safeguard Measures" as the main set of comprehensive trade remedy rules. At the same time, there are also individual rules of trade remedy in every country and region.

1.1 *Anti-dumping rules*

Long before the GATT, Australia, Canada and the US had already come up with anti-dumping legislation. In the regional integration process, regional anti-dumping rules were formed, with EU anti-dumping rules being the most typical. At the multilateral level, GATT Article VI, which was created in 1947, made provisions for anti-dumping. For the first time, anti-dumping rules were included in the scope of multilateral trade rules. With the further development of the multilateral trading system, the current multilateral WTO anti-dumping rules have become increasingly specific and comprehensive.

The anti-dumping rules of WTO come mainly from GATT Article VI in 1994 and the "Agreement on Implementation of Article VI of the GATT 1994" (hereinafter referred to as the "Anti-Dumping Agreement"). The "Anti-Dumping Agreement" provides three important conditions on anti-dumping measures: (1) imported products enter the markets of importing countries at dumping prices; (2) the material injury or threat thereof caused to like products in the domestic industry when imported products enter the country; and (3) the cause and effect link between dumping and the injury caused to the domestic industry. The investigation on anti-dumping typically includes the initiation, preliminary and final phases. The validity period of anti-dumping measures cannot be longer than five years from the start date, but through the sunset anti-dumping review, this time period may be extended for another five years each time.

1.2 *Countervailing rules*

The early countervailing remedies were implemented mainly through trade agreements and unilateral countervailing measures can be traced back to the US Tariff Act in 1890. In 1947, GATT provided the first multilateral prototypes of subsidies and countervailing rules. Further developments of the multilateral trading system led to the current subsidies and countervailing rules system of the WTO becoming increasingly specific and comprehensive. The main components of the system include: (1) the relevant provisions in GATT 1994; (2) "Agreement on Subsidies and Countervailing Measures" which interpret the relevant provisions of GATT 1994 so as to provide concrete basis and operation rules for subsidies and countervailing duty; and (3) the special provisions on subsidies and countervailing in "Agreement on Agriculture".

The subsidies in the "Agreement on Subsidies and Countervailing Measures" refer mainly to the financial contribution provided by a government or any public body, any price support given by the government and the benefits thereby conferred. The definition contains three basic elements: (1) financial contribution including grants, loans, investment shares, loan guarantees, fiscal incentives, provision of goods or services or purchase of goods other than the general infrastructure; (2) financial contribution is provided by governments or public bodies within the borders of the member country involved, the government can also entrust or direct private bodies to implement such support; and (3) the conferment of benefits. The agreement also includes the concept of "specificity", *i.e.* the subsidy is given to an enterprise of industry or group of enterprises or industries, or constitutes prohibited subsidies. Only when it constitutes specificity can a subsidy be countervailed. Subsidies are divided into two categories, namely prohibited subsidies and actionable subsidies.[1] According to members' knowledge on how subsidies may play an important role in the economic development of developing countries, more time was given to set out the special treatment of developing members in the "Agreement on Subsidies and Countervailing Measures". Similar to anti-dumping measures, countervailing measures cannot expire later than five years from its start date and its validity may be extended after the sunset review.

As a unilateral remedy measure taken against subsidies, countervailing measures and anti-dumping measures have many things in common. For

---

[1] Prohibited subsidies refer to the subsidies provided in accordance with the export performance, or subsidies given by using domestic products instead of imported products. These include export subsidies and local content subsidies. For prohibited subsidies, a member may resort to dispute settlement. For example, when there is material injury or threat thereof to a member's domestic industry, the subsidy can be countervailed. Actionable subsidies refer to all specific subsidies other than the prohibited subsidies. Such subsidies cover a very wide range of content unless they adversely affect the interests of other members. Such adverse effects include three kinds of situations: (a) injury to the domestic industry of another member, (b) nullification or impairment of benefits accruing directly or indirectly to other members under GATT 1994 in particular the benefits of concession bound under Article II of GATT 1994, (c) serious prejudice to the interests of another member. On the adverse effects of actionable subsidies, other members can seek multilateral or unilateral relief.

example, the two share some commonalities, such as "domestic industry", "damage" *etc.*, and a very similar investigation process. The anti-dumping and countervailing duties are borne by the companies. When anti-dumping measures are used to manage situations caused by subsidies, there may be an overlap with countervailing measures. The biggest difference between the two measures lies in the target of investigation. The target of anti-dumping investigations is the enterprise while the targets of countervailing investigations are both the enterprise and the government. This determines the greater differences between the two investigation procedures, of which the most important difference is whether intergovernmental consultations were conducted. Before importing members initiate countervailing investigations, they should consult the government of exporting members, which provide subsidies for the imported products. Throughout the whole course of investigation, the government of exporting members may request for consultations and the government of importing members should provide opportunities for consultation whereas in anti-dumping investigations, importing members are only required to fulfill obligations such as notifying exporting members and intergovernmental consultations are not statutory procedures.

1.3 *Rules of safeguard measures*

As compared to the rules of anti-dumping measures and countervailing measures, the rules of safeguard measures were constructed later. In 1943, the US and Mexico signed the "reciprocal trade agreement" which included provisions on safeguard measures for the first time. Article XIX of GATT (signed in 1947) discussed the "emergency actions on certain imported products" and this provided a prototype for multilateral rules on safeguard measures. With the further development of the multilateral trading system, the WTO now has a more specialized and complete set of multilateral rules on safeguard measures.

Safeguard measures are also called emergency actions. In free trade agreements, parties often refer to them as "global safeguard measures". When there is serious injury or threat thereof caused to the domestic industry by a surge in import, the importing country may take safeguard measures to provide relief to the domestic industry. The legal norms of safeguard measures in the WTO include Article XIX of GATT 1994 and WTO's "Agreement on Safeguards".

The WTO's "Agreement on Safeguards" provides the starting conditions, investigation methods, implementation procedures, types of measures and validity period for safeguards. It requires that the Party which implements safeguard measures against affected WTO members fulfill the obligation to notify and consult. Rights of compensation and rights to suspend concessions are given to other WTO members. It also set out provisions with regard to dispute settlement. According to the requirements of the agreement, the implementation of safeguard measures should meet the following conditions: (1) import surges; (2) serious injury or threat thereof caused to the domestic industry; (3) unexpected import surges; and (4) causal link between the surge in import and the injury done on domestic industry.

Compared to anti-dumping and countervailing measures, which are taken against unfair imports, safeguard measures are not taken against "unfair trade" practices. This means that safeguard measures can be taken against imports under normal trade. The "Agreement on Safeguards" puts forward higher requirements for rules setting and regulates even more severe consequences,[2] as compared to anti-dumping and countervailing measures.

In addition to the safeguard measures, which can be applied to imported products worldwide, there are also regional and bilateral safeguard measures. For example, in FTAs, many parties use WTO's "Agreement on Safeguards" to establish mechanisms for safeguard measures (also known as transitional safeguard measures). It is aimed at providing remedies such as suspension of tariff reduction or increasing most favored nation tariffs when the contracting parties' domestic industries suffer serious injury or threat thereof because of the surge in imports due to FTAs; there are also parties which use the agricultural special safeguard measures in WTO's "Agreement on Agriculture" to set up special safeguard mechanisms for bilateral agricultural products. Furthermore, in China's Accession to WTO Protocol, special safeguard measures were set up (hereinafter referred to as the Special Safeguards) and in the working report of China's accession to the WTO, special restriction clauses for

---

[2] Shown mainly in the following points: (1) the target of safeguard measures is the imported products from all sources. It is not directed against a specific exporting country or region. All countries and regions are to be treated equally without discrimination; (2) increased imports are required to achieve a high degree and the surge in imports is an unforseen development; (3) the industry injury criteria to take safeguard measures is more stringent than the anti-dumping measures and anti-subsidies measures in "Anti-Dumping Agreement" and "Agreement on Subsidies and Countervailing" in terms of injury or threat thereof; and (4) the establishment of trade compensation mechanism. According to this mechanism, the Party which takes the safeguard measures needs to provide equivalent trade compensation to the exporters in the case of specific conditions being satisfied. The relevant exporters can retaliate against the party taking the measures when the conditions are met.

textiles were established (hereinafter referred to as textile special limit provisions).

1.4 *The effects of rules*

Although the financial crisis led to a large number of trade remedy measures, it has not evolved into a global trade war. What has become evident are the effects of WTO's trade remedy rules.

First of all, rights and obligations coexist in this system, reflecting the various aspects of contest in rules between proponents of trade remedy measures and those who oppose the excessive usage of such measures. As a result of the contest, on the one hand, the members affected by imports can legally use trade remedy measures to provide the necessary protection for their domestic industries; on the other hand, the exporting members and their industries affected by trade remedy investigations may exercise the rights of these rules to protect their export rights. At the same time, due to the coexistence of rights and obligations, when the parties use trade remedy measures to protect their domestic industries, they have to be aware of the effects of their behavior and the chain reaction it might cause. We need to respect this set of rules to avoid trade protectionism.

Secondly, the WTO rules are set to resolve trade friction through dialogue and consultation. For example, the consultation provisions in the countervailing process, the price undertaking provisions in anti-dumping and countervailing processes, and consultation mechanisms of dispute settlements, *etc.* can be said to have provided relatively moderate friction-resolving mechanisms for members and their industries and enterprises. Again, the relevant monitoring mechanisms have provided certain platforms and assurance for compliance with this set of rules. These include:

(1) Supervision of Dispute Settlement Body (DSB), which is the "WTO's judicial supervising body". When the DSB deals with disputes between members, it has to clarify rules and ensure that members adhere to the rules. It provides an important platform against the abuse of all kinds of trade remedy measures. Through this platform, many acts of violation of trade relief rules have been addressed.

(2) The supervision of relevant trade committees and regular meetings. The three trade remedy measures committees established by the WTO trade remedy rule system, namely the anti-dumping measures committee,

Table 6.1 Number of trade remedy cases from the establishment of the WTO (1995) until the end of 2012.

Members	Total (1)	Total (2)	Anti-dumping (1)	Anti-dumping (2)	Countervailing (1)	Countervailing (2)	Safeguard measures (1)	Safeguard measures (2)
All members	4,786	1,160	4,230	968	302	101	254	91
India	707	182	677	167	1	1	29	14
United States	598	102	469	65	119	37	10	0
European Union	523	102	451	80	67	21	5	1
Argentina	312	80	303	80	3	0	6	0
Brazil	290	138	279	132	7	4	4	2
Australia	264	60	247	52	15	8	2	0
South Africa	233	14	217	11	13	2	3	1
China	207	59	200	53	6	6	1	0
Canada	202	37	166	24	33	13	3	0
Turkey	180	52	162	47	1	1	17	4

Source: Organized data released by the WTO.
Notes: Column (1) shows the data from the establishment of the WTO (1995) until the end of 2012; Column (2) shows the data from January 1, 2008 until the end of 2012 (mainly reflecting the situation after the financial crisis). The table also shows the 10 members with the most number of total cases since the establishment of the WTO till end 2012.

counter vailing measures committee and safeguard measures committee, provide an environment for supervising the compliance of trade rules. Moreover, although the WTO trade measures monitoring report and other relevant consensus reached by G20 Summit leaders to oppose trade protectionism are not included in the rules system, they provide a corresponding assurance for trade remedy rules to take effect (see Table 6.1).

2 Clarification and Improvement of Trade Remedy Rules

As the rules of trade remedy took effect, some of the problems that surfaced during the implementation also required closer attention. These problems reflected that the trade remedy rules system was somewhat lacking. It was necessary to clarify and improve the relevant rules, but the process was not a smooth one.

2.1 *The noteworthy issues in practice*

Since the establishment of the WTO in 1995, trade remedy measures have been used increasingly. Following the example set forth by developed countries, many developing countries have also begun using these measures frequently. On the one hand, this reflects that the demands of trade remedy measures in industries of various countries have increased in the context of globalization. On the other hand, this has also exposed some problems that require attention in practical application.

2.1.1 *Cases that highlight the power of trade remedy measures*

In practice, some members have been given great power in the case of trade relief measures. Some typical effects include:

(1) *A broad influence.* A typical example is the global safeguard measures investigation in the US, which involved a wide product range of more than 610 lines of steel products, with values up to USD17 billion in 2000, of which the EU was the biggest party involved with export of USD4 billion for the products concerned. In 2012, the EU launched the anti-dumping and countervailing case against China that was worth up to USD21 billion in exports of photovoltaic products. This case was the highest valued in history, whether as a single case or a single country concerned.

(2) *A high degree of impact.* During the implementation, the anti-dumping and countervailing measures of some countries include *ad valorem* levels, which are often very high, for example, levies of 50%, 100% or even 1,000%. This is very different from the tariff reduction that can be achieved for a single product during a tariff reduction negotiation.

(3) *The affected targets have increased.* In recent years, trade remedy measures in some countries have affected more products. High-tech products and new energy products continue to be the survey targets. In addition, the survey content has broadened from enterprise data involving cost price and government subsidies to the background and political identity of corporate executives, corporate party organizations and macroeconomic system in government, political party information *etc.*

2.1.2 *The expansion of trade remedy measures*

Trade remedy measures have mainly expanded in the areas of time, level, scope and geography. The expansion in terms of time refers to the extension of the implementation period of trade remedy measures through a variety of ways. The consequence is that cases of trade remedy measures that last for more than 10 years or even decades are common. For example, the EU's anti-dumping measures on bicycles originated in China have been implemented for more than 20 years. An expansion in level means increasing the level of trade remedy measures through review and other forms. With regard to the expansion in range, this may include the expansion of product range and sources, such as the components of anti-circumvention products and other sources of products, which are included in the range of anti-dumping measures. According to anti-circumvention legislation and implementation in some countries, after the anti-dumping or countervailing measures, if the exporter avoids anti-dumping duties through decentralization (for example, anti-dumping measures do not cover export of parts so parts might be imported and reassembled into a product) or goes through countries without measures to restrict re-export, the measures are also applicable to the parts or re-export of products. Geographic expansion mainly means that other countries can take anti-dumping measures for an unlimited number of times once a country has taken the same measures. In such cases, if the measure itself is not reasonable, then the expansion of ill effects can be further magnified.

2.1.3 *Alternating or accumulative trade remedy measures*

In the process of applying trade remedy measures, there are also cases in which some countries not only implement a single trade remedy measure but several of them in alternation or accumulation leading to more serious impact. For example, after a trade remedy measure ends, it is immediately replaced by another measure. When safeguard measures expire, anti-dumping rules replace them *etc.*, until the objectives are achieved. Another example is the use of a variety of trade remedy measures on the same product at the same time. It is typical to apply anti-dumping and countervailing measures simultaneously. In addition, there are also cases where anti-dumping rules and safeguard measures are applied simultaneously.

2.2 *The lack of trade remedy rules to some extent*

The aforementioned problem reflects, to a certain extent, flaws in the rules and institutions. Objectively, this creates the opportunity for some trade remedy measures to be used in excess.

2.2.1 *Lack of relevant rules basis to deal with problems*

Due to the lack of proper rules, it was difficult to find a basis from which to manage certain problems, especially the obviously unreasonable ones. For example, the WTO Anti-Dumping Agreement states that anti-dumping measures typically last five years, but in fact some of the anti-dumping measures have lasted for up to 10 years or even nearly 40 years. The five-year time frame has become the exception. This approach deviates from the objective of anti-dumping measures, which is temporary relief rather than long-term protection. It has gone beyond the anti-dumping "relief" function. Generally, it has been criticized on many occasions but the rules have not been successfully challenged.

2.2.2 *Power of discretion gives room for excessive use*

According to the WTO's "Anti-Dumping Agreement" and "Agreement on Subsidies and Countervailing Measures", importing members can take anti-dumping and countervailing measures against injurious dumping and subsidized imports. The agreements specifically state the rules of procedure of dumping, subsidized imports and the entities in the domestic industry which are injured. In the process of using anti-dumping measures and countervailing measures, it is necessary to use substantive and procedural rules for more stringent discipline on importing members. At the same time, these rules also give the authorities in the importing country greater discretion. The "Anti-Dumping Agreement" also states that in the event of anti-dumping disputes, if the WTO panel conducting the dispute proceedings find that there may be more than one acceptable interpretation of the relevant provisions, and the measures of the supervising organization in the importing country are in line with one of the acceptable interpretations, they should be regarded as consistent with the agreement.[3]

2.2.3 *Effect of procedural issues cannot be ignored*

It is noteworthy that procedural issues should be taken into consideration to understand the practical problems that exist in anti-dumping and countervailing measures because they tend to affect the substantive rights and obligations of the interested parties. For example, with regard to the anti-dumping and countervailing duty proceedings, if the investigating agency finds that certain exporters are uncooperative, higher anti-dumping and countervailing duties

---

[3]WTO "Anti-Dumping Agreement" Article 17, paragraph 6, subparagraph 2.

will often be imposed on such vendors than those not identified as uncooperative, even though they do not engage in dumping and subsidized export.

2.2.4 *Areas to improve for dispute settlement mechanism*

There are still gaps in the DSB with regard to disputes and enforcement proceedings. For example, even in a dispute case where rulings have been clarified by the DSB, a similar controversy could happen again. Another example is when the recommendations and rulings of the DSB are largely dependent on the autonomous implementation of the respondent party; some members do not fulfill their autonomous implementation, and even worsen the implementation by making more mistakes or delaying implementation.

2.2.5 *Discriminatory practices give rise to more unreasonable problems*

Some anti-dumping legislations or policies in certain countries distinguish between other countries and discriminate against certain countries. Some of these discriminatory practices are in the substantive aspects while some are in the procedural aspects. One of the most prominent is the approach taken by the US and the EU on non-market economies or countries with economies in transition. By integrating the substantive aspect and procedural aspect closely, these practices are capable of producing different results from the actual situation, and these results are not a violation of their domestic legislation or policy. It can be said that this is likely to be the purpose of their respective domestic legislation or policy or, at the very least, they are condoned by their domestic legislation or policy. The US Government Accountability Office (GAO) did a comparative analysis of the 25 anti-dumping measures that the US took against China and market economies. It pointed out that the average duty rate which was applicable to China was 61% higher than the "all others duty rate" for market economies (98% − 37% = 61%). According to analysis provided by the office, if the US had recognized the full market economy status of China, it would have greatly reduced the imposed anti-dumping duties on the Chinese enterprises.[4] An organization commissioned by the European Commission (EC) to analyze the effect of trade remedy measures of

---

[4] United States Government Accountability Office (GAO), "Eliminating Nonmarket Economy Methodology Would Lower Antidumping Duties for Some Chinese Companies: A Report to Congressional Committees," January 10, 2006; retrieved from http://www.gao.gov/new.items/d06231.pdf.

the EU also believed that the anti-dumping practices by the EC in non-market economies might have resulted in a situation with an analogue country price and higher cost price.[5] In safeguard measure rules, there were also similar problems. Besides the general rules of some members, they created a unique set of rules that were more convenient to use.

In addition, it is worth mentioning that the formulation and implementation of trade remedy rules were often mixed with a lot of political considerations. Trade friction include the ones caused by the use of anti-dumping and other trade protection measures. The cause of the problem is not simply the dumping and non-dumping measures, or fair and unfair trade. Some trade friction emerged due to a deeper level of economic and political reasons. To analyze the insufficience of trade remedy rules and improvement of rules, such a background must be considered.

2.3 *Efforts to clarify and improve trade remedy rules*

2.3.1 *The clarification of rules by the DSB*

The DSB supervises the members and ensures that they follow the rules of trade remedy for the WTO. This is useful to a certain degree as there is control over the misuse of rules and inappropriate discretion among the members. The supervision is through the interpretation of rules on a case-by-case basis, fulfilling the judicial interpretation functions of the WTO agency for the WTO's rules of trade remedy. In recent years, the agency has successfully solved a number of disputes in the field of trade remedy measures and played a very important role in clarifying the rules. According to the news on the WTO website, WTO members had filed a total of 454 trade disputes to the DSB from the time of establishment of the WTO (1995) until the end of 2012, of which 159 were trade remedy cases, accounting for 35% of the total cases. In the 159 cases, there were 11 cases involving both anti-dumping and countervailing disputes (hereinafter referred to as dual disputes). In the remaining 148 cases, the number of disputes with regard to anti-dumping, countervailing and safeguard measures were 88, 19 and 43 cases respectively. The anti-dumping disputes (including anti-dumping disputes as part of dual disputes) in trade remedy disputes accounted for up to 61% of the cases.

---

[5] Cliff Stevenson, *Evaluation of EC Trade Defence Instruments* (London/Brussels: Mayer, Brown, Rowe & Maw LLP, December 2005); retrieved from http://trade.ec.europa.eu/doclib/docs/2006/february/tradoc_127382.pdf, p. 25.

Through hearings conducted by the DSB, many acts of violation against the rules of trade remedies have been addressed. The misunderstanding of WTO trade remedy rules has been clarified among the different members and the misuse of trade remedy rules and inappropriate discretion of some members were corrected. Examples are anti-dumping dispute cases such as the complaint of India against the EC cotton bed linen in early days, and the later disputes that the EU, Japan, Canada, Ecuador, China, Vietnam and other members filed against the US concerning the zero practice.[6] In the early days, the EC used the zeroing practice in the method of "weighted average versus weighted average"[7] to get the dumping margin by comparing the normal value and export price. Specifically, the products were divided into different types and then the dumping margins of different product types were calculated. The negative dumping margins were changed to zero so it was not possible to offset the positive dumping margin of some types of products when the dumping margins were being summed up in the calculation. The result was that the total dumping margins of the products concerned were deliberately increased. The practice of the EC was ruled by DSB to be inconsistent with WTO regulations. Later, the EC (later the EU) abandoned the practice of zeroing and joined the bigger group to start challenging the practice of zeroing in the US. These members not only accused the US of using the zero practice in the method of "weighted average versus weighted average" to calculate the dumping margin, and thus, violating WTO rules, but also accused the US of using the zero approach in the method of

---

[6] The so-called zero practice refers to treating the negative dumping margins as zero dumping margin so it does not offset the positive margin of dumping, therefore the final sum of dumping of the product is generally positive and calculated to be higher than the dumping margin without using the zeroing practice. As a result, the "calculated" dumping products may not be originally considered as dumping products in which dumping exists; if the dumping margin is offset and the product is not "calculated" with a higher dumping margin, that dumping will not increase.

[7] In the process of determining the anti-dumping duty, the dumping margin must be calculated first, meaning that the export price is subtracted from the normal value of the product concerned. In the calculation process, there are three different kinds of calculation method depending on the situations. The first method is "weighted average versus weighted average" (W-W method), referring to the dumping margin that comes from the comparison between weighted average normal value and weighted average export price of different transactions; the second method is "single transaction versus single transaction" (T-T method), referring to the dumping margin that comes from the comparison between single normal value and single export price of different transactions; the third method is "weighted average versus single transaction" (W-T method), referring to the dumping margin that comes from the comparison between weighted average normal value and single export price of different transactions.

"single transaction versus single transaction" to calculate the dumping margin, which was inconsistent with WTO rules.[8] The practice of the US was also ruled by DSB to be inconsistent with WTO regulations.

Other examples were the "Byrd Amendment" dispute, which involved Australia, Brazil, Japan, Korea and other countries against the US, and the complaint filed by China against the US regarding four disputes over the anti-dumping and countervailing measures with repeated appeals. The early "Byrd Amendment" is a typical example of the pursuit of double remedy measures. On the one hand, the US imposed anti-dumping and/or countervailing duties on imported goods, therefore providing adequate protection for domestic manufacturers; on the other hand, the anti-dumping and/or countervailing duties collected were given to the domestic industries with anti-dumping and/or anti-subsidy complaints. This apparent repeated remedy was finally ruled by DSB to be incompatible with WTO rules.[9] With regard to the four anti-dumping and countervailing measures in the US, the background is that China was considered by the US as a non-market economy country. On the one hand, the dumping margins of the Chinese products were calculated and the alleged subsidies were a remedy. On the other hand, the same products with alleged subsidies may also enjoy countervailing measures so the alleged subsidies were "remedied twice". This obvious repeated remedying was eventually ruled by the DSB to be incompatible with WTO rules.[10]

Another example was the launching of investigations by the US on global safeguard measures of more than 610 lines of steel products tariff in 2000 and implementation of the safeguard measures in 2001. The case triggered a strong reaction among the countries and regions in the European community. The EU accused the US of practising a type of trade protectionism and unilateralism,[11]

---

[8] With regard to the meaning of "single transaction versus single transaction" (T-T method), please refer to the earlier footnote.

[9] Refer to WT/DS217. According to the US Continued Dumping and Subsidy Offset Act of 2000, also known as the "Byrd Amendment", the US customs authorities are mandated to distribute to the complaining domestic companies on an annual basis the proceeds of duties levied pursuant to a countervailing duty order or an anti-dumping order and so on.

[10] See the analysis presented in the third section of this chapter.

[11] Refer to EU press release "EU Adopts Temporary Measures to Guard Against Floods Of Steel Imports Resulting from US Protectionism" Brussels, March 27, 2002; "European Commission Calls on US Trade Representative Robert Zoellick to Avoid Unilateral Import Curbs", Letter from EU Ambassador to US Trade Representative Robert Zoellick, Washington, May 3, 2001; and, "We Must All Refrain from Unilateral Action," Speech by Mogens Peter Carl, Director General for Trade, European Commission, OECD High-Level Meeting on Steel, Paris, December 17–18, 2001.

and together with Japan, Korea, China, Norway and Switzerland and other countries, brought the matter up to the DSB. In the end, the US lost the dispute and had to terminate the measure.

In addition, the dispute settlement mechanism itself still needed to be improved. Paragraph 30 in the "Doha Ministerial Declaration" of WTO states that "Members agreed on the clarification and improvement on the 'Rules and Procedures on Dispute Settlement Understanding' (DSU)".

2.3.2 *Multilateral negotiations and efforts in rules clarification and improvement*

(1) Objectives of negotiations

The Doha Round negotiations included trade remedy rules as the topic of negotiation. Paragraph 28 in the "Doha Ministerial Declaration" of WTO authorized the anti-dumping and countervailing rules: "all parties agree to go through negotiations aimed at clarifying and improving the details in 'Anti-Dumping Agreement' and 'Agreement on Subsidies and Countervailing Measures' while keeping the basic concept, principles and effectiveness of these agreements and their aim, and considering the need of developing countries and least developed countries".[12]

(2) Overview of positions

During the anti-dumping rules negotiation, three main positions were formed due to the different interests of members. One of them is the conservative stance held by the US advocating the maintenance of the basic anti-dumping concepts and rules. The emphasis is on ensuring the effectiveness of anti-dumping measures in dealing with unfair trade practices. This stance opposes all substantive changes to the agreement and tries to overthrow the rulings of the DSB panel and Appellate Body through rules negotiation, such as the decision to prohibit zeroing practice and the decision on causal link issue.[13] Countries which hold another, more moderate position, are the EU, Canada, Australia and New Zealand. As their anti-dumping legislation and practice are more advanced, they actively promote their own anti-dumping legislation and

---

[12]"The Doha Declaration Explained," May 17, 2006, retrieved from https://www.wto.org/english/tratop_e/dda_e/dohaexplained_e.htm.

[13]Song Heping (ed.), *Research on the Anti-Dumping and Countervailing Rules in the Doha Round Negotiations* (China: Law Press, 2011), pp. 60–61.

experience on the multilateral level; another one is the "Friends of Anti-dumping"[14] represented by countries such as Japan, Korea and Norway. The team members are mostly export-oriented countries so they take few or even no anti-dumping measures on imported products. Their exports face repeated anti-dumping investigations in the markets of importing countries. They adopt a more aggressive stance and advocate the tightening of anti-dumping disciplines.[15] Most of the members from developing countries actively participated to clarify and improve the activities. They expressed their concern specifically for capacity building, technical support and differential treatment towards developing countries.[16]

During the subsidies and countervailing rules negotiation, three main positions were also formed. The first one is the conservative position held by the US and the EU. They advocate the tightening of subsidies regulations, including the scope expansion of prohibited subsidies (*i.e.* some subsidies which are not prohibited by the existing rules are also proposed to be included in the scope of prohibited subsidies) *etc.*, and support the increased effect on curbing subsidies through countervailing subsidies.[17] The second is the moderate stance, which countries like Australia and New Zealand have adopted, and the last main position refers to the opposition of limitations on the rational use of subsidies as well as the abuse of countervailing rules. Most developing countries expressed dissatisfaction towards the misuse of countervailing measures and restrictions on the rational use of subsidies to promote the development of domestic industries.

(3) Analysis of main issues

Since negotiations began in February 2002, the members have submitted a total of more than 400 proposals providing evaluation and suggestions to

---

[14] Known as "Friends of Anti-Dumping", the key members include 15 WTO members like Japan, Korea, Chinese Hong Kong, Brazil, Chile, Norway and Switzerland. Japan is the lead member of this team.

[15] Import and Export Fair Trade Bureau in the Ministry of Commerce, *Guide in Dealing with Foreign Trade Remedy Investigations* (China: China Commerce and Trade Press, 2009), pp. 6–7.

[16] During the rules negotiations, China also expressed its position to "clarify and improve the rules, strengthen discipline, prevent abuse, think of the interests of all parties". Refer to the third section of this chapter for more information.

[17] Even though they are considered as conservatives during the countervailing rules negotiations, the positions of the EU and the US are not the same. Refer to Song Heping (ed.) *Research on the Anti-dumping and Countervailing Rules in the Doha Round Negotiations* (China: Law Press, 2011), p. 62.

improve the "Anti-Dumping Agreement" and "Agreement on Subsidies and Countervailing Measures". The content covered a large number of substantive and procedural provisions of anti-dumping, and part of the substantive provisions of subsidies and countervailing subsidies. The WTO rules negotiating group chairman distributed three consolidated texts respectively on November 30, 2007, December 19, 2008 and April 21, 2011. Among the many proposals, the prohibition of zeroing in anti-dumping, the anti-dumping sunset review, anti-circumvention, transparency and procedural fairness, the review mechanism, the scope of prohibited subsidies, price controls of goods and services, external benchmark in calculation of subsidies, subsidy-allocation and other issues were the focus of various members.

(i) Issue on the prohibition of zeroing

As the zeroing practice specifically adjusts the negative dumping margin of investigated products to zero, it cannot offset the positive dumping margin. Therefore, the calculated dumping margin of the products has been deliberately increased. In the aforementioned WTO dispute case, zeroing practices by the members have been ruled as being inconsistent with WTO rules. If an agreement on the prohibition of zeroing practice can be reached, it will help ease the effect of anti-dumping measures. The measures should be used as "remedies" and they will help maintain the interpretation and ruling authority of the DSB. Thus, many push for such practices to be banned. Japan and members of the "Friends of Anti-dumping" alliance, and most of the other WTO members advocate or endorse the prohibition of zeroing. In the proposals and negotiations, the US resolutely opposed the prohibition of zeroing. On the contrary, it proposed to legitimize zeroing. The chairman consolidated the first draft which permits some zeroing, stating some situations where the practice should be allowed. However, the majority of members strongly opposed his views. In the chairman's second and third drafts, the parts of the content that permitted zeroing were labelled as content that members disagreed on.

(ii) Issue on the anti-dumping sunset review

Although the "Anti-Dumping Agreement" states that the period of implementation for anti-dumping measures is usually five years, the actual practice is that the anti-dumping measures are often maintained after the five-year period through the sunset review. The majority of the implementation periods is more than five years, some even decades (known as "the sun never sets"). The proposal to make an anti-dumping measure expire in due time through clarifying and strengthening the rules received more and more support. Canada, Japan, "Friends of Anti-Dumping", and China *etc.* proposed to restrict investigative bodies from initiating a sunset review investigation without the request of the applicant. They advocated the determination of a definite maximum time period for anti-dumping measures. In the first draft of the consolidated text of the chairman, parts of these proposals to strengthen the disciplines of sunset review were accepted, while allowing investigations to start quickly and temporary anti-dumping measures to be taken promptly after the original anti-dumping measures ended. In the second and third drafts of the chairman, the sunset review was labelled as content that members could not agree on.

(iii) Issue on anti-circumvention

Neither an informal anti-circumvention group nor WTO's rules negotiation team has come to an agreement on anti-circumvention. There is no clear definition for "circumvention" or "anti-circumvention". In the first draft, the chairman added a new, special anti-circumvention provision in the consolidated text. Under this provision, if investigations indicate that imported products with minor changes, products parts under investigation and products assembled in a third country have circumvented anti-dumping duties, the same anti-dumping duties can be applied to these imported products. Many members, especially the developing countries, opposed this new provision. Some members were concerned that this provision would lead to uncertainty and misuse of anti-dumping measures. In the second and third drafts, the chairman labelled the anti-circumvention content as content that members could not agree on.

(iv) Issues on anti-dumping transparency and procedural fairness

Members generally agreed to improve transparency and procedural fairness. However, many members felt that in considering the appropriateness of certain modifications, it was also very important to take into account the resource constraints of developing countries.

(v) Issue on the review mechanism of anti-dumping policy practices

In the first draft of the chairman's text, an annex with special provisions for the review mechanism of anti-dumping policy practice was added. This mechanism received strong support from many members. They opined that it was an important tool to improve transparency and provide technical support, and suggested enhancing it further. However, some members worried that it would increase the burden, especially for developing countries.

(vi) Issues on subsidies and countervailing

The chairman's text did not include the expansion of scope of prohibited subsidies, but included content that members greatly differed on, such as the specificity of subsidies for price regulated goods or services (*i.e.* financial contribution), the external benchmark in subsidy calculation and subsidy allocation *etc*. For example, with regard to the specificity of subsidies for the price regulated goods or services, a provision allowing "enterprise(s) which did not get subsidies" as a determining specificity consideration was added in the text of the chairman. The proposed change would completely change the existing specificity rule in the "Agreement on Subsidies and Countervailing". Under the existing rules, the presence of specificity in granting subsidies was determined by whether a group of enterprises received subsidies and not whether a few did not. However, this rule was changed by the chairman's text, allowing the "enterprise(s) which did not get subsidies" as a determining specificity consideration. This is to say if there were enterprise(s), such as two companies, which could not obtain subsidies, the subsidies given to all other companies could be considered as specificity subsidies. As a result, it is common to have financial contribution "to regulate the prices of goods or services". As there were individual enterprises which did not get the financial contribution, the financial contribution provided became one with "specificity". Therefore, the range of subsidies with specificity has expanded and the scope of countervailing has also increased accordingly.

It is worth noting that when rules negotiations were started 10 years ago, the WTO was not the one to start safeguard rules negotiation. That was the time when the US carried out the investigations for global safeguard measures on steel products. In the decade of rules negotiations, the use of safeguards by developed countries has dropped continuously. During this period, the disputes on safeguard measures that occurred basically ended with the users losing. In recent years, developing countries have become the main users of safeguard measures in the world. To this end, members like the US founded the "Friends of the Safeguards Procedures" group[18] in 2012 and expressed their concern at the WTO Safeguards Committee on October 22, 2012 in a regular session in autumn. Their concerns were the transparency and procedures of safeguards measures investigations. The US represents the "Friends of Safeguards" group to say that the members have made progress in the application of safeguards in

---

[18] "Friends of the Safeguards Procedures", also known as FSP, was established by 10 WTO members: Australia, Canada, the EU, Japan, Korea, New Zealand, Norway, Chinese Taipei, Singapore and the US.

the past few years and accordingly, no dispute settlement procedures was called in this regard. However, the increase of safeguards in the recent years is worth noting. Members should work together to address the systemic concern on safeguards procedures.[19]

2.3.3 *Changing trends in rules at the regional and national levels*

Although there have been disruptions to the WTO's clarification and improvements of rules, changes to rules have taken place frequently at regional and national levels. Many of the views expressed at multilateral rules negotiations are reflected on these levels and have been adopted and included among the changes made to relevant rules.

(1) Changes at the regional level

As a highly integrated economic area, the EU also activated trade remedy mechanisms. After amendments were made to the EU trade relief laws and regulations at the Uruguay Round negotiations, the laws and regulations have remained largely unchanged for more than 16 years. The EU believes that the world economic environment has changed greatly over the past 10 years and European companies are facing an economic environment that is increasingly strewn with difficulties. As such, in October 2011, the EU Commission decided to launch trade remedy modernization reviews to ensure the promotion of fair trade based on global trade liberalization, and to adapt EU trade remedy mechanisms to the new challenges brought about by the current international economic environment, keep up with the times and remain productive. On April 10, 2013, the EU Commission proposed amendments to legislation and relevant measures in order to modernize trade remedy mechanisms. The Commission's proposal for trade remedy modernization reforms included suggested amendments to legislation, guidelines for trade remedy investigation procedures and relevant non-legislative items.

The proposed legislative amendments made by the EU Commission include the following areas: First, increase the predictability of trade remedy measures by giving two weeks' advanced notice before the implementation of

---

[19]Refer to World Trade Organization, "'Friends of Safeguards' Urge More Transparency and Due Process in Investigations", May 9, 2013, retrieved from http://www.wto.org/english/news_e/news12_e/safe_22oct12_e.htm.

any provisional anti-dumping or countervailing measures. Second, if a trade remedy measure is reckoned, after a sunset review, to have expired after five years and no longer needs to be kept, the levies collected during the sunset review will be refunded. Third, where counter-threats exist, to protect European companies, the EU Commission may initiate trade remedy investigations in the absence of intra-industry complaints. Fourth, in the event of other partners using unfair trade subsidies or structural distortions caused to the raw materials market *etc.*, the EU may abandon its lesser duty rules. These proposals made by the EU Commission to modify legislation must be approved by the European Parliament and all EU member states in order to take effect. It is yet unknown whether the proposals will ultimately be adopted.

Relevant regional free trade negotiations also discussed the changing of trade remedy rules. Some advocated that content had to be more in-depth than the WTO trade remedy rules, partially achieving what some members advocated at multilateral rules negotiations. For example, the European Free Trade Association (EFTA) and Ukraine signed a free trade agreement in 2010 where both parties agreed to drop anti-dumping measures on the other party's products; and when conditions permitted, safeguard measures against the other party's products would be removed. The anti-dumping clause in the agreement reflects that the contracting parties do not wish to constrain bilateral trade with anti-dumping measures. This approach is consistent with the stance of free trade, opposition of anti-dumping or tightening of anti-dumping disciplines advocated among EFTA members and their role as members of the anti-dumping negotiating group on rules. Their agreement on safeguard measures reflects that contracting parties wish to minimize restrictions on bilateral trade due to safeguard measures. If conditions permit, the application of safeguard measures will simply be excluded. Another example is the free trade agreement signed by Australia and Malaysia in 2012. Both countries maintained their existing practices regarding the determination of dumping margin. Both negative and positive dumping margins were calculated and zero margins were not allowed, whichever dumping margin determination methodology was used. This agreement was consistent with the views against zero practice expressed by the majority of members in the WTO rules negotiations.

(2) Changes at the national level

Changes in rules occurred more frequently at the level of individual nations. According to statistics from the WTO Secretariat, from January 1, 2015 to February 5, 2015, the WTO members submitted a total of 167 legislative notifications to the WTO, among which 59 were on anti-dumping legislation, 51 were about subsidies and countervailing legislation and 57 were notifications about safeguard measures. The intensity of changes in rules is relatively greater. Some of the changes were aimed at clarifying and improving the rules to reduce unnecessary restrictions on trade. For example, Peru passed legislation to remove the anti-dumping provisions on non-market economies, indicating that all WTO members were market economies. This was really commendable, as it required political courage and boldness on Peru's part. Another example is New Zealand — it amended anti-dumping laws and made special provisions for refunding anti-dumping duties that had exceeded the dumping margins.

Other changes in rules were aimed at deregulation and promoting trade remedy measures. For example, the US launched a campaign to strengthen trade enforcement and set up a trade enforcement center. At the same time, amended legislation approving countervailing measures for non-market economies was passed in an extremely short amount of time. The US Department of Commerce announced 14 recommendations to strengthen trade remedy measures in 2010, including the "tightening of rules against enterprises from non-market economies receiving separate rate treatment". These recommendations strengthened the US' practices and rules on anti-dumping, anti-subsidy investigations, and in fact, favored anti-dumping rates and countervailing duties, increasing the burdens of respondents, increasing the difficulty of importing for importers and distributors, the time constraints of anti-dumping and countervailing measures for exporters *etc.*, and many of these were designed specifically against non-market economies. The US Department of Commerce claims that "unfair trade practices" by foreign governments and enterprises undermined the competitiveness of US companies, and to double exports, there was an urgent need to strengthen the effectiveness of US trade protection measures in many areas.

In addition, there are some rule changes designed to improve the operational efficiency of the trade remedy system. For example, in 2011, Australia announced the launch of the largest reform of the current trade remedy regime in the past decade. Australian officials noted that the existing Australian trade remedy system was not favorable for its domestic industry, especially SMEs, to take anti-dumping actions. This reform would focus on building a more modern, more rigorous and more effective anti-dumping system to change the above-mentioned situation. The WTO recognized that the unfair trade practices were major hazards, thus, they established the trade remedy system and the WTO members should ensure that unfair trade practices were effectively dealt with.[20] The specific measures cover five major areas including improving time efficiency.[21]

2.3.4 *Analysis and prospects of the evolution of rules*

The WTO began anti-dumping, subsidies and countervailing rules negotiations in 2002. The last rule negotiation discussion was held in the autumn of 2012 at the regular meeting between the WTO Anti-Dumping Committee and Committee on Subsidies and Countervailing Measures. The discussion has lasted 10 years as the scope of relevant trade remedy rules is extremely broad and content covered has been thorough such that members are able to clearly reflect and exchange their views and positions. There has always been a clash between those who advocate the tightening of trade remedy rules and those who wish to intensify trade remedy measures. The inherent problems and possible room for improvement are very obvious. As mentioned earlier, many members concurred with and welcomed the clarification and improvements to rules and the opposition of abuse of trade remedy measures, and some good trends have arisen in rules negotiations. For example, members have reached a common understanding on a number of related issues, a relatively wide range of response has also been collected on transparency and due process, the review mechanism that monitors members' trade remedy policies and practices has also creatively

---

[20] Refer to Hon Brendan O'Connor MP's media release, "*Government Combats Dumping and Helps Support Local Jobs*," June 22, 2011, retrieved from https://pk.awu.net.au/sites/pk.awu.net.au/files/government_combats_dumping_and_helps_support_local_jobs.pdf.

[21] The other four areas are as follows. (1) Improving the executive effectiveness of measures implemented including increasing resources, strengthening monitoring of implementation; combating the circumvention of anti-dumping duties. (2) Improving the decision-making process such as greater use of trade and industry experts; coming up with a more efficient application process, providing more resources to support domestic industry applications; clearer assessment of industrial damage factors; being flexible on time periods for complex cases. (3) Making it more convenient for the domestic industry to use the anti-dumping system including new specialized jobs, helping SMEs and mid- and downstream manufacturers in the investigation process; enhancing openness of imports and subsidies data, clearly stating application data requirements; clarify the range of stakeholders, relevant industry associations, trade unions and downstream industries included in anti-dumping investigations; requesting for more flexibility for relevant stakeholders in review investigations. (4) Improving coordination with other countries including conducting periodic reviews of the anti-dumping practices and decision-making processes of other countries; supporting Australian domestic industries in countering various subsidizing actions.

raised and received positive creative responses *etc.* Despite so, there is still great difficulty ahead in order to clarify and improve rules, and prevent the abuse of trade remedy measures.

At the regional and national level, some countries and regions achieved freer trade arrangements among regional members through FTA negotiations, and mutually excluded or tightened the application of trade remedies; some countries and regions improved upon their own rules to provide a more equitable environment for fair competition among different stakeholders; some rule changes focused on transparency and fairness of procedures, making corresponding substantive and procedural arrangements to protect the respective rights of stakeholders. At the same time, many of the rules transformations were mainly focused on strengthening trade enforcement, intensifying the crackdown on alleged unfair trade practices, including expanding the scope of alleged unfair trade practices, rarely involving tightened trade remedy rules and preventing the abuse of trade remedy rules *etc.* In a way, this reflected the tendency of some countries and regions to use trade remedy measures as a means to ease the pressure on the domestic industry since the financial crisis. However, the rule changes that were made during the crisis with trade protectionist tendencies were also very dangerous. Due to the rigid nature of rules, it would be difficult to adjust if rules had to be amended again after the crisis.

The current situation and trends show the following: (1) with regard to clarifying and improving rules with a view to being against the abuse of trade remedy measures and promote trade liberalization, there are already some actions taken but there is room for further work; (2) it is necessary and important to change rules at the multilateral and regional levels. If progress can be made in terms of clarifying and improving rules at the multilateral and regional levels, it will help reduce abuse of trade remedy measures and also facilitate the regulation and restriction of rules changes and trade remedy practices; and (3) there is considerable difficulty and resistance in the improvement of rules and prevention of abuse of trade remedy measures — some current activities have changed the rules and left room for trade protectionism, which in turn have resulted in the accumulation of negative effects.

3 China and Trade Remedy Rules

China has always advocated free trade, opposed trade protectionism, spoken against the abuse of trade remedy measures and actively participated in the development and improvement of rules at the WTO and G20 Summits as well as on other occasions. As a major user and party involved in trade remedy measures, China also needs to consider how to improve and better apply the relevant trade remedy rules in the future.

3.1 *China's practices in trade remedy rules*

Upon joining the WTO, China has truly become a maker of multilateral trade rules and user of multilateral mechanisms, and can make use of trade remedy rules to reasonably protect domestic industries. At the same time, it can improve the external regulatory environment and safeguard the rights and interests of export enterprises as far as possible.

3.1.1 *Becoming a rule-maker and a mechanisms user*

After becoming a WTO member, China simultaneously became a rule-maker in multilateral trade and played its role in promoting the comprehensive and continual development of multilateral trade rules. After joining the WTO, China could make use of the multilateral mechanism to upkeep rules and rights, for example, successfully lodging a complaint against US and EU trade remedy measures at the DSB; China could also monitor the unreasonable practices of other members and so on through the various committees of trade remedies measures and their regular meetings. In addition, because of the multilateral mechanisms, China obtained a new way to properly resolve conflicts with other members, avoiding the escalation of conflicts or taking unilateral confronting actions.

3.1.2 *Using rules to reasonably protect domestic industries*

After China joined the WTO, like other WTO members, it applied a unified set of trade remedy rules, conducted trade remedy investigations and applied trade remedy measures against imported products. Since joining the WTO, China has been prohibited or restricted from unilaterally using the traditional restrictive measures, such as quotas, against the imported products as before. Therefore, China has to resort to trade remedies to protect its domestic industries against imports while opening up its markets. China, following the WTO's trade remedy rules, constantly improves upon the relevant domestic legislation and mechanisms, and has achieved good results by reasonably using trade remedy measures to protect domestic industries. According to statistics, from the time anti-dumping investigations were first launched in 1997 until the end of 2012, 207 trade remedy investigations were launched by China — including 200 cases of anti-dumping, six on countervailing, and one regarding safeguard measures. Among them, the vast majority (177) of the trade remedy investigations were initiated after China joined the WTO.

3.1.3 *Changing the rule environment to safeguard export interests*

China's participation in the WTO negotiations is itself an excellent opportunity and platform for it to change previously unfavorable rule environment. The results of negotiations also show that China's overall external trade and economic regulatory environment has greatly improved. A typical example is the Section 301 that the US has persistently used against China,[22] and since China joined the WTO, the original unilateral advantage that the section had was replaced by DSB multilateral deals. In 2010, the US initiated Section 301 investigations on China's new energy policy measures and the conclusions of the investigation revealed that the subsidy policies on wind energy promulgated by a particular department in China were inconsistent with the WTO rules. In such a case, the US could not take unilateral retaliatory action against the policy and thus they resorted to lodging a complaint with DSB. In the end, the two sides resolved the dispute by consulting and under the dispute settlement mechanism.

It can be said that the outcome of negotiations specific to anti-dumping, countervailing and safeguard regulations mentioned in this chapter show that China is continually working towards being free from the burden of rules historically set by the US, EU and other developed nations and regions, and eventually achieving complete freedom. It is commonly understood that before China joined the WTO, the EU and the US had set up unilateral safeguard clauses, special textile limitations and non-market economic provisions for anti-dumping. Even though negotiations had not been able to completely abolish these clauses, China has set certain limitations in their Protocol of Accession and Working Group Report with regard to these provisions. Firstly, all three provisions were set a maximum legitimate period, among which special textile provisions expired in 2008 and special safeguard provisions lapsed in the end of 2013, and anti-dumping non-market economic provisions are set for 15 years, expiring at the end of 2016. Secondly, the specific content of the provisions were modified to include a number of constraints, restricting the members to some extent. Apart from some remaining issues in these three

---

[22] Section 301 refers to the relevant US legislation which allows the investigation of foreign trade barriers and appropriate measures to be taken. The name is derived from Section 301 of the "United States Trade Act of 1974". At present, the main legal provisions of the US Section 301 investigations are the "Section 301 provisions" amended after the "US Trade Agreement Act of 1979", "Trade and Tariff Act of 1984" and "1988 Omnibus Trade and Competitiveness Act", including the General 301, Special 301 and Super 301.

major areas, the China exports face essentially the same external trade remedy rules as other WTO members.

Comparing the time before and after China joined the WTO in 2001, there has undoubtedly been a great improvement in the Chinese exports' trade remedy rules environment, even if some discriminatory elements were still temporarily in effect. When these discriminatory content have been eliminated, Chinese exports will face an even better environment for trade remedy rules.

3.2 *Active participation in clarifying and improving rules*

Since joining the WTO, China has advocated free trade, opposed the abuse of trade remedy measures and taken various measures in different areas, being of one mind with other relevant members and working towards the further clarification and improvement of rules to create a better regulatory environment.

3.2.1 *Doha round negotiations*

China actively participates in the Doha Round multilateral rules negotiations and its negotiation capabilities and power have continually improved. China has gradually transited from a "passive recipient of rules" to being able to "push for rules to be made" and a member with important influence.[23] In the process, China has strived for "the clarification and improvement of rules, strengthened discipline, abuse prevention, and the reflection of all parties' interests" so as to "curb trade protectionism and achieve the goal of a fair international trade environment".[24]

China has successively submitted nearly 20 proposals, six working papers and more than 30 meeting addresses. With regard to anti-dumping, China has submitted or jointly submitted with other members, proposals to prohibit zeroing, reduce the implementation period of anti-dumping measures, and oppose anti-circumvention provisions so as to make recommendations for tightening anti-dumping regulations, enhancing the transparency of

---

[23] Refer to Zhou Xiaoyan, "The 'Core Negotiation Rights' China Earned A Decade after 'Joining the WTO' – A Series of Interviews in commemoration of China's Tenth Year of Accession to the WTO," retrieved from http://china.trade2cn.com/dataservice/economy/110831130917CNG.html.

[24] Refer to "Commercial Achievements since 16th National Congress of Communist Party of China, Series XII: Proper Handling of Trade Frictions and Effective Use of Trade Remedies," May 18, 2012, retrieved from http://www.mofcom.gov.on/aarticle/ae/ai/201211/20121108423879.html.

anti-dumping investigations, and preventing the abuse of anti-dumping measures. In terms of countervailing measures, China has submitted proposals against "regulated price" provisions, proposals on the prevention of abuse of "external benchmarks", proposals related to enhancing "negotiations before case-filing", preventing the abuse of "obtaining adverse facts" approaches as well as proposals on managing new subsidy programs, so as to limit the discretionary power of investigating authorities. The Chairman and members of the Negotiating Group on Rules have been paying much attention to China's stance and the content of certain proposals such as that of reducing the implementation period of anti-dumping measures *etc.* has been included in the Chairperson's consolidated reports.

3.2.2 *Regional trade agreement negotiations*

In regional trade agreement negotiations, China drafted elaborate negotiation plans and set up proper trade remedy provisions for distinct trade partners according to their respective trade characteristics and industrial competitiveness so as to effectively protect the domestic industry and avoid the abuse of trade remedy measures by trade partners, causing hindrances in the trade liberalization process.[25] For example, New Zealand, Korea, Iceland, Switzerland and ASEAN countries all recognize China's status as a full market economy, which has resulted in China's exports facing an anti-dumping rules environment that had further improved. Also, to facilitate and quicken the formation of a free trade agreement with New Zealand while easing the worries and concerns the domestic dairy industry has with regard to opening up the market, China and New Zealand set up a special dairy safeguard mechanism in their free trade agreement that played a relevant and practical role.

China has also set up bilateral safeguard clauses with free trade partners to prevent any party's domestic industries from being threatened or seriously injured by a surge in imports due to the free trade agreements. These safeguard clauses include the remedial measures such as suspending the decrease in tariffs or increasing the tariffs to the levels enjoyed by MFNs. These remedial measures have reassured the contracting parties. All of the above played a significant role in helping China and their free trade partners establish mutually open markets. They also provided some assurance for the early conclusion of other content areas in free trade agreements.

---

[25] *Ibid*, 239.

3.2.3 *Tracking and monitoring*

Tracking and monitoring the rules and practices of other countries is part of the daily work of Chinese government-related agencies. It is a long-term, arduous and extremely important job. Staying updated on the development of economic and trade-related laws and regulations, and evaluating and discussing the issues raised aids in preventing new, unfavorable rules from being established. Dealing with them on a case-by-case basis through active legal defense and negotiations, and maintaining pressure on investigating state authorities in terms of rules applications also helps to prevent rules from being abused. The combined, tireless efforts of industry and enterprises have also reaped good results and there are plenty of examples to show. For example, in cases such as when the US implemented double remedies on China's steel wire deckings and the relevant industries and enterprises actively responded by defending themselves with specific facts, data and rules and obtained a positive, no-injury ruling. Another example was a case initiated by Canada with regard to combined anti-dumping and countervailing investigations on certain copper pipe fittings. An enterprise whose annual export volume was lower than USD100,000 spent much more than that amount in hiring a lawyer to appeal the case and provided a defense backed with specific facts and data. In the end, the enterprise won the case with the ruling being a reduction of anti-dumping and countervailing duties to zero. In the province where this enterprise was, there were a total of 23 government departments that participated in the government's response towards countervailing measures and the company's initiative moved the hearts of the departments' representatives. When the general manager of the company knew that so many departments had responded and actively helped his enterprise in responding to the countervailing measure, he was very touched. Presently, the general manager has expressed that the company has developed rapidly in recent years and after responding to the trial and subsequent investigations in the years that followed, his understanding of anti-dumping and countervailing measures and awareness of how to protect personal interests according to the rules have deepened.

3.2.4 *Litigation*

After joining the WTO, China frequently went through the DSB to resolve trade remedy disputes, participating in the "game playing of rules", and by applying existing rules, not only did China clarify a number of issues with the rules, they also made the EU and the US amend their irrational domestic rules and practices, urged other countries to comply with the rules and promoted rule optimization. Among the cases settled by the DSB, the classic examples are the four double remedies cases China raised against the US (Case no. DS379) and the steel fastener anti-dumping measures case raised against the EU (Case no. DS397).

In case DS379, the DSB found that the US Department of Commerce's sole criterion for determining "public body" was government control, and thus classified Chinese state-owned enterprises as "public bodies". This was incompatible with US obligations under the WTO's "Agreement on Subsidies and Countervailing Measures". Enterprises ought to be endowed with government functions to be categorized as "public bodies". It was found that the US Department of Commerce, in taking both countervailing and anti-dumping measures against Chinese products while treating China as non-market economy, provided double remedies to US domestic industry, as such inappropriate countervailing duties were imposed on Chinese products and this was incompatible with the WTO rules.

In the D397 case, the DSB found that Article XV in the WTO Accession Protocol stated special rules for domestic prices and costs in determining price comparability, and was not without limitations or exceptions. The clause was only suitable for determining normal values and did not grant members the authority to give differential treatment to China in other areas. It also did not confirm that China was a non-market economy. Section 9(5) of "The EU Anti-Dumping rules" presupposed that all exporters and producers from non-market economies constituted a single entity together with their country, thus, to obtain separate duty rate, exporters had to bear the responsibility of proving that they satisfied the conditions in Section 9(5). Such a presumption lacked legal basis and was different from the general obligations set by Articles 6.10 and 9.2 of the "Anti-Dumping Agreement" (Articles 6.10 and 9.2 both required investigating authorities to provide separate duty rate for exporters and manufacturers, respectively). There was no basis for such a presumption in the WTO protocol as well.

Apart from using the multilateral dispute settlement mechanism, Chinese companies also frequently challenged the accusing country's domestic judicial proceedings with regard to their unreasonable rules and practices. The Chinese government also participated in the proceedings as *amicus curiae* or a third party in some cases. Typical cases included the US off-the-road tires double remedies case and the EU glyphosate anti-dumping case and other judicial cases.[26]

---

[26] For more details on cases, please browse the Ministry of Commerce website at http://english. mofcom.gov.cn.

For the earlier case, on December 19, 2011, the US Federal Circuit Court of Appeals found that in 1986, the Court of Appeal had made a clear decision in the case of Georgetown Steel that countervailing duties were not applicable to non-market economies and the US Congress had already approved this decision even when the "US Trade Law" was amended in 1988 and again in 1994. Therefore, countervailing duties should not be imposed on non-market economies. Before this, the US Court of International Trade had arrived at a verdict on this case on September 18, 2009, determining that the US Department of Commerce's practice of double remedies was likely to result in the double counting of tariffs, which was unreasonable. In the latter case, on June 17, 2009, the European Court of First Instance ruled that the European Commission's refusal to recognize the status of a Chinese enterprise's market economy was in violation of EU law.

3.3 *Related issues and thoughts*

There are two aspects to the trade remedy rules environment for China. One has to do with protecting the interests of the domestic industry, while the other aspect is related to the rules environment faced by exports. Both aspects could be improved and are worthy of further consideration.

3.3.1 *Rules environment for safeguarding the interests of domestic industries*

As mentioned above, after joining the WTO, trade remedy rules provided a basis for China to reasonably protect its domestic industries. After more than a decade of development, China has already established its own trade remedy laws and regulatory system as a well as a trade remedy investigation team. It can be said to be quite capable of handling this set of rules skillfully. In the future, three areas have to be seriously looked into.

(1) Stance on improving trade remedy rules

In multilateral rules negotiations, China adheres to "the clarification and improvement of rules, strengthened discipline, prevention of abuse, and reflection of the interests of all parties" and aims to "curb trade protectionism and strive for a fair international trading environment". This is China's stance on improving rules and maintaining export interests, as well as its position on improving rules to safeguard interests of domestic industries. This means that in multilateral rules negotiations, China hopes for more reasonable trade remedy rules for imported products as well as the prevention of abuse.

(2) Practical issues with the application of trade remedy rules

After a decade of development, China's investigative bodies have accumulated a wealth of experience in trade remedy investigations. Despite this, the relevant WTO members have also raised certain doubts with regard to the relevant practices of China's investigative bodies in specific case investigations, including issues of compliance. From the time of China's accession to the WTO until the end of 2012, the WTO members have filed 30 disputes against China, seven of which were about China's trade remedy measures, and relevant complaints were raised regarding the disclosure of information, determination of anti-dumping duties and others. The DSB has also ruled that some Chinese practices were inconsistent with the WTO trade remedy rules.

(3) Establishing trade remedy provisions in FTAs to protect domestic industries

The importance of trade remedy provisions in FTA negotiations is self-evident. Therefore, trade remedy provisions are often a key area that parties pay attention to so as to reach an FTA agreement as soon as possible. However, arrangements in FTA benefit some industries while hurting others, and all trade remedy provisions are applicable to only specific exports or imports. It is impossible to adjust the interests and please all players from all industries. As such, it can be said that the role the trade remedy provisions may play in facilitating the smooth implementation of FTA arrangements is still limited or cannot be expected to be greater.

For the two issues above, the relevant Chinese government, in particular the trade remedy investigations team, needs to continue to strengthen their awareness of the rules, deepen understanding, grasp and enhance their abilities to apply the rules, maintain an objective and fair attitude towards trade remedy investigations, and decide on rulings in accordance with regulations; for the latter issue, apart from establishing reasonable trade remedy provisions in FTAs, China probably also needs to consider the issue of balancing the various interests of domestic industries — for example, researching and learning more about the feasibility of the US Trade Adjustment Assistance System while keeping compatible with WTO rules. In addition, while safeguarding interests using rules, domestic industries need to carefully consider how to further strengthen their competitiveness against foreign imports.

3.3.2 *Rules environment faced by exports*

As mentioned earlier, when the special safeguard clause and non-market economy provisions lapse at the end of 2013 and end of 2016 respectively, it is expected that Chinese exports will face a trade remedy rules environment that is essentially no different from that faced by other WTO members, *i.e.* the application of rules will be of universal nature. Of course, attention should still be paid to two aspects in the process of applying universal rules. One being whether the situation is in fact disadvantageous for China, and the other being whether there is an improper or wrong interpretation of general rules. The problems are mostly related to the fields of anti-dumping and countervailing duties.

(1) Anti-dumping issues

It must be noted whether analogue country and "one country, one duty" practices will be continued to some degree and in certain areas. Take the EU for example, in the determination of normal value in accordance with EU laws, enterprises in market economies may face a problem with normal values not being entirely exporter's domestic prices in particular market situation. The costs of some of the constituent elements may be replaced by other representative market prices. People often term the representative market prices used in determining normal value as substitute cost.[27] In determining duty rates, the EU modified regulations after losing its appeal against China's complaint with regard to anti-dumping in the case of fasteners, such that duty rates were determined separately for each supplier; at the same time, they stated that the factors that ought to be considered in determining the duty rates include the structural or business relationship between suppliers and the country or between suppliers, whether the country controls or substantially influences the price or yield of certain exports, as well as the economic structure of the supplying country. Among these, "the economic structure of the supplying country" was the sole factor considered for separate duty rate, and in practical application, this could make it harder for companies to get a separate rate, thus there is the risk of a "one country, one duty" situation arising. Moreover, it is claimed that the WTO's universally applied trade remedy rules are the basis of these practices.

(2) Countervailing issues

This is mainly related to double remedies, expansion of the scope of those who supply the subsidy, increased scope of specific subsidies, rise in margin of subsidies

---

[27] Besides the EU, Australia, Peru and other countries also practice this.

and the use of adverse facts in investigation and determination procedures *etc.* When the anti-dumping non-market economy provisions expire, double remedy issues will mainly arise from the use of substitute costs. Using substitute costs to determine the costs of elements of companies involved in anti-dumping cases could also lead to double remedy provided by anti-dumping and countervailing. The expansion of the scope of those who supply the subsidy mainly affects the determination of public bodies such as the inclusion of Chinese state-owned commercial banks and state-owned enterprises, and even private companies (such as certain private enterprisc within which there is a party organization) into the scope of public bodies.

The main problem with the increased scope of specific subsidies is that of adopting a liberal scale to determine specificity, such that alleged subsidies that were originally not specific subsidies were now classified as having specificity. The rise in the margin of subsidies came about because of the cumulative growth in subsidies margin due to the enlarged scope of the subsidizing bodies and specific subsidies, and increased subsidy rates due to the use of external benchmark. This was an additional implementation of remedial measures on top of double remedies. Similarly, these issues exist also allegedly because the investigating bodies apply the WTO's general rules. In the area of multilateral development, unilateral policies and the trend of practices becoming more multilateral are worthy of attention. In particular, the most obvious problems are how to determine specificity and benefit thereby conferred in providing input with regulated price. If the relevant proposals become rules, it means that it would be easier to determine specificity of subsidies, inferring that more price-regulated goods or services would be identified as specific subsidies. External benchmarks that were treated as exceptions in the past would also likely be frequently used in the WTO countervailing rules system.

For this reason, it is necessary that the relevant parties enhance their awareness and knowledge of rules, and create a good regulatory environment safeguarding rules interests in multilateral and regional rules establishments and the application of related mechanisms. In particular, it is essential that trade remedy rules adaptation and convergence be conducted well after the market economy status provision expires, such that as China moves from a special status to a general position, they strive to enjoy the same set of rules and common treatment not just formally but in practice. Of course, the expiration of the provision does not mean that the problems that China's exports face currently will be resolved all at once.

At the same time, China also needs to reflect and examine the internal factors that led to trade frictions, including the flaws in the relevant institutional mechanisms, the inadequacy of market resource allocation, overcapacity in certain industries, over-reliance of some industries on the export market, the poor management of some enterprises *etc.* so as to rationally evaluate and handle trade frictions. It also needs to put in the utmost effort to nip the problem at the bud, and reduce and avoid trade frictions.

China must additionally make precise judgments and give careful thought to the major concerns reflected by overseas counterparts in terms of rules design and practical action. In reality, the anti-dumping "analogue country" practices, determination of public bodies and use of external benchmarks in countervailing issues, as well as the multilateral proceedings and monitoring taken against China's subsidy policies and measures (including counter-notifying the WTO, regular meetings of the WTO Committee on Subsidies and Countervailing *etc.*) all reflect concern regarding the Chinese government's relationship with the market. There are fears that the Chinese government will continue to intervene excessively with the market, distort the allocation of resources and that some enterprises (mainly state-owned enterprises) will continue to obtain unfair competitive advantages. Some of these concerns are not groundless. For example, since Chinese state-owned commercial banks are required by law to implement the national industrial policy, the US Department of Commerce finds that these banks thus constitute as public bodies, *i.e.* subsidy providers in countervailing measures. In litigation proceedings, the DSB also ruled that this call made by the US was not inconsistent with the relevant provisions of the WTO "Agreement on Subsidies and Countervailing Measures". Certain subsidies-related policies and measures introduced by the Chinese government, especially some local governments, had also been highlighted to the DSB and some of these policies and measures have been identified as inconsistent with the WTO rules. While clarifying the facts and defending China behaves according to rules, the Chinese authorities need to carefully examine and make objective comparisons to further clarify the relationship between the government and enterprises such that the market can play a more decisive role in the allocation of resources and the government can fulfill its role more adequately (such as making up for market failures). Not only will this help ease trade friction and tensions, it will also help promote the sustainable and healthy development of China's economy and society.

Chapter 7

Global Value Chains and Trade in Value-Added

I n the 1980s and 1990s, Chinese households were excited to have an imported TV or refrigerator. The terms "made in Japan" or "made in Germany" were a rarity in our lives and a symbol of quality. Today, when we get a new iPhone, it is difficult to say exactly which country it has been manufactured in. On the back of the phone, it is printed "Design by Apple in California; Assembled in China". It is hard to determine the origin of the phone although Apple is an authentic American company. According to statistics, the wholesale price of an iPhone 3G is USD178 but China gets only 3.6% of that amount. When the iPhone is assembled in the Foxconn factory in mainland China, and shipped from China to the US, the entire price of USD178 is included in China's export volume. The US, where the iPhone design was invented, has ironically become the importing country.

With the flourishing processing trade of China today, there are many situations similar to that of the production of the iPhone. Intermediate goods enter China to be assembled and the final products are often included in the export trade of China. Behind the large export volume, only a small amount of profit stays in the country. This undoubtedly distorts the trade balance and global division of labor between countries. There are many drawbacks in the traditional way of calculating total trade value in the increasingly globalized division today.

The proposed global value chains and trade in value added (TiVA) are the evolution of the traditional way of calculating international trade. It tries to keep to the real numbers in world trade, reform and improve the economic rules and standards, and promote international economic order more justly, reasonably and inclusively. The major countries in the world and international organizations gave full attention to this and put in efforts, using case studies, model analysis and other researches, to establish a number of databases that apply TiVA accounting. As the largest developing country that is a transforming economy, there are many enterprises in China engaged in general trade and processing trade. These Chinese enterprises have unique roles and characteristics with regard to import and export trade, employment and income distribution. According to these features, China, starting with the underlying data, makes its own development in statistical theory, method selection, policy interpretation among other areas.

1 Issues of Global Value Chains and Trade in Value-Added

1.1 *Background and concepts of global value chains*

Human society has undergone industrial revolutions and experienced technological innovation. Economic globalization has gradually emerged: under the influence of the free trade ideology of Ricardo and other classical economists, global trade led to country-based international division of labor and cross-border flow of products. By the late 1980s, the theoretical discourse on international division of labor was still characterized by division of labor according to the level of development between developed countries, and vertical disintegration of labor between developed countries and developing countries. It was clearly shown that developed countries conducted intra-industry trade while developed and developing countries were doing inter-industry trade. As multinational companies played an increasingly important role on the world stage, the two forms of trade, intra-company and intra-products, have gradually taken shape. The multinational companies subcontracted more and more of their production processes to independent companies in different parts of the world through equity or non-equity modes. The division of production spread to all parts of the value-added chain until intra-company trade accounted for one third of world trade.[1] The global sourcing strategies of multinational companies resulted in the phenomenon of international division of labor within the product. When the products were manufactured, production would be decentralized to chains which were cross-regional or cross-border in nature. More and more countries or regions have participated in the production or

---

[1] United Nations Conference on Trade and Development (UNCTAD), *World Investment Report 1995*, Transnational Corporations and Competitiveness (Geneva: United Nations, 1996).

supply activities in different aspects of the production process of a particular product. Division of production led to trade of intermediate inputs in different countries and production processes. Intra-product trade was created this way, and with the subsequent formation of global value chains, the benefits of trade between countries became more compatible.

The concept of a global value chains was developed and has continually improved based on the research of scholars. It probably went through four phases, namely value chains, value-added chains, commodity chains and global value chains. Professor Michael E. Porter from Harvard Business School pointed out in his book, *Competitive Strategy*,[2] that every business is a combination of process of various activities in the design, production, marketing, delivery and support of the product. All of these activities can be represented by a value chain. Professor Bruce M. Kogut from Columbia Business School believes that the value chain is basically a process with various inputs of technology, raw materials and labor. After assembling these aspects to form the final products, the cycle is completed through market transactions and consumption *etc*. In this continual value-added chain, the individual companies may only participate in a certain aspect, or the companies may include the entire value-added process in the corporate hierarchy system. Professor Gary Gereffi, a scholar from Duke University, combines the value chain analysis and industrial organization research, and proposes a global commodity chain analysis. In the context of economic globalization, the production process of goods is broken down into different stages. The formation of a transnational production system surrounds the production of a commodity, thus forming a global commodity chain. In 2001, Gereffi analyzed the process of globalization from the perspective of value chains. He believes that trade in goods and services should be regarded as a system of governance. Understanding the operation of the value chain is very important for business and policy-makers in developing countries since the formation of value chains is also the process that enterprises continue to participate in, in order to obtain the necessary technical capabilities and service support.

The report "Competing through Innovation and Learning" from the United Nations Industrial Development Organization (UNIDO)[3] points out that

---

[2] Michael E. Porter, *Competitive Strategy: Techniques for Analyzing Industries and Competitors* (New York: Free Press, 1980).

[3] United Nations Industrial Development Organization (UNIDO), "Competing through Innovation and Learning 2002/2003," retrieved from https://www.unido.org/fileadmin/user_media/Publications/Pub_free/Industrial_development_report_2002_2003.pdf.

"The metaphor of global value chains captures the links among enterprises spread across a variety of locations around the world. These enterprises perform a sequence of related dependent activities to bring a product or service from conception through the different phases of production to delivery to final consumers and to final disposal after use." It includes all participants and organizations that do sales and distribute profits. There is support given to institutional capacity and efficiency by linking suppliers, partners and customers through automatic business processes. This definition emphasizes that the global value chains are not formed by a large number of complementary companies but connect clusters of enterprises through a variety of economic activities. In order to enter the international market, companies must obtain basic technical skills. Once they enter global value chains, the learning effects caused by supply chains will appear. For this reason, enterprises which enter global value chains must improve their technical capabilities. They should also make the necessary preparations to move up the value chains.

The Institute of Development Studies at the University of Sussex in the United Kingdom did a more extensive study on global value chains. It defines global value chains as the entire life cycles of products across the globe from conceptual design to usage until they are scrapped, and all value-creating activities such as product design, production, marketing, distribution, user support and end-services are included. The composition of a value chain of activities may be kept within an enterprise or distributed among various enterprises. They can also be concentrated either within a particular geographic range or scattered around the globe.

Based on the above research literature, we can define global value chains as value creation and profit distribution chains where production, sales, recycling and other aspects, conducted internationally or regionally, are linked up in an orderly manner to realize the value of goods or services. The scale of global value chains is large and its structure is complex, involving both vertical and horizontal dimensions. Vertical refers to enterprises engaging in the processing of raw materials from start to the final products. This includes stages such as the division of labor, logistics management and value creation, involving design, product development, manufacturing, marketing, delivery, consumption, after sales service, finally recycling and other value-added activities. Horizontal refers to division of labor which is cross-country or cross-region.

Global value chains, supply chains and industry chains are currently popular concepts of international trade and investment. Although all three of them possess features of "chain" structure, the interpretation of the industrial organization and the analysis of enterprise resource capacities are different individually. Among them, value chains include the various stages or links in the process of forming a final good or service from the initial raw materials. The relationship of these links is an orderly chain. Each link forms part of the process of value creation and profit distribution, much like a life trajectory from the cradle to the grave. Supply chains focus on core businesses and begin from the procurement of raw materials to the formation of intermediate products, and then manufacturing of the final products through the control of logistics, information flow and capital flow. The sales network sends the products to consumers through a functional network chain structure that usually includes inventory, transportation, distribution, manufacturing, distribution, and other sectors. Industry chains are based on division of labor and collaboration. They include the entire process from raw materials to consumers. The relationships among the enterprises are interconnected due to technical linkages and input–output relations. It is believed that various industry sectors are based on certain technical and economic associations. The chain structure is formed by certain logical relationships and objective temporal distribution.

1.2 *Evolution of traditional international trade statistics accounting*

After the mid-19th century, the progress of the industrial revolution and further expansion of the world market have made it necessary to exchange and compare statistical systems among the countries. Back in 1853, the first session of the International Statistical General Assembly was held and the international statistical organization was formed. After World War II, the world economic system with the IMF, World Bank Group and GATT as pillars, was established. The System of National Accounts (SNA) which was the core of the entire economic statistics system was linked to this economic system. It included the balance of payments statistics and international trade (in goods) statistics. Currently, the relevant international organizations have developed a number of rules to regulate international trade statistics. They are included in several documents on international guidelines in existing publications that feature international trade statistics and accounting: "International Merchandise Trade Statistics" (IMTS), "Balance of Payments and International Investment Position Manual" (BPM) and "Manual on Statistics of International Trade in Services" (MSITS).

1.2.1 *International Merchandise Trade Statistics and "Harmonized Commodity Description and Coding System"*

The publication, *International Merchandise Trade Statistics: Concepts and Definitions* regulates the statistical concepts, standard measures and data collection methods of cargo volume and value, ownership of trading partner countries and commodity classification of cross-border trade in goods. As the impact of trade in services was not great during that time, people only perceived the trade in goods as "trade". The 1970 and 1982 editions were known as *International Trade Statistics: Concepts and Definitions*. Only in 1993 was it changed to *International Merchandise Trade Statistics: Concepts and Definitions*, and indicated that statistics only included trade in goods, that is flow of material resources: "Record all goods which add to or subtract from the stock of material resources of a country by entering (imports) or leaving (exports) its economic territory." The system is based on the data of actual goods crossing in and out of the customs of various countries. The statistical results generated is generally known as the customs data. Following the demands from various sectors, the national statistical offices then adjust, compile and disseminate the data on trade in goods and international balance of payments based on the customs data. The statistics from IMTS are then arranged according to the Standard International Trade Classification (SITC).

SITC is the standard classification for calculating and comparing the statistics of international trade in goods. In 1920, the League of Nations proceeded to develop the international trade terminology and commodities statistical catalog. They used the "tariff noun draft" as basis and revised the "compendium catalog of international trade statistics" for all member countries to use. In order to measure and analyze world trade statistics, the above compendium catalog was further amended to be the "Standard International Trade Classification". It was divided into 10 categories, 50 sub-categories, 150 classes and 570 sub-classes to be the common ground for national trade statistics and world trade system analysis. SITC uses economic classification criteria to classify raw materials, semi-finished products and finished products. This also reflects the industrial sector source and the degree of product processing.

For a more detailed merchandise description in external trade statistics, the Customs Cooperation Council approved the "Harmonized Commodity Description and Coding System" (HS) in June 1983. Since February 1993, different countries have adopted the HS and provided international trade statistics. There are 1,241 items and 5,113 sub-items, a combination of 97 chapters and 21 classes in HS. The goods are arranged sequentially according to the order of processing from raw materials, unprocessed products, semi-finished products to finished products. The overall structure is as follows: categories 1–4 are agricultural products; categories 5–7 are mineral products, chemical and related products, plastics, rubber and related products; categories 8–10 are animal products, wood, cork, wood pulp, paper and paper products; categories 11–12 are textile products, footwear, headgear; categories 13–15 are stone, plaster, cement, asbestos, mica and products of similar materials, ceramics products, glass, pearls, semi-precious and precious stones, precious metals, jewelry, base metals and their products; category 16 is machinery, mechanical appliances and electrical equipment; category 17 is vehicles, aircraft, vessels and related transport equipment; category 18 is optics, photographic, cinemato-graphic, measuring, testing, medical or surgical instruments and equipment, clocks and watches, musical instruments; category 19 is weapons and ammuni-tion; and categories 20–21 are miscellaneous products.

1.2.2 Balance of Payments and International Investment Position Manual (BPM) and Manual on Statistics of International Trade in Services (MSITS)

The international balance of payments (BoP) system is another main evidence that reflects the status of foreign-related economic development. For a long time, the BPM was written by the IMF, who had taken on the responsibility of overseeing and coordinating various countries' international balance of pay-ments. It has hence been the guiding document for countries in drafting their countries' BoP standards. The standards in BPM form the basic framework for international BoP of different countries. The various versions of "Balance of Payments Manual" were printed with "BPM" followed by their serial numbers respectively. There have been six BPMs beginning from 1947, followed by 1950, 1961, 1977, 1993 and 2008 from BPM to BPM2 and so on until BPM6. Comparing BPM5 and BPM6 — with services and trade in services playing a greater role in the international economy — there are four adjusted areas in two items "goods" and "services", under the part on "goods and ser-vices", to implement the ownership principles throughout international trade. They are as follows:

(1) Goods for processing: these are placed under trade in services instead of trade in goods. BPM6 no longer places goods for processing under goods but records them as services under "manufacturing services on physical inputs owned by others", and only the processing fees are recorded. They are further divided into goods processed by the compiling economy and

goods processed overseas. When goods are sent overseas for processing, but enterprises of the compiling economy provide raw materials, spare parts and commission foreign enterprises to process the goods, the processing fees are recorded as imports of services into the compiling economy. When goods are imported for processing, and enterprises of the compiling economy are entrusted by foreign enterprises to provide raw materials and spare parts in the course of processing, the processing fees are recorded as exports of services from the compiling economy.

(2) Merchanting of goods: these are placed under trade in goods instead of trade in services. BPM6 applies ownership principles and deems merchanting an import and export of goods. The gross profit from the resale is recorded as an export of goods, and the purchase of goods for merchanting is recorded as a negative export of goods.

(3) Tourists' purchase of high-value goods: this is placed under trade in goods instead of trade in services in the new manual.

(4) Repair of goods: this is placed under trade in services instead of trade in goods in the new manual.

Among them, the adjustment of statistical methods in processing trade has had a very significant impact in raising new awareness for actual development in trade in services of international goods under global value chains division.

Since the 1960s, service industries in developed countries have replaced manufacturing as the largest industrial sector in the national economy. Developed countries have begun entering the era of the service economy. During the 1970s, as the production and exchange of intangible goods increased in proportion, the barriers to production moving across borders were reduced. International trade then underwent major changes, with trade in services receiving more and more attention. The status and role of service industries and trade in services in the economic development of developed countries resulted in the growing needs for statistics of trade in services among the government, enterprises and related organizations. Whether the government develops more economic and trade policies, participates in international negotiations, invests in business plans or expands the market, it needs authoritative, accurate, comprehensive and timely statistics. This led to the establishment of a scientific and standardized international trade in services statistics system.

In January 1995, the General Agreement on Trade and Services (GATS) was established. It listed four ways to provide services and proposed a new definition for trade in services. The international community understood trade in services better and requested the introduction of a broad trade in services statistics system that was consistent with the new definition. Subsequently, the inter-organization working group of the main international organizations wrote the "Manual on Statistics of International Trade in Services" (MSITS). It summarized the four ways of providing services listed by GATS and took into account the features of the inseparability of service production and consumption, and the reality that the factors of service production stretched across borders. This constructed the mutually complementary framework of service statistics in balance of payments and trade in services statistics in GATS.

It should be noted that the economic statistics system, with the System of National Accounts (SNA) as its core, is adapted to the needs of world economic development and the international economic exchange situation after World War II, playing an important role in national economic development and international economic trade that cannot be underestimated. All the documents above related to accounting trade statistics are based on SNA.

1.3 *Further reform of international trade statistics due to the economic crisis*

Due to the impact of the economic crisis in 2008, the complementary industries and closely knit relationships in the value chains among various countries were highlighted. When there was unity, all parties benefited. When there was division, all parties suffered losses. IMF economist Rudolfs Bems[4] believes that in the presence of vertical specialization in international trade, trade and production chain are directly related. The effects of financial crisis now spread among countries faster than ever. One important channel that speeds up this impact is through domestically produced goods. For example, the US may reduce spending on US-made goods but the intermediate goods that produce these final products come from imports. If these intermediate products use the spare parts that come from US exports, the same reduction in imports will be transferred to the decline in exports in the US. The in-depth development of economic globalization and global value chains links the world economy more closely together. The economic crisis makes people more deeply aware of the value of the second chain in the crisis conduction effect.

This conduction process leads to unpredictability in global trade and regulatory environment, and further affects the real economy of production, trade,

---

[4] Bems R. *et al.*, "*Demand Spillovers and the Collapse of Trade in the Global Recession,*" IMF Working Paper (2010), WP/10/142.

employment, investment, innovation and other aspects. Even governments in many developed countries and international organizations are equally helpless in addressing the high unemployment rate and economic crisis. This exposes the defects of many who support the theory, statistics framework, regulatory system and regulatory approach of the global economy and trade.

The current method of measuring international trade statistics involves calculating gross import and export of goods at the customs. It does not take into full account the new changes under the economic globalization of international trade. They are mainly shown in the following.

Concealment of real trade flow. The traditional way of calculating trade statistics is to list the place of assembly and export of the final product as the country of origin. The trade value of the final product is simply attributed to the place of final assembly, and the trade at the place of product assembly is overvalued. The profitable trade value of the core components in the product value chain of the exporting country is seriously underestimated.

Distorting international competitiveness of countries. The traditional way of calculating trade statistics focuses only on the exporting country of the final product. It cannot accurately reflect the actual situation in which the different countries value add to the various production processes. The comparative advantages of the various trade parties are not reflected.

Exaggerated trade imbalance, causing trade friction. Using the traditional trade statistics accounting methods, the trade surplus of nations with large processing trade is exaggerated, resulting in many contradictions in trade deficit, exchange rate and other areas between countries with export of processing trade and importing countries. This leads to the implementation of trade protectionism by trade deficit countries, causing the intensification of trade friction.

In this context, there is a greater need to reform and innovate international statistical standards. Reforming and improving the world economic statistics rules and standards will enable the international order to be more just, reasonable and inclusive.

In 2010, the WTO and the French Senate Finance Committee jointly organized the international seminar for global value chains. Since then, WTO, UNCTAD, OECD, the Asian Development Bank and other international organizations and academic institutions have conducted in-depth research.

In 2011, the WTO Director-General Lamy proposed the "World Manufacturing Initiative" and called for improvements in international trade statistics from the perspective of global value chains to account for trade in value-added in order to make up for the shortcomings of the traditional trade statistics system. With this initiative, recent research on trade in value-added statistics and its extensive work have progressed rapidly and yielded fruitful results in the international arena. Due to world economic situations such as international fragmentation production and global value chains, major international economic organizations and scholars have proposed the use of TiVA to restore the original state of world trade and provide accurate data for various countries to establish policies, just as many countries generally accept the measurement of gross domestic product using value-added accountancy approaches.

TiVA is hidden in the traditional way of measuring total business flow. The added value is created by the countries producing exports. This includes the compensation of employees, taxes and profits in the production process. TiVA accounting attributes the value-added part of the exported product's production process to the different countries such that each country's export is only reflected as its own added value. This method is able to track the value added by each country in the production chain, reflecting the economic and trade relations among nations from the value-added perspective.

With regard to the research on global value chains, the attitudes of different countries vary. On the whole, developed countries invest more in research. The EU is especially active as the study will help promote the European market, but the US is leading in research methods. Although the government believes that some of the conclusions in the trade balance are in favor of China, it has officially expressed support for TiVA accounting. Japan and India are respectively more involved in trade in goods and outsourcing of services in global value chains. They are relatively proactive. Brazil and other resource-exporting countries are limited in their participation in global value chains. South Africa and other countries are worried that the developed countries may take the opportunity to put pressure on them so they are not very much in favor of the idea.

The issues of global value chains are closely related to the current economic globalization, regional economic integration and trend of opening up. This is not only about trade statistics but also about the formation of national trade policies. There is important significance in enhancing international competitiveness in national industries and promoting economic transformation. The research and discussion on this issue will affect the direction of the multilateral trading system and the formation of new international trade rules and standards. All parties will treat this competition with great importance, thereby increasing their right to speak and guiding it in the direction of development that is to their advantage.

2 A New Approach: Global Value Chains and Trade in Value–Added Accounting

2.1 *Latest developments in the research of global value chains and trade in value–added accounting*

In the late 1960s, Hungarian economist Béla Balassa[5] began to study the segmented distribution of a number of production processes in trade value chains. Later, Findlay,[6] a scholar from the US University of Columbia, Nobel laureate in economics, Paul Krugman,[7] and David Hummels,[8] a researcher from Purdue University, all studied the segmented distribution on international trade value chains. David Hummels proposed the concept of vertical specialization (VS) where the vertical specialized division of labor is defined as the value of imported intermediate inputs included in exports. He also proposed the "HIY method"[9] of calculating vertical specialization to reflect the country or region's participation in global trade value chains. The absolute value of imported goods used in exports would represent the value of vertical specialization, and the relative value of imported goods per unit of exports would represent the rate of vertical specialization.

The HIY method has gained wide recognition and application in trade value chains research; in 2008, Robert Koopman *et al.*,[10] scholars from the US International Trade Commission proposed extending HIY vertical specialization to multinational input–output models to study the value chains between

---

[5] Béla Balassa, *Trade Liberalization and Revealed Comparative Advantage* (United Kingdom: The Manchester School, 1965), pp. 33, 99–123.

[6] Ronald Findlay, "An Austrian Model of International Trade and Interest Rate Equalization," *Journal of Political Economy*, Vol. 86, No. 6 (1978), pp. 989–1007.

[7] Paul Krugman and Raul Livas Elizondo, "Trade Policy and the Third World Metropolis," *Journal of Development Economics*, Vol. 49, No. 1 (1996), pp. 137–150.

[8] David Hummels, Hun Ishii and Kei-Mu Yi, "The Nature and Growth of Vertical Specialization in World Trade," *Journal of International Economics*, Vol. 54 (2001), pp. 75–96.

[9] The HIY method refers to the theory put forth by Hummels, Ishii and Yi (2001).

[10] Robert B. Koopman, Zhi Wang, Shang-Jin Wei, "How Much of Chinese Exports is really made In China? Assessing Domestic Value-Added When Processing Trade is Pervasive," NBER Working Paper No. 14109 (August 2008).

the nine major East Asian economies and the US. Results showed that in the 1990s, the East Asian developing countries integrated more deeply into the East Asian production network and at the same time, heterogeneity in the various departments' value chains was found; in 2010, Kooperman *et al.*[11] proposed a conceptual framework for completely decomposing a country's gross exports into value-added components by source. This method combined the existing vertical specialization and TiVA measurement methodologies; in 2011, Erik Dietzenbacher,[12] a scholar from Groningen University pointed out the double counting flaw in the HIY method and proposed the appropriate trade metrics to avoid double counting. He also provided the direct empirical indicators between this approach and the existing incorrect method. Currently, WTO, OECD, UNCTAD, the US International Trade Commission, Japanese Institute of Developing Economies, the EU, the Chinese Academy of Sciences and other organizations are all conducting research on global TiVA, countries' and regions' mode of participation in global trade and their contribution and role in global TiVA.

In recent years, both domestic and overseas scholars have used a variety of quantitative methods and statistical approaches to reassess global value chains in international production, indicating the rapid developmental trends of international production and trade. The relevant research methods and advances are conducted at the following levels.

2.1.1 *Individual case analysis*

Individual case analysis is mainly a "sparrow dissection" mode of studying a single product's international production value chain, thereby indicating the changes in actual trade according to the value added to the production chain. After the 2008 economic crisis, trade imbalances drew widespread attention. The degree of imbalance became a research topic for some experts led by the WTO. Individual case studies were first conducted to gain better understanding of this area.

---

[11] Robert B. Kooperman, William Powers, Zhi Wang and Shang-Jin Wei, "Give Credit Where Credit Is Due: Tracing Value Added in Global Production Chains," NBER Working Paper No. 16426 (September 2010).

[12] Erik Dietzenbacher, Jiansuo Pei and Cuihong Yang, "Trade, Production Fragmentation, and China's Carbon Dioxide Emissions," *Journal of Environmental Economicsa and Management*, Vol. 64 (2012), pp. 88–101.

Case Study 1: Barbie Dolls

On September 22, 1996, the *Los Angeles Times* published an article titled "Barbie and the World Economy". In the US, a Barbie doll sells for USD9.99. Its price when imported from China is USD2, and the rest of the costs are added in the US, attributed to transportation, advertising, business profits *etc.* The doll has created thousands of jobs for the Americans. China's labor costs only account for 35 cents out of the USD2 import cost while the rest are respectively, 65 cents for raw materials, USD1 for freight and management, including the 10–20 cents profit received by the Hong Kong company managing the production of the toy. Of the 65 cents worth of raw materials, oil from Saudi Arabia is refined into ethylene in places such as Texas, US before being processed into plastic vinyl granules in Chinese Taipei, then made into the body of the Barbie doll; Japan provides the nylon that makes the hair of the doll; and the US produces the carton box packaging. China's labor costs of 35 cents only constitutes 3% of the Barbie doll's selling price in the States (see Figure 7.1).

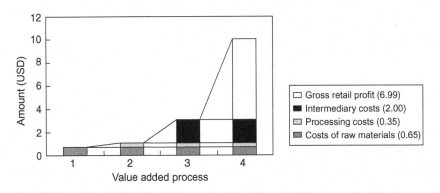

Figure 7.1 Distribution of value added of the Barbie doll.

Source: Authors' compilation of data.

Case Study 2: The iPod

Apple Inc. launched a digital music player called the iPod in 2001. The patent of the product belongs to Apple but Apple is not the producer. It is in fact assembled by manufacturers around the world.

The Apple fifth generation iPod consists of 451 pieces worth a total of USD299. The production value chain is formed across the world and its division of labor is distributed globally. Apple is not actually involved in the production and only earns USD80 from the total value of USD299. Toshiba

Corporation from Japan is a major player in the value chain. The key component, a 30G memory hard disk is provided by Toshiba but the actual production of the hard drive takes place in China while many components of the hard disk are provided by enterprises from other countries. Toshiba and the companies jointly producing the hard disk only obtain USD19 from the total value. Another key component, the chip worth USD13, is provided by an American company but the chip may or may not have been produced in the US. The countries receiving the least value from this chain are Korea and China. Korea provides the memory storage disk worth only a mere USD2. If the hard disk that is produced in China is not included, China only earns USD3.70 from the value chain. And this is earned by way of outsourcing through a Chinese Taipei OEM factory. It is unclear how much real value was created in mainland China.

Case Study 3: The iPhone

In November 2011, US computer scientist Andrew Hoog[13] broke down the costs of the iPhone according to its main components and researched the process of value added to the product along the product's international product value chain as well as the distribution of profits. He discovered that the production of the main components of the iPhone had been moved overseas, the parts that were produced in the States accounted for a relatively small proportion of the production, and the product value chain was shared by many companies in many countries.

On December 16, 2010, the Asian Development Bank Institute published the trade research report on iPhone 3G mobile phone.[14] The report showed that the wholesale price of an Apple phone was USD178.96 including labor costs and costs of parts, with Japan, Germany, and Korea receiving 34%, 17% and 13% of the costs respectively, while China received only 3.6% which was about USD6.5. However, under the existing trade statistical methods, the entire wholesale price was credited to China's export trade (see Table 7.1).

The iPhone is an important product of the US company, Apple. Its software and production are mainly designed in the States but the product is largely

[13] Andrew Hoog, "iPhone Forensics," (March 2009), retrieved from http://www.mandarino70. it/Documents/iPhone-Forensics-2009.pdf.

[14] Yuqing Xing and Neal Detert, "How the iPhone Widens the United States Trade Deficit with the People's Republic of China," Asian Development Bank Instittue Working Paper No. 257 (December 2010), retrieved from http://www.adb.org/sites/default/files/publication/156112/ adbi-wp257.pdf.

Table 7.1 Main components and costs of the iPhone.

Manufacturer	Parts	Cost (USD)
Toshiba (Japan)	Flash memory	24.00
	Display module	19.25
	Touch screen	16.00
Samsung (Korea)	Application processor	14.46
	Random access memory	8.50
Infineon (Germany)	Baseband	13.00
	Camera	9.55
	Radio frequency transceiver	2.80
	GPS receiver	2.25
	Power IC RF function	1.25
Broadcom (USA)	Bluetooth	5.95
Numonyx (USA)	Multi-chip package memory	3.65
Murata (Japan)	RF front-end modules	1.35
Dialogue Semiconductor (Germany)	Power integrated circuit application processor	1.30
Cirrus Logic (USA)	Multimedia digital signal codec	1.15
Costs of other materials		48.00
Costs of all materials		172.46
Assembly costs (Foxconn)		6.50
Total manufacturing costs		**178.96**

manufactured out of the US. Various parts are shipped to Shenzhen, China, assembled by Foxconn, and then re-exported to the US and other markets.

The iPhone is a typical high-tech product which prominently highlights the comparative advantage and absolute advantage of the US. At that point of time, there was not a single brand in China that was yet able to compete with them. According to the Ricardo and Heckscher-Ohlin theory of international trade, in such a case, the US should export iPhones to China; but the complete opposite is true. The American iPhone is manufactured in China, subverting the traditional trade theory. Instead of the US, the iPhone is produced globally through foreign direct investment, and international division of labor and supply chains: this is why developing countries such as China can export high-tech products and the origin of the invention, iPhone, has ironically become the importing country.

Table 7.2 iPhone trade and surplus between China and the US.

Year	2007	2008	2009
Sales in the US (millions of units)	3.0	5.3	11.3
China's export price (USD/unit)	229	174	179
China's exports (billions of USD)	0.687	0.922	2.022
China's trade surplus (billions of USD)	—	—	1.901
China's exports based on value added (billions of USD)	0.019	0.034	0.073
Value added/Total exports	2.8%	3.7%	3.6%
China's surpluses based on value added (billions of USD)	—	—	0.073

In 2009, China exported more than USD2 billion worth of iPhones, USD1.9 billion of which became China's surplus, accounting for 0.8% of China's surplus against the US that year (see Table 7.2). In 2011, Apple was expected to sell 21.3 million iPhones in the US, almost double that in 2009, meaning that the corresponding Chinese surplus also doubled.

However, the surplus earned from iPhone mobile phones did not end up in Chinese pockets. The value added in China is very low. Each iPhone's total manufacturing cost is about USD178.96 yet the assembly in China only accounts for 3.6% or USD6.5. To increase the value added, the surplus China has against the US due to the iPhone should not be recorded as USD1.9 billion but USD0.73 million.

2.1.2 *Analysis of intermediate goods trade using trade data*

The earliest quantitative study of global value chain was conducted as a trial measurement of trade in intermediate goods. Trade statistics were used to measure the scale of trade in intermediate goods, then further applied to measure the extent of a country's participation in international division of labor.

Statistics from customs would provide more comprehensive data on processing trade. João Amador and Sónia Cabral,[15] scholars from Portugal Central

---

[15] João Amador and Sónia Cabral. "Vertical Specialization Across the World: A Relative Measure," *The North American Journal of Economics and Finance*, Vol. 20, No. 3 (2009), pp. 267–280.

Bank pointed out that such processing trade data could give a narrow measure[16] of intermediate goods. Using this method, Deborah L. Swenson[17] found that offshore assembly trade in the States grew rapidly from 1980 to 2000. WBG economist Alexander Yeats[18] also studied various countries' and regions' share of international production using offshore assembly processing data and found that apart from the machinery and transportation equipment industries, textile and garment manufacturing, leather goods and other labor-intensive manufacturing industries were also core international production industries. Researcher at the University of Tennessee, Don Clark,[19] used offshore assembly data and found that American companies tended to shift simple assembly productions to unskilled labor-abundant countries. Professor Robert Feenstra[20] of the University of California, USA, found that the clothing and machinery, as well as transport equipment imported from industrialized countries through offshore assembly projects had rather intensive use of skilled labor. When Holger Görg[21] studied the EU's processing trade, he found that EU countries, particularly peripheral EU countries, recorded a significant increase in processing trade from the US from 1988 to 1994.

The measurement of the share of spare parts trade in trade in goods is another way to reflect the degree of international division of labor. This method is widely used due to the case of obtaining data and the comparability between different countries. Yates first used trade data from the Standard International Trade Classification (SITC) to study intermediate goods trade and results showed that in 1995, 30% of exports from OECD countries were parts and components and the proportion of such trade grew over time. Françoise Lemoine et al.[22] used imported intermediate goods data to examine the evolution of

---

[16] Narrow measure refers to the intermediate goods that are measured only under outsourcing and incoming (or import of raw materials) processing export conditions.

[17] Deborah L. Swenson, "Overseas Assembly and Country Sourcing Choices," *Journal of International Economics*, Vol. 66, No. 1 (2005), pp. 107–130.

[18] Alexander J. Yeats, "Just How Big is Global Production Sharing?" World Bank, Development Research Group (November 1999).

[19] Don P. Clark, "Country and Industry-level Determinants of Vertical Specialization-based Trade," *International Economic Journal*, Vol. 20, No. 2 (2006), pp. 211–225.

[20] Robert C. Feenstra and Gordon H. Hans, "Globalization, Outsourcing, and Wage Inequality," NBER Working Paper No. 5424 (January 1996).

[21] Holger Görg, "Fragmentation and Trade: US Inward Processing Trade in the EU," *Weltwirtschaftliches Archiv*, Vol. 36, No. 3 (2000), pp. 403–422.

[22] Guillaume Gaulier, Françoise Lemoine and Deniz Ünal-Kesenci, "China's Integration in East Asia: Production Sharing, FDI & High-tech Trade," *Economic Change and Restructuring*, 2007, 40(1–2), pp. 27–63.

East Asian trade; Athukorala and Yamashita used UN trade data classified by SITC to separate intermediate product trade volume from the total trade volume so as to analyze East Asian, EU and NAFTA trade. It was found that intermediate goods trade within East Asia grew relatively rapidly but when intermediate goods trade was removed from the equation, regional foreign trade had a greater impact on East Asia.

In addition, the Broad Economic Categories (BEC) database provided by the United Nations classified national trade products into the four categories of commodities, semi-finished products, components and capital goods, thus becoming a source of data for intermediate goods trade. Lemoine *et al.* also used the BEC classification to analyze the international division of labor for production within the East Asian region.[23] Stehrer and Ali-Yrkk also used the same approach to analyze the importance of intermediate goods and their changes in the EU-27.

Unfortunately, these approaches have their shortcomings. As international divisions of labor in other forms of trade are not reflected when measurement are made only with processing trade data, the extent of participation of various countries is underestimated. Moreover, the measurement of trade in parts relies heavily on the product classification in trade statistics. In addition, although the scale of trade in intermediate goods reflects the extent of international division of labor, intermediate goods are also manufactured from other inputs as well as intermediate goods, and several countries' value-added content has already been included, thus, the real value of value added in each country cannot be distinguished in the studies.

2.1.3 *Analysis using a single country's input–output tables*

The input–output model was proposed and founded by American economist Wassily Leontief around 1936. Following that, a number of economists extended studies upon the model. The checkerboard pattern of input–output tables is able to clearly reflect the production–consumption relationships among countries, regions and various product sectors. As such, it is a powerful tool used to track the flow of products and global value chains. A basic form of the table is shown in Table 7.3.

In the table, Z represents an intermediate flow matrix, V represents value added row vector, X represents total output column vector, F represents final demand column vector, C represents final consumption column vector, I represents gross capital column vector, E represents export column vector; in

---

[23] Lemoine *et al.*, "China's Integration in East Asia," *ibid.*

Table 7.3 Non-competitive input–output table.

Input/Output		Intermediate demand	Final demand				Total output and total imports
		Production department	Final consumption	Capital formation	Exports	Total amount	
		Department 1 Department 2 Department n					
Intermediate inputs of domestic products	Department 1 Department 2 ... Department n	Z^D	C^D	I^D	E^D	F^D	X^D
Intermediate inputs of imports	Department 1 Department 2 ... Department n	Z^M	C^M	I^M		F^M	X^M
Preliminary inputs		V					
Total inputs		$X^{D'}$					

Source: Authors.

addition, the subscript D represents domestic product, and the subscript M represents imports. In the input-output table, lines above indicate the flow of product distribution, and items in the columns represent product consumption. Take Z^D for example, the item z_{ij}^D refers to the production of j department against the consumption of i domestic goods; Z^M element z_{ij}^M refers to the production of j department against the consumption of i imported goods; C^D element C_j^D indicates the proportion of j department's domestic products used in the country's final consumption, C^M element C_j^M represents the proportion of j department's imported goods used in the country's final consumption; the other letters follow the same logic. Global value chains research using the single country input–output model is mainly conducted from two angles: studying the domestic value added (DVA, or domestic share) included in exports, and studying the imported goods (foreign share) included in exports.

The flaw in the single country input–output model is the assumption that there is no DVA in imports when measuring the impact of exports on value–added products. This is not true in reality. As such, these studies underestimate the DVA brought about by Chinese exports to a certain extent. In addition, it is hard to accurately determine, using the single country input–output model, which countries the foreign share included in exports belong to. When measuring vertical specialization, it is incorrect to assume that imported goods do not contain DVA. As international division of labor deepens gradually, it is very likely that a country's exports contains intermediate inputs that includes the country's value-added components. Thus, the above-mentioned assumption does not stand. Moreover, these studies can only analyze a single country's problems and do not clearly reflect the status and value allocation of each country in the GVCs. To resolve these problems, analysis must be conducted based on the international input–output model.

2.1.4 *Analysis using international input–output tables*

International input–output tables are able to clearly reflect the product flow and consumption relationships among various countries and different sectors. Not only can the model clearly demarcate the status of the various countries' individual industries in GVCs, it can also be used to measure important income factors such as labor, capital *etc.* as well as the value added by various countries in international division of labor. Currently, literature reviews on countries' value allocation from the global perspective has largely been conducted using the international input–output model. Research content includes mainly: (1) measurement of trade in intermediate goods among countries and regions; (2) measurement of vertical specialization levels in extending HIY methodology; and (3) measurement of the value added by trade. A sample of an international input–output table is as shown in Table 7.4.

In the above international input–output table which includes n countries and m industries, Z^{sk} refers to the Sth country's intermediate input matrix towards country k. F^{sk} refers to Sth country's products used as part of the Kth country's final demand. V^s and X^s refer to Sth country's value added row vector and total output column vector. Presently, there is substantial literature which uses these models, or has changed and modified these methods based on their needs, conducting further empirical analysis using international input–output tables.

2.2 *Efforts by international organizations to further promote value-added accounting methods*

In 2007, Professor Lawrence J. Lau of the University of Hong Kong and Professor Chen Xikang of the Chinese Academy of Sciences and others researched the China-US trade surplus issues[24] using the non-competitive input–output model and drew much attention. They used input–output technology and non-competitive input–output tables as well as existing customs data to measure the DVA of China-US imports and exports. WTO, UNCTAD, OECD, the Asian Development Bank and other international organizations and academic institutions subsequently carried out in-depth studies to improve the accounting method and gradually, an international consensus to use the input–output method to study TiVA was formed. Presently, there are still many issues to be resolved regarding the measurement of TiVA such as obtaining more accurate intermediate goods statistics and achieving greater coherence between trade and national statistics *etc*. As there are certain differences between various countries' trade statistical methods and national economic statistical methods, and these differences are not easily bridged, optimization approaches have to be taken to resolve this issue. A large amount of foundational research and work experience has been laid to this end.

The OECD and WTO have given considerable attention to TiVA and are continually working on it. The OECD input–output database has begun reflecting the relevant TiVA indicators and further enhancing the related construction thereof. Building upon the earlier heavily-financed research

---

[24] Lawrence J. Lau, Chen Xikang, Yang Cuihong *et al.*, "Non-Competitive Input–Output Model and Its Application – An Examination of the China-US Trade Surplus", *Chinese Social Sciences*, No. 5 (2007).

Table 7.4 International input–output table.

Input/Output		Intermediate demand				Final demand				Total output and total imports
		Country 1	Country 2	...	Country n	Country 1	Country 2	...	Country n	
Intermediate input	Country 1	Z^{11}	Z^{12}	...	Z^{1n}	F^{11}	F^{12}	...	F^{1n}	X^1
	Country 2	Z^{21}	Z^{22}	...	Z^{2n}	F^{21}	F^{22}	...	F^{2n}	X^2
	...	...	...	...	...	...	...	...	...	...
	Country n	Z^{n1}	Z^{n2}	...	Z^{nn}	F^{n1}	F^{n2}	...	F^{nn}	X^n
Initial input		V^1	V^2	...	V^n					
Total input		X^1	X^2		X^n					

projects, OECD and WTO are currently placing even more emphasis on the in-depth discussion and improvement of existing research results so as to promote TiVA accounting as part of the routine processes in the international and various national trade statistics systems. OECD and WTO also hope that more countries will increase funding for related research activities and make use of official statistics to conduct TiVA accounting.

Consistent international input–output tables need to be established as input–output matrices are applied in TiVA accounting. At the moment, five international input–output databases have been set up.

2.2.1 *OECD and WTO's global input–output database*

The OECD started research early and is a leader in this area. Its database covers 50 countries and regions. In March 2012, the WTO officially commissioned the OECD to conduct studies on TiVA accounting. On January 16, 2013, the OECD and WTO jointly issued the initial report on the global TiVA database. It was the first time that the value-added method was used based on input–output to estimate each country's trade data and reflect the actual situation of division of labor and benefits that each country was contributing and obtaining in the global value chains. The report included 18 industries (agriculture, manufacturing and services) from 40 countries (OECD members, the five BRICS countries and Indonesia). In May 2013, the OECD and WTO updated the database.

2.2.2 *The European Union's World Input–Output Database (WIOD)*

The EU invested 4 million euros in 2009 to construct this database. It covers the 27 EU members and 13 major countries and was opened to the world in April 2013. The EU Trade Commissioner Karel De Gucht said that the database estimates that the EU trade deficit with China was 36% lower than indicated by traditional statistics while trade deficits with Canada and Japan were correspondingly higher, and that the EU needed to re-evaluate its relationships with the major trading partners. 87% of the EU's exports are manufactured within the EU, while 13% are actually imports.

2.2.3 *The US Global Trade Analysis Project Database (GTAP)*

The database was developed in 1992 by Purdue University and 27 international organizations. In the entire GTAP system, the core and most valuable part is the global trade repository GTAP regularly provides. This repository that includes bilateral trade information, freight information needed for international trade, as well as various forms of trade protection policy information. It is based on data from individual countries' input–output tables and combines the tables together to show the relationships between various sectors and regions. After continuous expansion, version 7 of the 2004 GTAP database included 113 regions (94 countries and 19 mixed areas) and 57 industries. According to research by scholars from the US International Trade Commission, in 2004, the US trade deficit with China was 59% lower than indicated by traditional statistics while it was more than 140% higher for Japan and 130% higher for the EU.

2.2.4 *Japan's Asian international input–output database*

In the 1960s, the Japan Institute of Developing Economies (IDE) developed and proposed the Asian input–output model. In 1983, it came up with the first "1975 Asian International Input–Output Table" (AIIOT) which included eight economies. IDE publishes a new AIIOT every five years, providing a powerful analytical tool for studying the input–output connections, and changes and trends in industrial structures of the various industries and economies in the Asia Pacific region. In March 2006, IDE launched a new "Year 2000 Asian International Input–Output Table" which included the 10 countries and regions — Indonesia, Malaysia, the Philippines, Singapore, Thailand, China, Chinese Taipei, Korea, Japan and the United States. Data connections were done through analyzing imports and exports with Chinese Hong Kong, the EU and other regions around the world. In 2011, IDE jointly published the "Trade Pattern and Global Value Chains in East Asia" report[25] with WTO which attracted much attention.

2.2.5 *UNCTAD's global value chains database*

On February 27, 2013, the UNCTAD published a report entitled "Global Value Chains and Development: Investment and Trade in Value Added in the Global Economy", showcasing the preliminary results from its new global value chains database. This database greatly expanded data coverage based on existing data relevant to global value chains available internationally, and covers 187 countries and numerous industries in the world.

---

[25] WTO/IDE-JETRO, "Trade Pattern and Global Value Chains in East Asia: From Trade in Goods to Trade in Tasks," (2011), retrieved from https://www.wto.org/english/res_e/booksp_e/ stat_tradepat_globvalchains_e.pdf.

Although there are differences in the scope of countries covered and the time period in which each database was set up, generally, there are a few relatively consistent conclusions.

(1) The scale of trade in most countries decreased dramatically when measured according to value added. About 28% of global exports are imported by countries as part of the process of producing intermediate goods or services. Out of the USD19 trillion worth of global exports in 2010, about USD5 trillion were double-counted.

Trade imbalances were somewhat eased when measured according to value added. The TiVA accounting method only includes various states' pure value added and deducts all foreign value added segments from import and export values. According to existing statistical methods, countries that assemble at the low end of the value chain (such as China) have their exports severely overestimated, while countries at the low end of the value chain who provide components (such as Japan and Korea) have their exports seriously underestimated. Measured according to value added, China's trade surpluses against Europe and the US are generally lower while Japan and Korea's trade surpluses against Europe and the US are generally higher.

(2) The contribution of trade in services to exports is remarkable when measured according to value added. Trade in services account for 20% of global exports but the services industries contributed nearly half of value added in global exports. The services of developed countries such as the US, Britain, Germany, France and others constitute more than 50% of exports while services from developing countries including China constitute more than 30% of exports.

Currently, the issues with global value chains and TiVA accounting have become hot issues of common concern among countries in the world. In 2012, at the G20 Summit in Los Cabos, Mexico, Chinese leaders pointed out, "We should maintain and strengthen the multilateral trading system and continue to advance the Doha Round negotiations. We ought to focus on international trade value chain issues so that trade statistics more comprehensively and accurately reflect the benefits various countries receive from trade, and get a more objective and balanced view on the so-called problem of trade imbalance." At the first trade ministerial meeting at the G20 Summit in Mexico, the Doha Round negotiations and global value chains were discussed. In September 2013, the G20 Summit leaders issued a statement at the eighth G20 Summit held in St. Petersburg, Russia, to appeal against trade protectionism, ensure that regional trade agreements complemented the multilateral trading system rather than harmed it, and emphasized the role that building global value chains through trade had in the creation of employment.

3 China's Role in Global Value Chains

International trade accounting theory and its outcomes on global value chains have attracted great attention from international organizations and the western world, as well as become one of the topics of the 2013 G20 Summit. In the long-term, the reform of international trade statistics will be a strong trend and its process will be accompanied and supported by the battle for the rights to set international economic and trade rules. The majority of developing countries, especially the emerging powers, demand for an equal and fair voice in determining these. We hope that through the joint efforts of the international community, a fair and reasonable system of world economic rules and standards will eventually be established. This system must be able to scientifically reflect the value added and contribution of various countries in global value chains, restore the true state of global trade; it ought to be able to objectively reflect the development and interest demands of countries from the north to the south, and keep up with times; it must be able to promote the just and equitable development of international economic order, and thus contribute to global economic prosperity and stability.

Currently, with the joint efforts of the government, academia and research parties, China has caught up with the major developed countries in global value chains research and continues to participate in international cooperation and exchanges regarding TiVA accounting in global value chains. Using this as a point of breakthrough, China resolutely safeguards the liberalization and facilitation of the multilateral trading system, opposes all forms of protectionism, and actively participates in the development of accurate and fair international economic and trade rules and standards. This will bring more developmental opportunities, whether for a more open China or for the world.

3.1 *China's research progress and preliminary conclusions*

Since 2010, when the WTO called for international trade statistics to be improved from the perspective of global value chains, China, as the second largest trading nation, has been concerned about the value added content in its foreign trade and has actively promoted research in global value chains and TiVA. It has organized specialized research teams to augment its efforts to explore ways to make up for the flaws in the traditional trade statistics system using TiVA accounting. The Chinese Ministry of Commerce, Customs and other ministries have commissioned the Chinese Academy of Sciences to conduct topical research. Research groups separated processing trade from domestic production, proposed a systematic method of calculating Chinese value added in exports, and established a non-competitive input–output model that is appropriate for studying Chinese TiVA in exports. The main conclusions are as follows.

3.1.1 *Results of China's value-added exports*

- China's unitary exports contain low value-added content. In 2012, every USD1,000 worth of exports brought USD621 of DVA to China. This fully reflects the gradual integration of China into the global economy and its participation in international division of labor. China saw an increase in inter-industry, intra-industry and intra-company foreign trade (see Table 7.5).
- Processing trade exports had a relatively weaker stimulating effect on DVA than general trade exports. In 2010, only USD386 worth of DVA were brought to China for every USD1,000 worth of processing trade exports, which was less than half that of general trade exports. As the important feature of the processing trade is "processing", not only does it generate technological spillover effects, it also improves corporate governance and management capacity, promotes domestic brands and the construction of marketing channels, as well as creates a large number of jobs. In 2011, China's processing trade exports created employment for 18.58 million people. In addition, the "two foreign ends" characteristic of the processing trade precisely reflects the nature of China's foreign trade, that is, a more concentrated reflection of China's integration with the global economy,

Table 7.5 China's foreign trade value added data: USD in 100 millions.

	2002	2007	2010	2011	2012
Total product trade exports	3,256	12,205	15,778	18,984	20,487
DVA brought by product trade exports	1,685	6,963	9,405	11,457	12,721
Percentage of imports in total product trade exports (%)	48.2	43	40.4	39.6	37.9
Total trade in products and services			17,490	20,806	22,392
DVA brought in by trade in products and services			10,756	12,858	14,336
Percentage of imports in trade in products and services (%)			38.5	38.2	36.0

Source: Authors' compilation.

Note: In 2010–2011, the foreign trade value added was separated into general trade and processing trade according to input–output model measurements.

global value chains and international production networks. The processing trade is more integrated with the international market than general trade.

- The DVA content of China's exports from the textile industry, clothing and fashion accessories, leather and down products, processed wood, furniture manufacturing industries and other traditional labor-intensive industries as well as non-metallic minerals manufacturing industries is relatively high. Every USD1,000 worth of exports brings an average of USD700–800 worth of DVA to China. This reflects the status of Chinese industries' participation in global value chains, and also fully shows its international industrial competitiveness (see Table 7.6).

Table 7.6 DVA content for every USD1,000 worth of exports in 2010 according to industries: USD.

Industry	DVA	Industry	DVA
Agriculture, forestry, animal husbandry and fishing industries	925	Metal smelting and rolling industries	526
Coal mining and cleaning industry	856	Fabricated metal products	729
Oil and gas industry	853	General and special equipment manufacturing	604
Non-ferrous metal mining industry	867	Transportation equipment manufacturing	521
Non-metallic minerals and other mining industries	566	Electrical machinery and equipment manufacturing	523
Food products and tobacco industries	679	Communications, computers and other electronic equipment manufacturing	447
Textile industry	786	Instrumentation and office machinery manufacturing	409
Clothing, shoes and hats, leather and down product manufacturing industries	749	Crafts and other manufacturing	612
Wood processing and furniture manufacturing industries	732	Electricity, heat, gas and water production and supply industries	662
Paper-making, printing, education and sports product manufacturing industries	564	Construction industry	727
Oil processing, refining and nuclear fuel processing industries	211	Transportation and warehousing industries	787
Chemical industries	504	Wholesale and retail industries	941
Non-metallic mineral industries	796	Other service industries	880

Source: Authors' compilation.

- The value added from transportation and freight equipment, electrical appliances and instruments, communications equipment, computers and other electronic equipment, meters and measurement devices, cultural and clerical machinery manufacturing is relatively low. Out of USD1,000 worth of exports, the average DVA brought to China is less than USD550, reflecting the direction of China's industrial structure upgrading, which is also one focus of China's future industrial advantages.

3.1.2 *DVA of Chinese exports to major trading partners*

- The value added brought by China's product exports to India is the highest, followed by the EU, ASEAN, Japan, the US and Korea (see Table 7.7).
- The DVA from processing trade exports is relatively lower than that of general trade. In 2010, the DVA brought by China's processing trade to the US, the EU, ASEAN, Japan, Korea and India was 50.7%, 50.6%, 46.4%, 48.1%, 54.1% and 51.2% that of general trade to the same countries respectively.

3.1.3 *The value added to various countries by China's imports from major trading partners*

The data on value added brought to trading partners by China's imports shows that the US receives the highest value added while the value added brought to the EU, Japan and India are relatively close. However, there is a common feature, that is, the value added that China's imports bring to these four trade partners is much higher that the value added that exports from these countries bring to China. The value added brought to Korea is the lowest.

3.1.4 *Bilateral trade balance measured using value-added accounting methods*

- In 2011 and 2012, the China-US trade surpluses according to traditional trade statistics were USD202.4 billion and USD218.9 billion, respectively. However, measurements using value added revealed that China-US trade surpluses were USD92.6 billion and USD101.7 billion, a drop of 54.2% and 54.0% respectively.
- In 2011 and 2012, traditional trade statistics show that China-EU trade surpluses were USD144.8 billion and USD121.9 billion respectively, while according to value added accounting methods, the trade surpluses

Table 7.7 DVA of every USD1,000 worth of exports from China to major trading partners: USD.

| | 2010 | | | 2011 | | | 2012 | | |
	Total exports	Processing trade exports	General trade exports	Total exports	Processing trade exports	General trade exports	Total exports	Processing trade exports	General trade exports
Overall	615	387	781	618	384	776	621	386	792
USA	563	398	785	574	396	783	585	387	804
EU	651	392	774	656	390	773	631	392	805
ASEAN	608	351	756	625	355	753	661	363	791
Japan	565	378	786	575	379	779	599	395	818
Korea	558	394	728	561	387	720	587	413	779
India	652	371	725	658	371	727	695	377	778

Source: Authors' compilation.

were respectively lowered to USD80.3 billion and USD53.8 billion, a percentage decrease of 44.5% and 56.0% respectively.

- The China-Japan trade deficits measured using value added accounting methods compared with traditional trade statistics show that deficits grew by 41.8% and 71% in 2011 and 2012 respectively.
- China-Korea trade deficits decreased by 43.5% and 49% in 2011 and 2012 respectively, when measured using the value added accounting method. This is mainly because China's imports from Korea brought relatively low value added to Korea, and the value was lower than China's exports' value added to Korea in the same year.
- Traditional trade statistics showed trade deficits between China and ASEAN but using the value added accounting method, the deficits became surpluses. In 2010 and 2011, China to ASEAN trade balance transformed from USD −16.6 billion and USD −23.2 billion to USD2 billion and USD200 million respectively.

3.1.5 *The stimulating effect of China's imports on trade partners' employment*

Chinese imports from its major trading partners created a great amount of employment for these countries and regions. China's imports had the greatest stimulating impact on India's job market. In 2010 and 2011, for every USD1 million worth of products China imported from India, 228.4 and 268.1 jobs were created in India respectively. This was followed by Korea, the EU, Japan and the US which was the lowest. In 2010 and 2011, for every USD1,000 worth of products China imported from the US, the number of people employed was 0.0061 and 0.0060 respectively.

3.2 *China's future exploration of global value chains*

3.2.1 *Trade in value-added products can be a useful complement to the existing customs statistics system*

Currently, there are many constraints on the development of a comprehensive international trade statistics system that can fully reflect the changes in global value chains and the patterns of division of labor. First, it is challenging to harmonize the international statistical systems such as the trade in goods and trade in services statistics system, and the national economic accounting system *etc.* Second, it is expensive to implement a new product trade statistics system. The current statistics mechanism has been run, inspected, maintained and improved on for many years. It would be too costly to cast it all aside to start afresh. Third, the international organizations responsible for the existing mechanism will also hold onto their statistical authority and not go against themselves. Under the current circumstances, research in TiVA and statistical system design is more to complement the existing international trade statistics system.

A plausible method for consideration is to obtain intermediate goods trade statistics from existing trade in goods statistics, and deduct intermediate product volume from total trade volume to estimate trade in value added. By including national accounting data and bilateral trade in goods and services data in the international input–output tables, the sources and uses of intermediate products between countries and industries can be identified. Then using complex matrix computation, the proportion of a country's export value added in total export volume can be obtained. This approach produces different results due to the specific factors involved such as different input databases, different accounting methodologies, relevant assumptions and data adjustments *etc.* Currently, the Customs Department is also actively promoting research in TiVA accounting methods. Since the latter half of 2012, the department has carried out investigations on export trends and attempted to determine the final destination of imported products.

3.2.2 *Using the trade in value-added accounting method to evaluate the contribution of foreign trade to economic growth*

The existing accounting method has its shortcomings and can be, in some cases, misleading. For example, in evaluating the influence of foreign trade on economic growth, the indicator of "contribution of foreign trade to economic growth" is used and when net annual export volume is negative, the contribution of foreign trade is also correspondingly negative. Absurd conclusions will be achieved should foreign trade be explained with this method. The TiVA accounting method, in the context of global value chains, is able to establish the influence that exports have on domestic economic growth, income, and employment by way of an accurate analysis of exports' DVA, and arrive at a more objective evaluation of the economic contribution of foreign trade.

3.2.3 *Construction of China's global value chains and trade in value-added accounting database*

A large amount of national economic accounting data is required for developing global value chains and TiVA accounting work. Data on China's trade in products, trade in services, international balance of payments, national economic accounts and other information need to be collated and prepared to conduct TiVA accounting using input–output tables. Data on trade in goods are relatively simple to collect as the only source of information is import and export clearance of goods declarations and approvals. Trade in services information is relatively more complex as there are more departments involved, for example, the People's Bank of China and the State Administration of Foreign Exchange are responsible for financial services data, the China Banking Regulatory Commission is in charge of banking services statistics, the China Securities Regulatory Commission is responsible for data on security services, the Ministry of Communications and the Civil Aviation Administration of China are responsible for transport statistics, tourism statistics are under the charge of the National Tourism Administration, and computer and information services are under the jurisdiction of the Ministry of Industry and Information Technology. Thus, to establish a TiVA accounting system, a stronger statistical foundation needs to be in place, and work should start from areas such as basic statistics, survey systems, administrative records, statistical methods and legal concepts *etc.*

At the same time, national economic statistics and other data such as customs information should be integrated to construct a database that is open to the public, to make the TiVA accounting system available to all. Unlike the traditional industrial analysis and customs warning database, the construction of this database can be based on comparative advantages, and guide the transformation and upgrading of domestic industries, becoming the starting point for combining trade and industrial policies. With the TiVA database, historical data can be used to explore the reformation and upgrading of law and find a new pivotal point for a new round of opening up. This approach and the relevant data can also be used for in-depth studies on ways to transform and improve China's foreign trade.

3.3 Implications that global value chains have on China's trade policies

Global value chains have changed every nation's understanding of economic globalization. Due to the integration of production and trade, international trade is no longer a zero-sum game, that is, one party has to lose in order for another party to profit. Economic and trade relations between countries have transformed from singular competitive exclusion to coexistence through division of labor and competition, and parties become stakeholders in the same value chain. One country's restrictions or prohibitions on certain trade in products and services of another country will disrupt the operation of the entire value chain thus affecting its own interests. Countries have to shift from managing the balance of surpluses and deficits to supporting and encouraging trade, investment liberalization and facilitation policies.

For China, results from global value chains research have also supported the establishment of an open economy in a broader sense. The new perspectives and issues it has raised are largely consistent with the demands from various aspects such as the transformation and structural upgrading of China's current economic growth and the improvement of laborers' income. The re-evaluation and examination of existing trade perspectives, and adjusting of export-related policies according to the TiVA accounting method aids trade in promoting economic growth.

Firstly, global value chains concepts guide enterprises towards the two extensions of a "smile curve" to obtain more prominent competitive advantage. Participating in value creation of products based on the division of labor in global value chains allows developing countries to not be limited to traditional upgrading of division of labor from agriculture to industries to services, but facilitates the movement upstream and downstream along various parts of the global value chains in terms of division of labor. With the accurate assessment of the division of labor and competitiveness of various products and industries in the global value chains, the focus of upgrading and transformation of Chinese industries can be on utilizing the spillover effects of multinational corporations' advanced knowledge and technology. This can enhance design, development, marketing, services and other advanced production factors, and nurture international competitive advantage towards the two ends of the value chains so that while consolidating the position of "China Manufacturing" and "China Processing", "China Marketing" and "China Innovation" are also strongly promoted.

Secondly, the changes that global value chains have made in traditional production and international trade reveal that we are developing towards trade in services and production services in particular. Services closely link various segments in the production chain together and integrate and coordinate the various segments of independent and globalized production. At the same time, they also play an important part in value creation. In recent years, the proportion of trade in services in world trade has increased significantly. Currently, the value of services in intermediate input accounts for 30% of the total value added in manufactured products. In global value chains, services play an important role in every segment of production: the initial stages of feasibility studies, product concept design and development, market research, quality control, the rental, maintenance and repair of equipment, recruitment of staff and training and management, legal issues, transport and communications, insurance and finance aspects of the production process, the advertisements, distribution and circulation, transport and delivery, maintenance and other items required at the final stages of product sales. The liberalization of trade in services helps us to improve the competitiveness of the manufacturing industry in global value chains by streamlining services to improve their quality and efficiency.

Thirdly, the strengthening of cooperation with international organizations has led to active participation in the formulation of trade statistics rules. The TiVA accounting method has played a positive role in the objective assessment of areas such as China's trade balance, export dependence, industry position, international industrial participation, and industrial comparative advantage. The main priority now is to pay attention to and rely on international organizations' platforms to actively participate in international research on statistical methods and programs. This will allow China to join the countries using official statistics to conduct TiVA accounts early and, in turn, strengthen its voice in trade statistics reform.

As international organizations are promoting TiVA accounting work, China should seize the opportunity to initiate joint research projects with trade partners to analyze the issues of trade balance that exist among them using different statistical approaches. This would encourage parties to form a more objective and unified view of the issues, actively promote the improvement and implementation of China's use of TiVA accounting methods, and give better foresight when making foreign economic policies. On the other hand, China ought to also support international organizations' ways of coordinating national data and measurements, and actively participate in and support the relevant research conducted by WTO, UNCTAD and other important international organizations. China should encourage international organizations to share their data, and also reflect Chinese demands in international cooperation so as to contribute towards the establishment of a global, unified and standardized TiVA accounting system.

Chapter 8

Rules of Trade in Services

Among the materials for trade rules training compiled by the WTO Secretariat, there is a cartoon about a Spanish patient lying on the operating table in an operating theater in a German-owned hospital in Geneva, Switzerland. Standing around the operating table are a British surgeon doctor and several French nurses. The doctor looked perplexed and apparently encountered a difficult problem. He said to one of the nurses: "Search the internet quickly and enter the US website SURGERY.COM. Then click on the icon that says 'Are you totally confused?'"

This comic strip, which seems absurd, is actually a good reflection of the rapid development of the international trade in services in the context of globalization. This small surgical website actually contains all four modes of trade in services: cross-border supply (the US health website provides advice for Switzerland), consumption abroad (the Spanish patient receives medical services in Switzerland), commercial presence (German investors set up the hospital in Switzerland), presence of natural persons (the British doctor and French nurses provide medical services in Switzerland)! This operation can be achieved because of the liberalization of foreign direct investment, convenience of professional accreditation, ease of international travel, as well as the opening up of borders, common use of internet technology and other conveniences brought about by modern society. Imagine if Switzerland did not allow foreigners to open a local hospital and provide medical services, or blocked foreign medical sites and did not issue visas to foreign visitors or patients, then this comic strip, featuring a surgical procedure, would not exist.

But on the other hand, even if the Swiss authorities allow foreigners to establish hospitals and provide medical services in the country, there are still rules under Swiss domestic law that require foreign management staff and medical personnel to obtain business or work visas before entry. Their qualifications and academic background have to be reviewed and recognized. The specific standards of medical equipment and staffing of foreign hospital must be set in place and their service standards inspected and verified. In essence, it is the responsibility of government to ensure the quality of domestic medical services and protect the interests of patients and consumers.

Clearly, the global expansion of trade in services is inseparable from the opening up of the services market, movement of people and capital, scientific and technological progress, and also the regulation of the market and services of each country and the adjustment and implementation of relevant laws and regulations. So, what are the prevailing rules in international trade in services currently? How are negotiations progressing? How will it develop in the future? What are the impact and implications for China?

1 The Dilemma of Multilateral Rules of Trade in Services in Doha

1.1 *Brief description of multilateral rules of trade in services*

Trade in services refers specifically to the provision and trade in services between different countries or economies. Unlike trade in goods, the objects of trade in services are not physical goods but services provided by a person or organization. The processes of production or provision and consumption often occur simultaneously and are inseparable. In addition, although the various types of services must be produced or supplied by physically existing persons institutions or related equipments. Trade in services is in itself invisible and intangible, therefore trade in services is also often referred to as the "invisible trade". Currently, the international trade in services still lacks complete, reliable and timely statistical data. It is generally believed that the total amount of cross-border trade in commercial services is equivalent to about a quarter of total international trade in goods. According to data released by the WTO Secretariat in April 2013, the total trade in services in the world was about USD4.345 trillion in 2012.[1]

---

[1]WTO Press Release, "Trade to Remain Subdued in 2013 After Sluggish Growth in 2012 as European Economies Continue to Struggle," April 10, 2013, retrieved from http://www.wto.org/english/news_e/pres13_e/pr688_e.htm.

1.1.1 *The four modes of suppling trade in services*

From the literal point of view, the trade in services refers to "services" as the objects of trading. However, there is no recognized definition for "services" internationally. In the "General Agreement on Trade in Services" (GATS) of the WTO, definitions are only provided based on the different ways to trade in services.

According to the definitions given by GATS, trade in services can be supplied through four modes:

(1) The supply of a service from the territory of one Member into the territory of any other Member is called "cross-border supply" or Mode 1. In this mode, the service suppliers and service consumers are in different customs territories. However, the service crosses the border through modern communication technologies. For example, when a German architect provides architectural design services to a company in Switzerland via fax or e-mail; or a Swedish physician provides medical advice to a hospital in South Africa through a video call.

(2) The supply of a service in the territory of one Member to the service consumer of any other Member is called "consumption abroad" or Mode 2. In this mode, the service consumers are abroad and spend on the consumer services provided by local service suppliers. For example, when American tourists travel to Spain and enjoy local food and beverage, transportation, tour guide services; or when Chinese students study in Australia and receive local higher education services.

(3) The supply of a service by a service supplier of one Member, through commercial presence in the territory of any other Member is termed "commercial presence" or Mode 3. In this mode, the service suppliers enter the territory where the service consumers are and establish commercial organizations to provide services. For example, Citibank sets up branches and subsidiaries to provide services like deposits and loans; or the French Carrefour chain stores provide retail services in China.

(4) The supply of a service by a service supplier of one Member, through presence of natural persons of a Member in the territory of any other Member is known as "presence of natural persons" or Mode 4. In this mode, the service suppliers enter the customs territory where the service consumers are. They provide services as employees, contractors or individuals. For example, when a French company in Vietnam hires German experts to provide technical services in Vietnam; or an Indian dentist opens a clinic in the US and provides dental services as an individual.

1.1.2 *The basic principles of GATS*

GATS was one of the most important achievements in the Uruguay Round of multilateral trade negotiations. It was the first time that multilateral rules were established in trade in services internationally and the only framework agreement to regulate trade in services in the multilateral trading system. GATS set the framework for opening up and regulating international trade in services. The principles of progressive liberalization of trade in services among WTO members in accordance with their level of economic development and regulatory capacity were recognized. Moreover, the negotiating mechanism to promote the liberalization of international trade in services within WTO was set up through successive rounds of negotiations. Thus, the openness and transparency of the international service market have developed greatly, and the confidence of service suppliers in overseas investment and legal environment has increased. Hence, the trade in services worldwide has expanded.

There are a total of 29 articles and 8 Annexes in GATS. In addition, the schedual of specific commitment on services of each WTO member is also considered part of the GATS. This chapter will only describe some of the most basic rules in the GATS, including MFN, market access and national treatment, and transparency.

(1) MFN

The obligation of equal treatment to all other WTO members is generally applicable to all services sectors, including sectors in which a member has made commitments and those where commitments have not been made. In other words, whether WTO members implement relevant measures in its commitment to open trade sectors, or take open or restrictive measures in sectors without commitment, they must treat all trading partners equally.

There may be some temporary exceptions to MFN. Members need to list the "MFN exceptions" in their first submission of schedules in service trades, giving a particular sector of a specific member more favorable treatment. However, this exception can only be applied once and it cannot be re-applied or increased. There will be a periodic review for this and the period of exemption cannot be more than 10 years in principle.

(2) Market access and national treatment

The multilateral commitment of WTO members in trade in services is reflected in the Schedule of Specific Commitments. These schedules are reached through trade negotiations among members. They state the commitments of members on market access and national treatment, including open sectors, the level of market access to the sectors, as well as the retained market access and national treatment limitation. For example, if a member allows foreign retailers to operate in its territory, the retail services sector must commit to market access; if the member limits the foreign equity or number of stores that can be set up by foreign retailers, it is retaining market access restrictions; if a member requires foreign retailers to pay higher capital than similar domestic enterprises, it is withholding national treatment. WTO members are obliged to open their markets in accordance with the conditions listed in the schedule for foreign services and service suppliers (see Table 8.1). They may be challenged or sued by other members if they fail to do so and even face the rulings of the Dispute Settlement Body (DSB) in WTO.

It should be noted that GATS does not require members to provide services when the government is exercising authority or not operating on a commercial basis.

(3) Transparency

WTO members must promptly publish all laws and regulations affecting trade in services and establish inquiry points in government institutions. If there is

Table 8.1 Schedule of specific commitments on trade in services (sample table). Modes of supply: (1) cross-border supply, (2) consumption abroad, (3) commercial presence and (4) presence of natural persons.

Sectors or sub-sectors	Limitations on market access	National treatment limitations	Other commitments
C. Retail Services (excluding tobacco)	(1) None (2) None (3) Only joint ventures are permitted and majority foreign ownership is permitted for joint ventures; for chain stores with more than 30 branches, foreign equity shall not exceed 50%. (4) Unbound except as indicated in Horizontal commitment.	(1) None (2) None (3) There is no limitation except for the following: The registered capital of the joint venture is different from the domestic companies. (4) Unbound except as indicated in Horizontal commitment.	

Source: Author's compilation.

any change to legal measures affecting services trade in sectors with specific commitments, members need to notify WTO.

1.1.3 *The enabling provisions in GATS*

GATS is different from GATT and it has been in effect for a shorter period of time. There is less judicial interpretation and legal practice. The rules should be strengthened or revised. To solve this problem, the GATS itself also contains a number of enabling provisions, mandating members to negotiate on market access and related rules. The main provisions related to negotiation on rules are as follow: Article VI, paragraph 4 (regarding multilateral discipline on domestic regulation), Article X (emergency safeguard measures), Article XIII (government procurement) and Article XV (subsidies).

1.2 *Rules of trade in services in the Doha Round negotiations*

In theory, the Doha Round of trade negotiations on service trade can be divided into two parts. One is the negotiations on rules of trade in services. The other is negotiations on the market access of trade in services by means of "request" and "offer" based on the schedule of specific commitments on trade in services. But in fact, the two cannot be completely separated. Taking the example of a negotiation on the movement of natural persons, it is an indispensable element of market access negotiations. It can also be considered as part of the rules negotiations. Overall, the services trade rules negotiations and market access negotiations are closely related. The former provides the laws and rules of security for the latter while the latter enriches and inspects the practicality and effectiveness of the rules. The revision and improvement of existing rules, and the design and development of new rules are provided for ideas and direction. The Doha Round negotiations on rules of trade in services included domestic regulation, emergency safeguard measures, government procurement, subsidies and movement of natural persons and other issues. So far, little progress has been made in negotiations in the above-mentioned topics except in domestic regulation.

1.2.1 *Domestic regulation*

(1) Background of negotiations

The purpose of GATS Article VI (domestic regulation) is to ensure that WTO members make a commitment to implement general national laws, regulations and measures for the services sector in a reasonable, objective and impartial manner. In addition, members should provide appropriate procedures, so that the service suppliers can appeal for reconsideration of the administrative decisions affecting their trade. At the same time, the negotiating parties recognize that even non-discriminatory domestic regulatory measures are also likely to restrict trade in services. Therefore, GATS Article VI, paragraph 4 requests a continuation of negotiations in this area to establish multilateral regulations. This is to ensure that the qualification requirements and procedures, technical standards and licensing requirements of service suppliers are objective and transparent, and do not create unnecessary trade barriers. Before the formation of this multilateral regulation, members should also comply with the principles and targets in the implementation of their requirements and standards, so that the trading interests of other members are not affected. According to this mandate, WTO members have established the "Domestic Regulation Working Group" at the Council for Trade in Services to organize and develop relevant rules of negotiation. According to the consensus reached at the WTO Hong Kong Ministerial Conference in 2008, members would establish multilateral disciplines related to domestic regulation at the end of the Doha Round negotiations.

At present, domestic regulation is the only area in rules making that negotiations have made substantive progress. Members have basically agreed to develop multilateral disciplines to specify the regulatory measures in the domestic service sector judicial persons. This is to ensure the licensing requirements and procedures for qualification requirements and procedures for natural persons, as well as technical standards and other regulatory measures do not become trade barriers. The key to successful negotiations is to strike a balance between regulatory authority and take liberalization among the members.

(2) Overall progress of negotiations and focus of debate

The negotiations entered the text-based phase from 2007 and the draft text was completed in March 2009. The draft was an outcome of compromise from all parties. The emphasis was on regulatory authority and there were fewer constraints on members. Most of the provisions were soft disciplines which aimed for "best efforts".

At the moment, the biggest point of disagreement in the negotiations is whether the "necessity test" should be included in multilateral disciplines. The so-called "necessity test" refers to the evaluation of whether a trade policy measure taken by a member to achieve a reasonable goal recognized by WTO is consistent with the WTO rules and is "necessary", that is, if it can be replaced by another measure with lower trade restrictions. If the "necessity test" becomes part of the domestic regulation disciplines, it means that GATS will determine the domestic regulation of WTO members and the legitimate objectives WTO members. It can require members to achieve these objectives by taking measures which generate less impact on trade. The less impact the better, so as to not cause "unnecessary" restrictions on trade. Obviously, this will impose more stringent constraints on WTO member's policy space and regulatory discretion.

The main driving force for negotiations is small- and medium-sized open economies like Australia, Switzerland, and Chinese Hong Kong *etc.* They believe that the draft text is not ambitious enough and advocate changing most of the "soft disciplines" into mandatory and binding "hard clauses", including the "necessity test" clause. The US, Canada, Brazil, South Africa and other members request respect for the "regulatory power" of the members, and emphasize that overly-strict multilateral discipline will suppress the regulatory space and restrict the regulatory capacity. They are against the inclusion of the "necessity test" clause.

But on the other hand, the developed members generally require greater transparency and better discipline for licensing procedures and requirements. They encourage the developing members to increase the transparency of domestic regulation, lower the licensing requirements, and simplify licensing procedures to protect the interests of developed members in terms of service exports. The developing members, least developed countries, small and vulnerable economies *etc.* are more interested in the discussion the qualification requirements and procedures, and special and differential treatments related to natural persons.

Although negotiations on this subject have made substantial progress, they were hindered by the overall process of the Doha Round negotiations. The negotiations came to a halt. Some demanders stressed that the mandate of domestic regulation negotiations originates from the GATS itself, therefore, the negotiations should be independent of the process of the Doha Round negotiations and not be affected by its success or failure. However, due to the resistance by some members in recent years, the parties have not continued the consultation on the text.

1.2.2 *Emergency safeguard measures, government procurement and subsidies*

(1) Background of negotiations

Like domestic regulation negotiations, emergency safeguard measures, government procurement and subsidies are on the built-in agenda during the GATS negotiations. These are subjects that GATS has mandated members for negotiations in the text. The GATS only requires members to explore the possibility of establishing discipline in these three areas and does not require negotiations to achieve concrete results.

GATS Article X states "there shall be multilateral negotiations on the question of emergency safeguard measures based on the principles of non-discrimination". It shows that it does not directly authorize members to implement relevant measures or establish appropriate mechanisms, but treats such measures as an unsolved "problem" and requires members to carry on negotiations. Therefore, many WTO members including the US and European countries oppose the establishment of emergency safeguard measures in multilateral mechanisms, citing the reason of "unclear mandate". They are also against any member using emergency safeguard measures. Although GATS Article X also states that "the results of such negotiations shall enter into effect on a date not later than three years from the date of entry into force of the WTO Agreement" This mandate has been repeatedly postponed. From the establishment of WTO till now, the negotiations have lasted for two decades and have yet to yield any tangible results.

The negotiating mandate of government procurement in GATS Article XIII is "there shall be multilateral negotiations on government procurement in services under this Agreement within two years from the date of entry into force of the WTO Agreement". This mandate did not provide specific guiding principles for the framework and objectives of the negotiations.

GATS Article XV is also not clear in mandating negotiations on subsidies: "Members recognize that, in certain circumstances, subsidies may have distortive effects on trade in services. Members shall enter into negotiations with a view to developing the necessary multilateral disciplines to avoid such trade distortive effects". With regard to "what the certain circumstances are" and which subsidies may constitute "distorting effects", the negotiating mandate has yet to give guidance to members, resulting in many opposing the establishment of discipline in subsidies or unwilling to submit the information of their national subsidy policies.

Given the above situation, the WTO "Hong Kong Ministerial Declaration" in 2005 only required members to develop disciplines on domestic regulations before the end of the Doha Round negotiations. Concerning the other three issues, the only requirement is to strengthen the negotiations and discuss the "possible" multilateral disciplines. Looking at the current situation, even if the Doha Round negotiations finally conclude, it is only possible to achieve some results in the field of domestic regulation. The differences among members during the negotiations on emergency safeguard measures, government procurement and subsidies are too great. It is unlikely that multilateral disciplines will be established in the current round of negotiations.

(2) Overall progress in negotiations and the focus of debate:

Emergency Safeguard Measures: ASEAN is the main driving force for this subject. It recommends referring to the "Agreement on Safeguards" under the GATT framework to establish a similar safeguards mechanism within the service sector. When the import of services from other WTO members surges, a member can take restrictive measures on trade in services under this protection mechanism to protect the domestic industry from serious damage or threat of serious damage. ASEAN proposes step-by-step discussions to deal with the technical problems and establish the mechanism, paving the way for possible future multilateral disciplines. Currently, WTO members have had several discussions on related issues but there has been little progress. Moreover, most of the developed members like the US and European countries have questioned the necessity and feasibility of establishing an emergency safeguards mechanism in trade in services. In addition, the key questions such as how to define "domestic industry" and how to determine the existence of "damage" differ greatly among the members.

Government Procurement:[2] The EU is the main driving force for government procurement. Through negotiations, it hopes to reach an agreement as an annex of GATS to regulate programs related to government procurement. The major developing members like India, Brazil and South Africa oppose the idea. According to the EU plan, members should discuss in stages various aspects like the importance, market opening and market access. However, the idea has not been widely supported by the members.

The EU actively promotes government procurement negotiations with the intention of driving developing members to open up the markets of government procurement further and make commitments. South Africa and other developing members believe that the discussion should focus on how the service

---

[2]Currently, the WTO has plurilateral agreements which apply to a few members on government procurement, namely GPA (an introduction can be found in Chapter 9). The government procurement negotiations under the GATS framework aim to discuss whether and how government procurement rules can be developed and applied to all WTO members in trade in services.

providers from developing member states can enter the government procurement markets of developed countries.

Subsidies: Unlike the specialized disciplines on subsidies in the trade of goods under GATT (*i.e.* "Agreement on Subsidies and Countervailing Measures"), the GATS framework has not established specialized disciplines on subsidies in trade in services. When the WTO members use service subsidies, they only have to comply with MFN, transparency, and the principle of national treatment to a certain extent (*i.e.* unless there is a reservation or exemption, they should provide subsidies equally to domestic and foreign services and service suppliers alike). However, some WTO members consider that the subsidies in trade in services may distort trade and cause discrimination to foreign services and service suppliers. Therefore, the reference should be GATT and a set of countervailing regulations should be established in trade in services. Currently, the parties differ considerably in their opinions on the necessity and feasibility of establishing such disciplines. The discussions only focus on issues regarding the definition of subsidies on trade in services, exchange of information among members and so on.

The amount of subsidies in the service sector of the US is huge and there are many projects. Therefore, it has been stressed that there is no material impact of subsidies on trade in services and the US is against the general application of multilateral disciplines. There are many subsidies in services in the EU but the policies are more transparent. The EU is willing to share information about their subsidies in services with other members. India has been actively promoting the exchange of information on subsidies but most of the developing members are not proactive in submitting the information on subsidies. The main countries and regions driving the negotiations are small open economies like Switzerland, Chinese Hong Kong *etc.* Switzerland requests that negotiation of disciplines on subsidies and the exchange of information on subsidies happen at the same time. It also submitted a proposal to limit export subsidies for trade in services but did not receive support from the majority of members.

1.2.3 *Movement of natural persons*

(1) Background of negotiations

The negotiations on the movement of natural persons in trade in services mainly target Mode 4 as defined in GATS, that is the presence of natural persons. For the category of natural persons, besides the definition in GATS Article I, paragraph 2 ("the service supplier of a member provides service through any natural person of other members from their territories"), there are further requirements in the GATS Annex "regarding the movement of natural persons in providing services under this Agreement", namely the provisions of paragraph 2 in the Annex — "This Agreement shall not apply to the measures affecting natural persons seeking access to the job market of a member of the natural measures, nor shall it apply to measures with the permanent basis of citizenship, residence or employment measures". Under this agreement framework, GATS actually excludes foreigners seeking employment in the host country, as well as foreigners working for long periods of time in the host country. In other words, WTO members are loosening the restrictions on Mode 4 such that it does not apply to the foreigners seeking for employment opportunities after their entry into the countries. It is only applicable to approved foreigners with employee status granted by local foreign institutions or a service contract prior to entry. In addition, GATS does not apply to foreigners employed by local non-foreign-funded enterprises.

From the GATS schedule of current WTO members, the commitment of parties towards natural persons mainly covers two categories of natural persons. The first category refers to the service provided by foreign service suppliers through commercial organizations set up by foreign natural persons in the host country. This includes the foreign employees in the commercial organization, as well as the foreign natural persons who provide services in order to fulfill the contract prepared by their foreign employer or commercial organizations. The second category refers to foreign natural persons serving entirely in their personal capacity in the host country. It is worth noting that for these foreign natural persons, WTO members generally set higher qualifications and academic requirements, and require them to be senior management or experts. They could be service salespeople who do not get paid locally, or staff with professional qualifications or are highly educated.

After the conclusion of the Uruguay Round negotiations in 1993, follow-up negotiations were held as the WTO members were dissatisfied with the conditions of openness of the movement of natural persons. These had been extended till June 30, 1995, but they failed to achieve substantial breakthroughs. There was improvement in the promises of just a handful of members. According to the statistics of the WTO Secretariat, Mode 4 accounts for less than 5%[3] of the global trade in services now but due to the special status of the issue in trade in services, it has received a lot of attention from the developed and developing

---

[3] Andreas Maurer, Joscelyn Magdeleine, "Measuring Trade in Services in Mode 4," World Trade Organization, retrieved from http://artnet.unescap.org/tid/artnet/mtg/reformservice_bp3.pdf.

members and many stakeholders. With the new round of negotiations on trade in services and the Doha Round negotiations officially starting in 2000 and 2001 respectively, the improvement of the WTO members' commitment in terms of movement of natural persons, ways to promote the development of the members and better participation in the new round of negotiations have become important specialized topics in trade in services negotiations and Doha Round negotiations.

(2) Overall progress in negotiations and the focus of debate

Within the four modes of trade in services, the main concern of most of the developing members and least developed countries is Mode 4. This is because the other three modes are often at a competitive disadvantage while Mode 4 provides them with the opportunity to play to their comparative advantage. On the other hand, developed members like the US, the EU and Canada consider that it is necessary to promote their target markets and further reduce barriers on issues concerning the movement of natural persons that is related to commercial presence. This will aid their service suppliers in expanding business overseas.

Since the start of the Doha Round negotiations, the US, the EU, Canada, India, Colombia and other WTO members have raised proposals for the negotiations on the movement of natural persons. In July 2003, 15 developing members including China, India and Colombia also submitted a joint proposal for the negotiations on the movement of natural persons.

Overall, the developed and developing members of both camps have different emphases on issues regarding the movement of natural persons. Developed country members hope to further improve the commitments on natural persons by various parties related to commercial presence, particularly with regard to the movement of management in companies, senior employees, experts *etc*. Developing country members try to promote the improvement of commitments on natural persons unrelated to a commercial presence. They seek to achieve results in the areas of simplifying visa procedures, improving entry of persons, extending the validity of visas, facilitating accreditation as well as further expanding the scope of the GATS definition of natural persons to include more categories of people beyond the current definition which covers only highly skilled personnel.

The WTO Secretariat divides natural persons under Mode 4 into five types according to the current commitment of the various members and their negotiation proposals. They are intra-corporate transferees, business visitors and service salespersons, contractual service suppliers, independent professionals, and others. The first type refers to natural persons directly related to the presence of business. The other types are natural persons not necessarily linked to the presence of business.

Starting from 2003, more than 70 WTO members, including China, have submitted initial offers of trade in services and revised offer, of which the level of commitment of some members has improved in terms of movement of natural persons. This includes improvements in intra-corporate transferees and opportunities of market access for business visitors, increase of contract service suppliers and independent professionals in the natural persons category, extension in the validity of the visas, abolition or reduction of financial needs tests, and an increase in open sectors. But overall, there is still a big gap between the bids of developed and developing members. For example, the US essentially did not make an offer for Mode 4 and stuck to its level of commitment in the Uruguay Round. Although the EU, Japan and Canada have made improvements in their bids for Mode 4, these come with additional restrictions in sectors and qualifications and therefore, cannot meet the requests of most developing members.

1.2.4 *Troubled trade in services negotiations*

After the global financial crisis, the positions of developed members like the US and European countries have further declined in the international trade system. They feel that the original objectives and approach of the Doha Round negotiations have not adequately reflected the changes in international trade patterns. Therefore, they do not want to make substantive concessions in sensitive sectors. On the other hand, they urge China, India, Brazil and other emerging economies to assume more international responsibility to make more and greater trade concessions. There is a conflict between the above-mentioned position of developed members and the position of developing members which insists that "development" should be the core of negotiations and that the situation in developing countries should be fully taken into account, especially in agricultural and industrial market access negotiations. The two sides oppose each other strongly and negotiations have stalled. Due to the "package" approach of multilateral trade negotiations, market access negotiations of trade in services have come to a halt, which in turn hinder trade in services negotiations, causing consultations on each topic to be stalled.[4]

---

[4]On December 7, 2013, an "Early Harvest" agreement was reached during the WTO Ninth Ministerial Meeting in the Doha Round. However, the agreement did not involve trade in services negotiations, nor explicitly plan services trade rules negotiations for the future. Thus,

2 The Impact of the Financial Crisis on Negotiations of Trade in Services Rules

2.1 *The impact and implications of the financial crisis on international trade in services*

This financial crisis had a huge impact on international trade. There was a sharp decline in global trade volume of goods as well as the volume of trade in goods in the world's major trading countries. The decline in 2009 was particularly significant as it was as high as 23% and global trade in services of the same year also decreased by about 11%.[5]

After the financial crisis eased, international trade quickly recovered to its pre-crisis levels and global trade in services also saw a rapid rebound. In 2011, the total volume of global import and export trade in services had reached USD8.1942 trillion, comprehensively greater than the highest volume of trade in services before the crisis (which was 2008's USD7.5976 trillion).[6]

The US has a strong competitive advantage in service industries and in trade in services. Currently, the services sector accounts for more than 75% of the US GDP, and its contribution to employment is about 80%.[7] In addition, the US is the world's largest exporter of trade in services, with a huge annual surplus. In 2013, the volume of US trade in services exports was USD662 billion, accounting for 30% of the total US export trade; the trade in services imports amounted to USD432 billion, accounting for about 16% of total US import trade; the annual trade in services surplus was USD230 billion. Compared with the US, China's service industry only produces about 45% of its GDP and its trade in services exports was less than 10% of its total trade in services volume. Furthermore, its trade in services remained in year-round deficit (from 1995 to 2013, it had been in deficit for 19 consecutive years). In 2012, the deficit reached USD90.6 billion.[8]

---

it is still difficult to say whether the rules of multilateral negotiations on trade in services could make substantive progress in the next few years.

[5] WTO, "World Trade Report 2012," retrieved from https://www.wto.org/english/res_e/booksp_e/anrep_e/world_trade_report12_e.pdf, pp. 28–29.

[6] Refer to "China Trade in Services Statistics 2012," China Business Press 2012, Issue 1, p. 23.

[7] Coalition of Services Industry, "The Trade in Services Agreement (TISA)," available from https://servicescoalition.org/negotiations/trade-in-services-agreement.

[8] WTO, World Trade Report 2014, retrieved from http://www.wto.org/english/res_e/booksp_e/world_trade_report14_e.pdf, pp. 32–36.

Presently, China's capacity for trade in services exports is way below that of the US. In 2013, China's trade in services amounted to USD201.6 billion which was less than a third of the US. Moreover, the export of US companies' overseas branches were not included in the above US export figures. In 2010, the US announced that the amount[9] was USD1.1 trillion. If this data was included, the gap between China and the US would be even greater.

Because of the financial crisis, the US, on the one hand, recognized the importance of the real economy and began planning for a "regression to manufacturing" while, on the other hand, they recognized that their core competitiveness lay in their services sector including their strong information industry and their financial industry through which the US is acknowledged to be the global leader. In particular, the US information industry possesses Google, Microsoft, Oracle, Cisco and IBM, which are among the world's most powerful companies as well as having the most advanced technology and management experience and the most excellent talents. As such, in their planning for global trade in services distribution and signing of FTAs, the US pays special attention to the promotion of "free flow of data across borders", "neutral technology", "neutral modes", "competitive neutrality" and other principles and regulations which allow them to play to their strength in financial and information industries' business advantage and boost their services trade exports.

The impact of the financial crisis on the European economy is even more far-reaching. Many countries found it difficult to lift themselves out of the sovereign debt crisis. Apart from Germany, France and a few other countries, most EU member states continued to lose their advantage in the manufacturing sector and could not recover. In such a context, countries put more emphasis on the development of service industries and trade in services, hoping to increase employment, expand exports and get out of their troubled predicament as soon as possible. On the whole, the EU is the world's largest exporter of trade in services. According to data from the press release sent out by the European Commission on February 15, 2013 proposing plurilateral negotiations on trade in services,[10] trade in services made up ¾ of the EU's GDP and employment market, trade in services within the EU accounted for about 30% of intra-EU trade and the FDI of the services industry accounted for 70% of

---

[9] Refer to data released by the US Trade Representative's Office, retrieved from https://ustr.gov/countries-regions/china-mongolia-taiwan/peoples-republic-china#.

[10] European Commission Press Release, "European Commission Proposes to Open Plurilateral Trade Negotiations on Services," February 15, 2013, retrieved from http://europa.eu/rapid/press-release_IP-13-118_en.htm?locale=en.

the EU's FDI flow and 60% of FDI stock. Therefore, the EU believes that the establishment of a new international system of rules in trade, facilitating target markets in liberalizing their trade in services markets will help the EU utilize its existing competitive advantage and boost the export of their services.

As the world's two most important services exporters, the US and the EU are currently the main promoters of negotiations on the liberalization of global trade in services. Their allies include developed economies such as Canada, Australia, Japan, Switzerland, and Chinese Hong Kong, open economies such as Korea, Mexico, and Chile, as well as a few other developing economies who have signed FTAs with several developed economies, such as Turkey, Colombia, Panama *etc*. These economies call themselves the "Real Good Friends of Services" (RGF) and they believe that the promotion of the liberalization of trade in services in the world, and reduction of market access barriers of trade in services, are in line with their industrial interests and beneficial for strengthening their advantage in the trade in services field so as to expand their exports to other markets.

2.2 *The further accentuation of the importance and urgency of trade in services negotiations*

Since the beginning of the new century, the importance of trade in services and investment services in the global economy has become increasingly prominent. New service sectors and types of services emerge every day, and enterprises with service as their core business occupy the highest end of the world's industrial chains. The most classic example is Apple, the American company with one of the world's highest market value. Almost all of the products in its manufacturing process are outsourced while its core businesses are development, design, marketing and other service-related products.

However, GATS, the international legal and regulatory framework for trade in services, is a 20-year-old product that lies in stark contrast with the rapid development of the service industry and trade in services. GATS was established in 1993 and came into force in 1995. After many years, it has become increasingly difficult to deal effectively with the new emerging categories of services as well as the new technologies and problems related to trade in services. Take for example, social networking sites and cloud computing services which appeared in the 21st century. It is tough to clearly classify them under any current category of trade in services, thus WTO members are unable to determine whether their commitments include the above-mentioned services. In addition, with the development of information and communications technology (ICT), new services can often be provided directly across borders and many traditional services are also more readily available through the Internet. However, presently, several WTO members have yet to commit to fully opening up Mode 1 (cross-border supplies) and many service sectors have not been opened up citing "lacking technical feasibility" as a reason. This mismatch in regulatory framework and technological developments has made it challenging for governments to assess market liberalization and implement market regulation. It has also highlighted the inability of the current trade in services management and legal systems to deal with technological progress and market development of trade in services. In fact, the current systems may even be hampering the progress and development of trade in services.

GATS is quite different from the GATT in terms of stringency, comprehensiveness and constraints. As previously mentioned, GATS' negotiating mandate on whether or not emergency safeguard measures, export subsidies and multilateral disciplines of government procurement should be established within the field of trade in services is vague. Moreover, there are no clear negotiating objectives, thus WTO members have formed distinct and even completely opposite interpretations of the same negotiating mandate and text of agreement, resulting in much instability and inconstancy for future multilateral trade rule negotiations.

Furthermore, compared to the GATT, GATS provides much more practical flexibility in terms of national treatment and MFN obligations, allowing members to completely close various service sectors to foreign capital and not provide them with national treatment. GATS also allows members to maintain their MFN exemptions for the long term (the original 10-year period has, in actual fact, been extended indefinitely). Even developed countries such as the US, the EU, and Japan have retained several "non-negotiable zones". For example, the US refuses to make any commitment on maritime transport services; the EU refuses to commit to opening up their audiovisual services sector; and Japan is keeping strict limits on its hospital service sector. In addition, almost all developed members have extremely limited commitments under GATS Mode 4 and have set up extremely stringent requirements for foreign natural persons in terms of vocational qualifications, work experience, language abilities and others. Visa application procedures are also strict and residential periods limited as well. According to the GATS "Annex on movement of natural persons", natural persons are limited to small fields such as professionals, high-tech personnel and management staff, while non-professional and low-skilled workers are entirely excluded. Under the existing GATS framework and negotiating mandate, these trade barriers will not be removed in the foreseeable future.

As such, for both developed and developing members, the revision and improvement of existing GATS rules and on this basis, the reduction and removal of trade barriers bears strong practical significance. On the other hand, the outbreak and subsequent impact of the international financial crisis not only failed to effectively enhance global economic and trade cooperation, it even provided an excuse for a number of countries to implement trade protectionism. This also makes the revision and improvement of the existing legal trade in services framework and promotion of the liberalization process an even more urgent task.

2.3 *The origin and latest developments of TISA negotiations*

2.3.1 *Plurilateral services trade negotiations led by the US and Europe*

As the Doha Round negotiations remained in gridlock, plurilateral trade negotiations were stalled. Developed countries that had significant export interests such as the US, the EU, Canada, Australia and others finally decided to bypass the Doha Round and re-invent the wheel. They led some WTO members with common interests or that took similar stances, *i.e.* the previously mentioned "RGF Group", in launching plurilateral trade negotiations in Geneva, so as to substantively promote the liberalization of trade in services. Since the beginning of 2012, they have held seven rounds of plurilateral discussions in order to reach an agreement on the form of negotiation, objectives and framework for future agreements *etc.* They decided to begin internal negotiating mandate procedures in their respective countries and officially launch the "International Services Agreement" (ISA) negotiations from spring 2013. Later on, these negotiations were renamed TISA negotiations.[11] Till July 2013, a total of 23 WTO members had participated in the TISA negotiations. They included 11 developed countries such as the US, the EU, Canada, Australia, Japan *etc.* as well as 12 developing members such as Korea, Mexico, Pakistan, Turkey, Chinese Hong Kong, and Chinese Taipei.

---

[11] At the meeting of the Trade in Services Council in March 2013, the RGF Group announced that its goal for negotiations is to reach a "Trade in Services Agreement", and renamed the ISA negotiations as TISA. However, there are still a number of media reports that refer to the ISA negotiations as PSA (Plurilateral Services Agreement) negotiations.

According to the "Memo — Negotiations for a Plurilateral Agreement on Trade in Services"[12] released by the European Commission on February 15, 2013, the RGF Group is not an exclusive, fixed organization but a temporary consortium set up by WTO members who are committed to promoting trade in services negotiations. 2010 data reveals that the total volume of trade in services from the members of the Group account for two thirds of the world's total volume in trade in services (excluding intra-EU trade).

2.3.2 The establishment of TISA negotiation objectives and framework

TISA negotiating parties believe that the overall objective of TISA negotiations is to revise, supplement and improve upon existing rules of trade in services, so as to greatly reduce or eliminate market barriers and achieve a high level of liberalization in trade in services.

After TISA negotiations were officially launched, some of the participants, led by the EU, further clarified and proposed that TISA not be just a FTA between the members of the RGF Group but ought to aim to ultimately be included in the WTO system. To this end, TISA should be based on GATS, incorporate some of the core provisions of GATS, strengthen existing disciplines, implement some new disciplines, and achieve higher levels of liberalization. They stressed that TISA should attract the participation of more WTO members in order to become more multilateral at a later stage. However, the US did not seem keen on making the TISA multilateral but was more concerned about whether the TISA could reach a greater level of liberalization of trade in services.

With regard to the mode of commitment, TISA negotiating parties unanimously agreed to refer to the GATT model on the issue of national treatment, making it an obligation that is universally applicable to all services and service delivery models: should a participant wish to be exempted from this duty, it must go through the process of negotiation and be incorporated into its list of concessions. The various parties also agreed that the specific commitments made by a participant shall be reflected through the openness of its market in principle (*i.e.* the "Standstill Clause" is applicable), unless explicitly stated otherwise. Furthermore, any removal of discriminatory measures and practices

---

[12] European Commission, "Negotiations for a Plurilateral Agreement on Trade in Services," February 15, 2013, retrieved from http://europa.eu/rapid/press-release_MEMO-13-107_en. htm?locale=en.

in the future shall be automatically locked and recorded in the commitments of the participants and shall be irreversible (*i.e.* the "Ratchet Clause" is applicable).

As observed from the information TISA participants have disclosed to the public as well as relevant research and media reports, the TISA framework mainly includes the following elements:

(1) The main body of the agreement is based on GATS. New rules and new market access commitments are based upon GATS. The coverage is broad and no sectors or service delivery models are precluded.
(2) The agreement is composed of the text of the agreement, schedule of specific commitments and reservations, and the "new sectoral disciplines".
(3) The negative list was applied to national treatment, the positive list was applied to market access, and the specific concession lists of the various parties ought to reflect the state of openness of their markets.
(4) A section on "the interpretation of commitments" was established including items such as firmly locking the existing degree of openness, the irrevocability of autonomous liberalization measures once implemented in the future *etc.*
(5) In the establishment of "new sectoral disciplines", participants shall submit proposals which shall be incorporated into the final agreement when a consensus is reached. The areas that may be covered are domestic regulations and transparency, information and communication technology services, financial services, professional services, transportation and logistics services, maritime transport services, environmental services, energy services, movement of natural persons, regulation of state-owned enterprises, transparency in government procurement *etc.*
(6) To strive to reach a high level of agreement while maintaining openness, increase the number of participants and aim towards multilateralism.

3 Prospects for the Evolution of International Rules for Trade in Services

3.1 *TISA's exploration of new trade in services rules*

In order to achieve high standards of liberalized agreements, TISA negotiating parties were prepared to, on the basis of GATS, combine the current new trends and features of international trade in services to explore the development of a new set of rules for trade in services. The new rules mainly cover the following areas.

3.1.1 *Hybrid list of commitments*

TISA negotiations adopt a hybrid mode of commitment where members follow the negative list of commitment with regard to national treatment while adopting the positive list of commitment in the area of market access.

The negative list approach to commitment is a common practice of the US when signing FTAs. It means that the parties agree to open up all service sectors in principle, apply MFN treatment, national treatment, market access, cross-border free trade and other general obligations. If any party is unable to fulfill these obligations in certain industries or sectors, they must list the exceptions and detail the relevant regulations and measures, called "non-conforming measures". Once these sectors and non-conforming measures are listed, there shall be no other additions or amendments, otherwise, the relevant signatories have to obtain the consent of other signatories through consultation or dispute settlement mechanisms and make the appropriate trade compensation.

Presently, according to Articles XVI and XVII of GATS, WTO members take the positive list approach when fulfilling commitments in the field of trade in services, that is, members list out the service sectors in which they allow foreign participation in their Schedule of Specific Commitments, and clearly state the corresponding market access limitations and restrictions in national treatment. Foreign participation can be prohibited in sectors that are not listed in the schedule. Currently, most FTAs in the world take this approach to commitment in terms of trade in services. The FTAs that China has signed as well as the FTAs signed by the EU and other economic bodies mainly take such an approach.

In the early exploration stage of TISA negotiations, the US, Australia, and other developed members requested that all negotiating parties adopt the negative list approach to commitment but some members led by the EU opposed and requested that the current GATS' positive list approach be undertaken. After several rounds of consultations, the two groups finally reached a compromise and agreed to adopt a hybrid approach in TISA negotiations where the negative list approach is undertaken only for national treatment. Following this approach, unless a member clearly states that relevant sectors are excluded or that there are reservations in these relevant sectors with regard to national treatment, they are obligated to provide general national treatment for foreign services and service suppliers in all service sectors. However, members can still follow the GATS approach to commitment in terms of market access, and selectively open relevant service sectors and implement a number of restrictions.

On the whole, this means that unless the host country makes reservations or exceptions, foreign investors shall enjoy full national treatment upon meeting market access requirements, that is, enjoy "Post-Establishment National Treatment". Compared with the GATS approach to commitment, the greatest difference with this approach is that parties must be more open- and transparent in appling the principle of national treatment.

3.1.2. *Principle of competitive neutrality and discipline of state-owned enterprises*

Chapter 12 of this book is dedicated to introducing the principle of competitive neutrality and discipline of state-owned enterprises. As such, in this chapter, only the content related to TISA negotiations will be covered.

At the beginning of the negotiations, the US had considered allowing TISA to come up with a package of regulations for state-owned enterprises in trade in services. However, after a series of consultations, there have been signs that the US could forgo this goal and consider taking a "sectoral" approach during TISA negotiations to resolve the issues with state-owned enterprises. By doing so, it can apply the principle of competitive neutrality and regulate state-owned enterprises only in specific service sectors.

The reasons why the US considered adopting a "sectoral" approach to solve the problems of state-owned enterprises in TISA negotiations could be the following: (1) there was great resistance towards the attempt to comprehensively regulate state-owned enterprises in TPP, thus, the "sectoral" approach is more likely to be accepted by other participants in the negotiations; (2) the comprehensive regulation of state-owned enterprises will further reduce the opportunities for other developing countries to join in agreements; and (3) a "sectoral" approach fits in better with the GATS structure and there are also precedents of competitive regulations for telecommunications services under GATS framework.[13]

3.1.3. *Principle of technological neutrality and cross-border data flow*

To further promote the liberalization of trade in services, and play to their technological, human and financial advantage in trade in services, TISA negotiation parties hope to establish the principle of technological neutrality and

---

[13] "U.S. Mulls Sectoral Approach For SOE Disciplines In Services Plurilateral," *Inside U.S. Trade*, Vol. 31, No. 10 (August 3, 2013).

modal neutrality in its agreements, and requires that all participants commit to allowing free flow of data across borders.

(1) Principle of "technological neutrality"

The principle of "technological neutrality" is a concept that was proposed during the development of the EU legal framework for competitive policies. It suggests that when a service (such as telecommunications) can be provided via a variety of technological methods (for example, cable, wireless, satellite *etc.*), the objective for monitoring such services should be to protect consumers and ensure service quality rather than targeting any particular technology that provides the service so as to avoid discrimination against any technology and thus hinder technological innovation. Later, the content and extension of this principle began to evolve and was gradually introduced into the international regulatory regime which included the WTO framework. In 1999, a notice from the European Commission[14] listed "technological neutrality" as one of the five principles of the EU electronic communications regulatory framework and stated that "legislation should define the objectives to be achieved, and should neither impose, nor discriminate in favor of, the use of a particular type of technology to achieve those objectives."

From a historical point of view, if a country's industrial regulators are unable to apply and uphold the principle of "technological neutrality," and restrict or specify that certain types of services can only be provided through specific technological methods, fair competition in the market will be hindered, and technological innovation in that field will be curbed. This will also adversely affect the interests of consumers and international competitiveness of domestic industries.

The term "technological neutrality" is not clearly used in GATS and its annexes but some of the specific provisions apply and put the concept of "technological neutrality" into practice. For example, the GATS "Annex on Telecommunication Services" defines "telecommunications" as: "the transmission and reception of signals by any electromagnetic means". In addition, Article II Paragraph 2 of the Basic Telecommunications "Reference Paper" (Interconnection to be ensured) in Annex 1 of China's Schedule of Specific Commitments on Trade in Services for accession into WTO, states that: "Interconnection with a major supplier will be ensured at any feasible point

---

[14] EUR-Lex, "A New Framework for Electronic Communications Services," 1999, retrieved from http://europa.eu/legislation_summaries/internal_market/single_market_services/l24216_en.htm.

in the network"; Article I of Group on Basic Telecommunications "Note by the Chairman" in Annex 1 states, "unless otherwise stated in the sector column, any basic telecom services listed in the sector column (c) may be provided through any means of technology (*e.g.*, cable, wireless, satellite)" Many WTO members, including China, included these two documents in their Schedules of Commitments, and accepted the principle of "technological neutrality" embodied in basic telecommunication services.

Overall, "technological neutrality" in trade in services means that if a WTO member makes commitment in any service delivery mode, other members may supply this service via any feasible technological means under the same mode.

(2) Principle of "modal neutrality"

Essentially, the principle of "modal neutrality" in trade in services comes from the principle of "technological neutrality". One of the biggest differences between trade in goods and trade in services is the diverse supply modes, particularly diverse technological means. Due to the rapid development of information and communication technologies, many services that could not or found it difficult to be supplied across borders can now be directly provided via the Internet or telecommunications technologies. The share of trade in services supplied via the four modes is constantly changing, and there is more trade in services being supplied via Mode 1 (cross-border supply) and Mode 4 (presence of natural persons). Under such circumstances, some WTO members have begun to promote the principle of "modal neutrality" in trade in services, requiring other members to open trade in services and at the same time treat the four service delivery modes equally so as to avoid bias and discrimination against other supply modes. In particular, preference for the commercial presence mode where foreign investors are required to establish institutions should be avoided.

The goal of TISA negotiations includes the development of more specific and operational principles in the above-mentioned areas and requiring members to apply the principle of "modal neutrality" with regard to specific commitments. For this purpose, the final agreement also includes specific regulations developed for the various sectors of financial services, information and technology services, professional services, e-commerce, movement of natural persons and other fields. On the one hand, Mode 1 requires all parties to allow foreign service suppliers direct delivery of cross-border services without establishing business entities or organizations on the ground. On the other hand, Mode 4 requires that parties to provide greater market access for foreign technical personnel and professionals, that is, to make it more convenient for them in terms of entrance qualifications, residency and visa procedures *etc.*

(3) Cross-border data flow

This issue is closely related to the principles of technology neutrality and modal neutrality. With the deepening of the information technology revolution and the rapid development and popularity of Internet technology, cross-border supply of trade in services has become more convenient and accessible, dramatically changing the distribution of global trade in services across different sectors and modes. According to relevant data[15] released by the WTO Secretariat, compared to 1995, the current distribution of various service sectors in total trade in services has changed greatly, among which the share of tourism services has dropped from 34% to 26%; the share of the transport services sector decreased from 26% to 20%; while the share of "other business services" such as telecommunications, computer services, professional services, financial services and others increased from less than 40% to 53%. As market access conditions have not yet been greatly improved around the world, the significant increase of the share of these sectors is mainly due to the rapid growth of cross-border services provided by modern communications technology such as the Internet *etc.*

For this reason, developed economies which have clear advantages in cross-border services have, in recent years, vigorously promoted the opening up of the Internet, the free flow of data across borders and other concepts, and attempted to formulate relevant rules to limit the management of cross-border Internet communications by other states. At the end of 2011, the OECD Council, known as the "developed countries' club", specially published *Recommendation on Principles for Internet Policy Making*,[16] requesting that when states develop or revise policies and measures affecting the Internet economy, they consult stakeholders and follow the 14 proposed principles for promoting free flow of data, namely: (1) promote and protect the global free flow of information; (2) promote the open, distributed and interconnected nature of the Internet; (3) promote investment and competition in high speed networks and services; (4) promote and enable the cross-border delivery of services; (5) encourage multi-stakeholder cooperation in policy development processes; (6) foster voluntarily developed codes of conduct; (7) develop

---

[15] WTO, "Measuring Trade in Services: A Training Module," retrieved from https://www.wto.org/english/res_e/statis_e/services_training_pres_e.pdf, p. 9.

[16] OECD, "OECD Council Recommendation on Principles for Internet Policy Making," December 13, 2011, retrieved from http://www.oecd.org/internet/ieconomy/49258588.pdf.

capacities to bring publicly available, reliable data into the policy-making process; (8) ensure transparency, fair process, and accountability; (9) strengthen consistency and effectiveness in privacy protection at a global level; (10) maximise individual empowerment; (11) promote creativity and innovation; (12) limited Internet intermediary liability; (13) encourage cooperation to promote Internet security; and (14) give appropriate priority to enforcement efforts.

The US Peterson Institute for International Economics published the research report, *Framework for the International Services Agreement*,[17] in April 2012, proposing that nearly half of all cross-border trade in services is provided via information and communication technologies. These services include data processing, back office services, telecommunications, computer and related services, financial analysis, building and equipment design, processing of insurance claims, education, printing, medical services and various other professional services. The report claims that the most basic form of cross-border trade in services is the exchange of data, and restrictions on cross-border data flow hinders data exchange between service suppliers and consumers, thereby increasing transaction costs and affecting service efficiency. For cross-border trade in services to continue growing, all parties need to further reduce the barriers to cross-border trade.

It is foreseeable that TISA negotiating parties will vigorously promote the establishment of clear regulations for the free flow of data across borders. The relevant sections in the US-Korea FTA[18] is able to provide a point of reference in this regard. In the chapter on electronic commerce in the US-Korea FTA, the provisions for "cross-border information flow", stipulate the following: "Recognizing the importance of the free flow of information in facilitating trade, and acknowledging the importance of protecting personal information, the Parties shall endeavor to refrain from imposing or maintaining unnecessary barriers to electronic information flows across borders." The chapter on cross-border trade in services explicitly states that both parties shall abrogate the obligatory requirement for the establishment of a local institution, that is, "Neither Party may require a service supplier of the other Party to establish or maintain a representative office or any form of enterprise, or to be

---

[17] Gary Clyde Hufbauer, J. Bradford Jensen and Sherry Stephenson, "Framework for the International Services Agreement," from http://www.iie.com/publications/pb/pb12-10.pdf, pp. 41–42.

[18] Refer to the US-Korea Free Trade Agreement published by the US Trade Representative Office on the government's website, https://ustr.gov/trade-agreements/free-trade-agreements/korus-fta/final-text.

resident, in its territory as a condition for the cross-border supply of a service." If such is the basis, then relevant regulations established by TISA would likely require the parties to abolish any compulsory establishments or residency requirements for cross-border service suppliers, and reduce or eliminate cross-border transmission of electronic data limitations or barriers.

3.1.4. *Revision and improvements to sectoral regulations*

(1) Information and Communication Technology (ICT) services

Information and communication technology services are the organic combination of telecommunications, computers and related services. This is a concept promoted by the US and EU, based on their industrial interests, with the purpose of making use of their technological, capital and intellectual property advantages to encourage other countries to reduce trade and technological barriers, and promote global expansion of their industries. As GATS has only established sectoral regulations for the telecommunications industry (that is, the "Annex on Telecommunications Services"), and has yet to establish specialized regulations for computers, IT services and other fields, the main developed economies have been trying to promote the establishment of a broader-ranged set of multilateral ICT sectoral rules. In June 2011, the US and the EU submitted a joint proposal on the development and supervision of ICT services[19] to the WTO Council for Trade in Services and suggested the following 10 principles: (i) transparency; (ii) open networks, network access and use; (iii) cross-border information flows; (iv) local infrastructure; (v) foreign ownership; (vi) use of spectrum; (vii) regulatory authorities; (viii) authorizations and licenses; (ix) interconnection; (x) international cooperation.

Several principles among the 10 principles listed above coincide with or are closely related to the principles of "technological neutrality," "modal neutrality" and free flow of data across borders as brought up during negotiations with TISA participants. The inclusion of these principles into the final textual TISA agreement would mean that participants have to be highly committed to granting market access and national treatment, and implementing transparency, and domestic regulations among others. They would also have to allow foreign ICT service suppliers to employ a variety of business and service

---

[19] Refer to the joint proposal by the US and the European Union to the WTO Trade in Services Council on June 13, 2011, document no. S/C/W/338.

models and make use of various technological methods to compete fairly with similar service suppliers in the country on international and domestic platforms.

(2) Transportation and logistics services

The formation and development of global supply chains reflect the important features and trends in current and future economic globalization, and transport and logistics services are the most important pillars for the stability and efficient operation of global supply chains. In terms of coverage, transportation and logistics services include land, sea, and air transport, as well as warehousing, postal, courier and distribution services *etc.* Presently, there are no specific regulations for transport and logistics under the GATS framework, and the openness of WTO members in these sectors varies. In fact, a member that is open in a certain sector may be significantly less open in another service sector. As such, TISA promotes liberalization in this field so that the difference in members' level of openness may be narrowed and industrial segmentation may be less distinct, achieving sectoral interaction and thereby improve overall efficiency.

(3) Financial services

The main objective of TISA negotiations in the financial services sector is to integrate various parties' financial sector commitments in FTAs and further expand foreign capital access into the financial services' market, based on the plurilateral agreement "Understanding on Commitments in Financial Services" signed under the WTO framework (China has not yet signed this agreement). Specifically, participants will be required to provide national treatment to foreign investors in the financial services sector, allow the establishment of fully foreign-owned financial institutions, remove restrictions on the number of foreign financial institutions, allow mergers and acquisitions, grant access to the country's payment and settlement systems, so as to facilitate cross-border trade of financial services as well as free flow of financial information and data across borders, as well as allow foreign financial service suppliers to provide new financial services in its territories.

(4) New services

Due to technological developments in the field of trade in services, new service modes and sectors have continually emerged. It is becoming increasingly difficult for the old classification and trade management system to cope with such trends. Therefore, one of the objectives of TISA negotiations is to formulate relevant rules for these new services so as to encourage innovation and promote the opening of markets. In early 2013, US Trade Representative Ron Kirk expressed in his report to the US Congress with regard to TISA negotiations that "future agreements will cover the 'services that have yet to emerge'". Many trade experts have expressed doubts about this because only if negative lists are used can there be an agreement that automatically covers new services that may occur in the future. Currently, negotiating parties have already made it clear that "mixed lists" would be utilized, thus new services would not automatically be bound by regulations stated in the agreement. In this regard, some experts speculate that the US will push for more flexible schedule updating mechanisms to be used, allowing members to constantly update their schedules and incorporate new services as they emerge.[20]

In reality, the US has, at least in the financial sector, already established regulations for new services in some of their signed FTAs. This will also provide a reference for TISA to develop appropriate rules. Take the US-Korea free trade agreement for example, in the section on "Financial Services", a special clause was written for "new financial services", stating that: "Each Party shall permit a financial institution of the other Party to supply any new financial service that the Party would permit its own financial institutions, in like circumstances, to supply without additional legislative action by the Party". At the same time, "a Party may determine the institutional and juridical form through which the new financial service may be supplied and may require authorization for the supply of servcie". The content of the clause shows that if TISA establishes relevant regulations for new services, the parties in the agreement may not be required to open up all the new services but will rather require the signatories to grant foreign investors national treatment in the opening of new services sectors. Furthermore, regulatory agencies will be required to be open and fair in implementing their licensing systems.

(5) Strengthening of existing GATS regulations

(i) Domestic regulations

Based on the progress of domestic regulatory negotiations in the multilateral arena, some TISA participants requested that "necessity tests" be set up in the field of domestic regulations to ensure that there are no unnecessary barriers to

---

[20] 'USTR Says It will Seek to Cover New Services in Plurilateral Agreement,' *Inside U.S. Trade*, Vol. 31, No. 3 (January 18, 2013).

trade in all parties' domestic regulatory measures. As the US and Canada have always opposed the establishment of "necessity tests" in this area, the parties may find it difficult to reach a compromise on this issue. However, they would still strive to achieve transparency of domestic management systems, and simplification of licensing procedures and qualifications.

(ii) Emergency safeguard measures, government procurement and subsidies

Although TISA participants had suggested the possibility of advancing negotiations under GATS (including emergency safeguard measures, government procurement and subsidies as well as other issues), the current situation shows that due to opposition from most developed members, negotiations would not be conducted on emergency safeguard measures and mechanisms. In terms of government procurement and subsidies, some developed members may be asked to strengthen regulations and transparency of government procurement, and to avoid "trade distortion" in service subsidies.

3.2 *Prospects of international rules of trade in services*

The current situation of negotiations for trade in services in the Doha Round and the development of the TISA negotiations indicate that the following international trends are likely to occur in the future, that is, both the "old rules" from GATS and "new rules" from TISA will coexist and ultimately there will be a combination of the two.

3.2.1 *Prospects of GATS rules negotiations*

At present, affected by the slow overall progress of the Doha Round, GATS rules negotiations have also been stalled. However, a number of important WTO members, including China, are still striving to promote the progress of the multilateral negotiations. On December 7, 2013, at the WTO ninth ministerial meeting held in Bali, Indonesia, a consensus was reached on the "Early Harvest" agreement of the Doha Round.[21] The results were an important breakthrough for trade facilitation, and agricultural and developmental issues, and injected new vitality into the multilateral trade negotiations. Therefore, in the short term, the progress of multilateral rules negotiations on trade in

---

[21] PRC Ministry of Commerce, "The Ninth WTO Ministerial Conference Come[s] to A Close," December 8, 2013, retrieved from http://english.mofcom.gov.cn/article/newsrelease/significantnews/201312/20131200425962.shtml.

services among WTO members is still dependent on whether WTO members are able to move the outstanding issues of the Doha Round forward and practically implement the work plans so as to achieve substantive results. In the mid- to long-term, whether trade in services should be a part of the built-in agenda remains an important issue in the future of multilateral trade negotiations. On the whole, however, considering the vast difference in negotiating positions of WTO members on rules of trade in services, there is still a long and arduous path ahead for negotiations.

3.2.2 The impact of TISA on the international system of rules for trade in services

With it being difficult for there to be a positive outcome from GATS negotiations, should TISA negotiations succeed and a final agreement be reached within the next one to two years, two camps with different levels of open markets and unequal interests and benefits will form in the field of international trade in services. There will also be a situation where there are both high and low degrees of liberalization as well as loose and strict levels of restrictions as the old and the new systems coexist. If the US, Europe, Japan, Australia and other developed countries grow cold towards the liberalization of trade in services in the multilateral framework, the progress of including TISA in the multilateral WTO framework will once again be delayed. In addition, the US and EU are still promoting TPP, TTIP and other regional free trade agreements covering trade in services, thus the actual authority of GATS and the trade in services rules negotiations platform may be weakened to a certain extent.

3.2.3 Possible legal status of TISA and its path to multilateralism

TISA negotiations were launched by the US, EU and other developed economies after the crisis in a bid to fully exploit its competitive advantages, construct a new international trade order and lead in developing a new model of economic development. At the same time, it was also a response to the world economy's developmental trend from "globalization" toward "digitalization" and "service orientation". Once this is achieved, it will cover more than 70% of the total world trade in services,[22] and a new model of market access and rules establishment will be formed in trade in services.

---

[22] Shawn Donnan, "China Seeks Accession into TISA Negotiations," Financial Times [Chinese site], September 24, 2013, retrieved from http://www.ftchinese.com/story/001052637.

When plurilateral trade in services consultations were conducted in 2012, some members of the RGF Group such as the US and Australia suggested establishing a closed free trade agreement out of the WTO framework that applies only to negotiating parties and invokes Article V[23] of GATS (economic integration), exemption from fulfilling multilateral obligations such as MFN and open markets. Some members also believed that a plurilateral service agreement[24] could first be reached, modeling the GPA, so as to encourage more members to participate. However, other members, including the EU, believed that the agreement should ultimately be multilateral and incorporated into the WTO system, replacing GATS and becoming the new generation of multilateral trade in services rules. Later, when TISA negotiations were officially launched, on the surface, the parties seemed to have reached a tacit understanding on this issue, that is, to not fix the form and nature of agreement in the short term but to work towards the end goal of a multilateral TISA.

From the current agreement framework, progress and prospects of TISA negotiations, it can be observed that TISA may, in the short term, become a free trade agreement signed by some WTO members covering only trade in services, and not be incorporated into WTO's multilateral legal system. Yet TISA's mid- to long-term goal is definitely to attract more participants and go multilateral to become part of WTO multilateral rules. The European Commission pointed out in the "Plurilateral Agreement on Trade in Services" memo that in the first phase of negotiations, the agreement will only be binding for participants and thus is not a part of the WTO Doha Round negotiations. However, parties shall ensure that the structure of the multilateral agreements can provide a credible path for future multilateralism. This means two requirements have to be met: firstly, the commitments that participants make under this Agreement have to be consistent with those currently taken up under GATS so that the former can be easily incorporated into the GATS framework. Secondly, the number of participants must reach a certain "critical

---

[23] GATS Article V allows any WTO member to participate in or enter into an agreement liberalizing trade in services between or among the parties to such an agreement, without fulfilling MFN or opening up of markets and other multilateral obligations. This is provided that such an agreement has substantial sectoral coverage and the level of commitment is higher than that which participants commit to multilateral trade in services under the WTO framework.

[24] According to Article IX, Paragraph 3 of "Marrakesh Agreement Establishing the WTO", the consent of more than ¾ of WTO members needs to be obtained and the WTO Ministerial Conference shall make the decision for special exemptions. This is because such plurilateral agreements would only be applicable to participants so they are not required to fulfil multilateral obligations such as granting MFN and open market access *etc.*

mass" so that the benefits of the Agreement can be extended to all WTO members. To avoid "free riders" (that is, those who enjoy the outcome of negotiations without making any concessions), MFN treatment shall be temporarily suspended until the number of WTO members who join the Agreement reach its critical size. Therefore, a special "participant clause" shall also be included in the Agreement so that interested WTO members can join, and mechanisms and conditions for achieving multilateralism be established.

The "critical mass" concept is borrowed from a mechanism used and enforced under WTO's ITA. This agreement was signed by 29 WTO members in late 1996, but it was also stated in the agreement that the participants of the agreement must account for 90% of the world's trade in information technological products by April 1, 1997 in order for the agreement to come into effect.[25] This threshold of 90% was determined to be the "critical mass".

According to statistics provided by the WTO Secretariat in 2011, the trade in services exports from China, India and Russia accounted for 4.4%, 3.6% and 1.2% of the world's total volume of trade in services respectively, while their imports accounted for 6.1%, 3.4% and 2.3% respectively.[26] Based on the above data, should future TISA participants follow ITA's precedence and set its multilateral "critical mass" as 90% of the world's total volume of trade in services, it would be extremely difficult for TISA members to hit the "critical mass" benchmark in trade volume. This is due to large developing countries such as BRICS (China, India, Brazil, Russia and South Africa) not being included and it would, therefore, not be incorporated into the WTO multilateral framework. However, if the "critical mass" were lowered, to about 80% of world's total volume of trade in services, the figure would be easily achieved. [27]

If the BRICS countries including China and other major developing countries participate and sign the TISA, the TISA would eventually be incorporated successfully into the WTO system and on the one hand, it would replace GATS

---

[25] At the close of 1996, the 29 signatories only accounted for 83% of the world's total trade in information technology products, but with other WTO members subsequently joining in, the 90% benchmark was exceeded and ITA came into effect as planned. Refer to "Introduction to the Uruguay Round Agreements," WTO Secretariat [Translated by Suo Bicheng] (China: Hu Ying Law Press, 2000), p. 393.

[26] Refer to "China Trade in Services Statistics 2012", *China Business Press,* 2012, p. 22.

[27] Excluding China, the current total volume of trade in services of TISA participants is already more than 70% of the world's total volume. Should China and India's trade in services be included, the total volume would be about 80% of the world's total volume of trade in services.

to become a new international norm to be generally applied to the field of trade in services; on the other hand, as it greatly affects the rules of investment and competitive policies, it would also provide a point of reference for WTO in conducting multilateral negotiations and developing rules in the relevant areas.

4 China and the New Rules in Trade in Services

4.1 *The influence of the new rules of trade in services on China's development and management of trade in services*

On September 30, 2013, the Chinese government officially announced the intention to join in TISA negotiations.[28] This was yet another important step, apart from being deeply involved in the Doha Round negotiations on trade in services, where China actively participated in international rule-making for trade in services. China's participation will greatly increase the possibility and feasibility of TISA being incorporated in WTO's multilateral framework eventually. In view of TISA's high standards and active exploration in the development of new rules, it can be expected that new rules of international trade in services will have a profound impact on China's development and management of trade in services.

4.1.1 *The effects of the "hybrid list" and "negative list" on China's trade in services management system*

To date, China has taken a positive list commitment approach in signing multilateral and bilateral trade agreements with foreign countries. Therefore, the implementation of the hybrid list approach promoted by TISA, particularly on China's negative list approach to national treatment, will pose several challenges for China's existing trade in services management system and external trade negotiations mode.

In the long term however, there are no substantive legal obstacles to China's negative list approach for managing and promoting the liberalization of trade in services. Currently, foreign investment projects are classified into the four categories of "Encouraged", "Restricted", "Prohibited" and "Allowed" in

---

[28] On September 30, 2013, the Chinese government officially announced their intention to join in TISA negotiations. Refer to a Xinhua report, October 17, 2013 [in Chinese], retrieved from http://news.xinhuanet.com/fortune/2013-10/17/c_125555957.htm.

China's "Guidelines and Regulations for Foreign Investment", among which the first three are included in the "Catalogue for the Guidance of Foreign Investment Industries" while those in the "Allowed" category are excluded. This implicit mode of permitting yet not publicly listing is, in fact, already legally based on the negative list approach.

In addition, the commitments that China made upon its accession to WTO show that although market access in trade in services employs the positive list approach and only open sectors are included in the schedule, the specific commitments for each sector in the list actually follow the negative list approach, that is, all restrictive measures are stated in the schedule, and those that are not stated cannot be imposed. At present, all existing regulations and policies in China's service sectors involving foreign investment have been revised or developed according to these commitments; the specific conditions and restrictions on foreign investment access have also been listed.

Since 2013, China has successfully achieved breakthroughs in their exploration of carrying out economic and trade negotiations using the negative list approach. At the fifth China-US Strategic and Economic Dialogue held in July 2013, China and the US agreed to use a negative list as the basis for substantive negotiations for bilateral investment agreements (detailed in Chapter 11 "Rules of International Investment"). Furthermore, the China (Shanghai) Pilot Free Trade Zone launched officially in September 2013 also begun exploring the establishment of a negative list management model in the pilot zone, with the aim of gradually forming a foreign investment management system in line with international standards. In November 2013, at the third Plenary Session of the 18th CPC Central Committee, the CPC Central Committee announced "The Decision on Major Issues Concerning Comprehensively Deepening Reforms" which further clarified its arm to "make market rules that are fair, open and transparent; implement a unified market entrance system, with market players of all kinds able to enter equally and legitimately into areas that are not on the negative list" and "explore a management model for foreign investors with pre-entry national treatment plus the negative list".[29]

Thus, whether from the legal, technical or planning for future reforms' point of view, the conditions and basis for China to adopt a negative list

[29] "CPC Central Committee the Announces the Decision on Major Issues Concerning Comprehensively Deepening Reforms" (Approved by the 18th CPC Central Committee at the 3rd Plenary Session on November 12, 2013), Xinhua.net, November 30, 2013, retrieved from http://news.xinhuanet.com/politics/2013-11/15/c_118164235.htm. Refer to Part 3 Article IX which advocates the speeding up of improvements to the modern market system, which was published on November 15, 2013.

approach to promote the liberalization of the trade in services sector already exist. In the future, should China use this approach to conduct multilateral or bilateral trade negotiations and make commitments to opening up, the transparency, predictability and stability of open service policies will be greatly enhanced and foreign investors' confidence and interest in China's service industries will also increase. This will significantly boost China's attractiveness in terms of bringing in foreign investment, advanced technologies, experienced management, talents and other workers to China's service industries. However, it should be noted that this adjustment in policy will deeply and extensively change China's current investment management system. Therefore, it will be some time before concrete measures are developed and fully implemented.

4.1.2 *The impact of ICT services and rules on cross-border data flows*

China, the country with most Internet users, already had more than 560 million Internet users in 2012. In the same year, China's total volume of e-commerce transactions exceeded 8 trillion yuan,[30] and China is expected to overtake the US very soon to become the world's largest e-commerce market.[31] Developing ICT services as the core of the Internet industry is essential for China's future restructuring and industrial upgrading and regeneration. In response to the rapid development of technology and the market, revision and improvements to China's ICT services and Internet service management system are also constantly being made.

Given the extreme importance of the Internet and its related industries, the developed countries, led by the US and Europe, have been trying to dominate international rule-making for this field, hoping to boost the global expansion of their relevant industries in this area. The developing countries, in general, are more passive in this field. On the one hand, they do not have the ability to participate in rule-making, on the other hand, they are on the lower end of the industrial chain and at a disadvantage in global competition. However, in the face of challenges in the market, and technology and data competition, developing countries need to make their

---

[30] PRC Ministry of Commerce, *China E-Commerce Report* (China: Tsinghua University Press, 2013), p. 2.

[31] "Chinese E-Commerce Market Expected to Surpass the US," China International Electronic Commerce Network, July 9, 2013, retrieved from http://trade.ec.com.cn/article/tradedzsw/201307/1250825_1.html.

voices heard in the rule-making process to safeguard their vital interests and promote the development of domestic industries. Viktor Schoberger and Kenneth Cukier, authors of the book *Big Data* which explores the revolutionary impact of the Internet era's mass information and data on the human society, wrote in an article published in *Foreign Affairs*[32] that "Regulations governing big data might even emerge as a battleground among countries ... Diplomats should brace for fights over whether to treat information flows as similar to free trade." Shortly after the article was published, the "PRISM" incident[33] broke out and caused an uproar in the world, sparking multinational diplomatic wrangling and confirming the two authors' insights. It can also be predicted that negotiations and talks surrounding the Internet and cross-border data flow rules will become key issues in future multilateral trade negotiations, and will profoundly affect international trade patterns.

The developmental trend and overseas expansion potential of China's Internet-based enterprises, e-commerce companies and service outsourcing companies have to be comprehensively considered as a whole in order to deal with this challenge. In 2012, the scale of China's Internet services market had already exceeded 200 billion yuan, second only to the US. The market value of seven enterprises rose to the top 30 in the global Internet market,[34] becoming the industry's global leaders. In the same year, the total turnover of Taobao.com and Tmall.com hit 1.1 trillion yuan (about USD170 billion), more than Amazon.com and ebay.com combined.[35] In addition, China has come in after India to become the world's second largest service outsourcing country. The international service outsourcing contracts undertaken by China amount to

---

[32] Kenneth Cukier and Viktor Schonberger, "The Rise of Big Data," *Foreign Affairs*, May/June Issue, 2013.

[33] The PRISM incident refers to the leaking of information by Edward Snowden — then a private contractor working for Booz Allen Hamilton — which unveiled information about PRISM, a mechanism that allows the US government to collect user data from companies such as Apple, Google, Microsoft, Yahoo *etc.* This was largely part of the National Security Agency's surveillance programme, which had been shrouded in great secrecy since 2001. Refer to "America's 'PRISM' Incident," retrieved from http://xinhuanet.com/world/ljm2013/index.htm.

[34] "Turnover of China's Internet Services Market Exceeds 200 Billion Yuan," Finance QQ, December 28, 2012, retrieved from http://finance.qq.com/a/20121228/005848.htm.

[35] "The World's Greatest Bazaar," *The Economist*, March 23, 2013, retrieved from http://www.economist.com/news/briefing/21573980-alibaba-trailblazing-chinese-internet-giant-will-soon-go-public-worlds-greatest-bazaar.

USD43.85 billion.[36] B2C service companies, including Jingdong Mall, Vancl, Lashou.com *etc.* experimenting with overseas retail businesses while utilizing China's manufacturing advantages of products "made in China" also contributed to the rapid change towards industrial upgrading of "Services provided by China and Products invented in China", "Chinese services" and "Chinese creations". In addition, the Chinese government has established information consumption as a basic national policy,[37] and in the future, will accelerate the construction and upgrading of the country's Internet and communications network infrastructure, and vigorously promote home-based fiber networks and raising network speed. In December 2013, the Chinese government issued 4G licenses to three major telecommunications operators,[38] while domestic enterprises have also made a mark in 5G technological research.[39] Therefore, whether in terms of the domestic industrial layout, market size, level of development, future trends, performance of leading enterprises, technical capabilities, and developmental needs, China has great need to compete in the global information industry and also possesses the relevant conditions and capabilities to shape international rules.

The new rules for ICT services and cross-border data flows will pose particular challenges to China's existing regulatory system, especially with regard to expanding market access for foreign ICT service providers and promoting regulations for free flow of relevant electronic data across borders for trade in services. These will significantly influence China's existing information industry, Internet governance as well as domestic industries. At the same time, as these rules abolish or reduce barriers to cross-border trade in services on a global scale, improve the transparency of the regulatory system, curb market monopoly, enhance protection of consumer privacy and rights *etc.*, they are also in line with the further development of China's information technology, the Internet and related industries, as well as the need to open up overseas markets.

---

[36] "International Service Outsourcing Contracts Undertaken by China Hit USD43.9 Billion Last Year, Up by 34%," Renmingwang (People.com.cn), February 20, 2013, retrieved from http://finance.people.com.cn/n/2013/0220/c70846-20542691.html.

[37] PRC Government, "State Council Issued Several Opinions on Promoting Information Consumption and Expanding Domestic Demands," Official PRC Government website, August 14, 2013, retrieved from http://www.gov.cn/jrzg/2013-08/14/content_2466857.htm.

[38] "Three Major Telecom Operators Awarded 4G Licenses," Xinhua.net, December 5, 2013, retrieved from http://news.xinhuanet.com/2013-12/05/c_118423202.htm.

[39] "China and Korea Join Hands to Develop 5G Technology; Huawei Leads the Industrial Innovation by Investing USD600 million," Huanqiu, December 10, 2013, retrieved from http://tech.huanqiu.com/comm/2013-12/4644954.html.

On the whole, China should actively participate in the formulation of international rules in this field so as to gain advantages and eliminate disadvantages in global international competition and cooperation.

4.1.3 *Impact of new rules in transport and logistics services*

Presently, China has become the world's largest exporter of goods and the world's biggest trading nation. In sharp contrast, however, are China's current logistics costs which account for 18% of the country's GDP, double that of developed countries.[40] Therefore, the promotion of the integration and facilitation of logistics supply chains, opening up of relevant sectors, and introduction of competitive mechanisms and advanced technologies and management, will be helpful for reducing logistics costs and improving efficiency, which is in line with the overall interests of the state and society. In addition, the global reduction and removal of trade barriers to transportation and logistics services sectors and improving overall level of liberalization is beneficial for creating a fair, free and transparent trading environment, raising efficiency of global supply chains and injecting powerful vitality into global economic and trade development. China's maritime services are strongly competitive in the international arena, and with China's increasing overseas investment, and growing foreign trade and outflow of manpower, there is an increasing need for China's air and land transport, distribution and other courier services to venture abroad. In formulating new trade rules in the above-mentioned sectors, focusing on the reduction of trade costs and facilitating the global flow of goods and services are helpful to achieving the goals and interests mentioned above.

4.1.4 *Impact of other new rules*

New trade in services rules in fields such as financial services, energy services, maritime transport services, environmental services, movement of natural persons and other new service areas are designed to encourage all parties to lock in their current level of liberalization, greatly increase foreign access, improve transparency of the regulatory system, promote uniform implementation of standards, improve the efficiency of global industrial chains *etc.* In the short

---

[40] Refer to article on China Logistics and Purchasing Network, "China's Logistics Costs Account for 18% of GDP in 2010," China Wuliu, May 11, 2011, retrieved from http://www.chinawuliu.com.cn/zixun/201105/11/123338.shtml.

term, the implementation of these rules pressure China's market regulators and relevant enterprises to a certain extent; but in the long term, they fulfill the requirements for China to vigorously develop the service industries, increase domestic demand, reduce energy consumption and achieve economic restructuring and sustainable growth. Especially in areas such as the movement of natural persons, if the parties can further remove or reduce the numerical restrictions and arbitrary requirements, and improve procedures and requirements for application of visas and work permits, China will be able to draw on its strengths and promote the export of Chinese medicine, Chinese language education and other services which are characteristic of China as well as gain a competitive advantage in the overseas expansion of construction, shipping and other services.

Overall, as trade in services is not only a new growth point for the future development of international trade, but also an important means of adjusting China's economic and trade structure, China should take the initiative to be actively involved in the international competition in trade in services, as well as in the shaping and implementation of international rules.

4.2 Thoughts on China's response to the new international trade in services situation

4.2.1 China needs to continue expanding liberalization of service industries, and be deeply involved in international rule-making

The outbreak of the international financial crisis in the 21st century profoundly changed international trade and further accelerated the trend of expansion and liberalization of trade in services worldwide. After the financial crisis, developed countries paid more attention to utilizing their strengths in capital, technology, talents and institutions in services and trade in services fields. On the one hand, they actively boosted their superiority in global trade in services, and on the other hand, they further opened up the services market in developing countries through bilateral trade negotiations, promoting the export of services. The issues of trade in services in multilateral and regional economic and trade negotiations have become increasingly important. In such a context, developing countries also place increasing emphasis on the cultivation and development of trade in services, focusing their efforts on developing domestic services and enhancing the export competitiveness of the services sector. In recent years, the popularization and development of information and communication technologies and the Internet around the world has brought new opportunities for expanding services exports and increasing comparative advantages to a great number of developing countries, including China.

In 2012, China's volume of trade in services reached USD470.6 billion, making it third in the world.[41] However, compared to the volume of trade in goods in the same period, the scale of China's trade in services is still relatively small, amounting to only 1/10 of total foreign trade, equivalent to about half of the world average. It has huge potential for development.

China has fully recognized the importance of developing the service industry and trade in services, and has established this as an important means of adjusting the industrial and trade structure and promoting employment. In the "12th Five-year Plan", China pointed out that the development of trade in services must be expanded in an orderly fashion in line with the level of development of China's services and what is feasible. During the 12th five-year period, China will accelerate the development of its service sectors, steadily expand imports of modern services, support the introduction of advanced technologies and management experiences in design, development, marketing and other aspects, and encourage foreign investment in software development, cross-border outsourcing and logistics services. By 2015, the total import and export volume of trade in services in China is expected to reach USD600 billion, an annual increase of more than 11%.[42] To this end, China needs to further enhance the development of the services sector and its contribution to the national economy, continually improve policies to promote the development of services and trade in services, open up and expand the services sector steadily, introduce more international advanced management methods and business philosophies, and create more opportunities for good domestic service enterprises and individuals to obtain access to the foreign markets.

Therefore, whether in terms of changing their economic growth approach, adjusting economic structure, achieving sustainable development or the

---

[41] Refer to statistics announced by the Ministry of Commerce's Press Office published on the Ministry of Commerce website on April 19, 2013, "China's Total Volume of Trade in Services Ranks Third in the World in 2012", http://fms.mofcom.gov.cn/article/jingjigongtai/201304/20130400095477.shtml, 2013-06-28.

[42] Refer to "Development of Trade in Services in the Twelfth Five-Year Plan" (full text) published on China Trade in Services Guidelines website on March 1, 2012, http://tradeinservices.mofcom.gov.cn/a/2012-03-01-/186537.shtml, 2013-07-12.

current level of economic development, or consumers and domestic industrial needs, China needs to further expand service industries and promote the liberalization of trade in services. To effectively advance the competitiveness and development of the domestic trade in services market, and to create better conditions for good Chinese service enterprises to venture overseas, China must also take the initiative to actively participate in the formulation of new rules in international trade in services, and have a greater voice in global economic governance.

4.2.2 China already has a strong foundation for promoting liberalization of trade in services and in-depth participation in international rule-making

According to WTO classification methods, the services sector can be divided into 12 sectors and about 160 sub-sectors. When China joined the WTO, it made a commitment to open up to about 100 sub-sectors in nine of the 12 sectors, but did not make any commitments yet to about 60 sub-sectors of the other three sectors; and among the 100 sub-sectors, there are 46 where mejority or full ownership is prohibited, and in many other service sectors, China has maintained restrictions in terms of business scope. Therefore, there is still a lot of room for opening up China's service industries.

Since the start of the Doha Round negotiations, China has received requests from more than 20 WTO members requesting that China further open up telecommunications, finance, transport, audiovisual and other sectors, grant foreign investment national treatment, simplify approval procedures and increase transparency. China has also sent requests to almost 30 WTO members, and particularly requesting that developed members reduce Mode 4 trade barriers, providing greater market access for China which has a comparative advantage and large export interests in service sectors including construction and engineering, Chinese medicine, Chinese language education, satellite launching, maritime, nursing and others. To deal with these requests and take into consideration the level of openness of the domestic market, China submitted initial offer and revised offer in September 2003 and July 2005 respectively. In addition, the Chinese government adopted several FTA agreements, as well as signed and implemented the CEPA ("Closer Economic Partnership Arrangement" signed by Mainland China, Chinese Hong Kong, and Chinese Macau) and ECFA, further expanding the opening up of trade in services.

As a developing country, China is a late entrant and has not developed as far in trade in services. However, by pushing forward with various reforms in service industries, it has improved the level of openness in the services sector. In recent years, China has also gradually adopted a series of measures to promote further opening up of the market. At the end of 2011, China issued a new "Foreign Investment Industrial Guidance Catalogue" to encourage foreign investment in modern service industries and to support these industries which are largely the livelihood of the common folk. It also encouraged the use of foreign capital, greater liberalization and added nine policies to encourage service industries. Furthermore, according to the economic development needs, China also further implemented a series of initiatives to open up the securities, insurance services and other sectors. The China (Shanghai) Pilot Free Trade Zone which adopted the trial negative list management model approach, as well as the relevant plans from the "CPC Central Committee's Decision on Major Issues for Comprehensively Deepening Reform" mark the new heights that China has reached in opening up. The above-mentioned policies, measures and programs lay a solid foundation for China to further expand the liberalization of services and also fully reflect the determination of the Chinese government in further promoting the liberalization of trade in services.

China also possesses the strong foundation and conditions necessary for being deeply involved in international trade in services rule-making. Since joining the WTO at the end of 2001, China has comprehensively participated in trade in services market access and rules negotiations in the Doha Round, conducted countless rounds of bilateral and multilateral market access negotiations with several WTO members, been deeply involved in various negotiations organized by the WTO Trade in Services Council, submitted numerous negotiation proposals and documents, actively put forward and set up meeting and negotiation agendas, chaired discussions on relevant issues, and arbitrated the various stances of the members so as to promote the advancement of negotiations. In addition, apart from negotiations on market access, China has also completed and is in the midst of negotiating a number of FTAs, and has conducted in-depth negotiations and discussions with distinct opponents with regard to the various rules of trade in services. China has also carried out useful and innovative exploration on rules in e-commerce, movement of natural persons, mutual recognition, domestic regulations and other important trade in services sectors, and has seen a certain level of success. Therefore, when participating in international trade in services rule-making talks, China is able to take advantage of the experience it has accumulated in negotiations, and build upon outcomes already achieved to develop effective negotiation strategies and reasonable objectives to actively participate in rules-shaping, and maintain and strive for its national interests.

4.2.3 *Relevant policies and measures proposals*

To achieve the goals of vigorous development of the service industries, broaden the openness of service industries and be deeply involved in the establishment of international trade in services rule-making, it has been proposed that the Chinese government adopt the following policies and measures according to the actual needs of domestic economic restructuring, taking into account the new features and trends in international economic and trade development:

(1) Actively participate in the formulation of rules for international trade in services, and continue to promote an early conclusion of the Doha Round negotiations

The negotiations on trade in services are an important part of the Doha Round negotiations, involving more then 160 WTO members and the opening up of their services market, as well as the further revision and improvement of rules of trade in services. If the Doha Round negotiations can be successfully concluded, not only will barriers to trade in services be reduced and global trade in services expanded, it will also contribute to the establishment of a fair, free and transparent global services trade environment. At the same time, China should be deeply involved in the development of new rules of trade in services. It should also closely track the progress of important trade negotiations in TPP and TTIP led by developed countries like the US and European countries, and research extensively on innovation and the results of the service trade rules in these negotiations in order to take precautions and seek countermeasures.

(2) Promote further opening up of the domestic services market by facilitating the export of services through various multilateral and bilateral channels

In future trade negotiations, the Chinese government can integrate the balance of pros and cons according to the needs of current economic restructuring and services market development, and further expand the opening up of services sectors that are beneficial to the national economy. In return, it can broaden sectors of important export interests for major trading partners in China. While the current multilateral trade in services negotiations are stalled, more effort can be put in FTAs and other channels, such as the signing of supplementary agreements CEPA, ECFA, RCEP, China-Japan-Korea and China-Korea FTAs to continue to promote the opening up of trade in services. At the same time, China should attract much needed capital, technology and talent by opening up some inland areas of the country and introducing competition to improve the domestic market and strengthen domestic service industries.

(3) Strengthen the concept of opening up the services sector, reduce market access restrictions, and strengthen market supervision

Service industries are the focus of China's future industrial development and represent the general direction of China's economic structural adjustment. On the one hand, China has a huge market for services and there is a growing demand for services with its big population. On the other hand, developing services create employment so it is the best way to improve living standards. The economic growth trend in China is changing from investment-driven to consumption-driven. The opening up of services, with rules of law, and systematic and transparent regulatory procedures in place to manage foreign service suppliers operating in the market creates both consumption and employment. It fulfills the needs of a "low carbon economy" and "green economy", and is in line with the direction of China's future economic development.

(4) Actively establish and promote the mechanisms for mutual recognition of qualifications and academic background with other countries

As a large economy with high long-term growth, China has the world's largest population of internet users and the world's largest number of engineering students.[43] In future global trade in services competition, China has the market size, capital and talent that other countries do not have. In fields such as cross-border e-commerce, patents and technology exports, China has huge potential benefits. Establishing the mechanism to mutually recognize qualifications and academic backgrounds of professionals from economic trading partners and investing countries not only provides the institutional support for China to further open up, it also supports the expansion of China's foreign investment and trade in services, encouraging Chinese professional and technical staff to "go abroad" and bring about an even greater global distribution of Chinese capital and industry.

---

[43] See "Top in the World with 7 Million Engineering Students, China Wants to Become Power Nation of Engineers" Xinhua.net, December 15, 2010, retrieved from http: //news.xinhuanet. com/edu/2010-12/15 /c_12880350.htm, 2013-07-12.

(5) Prepare service industries to open up domestically and globally

Handling domestic and foreign relationships with regard to opening up should become an important topic for boosting the development of China's service industries. At this stage, China ought to earnestly implement the policies and measures from "Several Opinions of the State Council on Encouraging and Guiding the Healthy Development of Private Investment" (State Councile [2012] NO.13) and encourage more private investment in energy, mining, telecommunications, flow of commerce, culture, tourism, sports, finance, education and training, healthcare, transportation, social welfare and other trade-related services. Before opening up globally, it is important to open up domestically first or open both markets up simultaneously. Through the strengthening of the domestic service industries and the development of the domestic services market to improve the quality and level of services trade, sustainable development can be achieved.

Chapter 9

Rules of Government Procurement

On February 13, 2009, the US House and Senate passed a new economic stimulus plan which amounted to USD787 billion. This economic incentive plan, of which 35% was in tax cuts and 65% went into government investment, was hailed by the Obama administration as an important milestone that would lead the US to economic recovery and resulted in a powerful ripple effect. The US economic stimulus package immediately aroused widespread concern in the international community, not only because of the enormous size of the stimulus package, but also because of the blatant suggestion to "Buy American Provision" included in the stimulus program. This raised concerns over the rise of US trade protectionism. This provision imposed a general requirement that any public building or public works project funded by the new stimulus package must use only iron, steel and other manufactured goods produced in the United States, unless the federal government decide that purchasing iron, steel and other manufactured goods produced in the US would be damaging to public interest.

This provision was also immediately condemned by the UK, Canada, Germany, Australia, Japan, China, Brazil, India and other trading partners. Brazil was even prepared to turn to the WTO and OECD for assistance in facilitating resolution and there was a sense of uneasiness during the Davos Economic Forum. More people began to worry that if the US, being the world's largest economy, slid into economic recession, trade barriers might be erected to protect domestic jobs.

Some countries were ready to follow the US policy of purchasing domestic goods, thus further deepening the woes of the world economy which had been afflicted with both the financial crisis and economic crisis. Faced with a wave of condemnation from the international community, President Obama had to resist the pressure from Congress and promised that the US would "continue to" comply with the relevant provisions of the WTO and NAFTA. Before the final passing of the bill, a limiting clause which stated that "the bill should be implemented in ways compliant with US obligations under international agreements", was introduced.

Why did the US government's policy of "buy domestic goods" lead to so much backlash? And what are the international obligations that the US government should abide by?

To answer this question, one must understand the WTO's "Agreement on Government Procurement".

1 Agreement on Government Procurement (GPA) and Its New Developments

1.1 *How the GPA came about*

Today, governments are the world's largest consumers. In many countries, the total expenditure of public institutions on procurement of goods, services and works usually amount to 10%–15% of a country's GDP, while trade related to government procurement accounts for about 10% of total world trade.

To regulate the huge amount of government procurement activities, many countries usually establish stringent government procurement regimes and require centralization of procurement so as to ensure principle of value for money, improve efficiency of financial fund and prevent corruption through open and fair competition. Such a regime can be traced back to the Stationery Office established by the UK in 1782. However, government procurement is an exception in the international trade arena. Many countries regard government procurement as part of a country's public financial policy. In order to protect domestic industries, there is a clear distinction in the way domestic and foreign suppliers are treated in government procurement activities, and many feel that it is perfectly justifiable to adopt protectionist measures and purchase exclusively from domestic suppliers instead of foreign suppliers.

As early as the establishment stage of the multilateral trading system, the US intended to introduce the national treatment rule to the field of government procurement, but received general opposition. From the very beginning, government procurement policy had been an exception to the national treatment rule as stipulated in the multilateral trading system.[1]

---

[1] Gabrielle Marceau and Annet Blank, "History of Government Procurement Negotiations Since 1945," *Public Procurement Law Review*, Vol. 4 (1996).

The paragraph 8(a) of Article III of the GATT, clearly states, "The provisions of this Article shall not apply to laws, regulations or requirements governing the procurement by governmental agencies of products purchased for governmental purposes and not with a view to commercial resale or with a view to use in the production of goods for commercial sale". Government procurement does not have to abide by the rule of the national treatment and governments could give priority to domestic products in government procurement.

Nevertheless, the call of developed countries to mutually open government procurement markets has never ceased. In the early 1960s, the Organisation for Economic Co-operation and Development (OECD) began to focus on the government procurement issue. During the same period, EU member states mutually opened government procurement markets and the European Commission released the first directive on the procurement of works[2] in April 1965. OECD's discussions on government procurement regimes started in the 1960s and continued to the mid-1970s. In December 1976, OECD submitted a document entitled "Draft Instrument on Government Purchasing Policies — Procedures and Practices"[3] to GATT. This happened to coincide with the GATT Tokyo Round of multilateral trade negotiations.[4] Although the above-mentioned document was written by experts, it had an important impact on the ongoing negotiations on Agreement on Government Procurement. In April 1979, the US, the EC, Japan, Canada and a few other parties reached an agreement known as the "1979 Agreement on Government Procurement" (hereinafter referred as GPA 1979). Parties to the agreement committed to mutually open government procurement markets. This agreement is informally referred to as "Code on Government Procurement". Although GPA 1979 was binding only on its parties and its coverage was mainly limited to the contracts of the central entities in charge of procuring

---

[2] 65/187/CEE, J.O. 929/65, 13.4.65.

[3] Draft Instrument on Government Purchasing Policies, Procedures and Practices, OECD Doc. TC(76)27 and GATT Doc. MIN/NTM/W/81, January 28, 1977.

[4] In September 1973, the seventh round of multilateral trade negotiations presided by the GATT, was launched during the Ministerial Meeting of States held in Tokyo, Japan, hence the name Tokyo Round of multilateral trade negotiations. This round of negotiations, which ended in November 1979, employed the use of a Swiss formula to reduce industrial tariffs, leading to reductions up to 33%, resulting in a series of agreements on non-tariff measures and authorization provisions for developing countries.

public goods, it meant that the international rules governing the area of government procurement had finally surfaced.

Ever since GPA 1979 was introduced, it has undergone several revisions. During the Uruguay Round of multilateral trade negotiations, GPA parties began a new negotiation within the framework of an informal working group to further adjust and expand the scope and coverage of the GPA, and finally reached the "1994 Agreement on Government Procurement" in December 1993 (hereinafter referred to as GPA 1994). This agreement has become an integral part of the final act of the Uruguay Round, and is one of the four plurilateral agreements in the WTO legal system. On January 1, 1996, GPA 1994 came into effect. There are currently 15 parties covering 43 WTO members. The key members are the US, the EU, Canada, Japan and other developed members of the WTO.

1.2 *The basic components of GPA*

GPA 1994 established the basic framework of the GPA. The agreement consisted of two parts, the first part includes the preface and 24 articles, while the second part is the "Appendices".

The basic objective of the GPA is to achieve greater trade liberalization and improve the existing international trading environment by setting up an effective multilateral framework of rights and obligations with respect to laws, regulations, procedures and practices regarding government procurement.

GPA emphasizes the following three principles. The first is the principle of non-discrimination. This means that all parties should not prepare, adopt or implement laws, regulations, procedures and practices regarding government procurement so as to afford protection to domestic products or suppliers, discriminating against foreign products or suppliers. The second is the principle of transparency which means all parties should provide transparency of laws, regulations, procedures and practices regarding government procurement. The third is the principle of preferential treatment for developing countries which means all parties should provide special treatment towards the developing countries, in particular the LDCs. Examples of such assistance could include providing technical assistance to cater to the developmental, financial and trading needs of the developing countries.

The scope[5] of the GPA includes:

(1) Procuring entities: "An entity that is directly or substantially controlled by the government or other government-designated entities", includes not only government organizations, but also other entities, such as government agencies; includes not only central government entities, but also includes sub-central government procuring entities. All parties joining the GPA should provide an annex with a list of procuring entities. Only the entities listed in the annex would be bound by the GPA.

(2) Procuring objects: The goods, services and construction services covered by the agreement are applicable to contracting parties for goods of a specified threshold value, construction services (with the exception of concession contracts for basic construction projects) and services procurement. Among these, the minimum value of goods for which central level procuring entities is governed by the agreement is SDR130,000, while the threshold value of services for which central level procuring entities and the threshold value of goods and services for which sub-central procuring entities are governed by the GPA, are determined after consultations among the Parties, and included in the annexes to the Agreement. For procuring of construction services, the agreement covers the construction works listed in Section 51 of the United Nations Central Product Classification. However, GPA is not applicable to procurement involving national security, including procurement of weapons, ammunition, strategic materials; or joint procurement closely related to national security and defense, and involving the protection of public morals, order or safety, concerning the life or health of human, animals and plants, intellectual property, protection of organizations for disabled people, philanthropic institutions or prison labor.

GPA stipulates that procurement methods could be classified as open tendering, selective tendering, limited tendering and negotiation. GPA also clearly states the challenge procedures that suppliers could invoke. Article XX of the GPA states that in the event of a complaint by a supplier that there has been a breach of GPA in the context of a procurement, each party shall encourage the supplier to seek resolution of its complaint in consultation with the procuring entity. The interested supplier should initiate the challenge procedure within

---

[5] Zhong Xiaohong, "The Influence of the WTO's 'Agreement on Government Procurement' on Our Government's Procurement Regime," *Beijing Social Sciences*, No. 4 (2001).

10 days from the time when the basis of the challenge is known or reasonably should have been known, and he should also notify the procuring entity. Challenges should be reviewed by at least one impartial administrative or judicial authority that is independent of the procuring entities. To correct breaches of the GPA and to preserve commercial opportunities, challenge procedures could employ rapid interim measures. Such measures may result in suspension of the procurement process. The procedures may provide that the overriding adverse consequences for the interests concerned, including the public interest, may be taken into account when deciding whether such measures should be applied. At the same time, the challenge procedures should generally be completed in a timely manner so as to protect commercial and other interests.

1.3 *The birth of a new GPA during the 2012 financial crisis*

Looking back at the development of the GPA, it can be observed that the agreement is still moving towards expansion of its scope, strict disciplinary restraints and encouraging the opening up of government procurement markets. As early as 1997, one year after GPA 1994 took effect, the participating parties launched a new round of negotiations, and on December 8, 2006, a consensus was reached on the amended GPA 1994, resulting in a temporary agreed GPA-text. Thereafter, all parties bid and negotiated in accordance with the scope of their respective government procurement and an agreement was finally reached during the 8th WTO Ministerial Meeting in December 2011. In March 2012, the results of a new round of negotiations including "Revised Agreement on Government Procurement (GPA 2012)" and improved bids from all parties were approved. The results of the negotiations would take effect after approval from the legislative bodies of the parties.

While the Doha Round of negotiations reached an impasse, GPA 2012 could be regarded as a rare breakthrough in rules for global trade liberalization rules since the financial crisis. From the legal perspective, the new text is a revised and more comprehensive version of GPA 1994, rather than a new agreement.

First, it has expanded the objectives of implementing GPA. The main objectives of GPA 1979 and GPA 1994 were to achieve trade liberalization in the field of government procurement through eliminating discriminatory practices. The objective of GPA 2012 was not only limited to achieving non-discrimination, but also included improving the efficiency of public resource management and preventing corruption. These objectives were independent and unrelated to trade objectives. Paragraph 4 of Article IV of GPA 2012, clearly stipulates that a procuring entity should conduct procurement in a transparent and impartial manner to avoid conflicts of interest and prevent corrupt practices. This point is innovative, as anti-corruption has not been explicitly mentioned in the current WTO legal system.[6] From many other articles of GPA 2012, it can be seen that the corruption issue is emphasized.

For example, the agreement has enhanced the requirements on tendering transparency, and stipulated that the number of suppliers permitted to participate and the criteria for selecting the limited number of suppliers should be stated in each notice of intended procurement.[7] As modifying a contract that has already been awarded could lead to unfair competition and corruption, GPA 2012 has imposed restrictions on the modification of awarded contracts and stipulated that a procuring entity should not use options, cancel a procurement or modify awarded contracts in a manner that circumvents the obligations under this Agreement.[8]

Second, it has further expanded the coverage of the GPA. Overall, the coverage of GPA 2012 has been futher expanded, the level of commitment of its parties has increased and the form of commitment has also been improved. Under the new agreement, there is a total increase of about 500 government procuring entities in all parties. At the central government entity level, there is a total increase of 150 central government procuring entities among the EU member states; at the sub-central government entity level, Canada included its provincial local government within the coverage of the GPA for the first time, while Japan, Korea, Israel and other countries have expanded the degree to which their local entities are open. With regard to other entities, Israel, Japan, Korea and other parties have increased the number of state-owned enterprises. Some parties increased the number of goods and services covered by the GPA. For example, all parties have committed to include construction services in the coverage of the GPA. The US, Japan, Korea, Israel have also lowered the threshold value. Meanwhile, GPA 2012 has also classified some departures from the norm widely prevalent during actual operation as being an exception to government procurement rules.

Third, it further clarified the principles of special and differential treatment. To accelerate the accession of developing countries to the GPA, GPA 2012 has provided a series of "transitional measures" for developing countries, which

---

[6] Robert D. Anderson and Sue Arrowsmith, *The WTO Regime on Government Procurement: Past, Present and Future* (United Kingdom: Cambridge University Press, 2011).

[7] GPA 2012 Article II, paragraph 5, and Article VII, paragraph 2.

[8] GPA 2012 Article XV, paragraph 7.

includes discounted prices, compensation, the phased-in addition of specific entities or sectors and gradual reduction in the threshold value. The specific measures depend on the negotiations between the acceding member and the parties. The transition period is five years for LDCs and three years for the developing members.[9]

Fourth, GPA 2012 designed the plan for the future development of government procurement rules. During the negotiations of GPA 2012, parties have made preliminary plans on some unclear issues regarding GPA rules, arranging for related research and negotiations. These issues include: public and private partner relations and the coverage of the procurement projects, small and medium enterprises, collection of statistics and reporting, sustainable procurement and international procurement safety standards. These issues will be the main focus of future negotiations on government procurement.

Notably, besides the expansion of its contents and coverage in the GPA, there is also a trend of more members joining the GPA. As a plurilateral agreement, GPA has long been considered a rich countries' club, and the majority of its parties are either developed countries or wealthy developing countries. But this situation is changing. In 2004, 10 new EU member states — Czech Republic, Estonia, Cyprus, Latvia, Lithuania, Hungary, Malta, Poland, Slovenia, and Slovakia, officially joined in the "Agreement on Government Procurement". Chinese Taipei, Armenia and Croatia also subsequently joined the GPA in 2009, 2011 and 2013 respectively. Currently, there are 27 observers in the GPA, including India, Saudi Arabia, Ukraine, Malaysia and Bahrain. Ten WTO members, including China, New Zealand, Ukraine, and Albania are negotiating their accession. Another six members have committed to begin their accession negotiations soon, among them is Russia that made a clear commitment to submit its application to join the GPA four years after its WTO accession.

2 Government Procurement in Regional Collaboration

It had always been the developed countries' stand to promote multilateralism of government procurement rules. In the First Session of WTO Ministerial Conference in 1996, the issue of transparency in government procurement was added to the negotiation agenda and became one of the "Singapore issues". To this end, WTO established the "Working Group on Transparency in Government Procurement", with a view to a multilateral agreement on

---

[9]GPA 2012 Article V.

transparency in government procurement and therefore to provide the conditions for multilateralization of "Agreement on Government Procurement". Although the issues discussed did not involve the market access, it still met with widespread opposition from developing countries and this issue eventually failed to be included in the Doha agenda. In face of obstacles in the multilateral arena, the countries concerned continued to promote the expansion and improvement of plurilateral GPA and at the same time, introduce government procurement-related content in regional economic cooperation.

According to statistics, among the 139 regional trade agreements which were formed and still in force after 2000, 87 agreements included provisions or chapters on government procurement.[10] Among these 87 agreements, with the exception of nine which were signed among GPA parties, more than half were signed between GPA parties and non-parties. In fact, GPA parties have regarded regional trade agreements as an important means of promoting liberalization in government procurement markets. Those countries that are reluctant to join GPA in the near term are willing to gradually integrate GPA rules and selectively open up its government procurement markets through regional trade agreements.

The US, the EU and other developed countries are still the main proponents behind government procurement provisions. In their free trade agreements with developing countries, (*i.e.* the "North-South Cooperation" type of FTAs) they have established provisions or chapters regarding government procurement, and the demands on the degree of openness of government procurement markets are extremely high and the agreements are very detailed. In 2007, the US Republican and Democratic Parties reached an agreement known as the Bipartisan Trade Deal, which specified government procurement elements must be incorporated in future US free trade agreements and requested that US government procurement goods and services suppliers comply with US labor laws and observe protection of the environment.[11] The degree of liberalization and the extent of regulation of government markets in the Latin American countries, the Middle East, Singapore, Australia, Japan and Korea are relatively high. Thus, very often government procurement elements are incorporated

---

[10]Tu Xinquan and Hao Gang, "New Trends on Liberalization in Government Procurement Markets and Negotiations on China's Accession to GPA," *National School of Administration*, No. 5 (2012).

[11]Office of the United States Trade Represetative, "Bipartisan Trade Deal," May 2007, retrieved from http://www.ustr.gov/sites/default/files/uploads/factsheets/2007/asset_upload_file127_11319.pdf.

into the free trade agreements, with the form and content of the agreements being similar to the GPA.[12]

However, Southeast Asian countries and CIS countries (The Commonwealth of Independent States) maintained a conservative stance towards government procurement.

There are four kinds of approaches towards incorporating elements of government procurement in free trade agreements. First, to regard government procurement as an item for future negotiation, such as the "Canada-Costa Rica FTA". Second, to promote liberalization in government procurement only in principle, rather than including substantive content in the agreement, such as the "Australia-New Zealand FTA" and the "Korea-India FTA". Third, to include GPA elements in the FTA by making appropriate adjustments of the GPA content, such as the "US-Singapore FTA" and "Japan-Singapore FTA". Fourth, to add new obligations on the basis of the parameters of the GPA, for example, in the "US-Australia FTA", and the "EU-Chile FTA".

Government procurement provisions or chapters in the above-mentioned FTAs generally include the following elements: first, the mutual opening of government procurement markets between FTA partners; second, the adoption of the principle of national treatment towards foreign companies and products; third, the broader definition of government procurement activities, including central and local government agencies as well as various government actions; and fourth, the determination of the threshold value in government procurement. The agreement is only applicable to government procurement which attained or exceeded the threshold values.[13] It can be observed from the contents of the relevant FTA that the threshold value of government procurement is generally lower in the free trade agreements that the US signed with other countries. This implies that there is a greater demand for opening of markets. On the other hand the threshold values in EU's FTA agreements are generally closer to the GPA threshold values.

From the ongoing FTA negotiations, it can be observed that government procurement will be incorporated into more regional economic arrangements. For example, in TPP negotiations, ambitious standards are set on the government procurement issue even though only the US, New Zealand and Japan are GPA members. It is worth noting that while developed countries push for the opening of government procurement markets through regional economic cooperation on

---

[12] Zhang Xiaoyu, "Government Procurement in the FTA," *International Trade*, No. 2 (2008).

[13] Martin Khor, "Government Procurement in FTAs: An Outline of the Issues," Third World Network; retrieved from http://www.ftamalaysia.org/file_dir/58298860344cdb056ceb99.pdf.

the one hand, they also implement more stringent restrictions on government procurement on the other hand. One of the aims of this strategy is to coerce other countries to either open government procurement markets or join the GPA.

For example, the EU is a regional organization with the highest degree of economic integration; it has spared no efforts to promote the elimination of barriers in government procurement markets within the region and has achieved remarkable results. However, the European Commission believes that more than half of the world procurement markets are closed. Among the EU exports, only 10 billion euros of exports could enter foreign government procurement markets. Due to obstruction from restrictive procurement practices, at least 12 billion euros of exports did not materialize. According to European Commission data, out of the EU's government procurement of two trillion euros, 325 billion euros of the markets are open to non-EU enterprises. However, "EU enterprises and products are not always able to enjoy the same degree of openness in foreign government procurement markets". Compared to the EU, only 178 billion euros of the US's government procurement markets and 27 billion of the Japan's government procurement markets are open to foreigners while the Chinese procurement markets are even less open as compared to US and Japanese markets. Some countries even adopted protective measures during the economic crisis. In this context, the European Commission drafted a proposal on the regulation of government procurement entitled "Access of Third-Country Goods and Services to the Union's internal market in public procurement and procedures supporting negotiations on access of EU's goods and services to the public procurement markets of third countries"[14] (hereinafter referred to as the new EU regulation), and submitted to the European Parliament and the European Council for consideration. The new EU regulations aimed at strengthening the EU's position during negotiations with third party countries, clarifying the provisions for third country enterprises, goods and services to access the EU's government procurement markets, and thus ultimately improving business opportunities for EU companies worldwide, creating jobs and promoting innovation.

In comparison to the existing procurement policies, the most distinctive feature of the new EU regulation is that it limits the access of members that

---

[14] European Commission, "Proposal for a Regulation of the European Parliament and of the Council on the Access of Third-Country Goods and Services to the Union's Internal Market in Public Procurement and Procedures supporting Negotiations on Access of Union Goods and Services to the Public Procurement Markets of Third Countries", March 21, 2012, COM(2012) 124 final.

the European Commission perceived as "unqualified"[15] to access the EU's government procurement markets. In particular, the new EU regulation includes three provisions.

First, it stipulates the rules of origin for goods and services purchased by the government. It requires the origin of services to be determined by origins of the natural or legal persons who provide the services. Limits are imposed on "non-covered goods or services" (*i.e.* goods or services provided by "unqualified" members), such as excluding tenders which comprise of more than 50% of non-covered goods and services and imposing fines on the non-covered goods or services in tenders submitted. Upon requests from the contracting entities, the European Commission could also take restrictive measures, or even authorize the exclusion of tenders which include "non-covered goods and services".

Second, it imposes strict limits on low price tenders. The new regulation stipulates where entities in the fields of water supply, energy, transport, and postal sector carry out procurement for those tenders which the origins of the goods and services are outside the EU, and which consist of more than 50% of non-covered goods or services, the entities should notify the other tendering parties.

Third, the European Commission will carry out consultations with or take retaliatory measures against a third country for the restrictive market of the latter. The European Commission may initiate, or upon request, conduct external investigations into alleged restrictive government procurement measures. If the investigation finds the existence of such restrictive measures, the Commission shall engage in consultation with the country, to ensure that EU enterprises, goods and services would be able to participate in the country's public procurement tenders and receive national treatment. If the country refuses to engage in consultation with the EU, or a satisfactory outcome could not be reached within 15 months, the European commission would take retaliatory measures in a bid, to restrict the access of the country's goods and services into EU's government procurement markets.

It is obvious that the intention of the new EU regulation is to "take revenge" on those countries that have not opened their government procurement markets to EU enterprises. At the same time, the new regulation strives to rope in

---

[15] For example, the three type of restricted members mentioned in the WTO "Agreement on Government Procurement" are GPA parties, parties that have signed FTAs with the purchasers, and LDCs.

or force China and other emerging economies to join the GPA as soon as possible. According to the regulations, the Commission may end consultations with third countries and cease its retaliatory measures in the following situations: first, the third-country has joined the GPA; and second, the country has concluded bilateral agreements with the EU on public procurement. In addition, the new regulation also provides a temporary exception for countries that are in the middle of substantial negotiations with the EU on government procurement market access issues. The Commission may temporarily allow the country's goods and services to enter the EU market.

3 Negotiations on China's Accession to the GPA

3.1 *Overview of China's accession negotiations*

When China joined the WTO in 2001, it stated that "it would become an observer of the GPA, upon accession and would initiate negotiations for membership in the GPA by tabling an Appendix 1 offer as soon as possible, and begin negotiations on the accession to GPA". On December 28, 2007, China submitted its application and initial offer for acceding to the GPA (*i.e.* China's government procurement markets coverage list) to the WTO Secretariat and officially launched negotiation talks. Subsequently, China submitted revised offers in July 2010, November 2011, November 2012, December 2013 and December 2014 respectively.

Although the GPA parties welcomed China's initiation of the accession process, they were critical of the limited scope of the offer, noting that it would need substantial improvements to bring China's coverage to the level of the GPA parties. GPA parties requested that China significantly reduce its threshold value for the size of covered contracts, include more sub-central government entites and state-owned enterprises (SOEs), expand services coverage, shorten the implementation period and remove broad exclusions. Overall, the key differences between China's offer and the demands of GPA parties lie in the following aspects.

With regard to the coverage of procurement, China's Law on Procurement only specified that purchasing activities conducted with fiscal funds by government departments, institutions and public organizations under specific circumstances using fiscal funds are considered as government procurement. GPA parties requested that China's regime be consistent with the provisions of the GPA, that is, procurement undertaken for governmental purposes be regarded as government procurement.

In terms of the threshold value of contract which is open to bidding, GPA parties requested that China's regime be consistent with theirs, *i.e.* procurement of goods and services and procurement of construction works be reduced to SDR130,000 and SDR5,000,000 respectively. In terms of opening government procuring entities, with the exception of the central government, China offered to open up some provincial government procurement markets, but GPA parties requested that China open up more provincial government procurement markets, and incorporate procurement of state-owned enterprises under the coverage of government procurement.

As for the implementation period, China proposed a three-year transition period from the time it joins the GPA to the time it fulfils the agreement. GPA parties requested China to not set up a transition period from the time it joins the GPA to the time it opens up its procurement markets, with the exception of a few areas. In addition, GPA parties also requested that China should reduce the number of exceptional cases which are not covered by the agreement.

3.2 *Accession to the GPA is generally favorable to China*

Joining the GPA is an important commitment that China made when it entered the WTO. The GPA has a positive impact on opening up the international government procurement markets to China as well as accelerating the reform of China's government procurement regime.

3.2.1 *Accession to the GPA will eliminate the legal barriers to the GPA parties' government procurement markets*

GPA is a plurilateral agreement, and only the parties can enjoy the rights of mutual opening of government procurement markets. When competing in GPA parties government procurement markets, non-GPA parties often face many restrictions and do not receive legal protection of rights and interests. For example, the US government is unable to directly purchase goods and services from China as required by its laws. After China's accession to the GPA, such legal barriers for China's products to enter the US and EU government procurement markets will be eliminated, thus providing an important opportunity for Chinese enterprises to enter the developed countries' government procurement markets.

It is estimated that government procurement accounts for about 10%–15% of GDP in most countries in the world. Data shows that since 2005, US government procurement contracts had been maintained at more than USD2 trillion, and even exceeded the USD3 trillion in 2009,[16] accounting for more than 10% of its GDP and about 30% of its fiscal expenditure. In 2008, the EU's government procurement amounted to 2.16 trillion euros, accounting for 16.5% of the EU's GDP, of which 392 billion euros (which is 3% of GDP in EU) exceeds the threshold value.[17] If China became the first major developing country to join the GPA, it would be easier for Chinese products to gain an advantage while competing in the international markets. At the same time, this would also induce the US, the EU, Japan and other GPA parties to expand investment in China, capitalize on China's infrastructure and labor advantages and shift the production base of their government procurement products to China.

3.2.2 *Limited impact on China's government procurement markets upon accession to GPA*

Joining the GPA and the accession to the WTO is different in nature. After joining the GPA, there is no further reduction in tariffs rates; non-tariff measures will not be eliminated and there is no change in the degree of openness for trade in services. The essence of the GPA commitment is that when conducting procurement, central government entities, sub-central government entities, and other entities should allow the suppliers of GPA parties to take part in the tendering process where the procurement for goods, services or construction services exceeds a certain level (*i.e.* above the threshold value). Taking part in tendering does not necessarily mean that the tender will be necessarily awarded, neither is it an obligation to purchase. It can be observed from the actual situation that although China has not joined the GPA, the degree of openness of its government procurement markets is fairly higher, and thus China's accession to the GPA would not have a significant impact on its government procurement markets. In the field of goods, the vast majority of Chinese products are highly competitive and China needs to import mainly high-technology products whose market demands the domestic companies are unable to satisfy.

As the provision of services is subject to geographical restrictions, government procurement of services is mainly restricted to services within the country.

---

[16] Ma Tianming, "Analytical Report on the US Government Procurement Market," Sina.com, November 10, 2011, retrieved from http://blog.sina.com.cn/s/blog_48e8565a0100z0qm.html.

[17] WTO document GPA/102/Add.7, March 25, 2013.

For example, public construction services are limited by qualifications and construction costs and therefore foreign construction service providers do not have an advantage over local construction units.

3.2.3 *Accession to GPA is beneficial to promoting the reform of the government procurement regime*

For the case of China, the reason for joining the GPA is not only to access the global government procurement markets, but more importantly, to push forth deep reform of China's government procurement regime, promote fiscal transparency, break down industry monopolies and regional blockades and achieve reform through opening up its markets.

The GPA emphasized that adequate competition must be introduced into the markets during government procurement and required GPA parties not to discriminate against foreign products or service suppliers. All GPA parties should strive to be impartial and transparent with regard to the laws, regulations, procedures and practices on government procurement, and establish the challenge procedures and complaint mechanisms targeted at questionable actions during government procurement. Once China joins the GPA, China's government procurement should adhere to higher standards of transparency, which will be conducive for promoting "sunshine fiscal finance", avoid "black box operations" and in the long run, will help to eradicate corruption.

China's government procurement will abide by the principle of national treatment and treat both domestic and foreign-invested enterprises fairly. This will ensure fair competition for foreign-invested enterprises, strengthen fair rules for government procurement, break down regional and industrial monopolies, and provide fair competitive conditions for all enterprises, including private, small and medium enterprises. The introduction of the GPA's challenge and complaint mechanisms will also help to strengthen the supervision over government procurement activities, and provide opportunity for both foreign and domestic enterprises to make use of the relevant mechanisms in order to safeguard their own interests, which in turn will enhance the impartiality of government procurement. Some are concerned that once a country joins the GPA, the "xenophile" mentality in government procurement will cause a huge influx of foreign products. If the existence or seriousness of such a mentality is put aside for the time being, strict capital budget management, open cost performance and fair competitive mechanisms will not only correct the xenophilic attitude, but also improve domestic enterprises' product quality and performance, and enhance market competitiveness.

3.3 *China will still face major challenges upon joining the GPA*

In recent years, China has actively implemented the Law on Government Procurement to promote the reform of the government procurement regime, with open competition being its key strategy. The "separation of control and procurement" mechanism supports the gradual improvement of its government procurement regime, ensures that the government procurement regulatory approach is more complete, and that the scope and scale of government procurement continues to expand. During the negotiation process for opening its government procurement market, multilateral and bilateral international exchanges and cooperation continued to be strengthened. However, it should be observed from certain GPA rules and the demands from GPA parties that there is still a wide discrepancy in China's current government procurement regime. The differences are mainly in the following areas.

First, the GPA's definition of government procurement is based mainly on the US and European's definition of government procurement or public procurement, and specifies that all purchases for government purpose should be regarded as under the government procurement activities. According to this definition, all procurement (goods and services procured by the government) covered by China's Law on Government Procurement and some of the procurement covered by China's Law on Tendering and Bidding (*i.e.* public works and related purchase) fall into the coverage of GPA. During the negotiations, GPA parties feel that if the narrow scope of the Law on Government Procurement was adopted, the coverage of China's government procurement would be substantially smaller than the international level. Hence, they insisted that public works covered by the Law on Tendering and Bidding should be included in the coverage of government procurement. However, this will not only involve China's existing laws and regulations but also touch on China's current regime.

Second, the US, Europe and other developed countries intend to use GPA norms to restrict the procurement behavior of China's state-owned enterprises. Although the GPA did not explicitly specify that state-owned enterprises should be included in the coverage of government procuring entities, by observing each country's government procurement regime, many non-governmental organizations (NGOs) have public service functions or own public institution properties, accept government guidance, control or influence, and thus fall under the jurisdiction of China's government procurement regime. Therefore, many state-owned enterprises and public institutions in the field of public utilities have been incorporated into the coverage of some of the GPA parties. Due to such precedents, the US, the EU and other GPA parties have requested China to include so-called state-owned enterprises in the field of public utilities into the offer. For example, the EU requires that all entities engaged in commercial or industrial activities in China in the field of gas or heating, electricity, water supply, urban transport, airports, ports, telecommunications services, petroleum, coal and other solid fuel exploration and mining, postal services, and other areas, be included in the coverage of government procurement, as long as their procurement policy is substantially controlled, decided or influenced by the central, regional or local government. With this approach, 108 names of specific companies in the petroleum and petrochemical industries were enumerated. But it must be pointed out that China's economic system is different from that of the US and the EU. Public ownership is the main component of China's economy but state-owned enterprises are prevalent and operate in accordance with relevant laws. In its Working Group's report for WTO accession, the Chinese Government had committed that state-owned and state-invested enterprises would not be considered government procuring entities. If China were to accept all the restrictions that developed countries imposed on their state-owned enterprises, this would far exceed what China can tolerate and accept.

Third, GPA parties have set high demands on Chinese sub-central governments. They have not only requested for all provincial governments to be included, but also requested a list of 23 sub-provincial cities be included in the coverage. The EU even requested prefecture-level cities to be included. Although China has a unitary system, the central government keeps a loose rein on local fiscal and budget management. Under the system where administration is managed by different levels and local government procurement is essentially self-managed, the government procurement at sub-central levels are not yet aligned with international standards.

Faced with the above-mentioned challenges, China prepared to cope by accelerating the improvement of its government procurement regime. For example, China should increase the degree of openness and transparency in government procurement, restrict discretionary power at all levels of government and impose stricter management on public works procurement where there is currently a high incidence of corruption. On the other hand, China should actively and steadily push forward GPA negotiations to better safeguard its own interests. The GPA adopts the reciprocity principle, which can be understood as, "If you open the markets to me, I will open them to you; if you do not open the markets to me, I will not open them to you either." This principle must be made full use of during negotiations, to avoid non-reciprocity where China opens up its markets but GPA parties do not. For example, as for sub-central entities, the coverage of local procuring entities varies greatly among the GPA Parties. Some parties like Japan, Korea and the EU are more comprehensive and include all levels of sub-central government. Others cover a more limited number of entities: for example, the US only committed to include 37 state-level governments. Obviously, there is no reason for the US and the EU to require China to completely open its markets. As for state-owned enterprises, the EU's existing commitment does not include gas, heating, telecommunications services, oil, coal and other solid fuel exploration and mining, postal services and other areas of business. It is clearly unreasonable to expect China to be unilaterally open its market.

Through the GPA negotiation process, China should actively learn from its international experiences, deepen its reforms in accordance with their own goals, break down barriers for its own interests, accelerate the pace of reform of the government procurement regime and adhere to the principle of reciprocity. China should also fully utilize the GPA's special and differential treatment available to developing countries, seek advantages while avoiding disadvantages based on national conditions, and strive for early completion of a the negotiations on the basis of a balance of its rights and obligations.

In short, although China's accession to the GPA means that all levels of government in the country will face more external constraints during government procurement, this is conducive to promoting the establishment of a more open, fair, just and efficient government procurement regime, and it will help to improve fiscal transparency and legalization standards in China. On the whole, this is in line with China's basic objectives of promoting reforms of the financial systems. During the Third Plenary Session of the 18th CPC Central Committee, it was mentioned that the market should play a decisive role in resource allocation, deepen economic reform and accelerate the perfection of a modern market system. A government procurement market is not only related to the reasonable allocation of market resource, but it is also related to the restriction and supervision of the exercise of rights. China should assess the situation, formulate a top-level design, build up a solid foundation at the baseline, adopt both an offensive and defensive approach and an approach that is beneficial to itself, seize every opportunity, and join the GPA as soon as possible.

Chapter 10

Rules of Intellectual Property

In June 2010, the TRIPS Council in the WTO began debating on the level of global enforcement of intellectual property rights. The developing members pointed out that in recent years, developed countries have negotiated and signed bilateral or plurilateral agreements that sought to enforce standards of intellectual property higher than those required in the TRIPS agreement. This indirect violation of the TRIPS agreement had the potential of adversely affecting developing members. Developing members requested that the TRIPS Council ascertain the basic principles while the developed members opined that the TRIPS Agreement provided the minimum international standards for protection of intellectual property and did not prohibit members from establishing higher protection standards. Furthermore, seeking solutions for areas not covered under the TRIPS Agreement and the WTO's unresolved intellectual property issues apart from the TRIPS Agreement framework were not violations of the TRIPS Agreement or other WTO agreements.

Evidently, the above argument did not hinder the further development of rules of intellectual property. In October 2010, pushed forth by the US, the EU countries, Japan and other developed countries, ACTA[1] was signed, and the US-led TPP[2] was progressing rapidly. In June 2013, the US and Europe highlighted and publicized the launch of TTIP negotiations. In both the TPP and TTIP, the chapter on intellectual property rights is one of the important topics for contention. One wonders from TRIPS to ACTA, and from the TPP to TTIP, how will rules on intellectual property develop from here?

---

[1] Detailed in the later part of the chapter.
[2] *Ibid.*

1 Overview of Rules on Intellectual Property Rights before the Economic Crisis

Intellectual Property Rights (IPRs) refer to the intellectual proprietary rights accorded to a citizen, legal person, or other organizations in the arts and literature, science and technology and other fields creations of the intellect. In general, intellectual property rights currently include seven sections namely copyright and related rights, trademarks, geographical indications, industial designs, patents, layout-designs (topographies) of integrated circuits, and protection of undisclosed information.[3] There are distinct regional, temporal and exclusive features to IPRs. The objectives of IPRs protection should facilitate the promotion of technological innovation, transfer and dissemination, be of mutual advantage to producers and users of technological knowledge, contribute to social and economic welfare and help to balance rights and obligations.[4] It can thus be seen that IPRs form a civilized system of rules of intellectual property created by man and its primary goal is to achieve equilibrium between encouraging innovation and common usage. The protection of intellectual property rights and the prevention of abuse of intellectual property rules are two sides of the same coin.

Before the economic crisis, the development of rules on intellectual property rights had already been rather mature. From the initial domestic legislation, it had gradually expanded to the international level, and a large number of international intellectual property treaties had been formed. These international treaties had further developed from being simple IP regulations to a combination of IP and trade rules. In addition, IP rules had also been included in the content of bilateral and plurilateral agreements among countries. Human society had already seen the development of intellectual property rights from domestic regulation, the Paris Convention, the Berne Convention, the World Intellectual Property Organization (WIPO) rules to the WTO Rules.

1.1 *Domestic legislation of IPRs*

IPRs originated as a privilege from the feudal society. This privilege was granted either by a monarch, or the feudal state, or by local officials who represented the monarch.[5] Early legislation of intellectual property came from the capitalist

---

[3] Refer to TRIPS Agreement, Article 1, paragraph 2.

[4] Refer to TRIPS Article 7.

[5] For example, King Edward III bestowed John Kempe, the Flemish craftsman, with the "patent rights" to his sewing and dyeing technology. Refer to Zheng Chengsi, *Theory of Intellectual Property Rights* (Beijing: Law Press, 2003), pp. 2–3.

Table 10.1 Early IPRs legislation by major capitalist countries

Patent law		Copyright law		Trademark law	
Year	Country	Year	Country	Year	Country
1623	Britain	1710	Britain	1804	France
1790	The US	1790	The US	1862	Britain
1791	France	1793	France	1870	The US
1877	Germany	1837	Germany	1874	Germany
1885	Japan	1875	Japan	1884	Japan

Source: Authors' compilation of laws.

countries with more developed market economies, reflecting the proprietary rights and privacy of intellectual property (see Table 10.1).

In addition to specialized intellectual property law, the US also established the Section 337 targeting foreign companies that violated IP and Section 301 targeting inadequate protection of IP by foreign governments, in the 1930 "Tariff Act" and 1988 "Omnibus Trade and Competitiveness Act" respectively. The US was the first to establish binding rules of intellectual property and trade rules in domestic national legislation.

China's earliest legislation of IP which was similar to that of the West began in the late Qing Dynasty. Faced with internal and external threats, the Qing government tried to reform and in 1898, 1904 and 1910, issued the "Regulations on Rewards for the Promotion of Technology", "Interim Trademark Registration Regulation" and "Copyright Code of Great Qing Dynasty" respectively. At that time as the Qing Dynasty perished quickly, the legislation they promulgated was not truly implemented. After the Qing Dynasty was overthrown, in China's modern history, whether the Northern Warlord Era or the Republic of China Era, till the founding of New China and before the opening and reform, there had been relevant legislations related to IP but because of war and the highly unified planned economy after the founding of the People's Republic of China (PRC), IPRs, as a type of private rights, had not had the suitable fertile ground for growth. As reforms took place and the opening up and construction of the market economy continued to deepen, contemporary Chinese trademark laws, patent laws, copyright laws were adopted in 1982, 1984 and 1990 respectively. IP content related to foreign trade was also included in China's revised "Foreign Trade Law" in 2004.

1.2 *International convention system of IPRs*

In 1873, the International Exhibition of Inventions was organized in Vienna, but foreign exhibitors refused to participate in the exhibition for fear that their ideas would be stolen or used for commercial purposes in other countries and this was the first time international intellectual property protection issues were presented. As can be seen, the protection of the business interests of an IPRs holder in a foreign market is the endogenous driving force for the internationalization of IP rules. Subsequently, the "Paris Convention on the Protection of Industrial Property" (PCPIP) was birthed in 1883. This was the first international treaty created for the protection of a citizen's intellectual property in a foreign country, and thus, patent and trademark protection was brought to the international stage for the first time. In 1886, the establishment of the "Protection of Literary and Artistic Works Berne Convention" also set copyright protection on the international stage. The protection of intellectual property thus stepped from the domestic arena onto the international protection arena through the "Paris Convention" and "Berne Convention".

In 1967, the "The Convention on Establishing World Intellectual Property Organization" (WIPO) was adopted and came into effect in 1970 when the WIPO was officially founded. In 1974, WIPO became a specialized agency of the United Nations system of organizations and the international protection of human intellectual property entered the WIPO era. China joined the organization in 1980.[6] Currently, WIPO manages 28 international treaties. There are 10 international treaties with respect to trademarks and China is included in four of them.[7] There are 10 patent-related treaties and China has joined six of

---

[6]China joined the WIPO before its first legislation on intellectual property was passed (the 1982 Trademark Law), thus the alignment of Chinese intellectual property legislation with international standards is one of its characteristics.

[7]The 10 international treaties are as follows: (1) China became a member of the PCPIP which was concluded in 1883, on March 19, 1985. (2) The Madrid System of International Registration of Trademarks, namely the "Madrid Agreement Concerning the International Registration of Marks" signed in 1989 and the "Protocol Relating to the Madrid Agreement" signed in 1989. China became a member of the Madrid Agreement on October 4, 1989 and China joined the Madrid Protocol in December 1995. (3) The "Madrid Agreement for the Repression of False or Deceptive Indications of Source on Goods" concluded in 1891. (4) On August 9, 1994, China became a member of the "Nice Agreement Concerning the International Classification of Goods and Services for the Purposes of the Registration of Marks" which was concluded in 1957. (5) The "Lisbon Agreement for the Protection of Appellations of Origin and their International Registration" was signed in 1958. (6) The "Vienna Agreement Establishing an International Classification of the Figurative Elements of Marks" concluded in 1973. (7) In 1973, the Trademark Registration Treaty was concluded. (8) In 1981, the "Nairobi Treaty on the Protection of the Olympic Symbol" was signed. (9) In 1994, the "Trademark Law Treaty" was concluded. (10) On January 29, 2008, China signed the "Trademark Law Treaty" that concluded in 2006.

them.[8] There are eight associated with copyrights and China has joined four of them.[9]

Apart from the WIPO, there are three international conventions dealing with IPRs: the first is the "International Convention for the Protection of New Varieties of Plants"[10] (UPOV Convention), of which China became a member on April 23, 1999. This convention is managed by the International Union for the Protection of New Varieties of Plants. The second is the "Universal Copyright Convention" concluded in 1971, of which China became a member on October 30, 1992. This convention is managed by UNESCO. The third is TRIPS that concluded in 1995 and of which China became a member on December 11, 2001. TRIPS is managed by WTO.

---

[8] The 10 patent-related treaties are as follows: (1) On March 19, 1985, China became a member of the PCPIP which was concluded in 1883. (2) The "Hague Agreement Concerning the International Registration of Industrial Designs" was concluded in 1925. (3) On September 19, 1996, China became a member of the "Locarno Agreement Establishing an International Classification for Industrial Designs" which concluded in 1968. (4) On January 1, 1994, China became a member of the "Patent Cooperation Treaty" concluded in 1970. (5) On June 19, 1997, China became a member of the "Strasbourg Agreement Concerning the International Patent Classification" which concluded in 1971. (6) On July 1, 1995, China became a member of the "Budapest Treaty on the International Recognition of the Deposit of Microorganisms for the Purposes of Patent Procedure" which concluded in 1977. (7) In 1989, China became a member of the "Washington Treaty on Intellectual Property in Respect of Integrated Circuits" which concluded in 1989. (8) In 2000, the "Patent Law Treaty" was signed. (9) The "Vienna Agreement for the Protection of Type Faces and Their International Deposit". (10) The "Geneva Treaty on the International Recording of Scientific Discoveries."

[9] The eight copyright-associated treaties are as follows: (1) On October 15, 1992, China became a member of the "Berne Convention for the Protection of Literary and Artistic Works" concluded in 1886. (2) On April 30, 1993, China became a member of the "Rome Convention for the Protection of Performers, Producers of Phonograms and Broadcasting Organizations" which concluded in 1961. (3) The "Brussels Convention Relating to the Distribution of Programme-Carrying Signals Transmitted by Satellite" concluded in 1974. (4) In 1971, the "Geneva Convention for the Protection of Producers of Phonograms against Unauthorized Duplication of Their Phonograms" was concluded. (5) The "WIPO Copyright Treaty" (WCT) was concluded in 1996 and China acceded to the Treaty in 2006. (6) In 1996, the "WIPO Performances and Phonograms Treaty" (WPPT) was concluded and China acceded to the Treaty in 2006 as well. (7) In 1996, a treaty concerning a number of issues concerning the protection of literary and artistic works was adopted. (8) On June 26, 2012, the "Beijing Treaty on Audiovisual Performances" was signed (not yet in force).

[10] The Convention officially took effect on August 10, 1968 and was subsequently revised in 1972, 1978 and 1991. There are now two texts to the Convention, the 1978 version and the 1991 version. China only acceded to the 1978 version of the Convention.

It is noteworthy that the vast majority of international IP conventions mentioned above serve mainly to solve the issues of IP protection on when and how the rights are granted and how to protect these rights. This determines the mission of the international IP conventions from the outset to harmonize the differences between various countries' domestic IP legislation and unify the principle of IPRs protection. Only with the appearance of TRIPS were trade rules and intellectual property rules integrated for the first time, marking the growing importance and value of IP in the field of trade and economics, and the entrance of IP protection into the WTO era.

1.3 *Agreement on trade-related aspects of intellectual property rights (TRIPS)*

The launch of trade-related aspects of intellectual property rights (TRIPS) was mainly driven by the US — it had already proposed including the prevention of counterfeiting trade into negotiations during the Tokyo Round of GATT negotiations. Thereafter, during the Uruguay Round negotiations, the US further pushed for IP issues to be incorporated as new topics or they would not participate in the eighth round of negotiations. To this end, the US actively sought a two-pronged approach with the developed countries, communicating with them through governmental communications and industry channels; and with the developing nations, the US on the one hand used the tools of "Special 301" to put pressure on Brazil, Argentina, India, Thailand and other developing countries; and on the other hand, the US linked IP issues with the developing nations' common issues of concern such as textiles, agricultural products and others. Eventually, the US turned the IP content from NAFTA into the multilateral TRIPS and make it one of the three major areas of WTO rules.

TRIPS comprehensively established the minimum global obligations for international IP protection for the first time. This is mainly reflected in the following five areas. First of all, it achieved effective convergence with other international rules of IPRs. Article 2, paragraph 1 of TRIPS states that members shall comply with Articles 1 to 12 and 19 of the "Paris Convention" (1967); and paragraph 2 requires that nothing in Parts I to IV of this Agreement shall derogate from existing obligations that Members may have to each other under the "Paris Convention", the "Berne Convention", the "Rome Convention" and the "Treaty on Intellectual Property in Respect of Integrated Circuits". Secondly, all IP-related categories existing when TRIPS was launched are included in the scope of IPRs protection. Specifically, these included seven types of IP objects namely, copyright and related rights, trademarks, patents, industrial designs, geographical indications, layout designs of integrated circuits and undisclosed information. Thirdly, based on the provision of national treatment as part of previously concluded IP conventions, the trade rule of MFN shall be included under IP protection. Fourthly, in terms of legal protection of IP, the administrative, civil, criminal, customs and other enforcement measures are specified and the effectiveness and deterrence value of law enforcement are emphasized. Fifthly, the "weapon"[11] for trade retaliation in dispute settlement and sanctions for violating TRIPS has been established, making the implementation power of TRIPS much greater than those of the "Paris Convention", "Berne Convention" and "WIPO" in international IPRs protection.

1.4 *Bilateral or regional intellectual property rules*

Intellectual property rights are an important topic associated with the economic and trade relationships between countries. International IPRs rules are often conceived during bilateral or regional activities.

Take China-US IPRs relations as an example of rules arising from bilateral activities. In January 1979, provisions in principle on inventions and copyright protection were made for the first time when the "Agreement on High Energy Physics" was signed by China and the US. In July, the same year, the two countries signed the "Agreement on Trade Relations Between the United States of America and the People's Republic of China" of which Article 6 stated that: "Both Contracting Parties agree that each Party shall seek, tinder its laws and with due regard to international practice, to ensure to legal or natural persons of the other Party protection of patents and trademarks equivalent to the patent and trademark protection correspondingly accorded by the other Party". Earlier, the two parties had clashed severely on four occasions in 1989, 1991, 1994 and 1996 respectively, with regard to IPRs. This promoted the further improvement of China's IP legislation. Thereafter, during the China-US negotiations for China's accession to WTO, IP also became a key area of negotiations for a consensus to be reached on whether China could enter WTO bilateral agreements. The biggest conflict over IPRs between China and the US happened on April 10, 2007 when the US filed a request for consultations with the WTO dispute settlement mechanism on IP issues with China. This led to

---

[11] For example, in the case of US prosecuting India for violation of IP (DS50), India amended the relevant measures that were inconsistent with TRIPS under the WTO dispute mechanism. Another example is the 1999 EU versus the US copyright case (DS160). After the US lost the case, the EU sought for authorization to retaliate and forced the US to make concessions.

the first WTO litigation associated with IP enforcement[12] in history. After litigation, the inclination towards IP cooperation became more and more clearly. At the 22nd US-China Joint Commission on Commerce and Trade in 2011, the two governments signed the first Intellectual Property Rights Cooperation Framework Agreement. Due to the objective differences between the two in terms of social system, legal concepts and other developmental aspects, it can be seen that US-China IPRs cooperation will continue to alternate between conflict and cooperation. However, the current objectives for both China and US in IPRs is the same. Both parties face the same challenges on IPRs brought about by the rapid development of technology. As the level of IPRs protection increases in China, the cooperation between the two parties in terms of IPRs will become broader and broader.

At the regional level, APEC can be taken as an example. For many years, the US, Japan, Canada, Australia and other major economies have continually pushed for APEC to approve intellectual property rights bills through various platforms such as informal APEC leadership meetings, meetings of Ministers Responsible for Trade (MRT), Economic Senior Officials' Meetings (SOM), Committee on Trade and Investment (CTI) and the Intellectual Property Expert Group meetings (IPEG) *etc.* These bills include an initiative and five guidelines namely the "Anti-Counterfeiting and Piracy Initiative", the "Guidelines to Protect Against Unauthorized Copies", "Guidelines to Reduce Trade in Counterfeit and Pirated Goods", "Guidelines to Prevent Internet Sales of Counterfeit Goods", "Guidelines to Secure Supply Chains against Counterfeit and Pirated Goods", and the "Guidelines for Effective IPRs Public Awareness".

In addition, IP rules at the bilateral or regional level are also more evidently negotiated at various international FTAs, reflecting the further integration of IP and trade rules. For example, in 1994, the IP content in "NAFTA", signed by the US, Canada and Mexico, became a prototype for TRIPS. Another example is the TPP negotiations which is being pushed for actively. Its IP rules will also be of a higher standard. It is worth noting that some developed economies which have been unable to achieve higher standards of IP rules in the two multilateral platforms of WIPO and WTO have turned to bilateral or regional negotiations in search for greater protection. To some extent, it can be said that FTA negotiations now stand at the forefront of the era for opening up IP and their IP content also reflects the latest trends and changes in international IP rules.

---

[12]WTO Dispute Settlement (DS362). Refer to Chen Fuli, *US-China WTO Dispute of Intellectual Property Rights* (Beijing: Intellectual Property Publishing House, 2010).

2 Changes in Intellectual Property Rules since the Economic Crisis

Since the 2008 economic crisis, countries around the world have introduced new domestic and foreign economic development policies in order to overcome the crisis and step out of the shadows of the economic downturn as soon as possible. Developed economies have become clearer with regard to their apparent competitive advantage in intellectual property through the crisis, and have made it an important focal point in promoting economic recovery and innovative development. On April 11, 2012, the Bureau of Economic Analysis and the Patent under the US Department of Commerce and Trademark Office jointly issued the "Intellectual Property and the US Economy" report.[13] The report noted that in 2010, the IP-intensive industries in the US created a total value added of USD5.06 trillion, accounting for 34.8% of the year's GDP; IP-intensive industries directly or indirectly created 40 million jobs accounting for 27.7% of US employment in 2010; and the export volume from IP-intensive industries reached USD775 billion, accounting for 60.7% of total merchandise exports. On September 30, 2013, the European Commission Directorate General for Internal Market and the European Patent Office jointly issued the "Report on Contribution of IP-Intensive Industries to the European Economy and Employment". The report showed that the value produced by European IP-intensive industries was 4.7 trillion euros, accounting for 39% of total value of the EU; and 35% of EU employment came from IP-intensive industries. Due to the huge economic benefits and significant comparative advantages, the US has always been the staunchest defender of IP rules and the most active promoter of future rules.[14] The EU, due to internal economic development and foreign competition needs, is also continually strengthening IP rules, becoming another important force in promoting rule changes.

2.1 *Integration of the US domestic intellectual property rules*

The economic crisis intensified the competition between national economies. Faced with the development of new technologies and new IP infringements,

---

[13] US Department of Commerce Bureau of Economic Analysis and the Patent and Trademark Office, "Intellectual Property and the US Economy: Industries in Focus," March 10, 2012; retrieved from http://www.esa.doc.gov/Reports/intellectual-property-and-us-economy-industries-focus.

[14] It can be said that the current changes in IP rules are inseparable from US research studies. Studying the US is equivalent to revealing the most important aspects of changes in IP rules.

the US restructured and integrated IP rules to consolidate their strong IPRs comparative advantages.

First, the IP resources and organization prioritization method[15] was implemented. In 2008, the US passed the "Prioritizing Resources and Organization for Intellectual Property Act" (PRO-IP Act), further increasing the civil and criminal penalties for trademark, patent and copyright infringement, especially clarifying the responsibilities of secondary infringement of IPRs, and extended the enforcement of IPRs to the export sector for the first time, preventing the export of goods that violated copyrights or trademarks to be exported or forwarded by freight. In civil law enforcement, the statutory compensation of counterfeit goods was raised from USD1,000 to USD200,000, and repeat infringers could pay from USD1 million to USD2 million. In criminal law, those who committed felonies involving infringement of IPRs could be fined or sentenced up to 20 years in prison and crimes causing death were punishable by life imprisonment. In organization, the post of Intellectual Property Enforcement Coordinator (IPEC) was created at the White House, an independent IPRs law enforcement agency was established within the Ministry of Justice and more IPRs Ombudsmans were appointed and sent overseas.

Secondly, the first Joint Strategic Plan on Intellectual Property Enforcement was released. In June 2010, the US issued the first Joint Strategic Plan on Intellectual Property Enforcement coordinated by the IPEC. The plan proposed more than 30 measures comprehensively covering six aspects to improve the enforcement of IPRs including: actively ensuring the government uses legal software; increase IPRs information sharing with rights holders; identifying foreign piracy websites as part of the "Special 301" inquiry procedure; enhance communications to strengthen and broaden Section 337 enforcement; strengthen federal, state and local IP enforcement and coordination efforts; actively work to strengthen enforcement of IPRs internationally, combatting foreign-based and foreign-controlled websites that infringe American IPRs and promote enforcement of US IPRs through trade policy tools; stem out IPRs infringements in commodity supply chains; and encourage civilians to reduce network infringements through self-disciplinary actions.

Third, IPRs enforcement advisory bodies were set up.[16] On February 8, 2011, US President Obama signed the Executive Order 13565 announcing the establishment of the Senior Intellectual Property Enforcement Advisory

---

[15] http://www.gpo.gov/fdsys/pkg/PLAW-110publ403/pdf/PLAW-110publ403.pdf.

[16] The White House Press Room, "Executive Order 13565 — Establishment of the Intellectual Property Enforcement Advisory Committees," February 8, 2011; retrieved from http://www.

Committee and the Intellectual Property Enforcement Advisory Committee. Both committees would be chaired by the White House IPEC and the members would be from the State Council, Ministry of Finance, Ministry of Justice, Ministry of Agriculture, Ministry of Commerce, Ministry of Health and Human Services, Department of Homeland Security, the White House Office of Management and Budget, the Trade Representative's Office and other departments. The main responsibilities of the committees were confined to the study and the formulation of US IP enforcement strategies from the perspective of effective law enforcement and manage new problems and situations arising in IP law enforcement.

Fourth, a comprehensive revision of the Patent Law was completed. In September 2011, the US completed the most comprehensive revision of the Patent Law in 60 years. The main purpose of the revision was to ensure the validity of patent authorization and simplify the procedures of implementation, thereby strengthening the patent system.[17] The main adjustment was to change the US' "first to invent" principle to the "first to apply" principle and conduct new patent validation opposition proceedings including the post-grant review[18] and *inter partes* review.[19] In addition, the revision of the Patent Law clarified that certain types of subjects in dispute would no longer be eligible for a patent, such as applications related to human organs, or methods of tax reduction or tax evasion.

2.2 *The EU's strategy for intellectual property*

As the cradle of civilization of the IP system, IP is closely linked to huge economic benefits for the EU. Faced with the new changes in technology and market competition, particularly the huge increase in Internet commerce activity, the European Commission proposed the "A Single Market for Intellectual

---

whitehouse.gov/the-press-office/2011/02/08/executive-order-establishment-intellectual-property-enforcement-advisory.

[17] Patrick J. Coyne, "America's Inventions Act," BNA's Patent, Trademark & Copyright Journal [translated in Chinese], October 28, 2011; retrieved from http://www.finnegan.com/zh-CHS/resources/articles/articlesdetail.aspx?news=153b2651-ca27-409d-84e6-eac24f2ad3d1.

[18] Post-grant reviews mean that within nine months of the issuance of the patent, anyone may submit a petition for review and the petition may be published or publicly disclosed challenging the applicant's novelty and inventiveness, the enforceability by those in the field, the non-support of the manual, or the topics related to the protection thereof.

[19] Third parties may also submit petitions to challenge a patent nine months after issuance or after a review has been conducted, but such challenges can only be made with regard to the novelty and progress of the patent.

.

Property Rights boosting creativity and innovation to provide economic growth, high quality jobs and first class products and services in Europe" on May 24, 2011. This strategy introduced a series of short and long-term IPRs measures to further improve the EU's existing IP rules, encourage innovative development and achieve new global competitive advantage.

The first had to do with patents. The European Commission would continue promoting strong cooperation among member states to implement unified enforcement of IP protection. At the same time, proposals for the establishment of a unified specialized patent court in the EU were raised.[20]

Secondly, with regard to trademarks, the European Commission proposed that amendments be made to the Trade Marks Ordinance and the EU Trade Mark Directive legislation so as to speed up the modernization of the EU's trademark system, ensure the efficiency and unification of trademark registration at the EU and member states levels and meet the needs of the digital age.

The third measure dealt with geographical indications, targeting the lack of protection for non-agricultural products in the EU's geographical indication rules. The European Commission would study the existing legal framework of the member states protecting geographical indications, analyze the potential impact of non-agricultural geographical indications, protection on the economy and put forward relevant legislative proposals based on the research.

The fourth has to do with copyright licensing. To deal with the problem of copyright licensing rules only remaining at the national level in member states, the Commission would promote the establishment of a unified EU copyright license and rewards sharing system, make legislative proposals on EU copyright collective management organizations, particularly in the field of music and audiovisual products *etc.*

The fifth measure was created for the field of Digital Libraries, where the European Commission put forth legislative proposals concerning "orphan works",[21] to promote the digitization and retrieval of such works and at the same time, accelerate the establishment of digital library projects. This will enable the EU to progress further towards a common copyright rules system.

The sixth measure dealt with terms of law enforcement. The European Commission put forward legislative proposals to set up the "EU Observatory

---

[20] On February 19, 2013, the ministers of 24 EU member states signed an agreement in Brussels on the establishment of a Unified Patent Court (UPC), paving the way for the implementation of a single patent system in Europe.

[21] Refers to works whose authors or rights holders are unknown or cannot be determined but are nevertheless, copyrighted.

on Counterfeiting and Piracy" in the Internal Market Directorate General responsible for IP-related work. At the same time, the Commission also suggested making amendments to the IP enforcement directive issued in 2004 to increase IP protection in digital environments.

The seventh considered customs border protection measures. The European Commission proposed a new legislative draft concerning customs protection of IPRs, further strengthening IPRs protection at the EU customs, especially including small consignments of goods purchased online into the list of intellectual property protected by the customs.

2.3 *Improvements of IP rules by other countries*

After the crisis, the rest of the world also significantly strengthened their efforts to adjust domestic intellectual property rules. After four attempts, Canada completed their revision of the copyright laws, further expanding the content to combat online piracy. Brazil, India, Jamaica, the Philippines and Malaysia launched the revision of copyright laws as well. Japan, Panama and Pakistan adopted new copyright laws. Pakistan also adopted the "Intellectual Property Organization Act" to unify management of trademarks, patents, and copyrights. Korea launched revision of the "Trademark Law", and signed a so-called FTA including IPRs content with the US, comprehensively improving IP protection standards. Australia completed revisions to the "Patent Law" and "Trademark Law", among which the criminal penalty for trademark counterfeiting was increased from two years to five years. In 2012, Russia began developing a long-term intellectual property strategy to encourage more patents to enter the market. China also began making amendments to the "Trademark Law",[22] "Copyright Law" and "Patent Law".

2.4 *Anti-counterfeiting trade agreement*

Anti-Counterfeiting Trade agreement (ACTA) negotiations were originally envisioned and proposed in 2006 by the US and Japan. Canada, the EU[23] and Switzerland participated in the early stages of deliberation in 2006 and 2007 while Australia, Mexico, Morocco, New Zealand, Korea and Singapore *etc.*

---

[22] On August 30, 2013, at the fourth session of the 12th NPC Standing Committee meeting the "Decision to revise 'The People's Republic of China's Trademark Law'" was passed.

[23] The EU was both a party in the negotiation as well as the representative of its 28 member states.

joined in the negotiations later. After 11 rounds of intensive consultations, the negotiations finally concluded in Japan in October 2010. The signing of ACTA is a typical representation of the IP powers' plurilateral push for development of IP rules, reflecting the efforts of these countries to further strengthen trade-related IP rules upon TRIPS, and to a certain extent, ACTA can be called "TRIPS-PLUS" (Trade-Related Aspects of Intellectual Property Rights Agreement +). ACTA will come into effect with the approval of six countries. At present, apart from Japan who has officially given approval, ACTA's progress for approval by other negotiating parties has not been smooth. On July 4, 2012, the European Parliament voted against ACTA and Australia also delayed giving its approval for ACTA. This, undoubtedly, surfaces a challenge as to whether ACTA will officially be effected and also casts doubts on its "survival" prospects. Nonetheless, regardless of success or failure, ACTA is an attempt by man in search for strong global protection of intellectual property. In particular, as criticism against ACTA dies down, IP content is gradually appearing more in TPP and TTIP negotiations, it is yet to be seen if ACTA would eventually take effect or come back "in guise" (see Table 10.2).

2.5 *Intellectual property rights in the TPP*

The TPP originated from FTA talks between the four countries of Singapore, Brunei, Chile, and New Zealand. The US took the lead after joining the talks in December 2009 and intended to make TPP the "21st century model for FTA negotiations".

In terms of IP protection, TPP is, after ACTA, another attempt by the US to carry out a comprehensive reconstruction of future IPRs rules through regional trade. Officials responsible for negotiations at the USTR office have emphasized that "the IP chapter for the TPP would harmonize IPR obligations strictly upwards" and "would not consider anything that lowered IPR norms in the TPP negotiations, and only measures that raised norms".[24] In addition to changes in IP rule content, TPP also makes provisions for dispute settlement procedures to deal with problems in IP protection that will undoubtedly fortify and ensure the smooth implementation of a high level of IP protection (see Table 10.3).

---

[24]James Love, "Notes from Meeting with USTR on the TPP IPRs Chapter", December 13, 2010; retrieved from http://keionline.org/node/1035.

Table 10.2 Main differences between ACTA and TRIPS.

Item for comparison	TRIPS	ACTA	Analysis
Relationship with Other International Conventions	Article 2: Intellectual Property Conventions (1) With regard to Sections II, III and IV of the Agreement, the Parties shall comply with the provisions of Articles 1–12 and 19 of the "Paris Convention" (1967). (2) No regulation in Sections I to IV of this Agreement shall be detrimental to the existing mutual obligations the Parties have assumed in accordance with the "Paris Convention", "Berne Convention", "Rome Convention" and the "Treaty on Intellectual Property related to Integrated Circuits".	Article 1: This Agreement shall not derogate from any existing obligations the Parties have assumed to any other Party according to agreements, including the TRIPS Agreement.	ACTA does not specify the agreements included in "existing agreements", referring to all existing intellectual property agreements, including all above-mentioned treaties introduced in TRIPS, as well as "Madrid Agreement concerning the International Registration of Marks" (1989), "Budapest Treaty" (1977), "Treaty on the Protection of New Varieties of Plants" (1991), "Singapore Trademark Law Treaty" (2006) and the "WIPO Internet Treaties (1996)" *etc.*
Judicial Review	TRIPS Article 41.4: Parties to a proceeding shall have an opportunity for review by a judicial authority of final administrative decisions and, subject to jurisdictional provisions in a Member's law concerning the importance of a case, of at least the legal aspects of initial	Not specified	Lack of provisions on judicial review is one of the aspects for which ACTA is criticized by the international community. ACTA is criticized for solely seeking to expand the protection of rights holders without

(Continued)

Table 10.2 *(Continued)*

Item for comparison	TRIPS	ACTA	Analysis
	judicial decisions on the merits of a case. However, there shall be no obligation to provide an opportunity for review of acquitals in criminal cases.		regulating the balance of interests and security mechanisms, including judicial reviews.
Civil Prohibitions	TRIPS Article 44: Members shall have the authority to order a party to desist from an infringement, *inter alia* to prevent the entry into the channels of commerce in their jurisdiction of imported goods that involve the infringement of IPRs, immediately after customs clearance of such goods.	ACTA Article 8: Each Party shall provide that its judicial authorities have the authority to issue an order against a party to desist from an infringement, and *inter alia*, an order to that party, or, where appropriate, to a third party over whom the relevant judicial authority exercises jurisdiction, to prevent goods that involve the infringement of IPRs from entering into the channels of commerce.	ACTA provides that in appropriate circumstances, injunctions may be issued to third parties but does not define the scope of a third party, nor state what constitutes an "appropriate" occasion, leaving it to the Parties' discretion. Third-party providers may include product processors, providers of raw materials, warehouse providers, transporters, sellers or users *etc.*, who may be infringers, and users may also include end-users of products.
Point 1 of Civil Compensation, that is, Fault Liability	TRIPS Article 45.1: Infringers shall pay the right holder damages adequate to compensate for the injury the right holder has suffered because of an infringement of that person's IPRs.	ACTA Article 9.1: Infringers shall pay the right holder damages adequate to compensate for the injury the right holder has suffered as a result of an	The ACTA provision is more detailed than that of TRIPS, specifying the method of consideration in determining the estimated

value of the amount of damages. This more clearly protects the rights holder and has a stronger deterrent effect against violations.

infringement. In determining the amount of damages for infringement of IPRs, a Party's judicial authorities shall have the authority to consider, *inter alia*, any legitimate measure of value of the infringed goods or services, which may include lost profits, the value of the infringed goods or services measured by the market price, or the suggested retail price.

TRIPS Article 45.2:
Infringers may be ordered to return the right holder profits or pay for statutory damages, even where the infringer did not knowingly, or with reasonable grounds to know, engage in infringement activities.

In seeking accountability for liability without fault, TRIPS limits the cases to when appropriate and uses the word "may", so members can exercise discretion. ACTA, on the other hand, enforces the obligated return of profits for copyright and trademark infringement, even in the case of liability without fault, and further specifies the methods of calculation

ACTA Article 9.2:
At least in cases of copyright or neighboring rights infringement and trademark counterfeiting, each Party shall order the infringer to pay the right holder the infringer's profits that are attributable to the infringement. A Party may presume those profits to be the amount of damaged referred to in paragraph 1. At least with respect to infringement of copyright or related rights protecting works, phonograms, and performances,

Point 2 of Civil Compensation, that is, Liability without Fault

(Continued)

Table 10.2 (*Continued*)

Item for comparison	TRIPS	ACTA	Analysis
		and in cases of trade mark counterfeiting, each Party shall also establish or maintain a system that provides for one or more of the following: (a) Pre-established damages; or (b) Presumptions for determining the amount of damages sufficient to compensate the right holder for the harm caused by the infringement; or (c) At least for copyright, additional damages.	of profits. At the same time, apart from return of profits, it also provides three types of remedies namely statutory damages, pre-determined compensation and additional compensation, of which one or more can be applied together. ACTA is more mandatory and comprehensive in this regard.
Point 3 of Civil Compensation, that is, Costs of Rights Protection	TRIPS Article 45.2: The judicial authorities have the authority to order the infringer to pay the right holder expenses, which may include appropriate attorney's fees.	ACTA Article 9.5: Each Party shall provide that its judicial authorities, where appropriate, have the authority to order, at the conclusion of civil judicial proceedings concerning infringement of at least copyright or related rights, or trademarks, that the prevailing party be awarded payment by the losing party of court costs or fees and appropriate attorney's fees, or any other expenses as provided for under that Party's law.	ACTA provisions related to costs of rights are more favorable for rights defenders.

| Dealing with Infringed Goods and Their Raw Materials and Production Tools | TRIPS Article 46:
Goods that are found to be infringing, materials and implements used in the creation of the infringing goods shall be disposed of outside the channels of commerce. | ACTA Article 10:
At least with respect to pirated copyright goods and counterfeit trademark goods, each Party shall provide that, at the right holder's request, its judicial authorities have the authority to order that such infringing goods be destroyed, except in exceptional circumstances, and costs of destruction shall be borne by the infringer; judicial authorities shall further have the authority to order that materials and implements used in the manufacture or creation of such infringing goods be destroyed or disposed of outside the channels of commerce and these remedies shall be carried out at the infringer's expense. | With respect to infringing goods and the materials and implements used in manufacturing and creation, ACTA's priority is to have them destroyed. This is different from the provisions of TRIPS where the order of remedies is significantly different. ACTA further provides that the costs shall be borne by the infringer. |
| Customs Border Measures | TRIPS Article 51:
Members shall suspend the release of free circulation of imported goods reasonably suspected to be counterfeit or pirated; members | ACTA Article 16:
Each Party shall adopt or maintain customs border procedures with respect to allegedly infringing import and exports shipments. | ACTA made mandatory the selective customs border measures that TRIPS provides for members in dealing with infringing goods. |

(Continued)

Table 10.2 (*Continued*)

Item for comparison	TRIPS	ACTA	Analysis
	may provide for corresponding procedures concerning the suspension of the release of infringing goods destined for exportation from their territories.		In addition, ACTA also expanded the authority of customs correspondingly.
Criminal Procedures	TRIPS Article 61: Members shall provide for criminal procedures and penalties to be applied at least in cases of willful trademark counterfeiting or copyright piracy on a commercial scale. In appropriate cases, remedies available shall also include the seizure, forfeiture and destruction of the infringing goods and of any materials and implements the predominant use of which has been in the commission of the offence.	ACTA Article 23: Each Party shall provide for criminal procedures and penalties to be applied at least in cases of willful trademark counterfeiting or copyright or related rights piracy on a commercial scale, including at least those carried out as commercial activities for direct or indirect economic or commercial advantage. Each Party shall provide for criminal procedures and penalties to be applied in cases of willful importation and domestic use, in the course of trade and on a commercial scale, of labels or packaging, as well as in appropriate cases for the unauthorized copying of cinematographic works. Parties shall ensure that criminal	ACTA clarified the definition of commercial scale, increased the range of criminal offences, expanded the types of relevant goods to be investigated and seized, and prioritized the destruction of infringing goods and materials.

liability for aiding and abetting is available. The liability, which may be criminal, of legal persons for the offences specified shall be without prejudice to the criminal liability of the natural persons who have committed the criminal offences.

ACTA Article 25:

Parties shall have the authority to order the seizure of suspected counterfeit trademark goods or pirated copyright goods, any related materials and implements used in the commission of the alleged offence, documentary evidence relevant to the alleged offence and the assets derived from, or obtained, directly or indirectly through, the alleged infringing activity, and to order the forfeiture, destruction or disposal of the above mentioned items outside the channels of commerce.

(Continued)

Table 10.2 (*Continued*)

Item for comparison	TRIPS	ACTA	Analysis
Protection of IP in the Digital Environment	Not specified.	ACTA Article 27.	On the basis of the American "Digital Millennium Copyright Act" (DMCA), ACTA further refined the relevant content in the WIPO "Internet Treaties" (WCT, WPPT), and incorporated IP protection in the digital environment for the first time into trade rules. ACTA provides that, firstly, Parties ensure that both civil and criminal enforcement procedures be available so as to permit effective action against an act of infringement of IPRs which takes place in the digital environment which constitute a deterrent to further infringements. Secondly, without prejudice to the rights, limitations, exceptions or defenses to copyright or related rights infringements, Parties should provide civil

remedies against infringement by third-parties, that is, infringement for economic purposes, inducement or funding others to engage in infringing activities. Thirdly, internet service providers (ISP) are only exempt under the strictly defined conditions laid out by ACTA.

Table 10.3 Main differences between the TPP[25] and TRIPS.

Category	Relevant TPP provision	Comparative analysis with TRIPS
Obligations of International Conventions	Besides complying with TRIPS, parties have to ratify or accede to the following international conventions and treaties before the TPP takes effect: "Patent Cooperation Treaty" (1970, revised in 1979), "Paris Convention for the Protection of Industrial Property" (1967), "Berne Convention for the Protection of Literary and Artistic Works" (1971), "Convention Relating to the Distribution of Programme-Carrying Signals Transmitted by Satellite" (Satellite Convention, 1974), "Protocol Relating to the Madrid Agreement Concerning the International Registration of Marks" (1989), "Budapest Treaty on the International Recognition of the Deposit of Microorganisms for the Purposes of Patent Procedure" (1977, revised 1980), "International Convention for the Protection of New Varieties of Plants" (UPOV Convention, 1991), "Singapore Trademark Law Treaty" (2006), "WIPO Copyright Treaty" (WCT, 1996), "WIPO Performances and Phonograms Treaty" (WPPT, 1996). In addition, before the TPP takes effect, each Party should make every effort towards ratification or accession to the "Patent Law Treaty" (2000) and the "Hague Agreement Concerning the International Registration of Industrial Designs" (1999).	TPP effectively and comprehensively consolidates the existing international conventions on IP, and on this basis, makes provisions for the minimum obligations from international treaties and conventions that Parties should comply with. Compared to the TPP, TRIPS only makes reference to the four international conventions: "Paris Convention", "Berne Convention", "Rome Convention", and the "Treaty on Intellectual Property in Respect of Integrated Circuits".

[25] On March 11, 2011, the US draft for IPRs content in TPP was published on the Internet. As negotiations for TPP are still ongoing, this draft only serves for a comparative study with TRIPS; draft of intellectual chapter of the TPP Agreement (February 10, 2011) retrieved from http://www.bilaterals.org/spip.php?article19199.

Trademark Registration	As a condition for trademark registration, no Contracting Party must not require a registered mark be perceived visually. No Contracting Party shall deny the registration of a trademark that is identified only by sound or smell.	TRIPS Article 15: Members may require, as a condition of registration, that signs be visually perceptible. TPP greatly relaxes the conditions for trademark registration, and just sounds and smells *etc.* may also be registered as trademarks.
Well-Known Trademark Protection	Parties shall not determine whether a mark is well-known based on whether the mark was registered in its territory or in another Party's territory, or whether the mark was recognized beyond its service or product field. Parties shall not refuse to protect a well-known trademark because the mark was not registered in its territory or was not included in the directory of well-known trademarks or lack of awareness of the well-known trademark.	TPP draws on the provisions in Article 18.2.6 of the US-ROK Free Trade Area Agreement and introduced the conditions of "commercial use" trademark protection from the US "Lanham Act", expressly prohibiting the fulfilling of certain conditions as the premise for protecting well-known trademarks. These provisions are more relaxed compared with TRIPS Article 16 paragraphs 2 and 3, making it easier to protect well-known trademarks.
The use of trademarks	TPP rejects setting conditions on trademark licensing and assignment based on filing records.	TRIPS Article 21 states that members may determine conditions on the licensing and assignment of trademarks. TPP evidently further relaxed the requirements for trademark licensing and transfer, making it more convenient for right holders to exercise their relevant rights.

(Continued)

Table 10.3 *(Continued)*

Category	Relevant TPP provision	Comparative analysis with TRIPS
Geographical Indications[26]	TPP provides that any marks or combination of marks including names of places, names of persons, letters, numbers, metaphorical names, colors *etc.* can become geographical indications.	Compared with TRIPS Article 22.1, TPP evidently expanded the scope of recognition for geographical indications. As with TPP's protection of trademarks, the practice for protection of geographical indications is consistent with the US.
Copyright and Related Rights Protection Principles	TPP provides that each Party shall ensure that authors, performers and record producers have the right to authorize or prohibit any form of reproduction of their works, performances and recordings, whether permanent or temporary, including temporary storage in electronic form.	Compared with TRIPS, TPP gives copyright owners broader exclusive rights, that is, the exclusion of any form of reproduction, including permanent, temporary copies or short-term storage in electronic form. This alters the ordinary meaning of "copy".[27]
Term of Copyright Protection	The term of protection for works (including photographs), performance rights, or album rights, is calculated according to the life of a natural person, that is, the lifetime of the author and 70 years after the author's death; if not calculated based on the life of a natural person, then the term of protection shall be not less than 95 years from the end of the calendar year during which the publication, performance or album was first released, or if the publication or distribution	TRIPS Article 12 provides that besides photography or applied art productions, the term of protection is 50 years if not calculated according to the life of a natural person. TPP greatly extends the term of protection.

[26] In accordance with TRIPS Article 22.1, geographical indications refer to the logo identifying the product source as a Member's territory or a region or place within the territory. The specific quality, reputation or other characteristics of the product are primarily attributable to its geographical origin.
[27] The general meaning of "copy" is that the work is attached to a certain carrier, and that the carrier should be able to be perceived or copied.

of the work was not authorized within 25 years of the date of creation of the work or completion of the performance or music production, then the term of protection shall be not less than 120 years from its date of completion of the work, performance or album.

| Technological Protection Measures | Parties shall provide that any person who deliberately seeks commercial advantage or for the purpose of personal gain, undertakes the following acts,[28] be subject to criminal investigations and proceedings: First, the circumvention, without authorization, of effective technological protection measures that prevent access to a protected work, performance, music or other copyrighted works. Second, the manufacture, import, sale, offer to sell relevant facilities, products, components or providence of promotional, advertising, or marketing services, including designing *etc.* and other acts that facilitate the circumvention of or are aimed at circumventing any effective technological measures. | This section was not covered under TRIPS but is drawn and developed from the content of "US-ROK FTA", ACTA and the US "Digital Millenium Copyright Act" (DMCA). For example, TPP Article 4.9 is similar to Article 18.4.7 of the "US-ROK FTA" but in TPP, "knowingly or unknowingly" conditional requirements are removed; and distinct from ACTA Article 27.6, "knowingly or unknowingly" is not a condition in the identification of circumvention of technological protection measures in TPP; and also distinct from DMCA Article 1201(a)(2)(c), TPP includes "promotion, advertising" content. This makes TPP's protection of technological protection measures even more stringent. |

(Continued)

---

[28] Except for non-profit libraries, archives, educational institutions or public non-commercial broadcasting organizations.

Table 10.3 (*Continued*)

Category	Relevant TPP provision	Comparative analysis with TRIPS
Rights Management Information	No person shall, without authorization, knowingly or unknowingly, commit the following acts to induce, support, facilitate, or conceal an infringement of copyright and related rights: firstly, the knowingly removal or alteration of rights management information; secondly, the sale or importation for the purpose of sales of products containing rights management information, knowing that rights management information has been removed or altered without authorization; thirdly, the sales or import, broadcast or other forms of communication for the purpose of sales to provide copies of the relevant works, performances or album to the public, knowing that rights management information has been removed or altered without authorization. Parties shall provide for criminal procedures and penalties to hold anyone who intentionally commits the above mentioned acts for commercial profit or personal gain[29] criminally responsible.	TRIPS does not provide for this. This section is similarly drafted and developed from the "US-ROK FTA", ACTA and DMCA.
Granting of Patents	As long as an invention is novel, creative and practical, Parties should grant patents to this invention in all technological fields, whether to the product or its manufacturing processes. In addition, in conformity with the standards of the patent, Parties should also ensure that patents be granted to any new application forms or methods for the known product, even if these inventions do not increase the efficacy of the product. Parties should also grant patents to the diagnosis, therapeutic and surgical procedures done on humans, plants or animals.	TRIPS Article 27.3 provides that members may exclude from patentability diagnostics, therapeutic and surgical methods for the treatment of humans or animals; plants and animals and other than microorganisms while TPP provides that they should be patentable.

[29] Except for non-profit libraries, archives, educational institutions or non-commercial broadcasting organizations.

| Civil Injunctions | Parties shall carry out injunctions according to provisions under TRIPS Article 44 and provide bans on the export of infringing goods. | The TPP increased the mandatory requirement to implement a ban on the export of infringing goods. |
| Civil Compensation | Parties shall provide that its judicial authorities have the authority to at least order the infringer to pay the right holder damages adequate to compensate for the injury the right holder has suffered. At least in cases of copyright and related rights infringement, and trademark counterfeiting, judicial authorities have the authority to order the infringer to pay the right holder the infringer's profits that are attributable to the infringement. Judiciary authorities are to determine the specific amount for compensation according to the retail price of the infringed goods and services submitted by the right holder or other legitimate calculation methods, to recognize the value of the infringed goods or services. In civil judicial proceedings with respect to trademark counterfeiting and infringement of copyright and related rights, Parties shall also establish or maintain a system that provides for pre-established damages, which shall be available on the election of the right holder. The pre-established damages shall be set out in an amount that would be sufficient to compensate the right holder for the harm caused by the infringement, and with a view to deterring future infringements. For patent infringement, judicial authorities have the authority to order the infringer to compensate the right holder three times the amount of damage caused. Except in special circumstances, the judicial authorities have the authority to order the infringer to bear litigation costs and the right holder's reasonable attorney's fees. | Compared with the TRIPS, the TPP established a pre-established damages system for trademark and copyright infringement, as well as the triple damages payment system for patent infringement. The latter is not provided in ACTA. Meanwhile, TPP also clearly specifies the calculation method for determining the amount of compensation and content with respect to bearing the costs of intellectual property litigation *etc.*, which are also not specified in TRIPS. |

(Continued)

Table 10.3 (*Continued*)

Category	Relevant TPP provision	Comparative analysis with TRIPS
Disposal of Infringing Goods, Raw Materials and Manufacturing Implements	Parties shall provide that its judicial authorities have the authority to detain suspected infringing goods, raw materials and implements, and at the right holder's request, to order that materials and implements that have been used in the manufacture or creation of the infringing goods be, without undue delay and without compensation of any sort, destroyed or disposed of outside the channels of commerce in such a manner as to minimize the risk of further infringement; and in regard to counterfeit trademark goods, the simple removal of the trademark unlawfully affixed is not sufficient to permit the release of goods into the channels of commerce.	The TPP differs from TRIPS Article 44 as it prioritizes the destruction of infringing goods, raw materials and implements while TRIPS provides for the destruction or removal from channels of commerce.
Customs Border Measures	Parties should provide that its competent authorities may initiate border measures *ex officio* with respect to goods under customs control that are imported, destined for export, in transit, or in the free trade zone, and that are suspected of being counterfeit trademark goods or pirated copyright goods.	TPP transplanted the relevant content from ACTA and expanded the scope of protection from the TRIPS required imports to exports, transit and other areas.
Criminal Responsibility	With respect to criminal liability and protection, TPP clarifies the meaning of the term commercial scale provided in TRIPS criminal liability clauses; secondly, the intentional act of importing or exporting counterfeit or pirated goods, and pirated copying of a movie or cinematographic work at a public broadcast without authorization from the movie-maker or video rights holder *etc.* are included in the scope of	At the same time that TPP re-affirms the criminal liability obligations under TRIPS, it further clarifies the definition of commercial scale, and expands the scope and methods of criminal liabilities.

criminal liability. In investigating criminal activities, TPP requires that Parties ensure criminal liability for aiding and abetting IP crimes is available under its law. In terms of penalties for offences, Parties shall provide monetary fines or sentences of imprisonment sufficiently high to provide a deterrent to future acts of infringement, consistent with the level of penalties applied, and with crimes of infringement for commercial advantage or private profit, penalties with a corresponding gravity shall be imposed. With regard to initiating investigation, Parties shall provide that their competent authorities may initiate legal investigative actions regarding infringement *ex officio*.

| Enforcement Measures in the Digital Environment | TPP requires that Parties ensure that the same civil and criminal law enforcement procedures apply to violations of trademark, copyright and related rights in the digital environment, and also requires that governments utilize legal software. TPP is imposes relatively stringent limitations except on liabilities of Internet Service Providers. | There is no such content under TRIPS. |

2.6 *Impact of global governance platforms on changes in intellectual property*

For a long time, the WTO, WIPO, G8, APEC among others, have played a positive role in global governance. IP has also always been a topic of discussion on these international platforms but due to the differences in the respective platform capabilities, their impact on the development of IP rules has been different.

Since the WTO Doha Round negotiations, the TRIPS Council has been having a "tug of debating" with regard to the relationships between IPRs and public health, system of geographical indications registration and expansion of protection, IPRs and the Convention on Biological Diversity, IP and folklore as well as traditional folk literature *etc.* Faced with the changes in IP rules after the economic crisis, the TRIPS Council debated about IPRs enforcement standards and ACTA respectively in June 2010 and February 2012 but to no avail. In 2008, WIPO established the "Committee on Development and Intellectual Property" and classified the 45 recommendations received regarding the development agenda into six groups including technological transfer, rule-making, technical assistance *etc.* and launched a major discussion on IP and Development. In 2012, WIPO completed negotiations on the "Beijing Treaty on Audiovisual Performances" and basically completed the negotiations for "Treaty on the Protection of Broadcasting Organizations". These should be the most important contributions of the WIPO on IP rule development in recent years. However, on the whole, because of the multilateral character of WTO and WIPO, with 159 and 183 members respectively, their decision-making mechanisms require that the consent of multiple members be sought for before any changes in IP rules can be made. This undoubtedly hinders the efficiency and ability of the WTO and WIPO in creating new IP rules, thus objectively push the IP powers to focus more on bilateral or regional negotiations.

As there are numerous issues of discussion for G8 and APEC, discussions on IP protection have remained at the level of verbal promises. For example, at the G8 Summit in 2011, opinions with regard to strengthening dialogue between Internet companies and governments, establishing regulations for Internet use, protection of personal information and IP, combating cybercrime and other issues were expressed. In 2008, in the APEC informal leadership statement, leaders recognized the obligations of economies in strengthening IP protection and enforcement, reaffirmed the importance of establishing a comprehensive system of balance for IP, and continued to encourage economies to increase cooperation efforts between IP experts and law enforcement agencies. APEC leaders welcomed the implementation of anti-counterfeiting and piracy initiatives and improvements to the patent system, and look forward to further progress. Although G8 and APEC are forum-based and do not directly create new IP rules, strong political wills expressed by the leaders, often offer an important factor for promoting change in today's IP rules.

2.7 Controversies over changes in intellectual property rules

There are many discussions over changes in IP rules. They are mainly focused on the relationship between IPRs protection and public interest, standards of IPRs law enforcement, prevention of IPRs abuse[30] and others.

With regard to the relationship between IPRs protection and public interest: In January 2012, a massive anti-legislative protest took place in the US. For a period of time, more than 2 million Internet users collectively cried out through "Twitter", more than 8 million emails flooded the White House, more than 10 million Internet users signed petitions, and even Google, Wikipedia, and more than 200 Internet companies jointly launched the "Internet Blackout Day".[31] This massive operation was launched in resistance to the new Internet IP legislation making its way through Congress, namely, the "Stop Online Piracy Act (SOPA)" and "Preventing Real Online Threats to Economic Creativity and Theft of Intellectual Property Act (PROTECT IP Act or PIPA)". Eventually the pressure from all sides forced the lawmakers to give up controversial bills. On February 11, 2012, tens of thousands of Europeans took to the streets to protest against ACTA.[32] German Greens Party leader Thomas Pfeiffer appealed among the protesting crowd, "It's not acceptable to sacrifice the rights of freedom for copyrights." According to Reuters, more than 40,000 demonstrators braved the cold and marched in protest in major German cities on that day.[33] Thousands of people also gathered and carried banners despite snow and

---

[30] When right holders exercise their right beyond the limits allowed by law, emphasizing too much on private rights and harming the legitimate interests of others or the public, it constitutes to abuse. Abuse can be classified into two categories: Firstly, the exercise of IPRs by right holders beyond the statutory scope; secondly, the unreasonable restriction of fair competition, or opposition to public policy, although not beyond the legal scope.

[31] On January 18, 2012, more than 200 Internet companies turned their operational sites black, indicating that the Internet would go dark if the relevant law was passed.

[32] Refer to the following section for details.

[33] February 11, 2012 is known as "International Anti-ACTA Day".

freezing temperatures in various European cities such as Warsaw, Prague, Bucharest, Vilnius, Paris, Brussels and Dublin. Both examples reflect the controversies surrounding IPRs rules in today's digital environment and reveal the conflict between IPRs protection, personal privacy and public interest. American scholar Jerry Brito, in his self-edited and published book[34] *Copyright Unbalanced*, mentioned that while the US Constitution's requirement that Congress commit to developing balanced copyright laws while sufficiently encourages authors with protection for enthusiastic creativity, does not impede public access to information. The Congress should, originally, represent public interest, yet over the past half a century, has deviated from the equilibrium to meet the desires of special interest groups. Jessica Litman also suggested that the Congress has become the spokesperson for the copyright industry.[35] Timothy B. Lee [36] analyzes that the pursuit to hold Internet Service Providers criminally responsible in the digital environment is against the "due process" spirit of law in the US Constitution, and the high costs of criminal investigations impede innovation and development.[37]

With regard to IPRs enforcement standards: In June 2010, the TRIPS Council discussed the standard of enforcement under TRIPS. Developing members proposed that in recent years, developed countries had, through negotiations and signing plurilateral, regional or bilateral agreements, sought to set the standard of IPRs protection and enforcement higher than TRIPS Agreement requirements, and are suspected to be violating the TRIPS Agreement and potentially adversely affecting developing members. They requested that the TRIPS Council pay attention to this and ascertain basic principles for IPRs in the Agreement. Developed members responded to the above question by commenting that the TRIPS Agreement provisions on IP protection were the minimum international standard and did not prevent members from setting a higher level of protection. They also believe that seeking solutions outside the TRIPS Agreement framework for areas not covered by the TRIPS Agreement and IPRs enforcement issues unsolved by the WTO did

---

[34] Available through the Mercatus Centre George Mason University website (http://mercatus. org/copyrightunbalanced/) (United States: George Mason University, 2012).

[35] Jessica Litman, *Digital Copyright* (New York: Prometheus Books, 2006).

[36] Timothy B. Lee, "How the Criminalization of Copyright Threatens Innovation and the Rule of Law," in Jerry Brito (ed.) *Copyright Unbalanced: From Incentive to Excess* (United States: Mercatus Centre George Mason University, 2012), Chapter 4.

[37] Jerry Brito (ed.), *Copyright Unbalanced: From Incentive to Excess* (United States: Mercatus Centre George Mason University, 2012), pp. 68–70.

not violate the provisions of the TRIPS Agreement or other WTO agreements. In February 2012, the TRIPS Council launched discussions on the standards of law enforcement provided by ACTA. India expressed that ACTA prioritizes the interests of large corporations rather than the interests of consumers, and this could undermine TRIPS, restricting developing countries' access to afford-able medicines. China pointed out that many provisions in ACTA went beyond the provisions of TRIPS. Brazil claimed that a "one size fits all" approach is not feasible. WTO members participating in ACTA negotiations responded by stating that the main purpose of ACTA is to strengthen law enforcement to combat the proliferation of counterfeit goods and that ACTA did not target generic drugs nor interfere with legitimate access to the Internet. Researcher Aaron Shaw, at the Harvard University's Beckman Research Center for Internet and Society, believes that ACTA negotiations would establish inappropriately stringent legal standards that would not reflect the contemporary spirit of democracy, free market exchanges and civil liberties. Rather, ACTA would facilitate the violation of citizens' privacy by right holders without due process of law.[38] In June 2010, 90 scholars, practitioners and representatives of public interest organizations from six states gathered at the School of Law, University of Washington and came up with an "ACTA Emergency Communique" casting doubt on many of the issues during the negotiations.[39] WIPO Director General Francis Gurry also expressed his concern that ACTA is a sign of weakness in multilateral system and said, "Plurilateral ACTA negotiations and other such regional negotiations are a 'bad development' for multilateral agencies", signify-ing that the multilateral system is weakening.

On preventing the abuse of IPRs. On February 17, 2012, *Guangming Daily* published the article "Be Vigilant of the Abuse of Intellectual Property"[40] by Li Yifeng, who pointed out that while strengthening the protection of IP, the prevention of abuse of IPRs is as, if not more, important for China, which is actively involved in global competition. In April 2012, India enacted the first compulsory licensing of drugs, allowing Indian manufacturer Natco to pro-duce sorafenib (an anti-cancer drug patented by Bayer). In recent years, the US

---

[38] Aaron Shaw, "The Problem with the Anti-Counterfeiting Trade Agreement," retrieved from http://keionline.org/acta.

[39] Monika Ermert, "Scope of Anti-Counterfeiting Agreement Again a Big Issue in Round Nine," Intellectual Property Watch, June 26, 2010; retrieved from http://www.ip-watch.org/2010/06/26/scope-of-anti-counterfeiting-agreement-again-a-big-issue-in-round-nine/.

[40] Li Yifeng, "Be Vigilent of the Abuse of Intellectual Property," *Guanming Daily*, February 17, 2012; retrieved from http://sinoss.net/2012/0227/39570.html.

and the EU also launched anti-trust investigations regarding IP abuse against industry giants including Microsoft, Samsung and others. On the whole however, IPRs protection is held strongly amidst changes in IP rules, and there is insufficient regulation against the abuse of IPRs. Yet the dual nature of IPRs issues — protection of IP and prevention of rights abuse, determines the need of dialectical unity, like the two wheels of a bicycle or the two wings of a bird which must move in tandem.

3 The Evolution of Intellectual Property Rules and the Protection of Intellectual Property in China

From the establishment of domestic IP rules to international IP rules, from the pure international IP rules to the integration of IP rules and trade rules, and from the discussion on how the TRIPS differs from the ACTA and TPP, we can clearly observe that there has been a strong step by step evolution of IP rules, especialy with regard to "looking for an appropriate way to surpass other countries in the global regime, each community must determine how to define IPRs."[41] Currently, a central issue for IPRs protection in China is how to build a characteristically Chinese IPRs rules environment that is consistent with international practice and also adaptable to both present and future economic and social developmental needs.

3.1 *Evolutionary trends of IP rules*

In today's world, the pace of economic internationalization continues to accelerate and global economic competition is becoming more intense. Faced with the impact of the economic crisis and the challenges brought about by new technologies, the world urgently needs to find new economic growth points. The cultivation of new economic growth points is in urgent need of innovative breakthroughs, and innovative breakthroughs desperately require the protection that come with IP rules. Innovation-driven development, and future success brought by IPRs protection are increasingly becoming the consensus.

In such a context, the evolution of IP rules originated from the IP powers, rapidly developed via bilateral and plurilateral arrangements and on the whole, shows the trend of being a "three-in-one". The so-called "three-in-one" comprises the three features of "adaptation", "coordination" and "enhancement".

---

[41] Peter Drahos and John Braithwaite, *Information Feudalism: Who Owns the Knowledge Economy?* (New York: The New Press, 2005), p. 237.

"Adaptation" refers to the active adaptation of IP rule establishment and implementation to the new requirements of economic competition and new changes in global technologies; "coordination" means that the establishment and implementation of IP rules have to continually strengthen international coordination and cooperation; "enhancement" means that the content of protection has to be more prominent in the establishment of IP rules, and the implementation of IP rules has to be geared to show more practical results in protection. The so-called "three-in-one" means that the trend of international IP protection remains strong and continually developing in depth.[42] This is mainly reflected in five ways:

First, the standards are rising. ACTA and TPP exceed beyond the relevant provisions of TRIPS in many ways.[43] Even sounds and smells can be individually registered as trademarks, flora and fauna, and the diagnosis and treatment of human diseases can be patented, the term of copyright protection is repeatedly extended, and the administrative, civil and criminal procedures are increasingly specific and comprehensive.

The unified authorization of international IPRs "coordination" is continually strengthened. APEC proposed initiatives to cooperate on patent procurement procedures. On February 19, 2013, ministers from 24 EU member states signed an agreement in Brussels to establish the Unified Patent Court (UPC), paving the way for the implementation of unified patent procedures in Europe. The US, the EU countries, Japan, China, and Korea began five-countries cooperation projects, and are exploring trademark, patent applications and database-sharing issues.

Second, the fields are expanding. To "adapt" to the continual development of information technology, ACTA and TPP both made explicit provisions for IP protection in the digital environment. In addition to the seven types of IP objects provided for under TRIPS. The eighth IP object, the so-called "digital data information" seems to come up, on other hand, WTO also continues to discuss the relationship between IP and genetic resources, biodiversity, and traditional folklore. The integration of IP rules with economic and trade rules is even tighter. Since TRIPS integrated IP rules with multilateral trade rules for the first time, the current changes in international IP rules are mainly reflected in economic and trade rules as can be observed in the ACTA, TPP and numerous FTAs.

---

[42] In contrast, other aspects of IP rules such as the prevention and prohibition of IPRs abuse, protection of public interest *etc.* have not been developed in a balanced manner.

[43] Refer to Tables 10.2 and 10.3 for specific details.

Third, enforcement standards have become stricter. The evolution of IP rules constantly heightens law enforcement requirements, making law enforcement more specific and comprehensive,[44] practically pursuing better results,[45] and more convenience for rights holders.[46] In the evolution of rules, due to the powerful deterrence effect of criminal law enforcement, it is becoming the primary means of IPRs protection,[47] the ACTA and TPP further clarify criminal law protection of IPRs in international IP rules which were previously just conceptual, further expanding the scope and methods of criminal protection of IP, unifying the standards for IP criminal enforcement. Take US copyright protection for example, before the "Copyright Law" was implemented in 1976, copyright infringements had always been handled as misdemeanors. Now, as copyright interest groups continue to lobby, the Congress has revised the "Copyright Law" continuously such that there is a growing number of copyright infringements that are now incorporated as criminal offences. Fines for individual violation of copyright have increased from USD1,000 in 1975 to USD200,000 today, terms of imprisonment have been increased from a year to 20 years, and offences causing death are punishable by life imprisonment. The "Non Electronic Theft Act" adopted in 1997 extended the penalties to non-commercial infringements. In particular, the "Digital Millennium Copyright Act" (DCMA), adopted

---

[44] All seven objects of rights under TRIPS are included *i.e.* geographically, the physical market as well as the invisible networks are included. In terms of offenders, both direct and indirect infringers are included. In terms of behavior, violations in pursuit of direct economic interests as well as those motivated or not motivated by direct or indirect economic interests are included. All means of protection including civil, administrative, criminal and other protective measures are covered.

[45] The development of new technologies require more professionalism from IP enforcement teams; globalization of economic activity requires a greater emphasis on cooperation between countries in terms of IP law enforcement, including coordination between law enforcement departments, as well as cooperation among rights holders. In addition to law enforcement practice, there is a greater demand for transparency, countries are also continually exploring and introducing best practices for IP enforcement.

[46] First, not only should the costs borne by rights holders including litigation costs and attorney fees, be considered in the implementation of specific enforcement measures, but compensation for damages must also be considered; second, there must be an emphasis of cooperation with the rights holder during law enforcement, rights holder's burden of proof is limited to superficial evidence of the knowledge scope, and the requirements for rights holder's burden of proof should not lead to unreasonable slack enforcement; third, law enforcement agencies should share relevant infringement information with rights holders; and fourth, the opinion of rights holders should be sought in law enforcement, to seek for the best enforcement practices.

[47] To some extent, there has even been a trend of over-criminalization.

in 1998, extended criminal protection to the digital environment. In 2008, the "Prioritizing Resources and Organization for Intellectual Property Act" (PRO-IP Act) even became a watershed in digital copyright protection. Prior to this, criminal investigations were only focused on direct infringers who met certain conditions. Rights holders could only lodge civil suits against network service providers. However, this Act authorized federal judiciaries to initiate criminal investigations against network service providers, and granted them the authority to freeze relevant assets which included not just infringing copies but also any assets used in carrying out the infringing activity or assets intended for such use, as well as direct and indirect profits gained from infringements.

Fourth, coordination efforts are stronger. More international "coordination" is required in IP rules due to innovation across borders and the regional nature of IP protection. Especially in today's economic globalization, economic relationships are deepening, there is more interaction between international divisions of labor and cooperation, a move made by any country will inevitably affect other countries, further determining the need for the extension of international "coordination" of IPRs rules. From bilateral to multilateral, any establishment of IP rules is a result of "coordination". There are only 11 negotiating parties in ACTA and 12 in TPP, all the parties in both ACTA and TPP are members of the WTO and relevant international IP treaties. It is not unforeseeable in the future, base on that, it evolves into a plurilateral or even multilateral IPRs agreement.

Fifth, changes are increasingly rapid. IPRs encourage innovative development and thus IP rules must be open and inclusive. From the traditional industrial proprietary rights and copyrights to the seven object categories of rights under TRIPS, and with further innovative developments today and in the future, it is possible that there be new IP categories created with digital data information as an example. The unified authorization of IP at the international level contradicts the regional characteristic of IPRs, the extension of terms of copyright protection and post-transition period for pharmaceuticals patent protection[48] lends a certain elasticity to the temporal characteristic of IP. ACTA and TPP also further developed upon the IP proprietary content under TRIPS. The advancement of Internet technologies and vigorous development of e-commerce gave birth to IP rules in the digital environment. As innovations changes the world, objectively, IP rules must correspondingly evolve and progress. It can be asserted that the faster technology progresses, the more rapid the evolution of IP rules.

---

[48] Refers to the extension of exclusive rights protection of pharmaceutical patents after the 20-year patent protection expires. At present, this system has been implemented in some IP power countries.

3.2 *China's IP protection*

The Chinese government always attaches great importance to IPRs protection, fully understands that IPRs protection and waging war against counterfeits is the objective requirement for building an innovative country and accelerating the transformation of economic development, a domestic necessity for protecting and improving people's livelihood, as well as an inevitable choice for the expansion of international economic and trade cooperation. In recent years, China has achieved remarkable results in the protection of IPRs.

First, China has established IPRs as a national strategy. In 2008, China promulgated the "National Intellectual Property Strategy" by establishing the National IP Strategy Implementation Working Ministers Joint Meeting System with participants from 28 central departments who would work to launch the "National IP Strategy Promotion Plan" annually so as to carry out IPRs creation, operation, management and protection comprehensively.

Second, China has established a lead agency responsible for IPRs enforcement. In 2010, the State Council established a National Leading Group to combat IPRs infringement and sale of counterfeit and inferior goods, and also set up corresponding organizations in provinces and municipalities all over China. The State Council's leaders-in-charge held regular meetings every quarter to study and plan for IPRs protection in the following quarter. The National Leading Group unified and led the fight against infringement and counterfeiting, formulated policies and measures, supervised and inspected the work of localities and departments, and also oversaw the handling of major infringement and counterfeit cases. To secure the work, the Leading Group developed five systems: regular work meetings, focus on promotion, inspection and supervision, statistical reporting and performance appraisal systems which became long-term IP protection mechanisms.

Third, China has made further improvements to the IP legal system. Based on the needs of domestic economic construction and development, China continually revised and improved upon the relevant IP systems. In 2012, the State Council revised the "Regulations for Copyright Implementation", "Regulations on the Protection of the Right to Network Dissemination of Information", "Regulations for Computer Software Protection", "Regulations on Protection of New Varieties of Plants *etc.*, and substantially increased the fines for infringement of IPRs. In 2013, the third revision of the "Trademark Law" was completed. Currently, new revision work on laws such as the "Copyright Law"and "Patent Law" are ongoing.

Fourth, China has continually intensified its crackdown on IPRs infringements. In 2012, administrative enforcement departments recorded a total of 274,000 cases, raided 15,000 hideouts. Public security organizations solved 39,000 cases and arrested 57,000 suspects. Procuratorate organs strengthened supervisions for filing and investigating cases. In 2013, a total of 59,000 cases of criminal infringement and counterfeit were recorded, and 22,000 people were prosecuted.

Fifth, software legalization has been comprehensively promoted. Funds for procuring legal software were included into the government budget, software assets were included in asset management systems, and procurement and asset management were included into the scope of audits. Thirty-one provinces, autonomous regions, municipalities across the country and Xinjiang Production and Construction Corps completed the rectification and inspection work for copyrighted software, and software legalization work is also being carried out in an orderly manner across city and county government agencies. The central corporate headquarters also completed software legalization.

Sixth, China has established specialized IP courts. On August 31, 2014, the Chinese National People's Congress Standing Committee adopted the "Decision on the Establishment of IP Courts in Beijing, Shanghai and Guangzhou". The IP courts handle IP-related cases across administrative divisions, taking the roles of both the Court of First Instance and the Court of Appeal; and hear both civil cases as well as handle administrative cases. The establishment of IP courts is an important milestone in the protection of IPRs in China.

After three decades of development, China has rapidly grown to become an IP power. The number of patent and trademark applications in China increase every year. Now, China ranks top in the world. In 2010, copyright industries accounted for 6.57% of China's GDP.[49] China's IPRs work is receiving more and more recognition internationally. However, it should be noted that there is still much work to be done with regard to IPRs protection in China. In China, counterfeiting and piracy are still rampant. Various types of IPRs infringements are still prominent in certain fields and sectors. China has determined to complete plans to be an "Innovative Country" by 2020. According to the report "Global Innovation Index 2012" issued by WIPO, China was ranked

---

[49] Refer to results from the 2010 Study on Economic Contribution of Copyright-related Industries in China issued by the State Copyright Bureau on April 25, 2013.

No. 34, a great distance behind its established target. On the whole, China needs to further strengthen its awareness and enforcement of IPRs protection.

3.3 Active participation in the development of international IPRs

China is a latecomer in terms of participating in IPRs global rules, but it is a rapidly developing member. In constructing and developing a modern IP system, China has always taken reference and learned from international IP rules. In 1980, China joined the WIPO and the "Trademark Law" became China's first IP legislation only in 1982. China has already established an IP legal system covering all seven categories of IPRs and included almost all major international IP conventions and treaties. China has participated fully in WTO, WIPO, APEC and various multilateral and regional IP activities, and established several IP bilateral work mechanisms with the US, EU, Japan, Russia, Brazil, Switzerland *etc.* Faced with the new changes in external references and new demands in domestic development, China should adopt a more positive attitude to participate in the development of international IP rules. In the practice of building an IP rule system with Chinese characteristics, many complex relationships need to be handled appropriately. For example, in the actual relationship between IPRs protection and economic development in China, IPRs protection must truly become a powerful weapon against infringements, to encourage innovation and development of services. Another example would be the relationship between IPRs protection and construction of domestic law in China, where the construction of IP laws must be leveraged to improve the entire legal system. The resolution of these issues is bound to be an exploration process that is complex and arduous, where China continues to share and discuss its developmental experience with other countries and contributes to the improvement and transformation of future global IP rules.

Chapter 11

Rules of International Investment

On July 11, 2013, US President Barack Obama met with Vice Premier Wang Yang, the Special Representative of President Xi Jinping, during the fifth round of the China-US Strategic and Economic Dialogue in the White House in Washington, DC. This event coincided with the Edward Snowden incident. During the meeting, Obama looked gloomy and angry, and openly expressed his disappointment that Chinese Hong Kong had released Snowden earlier. Upon learning that the negotiations on the China-US investment agreement had made significant progress and that the Chinese government had agreed to engage in substantive negotiations with the US, based on the pre-establishment national treatment and the introduction of a negative list approach, Obama's tone improved quickly and he looked pleased. He applauded China's efforts to drive negotiations on the China-US investment treaty. On July 12, 2013, the Chinese Ministry of Commerce published a newsman's remarks in a prominent position on its website, stating that during the fifth round of the China-US Strategic and Economic Dialogue held in Washington, DC on 10 July to 11 July, the Chinese side had agreed to engage in substantive negotiations with the US on an investment treaty based on the pre-establishment national treatment and a negative list approach.[1] After seeing the news, an expert pointed out immediately that this means that the opening up of China's markets has moved on to a new historical phase and its significance is comparable to the year China joined the WTO.[2]

---

[1] Ministry of Commerce spokesman, Shen Danyang's remarks on China and US's active role in pushing forth negotiations of China-US investment treaty, retrieved from http://www.mofcom. gov.cn/article/ae/ag/201307/20130700196677.shtml (Interview conducted on July 17, 2013).
[2] China-US Strategic and Economic Dialogue Favorable to Many Industries, China's Management System for Foreign Investment Might Change Drastically, "*China Securities News*", July 15, 2013.

At this point, one may wonder what constitutes the rules for international investment? Why is there a need for negotiation of a China-US investment treaty? Why is a negotiation on investment treaty comparable to joining the WTO? What does the pre-establishment national treatment and a negative list refer to? Furthermore, as the multilateral trade system, WTO is an organization that is popular and familiar to China. So what is the situation in the area of international investments? Have multilateral and unified investment rules been formulated? In 2012, Sany encountered obstacles while investing in wind power projects in the US. The US's national security review faced by Chinese-invested enterprises is like the sharp razor suspended above China's foreign-invested enterprises and what is the mystery behind this problem?

This chapter tries to address all these questions through the introduction of "Rules of International Investment".[3]

1 Rules of International Investment

1.1 *The basic concepts of international investment rules*

Formally, international investment rules refer to the international bilateral treaties, regional agreements and multilateral agreements regulating cross-border investments, arrived at through negotiation and policy coordination among countries. From the content perspective, international investment rules is the collective term for various types of international rules which are intended to promote, regulate and protect cross-border investments. These rules do not focus on the issue of equality between the private investor and its partners, but rather on the legal issues of management and protection between the host country and private investors, arising from cross-border investment.

At present, the international investment rules are formulated in three forms. First, bilateral investment protection agreements or bilateral investment treaties.[4]

---

[3] Broadly speaking, investment rules include both the rules extended from the international treaties for regulating the rights and obligations of the Contracting Parties (Rules of International Investment) as well as the domestic legislation of the capital-importing countries regulating foreign investment. For the purpose of this book, this chapter will focus on international investment rules. Unless otherwise specified, "investment rules" mentioned in this chapter would refer to "International Investment Rules".

[4] The bilateral investment protection agreement originated in Europe , also known as " The European Style Agreement"; bilateral investment treaties originated in the United States, also known as "The American Style Agreement". For the difference between these two types of agreements, please see below.

Second, regional agreements in the form of free trade area (FTA) agreements. This type of agreement includes the rules on trade, in addition to the content of and provisions on investment rules. Third, multilateral agreements which contain investment rules on a multilateral basis.[5]

The existing international investment rules mostly regulate the rights and obligations between the host country and the investors. The rights and obligations between the investors and their home countries are rarely covered in the current international investment rule system.

1.2 *The history of international investment rules*

International investment rules have not always existed, they are the product of international economic and trade relations, particularly the development of cross-border investments to a certain historical stage.

1.2.1 *The embryonic form of international investment rules*

Historically, the earliest international rules related to investment do not exist independently, but were embodied in the once well-known "Friendship, Commerce and Navigation Treaty" (FCN). Starting in 1945, the US commenced a series of negotiations on the FCN. These treaties aimed at resolving commerce issues but also contained several asset protection provisions, such as providing fair and equitable treatment, on protection in accordance with customary international laws, and giving timely, appropriate and effective compensation on expropriation *etc*. Over the next 20 years, the United States and other developed countries, together with developing countries, concluded many similar agreements.[6] In the modern sense, the FCN is not an international

---

[5] It should be pointed out that, as of now, the world has yet to formulate multilateral investment rules which are similar to the WTO multilateral trade rules system. The multilateral agreements mentioned here refer to the ones formulated in specific areas, such as the "MIGA Convention" which specifies the rules for investment in insurance and the "Convention on the Settlement of Investment Disputes between States and Nationals of Other States" which specifies the resolution procedures for investment disputes *etc*. These multilateral agreements only involve the rules for specific areas of investment, and are far from being the comprehensive, systematic and all-encompassing multilateral rules that regulate cross-border investments. This will be elaborated in the chapter as follows.

[6] On November 4, 1946, the KMT government and the US government signed the "Treaty of Friendship, Commerce and Navigation between the United Satates of America and the

agreement that specializes in regulating cross-border investments, it only specifies the rules for protection of assets or overseas investment, and is fragmented and less comprehensive. Thus, the FCN could only be regarded as an embryonic form of international investment rules.

1.2.2 *The birth of international investment rules*

In 1959, Germany and Pakistan concluded a bilateral agreement with specific provisions for investment protection, which was later described as a landmark event of the birth of modern international investment rules. Shortly after, other Western European countries followed suit. Since 1960, Belgium, Denmark, France, Italy, Luxembourg, Netherlands, Norway, Sweden and Switzerland have concluded their first bilateral investment treaties. The implementation of these early stage international investment rules was significant and established the basic model which constituted the vast majority of international investment agreements in the subsequent decades. The basic model includes investment treatment (includes national treatment, MFN treatment, fair and equitable treatment), prompt, appropriate and effective compensation standards for expropriation; the rights to transfer investment funds freely and the provisions to settle the disputes between investors and the host countries as well as between parties in the agreement. Therefore, the international community consistently believes that international investment rules originated from Europe.[7]

During this period, international investment rules evolved and an important event occurred which led to a major milestone. In 1965, the World Bank submitted the "Convention on the Settlement of Investment Disputes between States and Nationals of Other States", also known as the "Washington Convention" to the various countries for signature. With this convention, the International Centre for Settlement of investment disputes (ICSID) was founded. Through this institution, investors could seek relief under international laws if the host country violated the rules and obligations under

---

Republic of China" in Nanjing, referred to as the "China-American Commercial Treaty of 1946". There are 30 articles and 68 paragraphs in the Treaty.

[7]This basic model had far-reaching influence and scholars called it the "European Style Agreement". In 1982, China and Sweden signed their first bilateral investment protection agreement and had been using the "European Style Agreement" model for a long time. In July 2013, China agreed to commence substantive negotiations with the United States on the basis of the approach of pre-establishment national treatment and a negative list, and since then, there was a change in the basic model.

international investment treaties and caused damages to their rights and interests. Article 25 in the convention states that the ICSID's jurisdiction is limited only to the legal dispute between one Party in the agreement and the nationals of another Party, which arise directly from investments. Such institutional arrangements are significant for investment protection. The international investment arbitration mechanism in the "Washington Convention" is now widely adopted in international investment agreements.[8]

Early on, international investment rules took on various forms. However, there was a common characteristic in the investment agreements, which essentially focused on the protection of the investments, whether the substantive provisions were related to the treatment of investments, expropriation, transfer *etc.* or the arbitration procedures for the settlement of investment disputes. The terms in the agreements focused on the protection of investment rights. The international investment rules in this period did not touch on investment access issues and the clauses in the investment agreement did not address environment, labor, state-owned enterprises, transparency, performance requirements and exceptions to essential security.

1.3 *The main components of international investment rules*

Investment rules are in a constant state of development and change, particularly the new issues in investment rules, such as state-owned enterprises, transparency, environment, labor and corporate social responsibility. Therefore it is difficult to ascertain if investment rules are already in a mature manner. The following introduction to international investment rules selects only the relatively mature rules which were formulated gradually after many years of development. This includes the definition of investment, investment treatment, expropriation, transfers, dispute settlement between the investor and the state, and other issues.

1.3.1 *Definition of investment*

The definition of "Investment" determines the scope of protection in investment treaties and forms the basis for jurisdiction over investment arbitration.

---

[8]On February 9, 1990, China signed the "Washington Convention" and officially became a member of the Convention in February 6, 1993. Since 1993, China has been adopting the arbitration mechanism for international investment disputes embodied in the "Washington Convention" while concluding international investment agreements with other countries.

Almost all international investment agreements include a definition of the concept of "investment". The early stage investment agreements emphasized the protection of foreign direct investment (FDI) and strictly defined the scope of investment through the definition of investment. With the development and change in international investment rules, the connotations behind the definition of investments in international investment agreements have also expanded, and currently, most investment agreements employ a "broad" definition of investment, and all assets with investment characteristics (comprising tangible assets and intangible assets) are included in the scope of protection. This includes not only direct investments, but indirect investments as well. The assets included are enterprise, equity, debt, financial derivatives, intellectual property rights, contractual rights, and other claims to money and other fulfillment rights. As to what constitutes "investment characteristics," a number of international investment agreements have listed down three characteristics, *i.e.* commitment of capital or other resources, the expectation of income or profit and the assumption risks involved in committing to the assets.

1.3.2 *Fair and equitable treatment*

The rules for the treatment of foreign investment is an important component of international investment agreements as it directly determines the legal status of foreign investors in the host country. The most striking aspect is whether the treatment of foreign investment meets fair and equitable standards, because this is not only a yardstick to assess the relationship between foreign investors and the host countries but also the host country's willingness to accept foreign direct investment after taking into consideration the fair and equitable interests of foreign investors. As an absolute standard of treatment, fair and equitable treatment standards have been widely included in international investment agreements. Take UNCTAD reports as an example, there are two explanations for the precise meaning of "fair and equitable treatment". First, the original intent approach, *i.e.* giving fair and equitable treatment to the definition of treatment of foreign investment. Second, treat "fair and equitable treatment" as being equivalent to the international minimum standards. In accordance with the original intent approach, "fair and equitable treatment" refers to the original meaning of the words "fair" and "equitable". When foreign investors received the commitment of "fair and equitable treatment", they could evaluate directly if the treatment they have received is "fair" and "equitable". If not, they could conclude that "fairness" and "equity" have been violated. Those who hold the second view regard fair and equitable treatment to be identical to the international minimum standards. The inference behind this view is that foreign investors are entitled to a certain level of treatment under customary international law and if the country's treatment of foreign investment is below that level then they should be held accountable.

1.3.3 *National treatment*

National treatment demands that a State treats foreigners in a manner comparable to the way it treats its nationals and that foreigners and nationals enjoy the same treatment. As there is a clear point of reference, treatment of foreigners became one of the most important elements in international investment agreements. Generally, the host country is required to treat the foreign investors and their investments, no less favourably than its own national investors during the life-cycle of the investment.[9] Through research conducted on bilateral investment treaties signed by the countries in the world and the free trade zone agreements, UNCTAD theoretically classified national treatment into pre-establishment national treatment and post-establishment national treatment. This distinction is very important as it is directly related to whether the international investment agreement has incorporated pre-establishment investment liberalization elements in the agreement. If pre-establishment national treatment is included in the international investment agreement, then this means that foreign investment and domestic investment must be treated equally during the entry phase (with the exception determined through negotiation). Therefore, the essence of pre-establishment national treatment is the market access issues encountered when foreign investment enters the host country. If the international investment agreements only specify post-establishment national treatment, this implies that the host country is only committed to national treatment after the foreign investment has entered the market. Before the foreign investment enters the markets, the host country could continue to maintain and adopt control measures and even strict screening and approval procedures on foreign investment, without directly impacting its market access obligations.

---

[9] The so-called life-cycle of investment refers to all aspects of the investment process, from the birth of the investment (often through the establishment of a company) to the date of its liquidation or dissolution, including the establishment of the investment, acquisition, expansion, operation, management, owning an interest in the business, disposition and other forms' disposition of assets *etc.*

With reference to the 2012 U.S. Model Bilateral Investment Treaty,[10] the national treatment provisions were stated as follows: Each Party shall accord to covered investments treatment no less favorable than that it accords, in like circumstances, to investments in its territory of its own investors with respect to the establishment, acquisition, expansion, management, conduct, operation, and sale or other disposition of investments. Among these, "establishment", "acquisition" and "expansion" are related to the investment access issues[11] and specifying the obligations of national treatment under these three areas, suggests that the Party is committed to pre-establishment national treatment obligation. The rest of the areas, such as "management", "operation", "sale", *etc.* belong to the post-establishment phase. Granting national treatment in these areas, is considered as post-establishment national treatment.

At present, China has not committed to grant pre-establishment national treatment[12] to other Parties in its investment agreements. Only post-establishment national treatment is stipulated in the agreements. For example, Article 138 in the "China and New Zealand Free Trade Agreement" specifies that all parties should treat the investment and investment-related activities of foreign investors in the areas of administration, management, operations, maintenance, use, proceeds or disposition, no less favourably than the investment and investment-related activities of its own national under similar conditions. This provision does not include "establishment", "acquisition" and "expansion", the

[10] During negotiations on bilateral investment treaties or free trade agreements, the US adopted a unified template for bilateral investment treaties. The latest version was released on April 20, 2012, thus it is known as the "2012 U.S. Model Bilateral Investment Treaty".

[11] "Establishment" refers to an investor of one country setting up a new enterprise in another country. "Acquisition" is also known as "merger and acquisition", and involves a foreign investor acquiring the entire or partial share capital of a domestic enterprise in the host country. This could take the form of purchasing existing shares from the current shareholders or through purchasing the additional shares issued by the enterprise, thus achieving foreign ownership in the domestic enterprise. It also includes the purchase of assets and land rights *etc.* "Expansion" involves increasing the scale of operations of the enterprise with more capital and shareholders exerting more control over the business via expansion of shares. "Expansion" could also be interpreted to mean the expansion of power after investments have been made, and it is also possible to violate the host country's industrial policy of restricting foreign ownership in some fields, thus it is also considered to belong to the pre-establishment phase.

[12] The "pre-establishment national treatment" in the China (Shanghai) Pilot Free Trade Zone is China's domestic policy of granting benefits to foreign investors, and is not based on bilateral investment agreements signed between China and foreign countries.

three phases of investment, which have pre-establishment investment implications.

It seems that more and more countries are adopting "pre-establishment national treatment", including developed countries and region like the US, the EU, Canada, Japan, Australia and others, and developing countries like Mexico, India, Thailand, South Africa, Russia, Vietnam and other countries. It should be noted that absolute national treatment, comprising both pre-establishment and post-establishment national treatment does not exist in the world and countries who adopted the full access approach would usually include exception clauses in the agreement. Typically, a list which states the fields for which the country intends to maintain restrictions on foreign investment, often cited as the negative list is included in the agreement,[13] as an exception to the principles of national treatment.

1.3.4 *Treatment of the most favored nation (MFN)*

Just like the principles of national treatment, the treatment of the most favored nation is one of the key provisions in international investment rules. This demands that the host country does not treat a foreign investor in a less favorable manner compared to a foreign investor from another country under the same circumstances. This is intended to prevent discriminatory treatment based on the nationality of the foreign investors. Just like the foregoing provisions on national treatment, the scope of coverage under the treatment of the most favored nation is very wide and generally applies to the entire life cycle of the investment, including the establishment of investments, management, maintenance, use, sale or liquidation of investments *etc.* However, the scope of the treatment of most favored nation are not consistent among the various international investment agreements.

In practice, there are also distinctions between "pre-establishment" and "post-establishment" for the treatment of most favored nation. If the MFN clauses in the international investment agreement include the three investment terms, *i.e.* "establishment", "acquisition" and "expansion", which have pre-establishment

---

[13]There is no exception even in a country like the US, where there is a high degree of market liberalization in its investment markets. The US included a negative list in its bilateral investment treaties and free trade agreements, listing down the measures or fields in which it maintains restrictions on foreign investment.

connotations, this means the Party has committed to give MFN treatment to the other Party in the pre-establishment phase, *i.e.* to grant investors and their investments pre-establishment treatment that shall not be less favorable than the treatment to third-Party investors and their investments. This is also known as the "pre-establishment MFN treatment". However, if the international investment agreement does not incorporate pre-establishment phase and only specifies the post-establishment stages of administration, management, operations and sales aspects of investment, this means that the Party has committed to give the MFN treatment in the post-establishment phase, also called the "post-establishment MFN treatment".

1.3.5 *Expropriation*

Expropriation in the international investment agreements refers to the host country's use of public power to deprive investors or their invested enterprises' ownership to the assets or the right to use the assets, including the expected returns on the assets. It is generally believed that states have a sovereign right under international law to nationalize all assets within their territories, including foreign private assets, subject to certain conditions. Although expropriation is worded differently in various bilateral investment agreements, different treaties basically specify similar conditions, *i.e.* expropriation has to be taken for a public purpose, adopt non-discriminatory treatment towards foreign investors, compensate foreign investors and must be carried out in accordance with due process of law.

In practice, most bilateral investment agreements do not define expropriation directly but include a general description of it. For example, the German Model Treaty adopts "any measures the effects of which would be tantamount to expropriation or nationalization..." The Netherlands Model Treaty defines expropriation as "any measure which directly or indirectly deprives the investment rights of nationals of the other Party". China's Model Treaty currently specifies that "a Contracting Party shall not adopt nationalization, expropriation or other measures equivalent to nationalization or expropriation (collectively referred to as expropriation) towards the other Contracting Party's investment in its territory. Measures which are equivalent to nationalization or expropriation are referred to as indirect expropriation".

Expropriation can be classified as direct expropriation and indirect expropriation. The former refers to openly and deliberately depriving the owner of his or her property through the transfer of title or outright seizure.

Direct expropriation occurred mostly in the middle of the 20th century, when there were national independence movements, decolonization movements and when old regimes were overthrown by revolutionary forces. It is noteworthy that there was an emergence of direct expropriation of foreign investors' investments in Latin American countries recently. For example, the President of Argentina announced that the Argentinian government had forcibly acquired the Spanish company, Repsol's 51% stake in the YPF oil company.

Indirect expropriation refers to the various regulatory measures that the host government takes to intervene in foreign investors' rights of ownership. The expropriation process is often gradual. Although these measures do not deprive the investors of their rights of ownership, the impact on investors' assets is sufficient to constitute a seizure of their interests, or restrict the management, use or control of investments or substantially impair the value of the investments. After World War II, the whole world entered a relatively peaceful and stable development stage. Direct expropriation was less frequent whereas the occurrence of indirect expropriation was on an upward trend. The international community thus paid increasingly more attention to the issue of indirect expropriation. For example, in October 2007, the Government of Ecuador announced a presidential decree to impose a special levy on foreign oil companies. The tax rate was 99% (commonly known as "windfall profit tax"). This news caused a great sensation worldwide. Although the taxes imposed did not deprive the foreign oil companies' ownership of oil assets, this led to a seizure of investment income, and was in fact tantamount to depriving the rights of ownership of foreign investors, and thus belongs to the category of indirect expropriation.

Expropriation is a core provision in international investment agreements, and is directly related to the protection of rights and interests of investors. It has become common practice in almost all international investment agreements for the host government to compensate foreign investors upon expropriation. However, compensation standards is an issue, *i.e.* amount of compensation and the mode of compensation. There has always been a great disparity in standards of compensation. Developing countries adhere to the "appropriate compensation" or "reasonable compensation" standards, while developed countries insist on giving "prompt, adequate and effective" compensation, *i.e.* Hull formula's high compensation standards.[14]

---

[14] The "Hull formula" is synonymous with "prompt, adequate and effective" compensation standards. It originated from the expropriation compensation standards mentioned in US

In the early stage of China's foreign international investment agreements with other countries, China had always insisted on the "appropriate compensation" or "reasonable compensation" standards and opposed the introduction of the Hull formula in bilateral investment agreements. However, in recent years, with continued increase in the scale of China's foreign investments, there is an increasing need to protect the rights and interests of Chinese enterprises' investments overseas. Although China does not abide by the "prompt, adequate and effective" standards fully in its treaty practice, the specific wording in the treaties is gradually changing and drawing closer to these standards. For example, the expropriation clause in the "Agreement Between the Government of Canada and the Government of the People's Republic of China for the Promotion and Reciprocal Protection of Investments" states that "Such compensation shall be equivalent to the fair market value of the investment expropriated immediately before the expropriation, or before the expropriation became public knowledge, whichever is earlier, shall include interest at a normal commercial rate until the date of payment, and shall be effectively realizable, freely transferable, and made without delay". From this provision, it can be seen that the compensation standards that China follows in its treaty practices recently is close to the high compensation standards of the Hull formula.

1.3.6 *Transfer clause*

For foreign investors, in addition to concerns that they might be unlawfully deprived of their overseas investment, assets will not be forcibly occupied or unlawfully expropriated, they are most concerned about two problems. Firstly, the question of whether the investment principal, profits and other legitimate income will be delivered in a currency which is freely usable. Secondly, whether they will be able to transfer the returns from investment (including profits and returns in kind) out of the host country. If these two problems are not resolved,

---

Secretary of State, Cordell Hull's diplomatic note to the Mexican ambassador in 1938. "Adequate" compensation means that the compensation amount should be equal to the full value of the expropriated asset (ie. the fair market value), and includes the interest until the date of compensation, and may even include the expected profits in some instances. "Prompt" compensation refers to timely payment of compensation. If the payment of compensation is made in the form of instalments, then interest on arrears must be paid as compensation. "Effective" compensation means that compensation should be made in a freely convertible currency or freely usable currency.

then the investors' rights and interests will be greatly affected. Therefore, the ability to freely transfer foreign exchange and the interests of foreign investors is closely related. For this reason, the clauses regarding the transfer of foreign exchange has always been an important element in the international investment rules, for both the early as well as current international investment agreements.

In transfer clauses, it is generally specified that the Parties of the investment agreement mutually allow the investors from the other country to freely transfer capital and investor funds, including profits, dividends, interests, royalties, fees and other investment income, all or part of the liquidation proceeds from investments; payment from investment-related loans; investment-related income of the nationals of the Party; expropriation of compensation payment *etc.* As the transfer issue typically involves the host country's exchange controls, international investment agreements tend to provide some exceptions to the obligations shouldered by the host country so as to take account of the host country's interests. This includes mainly the following three scenarios. First, the investors must abide by the laws and regulations or other formalities imposed by the host country. Second, through the implementation of relevant laws (such as insolvency laws, financial regulation, criminal penalties *etc.*), the host country could prevent the transfer of investors' investment returns through fair, just, non-discriminatory and good faith manner. Third, international investment agreements generally specify that if a Party's balance of payments is under serious difficulties or threats thereof, then the Party may implement the necessary measures to temporarily restrict the transfer of foreign exchange.

1.3.7 *Umbrella clause*

In international investment agreements, the "umbrella clause" is a unique arrangement in the system which strengthens the level of protection of the interests of investors. The typical statement in the agreements is: Each Contracting Party shall constantly guarantee the observance of the commitments it has entered into with respect to the investments of the other Contracting Party.[15] It demands that the Contracting Parties not only comply

---

[15] For example, article 10, paragraph 2 of the Agreement between the People's Republic of China and the Federal Republic of Germany on the Encouragement and Reciprocal Protection of Investments signed in 2003 states "Each Contracting Party shall observe any other obligation it has entered into with regard to investments in its territory by investors of the Other Contracting Party".

with their international investment agreements, but also comply with all the commitments made to the investors of the other Contracting Party, including franchise agreements and commercial contracts. This clause was first proposed by the eminent British jurist, Lauterpacht in the 1950s. In 1959, Germany and Pakistan signed the world's first investment protection agreement and the "umbrella clause" was incorporated into the agreement. According to statistics, there are currently nearly 3000 bilateral investment treaties, of which 40% contain the "umbrella clause" in various forms.[16]

In international arbitration practices investments, the umbrella clause is controversial. There are two main schools of thought. First, those who advocate strict interpretation of the umbrella clause. A classic example is the SGS[17] versus Pakistan case.[18] Although there was a breach of contract or written commitment, it did not constitute a breach of obligations under the international investment agreement. Second, those who advocate a broad definition of the umbrella clause. The classic example is the SGS versus Philippines case,[19] whereby a breach of the contract or written commitment constituted a direct breach of obligations under the international investment agreement. Currently, the mainstream view is that the restrictive interpretation is more reasonable. That is, the host country's breach of contract or written commitment should not escalate automatically to a violation of the treaty. It is only when the acts of the host country breach the obligations under the contract and at the same time, violate the obligations under in the bilateral investment treaties, should complaints be made based on the bilateral investment treaties. This interpretation maintains the effectiveness of the umbrella clause and also

---

[16] K. Yannaca-Small, Interpretation of the Umbrella Clause in Investment Agreement, OECD, Working Papers on International Investment, Number 2006/3, pp. 5–6.

[17] The company's full name is Société Générale de Surveillance S.A. and it is a Swedish company.

[18] The tribunal pointed out that a broad interpretation of the umbrella clause would include the numerous contracts between investors and the countries, as well as the commitments that the country makes to other investors in another country's domestic system. Any simple breach of these obligations is considered to be a violation of the terms of the international investment agreements. In this case, the other terms regarding the substantive treatment in international investment agreements would become "superfluous".

[19] The tribunal pointed out that Philippines failed to comply with its binding commitments, including the contractual commitments it had undertaken on specific investments, and had violated the bilateral investment agreements.

takes into account the balance of interests between the host country and the foreign investors.[20]

1.3.8 *Arbitration between investors and investment host states*

If the definitions of investment, treatment of investment, expropriation, transfer and other provisions specify the substantive rights enjoyed by investors, then the arbitration clause between the investor and the host state specifies the procedures in which investors could seek right relief. The international investment arbitration mechanism between investors and the host states is one of the most prominent features in the international investment agreements. The theory of public international law states, that sovereign states enjoy "jurisdictional immunity." Thus, any individual or entity shall not approach an organization to sue a sovereign state. The international arbitration mechanism introduced into the international investment agreements implies that a private investor could sue the sovereign state, which is also the investment host country, via the international investment arbitration body. This is a major breakthrough in the traditional view of the international law mentioned above. For investors, the introduction of these dispute resolution clauses is crucial as it ensures the protection of the investors when their interests are unlawfully infringed upon by the host country, and they are able to obtain fair and just means for relief.

It could be observed from the implementation of the international investment agreements that the majority of countries have adopted the arbitration rules in the "Washington Convention" and the "United Nations Commission on International Trade Law" (UNCITRAL) for international arbitration.

From the specific provisions in the agreements, it could be observed that the specifications on the international investments arbitration procedures vary among the different international investment agreements. For example, there is only one article on arbitration mechanism between the investor and the host state (Article IX, includes four paragraphs) in the "Agreement between the People's Republic of China and the Federal Republic of Germany on the Encouragement and Reciprocal Protection of Investments" signed in 2003. However, the "Agreement Between the Government of Canada and the Government of the People's Republic of China for the Promotion and

---

[20] Yu Jinsong, "Balance of Interests between the Investors and the Host Countries in the Arbitration of International Investment Treaties", *Chinese law,* , Issue 2 (2011).

Reciprocal Protection of Investments" concluded in 2012, covered the arbitration procedures extensively and included many pages on arbitration procedures (a total of 14 articles, accounting for one third of 35 articles of the entire agreement).

1.4 *The role of international investment rules*

1.4.1 *Protecting the interests of the investors*

The protection of investors' interests is the cornerstone and the main mission of international investment agreements. The key focus of the main provisions in traditional international investment rules, such as fair and equitable treatment, national treatment, most favored nation treatment, full protection and security, compensation for expropriation, transfer of foreign currency, umbrella clause, compensation for loss, subrogation *etc.* is on resolving and protecting investors' interests. When one Party in the treaty breaches the terms in the investment agreement, the foreign investors could employ the dispute settlement mechanism in the international investment rules as well as the international investment arbitration system to safeguard their legitimate rights and interests.

In addition, when it comes to disputes on the interpretation and application of international investment agreements, the Party concerned may request for consultations with the other Party of the treaty or submit to the international arbitration mechanism between the Parties (*i.e.* the international arbitration mechanism between the Parties of the treaty) for a resolution.

After decades of development of international investment rules, performance requirements, environment, labor and other articles are added into the investment agreements, in addition to the traditional provisions which are directly related to the protection of foreign investment. This gave rise to the current international investment agreements, which ensure fair competition between the investors and other competitors and protect the interests of the investors.

1.4.2 *Addressing market access issues for investments*

Investment liberalization or the market access issue is the new trend in the development of international investment agreements, as well as the new mission of international investment rules. In 2006, UNCTAD (United Nations Conference on Trade and Development) released a research report, pointing out that not only did the new generation of international investment agreements continue to provide protection for international investments but there was also a growing emphasis on liberalization of market access.[21] The study also showed that most of the economic integration investment agreements included specific obligations for investment liberalization between the Parties, as a means to deepen trade liberalization and market integration. Some regional agreements or FTAs primarily or almost totally focused on liberalization.[22]

On the mode of market access, the implementation of international investment agreements take on two forms regarding market access: the first model, "the pre-establishment national treatment and a positive list" model, lists down the fields where investment liberalization is realized or investment markets are liberalized in a positive list. The Parties in the treaty need to grant pre-establishment national treatment to only the industries and fields in the list, and they do not have to commit to liberalize the industries outside the positive list. The second model is "pre-establishment national treatment and a negative list" model, which includes the fields and industries where restrictive measures are adopted or foreign investment is prohibited. The Parties in the treaty need to abide by its investment liberalization obligations to the industries outside of the negative list and open up their investment markets. There are advantages and disadvantages to the two models. The former model is more accommodating towards the host country, and the industries and fields outside the positive list enjoy wider room for policy adjustments. The latter model is more favorable to investors, providing a stable, transparent and predictable investment environment for cross-border capital flows.

In contrast, since the "pre-establishment national treatment and a negative list" model fulfils the objective needs of cross-border capital flows for an institutional environment, it has been adopted by more and more countries, and has become the trend as international investment rules evolve. It is likely to become the prevailing international treaty practice. According to statistics, there are at least 77 countries currently, including more than 60 developing countries, which have adopted the "pre-establishment national treatment and a negative list model" and high-level investment liberalization provisions.

---

[21] See UNCTAD: "International Investment Arrangements: Trends and Emerging Issues", UN, New York and Geneva, 2006, p. 3.

[22] See UNCTAD: "Investment Provisions in Economic Integration Agreements", United Nations, 2006, p. 44.

1.4.3 *Creating a favorable investment environment*

Another important objective of international investment rules is to create a stable, transparent and predictable investment climate, and to dispel foreign investors' concerns about the safety of their investments and boost investors' confidence. In the 1980s, an increasing number of developing countries had changed their stance and were willing to conclude international investment agreements with developed countries, largely because they hoped to improve their investment environment and expand the inflow of foreign investment. For an enterprise that is about to embark on foreign investment, the existence of an investment agreement and the quality of the agreement, between its home country and the targeted investment country, and whether the substantive rights and procedural rights protecting the interests of the investment are of high standards, are important considerations during the assessment of its investment decision.

Since the reform and opening up, China has been firmly pursuing an active policy to attract foreign investment and has been ranked the most attractive country among developing countries for foreign investments for 21 consecutive years. Among the reasons for this are China's economic stability, huge market capacity, China's focus on advancing its legal system, as well as its construction of an open economic system. Another factor that should not be underestimated is China's active role in concluding bilateral investment treaties with other countries and its gradual acceptance of higher standards of investment rules in accordance with its actual development situation. Through this initiative, the investment environment for foreign investment was enhanced and China became one of the most preferred target countries for foreign investment for many consecutive years.

1.4.4 *Balancing the interests of the investor and the host country*

Historically, most international investment agreements were concluded between capital-exporting countries (investors' home countries, mostly developed countries) and capital-importing countries (investment host countries, mostly developing countries). The two sides differed in their demands of foreign capital, thus it is inevitable that there is a conflict of interests. The investor's home country demands that the host country provide sufficient protection for investors, including a high level of protection and allows the settlement of investment disputes through international arbitration while the host country is concerned that the protection of foreign investment may be detrimental to the economic development of its country, and reduces the room for policy adjustment in the host country. One of the important missions of international investment rules is to strike a suitable balance between maintaining the sovereignty of the host country for the regulation of foreign investment and protecting the interests of the investors. Balancing the rights and obligations between the foreign investors and the host countries is a key issue in most negotiations on international investment agreements, and will be the focus of debate in the future development of international investment rules.

2 The Historical Evolution and New Developments in International Investment Rules

2.1 *The historical evolution of international investment rules*

Since the birth of international investment rules, the signing of investment treaties around the world have become increasingly common, and the content and form of international investment rules have spread and expanded. To sum up, the historical context of the development of international investment rules has the following six characteristics.

First, there is a substantial increase in the number of agreements. In 1959, Germany and Pakistan concluded the first international investment agreement, which set the precedent for future agreements. For the next 30 years till 1989, less than 400 bilateral international investment agreements were concluded. However, in the subsequent 15 years, the number of bilateral investment treaties signed by the countries in the world reached a high of 2,000, averaging 11 agreements per month. According to UNCTAD statistics, as of the end of 2012, the number of investment agreements in the world had hit 3196, of which 2857 were bilateral investment treaties and the remaining 339 were free trade agreements and the investment rules in other regional arrangements.

Second, there is a upsurge of American-style agreements. Strictly speaking, the practice of negotiating international investment agreements in the early stage did not involve the US. During this time, the United States had always persisted in protecting the rights and interests of overseas investments through concluding the FCN. But the US government gradually realized that this approach did not achieve the desired effect. Firstly, the main task of the FCN is not for solving the issue of investment protection as the effectiveness of its investment protection function is often watered down and weakened. Secondly, the United States had consistently sought to protect its overseas investments through observation of customary international laws, but the protective effect is not satisfactory due to controversy with regard to the connotations and content of customary international laws among the international community. After much deliberation, the United States decided to implement its own bilateral investment treaty program. From 1977 to 1981, the United States prepared for its first template of bilateral investment treaty, and officially began the practice of negotiating bilateral investment treaties. The distinguishing feature of the US investment agreement template is the providence of high standards of investment protection rules, while being committed to the terms of market access of investment and promoting a high level of investment liberalization. As the US has had great influence at the international community for a long time, the American bilateral investment agreement had a significant and far-reaching impact on the development of international investment rules, and was subsequently adopted by Canada, Australia, Japan, Korea and many South American and Eastern European countries. International investment agreements signed in accordance with this model are called the "American Style Agreement". In contrast to the "European Style Agreement" which only emphasized the protection of investment, the "American Style Agreement" emphasizes the protection of investment, and is also concerned about the entry of investment. Thus, it is more comprehensive.

The third characteristic is the rapid increase in the number of countries involved in the treaty-making. In the 1980s, with the active participation of China and many other developing countries, there were more and more participants in formulating the international investment rules. Today, almost every country in the world is involved in at least one international investment agreement, with the majority of countries concluding a number of agreements.[23] Traditionally, capital-exporting developed countries were the advocates of bilateral investment treaties, out of consideration for their own interests and the protection of foreign investments. In contrast, developing countries were concerned that their obligations under bilateral investment treaties would restrict their regulatory sovereignty rights on foreign investment, and were generally not enthusiastic or were even resistant towards bilateral investment treaties. However, by the 1980s, this situation changed. Developing

---

[23] UNCTAD, International Investment Rule-Making: Stocktaking, Challenges and the Way Forward, 2008, p. 5.

countries gradually realized that "capital flows into a country would make the country prosperous." The extensive use of foreign funds would not only solve the financing problems for development but would also bring technological innovation, advanced management experience and create jobs — thus promote economic growth. And one of the effective means to promote and encourage foreign investors to invest in developing countries is through bilateral investment protection agreements as these help to boost investors' confidence and create a stable and transparent investment environment directly and effectively. It can be said that in developing countries, the signing of international investment agreements to attract foreign investment to help in their economic development, has gradually become a objective need. With the extensive and active participation of developing countries, the number of countries involved in international investment agreements has rapidly increased, with no country being an exception.

Fourth, the connotations of international investment rules are expanded. The main mission of the early international investment rules (or even the only mission) is to construct a system of rules to protect the interests of the investment. With the birth and development of the "American Style Agreement", the situation changed. In addition to ensuring a high standard of investment protection rules, the countries that used the "American Style Agreement" in their international investment agreements with other countries also included market access of investment and labor, the environment, performance requirements, transparency and other rules to further enrich the scope of international investment rules.

Fifth, there is expansion in the form of international investment rules. Traditionally, there were two forms of international investment rules. Firstly, the FCN advocated by the United States prior to 1980s and secondly, the bilateral investment protection agreements advocated by Germany and other western European countries.

In the 1990s, FTAs, of which NAFTA was an example, quickly became an important form of international investment rules due to the inclusion of elements of investment protection and investment liberalization in the investment agreements. For the US, in addition to the NAFTA, it had also signed free trade agreements with Morocco, Singapore, Chile, Dominican, the five Central American countries (Costa Rica, El Salvador, Guatemala, Honduras and Nicaragua), Peru, Oman, Colombia, Panama and Korea *etc.*, and investment chapters were included in the agreements. Currently, most free trade agreements or other regional trade arrangements no longer focus solely on trade issues. Investment rules are also included so as to achieve the objective of deep economic integration. According to the UNCTAD statistics, as of the end of 2011, as many as 311 free trade agreements or other regional trading arrangements have included investment chapters or new separate supplementary investment agreements to existing treaties.

Sixth, there is an increasing number of international investment disputes. As of the end of 2012, the number of cases of international investment disputes reached 514[24] and the total number of countries sued was 95.[25] The scope of the disputed government measures was very broad, including the revocation of the license, breach of investment contracts, violation of public bidding, amendment in national regulatory framework, withdrawal of approved subsidies, direct expropriation and taxation measures *etc.* The amount of compensation involved in these cases was huge, easily reaching tens of millions or even hundreds of millions. In 2012, the international arbitration tribunal[26] ruled that the Ecuadorian government compensate USD1.77 billion in the "American Occidental Petroleum Corporation versus Ecuador" case, which is one of the highest compensation amount awarded by the international investment arbitration tribunals.

2.2 *The current state and form of international investment rules*

After years of development, international investment rules now take on mainly two forms. First, bilateral investment treaties, and second, the investment provisions under regional trade arrangements.[27]

---

[24] In 2012 alone, there were 62 new cases, which as of now is the single year with the highest number of international investment disputes. This phenomenon demonstrated the trend that foreign investors were more and more willing to have recourse to the international investment arbitration mechanism settle the investment-related disputes.

[25] Among the countries which were sued, Argentina was the country that was sued most frequently (51 cases), followed by Venezuela (34 cases), Ecuador (23 cases) and Mexico (21). As of the end of 2013, China was faced with only one case of dispute under the international investment dispute framework, *i.e.* Malaysia's Ekran versus Government of China in 2011. The case was settled through consultations in May 2013.

[26] International investment arbitration is the third-party body, established on the basis of international investment agreements and arbitration rules, to deal specifically with disputes between the investors and states.

[27] A regional trade arrangement is a generalized formulation, referring a free trade area between different countries, customs union, economic integration agreements, economic partnership

It is worth noting that although bilateral investment agreements are still the most common form of international investment agreements, the number of bilateral investment treaties concluded has begun to decline since 2001. The 10-year period during the 1990s witnessed the strongest growth in the annual number of signed bilateral investment treaties, with an average of 147 per year. In 2011, the number of bilateral investment treaties signed declined to 33. By 2012, the number dropped further to only 20. With respect to the Contracting Parties, the countries which are most active in concluding bilateral investment treaties comprise Germany, followed by China at the second rank and Switzerland at the third. [28]

In contrast, regional trade arrangements represented by free trade agreements, are becoming an important part of the international investment system. Although the current proportion of free trade zones (slightly more than 10%) is low, the influence is growing steadily. Among free trade agreements, the most representative is the "North American Free Trade Agreement", which specified in great detail and length, a wide range of investment rules, among which are the investment liberalization provisions which the US has been actively promoting, pushing for the opening up of investment markets between Parties in the treaty, as well as specifying high standards of investment protection rules. This includes very detailed and specific dispute settlement clauses for investment disputes.[29] Currently, the US is actively pushing forth negotiations on TTIP, a regional agreement with far-reaching influence on the world. Implementation of high standards of investment rules will be among the key focus of the negotiation. It is foreseeable that once the agreement has successfully

---

agreements and bilateral or plurilateral agreements with regard to trade, investment and other rights and obligations.

[28] According to the UNCTAD 2007 statistics, the top 10 countries which most frequently concluded bilateral investment treaties were: Germany, China, Switzerland, United Kingdom, Italy, Egypt, France, the Netherlands, Belgium and Luxembourg, and Korea. In practice, Belgium and Luxembourg worked together as one Party in negotiating bilateral investment treaty with other Parties, and are known as "Benelux Union".

[29] Up to now, the US has signed 14 free trade agreements with 19 countries, including, Canada and Mexico (NAFTA), Israel, Jordan, Bahrain, Morocco, Singapore, Chile, Dominican and five Central American countries (Costa Rica, El Salvador, Guatemala, Honduras and Nicaragua), Peru, Oman, Colombia, Panama and Korea. Besides the agreement with Panama, the other 13 agreements have all started to take effect. Among the 13 agreements, the agreements with Bahrain, Israel and Jordan did not involve investment components whereas the remaining 11 contain specific investment provisions.

concluded, the elements and content in the agreement will profoundly impact the development of international investment systems.

In contrast with international trade, one of the greatest traits of international investment is the lack of an organization like the WTO, which could unify multilateral investment rules. Instead, international investment appears to be in a "fragmented" state. Foreign investment agreements concluded by different countries are different and there are even differences between the same country's investment agreements which concluded with different countries. This results in extremely fragmented and inconsistent content in international investment rules, making it messy and complicated, like a bowl of spaghetti,

From the content point of view, international investment rules have developed to the present state where there is co-existence of "convergence" and "diversity". "Convergence" refers to the trend of convergence of the content and discipline components in international investment agreements after more than half a century of development and mutual influence of investment treaties. For example, most of the international investment agreements include the preface, the definitions of investment and the investor, fair and equitable treatment, national treatment, most favored nation treatment, expropriation, compensation for civil strife, subrogation, umbrella clause, denial of benefits, arbitration mechanism between countries, arbitration mechanism between the investor and the host country, entry into effect, termination clause *etc.* "Diversity" means that despite the "convergence" traits mentioned above, some countries, especially developed countries represented by the US, included new elements into the traditional investment agreements, for example, clauses on environment, labor, transparency, performance requirements, taxation, financial services *etc.*,[30] resulting in distinct "diversity" traits in the agreements. On April 10, 2012, the EU and the United States jointly issued the "Shared Principles for International Investment", stating clearly their position of including rules governing the commercial conduct of multinational enterprises and national security review into the scope of the rules on international investment.[31]

---

[30] In addition to the United States, Canada, Japan and Australia do not adhere strictly to the traditional content while signing investment agreements or free trade agreements with third Parties and they gradually became staunch supporters and practitioners of "diversity" in international investment rules.

[31] See "Statement of the European Union and the United States on Shared Principles for International Investment, retrieved from: http://www.ustr.gov/webfm_send/3337, accessed on August 23, 2013.

In 2008, UNCTAD published a research report on "International Investment Rule-Making: Stocktaking Challenges and the Way Forward" pointing out that the core rules of international investment system reflects consistency, however there are increasing differences in other areas of the investment system. In other words, although a considerable degree of consensus has been reached on a number of key elements involved in the protection of investments, there are still many differences in other aspects related to international investment agreements.[32]

Driven by some developed countries, the international community began to promote the formulation of multilateral investment rules in 1948. This was known as the "Charter for International Trade Organization" (referred to as "The Charter"). The Charter was committed to multilateralism in international trade rules, and at the same time, incorporation of the rules regarding international investment, attempting to establish a multilateral framework for international trade and international investment. However, due to opposition from the US, the Charter's efforts to establish a blueprint for multilateral investment rules were in vain. After a long time, bilateral investment protection agreements gradually became the main source for international laws on cross-border investments after Germany and Pakistan signed the first bilateral investment protection agreement in 1959. During the Uruguay Round of negotiations (1986–1994) of the GATT, the United States tried to incorporate investment issues into the multilateral trade system but was opposed by developing countries, and finally reached an agreement only on "Trade-Related Investment Measures" (the IRIMS Agreement). Driven by the US, the Organisation for Economic Co-operation and Development (OECD) had launched the "Multilateral Agreement on Investment" (MAI) negotiations since 1995. This is by far the most ambitious initiative that the international community has taken on the rule-making of multilateral cross-border investments. However, as countries are unable to reach a compromise on some issues, with many NGOs and developing countries generally opposed to MAI's proposed high standards, the negotiations failed in 1998.[33] Subsequently, developed countries

---

[32] United Nations Conference on Trade and Development, *UNCTAD Series on International Investment Policies for Development*, retrieved from: http://unctad.org/en/Docs/iteiit20073_en.pdf, accessed on August 23, 2013.

[33] The most controversial clause in the MAI is the national treatment provision, which tried to achieve the objective of investment liberalization by applying the principles of national treatment to the establishment (*i.e.* investment establishment phase) of an enterprise, thus setting

hoping to include the investment issue in the WTO framework, set up a "Working Group on Trade and Investment" during the Singapore Ministerial Conference in 1996 and proposed to establish a "multilateral framework for investment" during the "Doha Ministerial Declaration" in 2001. Due to opposition from developing countries, the negotiations on investment ceased in the Doha round of WTO since the Cancun Ministerial Conference in 2003.

While it is difficult for the international community to reach a consensus on a comprehensive multilateral investment treaty in the short-term, or a multilateral investment treaty under the WTO framework, it is undeniable that under the push of developed countries, the process of multilateralism of cross-border investment rules was under constant deliberation and exploration, and partial results were achieved. For example, the World Bank launched the "Washington Convention" in 1965, which was signed by many countries and provided a comprehensive and convenient framework for the settlement of investment disputes. In 1992, WBG completed "Guidelines on the Treatment of Foreign Direct Investment", proposing a plan to guide host countries' protection and treatment of foreign investors.[34] In 1988, the Multilateral Investment Guarantee Agency (MIGA) was established, complementing national and regional investment guarantees multilaterally and strengthening the legal security of foreign direct investment. The Agreement on Trade-Related Investment Measures (TRIMS) under WTO prohibits certain trade-related investment measures; GATS provides disciplines for international trade in services through multilateral rules, of which Mode 3 under trade in services (*i.e.* commercial presence) is in itself an investment issue. This means that the investment disciplines between WTO members regarding the commercial presence have become a multilateral rule.

It is particularly noteworthy that in the past several years, the US has proposed to the OECD many times that vice-ministerial level officers should participate in informal investment policy meetings, to discuss the settlement of investment disputes, fair competition and other issues, with the intention of gradually promoting the formation of multilateral investment rules.

---

in place the basic principles for comprehensive openness and liberalization of investment, areas which are not open are only exceptions. This effectively requires the host country to relinquish power to review and reject the access of foreign investment. In this regard, there was considerable debate between the developing and developed countries.

[34] This refers to the "Guidelines on the Treatment of Foreign Direct Investment", specifying foreign investment market access, treatment, expropriation, and dispute resolution issues. The guidelines are not legally binding and are strictly for declaratory and guiding purposes.

2.3 *The impact of economic crisis on investment and its rules*

The outbreak of the financial crisis in 2008 left a profound impact on the world economy. The international financial system was shaken, and cross-border trade and investment was also severely affected. In 2009, global cross-border investment declined by 40%, of which the investment in developing countries fell by 35% after growing for six consecutive years prior to 2009. The inflows of foreign investment in Brazil decreased by 50%, Argentina by 41% and India by 19%. Among the developed countries, the inflows of foreign investment in the UK's fell by 93%, the US by 57% and Japan by 53%. To create new jobs, the developed countries shifted their focus to the real economy and took up measures such as taxation policies to attract capital flow back from multinational companies while slowing down the process of moving manufacturing overseas. At the same time, multinational companies restructured their global investments substantially in response to the crisis, resulting in more international capital flow among developed countries and a corresponding reduction in investment in developing countries. International capital flow underwent major changes.

Against the backdrop of the international financial crisis, the investment policies of various countries exhibited two parallel features — "advocacy of liberalization and ease of investment" to "investment protectionism". On the one hand, in response to the financial crisis, and to quickly reduce the impact on the national economy due to significant reduction of cross-border capital inflow, many countries further relaxed restrictions on market access of foreign investment, promoted liberalization of investment, introduced incentives for the ease of investment, implemented tax reductions and exemptions, and other incentive measures. The international competition in attracting foreign investment among countries intensified unprecedentedly. On the other hand, "investment protectionism" was evidently on the rise. In order to reduce the negative impact of the financial crisis, some countries adopted discriminatory practices and began using loopholes in the international rules to "disguise" the way they discriminated against foreign investors or their products. For example, products with high level of domestic contents were favored in government procurement (especially for large public infrastructure projects), banks were required not to issue loans to foreign businesses, a broad interpretation of definition of national security, were to be safeguarded by "national security exception" *etc.*[35] In view of

---

[35] Refer to UNCTAD, "World Investment Report 2009: Transnational Corporations, Agricultural Production and Development," New York and Geneva: United Nations, 2009, p. 31; retrieved from http://unctad.org/en/docs/wir2009_en.pdf.

this situation, during the G20 London Summit held in April 2009, the leaders recognized that the implementation of protectionism in trade and investment in the period of the financial crisis would severely affect the world economy. They made commitments not to establish new trade and investment barriers, and promised to ensure the free flow of global capital so as to resist financial protectionism. However, after the London Summit, actual international practices reflected that these declarations made at the London Summit were not practically effective. Some countries still seem to implement measures of trade and investment barriers in various forms.

Therefore, the impact of the financial crisis on investment policies could be categorized to two aspects: one was the further liberalization and ease of investment, the other one was to seek to strengthen investment regulations and safeguard the interests of the host countries. In the establishment of international investment rules, attention and concern were on these two points. Firstly, more and more countries changed their original stances. They were more willing to include the clauses on liberalization and ease of investment in their international investment agreements in order to expand the scale of foreign investment and alleviate the negative impact of the financial crisis on their economic development. Secondly, with regard to issues related to financial capital flow and foreign exchange control, many countries had tightened their practices when foreign investment agreements were signed so as to strengthen the regulation of financial capital and foreign exchange.

After the financial crisis, a new stage of development began in the international investment rules. To sum up, the new trends and features are as follows: first, restrictions on liberalization of investment have been continually reduced. Traditionally, IIAs mainly played the role of investment protection and promotion but did not cover issues of investment liberalization. However, in recent years, bilateral investment treaties and FTAs have broken away from the traditional functions of protection and promotion, and entered the era of promoting liberalization of investment. With regard to specific content, the scope of definitions of investment and investors has been expanded, so more investment and investors have been covered in the protection mechanisms in international investment agreements; national treatment and MFN clauses have also been extended from post-establishment to pre-establishment. In addition, a number of international investment agreements also included rules on performance requirements.

Second, investment rules have become more comprehensive and colified. From a structural point of view, current international investment agreements are generally divided into three parts: term definitions, substantive rules, and procedural rules. They are far more comprehensive and systematic than the treaties in the earlier years. From a content perspective, besides the traditional content of investment treatment, transfer of foreign currency, compensation for expropriation *etc.*, financial services, taxation and national security exceptions were also included to ensure that the Contacting Parties should not lower labor and environmental protection standards to attract foreign investment. Other aspects of content included not forcing foreign investors to transfer technology, implementation of requirements and transparency of export performance, state-owned enterprises, intellectual property and government procurement.

Third, investment rules have become more detailed. Primarily, the content of definitions has increased significantly. Using the US model BIT as an example, there were only 10 definitions in the 1994 version, but the 2012 version increased the number of definitions to 35. Next, the provision of investment treatment has become more detailed. The provisions of national treatment and most favored nation treatment for both investment and investors are specified separately. Moreover, there are detailed standards of fair and equitable treatment, standards and procedures of compensation for expropriation *etc.* in the new generation of international investment agreements. In addition, dispute settlement provisions are even more comprehensive. The dispute resolution in some international investment agreements account for nearly half of the total number of provisions in the agreement. In some comprehensive international investment agreements, there are a lot of annexes and footnotes besides the text, and these also have the same binding effect upon the Contacting Parties.

Fourth, protection for investors and investment has been strengthened. The scope of national treatment and MFN clauses has gradually expanded, thereby increasing the benefits for foreign investment gradually. Treatment does not only apply to the measures taken by the central government but also to those taken by the local government and international investment rules do not only apply to investment after the effective date but also to investment before the effective date. Hence, the protection on the scope of investment has been expanded. On the standards of compensation for expropriation, some developing countries which had consistently adhered to their position have changed their attitude in favor of high standards of "prompt, adequate and effective" compensation. On definition of investment, besides protecting direct investment in the traditional sense, investment via the third place and financial derivatives are also included in the scope of agreement.

Fifth, there is more attention on the balance between the interests of host country and protection for investors' rights. Historically, international investment agreements have emerged, evolved and developed as developed countries pushed for them. Initially, they were developed primarily to protect investments and investors of developed countries in developing countries. However, with the rise of developing countries and their development in outbound investment, developing and developed countries have changed from pure capital-importing or capital-exporting countries to countries with a mixture of both. Therefore, in the new model of international investment agreements of developed countries as representatives, the focus has been to balance the interests of the host country and investor protection. With regard to dispute settlement, the procedural provisions have become more detailed with the development and improvement of various mechanisms, not only leaving some space and room for the host country but also limiting the discretion of the international investment arbitration tribunal. In terms of exception clauses, an increasing number of countries have introduced national security exceptions, general exceptions, financial prudential exceptions, tax exceptions and even cultural exceptions. These are aimed at providing a high level of foreign investment protection while taking better care of the national interests of host countries.

Sixth, the developed countries are active in leading the formulation of international investment rules. On April 10, 2012, the EU and the US jointly issued the "Statement of the European Union and the United States on Shared Principles for International Investment" (referred to as "The Statement"). "The Statement" lists seven measures, namely an open and non-discriminatory investment climate (including pre-establishment national treatment), a level playing field among state-owned enterprises, provision of strong protection for investors and investments, fair and binding dispute settlement, robust transparency and public participation rules, responsible business conduct (including multinational social responsibility) and narrowly-tailored reviews of national security considerations. These reflect the unified position of the US and the EU in international investment rules.[36] The move of the US and the EU to set new standards and regulations in the international investment rules reflects their intention to jointly lead international investment rule-making. On April 20,

---

[36] See "Statement of the European Union and the United States on Shared Principles for International Investment," retrieved from http://trade.ec.europa.eu/doclib/docs/2012/april/tradoc_149331.pdf.

2012, the US completed the internal review procedures of the 2004 Bilateral Investment Treaty Model and published the 2012 version. Provisions like environment, labor, transparency and performance requirements in the new model are modified and improved. In addition, the US has been vigorously promoting the TPP and TTIP negotiations with a view to establishing the world's highest level of investment rules.

Seventh, the multilateral trend of international investment rules has been strengthened. International investment rules are still in a "fragmented" state. Not only is there a lack of comprehensive multilateral treaties but there is also no functioning international institution. What is most lacking is a judicial dispute settlement mechanism. In the face of the financial crisis, some countries and international organizations realized the necessity and urgency to establish and standardize multilateral investment rules when looking at how to get out of the financial crisis. In January 2013, the US government think tank, the Peterson Institute for International Economics, published a paper entitled "The World Needs a Multilateral Investment Agreement" and called on countries worldwide to reach a "Multilateral Agreement on Investment".[37] Former WTO Director-General, Pascal Lamy, said on various occasions that the establishment of a unified multilateral framework for investment will help improve the stability of the global investment environment and enhance its predictability and transparency. Currently, many countries have recognized that the multilateralization of international investment rules is necessary for economic globalization and increasing interdependence of national economies. The problems faced by the international community are becoming more and more common, especially in the areas of environment, health, labor, and so on. Instead of one or a few countries striving to solve these problems by themselves, the joint efforts of and comprehensive rule-making by the international community are required. The existing international investment rules, mainly based on bilateral investment treaties, is limited in scope, and cannot deal with these global issues. The only solution available is to change the current approach of international investment governance and approach to implement multilateral governance, forming a set of unified multilateral investment rules.

---

[37] Anders Åslund, "The World Needs a Multilateral Investment Agreement," *Peterson Institute for International Economics,* January 2013; retrieved from http://www.piie.com/publications/interstitial.cfm?ResearchID=2307.

3 International Investment Rules and Security Review

With regard to international investment rules, the issue of national security review of foreign investment has always been a hot topic. From the CNOOC acquisition of Unocal Corporation, to the Huawei acquisition of Australia's national broadband network project and the Sany acquisition of the US wind farm projects, cases of Chinese enterprise investments facing obstacles due to security reviews have frequently been reported in newspapers, causing widespread concern in the media and public. Whether in the past, present or future, one hurdle in the process of Chinese enterprises "going abroad" is security review of certain countries. It is thus natural to ask how international investment rules, a part of a legal system that regulates the relationship between investors and host countries, address this issue. Is there a system of rules to regulate the national security review practices of different countries? Is there a need for the international community to establish a unified system of rules for national security review?

3.1 *International investment rules and the security review system*

As of now, there are no internationally recognized, uniform rules for security reviews. In the framework of international investment rules, the issue of national security is generally an exception in international investment agreement and the Contracting Party may take measures to safeguard essential national security interests in its territory. There are three specific approaches.

The first is the absolute exception agreement. Some provisions in the international investment agreements state that the Contracting Party may take any action "it considers" necessary to protect its essential security interests, meaning that the measures adopted by the Party are "self-judgement" and not bound by the obligations of the agreement. The agreements are not subjected to the jurisdiction of the investment arbitration mechanism. The US is a representative of this approach as the above-mentioned "self-judgement" security exception is included in most of the international investment agreements they have signed with other countries. A similar approach was adopted in the US 2012 model BIT, and the 2004 model agreement of Canada for promotion and protection of investment agreement. The investment agreements signed by China in recent years (such as China-Japan-Korea trilateral investment agreement), and the existing model agreement also adopted a similar approach.

The second is the relative exception. Some security exception clauses do not include self-judgement terms. In this case, as respondent host countries can invoke the relative exception clause in the event of investment disputes, they defend themselves on the ground of protecting essential national security. The international investment arbitration tribunal will eventually make judgement on whether it is an issue of national security and if it is an effective defense based on national security. For example, although there are essential security exception clauses in the bilateral investment treaty between the US and Argentina, they do not include self-judgement terms such as "it considers". Therefore, among the disputed investment cases in arbitration under the treaty, the arbitration tribunal concludes and has the right to determine if the measure taken by the Argentine government to protect national security violates treaty obligations.

The third is the bilateral investment that does not include essential security exceptions. The treaties that China signed earlier fall into this category, such as the bilateral investment treaties with Britain, Germany, Kuwait, Israel and other countries. The treaties of Brazil, Italy, South Africa with other countries also fall into this category. In this case, if the Parties take measures for security reasons, they can only defend in accordance with the general principles of public international law, as cited in the United Nations Charter in order to fulfil the obligation to "maintain or restore international peace and security" or form a defense using the state of distress and necessity under customary international law (according to 2001 International Law Commission "Responsibility of States for Internationally Wrongful Acts").

In addition, with regard to the range of "essential security interests" or "national security", most international investment agreements neither explain nor define. Thus, the concept is broader so the arbitration tribunal usually defines with reference to customary international law; while some agreements include clear lists, such as the 2004 Model Agreement of Canada for Promotion and Protection of Investment which states that measures related to arms trade, engaging in war, wartime and other emergency situations and nuclear non-proliferation are security exceptions.[38]

---

[38] The Agreement Between the Government of Canada and the Government of the People's Republic of China for the Promotion and Reciprocal Protection of Investments signed in September 2012 listed related areas clearly. Article 33, paragraph 5 states: nothing in this Agreement shall be construed: (a) to require a Contracting Party to furnish or allow access to any information if the Contracting Party determines that the disclosure of that information is contrary to its essential security interests; (b) to prevent a Contracting Party from taking any

3.2 *Security review systems of major countries*

As of now, there is no investment rules for national security review in the world. Even in the negotiations of investment agreements, the issue of national security is only managed as an exception in the investment process, not to mention the constraints imposed by the mandatory rules on security review. At this stage, most countries in the world use their domestic legislation to regulate the security review system of foreign investment. Below is a brief introduction of the security review systems of four typical countries — the US, China, Canada and Australia.

3.2.1 *Security review system of foreign investment in the US*

The US national security review system was founded in the Exon-Florio Amendment in 1988. The US Treasury Department released the rules of implementation of the amendment called "Regulations on Mergers, Acquisitions and Takeovers by Foreign Persons" in 1991. The Foreign Investment and National Security Act (FINSA) which took effect in 2007 modified the provisions and formally acknowledged the status of The Committee on Foreign Investment in the United States (CFIUS) in the form of law, clearly defining its structure, tasks, procedures and duties. CFIUS also identified the specific components and functions of sectors and divisions in the process of reviewing transactions involving national security. In November 2008, the US modified and announced the "Regulations Pertaining to Acquisitions, Mergers, and Takeovers by Foreign Persons" as rules of implementation for FINSA based on the Exon-Florio Amendment in 1991. As a specialized agency responsible for national security review, CFIUS belongs to the Treasury Department and is an inter-departmental government agency. It is primarily responsible for assessing and monitoring

---

actions that it considers necessary for the protection of its essential security interests: (i) relating to the traffic in arms, ammunition and implements of war and to such traffic and transactions in other goods, materials, services and technology undertaken directly or indirectly for the purpose of supplying a military or other security establishment, (ii) in time of war or other emergency in international relations, or (iii) relating to the implementation of national policies or international agreements respecting the non-proliferation of nuclear weapons or other nuclear explosive devices; or (c) to prevent a Contracting Party from taking action in pursuance of its obligations under the United Nations Charter for the maintenance of international peace and security.

the impact of foreign investment on national security. CFIUS is chaired by the US Treasury Secretary. The Secretariat is located in the Treasury International Investment Bureau of Treasury Department and it takes charge of the daily affairs in the committee. The members of CFIUS include the heads of the following departments and agencies: (1) Department of the Treasury (chair), (2) Department of Justice, (3) Department of Homeland Security, (4) Department of Commerce, (5) Department of Defence, (6) Department of State, (7) Department of Energy, (8) Office of the U.S. Trade Representative, (9) Office of Science & Technology Policy. The following agencies also observe and, as appropriate, participate in CFIUS's activities: (1) Office of Management & Budget, (2) Council of Economic Advisors, (3) National Security Council, (4) Homeland Security Council.

From the perspective of being an object of review, the foreign security review of the US is only limited to an examination of foreign mergers and acquisitions. Greenfield investment is not subject to review. From the procedural point of view, there are three stages in the review — CFIUS review (30 days), a investigation (45 days) and Presidential Decision (15 days). From the institutional point of view, the CFIUS allows the transation be withdrawn. That means the parties to the transaction can submit a written request to withdraw the mergers and acquisitions, thereby terminating the merger due to political factors, commercial reasons, approval prospects and other considerations, before the president of the US announces his decision.

To sum up, the CFIUS system has three characteristics: First, the "national security" concept is vaguely defined and provides CFIUS much discretion. Second, there is a lack of transparency. For projects that did not pass the review, not only was the review process not disclosed, but explanations and justifications were not provided either. Third, the process of the US security review is vulnerable to the influence of the US Congress, media and public opinion, causing the merger and acquisition project which was originally economical in nature, to be political, directly or indirectly resulting in the failure of some transactions.

3.2.2 *Security review system of foreign investment in China*

On February 3, 2011, after learning substantially from the experience and practices of other countries, the State Council issued the "Circular of the General Office of the State Council on the Establishment of Security Review

System Regarding Merger and Acquisition of Domestic Enterprises by Foreign Investors" (State Council Issue [2011] No. 6, hereinafter referred to as "Circular") and formally established the Chinese security review system of mergers and acquisitions for foreign investments. The Circular clearly defined the scope, content, working mechanisms and procedures of the security review system for mergers and acquisitions. In August 2011, the Ministry of Commerce issued the "Provisions of the Ministry of Commerce for the Implementation of the Security Review System for Merger and Acquisition of Domestic Enterprises by Foreign Investors" and standardized the procedures for security reviews according to the responsibilities of the Ministry of Commerce. Regarding the scope of review, the Circular determined that the industries where foreign mergers and acquisitions were issues of national security, and had to be reviewed. Two categories were listed: first, the military and military supporting enterprises. Second, the acquisition of important domestic agricultural products, energy and resources, critical infrastructure, transportation services, key technologies, and major equipment manufacturing; items which are related to national security, by foreign investors. In essence, there is a need for security review when a foreign investor acquires a domestic enterprise in these industries and sectors and obtains actual control.

Regarding the specific review, they are divided into two types: general review and special review. General review procedures are simplified and are of a shorter duration. A written request is submitted to ask for a joint meeting with members of the departments concerned. If all departments deem that the merger and acquisition deal does not affect national security, the security review process is terminated. If member departments think that the deal could affect national security, they would start the special review process. During the special review process, the member departments participate in a joint meeting. If the opinions are basically the same, the decision is made at the joint meeting; if there are significant differences, the issue would be submitted to the State Council, which would then make the decision. Furthermore, in order to provide investors with the remedial opportunities, the security review procedures allow investors to apply for project modification or revocation of merger and acquisition transaction.

The Third Plenary Session of the Chinese Communist Party's 18th Central Committee adopted the "Decision of the Central Committee of the Communist Party on Some Major Issues Concerning Comprehensively Deepening the Reform", in which it was pointed out that the establishment of the National Security Council would improve the national security system and strategy to ensure national security. This important decision provides an important basis for China's national security review system on improving foreign investment, and making full use of the national security review in order to achieve effective regulation of foreign investment.

3.2.3 *Security review system of foreign investment in Canada*

The domestic legislation to implement Canada's national security review of foreign investment includes the "Investment Act Canada", "Investment Regulations Canada", "National Security Review of Investments Regulations" *etc.* The agencies in charge are the Investment Authority and the Competition Bureau of Department of Industry.

(1) General review

The starting point of review procedures differs depending on whether the countries are WTO members. For non-WTO members, the review process is necessary for a scale of investment of more than CAD5 million of direct investment or more than CAD50 million of indirect investment. For WTO members, a lower standard of review applies (except for sensitive sectors) and this standard will be adjusted annually based on nominal GDP (NGDP) growth data. In recent years, the standard of review has been about CAD300 million. Sensitive industries include the energy industries (*i.e.* oil and gas production, electricity, nuclear). For example, in uranium mining, the increase in the share of foreign uranium mining and processing enterprises must not exceed 49% but exceptions are allowed if the companies could prove they are controlled by Canadians. Other areas of foreign investment with federal and provincial legal constraints include oil, natural gas, mining, and so on.

The important elements of review include the role of investment affecting the level and nature of Canadian economy, such as how it impacts the provision of services and exports such as the level of employment, resource development, processing, and utilization area in Canada; the extent and significance of Canadians participating in the equity of foreign-invested enterprises; the impact on labor productivity, industrial efficiency, technological development, product innovation and product categories in Canada; the impact on competitiveness of industries and enterprises in Canada; the impact on industrial and economic policy objectives set by Canadian federal or provincial legislation; the contribution to Canada's ability to compete in the world market.

If the conclusion of the review shows that the foreign presence brings a "net benefit" for Canada, the project will be approved. Foreign investors can commit and provide guarantees to maintain production, labor, research and development and capital spending level in Canada for at least the next three to five years to demonstrate that Canada will gain net benefit so as to ensure that the project is approved by the Government of Canada.

(2) National security review

Under existing Canadian law, Canada may implement national security reviews on the foreign investment deals related to mergers and acquisitions that "endanger its national security", no matter the value or income level of Canadian business assets or enterprises, or the proportion of shares in the targeted enterprise to be acquired. The power to initiate the security review process lies with Canada's Security Department or Intelligence Agency. The industry minister has the authority to implement the review. Nineteen institutions participate in the investigation including the Ministry of Industry, Heritage, Public Safety and Emergency Preparedness, National Defense, Foreign Affairs and International Trade, Ministry of Justice, the Privy Council office, the Department of Natural Resources, the Ministry of Finance, and other departments. All the provinces, regions, municipalities and police agencies participate as well. Canada, however, did not define the scope of national security review explicitly. In practice, this may increase the discretion of the Government of Canada and the uncertainty of national security review. The final results of the national security review determine whether the projects are approved (which allows the implementation of investment projects), rejected (investment projects will not take place), or conditionally approved (*i.e.* there are conditions attached to the implementation of investment projects).

3.2.4 *Security review system of foreign investment in Australia*

Australia has implemented a conditional review system on foreign investment. On investing in sensitive sectors and huge amounts in foreign investment projects, the law states that the project must be reported. Only after the investment projects on acquisition are first vetted can the investing party carry on. The legal basis includes the implementation of the "Foreign Acquisitions and Takeovers Act" in 1975; the implementation of "Foreign Acquisitions and Takeovers Regulations" in 1989; and the review policies for foreign investment amended and approved by the Australian government.

The Australian Treasury is responsible for the development and approval of the management of foreign policy. Under the department, the Foreign Investment Division was set up to formulate foreign policy. The Minister of the State Treasury has the final power to approve foreign investment projects. The Foreign Investment Review Board (FIRB) was founded in 1976 and it is responsible for giving advice on government foreign policy and execution to the Federal Treasurer who decides if the foreign investment review is subject to judicial review or administrative reconsideration.

The scope of review includes the obtaining or holding of the equity or controlling power of an asset that meets the statutory standard amount of an Australian company, or foreign investment that acquires Australian urban land. For foreign investments that come from state-owned enterprises and sovereign wealth funds, all of them need to go through the prior approval of Australian government regardless of their scale of investment and the size of the targeted asset of the investment.

The "Foreign Acquisitions and Takeovers Act" authorizes the Federal Treasurer to decide cases based on whether the acquisitions and mergers violate the national interest, but it is not clearly defined and explained. The FIRB carries out the assessment of national interests based on the following factors: First, the national security factor — where the impact of a foreign investment on the protection of national strategies and security capabilities for Australians is measured and accessed. The findings are mainly based on the views of the Security Department. Second, the competitiveness factor: whether it will control the price of Australian goods or services. Third, the national policy factor: whether it is in line with the government's policy on taxation, environmental protection and other aspects. Fourth, the economic and community factor: the impact on employees, community, creditors, interests of public shareholders in the acquired company; and fifth, the characteristics of investors: whether the foreign investors operate on a transparent commercial basis.

3.3 *Should the rules of national security review be promoted to the international level?*

In recent years, there has been a growing trend where Chinese enterprises face security reviews for overseas investments. The impact is huge, especially for Chinese enterprises "going abroad". In this context, the Chinese government has undertaken many initiatives. One is to increase efforts to consult on specific cases by communicating through diplomatic channels and with foreign security review agencies. Another initiative that has been taken is the usage of various platforms for dialogue to express the concerns of the Chinese government. For example, on July 10 and 11, 2013, during the fifth round of the China-US Strategic and Economic Dialogue, after China made much efforts in consultations, the US made commitments in many areas of the CFIUS security review.[39] Third, the foreign investment agreements signed included a "essential security exception" clause is included in new BITs, leaving space and room for China to establish a security review system for mergers and acquisitions by foreign investors. For example, the China-Japan-Korea Investment Agreement signed in 2012 stipulates that Parties may take measures to protect their essential security interests and they are not bound by the obligations in the agreement.

The issue of security review is actually a double-edged sword for China. On the one hand, with China's foreign investment rapidly developing, the actions of review agencies are strictly bound and transparency of security review is enhanced to ensure impartiality in the process in order to establish a set of strict rules of security review for foreign investment. The goal that the Chinese government should work towards should be the creation of a stable, transparent and predictable environment for Chinese enterprises in international investment. With this in mind, it seems that the Chinese government should advocate the introduction and strengthening of national security rules in international investment rules to ensure there is no abuse of national security reviews. On the other hand, China has just established a security review system for foreign investment and needs to improve its implementation. In order to eliminate the impact of foreign investment on national security reviews, China seems to need to keep relatively lax rules on national security review at the international level to give enough room for policies to be adjusted while implementing and making improvements to the national security review system. It seems that with regard to this issue, the Chinese government's attitude is at odds.

---

[39] The US expressed specific commitments in the following: The US promised that the CFIUS review of all investments are limited to national security and not due to economic or other national policies. When a transaction causes national security risks, CFIUS will resolve as quickly as possible, including taking the targeted mitigation measures rather than prohibiting the transaction where possible. CFIUS will try its best to give an overview of the national security concerns based on the review of transactions in the annual public report, as well as the negative effects it considers the transactions will bring to the US national security or critical infrastructure. CFIUS will consider these negative effects in its next report.

At present, the international community has raised questions on the abuse of national security review by some countries. Some experts and think tanks have also proposed the establishment of international rules on security reviews. In the long run, the rules of national security reviews will be brought to the international level and become an integral part of international investment rules, which would be an irresistible trend.

In light of the growing internationalization of national security review rules, China needs to find an appropriate balance between promoting foreign investment and leaving space to conduct its own national security review. It is difficult to balance the two so accurately and objective conclusions cannot be drawn as yet. A comprehensive solution can only be found with more practice and experience.

4 China and International Investment Rules

4.1 *Overview and challenges of China's participation in rule making in international investment*

4.1.1 *Overall situation*

(1) The historical development of international investment agreements

Since China signed the first bilateral investment agreement with Sweden in 1982, it has signed bilateral investment treaties with 132 countries and regions, with addition of investment chapters in seven free trade zones[40] after over 30 years of practice. In terms of the number of bilateral investment treaties signed, China ranks second in the world after Germany. Compared with the earlier days, the content and structure of the investment agreements that China has signed have changed greatly. Overall, the international investment agreements that China signed can be divided into three stages.

The first-generation investment agreements (1982–1992): At the beginning of the period of reform and opening up, China recognized the positive role of attracting and utilizing foreign capital through signing foreign investment protection agreements. It used the investment agreement model text of former Federal Republic of Germany to develop a negotiating text for China bilateral investment protection agreements. At that time, China just started

---

[40] These seven FTAs are namely the China-ASEAN FTA, China-Chile FTA, China-New Zealand FTA, China-Singapore FTA, China-Peru FTA, China-Costa Rica FTA and China-Switzerland FTA.

using foreign capital. With the two-tiered system managing domestic and foreign capital, there was a risk of dispute between foreign investors and the government. When China negotiated international investment agreements with foreigners, it prioritized national interests and security. The Chinese emphasized maintaining control in their hands, and strengthened the supervision and control of foreign capital and relatively subordinated the interests of investors.

The second-generation investment agreements (1993–1998): In 1993, China formally joined the International Centre for Settlement of Investment Disputes (ICSID) Convention which was launched and signed in Washington on March 18, 1965. Since then, provisions allowing foreign investors to submit expropriation compensation disputes to ICSID for settlement have been included in China's bilateral investment treaties, greatly enhancing the legal protection of the interests of foreign investors. This is the main difference between the second-generation and first-generation investment agreements.

The third-generation of investment agreements (1998–present). Since 1997, a new situation has arisen with regard to bilateral investment agreements of China. It has become increasingly common for foreigners to request for the national treatment provisions during negotiations. In particular, after China's accession to WTO, China has developed economically and socially, and improvements have been made to the legal system and the level of foreign capital utilization has risen, and national treatment conditions given to foreign investment have also become more mature. In such a context, China has gradually made major adjustments to investment agreements. On the one hand, national treatment provisions began to be included in international investment agreements. On the other hand, in terms of provisions related to investment protection, such as expropriation, transfer, and investor-state arbitration mechanisms, a higher level of investment rules was gradually accepted.

In the wake of the financial crisis, China has accelerated the pace to negotiate investment agreements with key countries and regions. The important ones are the following three agreements: First, the China-Japan-Korea Trilateral Investment Agreement which was signed in May 2012. Second, Agreement Between the Government of Canada and the Government of the People's Republic of China for the Promotion and Reciprocal Protection of Investments which was signed in September 2012. Third, the Cross-strait Investment Protection and Promotion Agreement with Chinese Taipei which was signed in August 2012. Among them, the negotiations on investment agreement between China and Canada began in 1994 and the negotiation was finally completed in September 2012. This agreement covers the main elements and content which are included in investment protection agreements, with a total of 35 articles and six additional provisions. This includes all the important elements usually contained in international investment agreements. It is the most comprehensive BIT China has signed.

At present, China is negotiating two major agreements. One is the China-US investment treaty negotiations and the other is the China-EU investment agreement negotiations. China is working simultaneously with two of the largest economies in the world. The investment agreement negotiations have a great and far-reaching significance.

(2) Participation of China in multilateral investment treaties

With regard to multilateral treaties that are investment-related, China approved the Convention Establishing the Multilateral Investment Guarantee Agency (MIGA) on April 30, 1988, an initiative of the World Bank, thereby allowing China to become a founding member of the Convention. In addition to that, China also formally joined the "ICSID Convention" on July 1, 1992.

The MIGA Convention aims to establish an independent, international investment insurance agency, in order to encourage investors from developed countries to invest in developing countries. Established in accordance with the convention, MIGA is an independent legal entity that is relatively independent in terms of law and finance and mainly engaged in the investment of political risk insurance. The main task is to undertake the political risk of investment including individual insurance, re-insurance and co-insurance business. The agency bears four non-commercial risks: currency exchange risk, expropriation and risk of similar measures, breach of contract risk, war and civil strife risk. The MIGA insurance system also plays a positive role to improve the investment environment in China. It provides political risk guarantees for foreign investors in China, and continues to strengthen and promote the development of domestic legal and insurance mechanisms. Besides engaging in the insurance business, the agency also researches on the investment in various countries, exchanges national investment information and provides advisory services. It strengthens the cooperation of China with other countries in the area of investment and helps to improve the investment environment.

The purpose of the "ICSID Convention" is to provide mediation and arbitration convenience for the settlement of investment disputes between the government and the investor of another country. The mechanism of "International Centre for Settlement of Investment Disputes" (ICSID) (hereinafter, the "Center") is currently the only international arbitration institution to resolve such investment disputes. The Center has a comprehensive mechanism for dispute settlement. In accordance with the provisions of the convention, the Center is a voluntary jurisdiction rather than a compulsory jurisdiction. The State member may restrict the scope of jurisdiction of the Center. After China joined the convention, it informed the Center that China only agrees that disputes between the Chinese government and foreign investors concerning the amount of compensation for expropriation will be submitted to the Center. The "ICSID Convention" established a clear set of legally applicable rules. In the recognition and enforcement of awards, the obligation of the parties to willingly abide by and implement the rulings and the obligation of the State to undertake and implement the ruling were combined, thus solving the problems that may be encountered in the recognition and enforcement of foreign judgments under normal circumstances. This ensured the smooth implementation of the Center's awards.

The conclusion and accession of the above-mentioned bilateral and multilateral treaties have played an important role to further develop and improve the legal system of international investment protection and overall investment environment.

4.1.2 Challenges that China faces in participating in international investment rule-making

(1) The challenge of having a "mixed identity"

The position of a country signing investment agreements often depends on its status as host or investing country. The investing country tends to emphasize the protection of foreign capital and liberalization of investment, while the host country puts more emphasis on "maintaining control" to retain more space for policy adjustments. Before the late 1990s, China was mainly a country that attracted foreign capital (host country). Since the implementation of strategies to "going abroad", China has become a big investor with an increasing number of domestic enterprises investing overseas. According to statistics from the "World Investment Report 2013" by UNCTAD published in July 2013, China continued to rank first among the developing countries in attracting foreign investment, and was ranked second in the world for attracting investment in 2012, just behind the US. In foreign investment, Chinese enterprises were ranked third in overseas investment in the world in 2012. The US and Japan ranked the first and the second respectively. Thus, China has a great power on both ends to attract foreign capital as well as to make investment overseas. This led to a "mixed identity" and "mixed demand"; resulting in great challenges emerging for China when signing investment agreements. On the one hand, as the country continues to attract capital, China has to continue focusing on "maintaining control" to retain more space for policy adjustments. On the other hand, as an investing country, China urgently needs investment agreements of high standards to protect foreign investment. Such challenges have become increasingly apparent in recent years when China signed investment agreements with developed countries and regional suppliers such as the US, Europe, Japan and Korea. Of course, this challenge has also brought significant opportunities for the Chinese government to adjust its position promptly under the new situation. It is this "mixed identity" that helps China take more balanced, fair and objective negotiating strategies and stances while negotiating investment agreements and participating in the international investment rule-making process.

(2) The challenge brought about by the expansion of the connotation of international investment rules

In the 21st century, the content and terms of international investment rules have become increasingly complex and have gone beyond the scope of traditional investment protection agreements. First, regarding the substantive content, a growing number of countries require more details in the clauses of the investment protection agreements to increase their operability. For example, clarifying the features of the investment, the meaning and standards of fair and equitable treatment, including indirect expropriation and determination thereof, *etc*. Second, going beyond the traditional scope of investment protection agreements and increasing the content of investment agreements. On the one hand, issues related to investment liberalization and facilitation such as market access, transparency and prohibition of performance requirements, can be added to the agreement. On the other hand, some countries require other content related to investments to be included in the scope of agreement, such as competition policy, intellectual property, environmental protection, labor, taxation, finance and so on. Third, procedural provisions are becoming more complex. This is mainly reflected through the increasingly complex procedural provisions designed to resolve the disputes between the investors and the host country. The dispute settlement mechanism aims to increase the operability and transparency to prevent frivolous lawsuits by investors and limit discretion of the tribunal. For instance, the management of problems related to investors abusing their rights, third-party participation, release of awards and even the establishment of appeal mechanism are included. The above information goes beyond the scope of content covered in traditional Chinese foreign investment agreements. It is a huge challenge for China to take a firm position on these new issues while taking care of its own economic interests.

(3) The challenge brought about by international investment arbitration

Since the mid-1990s, investment disputes between investors and host countries have increased rapidly. International arbitration practices have become increasingly complex and uncertain due to the key provisions in investment agreements. For disputes of a similar nature, due to the different composition of the tribunal, the rulings are not consistent and may differ very much. Some tribunals ruled that the host country had to pay huge indemnities, raising concerns about the impact of such decisions on developing countries.

As the largest developing country in the world with a ranking of second place in the number of international investment agreements, China should have a clear understanding of potential risks in international arbitration. On the one hand, with the continuous development of international investment agreements, investors are increasingly invoking international arbitration as a means to safeguard their own interests. As the largest developing country that attracts foreign investors, there is always a potential risk of investors resorting to international arbitration against China. On the other hand, as China is on the way of negotiating international investment agreement with the US, the EU countries, and other developed countries, it is anticipated that if these agreements are reached, the investors in these countries not only have the right but also the experience in international arbitration. By then, the pressure that China faces in international investment disputes will be even greater.

4.2 China-*US bilateral treaty negotiations:*
The beginning of a new era

In the early 1980s, China and the US made attempts to carry out investment agreement negotiations. However, they were forced to stop because the differences between the two were too immense. On June 17 and 18, 2008, the fourth China-US Strategic and Economic Dialogue (SED) was held in Annapolis,

Maryland. Both parties officially announced the launch of negotiations on bilateral investment treaty through consultations. As of July 2013, China and the US had carried out a total of nine rounds of negotiations. Over the course of these rounds of technical negotiation, the two parties have clarified texts and exchanged views, setting the conditions to enter a substantive phase of negotiations.

On July 11, 2013, the fifth round of China-US Strategic and Economic Dialogue in Washington, which lasted for two days, came to an end. According to the "Joint U.S.-China Economic Track Fact Sheet of the Fifth Meeting of the U.S.-China Strategic and Economic Dialogue", China is to enter into substantive BIT negotiations with the United States. The BIT will provide national treatment at all phases of investment, including market access ("pre-establishment"), and be negotiated under a "negative list" approach. Prior to this, when China signed international investment agreements with other countries without touching upon issues such as investment liberalization or investment access. Pre-establishment national treatment had never been given to foreign investors before. A negative list was never used as a restrictive measure on foreign capital.

This new approach to substantive negotiations in investment agreements with the US reflects a major shift in China's stance in international investment rule-making. It strengthens China's voice in engaging in foreign investment agreement negotiations.

The new US model for BIT also establishes the world's highest standards of investment rules. Investment market access, rights protection, environment, labor, performance requirements, transparency, dispute settlement and other terms are more stringent in disciplinary requirements as compared to China's usual practice for foreign investment agreements. The beginning of investment treaty negotiations with the US signifies that China is moving into a new era of international investment treaties.

Pre-establishment national treatment and a negative list is the basis for substantive negotiations in bilateral investment agreements. This is not only one of the major outcomes of the fifth round of China-US Strategic and Economic Dialogue but also a milestone for China in the signing of international investment agreements and participation in international investment rule-making. This is a significant milestone and its impact is far-reaching.

First, it helps to promote investment agreement negotiations between China and the US. The major difference between China and the US has long been in terms of whether to include investment market access, that is, whether to introduce the pre-establishment national treatment and a negative list. The agreement to use this approach for next step negotiation means that both parties have successfully overcome a major obstacle. This promotes substantial progress in the China-US BIT negotiations and the negotiations are expected to eventually achieve a high-standard treaty.

Second, it helps to promote the reform and opening up of investment market. The management model of pre-establishment national treatment and a negative list requires that changes be made to the existing approval management system for foreign investment, and further opening up of investment. This approach not only conforms to the objective trend of development in international investment rules but it is also aligned with the current comprehensive national reform of establishing an open economic system. The introduction of this model is expected to contribute to greater reform and bring even more benefits after China joins WTO for 12 years.

Third, it enhances the protection of rights and interests of foreign investment, and promotes the implementation of "going abroad" strategies. The 2012 UNCTAD statistics revealed that China has become one of the biggest investor, coming in third behind the US and Japan. By the end of 2014, there were more than 20,000 Chinese enterprises abroad in more than 170 countries or regions. The cumulative non-financial direct investment overseas was as high as USD646.3 billion in non-financial sectors. If China and the US can reach a high standard of BIT using the model of pre-establishment national treatment and a negative list as a basis, China will continue to use high standards of investment protection and high levels of market access as a benchmark in the future. By signing new agreements or revising signed agreements worldwide, not only will the overall level of legal protection of rights and interests of Chinese overseas investment be raised and enhanced, a larger international investment market for Chinese enterprises will also be opened.

Fourth, it is beneficial for China to participate in the development of international investment rules with a more positive attitude. As mentioned previously, the WTO has yet to form a multilateral system of rules in the area of international investment. This shows a state of fragmentation. After the financial crisis, developed countries such as the US and European countries have paid more attention to the process of promoting multilateral investment rules. The change in position with regard to the market access of investments allows China to follow the development trend of international investment rules and be more proactively involved in the international investment rule-making process.

It is worth noting that although China has never been committed to granting pre-establishment national treatment and a negative list in treaty with a foreign party, there have been similar practices implemented in domestic reform. For example, the China (Shanghai) Pilot Free Trade Zone was established on September 29, 2013. One of the main tasks of the pilot zone was to implement the management model of pre-establishment national treatment and a negative list for foreign investment. The pre-establishment national treatment and a negative list in the China-US BIT agreement negotiations is different because it belongs to bilateral negotiation while the pilot project in Shanghai is unilateral in nature in terms of granting benefits to foreign investment in these areas. This means that such preferential treatment given to foreign investment was not reached through negotiations but was a Chinese initiative to implement reforms and other countries do not have to provide the same treatment to China.

The "Decisions from CPC Central Committee on Some Major Issues Concerning Comprehensively Deepening the Reform" passed by the 18th CPC Central Committee at its third plenary session pointed out that "We will implement a unified market access system; and on the basis of making a negative list, all kinds of market players may enter areas not on the negative list on an equal basis and according to law. We will explore a management model for foreign investors with pre-establishment national treatment and a negative list".

It also stressed "We will expedite negotiation of investment treaties with relevant countries and regions, reform the examination and approval mechanism for overseas investment.

This was the first time that these statements appeared in the document of the CPC Central Committee. This shows that the Chinese government has prioritized on the national strategy to implement the management model of pre-establishment national treatment and a negative list to accelerate the work of the China-US investment treaty negotiations. It also shows that since China signed the first bilateral investment protection agreement in 1982, it enters a new phase of signing international investment agreements after 30 years of practice and reflection.

4.3 Reflection on the participation of China in international investment rule-making

At present, the internal and external environment of China is undergoing profound changes. Externally, there is increasing pressure for China to open up further and treat foreign investors equally. Internally, the domestic economy is at the critical stage of restructuring and changing their ways of growth. Along with the "going abroad" strategy, what cannot be ignored is that the foreign investment in China is growing rapidly and companies generally require high levels of investment agreement to obtain a fair and transparent investment environment. In addition, with regard to the restrictions of investment market access in destination country, enterprises can make full use of two markets and two resources in the process, with the increasingly urgent demand for access to the international investment market. On the one hand, China cannot go beyond the current stage of economic development and level in its participation in international investment rule-making. On the other hand, it has to keep up with the new era. Overall, the high-level and standards of international investment rules are consistent with the objectives and long-term development interests of China's reform and opening up. Moreover, a series of problems encountered by Chinese enterprises when going abroad, such as its national security review of foreign investment, restrictions on capital flow by the host country *etc.*, require China to gradually explore possibilities of formulating international investment rules to address these issues.

Regardless of the international trends in recent years or the existing problems of "fragmentation" of international investment rules, multilateral investment rules is the general trend. In this regard, China should take initiative to participate. While it actively concludes high-standard investment agreements with other countries, it should strive for greater speaking rights for international investment rule-making and strongly promote the formation of multilateral investment rules which is conducive to the overall development of China.

Currently, China is actively negotiating investment treaties with the US and the EU, the two largest economies in the world. If the two agreements can eventually be reached, it means that the world's largest developing country and the largest developed economies would have reached a consensus on the international investment rules. This is bound to have a profound and positive impact on the development of global investment rules and even may unify existing multilateral investment rules.

It is worth noting that President Xi Jinping put forward the initiative to "explore and improve the global investment rules to guide the development of rational flow of international capital" at the G20 meeting held in St. Petersburg, Russia on September 5, 2013. This statement not only means that a Chinese leader made this solemn declaration for the first time, it also means that China will participate in the process of developing international investment rules in a more active manner. Meanwhile, the decision of the Third Plenary Session of

CPC that was passed in November 2013, clearly stated that China would "explore a management model for foreign investors with pre-establishment national treatment and a negative list", "relax market access for investment", "enhance overseas investment by enterprises and individuals", "expedite negotiation of investment agreements with relevant countries and regions" and so on. It can be foreseen that China will continue to play a more important role in the development of international investment rules in the future.

Chapter 12

Competitive Neutrality and State-Owned Enterprises

In 2011, the then US Under Secretary of State for Economic, Energy, and Agricultural Affairs, Robert Hormats, published many articles and gave speeches on different occasions, emphasizing the concept of competitive neutrality. He stated that existing international economic rules should be updated and adjusted so that competition would be free from the interference of external factors, and the weakness in existing international economic rules, which were unable to guarantee a level playing field for state-owned enterprises and private enterprises, would be mitigated. The concept of competitive neutrality spread like wildfire and became a hot international topic.

"What I am saying quite simply is that the U.S. is not passing judgment on whether or not China chooses to have state owned enterprises. Our concern is that to the extent they do, those SOEs should not receive benefits (e.g., preferred financing, exemption from anti-monopoly laws, generous export credits, etc) that put them at an artificial competitive advantage vis a vis private enterprises — of the U.S. or indeed any other country."

Since 2011, the US has included the issue of competitive neutrality between state-owned enterprises and private enterprises in the annual China-US Strategic and Economic Dialogue (S&ED). The US also discussed with China the issues of raising the dividend payment of state-owned enterprises, and ensuring non-discrimination among enterprises of various ownership in the areas of financing, taxation and regulatory policies *etc.*

Domestic scholars hold different views on the concept of competitive neutrality. Some feel that this complies with the laws of market competition, and is the way that Chinese enterprises, particularly state-owned enterprises, should reform; others feel that this is a new weapon to curb the development of Chinese state-owned enterprises and that China should exercise caution. Who is right? Is competitive neutrality the devil that Western countries specially devised to deal with China, or is it in itself "neutral"?

1 Issues Raised on Competitive Neutrality

What is competitive neutrality? As defined by the OECD, competitive neutrality means that state-owned and private businesses compete on a level playing field. From an economic point of view, this is essential to use resources effectively within the economy, so that the most efficient companies would be the ones providing the products and services. The concept of competitive neutrality regulates mainly the government and state-owned enterprises. The government should do what it needs to do *i.e.* ensure a fair competitive environment for commercial operators. State-owned enterprises should compete with private enterprises in an open and fair market environment for commercial activities and not discriminate against their transaction partners.

Competitive neutrality is not a new concept. In 1994, Australia introduced the competitive neutrality policy, requesting that the government's business activities should not enjoy net competitive advantages relative to the private sector competitors. The objective was to allow the market to allocate resources and enhance efficiency through competition. Australia had also established the corresponding complaint mechanism. The EU required its state-owned enterprises in postal services, energy, and transportation to distinguish between public service functions and commercial activities, and set up different accounts to take on their responsibilities separately.

The sudden interest in the competitive neutrality concept is closely related to the US Under Secretary of State, Robert Hormats. On May 5, 2011, Hormats published a report titled "Ensuring a Sound Basis for Global Competition — Competitive Neutrality"[1] on the US Department of State blog and subsequently made many speeches, expounding his views on competitive neutrality.

Hormats believed that since the 2008 financial crisis, the state had been playing a more important role in the economic development of a country. State-owned enterprises (SOE), state-supported enterprises (SSE) or National

---

[1] Robert D. Hormats, "Ensuring a Sound Basis for Global Competition: Competitive Neutrality," DIPNOTE (US Department of State Official Blog), May 6, 2011; retrieved from https://blogs. state.gov/stories/2011/05/06/ensuring-sound-basis-global-competition-competitive-neutrality.

Champions are emerging to become serious global competitors. However, many of the advantages of state-owned enterprises were derived through policies which distorted competition in the markets, so it was necessary to promote the establishment of international rules to ensure fair competition between state-owned enterprises and private enterprises.

Hormats also highlighted that the US would adopt the "two plus two" strategy to promote the rules of competitive neutrality in bilateral and multilateral situations. In bilateral situations, firstly, the US would promote the establishment of high standards of regulation of state-owned enterprises in the Trans-Pacific Partnership (TPP); and secondly, strengthen the rules on market access and national treatment in bilateral trade and investment agreements, and request state-owned enterprises delegated with governmental functions, to comply with governmental obligations in the trade and investment agreements. In multilateral situations, firstly, promote OECD guidelines on competitive neutrality and secondly, strive for the United Nations Conference on Trade and Development (UNCTAD) to participate in the discussions on competitive neutrality in order for more developing countries to support the US' views.

Why are developed countries, as represented by the US, increasingly concerned about the issue of competitive neutrality of state-owned enterprises in the wake of the financial crisis? Firstly, the share of state-owned enterprises in international trade and investments grew rapidly and secondly, the industries in the developed countries felt that state-owned enterprises affected their competitiveness.

In 2012, the Peterson Institute in the US published a research report entitled "Will the World Trade Organization Enjoy a Bright Future?" which analyzed the reasons for concerns over the issue of state-owned enterprises. Traditionally, the state-owned oil companies in the Middle East and emerging economies have exerted the greatest influence on international trade and investments. But now, the state-owned enterprises of China, Russia and other countries, are concentrated in the most profitable sectors of the economy — namely natural resources, telecommunications, chemicals and steel — and they have become global traders and investors.

In 2011, the UNCTAD analyzed the developments of overseas investments of state-owned multinational companies in the "World Investment Report". According to its statistics, although state-owned multinational companies only accounted for 1% of global multinational companies, their overseas investment amounted to USD146 billion in 2010, accounting for 11% of global direct investments. According to OECD statistics, among the Fortune 500 companies, the number of state-owned enterprises increased from 34 in 2000 to 95 in 2011. Among them, China's state-owned enterprises increased from 11 to 76, in India the figure increased from one to five, in Russia it increased from zero to three, whereas in Brazil the figure remained at two. From 1995 to 2007, the mergers and acquisition of state-owned enterprises accounted for 3% of global mergers and acquisitions. In the period 2008–2012, the private sector's investment in mergers and acquisitions declined, while the mergers and acquisitions of state-owned enterprises accounted for 11% of that of global mergers and acquisitions.

The US industries' concerns about their global competitiveness are undoubtedly the motivating factor behind the US government's emphasis on competitive neutrality. In articles on the US' push for regulations in state-owned companies, many analysts referred to a report with extensive impact,"21st Century Trade Issues: The Challenges to Services Trade and Investment from State-Owned/Assisted Enterprises, Restrictions on Data Flows, and Forced Localization".[2] In this report, the US Coalition of Services Industries (CSI) and the American Chamber of Commerce raised several issues which they thought would affect the competitiveness of US enterprises, one of which was the preferential policies that other countries gave to state-owned enterprises and state-supported enterprises, which distorted competition in the market, reducing the competitiveness of American companies. The US service sector was a competitive industry. According to WTO statistics, the exports of the US service sector in 2012 amounted to USD614 billion, which was a surplus of USD208 billion. The CSI is committed to raising the global competitiveness of the US service sector through promoting beneficial domestic and international policies. Its member enterprises include multinational corporations in the fields of courier services, telecommunications, insurance, banking and the software industry.

CSI reported that there were two sources of market distortions from state-owned enterprises and state-supported enterprises. The first source was regulatory favoritism; and the second was preferential government purchasing and finacial support. The report cited the regulatory policies that affected the competitiveness of private companies in the services industry, such as the limiting of industry access so as to exclude competition, state-owned enterprises are

---

[2] "'21st Century'. Trade Issues: The Challenges to Services Trade and Investment from State-Owned/Assisted Enterprises, Restrictions on Data Flows, and Forced Localization," by Coalition of Services Industries & US Chamber of Commerce's Global Regulatory Cooperation Project, at 2011 Global Services Summit: Engaging the Dynamic Asian Economies, Washington, DC held on July 20, 2011. Retrieved from http://www.esf.be/new/wp-content/uploads/2011/09/Global-Services-Summit-2011-Paper-on-21st-Century-Trade-Issues.pdf.

not to be bound by anti-monopoly law, technical standards to be in favor of state-owned enterprises, technology transfer as a condition for granting licenses *etc.* CSI believed that market distortions not only affect the competitiveness of American companies in the home markets of the state-owned enterprises, but as these state-owned enterprises entered the international markets, these distortions also affected the competitiveness of American companies in the US domestic market and third-country markets. CSI urged the US government to ensure market access and competitive neutrality during negotiations on trade and investment agreements, especially during the negotiations on the TPP, which is known as the Free Trade Agreement of the 21st century, thus resolving the market distortions caused by state-owned enterprises.

The US government has emphasized that it is only concerned if the competition between state-owned enterprises and the US companies is fair and does not make a judgment on whether the economic management of a country is good or bad in itself. The US is not advocating privatization by raising the issue of competitive neutrality, rather, it does not agree with the policy of raising a country's competitiveness by supporting state-owned enterprises. This is because this economic development model is unstable in the mid to long-term, resulting in inefficient resource allocation; preferential and discriminatory policies favoring state-owned enterprises would also lead to a loss of competitiveness in small and medium enterprises, which is detrimental to the interests of private enterprises and will affect innovation, economic growth and employment adversely.

After the financial crisis, the US increased efforts to promote the development of international rules to ensure fair competition for state-owned enterprises. Clearly, China's state-owned enterprises are its main concern. Statistics from the Fortune Global 500 show that state-owned enterprises account for more than half of China's foreign investment currently, so it is understandable that many people regard competitive neutrality and the regulation of state-owned enterprises as being specifically targeted at China. However, is this really so?

In reality, besides China, many countries have state-owned enterprises in industries such as energy, transportation and others. Among the 20 largest state-owned enterprises (non-financial sectors, ranked by revenue) in the list of Fortune Global 500 companies, nine are Chinese state-owned enterprises, the rest are oil companies from Russia, Brazil, Mexico, Norway, Malaysia and India, France's electricity company, Japan Post, USPS and German railway companies *etc.* According to the OECD's study of 4,500 cross-border mergers and acquisitions in the year 2012, the state-owned enterprises of France and Norway accounted for more than half of the foreign investment of their countries, just like China. Obviously, the form of the state-owned enterprise in each country and the specific circumstances of its foreign investment differ. For example in the case of Norway, most of the foreign investments of state-owned enterprises originate from Norges Bank Investment Management (NBIM), which is part of the Norwegian Central Bank, and is in charge of managing the government pension funds and Norway's foreign exchange reserves.

2 The Evolution of the Competitive Neutrality Policy and the Regulation of State-Owned Enterprises

Although competitive neutrality has become a hot topic in recent years, international dialogue on the issue of fair competition in state-owned enterprises has been going on for some time. Internationally, discussions on fair competition of state-owned enterprises (SOEs) mainly involved two aspects: Firstly, the OECD's research on how the domestic policy of a country could achieve competitive neutrality and secondly, the clauses regarding state-owned enterprises and fair competition in the international trade and investment rules.

2.1 *OECD's research on the issue of fair competition in SOEs*

2.1.1 *Prior to the financial crisis, research focused on the corporate governance of state-owned enterprises and emphasized that the government should ensure fair competition*

The OECD's research on the corporate governance of state-owned enterprises started in 2002. The backdrop is that some OECD member countries have considerable state-owned enterprises in the fields of public utilities and infrastructure, such as energy, transport and telecommunication. OECD member countries believed that good governance of state-owned enterprises would help improve the country's overall economic efficiency and competitiveness, and requested the OECD to conduct a study on the best practices of corporate governance in state-owned enterprises, hoping that the study would provide policy guidelines that would lead to reform in the state-owned enterprises in non-OECD member countries.

In 2005, the OECD published the "Guidelines on the Corporate Governance of State-owned Enterprises",[3] (hereinafter referred to as "Guidelines"), pointing

---

[3] OECD, "OECD Guidelines on Corporate Governance of State-Owned Enterprises," 2005, retrieved from http://www.oecd.org/daf/ca/oecd-guidelines-corporate-governance-soes-2005.htm.

out the challenges that the government encountered in the management of state-owned enterprises. The first challenge was to balance the exercise of ownership rights and intervention in operations. On the one hand, the country has the obligation to actively exercise their rights as owners, such as the nomination of the Board of Directors, and on the other hand, the application of undue interference in the daily management of the company should be avoided. Second, the government needs to ensure fair competition in the markets and not distort competition among various types of enterprises through its management and supervision. In other words, it is suggested that there be a strict distinction between the roles of the owners and the market regulators. As the owner, the government should manage state-owned enterprises in a transparent and accountable manner and avoid unnecessary interference in the company's daily operations. As the regulator, the government should ensure a level playing field in markets where state-owned enterprises and private sector companies compete in order to avoid market distortions.

The OECD Guidelines define state-owned enterprises as enterprises where the countries own significant controlling interests in the enterprises, including entire equity rights, majority stakes and important minority interests in the enterprises. They are applicable to state-owned enterprises that carry out commercial activities and exist as separate legal entities, regardless of whether they also simultaneously fulfill public policy objectives.

The Guidelines made policy recommendations in the following six areas:

(A) Ensure effective legal and regulatory system of state-owned enterprises

The legal and regulatory system regarding state-owned enterprises should ensure a level playing field for the private and state-owned enterprises, avoid market distortions, and fulfill OECD's principles of corporate governance.

There should be a clear separation between the role of the owners and the market regulators. The legal structure that governs the operations of the state-owned enterprises should allow creditors to press their claims and initiate insolvency proceedings. The law should clearly state the public service obligations of the state-owned enterprises, and the costs of public services should be transparent. State-owned enterprises should not be exempt from the application of general laws, and shareholders and competitors should have

The OECD updated, subsequently adopted, these guidelines in 2015; for more information please refer to http://www.oecd.org/corporate/ca/corporategovernanceofstate-ownedenterprises/34803211.pdf.

access to efficient redress through unbiased legal or arbitration instances when they consider that their rights have been violated. The legal and regulatory framework should provide the flexibility to adjust the capital structure of state-owned enterprises. The financing of state-owned enterprises should be competitive. The relationship between state-owned enterprises, state-owned banks and other state-owned enterprises should be based on purely commercial grounds.

(B) The State's role as an owner

The country should establish a clear ownership policy to ensure state-owned enterprises are governed in a transparent and accountable manner. The government should announce the ownership policy, clearly indicate the purpose of state-owned assets, the role of the government in corporate governance as well as how to implement the ownership policy. There must be a designated institution which could exercise the ownership rights in the government management system, and it would be best to centralize the ownership function. The institution responsible for exercising the ownership rights would be accountable to the Parliament.

The government should not be involved in the day-to-day management of state-owned enterprises. Instead, it should grant state-owned enterprises full operational autonomy and accord respect to the directors of state-owned enterprises who would carry out their responsibilities independently. The Government should exercise its ownership rights according to the legal structure of each state-owned enterprise. Its prime responsibilities include: attend the general shareholders meetings and effectively exercising voting rights, establish well-structured, merit-based and transparent board nomination processes in fully or majority-owned SOEs, and actively participating in the nomination of all SOEs' boards, set up reporting systems to regularly monitor, audit and assess the performance of state-owned enterprises. Where permitted by the legal system and the state's level of ownership, the government should maintain continuous dialogue with external auditors to ensure that the remuneration schemes for all SOE board members foster the long term interest of the company and can attract and motivate qualified professionals.

(C) Equitable treatment of shareholders

The State and the state-owned enterprises should ensure equitable treatment of all shareholders, and share company information. State-owned enterprises should communicate and consult all shareholders and maintain transparency. They should also facilitate minority shareholders' attendance of shareholder meetings and their participation in corporate decisions such as the election of the Board of Directors.

(D) Relationship with stakeholders

The state ownership policy should fully recognize state-owned enterprises' responsibilities towards stakeholders. The state ownership entities and state-owned enterprise should recognize and respect stakeholders' rights established by law or through mutual agreements. Publicly listed state-owned enterprises, large state-owned enterprises and state-owned enterprises pursuing important public policy objectives, should report on stakeholder relations. The Board of Directors of state-owned enterprises should be required to develop and implement internal codes of ethics in conformity with international commitments and country norms.

(E) Transparency and disclosure

State-owned enterprises ought to abide by the OECD's principles on corporate governance and comply with their high transparency standards. The ownership entity should publish the annual report of state-owned enterprises.

State-owned enterprises, under the supervision of the Board of Directors and the audit committee, should establish internal auditing procedures and report to the Board of Directors and the audit committee. Large scale state-owned enterprises should be subject to an annual, independent external audit in accordance with international standards. The high standards of accounting and auditing are applicable to state-owned enterprises, just as they are to listed companies. Listed state-owned enterprises and large scale state-owned enterprises should disclose financial and non-financial information based on internationally recognized standards.

In accordance with the OECD's principles on corporate governance, state-owned enterprises should disclose all significant items, such as the company's goals, ownership structure and voting rights, significant risk factors, financial help received from the state and significant transactions with related agencies *etc.*

(F) Responsibilities of the Boards of state-owned enterprises

The Boards of state-owned enterprises should fulfill its responsibility of providing strategic guidance and monitoring of management, have a clear mandate, be responsible for the company's performance and fully accountable to the owners of the enterprise, act in the best interest of the company, and treat all shareholders equitably. The Board of Directors should fulfill its responsibilities of providing strategic guidance and monitoring of management in accordance with the objectives established by the ownership entity and the Board has the right to appoint the CEO (Chief Executive Officer).

Board members should be able to make decisions independently and objectively and the Chairman of the Board of Directors cannot be appointed as the CEO. If employee representatives are required in the Board, it is important to ensure the effectiveness of the system. If necessary, the Board should set up specialized committees, particularly in audit, risk management and remuneration.

2.1.2 *Eight areas of domestic policy that ensured competitive neutrality after the financial crisis*

During the OECD Ministerial Meeting in 2011, it was suggested that ties with emerging economies should be strengthened and guidelines for fair competition between state-owned enterprises and private enterprises established. In April 2012, combining previous studies on the corporate governance of state-owned enterprises and the practices in Australia, the EU members and other countries, the OECD published a report, "Competitive Neutrality — Maintaining a Level Playing Field between Public and Private Business",[4] focusing on how the home country of state-owned enterprises could work towards a level playing field for both state-owned enterprises and private businesses through its domestic policies. This report proposed that at the domestic policy level, the government could adopt a policy framework to ensure competitive neutrality.

The following eight areas were included:

(A) Fine-tuning the operating system of state-owned enterprises

The objectives of public ownership and the areas where state-owned enterprises are providing public services should be explicitly listed down. There should be a distinction between the commercial operations and non-commercial (public services) operations of state-owned enterprises, and the commercial operations section which is engaged in market competition, should undergo company-wide

---

[4] OECD, "Competitive Neutrality: Maintaining a Level Playing Field between Public and Private Business, Report on OECD and National Best Practices in Competitive Neutrality," April 27, 2012; retrieved from http://www.oecd.org/daf/ca/corporategovernanceofstate-ownedenterprises/50302961.pdf.

reforms and its commercial activities should comply with market norms. If a state-owned enterprise is committed to specific public policy objectives while engaged in commercial operations, this could lead to a violation of market rules during the process of carrying out its commercial operations.

(B) Transparent accounting for public service obligations

Increase the transparency and disclosure obligations of state-owned enterprises with regard to the costs of providing public services, so as to ensure that the subsidies for the provision of public services do not cross-subsidize the commercial operations of state-owned enterprises. Audit organizations should be established to examine the costs of providing public services and the subsidies enjoyed.

(C) Achieve a commercial rate of return

Demand that the return on assets of the commercial operations of state-owned enterprises be similar to the rate of return on assets achieved by most of the companies in the same industry. If state-owned enterprises do not pursue commercial gains, then they may adopt an aggressive pricing strategy, like cutting prices to compete with the private enterprises. Setting a reasonable rate of return on the different types of commercial operations of state-owned enterprises would also avoid cross-subsidization among state-owned enterprises.

(D) Reasonable subsidies for the provision of public services

During the provision of public services, state-owned enterprises should avoid seeking compensation by causing market distortions. The government should provide sufficient subsidies to state-owned enterprises with public services obligations in a transparent manner. Preferably, these subsidies are to be paid directly from the financial revenue, rather than through cross-subsidization.

(E) Neutrality in tax collection

A similar tax system should be applied to the commercial activities of both state-owned enterprises and private enterprises. If a government agency is engaged in commercial activities but does not pay taxes, this would be detrimental to fair competition among the enterprises. The issue of neutrality in tax collection does not usually exist in state-owned enterprises which have undergone corporate reform.

(F) Neutrality in regulations

The commercial activities of state-owned enterprises and private enterprises are subject to the same legal regulations. Neutrality in regulations involves both the laws of the general business environment, as well as laws relating to regulation of specific industries. Competition laws and anti-monoply law should apply to state-owned enterprises.

(G) Neutrality in granting credit

Preferential credit should not be provided to state-owned enterprises, so that state-owned enterprises and private enterprises have the same access to financing and the same lending rates. When state-owned enterprises obtain a loan from the state or state-owned commercial banks, they should pay the market interest rate.

(H) Non-discriminatory government procurement

Government procurement policies and procedures should be non-discriminatory and transparent, and all enterprises who participate in the bidding process should enjoy fair treatment.

The OECD guidelines on competitive neutrality are non-binding and the core objectives of these guidelines are to ensure a level playing field between the state-owned enterprises and the private enterprises in the area of business activities. State-owned enterprises may engage in commercial operations, as well as be committed to their public service responsibilities. The government should try to distinguish between these two cases, and give transparent and adequate compensation to the public service area and avoid granting preferential treatment to state-owned enterprises in their commercial activities as this could lead to cross-subsidization of public services. The government should also ensure that the commercial operations of state-owned enterprises and private enterprises are given equal treatment in the areas of taxation, credit, procurement and other policies.

2.2 Multilateral trade rules and commitments of accession of state-owned enterprises

2.2.1 "Ownership neutrality" in multilateral trade rules

WTO multilateral trade rules do not mention state-owned enterprises separately but there are clauses directed at monopolies or priviledged enterprises, as well as rules specifying the regulation of government subsidies, which are aimed at achieving fair trade and fair competition.

(A) Clauses concerning monopolies or priviledged enterprises

(i) For trading of goods, Article XVII of "The General Agreement on Tariffs and Trade" (GATT) regulates state trading. State-trading enterprises are not the same as state-owned enterprises. They refer to enterprises that are awarded special privileges to import and export goods by the government and they could be state-owned enterprises or specially appointed private enterprises. Only designated state-trading enterprises may engage in the import or export of certain type of goods. For example, the Canadian Wheat Board was awarded the franchise rights to procure and export wheat produced in Western Canada under the Canadian law.[5] In Annex 2A of Protocol on the Accession of the People's Republic of China to the WTO, the goods to which China reserves state trading rights and the state-trading enterprises were listed.

Article XVII of GATT requires that state-trading enterprises act in a manner consistent with the general principles of non-discriminatory treatment, and decisions on purchase or sales be made solely in accordance with commercial considerations. In other words, state-trading enterprises with priviledged rights are required to determine which companies to buy from and sell to, entirely on the basis of price, quality and other commercial factors, so that other companies would have adequate opportunity to participate in market competition.

(ii) For trade in services, Article VIII of the General Agreement on Trade in Services (GATS) regulates monopolies and exclusive service suppliers. Monopolies and exclusive service suppliers may not necessarily be state-owned enterprises. GATS distinguishes two cases, firstly, the monopoly supplier of a service, which refers to an enterprise which is authorized or established to be the sole provider of a service irrespective of whether it is a state-owned enterprise or a private enterprise[6]; secondly, the exclusive service suppliers, which refer to a small number of enterprises which are authorized or established to provide a particular

---

[5] On August 1, 2012, the franchise of the Canadian Wheat Board was annulled after the amendment of the law.

[6] Refer to Article XXVIII of the GATS on the definition of "monopoly service provider".

service and restrictions are imposed on the competition among these enterprises.[7] GATS requires that WTO members ensure that these enterprises do not violate their commitment of granting the MFN treatment to members and mutual opening up of trade in services among members. In other words, monopolies or exclusive service suppliers ought to avoid discriminating against the enterprises of different countries. In addition, GATS also requires that members ensure that these enterprises do not abuse their monopoly position outside the scope of its monopoly rights.

In short, WTO rules demand that import and export enterprises or service suppliers which are granted monopoly power, do not abuse their monopoly position. These enterprises should adopt the principle of non-discrimination towards other enterprises, make decisions on purchases or sales based on commercial considerations and ensure that there are opportunities for other enterprises to participate in market competition.

(B) Clauses relating to government subsidies

"The Agreement on Subsidies and Countervailing Measures" (SCM) regulates governmental subsidy actions. Subsidies that are bound by WTO rules need to satisfy three conditions. Firstly, financial contribution, which includes the transfer of funds and tax exemption *etc.*; secondly, subsidy recipients receive benefits which essentially means they enjoy benefits which are more favorable than market conditions; thirdly, subsidies, referred to as specific subsidies, are granted to certain enterprises and industries. WTO only restricts specific subsidies, as providing subsidies to some enterprises would distort the allocation of resources. The SCM classifies subsidies into two categories. The first is that of prohibited subsidies, referring to the subsidies that are contingent on export performance or upon the use of domestic over imported goods, the second category refers to actionable subsidies. If the subsidized exports causes material injury to another country's competing industry, countervailing duties will be imposed on the subsidized exports, or a complaint about the subsidy policy could be filed to the WTO.

The purpose of WTO's regulation on the use of subsidies is to enforce fair trade, so that enterprises could compete fairly on the basis of market allocation of resources. Government subsidies to any ownership enterprise are subject to

---

[7] Refer to Article VIII, paragraph 5 of GATS.

the same regulations. "The Agreement on Subsidies and Countervailing Measures" is not directly related to state-owned enterprises. However, financial contribution could come from the government, or a public body, and public bodies could refer to institutions which exercise governmental duties, and do not necessarily refer to state-owned enterprises but could include state-owned enterprises delegated with governmental functions.

2.2.2 Clauses regarding state-owned enterprises in China's accession protocol to the WTO

In view of the status and role of state-owned enterprises in China's economy, the issue of state-owned enterprises could not be avoided during negotiations on China's accession to the WTO. WTO members expressed widespread concerns over the issue of China's state-owned enterprises and paid particular attention to whether the Chinese government influenced the purchases and sales activities of state-owned enterprises.

The clauses regarding state-owned enterprises in China's accession protocol to the WTO mainly revolved around the issues of non-discriminatory treatment and subsidies. This is directly targeted at state-owned enterprises with extensive exclusive privileges in the area of trading. China made a commitment to lift the controls over import and export operations. With the exception of a few products reserved for state trading, all enterprises can engage in foreign trading of their products.

China promised that its state-owned enterprises would make decisions on procurement and sales based solely on commercial consideration and WTO members would enjoy ample opportunities to compete with these state-owned enterprises in terms of procurement and sales, under non-discriminatory conditions. The Chinese government does not directly or indirectly affect the business decisions of state-owned enterprises.[8] In public utilities such as transport, energy, basic telecommunications and the supply of factors of production, the Chinese government committed to granting national treatment to foreign companies and foreign-invested enterprises, and state-owned enterprises also committed to non-discriminatory treatment of foreign enterprises and foreign-invested enterprises.[9]

---

[8] See "Working Group Report on China's accession," paragraph 46. This paragraph is introduced into the "Protocol on the Accession of the People's Republic of China to the WTO" as paragraph 1.2, and it also became part of the WTO rules.

[9] See "Protocol on the Accession of the People's Republic of China to the WTO," Article 3.

With regard to subsidies of state-owned enterprises, subsidies provided to state-owned enterprises will be viewed as specific, especially when state-owned enterprises were the dominant recipients of such subsidies, or state-owned enterprises received a disproportionately large number of such subsidies.[10] Under this clause, if the law only permits state-owned enterprises to enjoy a particular type of subsidy, then this subsidy would be regarded as a specific subsidy. Even if the law does not restrict the recipients of the subsidy to only state-owned enterprises, it could be determined that there is *de facto* specificity based on the circumstances listed above.

By fine-combing the WTO rules, it could be observed that ownership is not the starting point for multilateral trade rules. The main concern is that enterprises with exclusive privileges do not distort trade and market competition, whether they are state-owned enterprises or private enterprises. In addition, the control on government subsidies is not only directed at the subsidies that the government grants to state-owned enterprises. As specific subsidies granted to any enterprise would distort the market allocation of resources, they are subject to regulation under WTO rules. It could be said that the current multilateral trade rules is "ownership neutral", and the rules do not vary based on differences in the tenure of the business ownership.

2.3 *The issue of state-owned enterprises in international investment*

Unlike multilateral trade rules, international investment rules are currently still dominated by bilateral and regional agreements. The vast majority of investment agreements do not contain specific clauses on state-owned enterprises. Investments of state-owned enterprises are subject to the protection of investment agreements, but the host country may conduct special reviews of the investments of state-owned enterprises.

2.3.1 *Host countries' focus on investments of state-owned enterprises*

In recent years, there is increasing focus on state-owned enterprises, sovereign wealth funds and cross-border investments at the international level, particularly among developed economies. What exactly are they concerned about? In 2009, the OECD published "Foreign Government-Controlled Investors and

---

[10] See "Protocol on the Accession of the People's Republic of China to the WTO," Article 10.2.

Recipient Country Investment Policies: A Scoping Paper",[11] which could provide the answers to a certain extent. The foreign government-controlled investors are broadly defined in the report and include state-owned enterprises, public pension funds as well as sovereign wealth funds. The report concluded that the recipient countries' main concern over foreign government-controlled investments relates to whether these investors are driven by political or commercial objectives. Secondly, recipient countries are also concerned about competition, as private enterprises felt that the competition they face against state-owned enterprises is not fair.

2.3.2 Recipient countries conduct special reviews of the investments of state-owned enterprises

Some countries review the investments of state-owned enterprises and the investments of private enterprises differently. In most cases, the threshold for triggering a review of the investments of state-owned enterprises is lower. Since the review does not disclose information about the case, it can only be inferred from existing legal provisions and guidelines that the key focus of the review of the investments of state-owned enterprises is whether the investment arose from commercial objectives.

(A) The United States

Under the US law relating to national security review of foreign mergers and acquisitions, unless it is determined that the foreign government-controlled transactions would not harm the national security of the US, all foreign government-controlled transactions would enter the second phase of security review, that is, the investigation stage. According to the Guidelines Concerning the National Security Review conducted by the Committee on Foreign Investment in the United States (CFIUS), the acquiring firms controlled by foreign governments include foreign government agencies, state-owned enterprises, government pension funds and sovereign wealth funds. The guidelines pointed out that although foreign government control is clearly a national security factor to be considered, the fact that a transaction is a foreign government-controlled transaction does not, in itself, mean that it poses national security risk. The Committee needs to consider the specific circumstances of the case.

---

[11] OECD, "Foreign Government-Controlled Investors and Recipient Country Investment Policies: A Scoping Paper," Janaury 2009; retrieved from https://www.oecd.org/investment/investment-policy/42022469.pdf.

(B) Canada

In accordance with the "Investment Canada Act", foreign investments that exceed a certain amount would have to undergo a review of net benefit. Under the new standards in 2012, foreign investments which exceed CAD1 billion would be reviewed, but if the investment is from foreign state-owned enterprises, the threshold for review is CAD330 million instead.

In addition, Canada published the investment guidelines relevant to state-owned enterprises in 2007, which were subsequently amended in 2012. This modification expanded the definition of state-owned enterprises, which included not only enterprises directly or indirectly owned or controlled by the government, but also, enterprises which are directly or indirectly influenced by the government. The review focused on the corporate governance and the commercial nature of the activities of state-owned enterprises.

(C) Australia

In accordance with the "Foreign Acquisitions and Takeovers Act", the government needs to be informed when foreign private investors make investments exceeding AUD231 million, or acquire more than 15% interest in Australian businesses. All foreign governments and their related entities, regardless of the investment quantum, need to inform the Australian government and get prior approval before investing in Australia. During the review of investments from foreign state-owned enterprises, the commercial nature of the investment projects is also taken into consideration, in addition to the general factors for consideration. The review also takes into account whether investors' pursuit of broader political or strategic objectives could be detrimental to Australia's national interest and assesses whether the corporate governance structure of state-owned enterprises enables the foreign government to acquire actual or potential control over them.

2.3.3 Clauses regarding state-owned enterprises in investment agreements

Most existing international investment agreements do not contain specific clauses on state-owned enterprises. In the US investment agreement model, it is specified that one of the forms that investment takes is the establishment of enterprises, including private enterprises and state-owned enterprises. State-owned enterprises are defined as all enterprises which are owned or controlled by the government through ownership. The investments of state-owned enterprises and private enterprises are both protected by the investment agreement. This model also specifies that obligations assumed by the government under the investment agreement are also applicable to state-owned enterprises and other entities which are empowered to exercise governmental functions.

The above clauses are consistent with the principles of international laws and may be regarded as "ownership neutrality". Only state-owned enterprises that are supposed to perform governmental functions are requested to abide by treaty obligations like the government is. If other entities perform governmental functions, they will also be bound by the treaty. Ownership is not the main criteria for deciding whether an entity is bound by the treaty. The determining factor is the authorization of an entity to perform governmental functions.

2.3.4 *The US and Europe identified fair competition as one of the seven principles of international investments*

As more state-owned enterprises became international investors, especially Chinese state-owned enterprises, the US and Europe began to pay close attention to the impact of state-owned enterprises on international investment. In this context, the US and Europe issued a joint statement on April 10, 2012, stating the common principles behind international investment,[12] one of which is a level competitive playing field. The US and Europe proposed that the challenges brought about by the state's influence on commercial enterprises should be taken seriously, and measures should be coordinated to address these challenges. To this end, the US and Europe supported the OECD's initiatives in working towards competitive neutrality, stating that the goal is to enable state-owned enterprises and private enterprises to compete fairly in the same external environment.

---

[12] The seven principles include a commitment to open and non-discriminatory investment policies, a level competitive playing field, strong protections for investors and their investments, neutral and binding international dispute settlement, strong rules on transparency and public participation, responsible business conduct, and narrowly-tailored reviews of national security considerations.

2.4 *Regional trade agreements became the main battlefield for regulations on state-owned enterprises*

2.4.1 *Prior to the financial crisis, regulatory clauses on state-owned enterprises were already included in bilateral free trade agreements*

According to statistics on the WTO website, there are more than 500 regional trade agreements currently. Issues raised with regard to regional trade agreements in recent years go beyond the traditional issues of trade in goods. A number of new issues, especially investment issues, are introduced, besides trade in services and trade-related intellectual property issues. Before the financial crisis, the US and other developed economies, as well as other economies with more state-owned enterprises, had incorporated elements regarding the regulation of state-owned enterprises in their free-trade agreements.

(A) The US-Singapore Free Trade Agreement

In chapter 12 of the 2003 US-Singapore FTA, three areas were mentioned: anticompetitive business conduct, designated monopolies, and government enterprises. Among them, government enterprises should refer to state-owned enterprises. Under the influence of the US, two definitions for government enterprises came about. To the US, government enterprises are enterprises that are owned or controlled by the government. In Singapore, government enterprises refer to enterprises which are subject to effective government influence.

Singapore made a commitment that any government enterprise acts solely in accordance with commercial considerations in its purchase or sale of goods or services and provides non-discriminatory treatment to goods of the United States, to service supplies and to covered investments of the Untied States. State-owned enterprises should not limit prices and competition in production or demarcate customers, either directly or indirectly through transactions with their parent company or subsidiaries. Neither should they adopt measures which are detrimental to the interests of the customers or lessen competition in Singapore markets with exclusionary practices.

Singapore is also committed to not influencing the decision-making of its government enterprises either directly or indirectly, but it may exercise its voting rights in government enterprises. It would also publicize the annual reports of government enterprises, stating clearly the percentage of shares that Singapore and its government enterprises cumulatively own, voting rights, special voting or other rights. Information regarding government officials who are board members in state-owned enterprises, and the annual revenue and total assets of government enterprises would also be listed.

In the US-Singapore FTA, the regulations of state-owned enterprises can be classified into three types. The first type being regulations requiring government enterprises to make decisions based on commercial considerations and grant non-discriminatory treatment to other enterprises; the second type are regulations regarding government's commitments to not interfere in the business decisions of government enterprises and the third type covers transparency requirements.

The US-Singapore FTA defines which Singapore government enterprises are bound by the agreement. The bound enterprises are referred to as covered entities and there are three categories. First, enterprises established in accordance with Singapore laws and effectively influenced by the government, whose annual revenue is greater than SGD 50 million. Second, enterprises established in accordance with Singapore laws and effectively influenced by the government, whose total assets are greater than SGD 50 million. Third, any entity organized under the laws of Singapore in which the Government of Singapore owns a special voting share with veto rights relating to such matters as the disposal of the undertaking, the acquisition by any person of a specified percentage of the enterprise's share capital, appointments to the board of directors or of management, winding up or dissolution of the enterprise etc. Government enterprises which are excluded from the scope of the agreement include: enterprises and their holding companies which were established simply for the investment of Singapore's foreign reserves in the foreign markets and Temasek Holdings (state investment company). The so-called effective influence refers to owning more than 50% of the voting rights, or having material influence over the following matters: the formation of the Board of Directors and the Management Committee, strategies, finance, operating policies, and planning. When the government and the government enterprises own more than 20% of a company's voting rights and the government has the greatest voting rights, it can be presumed that the company is under effective influence from the government.

(B) Singapore-Australia Free Trade Agreement

Chapter 12 in the Singapore-Australian FTA contains provisions on competition policy. In this chapter, paragraph 3 states that all businesses registered or incorporated under their respective domestic laws are subject to competition laws. Paragraph 4 states the terms on competitive neutrality and requires parties to take reasonable measures to ensure that governments at all levels do not provide any competitive advantage to any government-owned businesses in their business activities simply because they are government owned, and the obligations under the competitive neutrality terms do not apply to their non-business, non-commercial activities.

2.4.2 More countries introduced clauses on regulation of state-owned enterprises in FTAs after the financial crisis

After the financial crisis, developed economies incorporated more clauses on state-owned enterprises in their free trade agreements. For example, in the free trade agreement between the US and Korea, the regulations on designated monopolies and state-owned enterprises were incorporated as before, and the detailed provisions on the information that parties should provide were stated in great detail. The EU also began to incorporate regulatory clauses on state-owned enterprises in its trade and investment agreements with third parties.

In 2010, the EU and Korea signed a free trade agreement. Chapter 11 in the agreement covered rules on competition of which paragraph 4 and paragraph 5 were related to public enterprises and state monopolies respectively. Under paragraph 4, any public enterprises and enterprises that were entrusted with special rights or exclusive rights, are subject to competition laws, and must not cause distortions to trade. Special rights are granted by the government when it designates or limits to two or more the number of enterprises authorised to provide goods or services, or confers on enterprises legal or regulatory advantages which substantially affect the ability of any other enterprise to provide the same goods or services. The public enterprises should refer to state-owned enterprises. Under paragraph 5, any state monopolies of a commercial nature must ensure that they do not practice discriminatory treatment at the point of purchase or sale.

The EU-Korea FTA requires that state-owned enterprises and enterprises with special rights or exclusive rights ensure fair treatment of other enterprises in their commercial activities and any acts of unfair competition would be subject to the law. Currently, one of the important occasions in which the US is promoting the regulation of state-owned enterprises is during TPP negotiations. The US industries strongly urge the government to establish high standards for state-owned enterprises through TPP negotiations. Although TPP negotiations are still ongoing, it is foreseen that the US will be pushing for the incorporation of more regulations on state-owned enterprises. Perhaps, some clues could be gathered from the previously-mentioned Peterson Institute report. The report pointed out that privatization should not be the prerequisite for the development of rules on state-owned enterprises. Neither should the objective be to restrict the growth of state-owned enterprises. Future rules on state-owned enterprises should include five aspects: Firstly, state-owned enterprises which are bound by these rules should include all enterprises which are engaged in commercial transactions and competition with private enterprises, and those enterprises which are controlled by the state; secondly, state-owned enterprises should commit to making transactions based solely on commercial considerations; thirdly, the shareholders, organization structure and other information in state-owned enterprises should be transparent; fourthly, the government should not discriminate against the private sector and should be fair to both state-owned enterprises and private enterprises and fifthly, state-owned enterprises should respect the national treatment principle.

From the evolution of competitive neutrality and the regulation of state-owned enterprises, it can be observed that after the financial crisis, the importance of state-owned enterprises in global trade and investment activities has increased and concerns on state-owned enterprises and fair competition have mounted. The core of competitive neutrality and the regulation of state-owned enterprises is fair competition between commercially-operated state-owned enterprises and private enterprises. Not only is the government responsible for ensuring a level playing field, state-owned enterprises are also requested not to discriminate against their business partners. The regulations of state-owned enterprises may be incorporated in more regional trade and investment agreements in the short run, and then gradually gain acceptance in more economies in the long run. At the same time, the best practices and guidelines recommended by the OECD and other international organizations may have an impact on the policy directions of all countries.

3 The Trends and Thoughts on Regulation of State-Owned Enterprises

3.1 *The trends, main characteristics and impact of the regulation of state-owned enterprises in the future*

3.1.1 *Development trends*

The US and Europe felt that the existing rules on international trade and investment were inadequate. In order to resolve the issue of fair competition between state-owned enterprises and private enterprises, new regulations and obligations of state-owned enterprises should be established by pushing for high standards in regional trade and investment agreements. Considering the evolution of competitive neutrality and regulations on state-owned enterprises mentioned above, future rules on state-owned enterprises and fair competition might develop in the following aspects:

(A) Governmental obligations

The core of competitive neutrality is that governments do not provide competitive advantages to the commercial operations of state-owned enterprises, so as to ensure a level playing field between state-owned enterprises and private enterprises. Future rules may require governments to supervise neutrality and adopt the same regulatory laws towards state-owned enterprises and private enterprises, including generally applicable laws such as competition laws, as well as specialized supervision rules for any particular industry. The government is also requested not to subsidize the commercial operations of state-owned enterprises which include providing favorable financing, goods, services *etc.* In addition, even though market access, national treatment and other traditional trade and investment issues are not directly related to state-owned enterprises, they will reduce the monopoly and priviledged position of state-owned enterprises in specific industries and would also be seen as an important means of achieving fair competition.

(B) The regulation of state-owned enterprises

Another trend in the development of rules is the direct specification of obligations that state-owned enterprises should assume, which could include two aspects. First, when state-owned enterprises perform governmental functions, such as licensing and establishment of quotas, they should abide by the international treaty obligations, just like the government. Second, when state-owned enterprises are engaged in commercial activities, they should not discriminate against any company and should take action solely according to commercial considerations when making purchases or providing goods or services. The obligations mentioned here are not new. In accordance with international laws, the behavior of any organization which performs governmental functions (regardless of ownership) is attributed to the government, and it should thus comply with the same obligations as the government. On non-discriminatory treatment, GATT and GATS requires priviledged enterprises (regardless of ownership) to make decisions on sale of goods or services based on commercial considerations alone and provide non-discriminatory treatment to other businesses. Our country made the above commitments when we joined the WTO.

As many state-owned enterprises are the restricted operators within specific industries, commercial considerations and non-discriminatory treatment are essential to ensure fair competition in the downstream market.

(C) Transparency

The government is requested to publish the list of state-owned enterprises, and provide information about the governance of state-owned enterprises as well as the subsidies they enjoy.

3.1.2 *Special characteristics and impact*

Several special characteristics can be observed through the evolution of competitive neutrality and the regulation of state-owned enterprises. Firstly, the transformation from self-policy to multilateral policy guidelines. After the competitive neutrality policy was practiced in Australia, the EU and other countries, and the OECD and other international organizations completed their research summaries, the policy gradually became the guideline for many countries. Secondly, the change from non-binding guidelines to binding rules by including clauses on state-owned enterprises in regional trade and investment agreements, made these clauses binding obligations under international law. Thus, any violation of these obligations could lead to disputes between States. Thirdly, the progression from regional to multilateral arrangements. As the terms on state-owned enterprises were introduced into more regional agreements, and large-scale, influential regional trade and investment agreements were developed, in particular the TPP and TTIP, as well as TISA, more countries became receptive towards the terms for state-owned enterprises, paving the way for the future of multilateralism and binding international rules. Fourthly, when the competitive neutrality issue was mentioned by the West and the OECD in the early stages, the move was not directed at China, as there were a considerable number of state-owned enterprises in various fields in developed countries and China's state-owned enterprises had yet to participate in international competition on a large-scale. However, the increase in the foreign investment of state-owned enterprises could be a significant reason for the current emphasis on competitive neutrality in the reconstruction of international rules, which increases the perception that this was targeted at China, thus a clear understanding of international rules is necessary. If this is not clearly understood, it may result in the failure to recognize the need and urgency for reforms of state-owned enterprises and the daunting task of fighting against ownership discrimination in international rules may be neglected.

Therefore, in assessing the impact of the development of regulations of state-owned enterprises, it is necessary to study the issue in a comprehensive, objective, rational, dialectical manner and look at the issue from different perspectives. One should not view these regulations simply as a scourge or insurmountable barrier system, and feel that the objective of all regulations on state-owned enterprises is to weaken China's competitiveness. We should also not ignore the West's concerns and their containment psychology toward state-owned enterprises as a result of China's rising international position. Instead, we should see the need for internal reforms of state-owned enterprises, which have a lot in common and coincide with the demands of competitive neutrality, as well as the challenges that competitive neutrality and regulations on state-owned enterprises present to our country. Not only should we assimilate reasonable rules on competitive neutrality, but we should also oppose discrimination due to ownership of an enterprise. It is necessary to consider the impact of competitive neutrality on Chinese state-owned enterprises, and its impact on the overall development of China; it is also pertinent to take into account both the short-term as well as long-term impact.

As such, we need to reflect deeply on this matter. If the key reason behind the US and Europe's proposition of the competitive neutrality issue is industrial competitiveness, then China should examine this problem by raising its industrial competitiveness on the global level, and then evaluate if this is contrary to China's independent reforms. We should also determine which areas we can draw on international rules for the improvement of our own institutional mechanisms and which are the areas in the development of international rules we could actively influence, so that the rules would be more fair and reasonable and not become a stumbling block to China's long-term development. There is a reasonable side to competitive neutrality, as it creates an equitable competitive environment, which does not go against China's independent reforms, and lays the foundation for the market to play a decisive role in the allocation of resources. Competitive neutrality is not the devil. In fact, it could positively force a reform of our market orientation. On the other hand, in view of the relatively high proportion of state-owned enterprises, coupled with an imperfect market economy system, it is inevitable that in practice, there will be occasions where our policies and methods still violate fair competition. Accepting greater restrictions would have a greater impact on China as compared to other countries, and may even lead to new trade disputes.

3.2 *Implication of competitive neutrality in the reform of state-owned enterprises*

The topic of state-owned enterprises has never been far from the heated debate of the public and experts in China. On February 27, 2012, the World Bank and the China Development Research Center of the State Council jointly issued a report entitled "China 2030: Building a Modern, Harmonious and Creative Society" (hereinafter referred to as "joint report"), and the section on state-owned enterprises caused a lot of controversy. Needless to say, the reason why the concept of competitive neutrality has drawn attention in recent years is closely related to the issues of state-owned enterprises, thus causing the wide-spread debate in China. Objectively, based on the concept of competitive neutrality and content of the previously mentioned analysis, the policy frame-work has implications on certain aspects of the reform of state-owned enterprises in China.

3.2.1 *Fair competition in line with the direction of reform in China*

Internationally, an important aspect related to competitive neutrality and the regulation of state-owned enterprises is the government providing fair competition for all businesses and this is one of the clear objectives of our economic reform.

The report at the 18th National Congress of the CPC pointed out that to deepen the reform of the economic system, China must unswervingly consolidate and develop the public sector and intensify the reform of state-owned enterprises; give unwavering encouragement, support and guidance to the non-public sector to ensure that all sectors of the economy use production factors justly in accordance with the law and participate fairly in market competition. The Third Plenary Session of the 18th CPC Central Committee decided to further reinforce the decisive role of market in allocating resources and the concept of fair competition for all sectors of the economy, for example, the state protects all economic sectors in property rights and legitimate interests, and ensures that all kinds of economic sectors use production factors equally, participate in market competition publicly in a fair way, and receive protection by law impartially ... the state adheres to equal rights, opportunities and regulations, abolishes unreasonable provisions for the various forms of non-public sectors and eliminates various invisible barriers. Clearly, the main purpose of reform of state-owned enterprises in China is to allow the market to play a decisive role in the resource allocation process. This is based on the objective understanding of the situation where China recognizes and says "I want to change", rather than being "obligated to change" by external forces. Further study of the direction of reform of state-owned enterprises as stated in the Third Plenary Session of the Eighteenth CPC Central Committee reveals that there is a great overlap between such an attitude and the principle of competitive neutrality.

Why was the reform direction put forward in such a way? Perhaps "The joint report" presented a possible explanation. The "The joint report" said that China needs to reform its allocation of resources and encourage competition in order to improve productivity. An active and efficient corporate sector is the key to maintaining rapid economic growth in China over the next 20 years and upkeep the international competitiveness and innovation capacity of enterprises. "The joint report" suggested that one way to reform the state-owned enterprise sector is to reduce monopolies and increase competition between state-owned enterprises and private enterprises — thus improving technical efficiency and resource allocation efficiency. Another approach is to enhance the fairness of the competitive environment and improve resource allocation efficiency. The advice of "The joint report" could be summed up as two core ideas: increase competition and fair competition. Through competition, the efficiency of non-state-owned enterprises and state-owned enterprises will improve.

With regard to the increasing competition, the state council issued "Several Opinions of the State Council on Encouraging, Supporting and Guiding the Development of Individual and Private Economy and Other Non-Public Sectors of the Economy" as early as 2005. In 2010, the State Council issued "Several Opinions of the State Council on Encouraging and Guiding the Healthy Development of Private Investment". After five years, there has been a more profound understanding on the increasing competition and importance of fair competition. This not only increases employment and improves the living standards of people but also achieves sustainable development in economy by perfecting the guarantee mechanisms in the socialist market economy system.

3.2.2 Positioning of China's state-owned enterprises

Competitive neutrality requires fair competition between the commercially operated state-owned enterprises and private enterprises. For the analysis of fair competition in state-owned enterprises, the state-owned enterprise must first be providing public products and services, or be in commercial operation. The answer seems simple, but it can be complicated in reality.

Take the 115 state-owned enterprises managed by state-owned Assets Supervision and Administration Commission for example. Some of them are in the field of tourism and business and seem to be operators in a fully competitive market; some are state-owned reserves companies with the function of adjusting to the market. Is the nature and position of these state-owned enterprises the same? Are these state-owned enterprises purely commercial operators, or are they serving public policy objectives in some way?

"The joint report" suggested state-owned capital as a kind of public resource should mainly be used to provide public products and deal with pressing social problems. Public products may include national defense, social security and infrastructure. They may also include reliable energy supply, transportation, postal and other fields of general service. Obviously, not all public products are necessarily provided by state-owned enterprises and the government can allow non-state enterprises to participate in government procurement of public products or services through market competition to reduce costs and improve quality. Of course, there is also the view that state-owned capital can also be used for commercial activities, as long as its day-to-day operations conform to the principle of competitive neutrality and abide by the regulation of state-owned enterprises. They are also entities of fair competition in the market.

The Third Plenary Session of the 18th CPC Central Committee stressed to define the different functions of state-owned enterprises. "There will be more investment on public welfare enterprises from the state-owned capital, making greater contributions in terms of providing public services. According to the Decision of the Third Plenary Session, in "natural" monopoly industries, such as public utilities, minerals and railroad networks, reforms will be introduced to separate the government's regulatory functions from business management and operations to be conducted by the state. In addition, a charter or franchise system will be implemented so that the natural monopoly sectors will be operated by franchisees independent of government agencies, but in compliance with relevant state regulations. It also stressed to promote the marketization in the allocation of public resources according to the characteristics of different industries and by opening up the competitive business. This further breaks down the various forms of monopoly in administration. There is improvement in the coordination of operation and also in effective checks and balances of corporate governance structure." It is clear that the direction of reform of state-owned enterprises in China is in accordance with the rules of market economy. As for the issue of fair competition which has drawn a lot of attention, on the one hand, the historical burden of state-owned enterprises has not been entirely lifted and the operating loss has not been completely compensated in the implementation of macroeconomic regulation and control policy. On the other hand, monopolies, hidden support policy and profit distribution have caused a lot of criticism. They should be in accordance with the requests of "clearly-defined functions of different state-owned enterprises" and distinguish themselves from the functions of public service of state-owned enterprises and commercial activities. In the field of competitive business, the market should be allowed to play a decisive role in the allocation of resources to ensure competitive neutrality. To gradually enhance the global vision of strategic adjustment, one must think deeply about other deep-seated issues such as what one "has, does and uses" in the state-owned enterprise system.

In fact, the country is speeding up its accurate definition of different functions of state-owned enterprise,[13] distinguishing between public and commercial activities, improving classification and evaluation methods, and setting different development goals for different types of enterprises at different development stages. There is no longer intervention in the specific business activities, legal property rights and operation autonomy of the enterprises.

3.2.3 *Competitive neutrality with mixed identities*

The OECD Guidelines on Corporate Governance of State-owned Enterprises show that state-owned enterprises can serve the non-commercial purposes and stress that if state-owned enterprises can serve the non-commercial purposes, the government should remain transparent. As a state-owned enterprise may have a mixture of businesses, three of the eight policy frameworks set by OECD concerning competition are about how state-owned enterprises with mixed identities can maintain fair competition. First, the government should carry out corporate reform to the business part of state-owned enterprises participating in competition. Second, the transparency of public service costs provided by state-owned enterprises is to be improved. Audit cost calculation is supervised to avoid the use of subsidies for state-owned enterprises to provide public service as cross-subsidies for state-owned enterprises in the competitive field of business. Third, there are reasonable subsidies to cover part of the costs of public services in a transparent manner. The most transparent approach is to use direct subsidies from fiscal revenue, rather than have state-owned enterprises participate in other

---

[13] Huang Shuhe's remarks on deepening the reform of state-owned enterprises and other situations when he was interviewed by a reporter on December 19, 2013; retrieved from http://news.onedow.com/eview/nodj0.html.

market competition and distort market competition to provide cross subsidies for state-owned enterprises. The country ensures to realize fair competition for state-owned enterprises and private enterprises in the competition fields.

Previously, a social hot topic was the collection of universal postal service funds[14] from courier companies and this was an example of ensuring fair competition with "mixed identity" state-owned enterprises. There were many controversies surrounding this topic but only one thing was for sure — the postal company was a state-owned enterprise with "mixed identities".

According to the regulation of Postal Law, postal enterprises take on the responsibility for providing universal postal service in accordance with the provisions of the state (that is according to the business scope, service standards and cost standards set by regulations of the State to continue to provide postal service for all users in the territory of the People's Republic of China). This is obviously a public service. The law stipulates that the State subsidizes postal enterprises for providing universal postal services and sets up a Universal Postal Service Fund. The Postal Law also stipulates that the universal postal service and competitive business of the postal enterprises should be operated separately. The universal postal service charges are determined by the state and the other business capital standards of postal enterprises are determined independently.

The universal postal service is a public service and its nature is clear. The law stipulates that the state subsidizes the providence of this public service. The key is while the postal enterprises with mixed identities provide public services and also participate in the competitive business operation (such as express delivery), they have to ensure that the subsidy is given in a transparent manner and does not cause negative effects on the competition in other similar markets (such as the express delivery market).

While discussing the specific ways of establishing a Universel Postal Service Fund, two aspects of information are very important. One is the costs of providing universal postal service by state-owned enterprises with "mixed business"; and secondly, how the current government provides subsidies (including benefits apart from subsidies). With this as the basis, it is possible to analyze how much capital support is needed to provide universal postal service and in what ways it can be given. Both the for and against viewpoints of collecting money from courier enterprises are looking for support from international practices, but it is more important to analyze China's situation and find a convincing solution for China.

---

[14] According to reports in early 2013, the Ministry of Finance and the State Post Bureau held a meeting with courier companies and sought the advice in "Interim Measures for the Usage and Management of Universal Postal Service Fund".

3.3 *Reflection on China's participation in international dialogue regarding state-owned enterprises*

The core concept of competitive neutrality is fair competition. From this perspective, this is not a new topic. Competitive neutrality is not specifically targeted at China but its effect on China may be greater. With China's strong emphasis on fair market competition, China actively participates in international dialogue on competitive neutrality and develops international cooperation with a constructive attitude. This will create a better international environment for a variety of ownership enterprises in China and a greater space for development.

3.3.1 *Not avoiding discussion with regard to issues on state-owned enterprises*

State-owned enterprises in China have begun to internationalize, from the past when they mainly sold products overseas to overseas investment in global resources allocation. In particular, we clearly put forward the strategy of "going abroad", hoping to encourage all enterprises to make full use of two markets and two kinds of resources to enhance the ability of international operation of enterprises. "Going abroad" is the inevitable choice for China's economic development with economic globalization. There is also an urgent need for Chinese enterprises to participate in international competition. In 2012, China's foreign direct investment reached USD87.8 billion and quite a part of it came from state-owned enterprises. As our country has a larger proportion of state-owned enterprises in overseas direct investment, the higher proportion of resource and energy industry is likely to catch the attention of relevant countries.

If commercially-operated state-owned enterprises cannot improve the enterprise competitiveness of fair market competitors domestically, not only will the efficiency of domestic resource allocation be restricted but it will be difficult for them to take off internationally. If the state-owned enterprises do not have a clear goal on overseas investment, corporate governance will not be highly transparent. Foreign governments and industries will then focus and speculate on unfair competition, leading to more restrictions and risk for China's state-owned enterprises in the world.

At present, with regard to the special review of state-owned enterprises from overseas investment which is mainly concentrated in the field of national security, some countries are concerned about the transparency of state-owned enterprises' management and whether the investment is for commercial purposes which extends to the extent of influence on the state-owned enterprises by the government. However, with increasing attention on the problems of competitive neutrality, especially when they think that state-owned enterprises have unresolved problems on competitive neutrality in their domestic market in the home country, the host countries do not rule out the possibility of more reviews on competition relations in the future. On May 9, 2013, the United States Economic and Security Review Commission held a hearing to discuss issues regarding China's trade and investment. When commenting on how China's investment had affected the US, lawyers representing the interests of the US industry suggested that the US should adjust the existing policies to respond to the investment from China's state-owned enterprises. The US industry thinks that the existing anti-monopoly laws and international trade rules cannot solve the issues of state-owned enterprises enjoying subsidies in their home countries and the low price competition in the US market. Investment reviews should include not only national security concerns, but also address economic considerations with regard to competitive neutrality. The US government should require China to ensure its state-owned enterprises establish foreign investment on the basis of competitive neutrality. As the host country develops its investment policy along this direction, the review on the investment of state-owned enterprises will become more uncertain and state-owned enterprises may face more barriers in foreign investment. China should strategize and prepare to respond earlier. As China's state-owned enterprises become more global, it is unrealistic to avoid the international discussion on the regulation of state-owned enterprises.

3.3.2 *Ideal goal: Domestic competitive neutrality and international ownership neutrality*

In the international dialogue on the issues of state-owned enterprises, China put forward its own demands which are: to ensure an environment of fair competition in the country and to ensure state-owned enterprises are not discriminated because of different ownership at the same time.

The economic committee of the CPPCC held a symposium "to promote coordination and development between state-owned enterprises and private companies". According to the workshop report, participants think that "ownership discrimination is the biggest obstacle". Whether state-owned or private, the participating enterprises are looking forward to remove ownership labels which make enterprises and governments clearly distinct. *People's Daily* reported on the workshop and quoted an entrepreneur, "We hope for a legal and fair institutional environment. Whether state-owned enterprises or private companies, every enterprise can have equal chance of entering the market. There should be equality in obtaining production elements and participating in fair competition. They should also accept the market elimination mechanisms". The fair framework of international rules should be "domestic competitive neutrality and international ownership neutrality". Specifically, when commercially-operated state-owned enterprises compete equally with other enterprises within the country, state-owned enterprises practically become the market players in market competition. Internationally, the rules on trade and investment do not distinguish ownership as the standard and discriminate state-owned capital. This is the common voice of state-owned enterprises and private enterprises in China as mentioned in the report above. China must adhere to this principle in international dialogue and negotiations.

The next step, that is, the establishment of international rules of competitive neutrality is still a very arduous task. On the one hand, competitive neutrality should not involve ownership evaluation and it should only require that countries ensure that commercially-operated state-owned enterprises compete fairly with private enterprises. There are no objections to the existence of state-owned enterprises but they should be regulated. It can be said that competitive neutrality does not challenge the basic existing economic system in our country. Therefore, the discussion of rules on competitive neutrality should not be politicized. If the state-owned enterprises can achieve competitive neutrality at home, the international community should not discriminate against them. On the other hand, if the competitive neutrality rules are abused, there will be discrimination and excessive examination against the trade and investment of state-owned enterprises. This can easily trigger counter measures and friction, leading the home country of the state-owned enterprises to review the investment motives and preferential treatment of foreign enterprises. Thus, this will cause great negative impact to international capital flows. The proportion of China's state-owned enterprises is relatively large in the economy, so reform will be a gradual process. There must be a reasonable transition period to distinguish the two functions of state-owned enterprises which are namely commercial and public services. A classification management system should be set up for modern enterprises. If external constraints are applied too fast and too hard, it is not conducive for the comprehensive deepening of reform and domestic competitive neutrality. Therefore, in the active participation of establishing international rules concerning competitive neutrality and regulation of state-owned enterprises, the abuse of rules should be prevented and "ownership neutrality" should be adhered to. The legitimate rights and interests of Chinese state-owned enterprises should be protected too. This requires good understanding of both China and the world, and more hard work in negotiation efforts.

Chapter 13

Rules of International Development Cooperation

On November 29, 2011, the grand opening of the Fourth High Level Forum on Aid Effectiveness was held in Busan, Haeundae, Korea. More than 160 countries and over 30 international organizations sent high-level delegations to the forum including UN Secretary-General Ban Ki-moon, OECD Secretary-General Angel Gurria, Korean President Lee Myung-bak, Rwandan President Paul Kagame, Ethiopian Prime Minister Meles Zenawi and several other leaders of nations and multilateral agencies. Their participation reflected the international community's great concern with regard to international development cooperation in the context of the economic crisis. At the opening ceremony, UN Secretary-General Ban Ki-moon called on traditional donor countries to honor their official development assistance commitments as soon as possible, for recipient countries to strengthen their capacity for independent development, and for emerging economies to play a bigger role in the field of international development cooperation.

At the meeting, the parties came to a basic conceptual agreement on establishing a "Global Partnership for Effective Development Co-operation" but the developed countries and emerging economies such as China, India and others disputed the nature of South–South cooperation, and the responsibilities and rules of international development cooperation. The developed countries stressed that traditional North–South cooperation no longer reflected the new changes in international development cooperation; that emerging economies ought to take up more responsibility for development aid, and that they should accept unified monitoring and using evaluation criteria together with developed countries. The emerging economies believed that under the current circumstances, North–South cooperation was still the mainstream international development cooperation; as such developed countries ought to bear the primary responsibility for international development cooperation. They expressed that South–South cooperation was a useful complement for North–South cooperation and new emerging economies still faced serious developmental tasks and thus, should not share in the duties of the developed countries. Furthermore, South–South cooperation was also of a different nature from North–South cooperation, and as both had their individual characteristics, developed countries should not impose the standards and rules of international development cooperation that were suited to their needs on the emerging economies. Both camps refused to concede and negotiations reached a deadlock.

This conundrum leads us to certain questions such as: What is international development cooperation? What are the differences between South–South cooperation and North–South cooperation in nature and features? What are the rules of international development cooperation? Why do emerging economies not want to follow the same rules applicable for developed countries? To find the answers to these questions, the history and evolution of the relevant rules of international development cooperation must first be discussed.

1 Rules of International Development Cooperation before the Economic Crisis

International development cooperation, also known as international development assistance, refers to the financial, material, and technical support provided by the international community to the economic and social development of developing countries. Currently, the main bodies giving development aid are developed countries and international organizations, and the aid they provide is generally referred to as Official Development Assistance (ODA).[1] At the same time, China, India and some developing countries have provided forms of economic and technical assistance to other developing countries that promote a general message that "the poor are helping the poor". Some non-governmental organizations, foundations, enterprises and even individuals have given a certain amount of development assistance to recipient countries.

The international development cooperation system today was first established after the end of World War II. Development assistance was greatly

---

[1] ODA generally refers to economic aid with a grant ratio of no less than 25%, given by Development Assistance Committee (DAC) member countries or multilateral development organizations to developing countries. The main purpose of ODA is to boost economic development and welfare in the recipient countries.

successful in helping post-war European countries in economic recovery and reconstruction. However, it was not as effective in helping Third World countries to develop their economies or reduce poverty. Thus, the international development cooperation rules proposed by developed donor countries continue to be questioned and challenged. The UN Millennium Development Goals pushed for the reform of international development cooperation rules, building upon a new set of development cooperation rules that were focused on aid effectiveness.

1.1 *Post-World War II international development cooperation system and rules*

After World War II, the US provided substantial economic assistance to the reconstruction of Europe by implementing the Marshall Plan.[2] At the same time, through the implementation of the Point Four Program in 1949,[3] the US began to provide economic and technical assistance to Asia, Africa, Latin America and other developing regions. Meanwhile, the Soviet Union was the main provider of economic assistance to those in the socialist camp. All these marked the beginning of international development cooperation. In the early 1960s, the European economies that had recovered began joining the rest as donor countries. The western donor countries formed the DAC[4] within the framework of the OECD to coordinate foreign aid policies among various nations. The organization gradually evolved and became the advocates and developers of rules related to international development cooperation. From a multilateral perspective, the UN, WBG, and IMF were subsequently established

---

[2]The Marshall Plan, named after the then US Secretary of State George Marshall, is formally known as the European Recovery Program. It is the economic and reconstruction assistance program provided by the US to war-torn western European countries after World War II. The program started in July 1947 and lasted four fiscal years. The western European countries received financial, technological, equipment and other assistance amounting up to a total of USD1300 billion dollars from the US.

[3]The Point Four Program was a technical assistance program for "developing countries" announced by United States President Harry S. Truman in his inaugural address on January 20, 1949. It took its name from the fact that it was the fourth foreign policy objective mentioned in the speech.

[4]The OECD Development Assistance Committee became part of the OECD by Ministerial Resolution on 23 July 1961. It is a unique international forum of many of the largest funders of aid, including 29 DAC Members. The World Bank, IMF and UNDP participate as observers.

after the war and the multilateral development assistance system was gradually developed and improved. As external assistance from developed countries formed the mainstream of international development cooperation, and multilateral aid funds were also mainly derived from developed countries, the international development cooperation system and its related rules are mainly led and dominated by developed countries. Although South–South cooperation began and gradually developed from the 1950s onwards, it was of a small scale and it had a limited impact on the development of international development cooperation rules. Of course, the so-called international development cooperation rules were simply some consensus and practices shared by the developed donor countries and they were not mandatory — yet western donor countries tended to impose the rules on recipient countries.

Western developed countries provided continous development assistance to the developing countries to help them along the path of rapid economic development since the 1960s. Inspired by the success of the Marshall Plan and influenced by modernization theory, development assistance was regarded as an economic booster for developing countries during that era. Recipient countries used the financial assistance to promote industrial development and economic growth, but the effects were not obvious. With the exception of a few countries, not only did the development gap between the developing and developed countries not shrink on the whole, it even expanded. In the 1970s, poverty was severe among the developing countries and one of the worst famines in history took place in Africa. Driven by the WBG and UN, the focus of international development cooperation turned towards extreme poverty, and aid resources were mainly invested in agricultural production, basic education, public health, rural roads, and drinking water. In the 1980s, due to missteps in development strategies and the impact of the oil crisis, many developing countries fell into serious debt crises. Western donor countries, the WBG, IMF and other multilateral aid agencies began launching economic structural adjustment reforms focused mainly on economic privatization, tariff reduction, public expenditure, and reduction of fiscal subsidies *etc.* in developing countries, and raised these as conditions for providing assistance. As the structural adjustment programs departed too far from the basic national conditions of the developing countries, many of these countries paid heavy economic and social costs. For example, the national industries suffered, food production decreased, citizens' income levels fell, and education, healthcare and other social benefits dropped dramatically while unemployment remained high. The structural adjustment programs continued into the 1990s and generally failed, thereby exacerbating the plight of the developing countries. According to WBG statistics, the per capita gross national product of sub-Saharan African LDCs fell from USD640 in the early 1980s to USD510 in the early 1990s; the gap with developed countries grew from 16.3:1 to 51.7:1.[5] In the 1990s, as the Cold War ended, the competitive factors[6] in international assistance diminished. The people of donor countries also began to doubt the effectiveness of providing assistance, thus the so-called developed countries began to experience "aid fatigue", and official development assistance continually declined. With the advance of globalization, the wealth gap between developing and developed countries continues to expand.

On the whole, Western ODA, which lasted nearly half a century, achieved some success. In the fields of social development such as health, basic education *etc.* the effect was significant. For example, the average life expectancy of people in developing countries has greatly increased and illiteracy rates have been cut by more than half. However, in terms of helping developing countries achieve economic modernization and poverty reduction, the result has been far from satisfactory. Apart from a few countries (such as Korea), which have achieved rapid economic development through international assistance and their own efforts, the majority of developing countries have not shown expected growth despite receiving years of international development assistance. In the early 21st century, 4/5 of the world's population still lived in developing countries. Among the six billion people on the globe, 2.8 billion live on less than USD2 a day, among whom 1.2 billion earn less than USD1 a day. Several developing countries, especially the sub-Saharan African countries that received the most assistance, are still experiencing slow, stagnant or even regressive economic growth. Poverty continues to rise and development assistance has not helped, and sometimes, even makes the situation worse.[7] Such phenomenon has drawn international attention to the effectiveness of assistance.

The international community generally believes that the main reason for ineffective assistance is the serious shortage of investment in development assistance and some unfair and unreasonable rules in international development cooperation. As early as in 1970, the United Nations had requested that developed countries increase ODA to at least 0.7% of each country's gross

---

[5] According to data released by the World Bank.

[6] After World War II, due to the needs of the Cold War, the US used development assistance as a means to compete with the Soviet Union for greater influence over developing countries. After the Cold War, international development assistance lost its political power and drive.

[7] Ian Goldin, Halsey Rogers, and Nicholas Stern, "The Role and Effectiveness of Development Assistance: Lessons from World Bank Experience," *The World Bank Research Paper*, March 2002.

national income (GNI), and it has repeatedly reiterated this request. However, most developed countries have not achieved this goal. From 1961 to 2000, although total ODA expenditure of DAC member states rose from USD40 billion to USD80 billion, the proportion of ODA in GNI fell from 0.5% to 0.22%. In a sense, developed countries have not been able to follow the critical rule of ensuring scale of assistance.

In addition, when western developed countries provided development assistance, they were influenced by the Cold War mentality and driven by the need to safeguard their own political and commercial interests. As a result, they developed a series of inappropriate and unreasonable rules and imposed them upon the recipient countries. Firstly, the development and implementation of international development cooperation programs, whether at the national or international level, were dominated and directed by the developed countries — with limited participation by the recipient countries. Western countries generally developed foreign assistance programs based on abstract Western development theories and their own developmental experience without taking the recipient countries' basic national conditions and development conditions into account. As a result, the execution of development assistance was not suitable for the receiving countries, achieved little success and at times, was even counterproductive. Furthermore, development assistance easily led to recipient countries becoming dependent on donor countries; it suppressed the autonomy of recipient countries and made it impossible for the recipient country to independently formulate development strategies that were more suitable for their national conditions. Secondly, when providing assistance, developed countries and multilateral organizations usually attach certain conditions that give them some leeway to interfere with the internal affairs of the recipient countries, such as the implementation of Western-style democracy or economic structural reforms *etc.* The ownership and wishes of the recipient countries are often not respected. To make matters worse, some Western countries take advantage of the situation by attaching conditions to influence or control domestic and foreign affairs of developing countries, seeking their own interests at the expense of the recipient countries.[8] Third, the developed countries consider their own economic interests above that of the recipient countries and provided a great amount of "tied aid", *i.e.* when a recipient country receives assistance, it has to purchase goods and services from

---

[8] Huang Meibo and Tang Luping, "Foreign Assistance: South–South Cooperation and North–South Assistance," *International Outlook*, Issue 3, 2013.

the donor country. Such methods of providing assistance hinder the recipient countries' economic development and self-development capabilities.[9]

Western countries claim that the developing countries account for the ineffectiveness of development aid. Western countries tend to believe that the governments of many developing countries are poor in governing, corrupt, and have poor institutional capabilities and these are the reasons for low aid effectiveness. Driven by the DAC, Western countries have also begun conducting internal reviews of their approaches in providing assistance. In 1996, DAC published a report entitled "The Role of Development Cooperation in Shaping the 21st Century". The report summarized the achievements and experiences of ODA since World War II and also pointed out the main problems that existed with Western aid.[10] The report initially put forward concepts of aid effectiveness, and emphasized that international development cooperation modes should shift from being donor-centered to recipient-centered.

1.2 *The impact of the United Nations Millennium Development Goals on international development cooperation*

Faced with the grim state of development of human society in September 2009, the UN held its Millennium Summit and the 189 member states adopted the "Millennium Declaration". The "Millennium Declaration" set a series of specific objectives, collectively known as the "Millennium Development Goals", for human economic and social development over the next 15 years. The Millennium Development Goals include eight major areas: eradicating extreme poverty and hunger; ensuring universal primary education; promoting gender equality and empowerment of women; reducing child mortality rates; improving maternal health; continuing the fight against AIDS, malaria and other diseases; ensuring environmental sustainability; and strengthening global cooperation to promote development. Under the eight overall goals, there are 18 specific objectives and 48 quantitative indicators. Most of these targets were set with 1990 as the base year and 2015 as the deadline for completion. The

---

[9] In 2001, the DAC adopted an initiative, calling for member states to stop providing "tied aid" to the LDCs.

[10] These problems include recipient countries' low participation and dependence on assistance, insufficient long-term assistance, excessive aid conditions, lack of effective coordination among donors. Refer to DAC, "Shaping the 21st Century: The Contribution of Development Cooperation," OECD, May 1996.

Millennium Development Goals marked the first time a specific, systematic, time-bound target system was put forward to resolve global developmental problems. To date, it is the greatest collective effort by the international community to address developmental issues.

The Millennium Development Goals had a significant impact on the international development cooperation system. First, helping developing countries achieve the Millennium Development Goals became the mid- to long-term objective for international development cooperation. The main focus of international development cooperation returned to poverty reduction. Secondly, the areas covered by Millennium Development Goals such as poverty reduction, basic education, basic healthcare, safe drinking water, environmental sustainability *etc.* became the focal areas of international development cooperation. Finally, the Millennium Development Goals set specific requirements on international development cooperation. For example, the eighth objective proposed that developed countries had to help developing countries (particularly the LDCs, landlocked countries and small-island developing states) achieve the first seven specific objectives by increasing development assistance, improving market access and reducing debts. It can be said that the Millennium Development Goals provided a new policy framework for international development cooperation, as well as promoted and guided the reform and restructuring of international development cooperation rules.

1.3 *The formation of new rules for international development cooperation*

In the 21st century, a vast number of developing countries called for changes to be made to unreasonable rules of international development cooperation so that their ownership is respected, and political and economic conditions attached to assistance be reduced. Particularly after the UN Millennium Development Goals were rolled out, much attention was drawn to the effectiveness of international development cooperation. The international community realized that for international development cooperation to effectively promote the Millennium Development Goals, there was an urgent need to resolve two issues: Firstly, development funds had to be increased to turn the long-term decline in ODA around; secondly, the existing rules of assistance had to undergo major reform to enhance the effectiveness of development assistance. As such, the international community conducted in-depth discussions on the two issues and pushed for a consensus to be reached on new rules for international development cooperation.

1.3.1 *The "Monterrey Consensus" on finance for development*

In March 2002, the United Nations held a conference on finance for development in Monterrey, Mexico and adopted the "Monterrey Consensus of the International Conference on Financing for Development". At the meeting, participants recognized the huge lack of capital for achieving the Millennium Development Goals and acknowledged that all possible domestic and international resources should be actively deployed towards development. For many African countries, LDCs, small-island developing states and landlocked developing countries, ODA was still their largest source of foreign capital and crucial to their implementation of the development goals in the "Millennium Declaration". Therefore, ODA had to be greatly augmented. The "Monterrey Consensus" urged developed countries to make specific effort to allocate 0.7% of their GNI as ODA for developing countries, and give 0.15%–0.2% of their GNI to LDCs so as to help them achieve their Millennium Development Goals. At the same time, the "Monterrey Consensus" called for measures that would enhance aid effectiveness, and requested that donor countries provide assistance according to the developmental needs and goals of recipient countries, increase recipient countries' participation in assistance programs and reduce assistance administrative costs, relieve the bondages on assistance (*i.e.* remove business conditions for assistance), and strengthen assistance policy coordination and evaluation of results.

1.3.2 *The Paris Declaration on Aid Effectiveness*

In February 2003, the OECD and WBG jointly organized the inaugural high-level forum on aid effectiveness in Rome. The participants mainly discussed how coordination between donor countries could be enhanced so as to increase aid effectiveness. After the forum, more than 40 multilateral aid organizations and 28 recipient countries adopted the "Rome Declaration on Harmonization" together.

In March 2005, the second high-level forum on aid effectiveness was held in Paris. High-level representatives from 91 countries and 39 multilateral development agencies and NGOs gathered together to discuss aid effectiveness measures and new rules for raising the quality of aid. The "Paris Declaration on Aid Effectiveness" (hereinafter referred to as "Paris Declaration") was adopted as a result of the meeting. The "Paris Declaration" proposed major reforms with regard to provision and management of assistance, and emphasized partnerships between donor and recipient countries so as to work together towards poverty reduction and sustainable development. In the "Paris Declaration", participating donors (including donor countries and multilateral development agencies) and recipients made five commitments for improving aid effectiveness.

Ownership

Partner countries commit to exercise leadership in developing and implementing their national development strategies through broad consultative processes...Take the lead in co-ordinating aid at all levels in conjunction with other development resources in dialogue with donors; donors commit to respect partner country leadership and help strengthen their capacity to exercise it...

Alignment

Donors commit to base their overall support — country strategies, policy dialogues and development co-operation programmes on partners' national development strategies and periodic reviews of progress in implementing these strategies...Partner countries commit to carry out diagnostic reviews that provide reliable assessments of country systems and procedures...Undertake reforms, such as public management reform, that may be necessary to launch and fuel sustainable capacity development processes...

Harmonization

Donors commit to implement, where feasible, common arrangements at country level for planning, funding (e.g. joint financial arrangements), disbursement, monitoring, evaluating and reporting to government on donor activities and aid flows ... Work together to reduce the number of separate, duplicative, missions to the field and diagnostic reviews...

Managing for Results

Partner countries commit to endeavour to establish results-oriented reporting and assessment frameworks that monitor progress against key dimensions of the national and sector development strategies; and that these frameworks should track a manageable number of indicators for which data are cost-effectively available...

Mutual Accountability

Donors and partners are accountable for development results. A major priority for partner countries and donors is to enhance mutual accountability and transparency in the use of development resources...

Twelve quantitative evaluation indicators based on the above-mentioned principles were stated in the "Paris Declaration". The goals to be achieved by 2010 were also set (see Table 13.1).

The "Paris Declaration" established a new code of conduct for international development cooperation, and together with the Millennium Development Goals and the "Monterrey Consensus", formed the new international development cooperation policy and rules framework, jointly guiding the new era of international development cooperation. Developed countries, multilateral development organizations, and developing countries have begun adjusting and reforming the relevant policies with regard to the provision and receipt of development assistance, so as to implement and fulfill the commitments they made in the "Paris Declaration". With the joint efforts of the international community, after several years of decline, the ODA rose from USD80 billion in 2000 to a record high of USD123 billion in 2005.

2 Evolution of International Development Cooperation Rules since the Economic Crisis

Just as international development cooperation embarked on the right track — where there was substantial growth in assistance funds and aid effectiveness began being taken seriously — a financial crisis that originated from the developed countries spread rapidly from the Western world across the globe. The financial crisis hit the economic and social development of developing countries severely, and also had far-reaching implications for international development cooperation. The inadequacy of developed countries in international development cooperation and the vigorous development of South–South cooperation brought about changes in international development cooperation and also contributed to the further evolution of relevant rules of international development cooperation.

Table 13.1 Twelve Indicators of Progress in the "Paris Declaration".

Ownership	Target for 2010
1 *Partners have operational development strategies* — Number of countries with national development strategies (including PRSs) that have clear strategic priorities linked to a medium-term expenditure framework and reflected in annual budgets.	**At least 75% of partner countries** have operational development strategies.
Alignment	
2 *Reliable country systems* — Number of partner countries that have procurement and public financial management systems that either (a) adhere to broadly accepted good practices or (b) have a reform programme in place to achieve these.	(a) **Public financial management** — Half of partner countries move up at least one measure (*i.e.*, 0.5 points) on the PFM/ CPIA (Country Policy and Institutional Assessment) scale of performance.
	(b) **Procurement** — One-third of partner countries move up at least one measure (*i.e.*, from D to C, C to B or B to A) on the four-point scale used to assess performance for this indicator.
3 *Aid flows are aligned on national priorities* — Percent of aid flows to the government sector that is reported on partners' national budgets.	**Halve the gap** — halve the proportion of aid flows to government sector not reported on government's budget(s) (with at least 85% reported on budget).
4 *Strengthen capacity by co-ordinated support* — Percent of donor capacity-development support provided through co-ordinated programmes consistent with partners' national development strategies.	**50% of technical co-operation flows** are implemented through co-ordinated programmes consistent with national development strategies.

Table 13.1 (*Continued*)

	Percentage of donors	
5a *Use of country public financial management systems* — Percent of donors and of aid flows that use public financial management systems in partner countries, which either (a) adhere to broadly accepted good practices or (b) have a reform program in place to achieve these.	**Target**	**Score***
	All donors use partner countries' PFM systems.	5+
	90% of donors use partner countries' PFM systems.	3.5 to 4.5

	Percentage of aid flows	
	Target	**Score***
	A two-thirds reduction in the % of aid to the public sector not using partner countries' PFM systems.	5+
	A one-third reduction in the % of aid to the public sector not using partner countries' PFM systems.	3.5 to 4.5

	Percentage of donors	
5b *Use of country procurement systems* — Percent of donors and of aid flows that use partner country procurement systems which either (a) adhere to broadly accepted good practices or (b) have a reform program in place to achieve these.	**Target**	**Score***
	All donors use partner countries' procurement systems.	A
	90% of donors use partner countries' procurement systems.	B

	Percentage of aid flows	
	Target	**Score***
	A two-thirds reduction in the % of aid to the public sector not using partner procurement systems.	A
	A one-third reduction in the % of aid to the public sector not using partner countries' procurement systems.	B

(*Continued*)

Table 13.1 *(Continued)*

6 *Strengthen capacity by avoiding parallel implementation structures* — Number of parallel project implementation units (PIUs) per country.	**Reduce by two-thirds** the stock of parallel project implementation units (PIUs).
Alignment	
7 *Aid is more predictable* — Percent of aid disbursements released according to agreed schedules in annual or multi-year frameworks.	**Halve the gap** halve the proportion of aid not disbursed within the fiscal year for which it was scheduled.
8 *Aid is untied* — Percent of bilateral aid that is untied.	**Continued progress over time.**
Harmonization	
9 *Use of common arrangements or procedures* — Percent of aid provided as programme-based approaches.	**66% of aid flows** are provided in the context of programme-based approaches.
10 *Encourage shared analysis* — Percent of (a) field missions and/ or (b) country analytic work, including diagnostic reviews that are joint.	(a) **40% of donor missions** to the field are joint. (b) **66% of country analytic work is joint.**
Managing for results	
11 *Results-oriented frameworks* — Number of countries with transparent and monitorable performance assessment frameworks to assess progress against (a) the national development strategies and (b) sector programs.	**Reduce the gap by one-third** — Reduce the proportion of countries without transparent and monitorable performance assessment frameworks by one-third.

Table 13.1 (*Continued*)

Mutual accountability

Mutual accountability	
12 **Mutual accountability** — Number of partner countries that undertake mutual assessments of progress in implementing agreed commitments on aid effectiveness including those in this Declaration.	**All partner countries** have mutual assessment reviews in place.

Important Note: In accordance with paragraph 9 of the Declaration, the partnership of donors and partner countries hosted by the DAC (Working Party on Aid Effectiveness) comprising OECD/DAC members, partner countries and multilateral institutions, met twice, on 30–31 May 2005 and on 7–8 July 2005 to adopt, and review where appropriate, the targets for the twelve Indicators of Progress. At these meetings an agreement was reached on the targets presented under Section III of the present Declaration. This agreement is subject to reservations by one donor on (a) the methodology for assessing the quality of locally-managed procurement systems (relating to targets 2b and 5b) and (b) the acceptable quality of public financial management reform program (relating to target 5a.ii). Further discussions are underway to address these issues. The targets, including the reservation, have been notified to the Chairs of the High-level Plenary Meeting of the 59th General Assembly of the United Nations in a letter of 9 September 2005 by Mr. Richard Manning, Chair of the OECD Development Assistance Committee (DAC).

*Note on Indicator 5: Scores for Indicator 5 are determined by the methodology used to measure quality of procurement and public financial management systems under Indicator 2 above.

Source: The Paris Declaration.

2.1 *The international financial crisis accelerated the process of diversification of aid*

In 2008, the financial crisis which erupted from the West quickly evolved into a global economic crisis. It dealt a serious blow to the development of developing countries, particularly the low-income countries. Firstly, global trade experienced the most severe decline since the Great Depression, when export commodity prices in developing countries fell significantly, resulting in a substantial drop in income. Secondly, there was a sharp decrease in capital flows to developing countries. Since 2003, net capital flows to developing countries had maintained an upward trend, reaching USD1.222 trillion in 2007 but in 2008, it suddenly plummeted 36% to USD780 billion. Due to the combined effect of the above factors, poverty in developing countries was exacerbated, and public education and health levels dropped significantly. In 2008, economic growth in developing countries dropped from 8.8% in the previous year to 6.1% and further declined in 2009 to 2.7%.[11] Evidently, the economic crisis made the development problems even more pressing. In addition, since 2007, food and energy crises broke out in developing countries, and natural disasters caused by global climate change also increased significantly. The combined impact made it even more difficult for developing countries, especially LDCs, to achieve their Millennium Development Goals.

The outbreak and spread of the international financial crisis made development assistance seem all the more important for developing countries. After the crisis broke out, the UN, WBG and other international organizations continuously appealed to donors not to cut budgets for foreign assistance. At the DAC ministerial meeting held in May 2009, developed donor countries stated that they would overcome the pressure brought about by the financial crisis and continue to honor the ODA commitments they made previously. ODA was USD120 billion in 2008 and by 2010 had hit a record high of USD128 billion. Nevertheless, donor countries have not been able to fulfill their previous commitments.[12] In addition, in 2005, 15 DAC EU member states committed to achieving 0.51% ODA/GNI by 2010 yet only eight countries managed to

---

[11] Refer to IMF, "World Economic Outlook," April 16, 2013; retrieved from http://www.imf.org/external/pubs/cat/longres.aspx?sk=40201.

[12] At the 2005 G8 Summit held in Gleneagles, donor countries pledged to increase ODA annually to reach USD130 billion by 2010 (calculated according to 2004 rates), yet according to comparable USD Rates in 2010, the actual increase in ODA was less than that committed by USD19 billion.

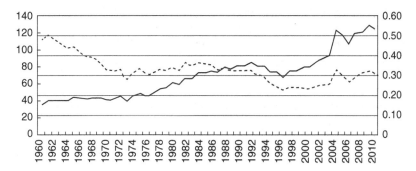

Figure 13.1   1960–2011 net ODA from DAC countries.

Source: DAC, "2012 Development Cooperation Report," calculated according to 2010 constant USD prices.

Note: The solid line represents net ODA, Unit: USD 1 billion; the dotted line represents ODA/GNI percentage (unit: %).

honor their commitments. With the further development of the global economic crisis, particularly the outbreak and spread of the debt crisis, the assistance budgets of developed countries began to be increasingly constrained by national austerity policies. Instead of growing, ODA began to decrease. In 2011, DAC member countries gave a net amount of USD125 billion of ODA, declining 2.7% as compared to 2010. In 2012, the amount dropped by another 3.9%, of which bilateral assistance in sub-Saharan African countries fell by 7.9% (see Figure 13.1).[13]

As North–South cooperation declined in scale, South-South cooperation grew rapidly and international development cooperation began to diversify. Since the beginning of the new century, China, India, Brazil, South Africa and other emerging economies have continued to increase spending on foreign assistance (see Table 13.2). In this economic crisis, the impact on emerging economies was relatively small. After the crisis broke out, they increased foreign assistance considerably. This was a stark contrast to the constrained assistance budgets of the developed countries. In addition, various organizations such as NGOs, private enterprises, philanthropic institutions *etc.* have actively been involved in development assistance. Their contribution to global development assistance is gradually growing.

The diversification of aid organizations, especially the continued expansion of foreign assistance from China and other emerging economies, has impacted the traditional international development cooperation system.

---

[13] According to data from OECD website.

Table 13.2 The BRICS' net ODA contribution (USD billions).

	2005	2006	2007	2008	2009	2010
Brazil	0.158	0.277	0.292	0.337	0.362	—
China	0.912	1.033	1.467	1.808	1.948	2.011
India	0.415	0.381	0.394	0.610	0.488	0.639
Russia	0.101	0.102	0.211	0.22	0.785	0.472
South Africa	0.042	0.049	0.085	0.089	0.120	0.094

Source: OECD/DAC website.

Note: China's figures are obtained according to the foreign aid fiscal accounts for the year converted into USD, as published on the Chinese Ministry of Finance website, but this does not include China Export-Import Bank's concessional loans disbursement. The rest of the data are DAC estimates, except for the 2010 Russian figures that Russia reported to DAC.

First of all, the absolute dominance of developed countries in the international development cooperation system has been challenged. According to WBG estimates, in 2009, assistance funds provided by donors other than DAC countries reached USD63.5 billion, accounting for 34% of total international development assistance. Furthermore, in the past decade, the proportion of ODA in total incoming assistance funds to recipient countries dropped significantly, from 50% in the 1960s to 20% in recent years. The diversification of development finance channels gave recipient countries more opportunities for comparison and selection, and it showed that the domination of recipient countries' aid channels by Western countries is changing.

Secondly, the concept and rules of Western-led development assistance are under attack and South–South cooperation model has been widely welcomed. The unique assistance concepts of respecting the sovereignty of recipient countries and non-interference in the internal affairs of recipient countries *etc.* by China and other emerging economies are readily accepted by recipients. The ones who launched South–South cooperation are also developing countries thus there is a mutual understanding of each nation's stage of development and characteristics of their political and economic systems, making it easier to build a truly equal and mutually trusting partnership. Generally, South–South cooperation developed mutually beneficial cooperation considering the developmental needs of the recipient countries, emphasizing project assistance, technical cooperation and personnel training. It is highly focused, and the effect on poverty reduction and promotion of economic and social development is more evident.

Thirdly, the Western developmental theories governing development assistance have been challenged. The development experience of emerging economies, particularly China, has drawn widespread attention of other developing countries, and has set off a "Look East" trend in the African countries. Many developing countries no longer referred to the "Washington Consensus" when developing their national development strategies and programs. Instead, they looked to and actively learned from the development experience of China, India and other emerging economies. This has, to a certain extent, shaken the dominance of Western development concepts in the international development cooperation system.

2.2 The establishment of "Global Partnership for Effective Development Cooperation"

As international development cooperation diversifies, the rules of international development cooperation have also diversified correspondingly. In particular, China's independent foreign assistance policy had a strong impact on Western-led international development cooperation. Western countries felt that the "aid effectiveness" rules built upon traditional North–South cooperation were not adaptable to new development trends. For this reason, Western countries began promoting the principles of aid effectiveness in South–South cooperation and other forms of development cooperation, and gradually established a framework for Global Partnership for Effective Development Cooperation, unifying the various forms of development cooperation. The rules of aid effectiveness further evolved to become "rules of effective development".

2.2.1 "Accra Agenda for Action"

In September 2008, the Third High-level Forum on Aid Effectiveness was held in Accra, Ghana. At the meeting, a mid-term assessment on the implementation of the "Paris Declaration" was conducted where it was stated that the "Paris Declaration" did make some progress such as improvements in the management of public funds by many developing countries, and donor countries have gradually strengthened the coordination of assistance. However, it was also concluded that the pace of implementation was too slow and reform had not progressed sufficiently. The "Accra Agenda for Action" (AAA) was adopted at the meeting. The AAA suggested that implementation of the "Paris Declaration" be accelerated, and that the relevant principles of the "Paris Declaration" be further developed and refined at the same time. First, it advocated strengthening the ownership of developing countries. Donor countries ought to make maximum use of the recipient countries' systems to implement assistance projects. Also, governments of developing countries should work closely with parliaments, local governments and civic organizations when formulating national development policies, as well as implementing and monitoring national development plans. Second, it called for more effective and inclusive development partnerships. Donors should improve the division of labor, reduce project overlaps, and lower management costs. Donor countries ought to make greater efforts to promote the progress of untying aid. The AAA recognized the modalities and characteristics of the South–South cooperation for the first time and considered the South–South cooperation a useful complement to the North–South cooperation. It also welcomed the diversification of assistance bodies, particularly the civil society organizations (CSO), and encouraged all development assistance participants to refer to the relevant principles in the "Paris Declaration" when implementing development cooperation. Third, it focused on development results. Both donors and recipients ought to enhance transparency, conduct mutual assessments and evaluations, be mutually accountable for development results and at the same time, be responsible to their citizens. Donors should increase aid predictability, and provide three to five years' worth of assistance funds and implementation plans to developing countries.

2.2.2 *The establishment of Global Partnership for Effective Development Cooperation*

With the further development of the global economic crisis, developed countries began to feel that it was becoming more and more difficult for them to dominate the international development cooperation. At the same time, the flourishing of the South–South cooperation brought unprecedented challenges for the developed countries. They believed that the promotion of the aid effectiveness principle only in the traditional North–South cooperation system would achieve a limited effect, and that efforts ought to be made to include South–South cooperation and other forms of development cooperation in the system of development assistance they led. The developed countries used two main approaches to reach and influence South–South cooperation. The first approach was to develop exchanges. Since 2007, the US, EU, Britain, France, Australia, Japan, and other countries have requested for exchanges with China in the field of development assistance, and also included the issues of development assistance as important issues for dialogue on high-level bilateral visits. In the exchanges and dialogues, Western countries strongly recommend the concepts of aid effectiveness and principles of the "Paris Declaration". OECD named China, India, Brazil, South Africa and Indonesia, the five emerging economies, as its "Enhanced Engagement Nations" and repeatedly invited them to participate as observers in high-level development cooperation meetings. In April 2011, DAC held a high-level meeting and adopted the suggestions put forth in the report, "Welcoming New Partnerships in International Development Cooperation". The report recognized the important role played by several non-member countries in international development assistance, and DAC welcomed their participation, and hoped to established contact with these new partners through open dialogue to share experiences in development assistance and look into launching development cooperation. Secondly, they began tripartite assistance cooperation and influenced South–South cooperation practically. As some developing countries such as Brazil, South Africa, Mexico, Chile, Malaysia, and Columbia did not have a long history of conducting development cooperation, they had limited assistance funds and were more positive about the suggestion of tripartite cooperation. China also held an open attitude when exploring development assistance cooperation with some Western countries.

In order to integrate South–South cooperation and other forms of non-traditional development cooperation with the Western-led North–South cooperation rules system as quickly as possible, developed countries hoped to reach a consensus with the various parties at the new High-Level Forum on Aid Effectiveness in 2011 to apply aid effectiveness principles to all forms of development cooperation and on this basis, establish a global partnership for development. Thus, the scene described at the beginning of this chapter took place.

Actually, before the forum, parties had already begun consultations on the outcome documents. OECD especially set up a consultative group for this purpose. As China, India and other countries clearly did not agree with content such as the nature and obligations of South–South cooperation as well as the acceptance of the same monitoring and evaluation criteria as the developed countries, the parties were unable to reach an agreement on the outcome document. At the Busan meeting, the consultative group, developed countries and China, India *etc.* conducted several rounds of discussions on the draft. Finally, the revised draft jointly proposed by China and India was accepted. "The Busan

Partnership for Effective Development Co-operation" (henceforth referred to as the "Busan Partnership") was adopted at the meeting. The outcome of the "Busan Partnership" mainly reflected in the following aspects:

(1) A final evaluation was conducted on the progress of aid effectiveness since the "Paris Declaration". The DAC had been evaluating the implementation of the "Paris Declaration" from 2007 until the end of 2011. The assessment included 22 recipient countries and 18 donor countries. The assessment report noted that the five principles and 56 commitments of the "Paris Declaration" were pragmatic and after being implemented, development cooperation improved in quality and the relationship between aid partners also tightened. Compared to 20 years earlier, donor countries intervene much less in the process of implementation of assistance, and aid practices are also more transparent. However, the implementation of the principles of aid effectiveness is "neither fast nor far-reaching enough". Out of the 12 quantitative assessment indicators, only two items, the strengthening of coordination and untying aid, achieved the targets set. The others items saw varying degrees of progress. The "Busan Partnership" called on the parties to make every effort to reach a consensus on the implementation of aid effectiveness.

(2) The concept of "aid effectiveness" was expanded to the "effectiveness of development cooperation". The "Busan Partnership" pointed out that assistance can only play a limited part in solving development issues. Developing countries' own revenue can play a greater role in satisfying their developmental needs. For this reason, the strengthening of developing countries' key departmental mechanisms and institutional construction must be supported. Necessary reform measures should also be undertaken so as to more effectively mobilize resources and provide services. Besides enhancing the effectiveness of development assistance, measures should also be taken to raise a variety of funding sources including tax collection, domestic funds, private investment, aid for trade, charitable funds, non-concessional public funding and climate change funds *etc.* so as to promote sustainable and inclusive development.

(3) A global partnership for effective Development Cooperation was established. The "Busan Partnership" pointed out that the current development cooperation framework is more complex than before. There are many parties involved — South–South cooperation, tripartite cooperation, public–private sector cooperation as well as other development cooperation modes are becoming increasingly prominent, complementing North–South

cooperation model. As such, it is necessary to build a new, inclusive "Global Partnership for Effective Development Co-operation" (referred to as "GPEDC"). This partnership is built based on the principles of a common goal and sharing. The common goal is to achieve sustainable development. The principle of sharing covers four aspects: First, developing countries enjoy the ownership to prioritize national development. Development partnerships are led by developing countries and implementation methods must correspond with specific national conditions and development needs; second, it is results-oriented. Development assistance must have a far-reaching impact on eradicating poverty and reducing inequality, promoting sustainable development and strengthening the capabilities of developing countries *etc.*, and should be consistent with the development priorities and policies set by developing countries; third, there is inclusive development partnership. Partnerships are based on openness, trust, mutual respect and mutual learning, recognition that there are differences between the various bodies yet they play complementary roles; fourth, transparency and mutual accountability. Development partners are mutually accountable to each other, and also to the beneficiaries of development cooperation, the citizens of their respective countries and relevant organizations.

(4) The nature of South–South cooperation and the development responsibilities assumed were clarified. The Busan conference discussed South–South cooperation in depth, recognized the nature, modalities and responsibilities of South–South cooperation as different from those of North–South cooperation, but at the same time, expressed that South–South cooperation and North–South cooperation could promote effective international development cooperation based on the principles of common objectives and sharing. The countries involved in South–South cooperation could make differentiated commitments according to their national circumstances. South–South cooperation could also voluntarily refer to the document of Bushan Forum agreed in the outcome.

After the Busan Forum, the OECD formed the "Working Group for Following Through after the Busan Forum" which lasted for six months. The group was formed to drive the official launch of GPEDC. In July 2012, the GPEDC was officially in operation and strove to become the new international mechanism for the development and coordination of international development cooperation policies and rules. It was also interested in working together with the UN and G20 to form the basic platforms for the global governance in development cooperation. Compared to the aid effectiveness, the GPEDC was aimed at establishing a multilateral platform at a higher level, and being more compatible and more institutionalized.

2.3 *Reflections on the rules of international development cooperation*

Since the beginning of the new century, the international community has worked hard on the two aspects of financing development and increasing aid effectiveness to facilitate the achievement of the Millennium Development Goals. At the Rome Conference, the agenda of enhancing aid effectiveness was explored. At the Paris conference, the five basic principles were established and at the Accra conference, they were refined. Then at the Busan Conference, the issue evolved into development effectiveness and the framework of global partnership for effective development cooperation was established. The relevant rules continue to be developed and improved upon. It can be said that the "Paris Declaration", the "Accra Agenda for Action (AAA)", and the "Busan Declaration" have become the bases and framework documents for today's international development cooperation. Developing countries have actively participated in previous aid effectiveness forums. In particular, China, India and other emerging economies have played a positive role, prompting for amendments and adjustments to be made to traditional developmental assistance rules in outcome documents. Some of the fundamental concerns of developing countries have been taken seriously into account.

Firstly, the principles of aid effectiveness emphasize the ownership and leadership of recipient countries in national development strategies as well as in the execution and coordination of external aid. This is the most significant progress and reconstruction that new principles have made to traditional rules, changing the long-running passive receiving condition of developing countries, and has a certain deterrent effect on the way developed countries compel recipient countries to accept Western development concepts. At the same time, it has also improved the ability of recipient countries to set their own development strategies. Developing countries have made significant progress in setting national development strategies and improving the standards of governmental management. African countries, especially, have greatly grown in their ability to lead national development and have effectively promoted economic development. In recent years, six out of 10 of the world's fastest growing economies are African nations. From 2002 to 2010, the average economic growth of Africa was 5.5%. Africa was also one of the few regions of the world that demonstrated great resilience in the face of the global economic crisis. Secondly, the principles of aid effectiveness stress that donor countries reduce the commercial conditions tied to assistance, "untied" assistance to a great extent, helping to increase the autonomy of recipient countries in procurement, effectively decreasing the costs of assistance projects and raising the effectiveness of aid funds. Moreover, aid effectiveness principles emphasize the results of providing aid, the planning and predictability of aid, and stress the evaluation of results. These rules help to increase the relevance and effectiveness of aid. Lastly, aid effectiveness principles have gradually grown in recognition of the diversity of aid organizations, particularly affirming the importance of South–South cooperation in international development cooperation, recognizing the beneficial and complementary nature of various types of development cooperation, including South–South cooperation, to traditional North–South cooperation. This helps to mobilize more resources for development assistance. At the same time, it promotes the diversification of methods of international development cooperation and democratization of international development cooperation rules.

However, the aid effectiveness agenda has always been dominated by developed countries, and reflects more of the ideas of developed countries. Although developing countries participate actively, their voice and influence is still limited, most of the rules are still developed by the developed countries. Therefore, there are still many limitations and controversies in the general application of the rules, which are mainly manifested in the following areas:

(1) The situation of developed countries interfering in the internal affairs of aid recipient countries through aid providing remains fundamentally unchanged.

The "Paris Declaration" advocates that recipient countries have greater autonomy in the use of aid resources, and that donor countries ought to utilize the systems of the recipient countries in implementing aid projects as far as possible, yet requires that recipient countries take reform measures with the "help" of donor countries, and improve governance. Donor countries also participate in evaluating the improvement of governance of recipient countries. In this sense, developed donor countries have not transferred development assistance leadership unreservedly to recipient countries. In practice, some major Western countries have never stopped using assistance as a means of interference in the internal affairs of recipient countries and often pressurize "disobedient" developing countries.

(2) Principles of aid effectiveness do not emphasize the importance of the amount of assistance strongly enough.

In discussions on development assistance at various international forums, the developing countries are most concerned about whether developed countries are able to honor their aid commitments, when the provided assistance can reach 0.7% of donor countries' GNI, the target scale and amount advocated and called for by the UN. However, developed countries have always taken an evasive attitude towards this issue. Outcome documents of aid effectiveness forums do not pay enough attention to increasing the scale of assistance and no targets or deadlines for meeting the goals have been set. Since 2005, the proportion of ODA has hovered around 0.3% of developed donor countries' GNI, way below the 0.7% goal set by the UN.

Since the international economic crisis, developed countries' motivation to honor aid commitments and increase development aid has diminished. In the Busan Forum on Aid Effectiveness the developed countries proposed the concept of development effectiveness, to reduce the role of development assistance, and stressed the importance of recipient countries using domestic financial resources to meet their own developmental requirements, requesting that middle-income countries assume more responsibility for development aid, stating that private capital should contribute more to development. In a way, this also reflected that the intent of the developed countries was to shirk and transfer the responsibilities of international development assistance.

(3) There is a lack of practical binding power.

The initiatives and rules put forward in the "Monterrey Consensus" or various declarations from aid effectiveness forums do not have any legal force and have no real binding power on the signatories. Thus, when implemented in the signatory country, the relevant aid effectiveness rules do not receive strong support from domestic politics and hence, progress slowly. Some indicators, in fact, show a reverse effect. For example, since 2005, aid administrative costs have not effectively lowered, the main reason is that although developed countries commit to "loosen" aid, they send a substantially large amount of soft assistance mainly in the form of experts, leading to expensive services, so as to offset the "loosening" effect. The Western countries overemphasize interference in the areas of governance and democracy, among others, in the recipient countries yet their investment in priority areas such as infrastructural construction and agricultural development *etc.* has continued to shrink. According to incomplete statistics, between 1985 and 2010, the proportion of ODA that Western countries allocate to infrastructure fell from 25%–30% to less than 15%, and ODA allocated to the agricultural sector dropped from 19% to 4%. This figure is sharply contrasted with the recurring food crises and famines in Africa in these years.

(4) The DAC and Western countries have been trying to apply aid effectiveness principles to South–South cooperation but the move has been questioned and resisted by India, Brazil, China and other emerging economies.

Emerging economies believe that aid effectiveness principles are focused on the characteristics of North–South cooperation. They mainly reflect the viewpoints of traditional donor countries, and several principles do not take into adequate consideration the characteristics of South–South cooperation. Neither are the concerns of the countries in South–South cooperation adequately reflected. Therefore, they are not applicable to South–South cooperation. Many developing countries, especially the emerging countries, expressed their doubts about the authority and representation of aid effectiveness principles. They note that the aid effectiveness agenda is not a UN agenda nor has it been authorized by the UN. As such, the principles of aid effectiveness do not bear universal significance. Some developing countries explicitly oppose the inclusion of principles of aid effectiveness in UN outcome documents.

3 Rules of International Development Cooperation and China's Foreign Aid Policy

China has participated in South–South cooperation for more than 60 years. Over the years, China has insisted on mutual respect, equality and mutual benefit to provide a variety of forms and flexible ways of economic and technical assistance without attaching any political condition. This is widely accepted by developing countries. Since entering the new century, China has committed to achieving economic and social development goals domestically while increasing foreign aid to actively promote the Millennium Development Goals globally. Moreover, China shows openness in extending foreign aid for international exchanges and actively participates in the reform of rules of international development cooperation, learning from the good practices of international development cooperation and constantly improving the mechanisms of its foreign aid management system to further increase the effectiveness of foreign aid. In the current context where the development cooperation is constantly infused together, China should seize the opportunities while the South is on the rise and the North is losing power in the international political and economic arena. China should be more proactive in South–South cooperation and promote the rules of international development cooperation towards fair, reasonable and practical development.

3.1 *China has actively participated in the process of reform of international development cooperation rules*

The early assistance discussion focuses on the effectiveness of traditional ways of assistance which is a problem that exists in North–South cooperation, and China's involvement in the early assistance discussion is limited. The second High-level Forum on Aid Effectiveness was held in Paris in 2005 and China sent its department and bureau delegates for the first time. At the conference, China only participated in the discussion as a recipient country and signed the "Paris Declaration". The "Paris Declaration" was not very pressurizing for China as a recipient country. China has done very well on the rules as a recipient country, reaching or even surpassing many indicators. Since the reform and opening up of China, the governance capabilities of Chinese authorities have continued to improve. China has effectively exercised owner-ship of international development assistance and used it scientifically in the economic and social development plan of the country, playing a good sup-porting role. The international community recognizes China as one of the most effective and successful developing countries in utilizing international development assistance.

With the rapid development of China's economy and increase of foreign aid, developed countries began to pay close attention to China's foreign aid policy and influence. In November 2006, during the Beijing Summit of Forum on China-Africa Cooperation, the Chinese government announced a package of measures to strengthen China-Africa development cooperation, causing a strong impact on the international community. Western donors and DAC began to strengthen dialogue and exchanges with China in the field of foreign aid, and invited China as an "emerging donor" to participate in the discussion on aid effectiveness. China did not acknowledge the name of "emerging donor" but agreed to participate in the discussion on aid effectiveness as a traditional South–South cooperation partner. In 2008, Chinese delegations participated in the third High-level Forum on "Aid Effectiveness in Accra". They took the initia-tive to coordinate viewpoints with big developing countries such as Brazil, India, South Africa, and Mexico, putting forward changes to the AAA and making it recognize the important position and uniqueness of South–South cooperation in international development cooperation. China further proposed several ideas for improving the aid effectiveness: Firstly, China agrees that developing countries should direct their domestic development. The donor assistance scheme should be consistent with the development strategies of developing countries so as to improve their independent development capabilities. Secondly, the key to ensuring aid effectiveness is to respect the wishes of developing countries and emphasize the different conditions of various countries without attaching political conditions. The satisfaction level of developing countries towards the aid is used as one of the basic standards of evaluation for aid effectiveness. Thirdly, aid effectiveness is determined according to the sufficiency of aid provided, and developed countries should earnestly fulfill their commitment to aid. Fourthly, the diversity of developmental aid organizations and diversification of assistance should be encouraged. This was the first time that the Chinese government fully expressed its views and opinions on the principles of aid effectiveness. During the Busan meeting in 2011, China and India joined efforts to enable the outcome document consultative group to accept a revised text from the two countries. China's efforts helped to maintain the independence of South–South cooperation and showed consideration for low-income countries. China has played a positive role to promote fair and reasonable rules of international development cooperation.

3.2 Impact of principles of aid effectiveness on China's foreign aid work

China began providing foreign aid in 1950. At the beginning, China only provided financial assistance to countries in the socialist camp like the Democratic People's Republic of Korea, Vietnam, Mongolia, and Albania and so on. Since the Bandung Conference in 1955,[14] China has actively supported and promoted South–South cooperation, and begun to extend a wide range of assistance to developing countries. The Chinese government has always attached great importance on the effectiveness of foreign aid. In 1964, the Chinese government put forward the famous eight principles of foreign economic and technical assistance to guide foreign aid. In the eight principles, much content is consistent with the principles of aid effectiveness in the "Paris Declaration", such as the first principle of "equality and mutual benefit" and the eighth principle of "equal treatment"

---

[14] In April 1955, the first Asian-African Conference was held in Bandung, Indonesia. Premier Zhou Enlai led the Chinese government delegation to attend the meeting. According to the "Final Communiqué of the Asian-African conference of Bandung", "The participating countries agreed to provide technical assistance to one another, to the maximum extent practicable".

Table 13.3 China's eight principles for economic aid and technical assistance to other countries (January 1964).

(1) The Chinese government always bases itself on the principle of equality and mutual benefit in providing aid to other countries. It never regards such aid as a kind of unilateral alms but as something mutual.

(2) In providing aid to other countries, the Chinese government strictly respects the sovereignty of recipient countries, and never attaches any conditions or asks for any privileges.

(3) China provides economic aid in the form of interest-free or low-interest loans, and extends the time limit for the repayment when necessary so as to lighten the burden on recipient countries as far as possible.

(4) In providing aid to other countries, the purpose of the Chinese government is not to make recipient countries dependent on China but to help them embark step-by-step on the road to self-reliance and independent economic development.

(5) The Chinese government does its best to help recipient countries complete projects which require less investment but yield quicker results, so that the latter may increase their income and accumulate capital.

(6) The Chinese government provides the best-quality equipment and materials manufactured by China at international market prices. If the equipment and materials provided by the Chinese government are not up to the agreed specifications and quality, the Chinese government undertakes the responsibility to replace them or refund the payment.

(7) In giving any particular technical assistance, the Chinese government will see to it that the personnel of the recipient country fully master the technology.

(8) The experts dispatched by China to help in construction in recipient countries will have the same standard of living as the experts of the recipient country. The Chinese experts are not allowed to make any special demands or enjoy any special amenities.

reflecting the true "partnership". The second principle, to "strictly respect the sovereignty of the recipient countries" embodies the first principle of the "Paris Declaration" — "the principle of ownership". The fifth principle, to "help projects which require less investment but yield quicker results" and the seventh principle, to "provide technical assistance by imparting the relevant technology fully" are consistent with the "principles of performance management" advocated in the "Paris Declaration" (see Table 13.3).

After the eight principles of China's foreign aid were put forward, they were widely welcomed by developing countries. Some countries even recommended that China propose these eight principles to the UN as the basis for countries to carry out economic and technical cooperation.[15] Over the years,

---

[15] Shi Lin (ed.) *Contemporary China's Foreign Economic Cooperation* (China: China Social Sciences Press, 1989), p. 44.

the eight principles have guided China's foreign aid practice, and they have been constantly developed and improved on. Some of these principles such as equality and mutual benefit, mutual respect, not attaching political conditions *etc.*, have become the general guiding principles for developing countries in launching South–South cooperation.

Clearly, the principles of China's foreign aid are mainly based on South–South cooperation practices, and are very different from the "Paris Declaration" which is based on the practices of North–South cooperation. One of the greatest differences is that the "Paris Declaration" advocates ownership in the recipient countries but sets western democracy, human rights and good governance as prerequisites at the same time, while the core principle of China's foreign aid is China does not attach political conditions to its foreign aid and does not interfere with the internal affairs of the recipient countries by means of foreign aid.

Some Western media have accused China of using the principle of providing aid without political conditions to support dictatorship, which goes against Western democracy and human rights, and objectively condone the corruption and bad governance of these governments. This accusation is neither fair nor valid. First, the UN Charter advocates the principle of mutual respect and non-interference in the internal affairs among countries. China is a responsible developing country and follows the five principles of peaceful coexistence that deal with relationships among countries, so it certainly cannot go against this principle when it provides external assistance. China is a global development partner and there are about 120 countries that often accept Chinese assistance. If one counts the number of officials and technical personnel from developing countries that come to China to participate in training, the number of countries that carries out economic and technical cooperation exceeds 170 and includes the vast majority of developing countries. When China started economic and technical cooperation in these countries, they were treated equally, in accordance with the principle of non-interference in internal affairs. Second, the understanding of China towards democracy, human rights and governance is very different from the West. Obviously, the Chinese government cannot judge the recipient government in accordance with Western standards of democracy and human rights. China believes that for developing countries, especially low-income developing countries, the right to survival is the most basic and important human right. The development assistance for meeting basic survival needs can be the most effective in low-income countries. Many low-income countries that need international development aid are at low level of democratization. For these countries, the increase in aid will not only improve the basic rights of people but also promote the progress of democracy. Third, China's assistance mainly applies to the people's livelihoods in areas such as agriculture, health, sanitation, and drilling of wells for water supply. The Chinese government generally does not provide aid directly to the recipient governments but assists the people in recipient countries directly through construction projects, delivery of supplies, training and other forms of assistance. In this way, corruption can be effectively prevented in the recipient countries. Meanwhile, China's provision of foreign aid follows the concept of "teaching them to fish instead of giving them fish". Experience sharing, personnel training, and capacity building are highly valued and these help to enhance the management level of recipient governments. Fourth, it is not that China does not care about human rights, democracy, and good governance of the recipient countries. In fact, besides using parliamentary and civilian channels to extend democratic rights and multilateral exchanges, China holds foreign aid seminars and workshops on themes like democracy, the governance philosophy, administration, anti-corruption and establishment of law to train a large number of government officials for developing countries every year.

After the "Paris Declaration", the "Accra Action Plan" and the "Busan Declaration" further promoted several approaches based on the practices of North–South cooperation, which are also different from China's existing foreign aid approaches. For example, in the "Paris Declaration", the recipient countries were required to implement the aid projects according to the management and procurement systems of the recipient countries as far as possible, *i.e.* recipient countries direct the implementation. Generally, China implements aid projects based on the requirements of recipient countries and the consensus reached by both parties. The projects will be transferred to the recipient countries after they are finished. The "Paris Declaration" and AAA require donor countries to include the development strategies of recipient countries in drafting and publishing long-term, predictable assistance programs. As China's foreign aid is limited in scale in the past years, the annual assistance plan is generally based on the temporary requirements of the recipient countries and progress of the project. Both the "Paris Declaration" and AAA stress the strengthening of collaboration and cooperation among donor countries to avoid assistance duplication, and advocate tripartite cooperation. China is used to determining aid projects by consulting with recipient countries directly. The Busan Declaration actively promoted the diversification of international development cooperation bodies, called for private sectors, civil society organizations and charitable institutions *etc.* to be involved in international development cooperation, and supported the development of innovative financing through public–private partnerships (PPP). At present, China's foreign aid projects are still mainly government-led. The main aid implementers and methods of implementation are not very diversified. It can be said that Western aid is large-scale, dominating mainstream international development cooperation for many years, and has also accumulated a lot of practical and effective experiences over the years. China can learn from some of these good experiences, such as the development of long-term development assistance plans and assistance programs that have a duration of three to five years for respective countries, the extensive use of non-governmental organizations (NGOs) to implement community poverty reduction and development projects, and the active execution of PPP *etc.*

With the evolution of international development cooperation and continuous growth in scale of foreign aid, China's existing management system and mechanism for foreign aid cannot cope with the new situation. China began to adjust and reform foreign aid management and implementation methods, and actively learn from the experience of Western countries, and take into account reasonable content of the "Paris Declaration" and AAA. In 2010, the Chinese government summed up the achievements of participating in foreign aid for 60 years and on this basis, proposed a series of specific measures to further strengthen and improve foreign aid. The first is the optimization of foreign aid structure, which includes putting the focus of the assistance on LDCs, inland developing countries and small islands developing states. Assistance projects give priority to livelihood sector, such as hospitals, schools, water supplies, clean energy, *etc.* so as to meet the urgent development needs of the recipient countries and to benefit a vast number of people. There should be reasonable arrangement for the scale and proportion of grant, interest-free loans and concessional loans to increase the overall impact of using the funds *etc.* The second is the enhancement of recipient countries' self-development capacity, including the further strengthening of agricultural cooperation with recipient countries. This can be done by constructing appropriately scaled agricultural demonstration centers, imparting agricultural experience, training technical personnel and increasing the agricultural development abilities of recipient countries. The field of human resources training in recipient countries can be broadened to enhance training effectiveness. Recipient countries can increase their level of participation in decision-making, implementation, evaluation, post management, and other aspects in foreign aid projects. The third is the acceleration of the construction of dynamic, highly efficient and more open institutional mechanisms for foreign aid. This includes fully mobilizing local government and civil forces to support foreign aid work and promoting international exchanges and cooperation actively and steadily. The fourth is the use of foreign aid as a means to encourage Chinese enterprises to invest in recipient countries and help them develop their national industry, thus creating jobs and improving people's well-being.

In April 2011, China issued the first "China's Foreign Aid" white paper. The white paper summerizes China's experience of 60 years' foreign aid practice and puts forward the basic principles of China's foreign aid policy in the new era. The first is unremittingly helping recipient countries build up their self-development capacity. Practice has proved that a country's development depends mainly on its own strength. In providing foreign aid, China does its best to help recipient countries to foster local personnel and technical forces, build infrastructure, and develop and use domestic resources, so as to lay a foundation for future development and embarkation on the road of self-reliance and independent development. The second is imposing no political conditions. China upholds the Five Principles of Peaceful Coexistence, respects recipient countries' right to independently select their own path and model of development, and believes that every country should explore a development path suitable to its actual conditions. China never uses foreign aid as a means to interfere in recipient countries' internal affairs or seek political privileges for itself. The third is adhering to equality, mutual benefit and common development. China maintains that foreign aid is mutual help between developing countries, focuses on practical effects, accommodates recipient countries' interests, and strives to promote friendly bilateral relations and mutual benefit through economic and technical cooperation with other developing countries. The fourth is remaining realistic while striving for the best. China provides foreign aid within the reach of its abilities in accordance with its national conditions. Giving full play to its comparative advantages, China does its utmost to tailor its aid to the actual needs of recipient countries. The fifth is keeping pace with the times and paying attention to reform and innovation. China adapts its foreign aid to the development of both domestic and international situations, pays attention to summarizing experiences, makes innovations in the field of foreign aid, and promptly adjusts and reforms the management mechanism, so as to constantly improve its foreign aid work.[16] These policies and principles are not only in line with the eight principles of China's foreign aid, but also embody the spirit of South–South cooperation.

---

[16] People's Republic of China, State Council Information Office, *China's Foreign Aid* (China: People's Publishing House, 2011).

3.3 *Active involvement in rule-making to increase the international status and influence of South–South cooperation*

After the "Global Partnership for Effective Development Co-operation" (GPEDC) was launched, countries and international organizations that supported the Busan outcome document were generally regarded as members. Donor countries, recipient countries, emerging economies, international organizations, non-governmental organizations and private sectors were encouraged to participate and accept supervision and evaluation. Their intention to exert influence on South–South cooperation was evident. On the other hand, a growing number of developing countries began to recognize and accept the concepts and rules of aid effectiveness and development effectiveness, following the above rules in implementing assistance. Some developing countries like Colombia, Indonesia and Nigeria actively participated in the work of promoting aid effectiveness. Indonesia, Nigeria, and the UK each sent ministers to co-chair the Global Partnership. The WBG, UNDP, and other multilateral organizations were also important participating agencies, of which the UNDP and OECD jointly undertook the secretariat functions of Global Partnership. The mechanism is likely to become one of the leading platforms for global development policy discussions in the future. As the world's second largest economy and main partner in South–South cooperation, China should seize the favorable opportunity of the rise of the South and the stagnancy of the North in international cooperation, and adopt a more open attitude to actively participate in the formulation of aid rules so as to gain greater voice and influence, thus promoting the healthy development of rules in international development cooperation towards a more fair, reasonable and pragmatic direction.

First, China should clarify its position in the system of international development cooperation with dual identity as a recipient country as well as a party of South–South cooperation. It can participate and promote the development of the existing international system of cooperation and rules reform, and play an appropriate and constructive role. China should participate in Global Partnership discussions more actively, such as joining in the annual ministerial meeting of the Global Partnership, to present its positions and propositions on aid effectiveness and development effectiveness. Meanwhile, China should adhere to its position as a developing country and the development assistance nature of South–South cooperation, and manage its respective responsibilities and rights well. While gradually increasing foreign aid in line with its economic development, China should promote the objective under-standing of its stage of development and strength by the international community and other developing countries. This will help them understand the difficulties and other challenges of China in the economic and social development process more adequately so that they can maintain a rational understanding of China's ability to provide practical assistance.

Second, China should safeguard the basic position of South–South coop-eration in international development cooperation agenda. China should per-sist in the differences in nature between South–South cooperation and North–South cooperation, and emphasize that North–South cooperation is still the main international development cooperation. The developed coun-tries should bear the primary responsibility of increasing development fund-ing and enhancing effectiveness of development assistance. China should be clear in pointing out that the current aid effectiveness principles apply mainly to traditional North–South cooperation and it is not possible to indiscrimi-nately use them to regulate, monitor and evaluate South–South cooperation. China should first uphold traditional principles of South–South cooperation and effective practices like equality and mutual benefit, non-interference in the internal affairs *etc.* in providing foreign aid, and at the same time adopt an open attitude to refer to and learn from relevant principles and indicators of aid effectiveness. Obviously, China should strengthen unity with developing countries, improve coordination with the group of 77 countries as well as India, Brazil, and other large developing countries and together, play an active role in the UN, and maintain the basic position and principles of South–South cooperation.

Third, China ought to strengthen research on the effectiveness of South–South cooperation. China can work with other countries in South–South cooperation such as India, Brazil and South Africa, as well as international agencies like the UNDP, to strengthen research on the effectiveness of South–South cooperation. Relevant ideas and principles can be proposed to further enhance the effectiveness of South–South cooperation in order to maintain its independence and uniqueness and increase its influence and right of voice.

Fourth, China should actively learn from reasonable rules of international development cooperation and promote the reform of foreign aid. Although South–South cooperation and North–South cooperation are different in nature, the planning arrangements, management tools, implementation meth-ods, performance evaluation and other technical aspects share common ground. The outcome documents of the "Paris Declaration", AAA, and "Busan Declaration" contain a lot of ideas and principles that have certain significance on China's foreign aid work. China can learn the principles of aid effectiveness and promote the following reforms:

(1) Strengthen mid- to long-term planning for foreign assistance. The "Paris Declaration" promotes the development of mid- to long-term assistance programs and the aid program must be consistent with the national development strategies of partner countries. With the expansion of the scale of China's foreign aid every year, the forms of assistance have become increasingly diversified so the preparation of forward-looking and mid- to long-term assistance plans has been put on the agenda. In the preparation of mid- to long-term policy planning, the current international development cooperation system and the development process should be taken into consideration, for example, the progress of Millennium Development Goals, the requirements of sustainable development, the G20 consensus on development priorities and the post-2015 consensus on international development agenda *etc.* While considering the people's livelihood issues such as food security and health education first, due attention should be given to sustainable development, climate change, Aid for Trade and other areas. In formulating mid- to long-term assistance plans for various countries, the national development strategies of recipient countries should be taken into account. Opinions and suggestions should be fully solicited from the recipient countries so that the guidance for assistance reflects and satisfies the needs for development, thus promoting bilateral mutual benefit.

(2) Increase participation of recipient countries. China fully respects the wishes of recipient countries in giving foreign assistance. Recipient countries have a high level of ownership over project selection and scale. Aid effectiveness principles advocate that donors maximize the use of recipient countries' procurement systems in implementing assistance projects. In recent years, more and more recipient countries have suggested to China that they hope to become more involved in the implementation of China's foreign aid projects or allow recipient countries to direct the implementation of these projects. In this regard, China intends to adapt to the situation and go with the times to make necessary adjustments in the implementation of traditional foreign aid projects, further improve the degree of involvement of recipient countries, and allow countries with stronger management and implementation capabilities to try organizing and implementing assistance projects on their own. In addition, companies

that implement foreign aid are encouraged to subcontract part of the project to local enterprises, and employ local workers as far as possible.

(3) Improve the overall effect of aid. First, the current situation where there are only independent projects must be changed, to try to develop and promote more coordinated assistance programs. For example, while building agriculture demonstration centers, it is possible to reconstruct local roads, water supply, schools, hospitals and other projects to improve the overall result of helping the poor. Second, aid projects for multiple categories in the same field can be implemented in a coordinated manner to promote the improvement of that area on the whole. For example, in the field of healthcare, the provision of medical equipment and medicine to hospitals, training of medical staff, medical teams dispatch, medical technical cooperation or hospital management cooperation can be all conducted at the same time. Third, the level of technical cooperation can be enhanced from the existing general transfer of knowledge and technology to the establishment of development plans and building of institutional capacity in recipient countries. The "software" aid in the field of economic and social governance helps them understand the national conditions of China and learn from its development ideas and reform experience. Fourth, the value chain of assistance project is extended. For example, agricultural aid projects may be extended from plantations to processing and trade.

(4) Appropriate coordination of assistance operations with other aid providers. Aid effectiveness principles emphasize that aid providers strengthen coordination and cooperation, in order to reduce overlapping of assistance projects. China's foreign aid supports and promotes South–South cooperation, and conditions for other developed countries to adopt the same implementation framework for assistance projects have yet to be created. However, on the premise that recipient countries manage aid projects in their various countries, it is possible to coordinate appropriate action with other aid providers and exchange necessary information, or for China to participate in and provide certain part of the assistance according to the requirements of the recipient countries. With recipient countries that show greater and clearer will, have relatively strong coordination capabilities, and where research shows feasibility, China can consider participating actively in tripartite projects that will effectively promote the development of recipient countries.

Chapter 14

Rules for Trade and Sustainable Development

On April 24, 2013, a garment factory building in Dhaka, Bangladesh, the world's second largest clothing exporting country, collapsed — resulting in the deaths of more than 1,000 textile workers. This tragedy triggered a wave of global shock and reflections. The International Labor Organization (ILO) urged Bangladesh to close down garment factories that lacked safe production conditions. The EU considered imposing trade sanctions on Bangladesh to force it to improve the production environment for workers. Retail giants in Sweden and the UK agreed to purchase clothing and other goods only from Bangladeshi factories that met safety conditions.

On October 4, 2013, the International Civil Aviation Organization (ICAO) concluded its 38th Assembly in Montreal. After 10 days of intense debate, 191 ICAO member states finally agreed to develop a global market based measure (MBM) for international aviation in 2016, to address and reduce the carbon emissions of each member airline, and these would take effect in 2020. The President of the ICAO Council then, Mr Roberto Kobeh Gonzalez said excitedly: "This MBM agreement is an historic milestone for air transport and for the role of multilateralism in addressing global climate challenges." For passengers and traders around the world, this does not seem to be a piece of good news, as it implied that airfare and transportation costs were likely to rise significantly after a few years.

The two cases mentioned above occurred at two ends of the world and appear seemingly unrelated. But they actually reveal the trend of a continual expansion of trade. Environmental protection, climate change, labor rights and other sustainable development issues[1] have become important factors which

---

[1] In 1987, the World Commission on Environment and Development formally mentioned the concept of "sustainable development" in the report "Our Common Future", and defined sustainable development as "meeting the needs of the present without compromising the ability of future generations to meet their own needs". The connotation and extension of the

could affect international trade. What is the relationship between international trade and the issues on environmental protection, climate change, and labor rights? Is there a difference between the stand of developed countries and that of developing countries? Is there more common ground or are there more differences? How do the rules evolve and what are the future development trends? What should China do?

1 Ecological Dumping or Green Barriers?

In recent years, with deepened economic globalization and sustained, rapid development of international trade, environmental issues have become increasingly prominent. There are diverse opinions on the relationship between international trade and environmental issues. Trade liberals believe that trade itself does not harm the environment and government failure is the root cause of environmental deterioration, while environmentalists believe that free trade is the major cause of environmental destruction. Developed and developing countries hold different opinions on this issue, resulting in acute conflicts between them.

Developed countries believe that by adopting lower environmental standards, some developing countries' products have enjoyed greater competitive advantages in the markets of developed countries, thus constituting "ecological dumping" on developed countries. Developed countries should take appropriate trade restrictive measures to correct the "market failures" due to environmental externalities, so that competition takes place on a level playing field. However, for many developing countries, environmental resources are a factor of production and permitted by the environment to an extent. A low cost environment is therefore an important condition for their access to foreign capital and export competitiveness. Disregarding differences in the stage of development, developed countries tied in trade with environment issues, on the pretext of "ecological dumping", and attempted to coerce developing countries to significantly improve environmental standards, when in reality, they are implementing a form of green barriers and trade protectionist measures.

---

sustainable development concept have expanded continually. Currently the UN, the EU and other international NGOs have defined sustainable development as an integrated concept that includes economic development, labor standards, environmental protection, human rights, and anti-corruption measures.

1.1 *Multilateral rules on trade and the environment*

1.1.1 *Evolution of the multilateral trading system*

During the inception of the multilateral trading system in 1947, there was little emphasis on environment protection issues as environmental problems had yet to occur on a global basis. After the 1970s, trade and environmental issues gained the world's attention and environmental issues began to surface in the multilateral trading system, but no consensus had been forged on the issue. It was not until the GATT Uruguay Round of Negotiations in 1994, coinciding with the establishment of the WTO, that a final agreement was reached and all parties began comprehensive work on trade and the environment. In 1995, the WTO became formally operational, and the Committee on Trade and Environment (CTE) was set up. The role of the committee was to fully understand the relationship between trade and the environment in order to promote sustainable development, as well as to further promote the integration of the environment and multilateral trading system through research and recommendations.

At the Doha Round negotiations in 2001, the negotiations on trade and the environment were an important item on the Doha Development Agenda. The negotiations focused on three aspects: the relationship between WTO rules and Multilateral Environmental Agreements (MEAs),[2] the collaboration between the WTO and MEA Secretariats and the elimination of tariffs and on environmental goods and services. Due to differences in each nation's environmental standards, environmental goods and competitiveness of services, and differing and even opposing views on the definition of environmental goods between developed and developing countries, the WTO failed to achieve significant results during the negotiations in these areas.

1.1.2 *Existing provisions*

Although GATT and the WTO have yet to establish clear and uniform regulations on trade and environmental issues, there are scattered provisions in practice, touching on the relationship between trade and the environment, which could meet the rising demands on environmental protection. For example,

---

[2]MEAs refer to multilateral treaties whose objectives are to protect the environment. There are currently 250 effective MEAs in the world, of which about 20 contain trade restrictions. These treaties include the "The Basel Convention", "Convention on Biological Diversity", "International Tropical Timber Agreement", "Montreal Protocol on Substances That Deplete the Ozone Layer", "United Nations Framework Convention on Climate Change" and so on.

the provisions in Article XX (b), (g) of the GATT 1947 are commonly regarded as the most important provisions on tackling the issues of trade and the environment.[3] The article states that: "Subject to the requirement that such measures are not applied in a manner which would constitute a means of arbitrary or unjustifiable discrimination between countries where the same conditions prevail, or a disguised restriction on international trade, nothing in this Agreement shall be construed to prevent the adoption or enforcement by any contracting party of measures; (b) necessary to protect human, animal or plant life or health; (g) relating to the conservation of exhaustible natural resources...." In the implementation of WTO laws, this has become the most important legal basis for WTO members to adopt restrictive trade measures due to environmental reasons. In addition, the provisions on environmental issues are also scattered in a number of other agreements in the WTO. For example, the preface in the "Agreement Establishing the World Trade Organization" mentioned "sustainable development", advocating that the use of world resources must take environmental protection issues into reasonable account. The foreword in the "Agreement on the Technical Barriers to Trade" specified that members should refrain from taking unnecessary or inappropriate measures to use technical regulations and standards as a means of protecting the environment.

In the "Agreement on the Application of Sanitary and Phytosanitary Measures", it is stated that when sanitary and phytosanitary measures are taken to protect human, animal and plant life and health, they must not "constitute a means of arbitrary or unjustifiable discrimination" or "constitute a disguised restriction on international trade". In "The Agreement on Trade-Related Aspects of Intellectual Property Rights" (TRIPS), Article 27 specifies that patents shall be available for any invention, but "Members may exclude from patentability inventions, the prevention within their territory of the commercial exploitation of which is necessary to protect ordre public or morality, including to protect human, animal or plant life or health or to avoid serious prejudice to the environment, provided that such exclusion is not made merely because the exploitation is prohibited by their law".

It should be said that GATT and WTO provisions, as mentioned above, indicated that the multilateral trading system had begun to touch on the relationship between trade and the environment. However the provisions, though strong in principles, are worded in a flexible and vague manner, and are

---

[3] Li Shouping, "New Trends in Trade and Environmental Issues under the WTO Framework," *Modern Law*, Vol. 18, No. 1 (2005), pp. 32–38.

thus prone to ambiguity. Moreover, the trade restrictions, which the MEAs recognized, are often in conflict with the market access commitments in the multilateral trading system. WTO has yet to address this critical issue. Thus, between trade and environmental issues, which is more important? Where is the equilibrium point between trade liberalization and environmental protection measures? The answer is not apparent just looking at provisions alone. Fortunately, the GATT/WTO dispute settlement systems have made legally binding decisions on a number of environment-related trade disputes. Through analyzing these cases, we observed that the scales have gradually tilted towards the side of environmental protection.

1.1.3 *Observations of changes in trade and environmental rules through case studies*

GATT experts insist that trade liberalization take absolute priority. For example, Mexico filed a complaint against the United States in 1991 on the "tuna" case. Based on US domestic law, US banned import of tuna and tuna products from Mexico as Mexico fishermen used purse seine nets while harvesting tuna, resulting in the deaths of many dolphins. The GATT panel finally concluded that the US lost the case, and that the US had violated GATT's rules on abolishing quantitative restrictions and national treatment principles, and that this case did not belong to the two exceptional circumstances in GATT Article XX (b, g).[4] From the verdict, it can be observed that GATT adopts very stringent standards to assess the legality of environment and trade measures, refusing to adopt relevant international environmental treaties in interpreting GATT Article XX, and also denying the protection of domestic laws towards extraterritorial areas, and feels that the US should not impose its domestic standards on the production process outside the US. The panel was concerned that if processing and production methods (PPM) are recognized as the major cause of environmental problems, the MFN treatment would be rendered useless and free trade would be restricted, thus it refused to distinguish among "similar products" based on production methods. This decision protected the liberalization of trade, but the WTO was unable to impose sanctions on members who caused damage to the environment.[5]

---

[4] Zhang Lei, "Discussion on the Trend of WTO's Easing Trade and Environmental Measures," *WTO Focus*, Issue 1, 2009.

[5] Lang Ping, "New Round of Multilateral Trade Negotiations on Trade and Environment issues," *World Economics and Politics*, Issue 3, 2003.

After the establishment of the WTO, several decisions made gradually departed from the above principles established by the GATT panel. Compared with the GATT panel, the WTO dispute settlement body seemed to pay more attention to environmental protection issues. In the 1996 standards for gasoline case, the 1998 turtle/shrimp case, 1998 hormones in beef case as well as the 2001 asbestos cases *etc.,* the WTO dispute settlement body ruled in favor of the environment. For instance, in the standards for gasoline, turtle/shrimp as well as asbestos cases, the WTO dispute settlement body chose a broad interpretation of certain terms in GATT Article XX, such as "exhaustible natural resources" and "necessary" and other terms, so that environmental protection became a legal exception to liberalization of trade. The dispute settlement body pointed out that in the turtle/shrimp case, as long as it could be proven that there was a connection between the opposite party and its own jurisdiction, its domestic environmental measures would have extraterritorial effects. On the PPM issue, the dispute settlement body agreed that it is possible to distinguish the products based on PPM, and adopt restrictive trade measures towards products whose production methods cause environmental pollution.[6]

On the whole, the heightened attention that countries have paid to environmental issues have led to more in-depth discussions on the link between trade and environmental issues in the WTO. Overall, attitudes are also more relaxed and open, and the multilateral trading system has moved on from putting absolute priority on trade to one of coordination and mutual support between trade and environment. Although the parties have not established clear multilateral rules, from the dispute settlement bodies' verdicts on cases that involve the environment and trade, we can clearly see WTO's inclinations.

1.2 *Regional rules on trade and the environment*

1.2.1 *Rapid development of regional rules*

As the multilateral trading system was unable to include clear provisions on trade and environmental issues, some countries accelerated the pace of dealing with trade and environmental issues through regional economic cooperation. Presently, regional rules on trade and environment are evolving rapidly in regional economic cooperation forums and/or FTAs, and could become an important source of reference for the development of multilateral rules in the future.

---

[6]Zhang Lei, *ibid*, p. 525.

As a regional economic cooperation forum based primarily on policy dialogue, APEC plays an important role in promoting the establishment of trade and environment rules. For example, the liberalization of trade in environmental goods and services was the focus during the Doha Round of negotiations on trade and environment issues. In 2001, this issue was formally included in the WTO agenda and negotiations were launched in 2002. However, as members of developed countries had an edge in the competitiveness of environmental goods, and members of developing countries were on the defensive, opinions differed greatly and it was difficult to reach an agreement. Under this context, the US moved the battleground for liberalization of trade in environmental goods and services from the WTO to the APEC. After intense exchanges and consultations, the 21 members of the APEC committed to "reducing the tariff rates on environmental goods to 5% or less by 2015" at the 2011 APEC Summit. At the same time, they also resolved to eliminate non-tariff barriers, including local content requirements that distorted environmental goods and services trade. In 2012, APEC members also successfully worked out a list of 54 environmental goods, classified by six digit subcategories, and promised to reduce tariffs on these products to 5% or less by 2015.[7] APEC's move was an important motivating force that drove the resolution of the long-lasting stalemate on environmental goods and services in the WTO Doha Round of negotiations. In June 2013, the Obama administration made clear that the APEC list of environmental goods agreed to in 2012 would serve as a foundation for expediting the multilateral negotiations on liberalization of environmental goods and services.[8] In October 2013, APEC leaders pledged to explore ways to liberalize trade in environmental goods and services under the WTO framework, on the foundation of the APEC list of environmental goods.[9] On January 24, 2014, 14 WTO members, including the US, China and the EU, announced in Davos that negotiations on environmental goods would be officially launched, on the basis of the APEC list of environmental goods.[10]

---

[7] APEC, "APEC List of Environmental Goods," September 8, 2012; retrieved from http://www. apec.org/Meeting-Papers/Leaders-Declarations/2012/2012_aelm/2012_aelm_annexC.aspx.

[8] USTR, "President Obama Announces Actions to Address Climate Change," June 25, 2013; retrieved from https://www.whitehouse.gov/the-press-office/2013/06/25/fact-sheet-president-obama-s-climate-action-plan.

[9] APEC, "Supporting the Multilateral Trading System and the 9th Ministerial Conference of the World Trade Organization," October 7, 2013; retrieved from http://www.apec.org/Meeting-Papers/Leaders-Declarations/2013/2013_aelm/2013_aelm_mts.aspx.

[10] EU, "Joint Statement Regarding Trade in Environmental Goods," January 24, 2014; retrieved from http://trade.ec.europa.eu/doclib/docs/2014/january/tradoc_152095.pdf.

Free trade agreements are another important regional platform for the formation of trade and environmental rules. The US and the EU are the forerunners who have incorporated environmental issues in their free trade agreements, and have consistently linked trade and environmental issues. Both parties' treatment of trade and environmental issues in free trade agreements are way ahead of other countries.

The US had clearly stipulated environmental protection elements in the agreement as early as during the NAFTA agreement with Canada and Mexico in 1992. As such, the NAFTA became the first free trade agreement to include a specific category on the environment. As an advocate and pioneer of sustainable development, the EU specially included "trade and sustainable development" sections in free trade agreements in recent years to deal with the issues regarding trade, the environment and labor.[11] Through actual implementation of free trade agreements, the US and Europe formulated the "NAFTA model" and the "EU model" to manage trade and environmental issues, which served as a source of reference for future multilateral and regional rules on trade and environment issues. Therefore, it is necessary to conduct a comparative analysis of these two models.

1.2.2 *Comparison of the NAFTA and EU models*

It was observed from the form of NAFTA that it adopted "a combination of the main agreement and supplementary agreement" approach to the trade and environmental problem. In the main agreement, NAFTA did not include uniform specifications on the relationship between trade and the environment, and the relevant provisions on trade and the environment were scattered throughout the agreement, for example in the preface, and sections on sanitary and phytosanitary measures and standards-related measures. In addition to the main agreement, the three members of NAFTA signed a supplementary agreement in 1993, known as the "North American Agreement on Environmental Cooperation" (NAAEC)[12] as a supplement to the main NAFTA agreement, and both agreements took effect at the same time.

In the EU model, the EU set up a separate section in the body of the agreements, incorporating detailed provisions on trade, environment and labor issues. In terms of the effectiveness of law, the EU model seems to be more restrictive than the NAFTA. Perhaps it was this factor that led the US to adopt

---

[11] For example, the EU-Korea FTA which became effective in 2011, included separate chapters on "Trade and Sustainable Development".

[12] For the full text of the NAAEC, refer to http://www.cec.org/about-us/NAAEC.

separate chapters on trade and environmental issues in the main body of free trade agreements signed after the NAFTA. For example, in the US-Korea FTA", which took effect in 2012, both parties included separate sections on the "environment". Therefore, the NAFTA and EU models have demonstrated through this issue that the two models draw on each other's experience and are slowly integrating.

The NAFTA model is more detailed in content and "rigid" compared to the EU model. In terms of objectiveness, it is noted that NAFTA clearly stated its goal of promoting sustainable development, stressing that economic growth should not be pursued at the expense of the environment. With reference to specific measures, NAFTA allowed its member states to adopt restrictive trade measures when they felt that the import of a product or service could pose environmental hazards and prohibit the imports on a non-discriminatory basis. Member states may not seek to attract foreign investment through reducing environmental standards. With regard to MEAs, if NAFTA's clauses on trade were in conflict with those in existing MEAs, then the clauses in MEAs would take priority.

The relevant provisions of the EU model were relatively weak. In terms of objectiveness, the EU model specified that environmental protection could not be used to justify trade protection, and clearly promoted the liberalization of trade in environmental goods and services. However, in terms of specific measures, the EU's only requirement was that member governments should not lower the enforcement of environment protection to boost investments and trade. Unlike the NAFTA, there were also no provisions that restricted imports in the EU model, and the relationship between FTAs and MEAs was not explicitly stated.

With regard to the implementation mechanism and public participation, both the NAFTA and EU models advocated the establishment of mechanisms to enhance the level of environmental protection through strengthening the cooperation among members, as well as focused on the protection of the public's right to information and participation so as to ensure the implementation of agreements was in line with the interests of society. The three member countries in NAFTA established the Commission for Environment Cooperation (CEC) under the NAAEC framework.[13] The CEC's role was to raise public awareness of environmental protection, provide recommendations to the trade

---

[13] For more information, please visit the CEC official website (http://www.cec.org/Page. asp?PageID=1115&AA_SiteLanguageID=1).

representatives from the three countries and ensure that the implementation of environmental legislation and the implementation process were transparent.

It is worth mentioning that the NAFTA model included "rigid" provisions for public participation, allowing citizens or organizations of a member state to bring the accusations directly to the CEC if the member state failed to implement environmental regulations effectively. Although this did not result in binding restrictions on the government of the member state used and the member state sued need not fulfill its obligations, public pressure played a supervisory role in restraining the behaviors of member states in violation.[14]

In the EU model, the EU and its FTA partners established a Committee of Trade and Sustainable Development to implement the relevant provisions of the Agreement, and at the same time, set up a Domestic Advisory Group, comprising of individuals, NGOs and representatives of business organizations, to make recommendations on the implementation of sustainable development, thus ensuring public participation through the domestic advisory group.

With regard to dispute settlement mechanisms, the NAFTA model stated that if a Member State persistently failed to abide by its environmental regulations, other Member States may turn to sanctions as a last resort. According to NAFTA, the three members were required to submit a report on their enforcement of obligations annually. If a Member State was unable to enforce its regulations effectively, NAAEC specified that governmental consultations should take place and if negotiations fail, either party may request the Commission to convene a special session. If the Commission was unable to resolve the issue, the prosecutor might request setting up a panel. If the panel established that the Member State was guilty of not implementing the environmental legislative regulations, the Member State would be required to formulate a plan to resolve the issue. If the Member State failed to fulfil its specified obligations under the plan, the panel could impose a certain fine on the Member State, amounting to not more than 0.007% of the total trade in merchandise for the parties in dispute in the most recent year. All fines would go to a fund which was used for environmental protection or the implementation of environmental regulations.[15] If the member failed to pay the fine, the plaintiff would suspend the

---

[14]Xiao Man and Zhou Ning-hua, "NAFTA's Environmental Problems and their Implications to China," *Jiangnan University Newsletter*, June Issue, 2004.

[15]Li Shouping, "How NAFTA Coordinate the Issue on Environment and Trade and Its Enlightments," *Presentday Law Science*, Issue 5, 2005.

FTA preferential tariff rates and resume the implementation of the MFN tariffs.

In the EU model, dispute settlements are resolved entirely through consultations with the government, rather than through the dispute settlement mechanism in the agreement. If necessary, the advice of the "domestic advisory group" may also be sought. When a dispute occurs, the parties to the agreement can set up a panel, to provide relevant suggestions and recommendations to resolve the conflict. The parties should endeavor to implement these suggestions and recommendations. However, as these suggestions and recommendations were not mandatory, no sanctions would be imposed if they were not adopted.

1.2.3 *Development trends of the NAFTA and EU models*

Overall, the NAFTA model is more flexible than the EU model. The contents of its agreement are more extensive and involves greater public participation and mandatory dispute settlement elements. NAFTA is also quasi-judicial in nature and more "rigid". As the standards of the NAFTA model are higher and more restrictive than the EU model, this also means that it is more difficult to promote the NAFTA model. From observations of the participation of countries in FTAs in recent years, it is noted that despite more and more countries, in particular OECD members, agreeing to incorporate environmental protection issues in the FTAs, the form and content are closer to the EU model with its lower standards.[16] For example, the European Free Trade Association (EFTA), (comprising four members: Switzerland, Norway, Iceland, and Liechtenstein), is an important regional organization in Europe and is greatly influenced by the EU. After 2008, the EFTA has requested to include separate chapters on trade and sustainable development issues, based on the EU model, in its FTAs with other parties.[17]

The current situation shows that the US proposals in the Trans-Pacific Partnership (TPP) negotiations on trade and the environmental rules consist of three main parts: First, protection clauses, involving illegal logging, ocean fishing, illegal trade of endangered species, plants and animals; second, core com-

---

[16]OECD, "Regional Trade Agreements and the Environment: Monitoring Implementation and Assessing the Impact," September 2014; retrieved from http://www.oecd.org/tad/events/joint-working-party-trade-environment-workshop-vietnam-2014.htm/.

[17]EFTA, "Conclusion of EFTA Work on Trade, Environment and Labor Standards," retrieved from https://www.seco.admin.ch/seco/en/home/Aussenwirtschaftspolitik_Wirtschaftliche_Zusammenarbeit/Wirtschaftsbeziehungen/Freihandelsabkommen.html.

mitment clauses, requiring all parties to abide by their commitments in the MEAs — that is, the commitments under the MEAs take precedence over the market access commitments under the trade agreements. Third, public participation provisions, which allow the public to scrutinize if the parties in the agreement have abided by their commitments and resolve disputes through the dispute settlement mechanism.[18] Objectively speaking, these views are essentially the same as the core requirements in the NAFTA model, and involve very high standards, particularly the mandatory nature of the dispute settlement mechanism.

2 "Hot" Trade and Environment Issues: Climate Change

Intrinsically, climate change belongs to the category of environmental issues, but due to the huge and wide-ranging effects of climate change, it has superseded other environmental issues and became the "hottest" issue in international political economy in recent years. As defined by the United Nations Framework Convention on Climate Change (UNFCCC), climate change means "a change of climate which is attributed directly or indirectly to human activity that alters the composition of the global atmosphere and which is in addition to natural climate variability observed over comparable time periods". According to this definition, human activities, in particular human activities since the industrial revolution, are the main reasons behind climate change (which is characterized mainly by global warming) because, production and other human activities have led to the emission of carbon dioxide and other greenhouse gases, land use, and urbanization. According to the UN study, if greenhouse gas emissions continue to increase, the average temperature in this century may rise by 4°C, resulting in a rapid increase in sea levels, an influx of 200 million climate refugees, the extinction of a large number of species, and other disasters.[19]

The key strategy to addressing climate change is to exert full control over the emission of carbon dioxide and other greenhouse gases. According to the UNFCCC and Kyoto Protocol (KP), developed countries should take the lead to adopt measures to reduce their greenhouse gas emissions, undertake mandatory

---

[18] Ian F. Fergusson, William H. Cooper and Brock R. Williams, "The Trans-Pacific Partnership (TPP) Negotiations and Issues for Congress" March 20, 2015; retrieved from http://photos.state.gov/libraries/vietnam/8621/pdf-forms/tpp-crsreport032015.pdf.

[19] Global Policy Forum, "Climate Change," retrieved from https://www.globalpolicy.org/social-and-economic-policy/the-environment/climate-change.html.

emission reductions, and provide relevant funds and technology to developing countries. In accordance with the "common but differentiated responsibilities" principle, developing countries, upon receiving technology and financial support from developed countries, should take measures to mitigate or adapt to climate change. Under this principle, China as a developing country is only obliged to make voluntary reductions in emission, rather than undertake mandatory emission reductions.

It is the responsibility of all countries to respond actively to climate change and protect the environment that we live in. The reduction of greenhouse gas emissions is not only closely related to environment issues, but also to the energy structure of each country, the manner of economic growth *etc.*, and involves the restructuring of the economy and future developments. All this would inevitably lead to readjustment and distribution of domestic and international interests, reshape international trade patterns, and is in essence, an important political and economic issue in the international arena.

In this context, "carbon tariff", "carbon labelling", "carbon certification", "carbon footprint", "aviation/shipping carbon tax" and other issues emerged repeatedly, bringing about mixed reactions among the countries.

2.1 *Huge dispute over carbon tariffs*

2.1.1 *Concept and theories behind carbon tariffs*

Carbon tariffs refer to taxes and other border adjustment measures that a country imposes on imported goods during the import stage, based on their carbon emissions. Carbon tariffs and carbon taxes are different. Carbon taxes refer to domestic tax measures that the government imposes on domestic enterprises or industries that emit greenhouse gases, while carbon tariffs are levied on imported products. However, the two are closely related and currently, some countries have used carbon taxes as an excuse for imposing carbon tariffs.

Since the 1990s, more than a dozen countries, including Denmark and Sweden in Europe, have successively imposed domestic carbon taxes. Some states in Europe and US have established limits on emissions for transactions, which is equivalent to the effects of imposing domestic carbon taxes to reduce emissions.[20] As such, the US and EU proposed two reasons for imposing

---

[20] Su Ming, Fu Zhihua and Xuwen, "Recommendation of a Timely Introduction of a Carbon Tax," *China Economic Times*, August 5, 2013; retrieved from http://tax.hexun.com/2013-08-05/156796273.html.

carbon tariffs: First, by adopting mandatory emission reduction measures, the production costs of developed countries have increased, affecting the international competitiveness of the related enterprises. As a result, domestic products are at a disadvantage when they compete with imported goods. Second, as committed countries adopted mandatory measures to reduce emissions, a large number of domestic industries shifted to developing countries which are not committed to reducing emissions, resulting in the emergence of "pollution havens" in these countries, effectively raising rather than reducing the level of carbon emissions globally, thus resulting in a "carbon leakage" phenomenon. In order "to level the competition platform" and avoid "carbon leakages", it is necessary to impose carbon tariffs on the imports from countries which have not adopted similar emission reduction measures.[21]

2.1.2 *The US and Europe's push for carbon tariffs*

Based on the above theoretical reasons, the US and Europe have actively pushed for the implementation of carbon tariffs. Among the EU member states, France is the most active advocate of carbon tariffs, but in the face of opposition from the UK and other countries, which are supporters of free trade, the EU has failed to introduce the relevant policies. The US has made faster and greater progress. In June 2009, the US House of Representatives passed the "American Clean Energy and Security Act", proposing a cap and trade system, authorizing the US government to impose carbon tariffs on the imports from countries which have not taken measures to reduce emissions, and designing a specific operating plan concurrently. A number of international organizations actively supported the carbon tariff concept. In June 2009, the WTO Secretariat and United Nations Environment Program (UNEP) jointly published a report, stating clearly that under the existing WTO rules, there are provisions which allow the implementation of carbon tariffs, and even if these rules are inconsistent with general trading rules, as long as they meet the requirements of "general exceptions" under GATT Article XX, they could be regarded to be in line with WTO rules.[22]

The US and Europe's position on carbon tariffs were strongly criticized by developing countries. The former Director-General of WTO, Pascal Lamy,

---

[21] Wang Xin and Chen Ying, "Disentangling Carbon Tax: An Analysis of the European Policy," *Chinese Journal of European Studies*, Issue 6, 2010, pp. 44–58.

[22] Zhou Xinyi, "The Onslaught of Carbon Tariffs," *21st Century Business Herald*, January 7, 2010; retrieved from http://www.21cbh.com/HTML/2010-1-7/160933.html.

clarified later that the report only represented experts' opinions. During the Copenhagen Conference on climate change in 2009, the participants engaged in fierce debates on unilateral trade measures like carbon tariffs. There were serious differences in opinions between developed countries and developing countries, and the countries failed to reach an agreement. Within developed countries, there was also serious contention on carbon tariffs, and domestic legislation on carbon tariffs was blocked. France tried to lay the foundation for carbon tariffs on imported goods through the introduction of domestic carbon taxes, but the Constitutional Council rejected the bill, stating that the bill violates the principle of equality in taxes and runs counter to the aim of fighting climate change.[23] Due to opposition from energy states and the energy industries, the US' "American Clean Energy and Security Act" was not passed in the Senate.

2.1.3 *The development prospects for carbon tariffs*

The controversy on carbon tariffs can be explained through two main aspects. From the legal perspective, carbon tariffs are in conflict with the provisions of WTO and UNFCCC. There exist discrepancies between carbon tariffs and provisions like the WTO's border adjustment taxes, the national treatment principles and MFN principles. Even invoking the general exception clause in Article XX of the GATT would be difficult. Carbon tariffs also violate the basic principles of UNFCCC, which stated that developed countries and developing countries should bear "common but differentiated responsibilities" as well as the stipulated rule that "measures taken to combat climate change, including unilateral ones, should not constitute a means of arbitrary or unjustifiable discrimination or a disguised restriction on international trade". From the implementation point of view, there are technical obstacles to the implementation of carbon tariffs. Comparisons of the climate policies of two countries through the evaluation of the costs of reducing emissions between their enterprises and assessment of the carbon emissions of specific products, in particular measuring the carbon emissions over the product life cycle, is especially difficult on the technical front, and involves high administrative costs.

Due to strong resistance from developing countries, carbon tariffs are almost unheard of in recent years. However, as carbon tariffs could raise the competitiveness of domestic high-carbon industries in the US and Europe, and raise the

---

[23] China Daily, "French Constitutional Council Rejects 'Carbon Tax Bill'," retrieved from http://www.chinadaily.com.cn/china/2009copenhagenclimate/2009-12/30/content_9247252.htm

development costs for developing countries externally, and at the same time, enable the US and Europe to take the lead in the international division of labor and the implementation of "re-industrialization" strategy, the US and Europe would not easily give up the deterrent carbon tariff strategy. It is expected that the US and Europe would continue to use carbon tariffs as a backup "weapon", brandishing it occasionally and coercing developing countries to accelerate the pace of reducing emissions.[24] At the same time, the developed countries are seeking alternatives to carbon tariffs, for example through promoting carbon labeling, carbon footprint, and carbon certification actively or imposing "carbon tariffs" on trade in services in the international transportation industry. These alternatives encourage various industries to make changes to the high-carbon trade methods, consumption patterns, and lifestyles, thus contributing to the localization of production and import of low-carbon products, in order to achieve the strategic objective of carbon tariffs.

2.2 The rapid development of carbon labeling, carbon footprints and carbon certification

2.2.1 The concepts and essence of carbon labeling, carbon footprints and carbon certification

At present, among the various schemes to promote the reduction of carbon emissions, carbon labeling and certification, which focus on influencing consumer preferences, have become increasingly active. This method makes use of labeling and certification to inform consumers of the greenhouse gas emissions during the whole or part of the life cycle of the product, changing consumers' preferences for high-carbon products, therefore establishing demand for low-carbon products and leading to greater impact on international trade.

Specifically, carbon labeling involves indicating the carbon emission quantity during the production process of the good on the product label, thus providing consumers with information on carbon emissions of the product. Carbon certification, *i.e.* certification of low-carbon products, is achieved through putting a label on the product, promoting the purchase and consumption of consumer-oriented low-carbon products. In this way, the whole society

---

[24] ICTSD, "France to Re-Launch EU Carbon Tariff Proposal: Official," May 23, 2012; retrieved from http://www.ictsd.org/bridges-news/bridges/news/france-to-re-launch-eu-carbon-tariff-proposal-official.

contributes towards addressing the climate change issue through the production and consumption segments. These two concepts are built on the foundation of carbon footprints. Carbon footprints refer to the total amount of carbon dioxide emitted throughout the life cycle of a product or service (from the acquisition of raw materials to production, distribution, use and treatment after the product is disposed).

2.2.2 *Development and trends of carbon labeling and carbon certification*

Today, various countries continue to introduce different calculation methods for carbon emissions. Britain was the first to introduce "PAS 2050 Specification for the Assessment of the Life Cycle Greenhouse Gas Emissions of Goods and Services", recommending that organizations indicate the carbon emissions of the product in the production, transportation, delivery and other processes, thus informing consumers of the commodity's impact on global warming. The PAS 2050 standard is currently the standard with the greatest influence in the world. In 2009, Japan introduced TSQ0010, which not only indicated the carbon footprint of the commodity in its entire life cycle, but also the proportion of carbon footprint at every stage.[25]

Many developed countries have begun the carbon labeling and carbon certification work at the government and enterprise level. From the government perspective, Britain first launched the carbon labeling system, and verified the carbon footprints for more than 5,700 kinds of products. In 2007, Sweden built a more comprehensive "Environmental Product Declaration" database, recording the carbon footprints of many products and services. The Korean CFP (carbon footprint) labeling system was introduced in February 2009, stipulating carbon certification laws, which included "carbon labeling and the relevant provisions on carbon certification". From the enterprise level, Britain's supermarket, Tesco, started a pilot program on carbon labels for more than 20 kinds of commodities. The US retailer, Walmart, also required suppliers to verify carbon footprints, through a carbon scoring system, and gradually translated the carbon footprint data into carbon labels, which consumers could easily understand.[26]

---

[25] Huang Wenxiu, "Evaluation of Carbon Footprints for Domestic and Foreign Products and the Development of Carbon Labeling System," *Electrical Appliances*, Issue 4, 2012.
[26] Xu Qingjun, "New Trends in Carbon Tariffs, Carbon Labeling and Carbon Certification," *International Business*, Issue 7, 2011.

Development trends show that as carbon abatement gained greater popularity, product and service providers gradually accepted the use of carbon footprints to quantify the impact of carbon emissions on the environment, and made environmental information publicly available. Regulations on carbon footprints are likely to evolve from voluntary implementation currently to mandatory compliance in the future. For international trade in the future, more and more importers would require the exporters to provide carbon labels indicating the impact of their goods or services on the environment, providing information on carbon footprints, thus ensuring that it is easier for merchandise with carbon labels to enter the international trading markets, and gain consumers' acceptance. In addition, stronger mandatory carbon abatement requirements would give rise to the rapid development of low-carbon certification services and the formation of a carbon certification industry which reaps enormous benefits.

2.2.3 *Looming aviation and maritime carbon taxes*

2.2.3.1 Background to the introduction of aviation and maritime carbon taxes and coverage of the carbon taxes

When the Kyoto Protocol was signed in 1997, the parties in the agreement had yet to stipulate requirements on carbon emissions in the aviation and maritime fields. With the rapid development in international trade, carbon emissions in the transportation segment of aviation and maritime fields increased quickly; even though the current emissions accounts for only a small portion of total global emissions, but the growth rate is faster than that in other fields. The International Civil Aviation Organization (ICAO) forecasts that by 2050, the aviation emissions could increase by 3–7 times of its level in 2005.[27] The data from the International Maritime Organization (IMO) showed that the international shipping industry accounts for around 3% of global greenhouse gas emissions; if further measures are not taken, this proportion could rise to 18% by 2050.[28]

As an active proponent making recommendations on climate changes, the EU issued an order in February 2009, requesting that with effect from January 1, 2012, emissions from all flights from, to and within the European

---

[27] EU, "Reducing Emissions from Aviation," retrieved from http://ec.europa.eu/clima/policies/transport/aviation/.

[28] "EurActiv: IMO on Collision Course with EU Over CO_2 Emissions," retrieved from http://www.euractiv.com/section/climate-environment/news/imo-on-collision-course-with-eu-over-co2-emissions/.

Economic Area be included in the EU Emissions Trading Scheme (ETS). The EU specified that based on the average annual emissions in 2004–2006, the EU would set a free aviation allowance for each airline according to a specified discount rate and share, airlines which exceed the allocated aviation allowance need to purchase the corresponding emission amount from the ETS through auction. By 2020, there would not be free aviation allowances and all allowances would be obtained through auctions.[29] For airlines that failed to abide by the guidelines, punitive measures such as fines, detention, forced sale of aircraft equipment and route embargo *etc.* could be taken.

As the main mode of transport in international trade, the maritime industry has currently begun to follow the aviation industry's approach of mandatory abatement of emissions. In February 2012, the EU expressed that if the IMO was unable to reach a consensus on maritime carbon emissions at the multilateral level, the EC would pass a legislation modeled after the aviation carbon tax, and unilaterally impose a carbon tax directive and push forth abatement in maritime carbon emissions globally.[30] Taking into account that 90% of international trade is conducted via the sea, the EU move is likely to have a significant impact on international trade patterns.

2.2.3.2 Controversies over aviation and maritime carbon taxes

From the perspective of developing countries, the EU's unilateral measures are highly contentious on many levels. Firstly, the reduction of emissions in the aviation transport industry is an important component of the global action on climate change, and should thus follow the "common but differentiated responsibilities" principle, *i.e.* the reduction in aviation emissions should begin with developed countries. The EU aviation carbon tax does not distinguish between developed and developing countries, and include all carriers that take off and land within the European Economic area equally in its emissions trading scheme. In reality, developing countries are bearing mandatory emission reduction obligations. Therefore, the EU's approach clearly follows the "common" rather than "differentiated" principle.[31]

---

[29] EU, "Reducing Emissions from Aviation," *ibid.*

[30] Gongxin, "Aviation Carbon Tax Pending, the EU Moves On to the Shipping Industry," *China Economic Herald*, October 27, 2012, C01 edition.

[31] Yan Shipeng, "The Legality of the EU Aviation Carbon Tax and the Chinese Legal Response," *Journal of Jiangsu University*, Issue 6, 2012.

Secondly, the EU aviation carbon tax does not comply with the provisions of "The Convention on International Civil Aviation". The first article in the Convention states clearly that the contracting States recognize that every state has complete and exclusive sovereignty over the airspace above its territory. The EU carbon tax regulates the emissions of flights when they are in the airspace of member states, and is a violation of their national sovereignty.[32]

In addition, the EU issued free aviation allowances based on the annual average emissions in the period 2004–2006, which means that countries that produced higher historical emissions would benefit. For developing countries that produced low emissions in the past, but are undergoing rapid economic growth and a flourishing aviation industry, these aviation allowances are very unfair. For example, due to slow growth in the EU aviation industry, the growth in demand for aviation allowances is limited and the 27 EU inbound and outbound airlines only need to pay 15% to 18% of the carbon tax, whereas the rapidly developing Chinese aviation industry needs to purchase more than 60% of the aviation allowances for its airlines that are bound for Europe, reaching four times the amount of EU companies.[33]

The EU's unilateral restrictive measures of imposing aviation carbon taxes and launching maritime carbon taxes amounts to a disguised form of carbon tariffs in the transport service industry and the affected countries strongly opposed it. In 2011–2012, a number of countries, including China, held international conferences successively, strongly opposing the EU's violation of the sovereignty of non-EU countries and unilaterally including the international aviation in its emissions trading scheme. Some countries even issued trade retaliation threats.[34]

Faced with strong opposition, the EU was forced to announce in November 2012 that it would suspend its strategy of including the global aviation industry in its carbon emissions trading system. It continued negotiations on aviation emissions issues at the ICAO level, striving to reach a multilateral agreement with the parties. However, EU officials made it clear that if the ICAO failed to reach an agreement on international aviation

---

[32] Yan Shipeng, *Ibid*, p. 539.

[33] Qin Changbo, Ge Cha-zhong, Li Xiaoqiong and Liu Qianqian, "Impact of EU Aviation Carbon Tax on China and Recommendations," *Environment and Sustainable Development*, Issue 6, 2012.

[34] Chen Hui, "EU Aviation Carbon Tax and Countermeasures," *Power & Energy*, April 2012.

emissions by the end of 2013, the EU would resume its original strategy on January 1, 2014.[35]

2.2.3.3 Prospects for the implementation of aviation and maritime carbon taxes

In October 4, 2013, the ICAO agreed to develop a global market-based measure (MBM) for international aviation.[36] This seemed to imply that the debate over the EU aviation carbon taxes was coming to an end. However, the EU seemed to have tasted the fruits of unilateral measures and was unwilling to give up the implementation of aviation carbon taxes.

On October 19, the EU suggested modifying the original implementation plans of aviation carbon taxes, adjusting the scope of the aviation taxes, applying carbon emissions taxes on flights over the EU airspace during the period of 2014–2020, and exempting more than 70 countries from the carbon taxes. These countries include the least developed, low-income developing countries which are enjoying EU's Generalized System of Preferences (GSP),[37] and whose international air traffic is less than 1% of the global air traffic. China is not on the list.[38]

The EU argues that the implementation of the above scheme does not infringe the sovereignty of a third country, and is therefore a legitimate measure,[39] to which India and other emerging economies strongly opposed.[40] It is foreseeable that as the EU continues to push forth unilateral measures, the

---

[35] AFP, "EU Freezes Controversial Aviation Carbon Tax," November 13, 2012; retrieved from http://www.eubusiness.com/news-eu/aviation-tax-global.koj.

[36] ICAO, "Dramatic MBM Agreement and Solid Global Plan Endorsements Help Deliver Landmark ICAO 38th Assembly," October 4, 2013; retrieved from http://www.icao.int/Newsroom/Pages/mbm-agreement-solid-global-plan-endoresements.aspx.

[37] GSP refers to the universal, non-discriminatory and non-reciprocal tariff treatment that developed countries give to the imports from developing countries or regions, especially manufactured and semi-manufactured goods.

[38] For the list of countries, see http://ec.europa.eu/clima/policies/transport/aviation/docs/country_list_en.pdf.

[39] EU, "Aviation included in EU ETS," retrieved from http://ec.europa.eu/clima/policies/transport/aviation/.

[40] Dave Keating, "EU to Offer Concession on Aviation Emissions", *European Voice*, February 9, 2013; retrieved from http://www.europeanvoice.com/article/2013/august/eu-to-offer-concession-on-aviation-emissions/78082.aspx.

intense battle over aviation and maritime carbon taxes will persist over the long term.

3 Social Dumping or "Blue Barrier" Protectionism?

With nearly six billion people in developing countries joining the economic globalization process, one billion people in developed countries face fierce competition for jobs due to differences in labor costs.[41] Some developed countries believed that labor costs in developing countries are lower due to non-compliance with international labor standards:[42] some companies used child labor and prisoners to manufacture products for exports, some countries prohibited workers from forming associations freely, resulting in weak collective bargaining power, harsh working conditions and arbitrary reduction in wages. Export competitiveness achieved based on the above reasons constituted unfair competition and resulted in social dumping. Developed countries requested that trade and labor issues should be linked and trade restrictive measures should be imposed on the labor-intensive products from developing countries.

Developing countries are not opposed to the concept of labor standards. However, some countries believe that cheap labor is a necessary stage in a country's economic development and that there is no intrinsic relationship between trade and labor standards. This is essentially a form of "blue barrier" trade protection that developed countries created.[43] Through accusing developing countries of violating labor standards, developed countries adopted various measures to draw connections between trade and labor standards and included labor standards in bilateral and multilateral trade agreements. In actual fact, developed countries are denying developing countries of their comparative

---

[41] Zhu Min, "A Changing World," *International Economic Review*, Issue 6, 2012; retrieved from http://en.cnki.com.cn/Article_en/CJFDTOTAL-GJPP201206002.htm.

[42] International labor standards, also known as "core labor standards". These are the four basic principles identified in the "International Labor Organization Declaration on Fundamental Principles and Rights at Work and Its Follow-up" adopted during the 1998 International Labor Conference. The four principles are freedom of association and the effective recognition of the right to collective bargaining, the elimination of all forms of forced or compulsory labor, the effective abolition of child labor and the elimination of discrimination in respect of employment and occupation. See "ILO Declaration on Fundamental Principles and Rights at Work and Its Follow-up," retrieved from http://www.ilo.org/declaration/thedeclaration/textdeclaration/lang--en/index.htm.

[43] "Blue barriers" are blue, in comparison to "green barriers" which protect the environment, because they represent states' protection of blue-collar workers' interests.

advantage based on cheap labor and thus undermining the international competitiveness of products from developing countries.

3.1 *The issue of labor standards in the WTO*

3.1.1 *Evolution of multilateral labor standards*

The US is the first country to link trade and labor standards together. As early as during the GATT Tokyo Round and the Uruguay Round of negotiations in the 1970s, the US had advocated that the issue of labor standards be included in the relevant provisions in the GATT, but the idea was dropped due to opposition from many countries.[44] During the 1994 GATT ministerial meeting in Marrakesh, with the support of France and other EU countries, the US requested to link trade and labor issues, on the pretext of "social clauses", and to impose trade sanctions on the grounds of labor standards, so as to spur all parties to raise labor standards, but this was once again unsuccessful due to opposition from the majority of developing countries.[45]

During the WTO Ministerial Conference held in Singapore in 1996, the US — with the support of France, other EU members, Japan, and Canada — once again suggested including labor standards in WTO negotiations. When the US threatened that it would veto the entire Declaration if the "Singapore Ministerial Declaration" did not make mention of labor standards, developed countries and developing countries finally agreed to make the following statements in the Declaration after intense debate and negotiations: "We renew our commitment to the observance of internationally recognized core labour standards... We believe that economic growth and development fostered by increased trade and further trade liberalization contribute to the promotion of these standards. We reject the use of labour standards for protectionist purposes, and agree that the comparative advantage of countries, particularly low-wage developing countries, must in no way be put into question."[46]

However, the parties did not agree to ensure the implementation of the above commitments by imposing trade sanctions, nor was it specified if the

---

[44] Wang Weimin, "The Labour Standards Issue in the Recent American Free Trade Agreement," *Anhui University Law Review*, Issue 1, 2009.

[45] Qin Encai, "Discussion on the Legal Regulations on Labor Rights Protection in International Trade," *China Economist*, Issue 7, 2006.

[46] WTO, "Singapore Ministerial Declaration," retrieved from http://www.wto.org/english/thewto_e/minist_e/min96_e/wtodec_e.htm.

WTO should adopt follow-up measures. The only requirement was that the WTO should strengthen cooperation with the International Labor Organization. Therefore, the above Declaration effectively did not create binding commitments. There was no mention of labor issues in subsequent WTO ministerial meetings and it was only until the Doha Ministerial Conference held in 2001, that the WTO re-affirmed the Declaration on the international "core labor standards" reached at the Singapore Ministerial Conference, and mentioned the ILO's ongoing work on the social impact of globalization.[47] In fact, this statement excludes the labor issue from the Doha Round of negotiations.

3.1.2 *Existing provisions*

WTO parties are currently still divided on whether trade and labor issues should be linked. But under the WTO legal framework, there are some specific rules applicable to labor issues. These rules are stated in abstract terms, scattered among various WTO agreements, and provide room for linking trade and labor issues. For example, in the preface of the WTO agreement, it is mentioned that "recognizing that their relations in the field of trade and economic endeavour should be conducted with a view to raising standards of living, ensuring full employment and a large and steadily growing volume of real income and effective demand ... seeking both to protect and preserve the environment and to enhance the means for doing so". The statements clearly indicate that promoting and protecting labor rights are among the WTO's aims, and this is closely related to labor standards.

In addition to the above principles, the provisions in the WTO which are applicable to labor issues are the general exception clauses of GATT Article XX. Of which, subsection (e) "relating to the products of prison labour". This clause specifies that as an exception to the WTO nationa products of l treatment principle and MFN treatment principle, WTO members may adopt measures to restrict or prohibit the import of products made by prison labor. This is because many countries agree that allowing prisoners in jail to manufacture products for the international markets is an act of unfair dumping, as prisoners do not receive benefits or regular wages and other labor rights, and thus the production costs are lower than similar products.[48] In addition, broad interpretations of clause XX(a) "necessary to protect public

---

[47] Chen Hang and Liu Yong, "Discussion on the Necessity and Feasibility of the Establishment of "Core Labor Standards" under the WTO System," *WTO Focus*, Vol 17, No. 3 (May 2010).
[48] *Ibid.*

morals" and clause XX(b) "necessary to protect human, animal or plant life or health", could be applied to labor issues. For example, forced labor or the use of child labor and other acts, violate public morality and is bound to pose a threat to the life and health of workers, therefore these two clauses are applicable to trade restrictive measures which are against these acts.[49]

3.2 *Issues on FTA labor standards*

Unlike the WTO, some FTAs signed with the US and the EU already included labor rights protection related to trade or relevant terms on labor standards, and they were very specific. As the pioneers of trade and labor issues in FTAs, the US and the EU tend to be in unequal negotiation position with their partners because of their stronger bargaining power. They are able to force their negotiation partners to accept the requirements related to trade and labor. Due to the differences in the specific operation methods in negotiations between the US and the EU, the respective foreign negotiation practices formed are called the "NAFTA model" and the "EU model". In general, the NAFTA model is a more radical model with higher standards and stronger binding power. The EU model is more pragmatic and flexible. It takes care of the participants at different development levels appropriately and has weaker binding power.

3.2.1 *The NAFTA model*

NAFTA is the first FTA with clear and specific provisions related to labor rights and interests in the world.[50] In the NAFTA model, the parties mainly process the trade and labor issues through the North American Agreement on Labor Cooperation (NAALC) which is a subsidiary agreement of NAFTA. There are mainly three aspects of content in NAALC, namely the objectives and obligations, organization and dispute settlement mechanism of members.[51]

In terms of objectives and obligations, the NAALC broadly defines the labor rights provisions that need protection. It does not only cover the four "core labor standards" that ILO identifies, but also other economic labor standards.

---

[49] E Xiaomei, "Unilateral Trade Measures and WTO Rules Based on Labor Standards — New Trends in Trade Barriers and Countermeasures by Developing Countries," *Global Law Review*, Issue 2, 2010.

[50] CLC, "The North American Agreement on Labor Cooperation" retrieved from https://www.dol.gov/ilab/trade/agreements/naalc.htm.

[51] Refer to NAALC, retrieved from https://www.dol.gov/ilab/trade/agreements/naalc.htm.

There are a total of 11 labor rights provisions. NAALC states that members should include these provisions on labor rights through domestic legislation and ensure that the relevant laws and regulations are fulfilled and effectively implemented. These 11 labor rights include the freedom of association and organization, collective bargaining, striking, abolition of forced labor, protection of child and youth workers, minimum employment standards, elimination of employment discrimination based on race, religion, age, gender and other aspects, equal pay for both genders, prevention of occupational injuries and diseases, compensation for those who suffer occupational injuries and diseases, and the protection of migrant workers.

With regard to building mechanisms, the NAALC has established a relatively sound mechanism to ensure the effective implementation of agreements. The NAALC established the Commission for Labor Cooperation (CLC)[52] which is led by the Council of Ministers consisting of labor ministers to oversee the agreement. In addition, the agreement also requires that each country set up a National Administration Office (NAO) to receive request from interested groups and individuals on the enforcement of labor for other members. After review, a decision is made on whether further action should be taken.

In dispute settlements, NAALC "is usually sharper" and can clearly guarantee the fulfilment of agreement obligations by trade sanctions. NAALC states that after a dispute, the first review is done by the NAO and consultations are conducted at the ministerial level. If the problem cannot be resolved after the ministerial consultations, the disputing party can request that the Council of Ministers establish an Evaluation Committee of Experts (ECE) to make a decision. For a member with the pervasiveness and duration of the Party's persistent pattern of failure to effectively enforce its occupational safety and health, child labor or minimum wage technical labor standards, the panel can demand that the member pays a certain fine not more than 0.007% between the disputing parties' total trade in goods.[53] It can be said that the NAALC panel is similar to the WTO dispute settlement panel with quasi-judicial functions.

3.2.2 The EU model

The evolution of the EU model took place in two stages. Prior to 2008, the EU stipulated comparative principle on labor issues in trade agreements stressed only the promotion of various social development goals on labor and other

---

[52] See the CLC official website at http: //www.naalc.org/commission.htm.
[53] Refer to Annex 39, Article 1 in the NAALC "Monetary Enforcement Assessments"; retrieved from https://www.dol.gov/ilab/trade/agreements/naalc.htm.

issues through cooperation. However, since the start of the EU-CARIFORUM EPA in 2008, the EU mentioned the labor issues in the Preamble and also set up chapters on social aspects separately, dealing specifically with trade and labor issues. After the EU further improved the model, it created "Trade and Sustainable Development" chapters independently in trade agreements to manage trade, labor, and environmental issues.[54]

In the scope of protection, the area in which the EU model clearly protects labor rights is narrower than the NAFTA model and mainly focuses on four "core labor standards". For example, in the EU-Cariforum EPA, the two sides apparently focus on the implementation of "core labor standards" of the ILO. In the "EU-Korea FTA", both parties included provisions in their respective legal fight to achieve the four basic rights identified in the "ILO Declaration on Fundamental Principles and Rights at Work and Its Follow-up" which was passed during the International Labor Conference in 1998. They are namely the freedom of association and the effective recognition of the right to collective bargaining, the elimination of all forms of forced or compulsory labor, the effective abolition of child labor and the elimination of discrimination in employment and occupation.[55]

There is no compulsory dispute settlement mechanism applied to the labor disputes in the EU model. This is the biggest difference between the EU model and the NAFTA model. Before 2008, there were no mechanisms dealing with disputes on labor issues explicitly established in the FTAs signed between the EU and other countries. By 2008, when the EU and the Cariforum countries signed the economic partnership agreements, no appropriate mechanism was appropriately established despite both sides stating that disputes would be resolved through negotiations rather than trade sanctions. But in 2011, the provisions on the relevant mechanisms and procedures have become more complete in the "EU-Korea FTA". The EU and Korea should resolve the disputes via clear consultations between the governments. When necessary, they can seek advice from the "national advisory group" composed of non-governmental members. When a dispute arises, the agreement parties can set up a group of experts to put forward opinions and suggestions related to the dispute resolution. The countries of these parties shall endeavor to implement these suggestions and recommendations but they are not mandatory.

---

[54] Lorand Bartels, "Human Rights and Sustainable Development Obligations in EU Free Trade Agreements," retrieved from http://papers.ssrn.com/sol3/papers.cfm?abstract_id=2140033.
[55] Full Text of EU-Korea FTA, retrieved from http://www.customs.go.kr/kcshome/main/content/ContentView.do?contentId=CONTENT_ID_000002363&layoutMenuNo=23271.

3.2.3 *Development trends of the NAFTA model and the EU model*

The US and the EU are resolute in including labor issues in the FTAs, and strongly implementing them. It has become a prerequisite for countries to sign FTAs with them. All the FTAs that the US signed after the NAFTA are clearly related to trade and labor issues. The structure is also changed as there is no longer emphasis that the issues are resolved in the form of a subsidiary agreement. It follows the EU's practice of including the provisions on trade and labor standards in the text of the agreement. Through these FTAs, the US has successfully encouraged Jordan, Chile, Morocco, Guatemala, and other countries to refer to relevant international labor standards to make substantial changes in their domestic labor laws, thus improving the level of protection on the labor rights in these countries.[56]

Currently, issues related to trade and labor are still very sensitive. Even among the developed countries, there are also big differences. For example, besides signing a FTA that includes labor issues with the US, Australia has refused to include trade and labor issues in other FTAs that it has signed. Japan and the EFTA countries are more passive and do not insist on including the trade and labor issues in free trade agreements.[57]

The US and European countries encourage more countries to link trade and labor standards in free trade agreements, hoping to form multilateral rules as a result. However, it is difficult for the parties to reach a consensus in the short term.

4 China and Rules of Trade and Sustainable Development

From an international perspective, the global sustainable development situation has undergone profound changes since the United Nations General Assembly on Environment and Development in 1992. Sustainable development has gradually become an international consensus, with international and regional cooperation to promote it further. All the countries in the world, especially the developed countries, are placing an increasing emphasis on sustainable development. On the one hand, they emphasize facilitating

---

[56] Wang Weimin, "Labor standards issues in the recent American Free Trade Agreement," *Anhui University Law Review*, Issue 1, 2009.

[57] Lorand Bartels, "Social Issues: Labour, Environment and Human Rights," July 7, 2014; retrieved from http://papers.ssrn.com/sol3/papers.cfm?abstract_id=988639&download=yes.

economic development through international trade. On the other hand, they take environmental protection, labor standards and other issues into consideration under sustainable development. At the moment, it has become an important trend that cannot be ignored in international trade and economic development.[58]

Domestically, China has seized the opportunities in the global industrial transfer since the reform and opening up 30 years ago. It has taken advantage of factors like lower labor cost and land to vigorously develop an open economy. The foreign trade volume has increased by 100 times[59] and driven its national economy towards remarkable achievements in social development. During the rapid development of trade in the Chinese economy, the imbalance and incoordination under the requirements of sustainable development, like the construction of civilized ecology, environmental protection, and social development, have become increasingly prominent. With the new situation evolving, it seems that China should be more comprehensive in understanding the relationship between trade and sustainable development. Moreover, China should be more active to participate in regional and global trade and the establishment of sustainable development rules on the basis of exploration and practice of the rules.

4.1 *A more comprehensive understanding of the relationship between trade and sustainable development*

4.1.1 *Integration of trade and sustainable development is becoming an international trend*

During the six decades that followed after World War II, international trade has achieved unprecedented development and has grown to become the engine of world economic growth. From 1950 to 2012, the total value of world merchandise exports has increased from about USD61 billion to USD18.2 trillion in 62 years. This is an increase of nearly 300 times and is far more than the growth in industrial revolution or any other time in history. The rapid development of international trade has brought about unprecedented economic benefits for mankind. However, the unbridled use of natural resources by some countries and transnational corporations have resulted

---

[58] Lorand Bartels, "Human Rights and Sustainable Development Obligations in EU Free Trade Agreements," September 1, 2012; retrieved from http://papers.ssrn.com/sol3/papers.cfm?abstract_id=2140033.

[59] According to national statistics database data collation, the National Bureau of Statistics website at http://data.stats.gov.cn/english/.

in increasing pressure on the capacity of the world's natural environment. At the same time, the rapid development of international trade and economic globalization has promoted the global optimal allocation of capital, labor and other production factors. But due to marginalization, poor management, lack of security and other reasons, there is an increase of poverty, unemployment, wealth gap, and other social problems in some countries. Therefore, the rational use of natural resources and optimal allocation of labor and other factors of production on a global scale to expand production and consumption, while promoting a stable and harmonious social environment to achieve sustainable development, has become a current global issue that people are very concerned about.

At present, a growing number of countries support the inclusion of environment, labor and other sustainable development issues during trade negotiations. During the foreign trade negotiations with the US, although the environmental protection and labor standards are basically included at the start of NAFTA, this is not mandatory practice in the implementation. On May 10, 2007, the US Republicans and Democrats reached a "Bipartisan Trade Deal", stating that US' FTAs must include environmental and labor provisions from then on. Moreover, there must be details stated for specific provisions.[60] At the beginning of this century, the EU clearly stated that sustainable development is an important part of its foreign policy. There was a need to promote global sustainable development through trade agreements and it even demanded that all trade agreements include a "human rights clause".[61] Besides the US and the UN, other countries are also more open to trade and sustainable development. According to incomplete statistics, only four FTAs included the labor provisions in 1995. By 2005, the figure rose to 21. By 2011, it grew to 47.[62] This shows that the mutual integration of trade and sustainable development issues is strengthened. To a certain sense, this meets the needs of human development.

Clearly, due to the differences in the development level, cultural traditions, and social systems of developed and developing countries, it is normal for countries to have different understandings of trade and sustainable development. Overall, the developed countries cannot abuse the rules of trade and

---

[60] USTR, "Bipartisan Trade Deal," May 2007; retrieved from http://www.ustr.gov/sites/default/files/uploads/factsheets/2007/asset_upload_file127_11319.pdf.

[61] EU, "Human Rights," retrieved from http://europa.eu/pol/rights/index_en.htm.

[62] WTO, "Labour Standards: Consensus, Coherence and Controversy," retrieved from https://www.wto.org/english/thewto_e/whatis_e/tif_e/bey5_e.htm.

sustainable development and move towards extreme trade protectionism. When developing countries accept the rules of trade and sustainable development, it is impossible for them to go beyond their level of economic and social development, and make a commitment beyond their capabilities. Bridging the difference in position of developed and developing countries is a long and gradual historical process.

4.1.2 *China's development needs*

China's economy on the whole is at the mid- to last stage of industrialization, which is the heavy industrialization phase. It is difficult for the economic and trade development to stop depending on environmental resources in the longer term. However, the characteristics of inadequate environmental carrying capacity at present has become more and more obvious. The phenomenon of disorganized development and utilization of resources has been unsustainable. This is primarily because of the weak foundation in China's resources. There are inadequate resources per capita — fresh water, arable land, forest resources per capita have only reached 28%, 40% and 25% of the global average level respectively. Oil, iron ore, copper, and other important mineral resources per capita for recoverable reserves are only 7.7%, 17% and 17% of the world average respectively.[63] The more important reason is environmental pollution is becoming more serious, which leads to resources becoming scarcer. There are severe haze, groundwater, and soil pollution in Beijing and a large area of the country. This is alarming for the ecological environment. Currently, China has become the country with the most carbon emissions in the world. The carbon emission per capita is higher than the world average.[64] According to the research of the Chinese Academy for Environmental Planning of the Ministry of Environmental Protection, the degradation of China's ecological environment in 2010 cost up to USD230 billion, accounting for 3.5% of the GDP that year.[65]

---

[63] NDRC, "People's Republic of China National Report on Sustainable Development" official release; retrieved from http://www.china-un.org/eng/zt/sdreng/.

[64] *People's Daily* website "Pan Jiahua: A Dialectical and Objective Analysis on the 'World's Largest Emitter'," November 30, 2011; retrieved from http: //env.people.com.cn/GB/13356431.html.

[65] Wang Erde, "China Ecological Environmental Cost 1.5 trillion in 2010," *21st Century Business Herald*, January 15, 2013, retrieved from http: //epaper.21cbh.com/html/2013-01/15/content_42531. htm? div = -1.

At the same time, although there are still outstanding contradictions in China's labor supply and demand structure, employment turnover, youth employment, rural to urban employment and other pressures are still relatively high. But with the rapid rise in the proportion of aging population, the older population in China has exceeded 200 million.[66] The gradual decay of China's demographic dividend has become an irreversible trend. This will bring greater pressure on future economic growth. With China's labor laws and regulations improving steadily, the level of labor rights protection has gradually increased and awareness of citizens' rights is strengthening day by day. To a certain extent, labor costs have risen. As supply and policy factors work together to influence China, China's participation in international division of labor and international trade by relying on its traditional advantages of cheap and abundant labor may not work for long.

Looking toward the future, with growing constraints of environmental resources on economic development, the effect of demographic dividends will gradually reduce. Over the past 30 years, China has emphasized quantity over quality and speed over efficiency. This kind of rough and extensive growth method was unsustainable. Economic, social, and environmental factors must be organized to promote comprehensive, balanced, coordinated, and sustainable development. Therefore, managing the relationship between trade and the environment, labor, and other issues well in the mid- and long-term, is in line with the requirements of China's strategy to achieve sustainable development.

4.1.3 The challenge of sustainable development that China faces in international trade

Take carbon tariffs as an example. According to expert estimates, the embedded emissions[67] of Chinese exports are respectively 1.64 billion tons and 1.92 billion tons of carbon dioxide in 2007 and 2008. If embedded emission is used as the basis, an equivalent of USD35, 50 and 60 per ton of carbon dioxide is calculated as tax rate respectively on carbon tariffs and the tariff level of China's exports will increase by 3.4%–6.6%.[68] In addition, China's

---

[66] Reuters, "In China, Signs that One-child Policy May be Coming to An End", retrieved from http://www.reuters.com/article/us-china-population-idUSBRE90K0UV20130122.

[67] Embedded emissions are the sum of emissions throughout the product life cycle as a result of its various production processes.

[68] Gu Alun and Zhon Lingling, "Carbon Tariffs on China's Export Trade and Policy Recommendations," *China Economic & Trade Herald*, August 2012.

export products are generally low in technological content, high in energy consumption and intensive in labor and resources. In particular, the coal-dominated energy structure has led to exports releasing more product emission than some developing countries. Therefore, China may become the main target for international carbon tariffs to be implemented. For example, if USD30 per ton of carbon emissions is the standard carbon tariff for the same kind of imported goods, the actual tax for China commodities can be 20% of the unit value of goods while the actual tax of Brazilian goods which rely on clean energy may be 5%,[69] since there is different national energy structure.

Take the carbon tax in aviation as another example. China's civil aviation industry is in a period of rapid development: Over the past 10 years, the transportation of air passengers has maintained an average annual growth rate of 15.3%, about three times the growth rate of world air transport in the same period of time. Once the EU aviation carbon tax is implemented, Chinese airlines will have to invest a lot of money to reach the carbon emission targets of the EU for China-Europe flights, thus transport costs will rise drastically. According to preliminary estimates, after the first year of carbon tax in aviation, the cost of Chinese airlines that fly to and from Europe will likely increase by 800 million yuan. It will increase every year thereafter until 2020 when it will reach 3 billion yuan. The cumulative expenditure over this nine-year period totaled approximately 17.6 billion yuan.[70] If the cost is distributed to the consumers, the price of each international air ticket from Beijing to Europe may increase by 200–300 yuan.[71]

In the labor field, the introduction of a number of international standards will likely increase production costs. For example, the US launched the SA8000 (Social Accountability 8000 International Standard) which has become a standard that more and more international buyers require suppliers to meet. The standard includes the following: provisions on the minimum working age of workers; prohibition of compulsory labor on workers; health and safety regulations of workers; freedom of association and right to collective

---

[69] Xie Laihui and Chen Ying, "Is China Over Concerned about the Issue of Carbon Tariffs?" *International Economic Review*, Issue 4, 2010.

[70] Liu Manping, "Our Countermeasures to Respond to the Carbon Tax in European aviation," *Macroeconomic Management*, Issue 3, 2012.

[71] China Civil Aviation Information Network, "From January Next Year, Air Tickets to Europe May Increase by Two or Three Hundred Yuan due to 'Carbon Emission Tax'," March 22, 2011; retrieved from http://www.caacnews.com.cn/2011np/20110322/160443.html.

bargaining; elimination of different races, ethnicity, religion, and gender receiving discriminatory treatment; prohibition of disciplinary practice against the workers; regulations on workers working time; minimum standards for workers' wage provisions; implementation of the above management system by enterprises *etc.*[72] The implementation of these standards may put pressure on the cost of Chinese exports of textiles, garments, cosmetics, agriculture, toys, and other labor-intensive enterprises in the short term.

Overall, there are many factors like the international division of labor, trade status, energy structure, and population structure that determine if labor-intensive products with higher emission will remain as China's major export products for a longer period of time in the future. With the emergence of international green and blue trade barriers, China needs to promote energy saving technology, improve energy efficiency and optimize the energy structure. It can facilitate the export of products to accelerate the transformation and upgrading towards value chain development. It should also participate actively in the multilateral and regional levels in the establishment of rules on trade and sustainable development, achieving and maintaining domestic industrial development by using the relevant rules to ensure that the domestic industry accelerates towards the goal of transformation.

4.2 China's recent exploration and practical application of sustainable development rules in economic and trade fields

4.2.1 China's exploration of the concept and practices of sustainable development

China continues to develop and enrich the meaning of sustainable development. For example, the Chinese government participated in three major conferences — Conference on the Human Environment in Stockholm, Environment and Development Conference in Rio de Janeiro and Sustainable Development of the General Assembly Summit in Johannesburg, South Africa — that were milestones that formed and developed upon the concept of sustainable development. China was one of the countries that first proposed and implemented sustainable development strategies. After the

---

[72] Han Jinghua and Zhao Ru, "SA8000 Standard and Its Impact on China's Export Trade," *Special Zone Economy*, January 2013.

UNCED in 1992, the Chinese government issued "China's Agenda 21 — White Paper on 21st Century China's Population, Environment and Development" in March 1994. The sustainable development strategies were promoted to national level and fully implemented in 1996. In the new century, China has further deepened the understanding of sustainable development. In 2003, the sustainable scientific development which is people-oriented and comprehensively coordinated was put forward. Under the guidance of the scientific concept of development, China's economic restructuring and development pattern, construction of ecological civilization and harmonious society, resource conservation, and environmental protection had achieved results in the initial phases.[73] In 2007, the Party's Congress clearly stated the concept of "ecological civilization" in its 17th report, and improved the content of building a comprehensive well-off society. With the understanding of the importance of ecological civilization deepening, the report at China's 18th Party Congress in 2012 specifically proposed the construction of ecological civilization on the basis of "four building blocks" — economic construction, political construction, cultural construction, and social construction. This required the full implementation of "five-in-one overall layout to promote the modern construction of all aspects in coordination". In 2013, there was a special chapter in "The Decisions of CPC Central Committee on Some Major Issues Concerning Comprehensively Deepening the Reform" called "Acceleration of the Construction of the Ecological Civilization System" to discuss the specific content of constructing the ecological civilization in details. This shows that the construction of an ecological civilization has caught the attention of the party and the country.

On trade and sustainable development issues, the Chinese government has put these on high priority and achieved a lot of results. Domestically, China's National Development and Reform Commission approved Beijing, Tianjin, Shanghai, Chongqing, Hubei, Guangdong, and Shenzhen to carry out pilot projects on carbon emissions and trading on October 29, 2011 in order to promote the use of low cost market mechanisms to fulfill the target of Chinese control of greenhouse gas emission in 2020.[74] At present, all the

---

[73] China.org.cn, "China's National Report on Sustainable Development," June 1, 2012; retrieved from http://www.china.com.cn/zhibo/zhuanti/ch-xinwen/2012-06/01/content_25541073.htm.

[74] National Development and Reform Commission, "Notice of National Development and Reform Commission Regarding the Pilot Project on Carbon Emissions and Trading," retrieved from http://www.sdpc.gov.cn/zcfb/zcfbtz/.

cities have introduced the management approach of trading with carbon emissions. A number of provinces and cities are emerging in the carbon market. China also takes the initiative to cancel the export tax rebate for some commodities and control products that consume high energy and result in serious pollution to ensure that the targets of emission reduction are met.[75] With regard to foreign affairs, Prime Minister Wen Jiabao made clear commitment at the Copenhagen Climate Change Summit on December 18, 2009 that the Chinese carbon dioxide emissions per unit of GDP in 2020 would decrease by 40% to 45% as compared to 2005. Meanwhile, China actively supports developing countries in addressing climate change issues through South–South cooperation. In response to global climate change, China has tried to contribute to the best of its ability. On September 24, 2013, Chinese Foreign Minister Wang Yi made a commitment at the United Nations High-Level Political Forum on sustainable development that China would provide 200 million yuan to support Africa in tackling climate change.[76]

4.2.2 *The practice of sustainable development in China's FTAs*

So far, China has signed 14 FTAs involving 22 countries and regions. From these FTAs, China has been cautious with trade and labor, and environmental issues. In the FTAs that China signed before 2013, the parties generally mentioned principles in the Preamble that the FTAs were signed with the goals of "creating new jobs and protecting the environment for sustainable development", but specific terms and content were not established appropriately. In three separate FTAs that China made with Chile, New Zealand and Peru, respectively, the parties set up a special labor and environmental cooperation clause, citing relevant content in a memorandum of understanding signed between both supervising government departments to deepen bilateral economic and technological cooperation. However, the memorandums of understanding are at a lower level and are just working documents. They do not have strong binding international legality. Furthermore, the above content does

---

[75]Ministry of Commerce, "Interview with the Ministry of Commerce on the Abolition of Export Tax Rebate for Some Commodities," retrieved from http://english.mofcom.gov.cn.

[76]Speech by Wang Yi, "Sustainable Development — The Road to Achieve Chinese Dream and Human Progress," September 24, 2013; retrieved from http://www.fmprc.gov.cn/mfa_eng/wjb_663304/wjbz_663308/2461_663310/t1081238.shtml.

not mention if relevant disputes are brought for settlement by FTA dispute settlement mechanisms.[77]

On July 6, 2013, China and Switzerland signed a bilateral FTA.[78] In this important FTA that China signed, China took a major step forward in trade and sustainable development and achieved a lot of breakthroughs. In terms of structure, China agreed to set up a separate chapter on environmental issues in the FTA for the first time and sign an intergovernmental agreement on cooperation in labor and employment outside of the FTA. This is much higher in legal position than the memorandum of understanding signed in an FTA. In terms of content, both China and Switzerland defined clearer and more specific provisions on trade and sustainable development. For example, the parties refer to objectives like social progress and harmony in the preamble and encourage enterprises to comply with the internationally accepted principles and rules within good corporate governance and corporate social responsibility of both parties. Generally, these principles and rules include contents on environment, labor and even human rights, anti-corruption, and so on. In the environment chapter, the main content of both sides is to carry out practical economic and technical cooperation. It also draws on the FTA terms that the EU signs externally, stating clearly that the two sides should not attract investment and promote trade by encouraging to reduce the level of environmental protection. At the same time, environmental standards cannot be used for trade protection purposes. It is noteworthy that in the China-Switzerland FTA, both sides agreed the disputes under the environment chapter were not applicable to dispute settlement mechanisms. They can only be settled through friendly consultations between the governments.

4.3 *Participate more actively in the establishment of rules on trade and sustainable development*

Since the developed and developing countries have different positions in the WTO multilateral trading system, all the parties have debated on linking trade with environment and labor issues. It is difficult to reach an agreement. A long

---

[77] According to the compilation of free trade area service website of Ministry of Commerce. Related texts can be retrieved from http://fta.mofcom.gov.cn/index.shtml.

[78] Ministry of Commerce, "Gao Hucheng signed the China-Switzerland Free Trade Agreement with Johann Schneider-Ammann', " July 10, 2013; retrieved from http://english.mofcom.gov.cn/article/newsrelease/significantnews/201307/20130700192882.shtml.

protracted process is expected to form relevant multilateral rules. In this case, taking into account that the risks in negotiating FTAs with relevant countries and regions are controllable with less influence and difficulty, China can use these FTAs as "experimental fields" to deal with sustainable development issues such as trade and environment, labor *etc.* This is different from the multilateral stance as internal and external linkage can be used appropriately to participate actively in the establishment of regional rules on trade and sustainable development.

In China, the improvement of the legal system on environmental protection should be accelerated. The level of environmental protection should be increased and the implementation of restrictions on carbon emissions should be more stringent. The domestic carbon tax system can be introduced promptly[79] so that the tax benefits remain in the country. This eliminates the basis of carbon tariffs imposed by developed countries. For labor standards, China has currently approved international labour conventions related to two "core labor standards", *i.e.* the elimination of discrimination in employment and occupation, and ban of child labor. The collective contract system can be improved in the future by gradually adopting the standards like SA8000. Based on the complete abolition of the labor education system by the Third Plenary Session of the 18th CPC, the level of labor protection can be improved steadily.[80]

Externally, China may use the FTA as a key testing ground for promoting the establishment of rules on trade and sustainable development. Based on the China-Switzerland FTA, it can move forward in accordance with the new requirements, "confident path, confident concept, confident institution". It can take a more proactive stand during FTA negotiations, taking due consideration to link trade and the environment with labor issues appropriately. It can continue innovating concepts and systems according to the current new situation at home and abroad. Specifically, it can refer to the EU model and gradually include a chapter on sustainable development in FTAs to deal with trade and the environment, and other issues. However, the focus is on content such as the declaration of principles, pragmatic cooperation, capacity building, and public participation. It is only through amiable intergovernmental discussion

---

[79] Li Bin, "The Timing of Introducing Carbon Tax has Become the Focus," The *People's Political Consultative Daily*, June 8, 2010, B01 edition.

[80] Zhang Dongmei and Chen Jianfeng, "Legal Participation in Union Under Global Governance — Union's Role in Fulfilling Core Labor Standards," *Journal of China Institute of Industrial Relations*, Vol. 26, No. 4, August 2012.

to settle disputes that a transition and grace period is given to the domestic industry. Through this gradual approach, a solution that takes into account the sustainable development trend in the world situation and the development conditions of the country can be found. There must be a steady and continuous improvement in environmental protection and labor standards in China so as to make greater contributions to construct an ecological civilization and improve labor well-being and implement the strategy of sustainable development.

Chapter 15

Reconstruction and Prospects of Global Economic and Trade Rules

"Throughout history, real revolutions have often broken out quietly and calmly, such that those involved or in that generation never realized they were making history." In early 2013, a Chinese economist solemnly pointed out that the so-called "revolutions" actually refer to the reconstruction of global economic and trade rules triggered by the 2008 financial crisis.

The once-in-a-century financial crisis broke the previous trends of the world economy, strengthened the driving force behind the evolution of the global governance structure, and accelerated the pace of reconstruction and adjustment of global economic rules. On the one hand, the governance platform represented by the G20 and the relevant international organizations, faced with the problems exposed by the crisis, introduced a series of remedial actions — such as strengthening financial regulation — to actively improve existing rules. Emerging economies and most developing countries hope to establish a more balanced pattern of international governance and increase their right of voice. On the other hand, to seize future competitive advantage in the global competition presented after the crisis, the US, Europe and other developed countries put in all efforts to create a new generation of international economic and trade rules in a broader field. The US strongly pushed for the TPP, and the EU and the US launched TTIP negotiations, claiming the negotiations were representative. The two FTA negotiations not only sought to establish high standards of market access, they also focused on the exploration to establish new rules that covered various aspects including trade, investment, IPR, competitive neutrality, the environment, labor *etc*. It is no exaggeration to say that international economic rules are facing the most profound and comprehensive adjustment, improvement, and reconstruction since the 1990s, covering a wide range of areas in unprecedented intensity of change. A new blueprint for global trade rules is emerging from the turbulent battlefield.

If we look back at this point of time years later, we could be at a turning point in history.

1 The Direction, Battle, and Path of International Economic and Trade Rule Reconstruction

There are three basic characteristics of international economic and trade rule reconstruction after the financial crisis: First, the promotion of the opening up of the market and liberalization of investment and trade are still the main directions of the new round of international economic and trade rule reconstruction. The new rules will further emphasize high standards and levels, and the range of rule adjustment will extend from the traditional border measures to behind-the-border measures, striving to remove all obstacles, and substantially increase the degree of mutual openness in the global market. Second, various interest groups are battling intensely over the rule reconstruction, competing to introduce various new issues, and the scope of rule reconstruction has expanded way beyond that of the past. Developed countries emphasize fair competition and still dominate the setting of the agenda. Third, the path of rule reconstruction shows a diversifying development trend. Apart from the global governance platform, all kinds of regional cooperation are vying to create a new version of rules suitable for themselves and seizing the opportunity to try to lead the change in global economic and trade rules.

1.1 *The main direction of rule reconstruction points towards the promotion of liberalizing the market and trade investment*

The outbreak of the financial crisis made people reflect profoundly on its causes. International economic imbalances in the context of globalization was considered one of the deep-seated causes of the crisis. Some put forth the rhetoric of "anti-globalization", believing that uncontrolled capital expansion in the world must come to an end. Developed countries proposed a "return to industrialism" and promoted the reflux of the manufacturing sector. Trade protectionism rose and was regarded as evidence for "de-globalization" in the world economy. Some people even tried to discredit Neoliberalism which had grown in popularity since the generations of Reagan and Thatcher. Although these accusations were more rooted in criticizing the domestic macroeconomic policies of the developed countries, they also registered disapproval of the emphasis on liberalism and opening up in international trade and investment issues.

In terms of the rule reconstruction practices since the crisis, some people thought that emerging economies which benefited most from the globalization process did not strictly follow the rules but rather made use of loopholes in the rules to gain unfair competitive advantage. Therefore, they put stronger constraints and fair trade at the top of rule reconstruction agenda. In the face of environmental, labor, and other ecological problems brought about by globalization, the issues of sustainable development have become an important part of the new round of rule reconstruction and will inevitably create new restrictions on trade and investment behavior.

So did the financial crisis reverse the trend of globalization? Will international rule reconstruction restrict the opening up of the market and liberalization of investment and trade which had been brought about by globalization in any way?

Clearly, although globalization suffered a setback due to the crisis, it continued to gain momentum. Over the years, driven by international economic activities in finance, trade, investment, and great efforts made by multinational companies, global industries have formed an interdependent division of labor system. A global value chain that holds countries around the world together has been established, and the allocation of goods, services, capital, and technology on a global scale has become an irreversible norm. The progress of science and technology is another inexhaustible driving force behind globalization, the new Internet-based technological revolution has pushed global exchange of information to an unprecedented level of comprehensiveness and convenience. The market is naturally a mechanism based on the full docking of supply and demand information. The increasing dissemination of information makes achieving a complete market with global coverage more possible and clearer, resulting in declining transaction costs, and the blending together of economies has become an irreversible trend. In fact, despite the severe impact of the crisis, global trade rebounded quickly and in 2012, global trade in goods grew by 13.6% compared to 2008, the year that the crisis broke out.

The economic base determines the superstructure. As long as the trend of economic globalization has not changed, international economic and trade rules adjustment will inevitably follow such a trend. According to economic theory, the promotion of the opening up of the market and the liberalization of trade and investment, and the deepening and refinement of the international division of labor and driving international trade and economic development are not exclusive goals of neoliberalism, but basic principles of the market economy. The free allocation of various resources and elements in a broader field is an inevitable choice in order to improve efficiency.

History tells us that international economic and trade rules took shape in the global context of increasingly close economic and trade exchanges are products of globalization. When international economic and trade rules were first established after World War II, their main task was to address the economic and trade disputes between countries, and maintain international economic and trade order. However, as more and more people implemented the rules, they gradually realized that adherence to mutually open markets and safeguarding fair competition were the right ways to promote world economic and trade development the best interests of all countries. Therefore, from a relatively static and passive mediator of economic trade interests, international economic and trade rules have evolved into a powerful tool to promote the opening up of global markets and liberalization of trade and investment. In other words, since the birth of international economic and trade rules, the mission has been to promote international economic and trade development, and the promotion of mutually open markets and liberalization of trade and investment is in line with the inherent nature and principle of this mission.

Take multilateral trade rules for example. In the 1920s and 1930s, a severe economic crisis hit the capitalist world. To protect themselves, the US implemented the infamous Smoot-Hawley Tariff Act, collecting an average of up to 53% in tariffs on imported products. European countries subsequently followed suit, causing world trading to decline substantially by 70%. This short-sighted beggar-thy-neighbor move seriously exacerbated the global economic crisis. People reflected on the painful lesson and proposed the building of a worldwide multilateral trading system to ensure the normal development of international trade. When World War II ended, this idea was put into practice. In 1947, the General Agreement on Tariffs and Trade (GATT) was concluded, becoming the first multilateral system of global trade rules. After GATT was established, eight rounds of multilateral trade negotiations were conducted where tariffs were reduced and non-tariff barriers were removed, promoting extensive and important outcomes such as the opening up of trade in services and investment liberalization which in turn, contributed greatly to the post-war global trade and economic development.

Since World War II, despite repeated outbreaks of economic crises worldwide, nothing like the vicious trade war of the 1930s ever happened again. After the financial crisis, there was a rise in various types of protectionist practices. Existing international economic and trade rules still serve as breakwaters to curb the spread of protectionism. Successive G20 Summits all raised clear calls against protectionism. The WTO strengthened supervision and review over national trade policies and criticized the practice of trade protectionism. On the whole, there was no significant increase in the total number of global trade remedial cases during the five-year periods of 2003–2007 and 2008–2012, but the amount involved had increased greatly and was a great improvement over the period of beggar-thy-neighbor trade practices after the great recession.

Facts on the ground indicate that existing international economic and trade rules are still effective for maintaining an open international trade and economic system. Since the crisis, with the adjustment and reconstruction of international trade rules, macro-coordination has been introduced and strengthened: financial supervision, strict rules of competition, and attention to issues such as environmental protection and labor have also been enhanced. However, the basis and main objective is still in maintaining a free and open international trade system so as to promote the opening up of the market and investment and trade liberalization.

Despite the stalemate in the Doha Round negotiations, no country was willing to take responsibility for the stalled negotiations. The Ninth Ministerial WTO Conference in Bali took several twists and turns before finally reaching an Early Harvest with trade facilitation as the main outcome. This was the first worldwide agreement reached after the establishment of the WTO in 20 years, since the end of the Uruguay Round. This agreement can be described as the life booster injected to the Doha Round at a life-and-death moment. While overall negotiations faced resistance, a number of plurilateral negotiations moved doggedly forward. The Information Technology Agreement (ITA) was one of the extended negotiations. There are currently 78 members in this agreement, accounting for more than 97% of global trade in information technological products. The objective of the negotiations was to further expand the range of products with reduced tariffs, limit non-tariff barriers more strictly, and push for Brazil, Mexico, South Africa, and other important IT market players to join in the agreement. The US, the EU, Canada, Australia, and some other WTO members were also actively promoting the TISA plurilateral negotiations which aimed to significantly reduce or eliminate market barriers for trade in services. Its aims were much more ambitions than those of the GATT and Doha Round negotiations.

At the same time, regional economic cooperation was more active than ever. Since 2008, the WTO has been informed of 69 FTAs that have come into effect, accounting for 32% of the total number of FTAs. Large numbers of FTA negotiations are also taking place, especially the TPP and TTIP entities with a huge size of economy, advertisement of high liberalization and a goal to reduce tariffs on almost all products gradually to zero and substantially liberalize the trade in services market. The Regional Comprehensive Economic Partnership (RCEP) consists mainly of regional cooperation among emerging economies. Although the degree of openness is limited by various emerging economies, and it is not as ambitious as the TPP, it still aims for more openness than the existing commitments in the multilateral system and has a bigger market with higher expectations for growth. From the global and multilateral system's perspective, the open areas of regional economic cooperation are limited but its flourishing development precisely reflects countries' recognition and pursuit of higher levels of open market environments. Regional economic integration is a special manifestation in the process of deepening globalization, paving the way for the further opening up of the global market in the future.

In the area of investment, traditional international investment agreements focus more on investment protection and promotion while the new generation of investment agreements places more emphasis on promoting investment liberalization. Approaches that favor pre-establishment national treatment and a negative list are more and more widely accepted, and liberalization of international investment will also be further enhanced.

In short, as economic globalization deepens, although the reconstruction of international trade rules reflects the competition and readjustment of interest relationships among members at different phases of development, it will not deviate from the original intention of promoting the development of globalization. Whether the emphasis is on fair trade theory or sustainable development, the foundation lies in the liberalization of trade and investment. Any country that wishes to compete for the right to be heard in establishing international economic and trade rules must understand this fully in order to know the right direction to take with international negotiation strategies and the formulation of domestic policies.

1.2 *The complex battle among different interest groups influenced the direction of international economic and trade rules*

The fight for dominance in establishing international economic and trade rules is the strategic high ground for safeguarding national economic and trade interests. Since the crisis, the various parties have battled intensely over the reconstruction of international economic and trade rules. Differentiated and intertwined interests have made the battle more complex. One of the most important debates took place between developed countries and emerging economies.

Since the crisis, the world economy has undergone profound changes: Western developed countries have relatively declined in power while emerging economies have grown in influence. It is estimated that in the 1990s, emerging economies, as a whole, contributed approximately one fourth of the world's economic growth. In the first seven years of the 21st century, their contribution to world economic growth rose to about half. From the outbreak of the crisis to date, emerging markets have contributed as much as three fourths of world economic growth. From the international trade perspective, developing countries only accounted for 15% of the world's total 25 years ago but today, the proportion is close to 40%.[1] However, the sustainability of emerging economies remains uncertain. Developed countries will still continue to lead in the field of international trade for a long time. The world economy shows trends that the South is rising in power and the North is declining, yet the situation with a powerful North and a weaker South in global governance has not fundamentally changed. Developing countries hope for more institutional rights in global governance and rule-making, while developed countries hope that new issues will be brought to attention in the new round of international economic and trade rule reconstruction, and that emerging economies will assume more responsibilities and obligations. From this perspective, developed countries are still ahead of the developing countries, in both power and action in this round of international economic and trade rule reconstruction. They are the main driving force for rule reconstruction.

The impact of this struggle firstly highlights the fact that developed countries more prominently emphasize fair trade in the establishment of international economic and trade rules to safeguard their interests. Historically, the US, Europe, and other developed countries have committed to free trade theory for a long time and are using the international economic and trade rules they dominate to demand other countries to open up their markets, paving the way for their competitive industries to enter these countries. As developed countries decline in competitive advantage in the world economy and international trade, many Western politicians and scholars have stressed repeatedly since the crisis that the benefits of economic globalization are imbalanced. China and other emerging economies, whose rapid rise owes much to the global political, economic and security system established by the US and other Western countries, have contributed little to global and regional public goods and often

---

[1] Lin Jianhai, "Strategic Response to Challenges in the Global Economy," *China Business News*, September 2, 2013.

taken an opportunistic approach with existing international economic rules, gaining competitive advantage by way of currency manipulation, subsidies, forceful technology transfer, intellectual property infringement, supporting state-owned enterprises *etc.*, and underming the principle of fairness. The US must strengthen trade enforcement to ensure fair trade while the new generation of international economic and trade rules must help reverse this situation of unfair competition.[2]

Guided by this thought, in February 2012, the US government established a special trade law enforcement agency to urge nations to comply with international trade rules. At the same time, during TPP, TTIP and other FTA negotiations, the US strengthened fair trade rules across the board. On the one hand, they requested for more stringent intellectual property rights (IPR) protection, labor, environmental and safety standards, and other social provisions. Once formed, these rules would increase the obligations and costs borne by developing countries. On the other hand, they heightened the focus on competitive policies to promote the development of more stringent standards, restrict governmental support and limit the development of state-owned enterprises, proposing and emphasizing competitive neutrality, modal neutrality, technological neutrality and other concepts. With the US and the EU driving competitive neutrality, relevant rules gradually emerged. Compared to past FTA negotiations which focused on lowering tariffs, removing non-tariff barriers, increasing access to service markets, facilitating of trade and investment *etc.*, these new rules cover broad areas and hold strict standards, reflecting their strong, offensive and targeted nature. They have become the benchmark for the new round of rules reconstruction.

The outbreak of the financial crisis enhanced the voice of the developing countries in international governance. The G20 replaced the G8 and became an important platform for global governance. Developing countries are working hard to change their original role as passive recipients of international economic and trade rules, and seeking for greater institutional rights in rule-making and other areas. The IMF adjusted capital shares. The International Financial Stability Forum was renamed the International Financial Stability Board as China and other emerging economies joined in and rolled out various measures. This reflected a change of trends in the new round of rule adjustments, yet development countries are still generally on the defensive. In particular, emerging economies face even greater challenges.

---

[2]Zhang Yuyan, "Re-Globalization: China's Opportunities and Challenges," *Oriental Morning Post*, January 8, 2013.

Offering some special differential treatment for developing countries is a fundamental principle in existing international economic and trade rules. In the 1950s, with the growing number of independent nation states, the developing countries requested for the reform of international economic and trade rules, and the call for the establishment of a new international economic order grew stronger. After unremitting efforts, in 1964, the "Trade and Development" chapter was added to GATT, establishing the legal basis for providing special and differential treatment to developing members. This practice is still applied today. This principle is also widely applied in the development of other international rules. For example, the emphasis on "common yet differentiated responsibilities" in response to climate and other global environmental issues. However, internationally, there is only a general understanding and no clear definition of what constitutes a developing country. As proposed by the UN, the WTO only identified "Least developed countries" (LDCs). As some developing countries grow in strength, the US, the EU and other developed ones are singling them out in the game of international rules. For example, in the Doha Round negotiations in 2003, the US and Europe had already put forward the concept of "advanced developing country", requiring that China, Brazil, India, and other emerging economies not be regarded as equal to other developing countries in general and take on more responsibilities. On some international issues, the developed countries even contact and work together with some developing countries and LDCs to put pressure on emerging economies. For example, the Alliance of Small Island States (AOSIS) has, to some extent, joined hands with the developed countries in exerting pressure on the emerging economies with regard to climate change issues.

In the multilateral arena, emerging economies and other developing countries, using the power of consensus, stopped developed countries from introducing new issues that were advantageous for them and selectively promoting new rules. Thus, the developed countries sought other means and turned to economic cooperation and plurilateral agreements *etc.* to bypass differences in opinions and create a new version of international economic and trade rules in an attempt to force emerging economies into acceptance. Due to differences in levels of development, it is still difficult for emerging economies to develop sufficient agenda-setting power to compete with developed countries in the short term. In international rule-making, overall speaking, they still face a reality of defensive interests outnumbering offensive ones. In this sense, developing countries represented by the emerging economies encounter both challenges and opportunities in the new round of international economic and trade rules. It would not be surprising that the challenges are greater than the opportunities.

The battle over rules is complex with intertwining relationships: not only is it a struggle between developed and emerging economies, among developed countries, between emerging economies and the other developing countries, among emerging economies, governmental organizations and NGOs, there also exist varying extents of interest differentiation in various fields, with each party advocating for their own interests. For example, the EU and the US have differing opinions on rules of origin; Brazil and India take opposing offensive and defensive stances on agricultural issues; and in the Doha Round, the developing countries do not have a common stand on issues such as deep-sea fishing and cotton.

At the same time, multinational companies and trade organizations are also important forces in the battle over rules. Multinational companies have always been a main force in economic globalization. As strong market players, they have both vital interests as well as powerful influence in international economic and trade rule-making often by influencing the decisions of governments. The reason for the weak momentum and slow progress of the Doha Round negotiations is related to the multinational corporations' lack of interest in development and agricultural issues. In the new round of rule reconstruction, developed countries emphasize competitive neutrality and demand expansion of liberalization of services, strengthening of IPR protection, tightening of supervision over state-owned enterprises *etc*. All these directly reflect the interests and demands of Western multinational corporations. Civil organizations are also actively involved in the reconstruction of international economic and trade rules, exerting their own influence on certain industrial interests or advocating certain concepts, practices and perspectives. At important international conferences such as the G20 and WTO, various NGOs gather and compete to make their voices heard. During climate negotiations, the World Wildlife Fund, Greenpeace, Friends of the Earth and other climate-related NGOs have become very important off-site powers. Many country representatives have taken the initiative to convene aside and hold specialized dialogues with these NGOs.

In short, there are extensive and diverse forces with complex and varied interest demands at play in the new battle over international economic and trade rules. This situation with conflict and cooperation interwoven is a vivid portrayal of "game theory" at work. In order to avoid a zero-sum outcome, the current round of rule reconstruction will not depart from the basic trend of opening up markets and promotion of trade and investment liberalization.

However, in the new round of rule adjustments, parties will need to have strength and good strategies to gain more advantage.

1.3 *Regional and plurilateral agreements driving multilateral process may become one of the main paths of reconstruction*

Strictly speaking, international economic rules are a broad concept lacking precise definitions. Judging from the point of view of effectiveness, they include international treaties with both stringent rights and obligations as well as coercive constraints, generally accepted international practices, non-mandatory binding international consensus and the like. In terms of content, international economic and trade rules represented by GATT and WTO are included together with exchange rates and capital flow rules established by IMF as the representative, as well as aid and development rules established by representatives such as the World Bank and other relevant UN bodies, as well as special rules and a range of international standards developed by various specialized international organizations. In addition, the OECD also made important rule recommendations for reference in many areas.

The formation and adjustment of international economic rules is the result of a broad coordination and battle at various international forums. Since the crisis, G20 has become an important platform for global governance. It has reached a number of important consensus for improving global governance and international economic rules, established various important initiatives, and helped relevant international organizations to complete a series of rule adjustments and improvements. Yet, in general, in the process of rule reconstruction, multilateral mechanism is impeded from moving forward by conflicting interests and opinions while is easier to reach an agreement to reconstruct rules on the regional platforms because interest demands are similar. Although the new rules introduced by the regional platforms were only effective for members participating in regional cooperation, the ultimate goal of some large countries pushing for the establishment of new rules in regional cooperation is to extend these rules to the world, upgrading them to become generally binding international rules. This roundabout way of driving multilateral process by going regional has become particularly evident in the reconstruction of international economic and trade rules. One reason why this route has been successful is that the deepening of open markets and strict discipline allows a bigger "slice of cake" of regional cooperation so that cooperating members can each get a different-sized piece of cake, and with multilateralization, the majority of LDCs can enjoy free cake.

The multilateral trading system represented by the WTO is the main maker of international economic and trade rules, and conducting multilateral trade negotiations is the main way the WTO pushes for rule reconstruction. The WTO has discussed the Doha Development Agenda (DDA) for more than 10 years, but an agreement has yet to be reached. The emphasis for this new round of negotiations launched at the start of the century was development but as negotiations progressed, developed countries tended to focus on themselves and received more than they were willing to give in the multilateral arena, showing no intention to invest more in development. Instead, they turned to implementing differentiation strategies on developing countries and stressed that emerging economies had to assume greater responsibilities in negotiations. Most emerging economies still faced several problems with their own development and were unable to fulfil more international obligations, thus were reluctant to make concessions. In addition, the WTO "consensus" principle was inefficient; this led to a stalemate in multilateral negotiations and made it difficult to accomplish anything. Although the "Early Harvest" agreement of DDA was reached at the Ninth WTO Ministerial Conference (MC9), and the newly-appointed Director-General aspired to new negotiation path and strategies in 2014 when the iron was still hot, there remains a long road ahead before the Doha Round can come to a proper conclusion.

While multilateral negotiations stagnated, regional economic cooperation went ahead in full swing, at a quicker pace, featuring dominance by major powers and deeper expansion *etc*. Many countries, due to political, economic and other considerations, made efforts to forge regional cooperation so as to unite with countries that had similar interest demands, and explore new versions of international economic and trade rules more suitable for them in regional cooperation. In particular, the "two-ocean strategy" of the US which promoted the TPP and TTIP negotiations that stretched across the Pacific and Atlantic Oceans, not only emphasized the high standards of opening up of markets, but also introduced a broad range of new issues and established new rules. If both negotiations are implemented as planned, they will account for about 70% of global GDP and trade upon completion, undoubtedly becoming an important model and new benchmark for reconstruction of global trade rules.

Faced with aggressive regional cooperation in rule reconstruction, people cannot help wondering: Is the multilateral trading system in danger of being "outweighted" or "deconstructed" by regional economic cooperation?

Needless to say, the long-standing stalemate of the Doha Round negotiations seriously hurt the leadership position of the multilateral trading system in rule reconstruction. However, the Doha Round negotiations is not equal to the multilateral trading system. The existing multilateral trading system is the result of 60 years of post-war efforts. It now has 159 members, covering all of the world's major economies, and the various rules system and corresponding dispute settlement mechanisms it established are the cornerstone of the global trade order. Its fundamental role remains irreplaceable.

Although some countries have lost confidence in the "packaged" approach that the Doha Round is taking with negotiations and have steered towards regional cooperation, they still value the multilateral trading system's great influence in shaping rules and the MC9 which was described as "can't afford to fail" is sufficient evidence for this. The US, the EU, and other developed countries still show strong interest and determination to participate in plurilateral negotiations such as the ITA expansion negotiations, new GPA negotiations with new participants, TISA *etc.* under the multilateral framework. History has shown that plurilateral agreements can be converted into multilateral rules via triggers such as reaching a critical mass.

In short, whether in regional economic cooperation or plurilateral negotiations, participants are simply trying to bypass other negotiating parties who have differing opinions, gather trade partners to come to a consensus and grasp opportunities to establish rules. The establishment of a universal system of rules in the multilateral arena remains the ultimate goal.

The history of international economic and trade rules shows that plurilateral, multilateral and regional cooperation and negotiations are intertwined and take turns to lead the rule-making process. There have been numerous accounts of regional and plurilateral negotiations driving the multilateral process when the latter hits an obstacle. The GATT Tokyo Round negotiations beginning in 1973 attempted to reduce the various types of tariff barriers. A total of 106 members participated in the negotiations and a large number of negotiation outcomes were achieved through plurilateral agreements made by some members, including subsidies and countervailing measures, technical barriers to trade, import licensing procedures, government procurement, customs valuation, anti-dumping, beef agreement, International Dairy Agreement, civil aircraft trade agreement *etc.* More than half of these agreements were multilateralized before the WTO was formed, becoming the prevalent rules. It was also very difficult for the Uruguay Round negotiations launched in 1986 to make progress, especially as the developed countries attempted to introduce trade in services into the GATT and there was enormous resistance against the new issues of foreign investment, government procurement, IPR, and others. The US was frustrated with the progress and showed signs of giving up on GATT multilateral negotiations, turning their attention to the US-Canada FTA negotiations. The US and Canada signed the FTA in 1988 which resulted in a great increase in cross-border trade. With the addition of Mexico in 1994, the Canada-US FTA was superseded by the NAFTA. Many of the new topics envisaged by the US were accomplished first through this free trade zone. The establishment of NAFTA also added impetus to the Uruguay Round negotiations and some new issues which were eventually included in the Uruguay Round negotiations which were completed in 1994.

History often repeats itself. Today, with the stalemate in the Doha Round negotiations, FTA negotiations represented by TPP and TTIP are revealing new ambitions in rule reconstruction. Every country has to avoid being marginalized in the new round of rule reconstruction.

Although the multilateral trading system faces severe trials, it is not entirely impossible for it to gain renewed vigor. On the one hand, the regional negotiations promoted by the major countries, because of their inherent exclusiveness, eroded the potential global economic and trade interests and practically exposed weaknesses such as the "spaghetti" effect, evoked political distrust and dissipated bargaining power. As there were still domestic differences between the interests in the participating countries, if regional negotiations were too delayed, this could prompt a possible return to the multilateral platform. On the other hand, if the multilateral trading system could accelerate its reform to adapt to the complex pattern of interests in negotiations by making some changes to its decision-making mechanism, and include some issues that had been debated more thoroughly at regional levels, the core countries could correspondingly display political will and flexibility, and it would still be possible to find a balance of interests and consensus in multilateral negotiations.

2 Main Areas of International Economic and Trade Rule Reconstruction

In the evolutionary history of international economic and trade rules, it is not hard to find that with the in-depth development of globalization, the content of international trade and economic activities has continued to expand, and the fields involved in rules and range of adjustment also show a growing trend: From trade in goods to trade in services; from simple trade to trade-related investment rules and IP protection; from tariff reductions to reducing non-tariff barriers. The reconstruction of rules since the crisis in 2008 also had this characteristic. On the one hand, the opening up of markets was continually promoted, and on the other hand, a wider range of topics was introduced. These topics partly took the place of traditional tariff concessions and market access to become the focus in the battle of rule reconstruction.

2.1 *More attention will be paid to macroeconomic policy coordination in the reconstruction of international economic and trade rules*

International macroeconomic policy coordination refers to the consultation and coordination made by relevant countries, regional governments or international economic organizations in terms of macroeconomic policies such as fiscal, monetary, exchange rate and trade, either by appropriate amendments to the existing economic policies or by joint actions to intervene in market, with a view to mitigating impacts of emergencies and economic crises and upholding and promoting stable growth of national economies.[3] Since World War II, countries have become increasingly interdependent as economic globalization continued to develop; the spillover effect of a country's macroeconomic policy became even more obvious and the importance and necessity of coordinating international macroeconomic policies became more prominent. Since the 1970s, the Group of Seven (G7) have strengthened fiscal, monetary, exchange rate, and other policy coordination through platforms such as top leadership summits, meetings between finance ministers and central bank governors *etc.* For example, they achieved some success by implementing a common expansionary fiscal and monetary policy, launching the "co-growth plan" together, and jointly intervening in currency markets.

When this crisis broke out in 2008, the G7 mechanism among the developed countries was no longer able to cope with the impact of the global crisis by itself, thus it attracted more emerging economies and developing countries to form the G20 mechanism which became an important platform for global governance. More broadly-representative macroeconomic policy coordination was thus developed. Numerous appeals were made at several G20 Summits for countries to implement more coherent fiscal and monetary policies, financial

---

[3] Wan Hongxian, "International Coordination of Macroeconomic Policies of Western Countries," *Truth Seeking*, April 2006.

regulations, exchange rate and trade policies. Among these, some gradually turned into new international rules by consensus, for example, contributing to the reform of the international financial system, introducing the "Basel III" accords and prompting transformation of financial regulations from micro-prudential to macro-prudential supervision. With regard to different stances that countries take in terms of economic imbalance, after intense debate, the G20 launched the Reference Guide as an important indicator for measuring a country's economic balance. In countering hot issues of global concern such as competitive currency devaluation, uncontrolled monetary easing policies and excessive fiscal expansionary policies, G20 is also actively coordinating various positions and striving to make recommendations that are acceptable to all. Objectively speaking, such macroeconomic policy coordination only provides limited appeal and guidance at the moment. Even if some consensus is found and a corresponding evaluation mechanism constructed, it has no binding force as it cannot enforce compliance across countries or influence stringent international economic and trade rules. However, it is expected that with the continuous in-depth development of economic globalization, international economic and trade rules will inevitably move from operating by a micro-management approach towards a macro-management approach. In time, it is not impossible that some concepts that are generally consensual now gradually evolve into stricter, more significant rules.

Meanwhile, in the arena of highly integrated but individualistic regional economic cooperation, the transformation of such macroeconomic policy coordination into stringent rules and regulations has become a reality. In this most recent crisis, some EU countries experienced a severe hit of debt crises, leading the EU to reflect on the systemic weaknesses that exist between the one-currency policy and decentralized fiscal policy. As a result, it developed a financial contract with serious consequences such as terminating intergovern-mental treaties in order to strengthen fiscal discipline.

2.2 More attention will be paid to behind-the-border measures in the reconstruction of international economic and trade rules

The early international economic and trade rules paid more attention to so-called "border measures" and were committed to promoting tariff concessions and open market access. Relentlessly driven by the multilateral trading system, the level of tariffs around the world declined generally, and various trade quotas and quantitative restrictions were also significantly reduced. In contrast, countries implemented various types of management measures after goods crossed borders and these gradually became the main barriers to the process of international trade investment liberalization. At the same time, some countries' domestic policies were also regarded as the root causes of unfair competition and needed to be regulated. Thus, in the new round of trade negotiations and rule reconstruction, although tariff reduction and the opening up of markets are still important, "behind-the-border measures" are increasingly becoming the focus of attention and dominating the agenda of negotiations. In comparison, traditional tax cuts and other such issues are being discussed within the framework of existing rules while the control of behind-the-border measures are not only extensions of existing applicable rules but also innovations to modify current rules.

These behind-the-border measures include domestic regulations, technology, health, labor, environmental standards, IP protection, competition policy, regulatory approach, law enforcement *etc.*, and cover a broad range of areas. Because some traditional social policies have a relatively great impact on international trade and economic activities, they were also incorporated into the area of adjustments and restrictions. In reality, the strengthening restrictions on behind-the-border measures is to develop new international rules and extend them to each economic body's domestic economic policies and management, so as to eliminate potential barriers to trade and investment, and create a fair competitive environment both domestically and internationally. Compared with traditional border measures, the promotion of behind-the-border measures to form unified international rules has a more obvious requirement for states to relinquish a portion of their sovereignty. As the social system and developmental level of each country is different, it is still difficult to achieve a consensus on issues. There are also many controversies and differences in opinion among various interest groups within the countries, making the challenges greater and the process lengthier.

American scholar William Olson once noted that the sovereign state system separated people into individual cocooned political entities but economic prosperity required people to exchange goods and invest. This had always been a fundamental thorny problem of the sovereign state system.[4] However, a historical review of the development of globalization will show that many traditional attitudes are changing. In exchange for a more favorable external environment for development, it is now more common for states voluntarily

---

[4]William Olson, *The Theory and Practice of International Relations* (China: China Social Sciences Press, 1989 edition).

give up part of their sovereignty to further their own interests. The range of adjustment and fields involved in international economic and trade rules continue to expand and this is the historical logic behind-the-border measures gradually becoming the focus of international economic and trade rule reconstruction.

2.3 *Trade in services and investment rules will become more prominent in the reconstruction of international economic and trade rules*

International economic and trade rules were originally formed to regulate trade in goods. It was only in the 1990s at the Uruguay Round negotiations when trade in services and trade-related investment rules were introduced into the multilateral trading system. With the deepening development of globalization and continual advances in science and technology, trade in services has become increasingly prominent in international trade, and multinational investment has become an important driving force for the development of globalization. Thus, in the new round of rule reconstruction, trade in services and multinational investment, rather than trade in goods, have become topics of attention.

When the Doha Round negotiations deadlocked, some members of the US and EU delegations with similar positions launched trade in services negotiations and attempted to seize the opportunity to promote new trade in services rules. In a way, the US and EU strongly promoted trade in services negotiations because the field was an apparent advantage that developed countries possessed. The opening up of the trade in services market was beneficial for them. Objectively speaking, since the launch of GATS almost 20 years ago, trade in services has changed tremendously, e-commerce has developed rapidly, the cross-border flow of data has increased, and Internet-based technologies continue to emerge. The traditional mode of trade in services rules are no longer sufficient to cover the new developments in trade in services and must be further enriched. Presently, members participating in TISA account for 70% of the global trade in services market. China has also announced its desire to join the negotiations. TISA negotiations are very likely to temporarily replace the Doha Round negotiations and become the cradle of new trade in services rules.

Compared with multilateral trade rules, the rules of international investment have always been fragmented. According to UNCTAD statistics, as of the end of 2011, there were a total of 3,164 international investment agreements signed by the countries in the world, of which 2,833 were bilateral investment agreements and 311 were investment chapters in FTAs. Covering a narrow range of investments, these agreements were quite different from each other and unable to become true multilateral investment rules. Multinational investment is one of the main drivers of deepening economic globalization. After the financial crisis, countries competed to attract international capital. Developed countries put forward ideas such as "return of capital flow" and "reshoring", and many countries adopted approaches including tax cuts, simplifying approval procedures, breaking up of monopolies *etc.* to raise the level of investment liberalization. However, some countries still set up investment barriers in the name of national security, public interest, protecting employment *etc.* They not only implemented strict reviews on foreign investment but also placed various restrictions such as banning the spillover of advanced technology, among others, on foreign investments from their own countries. Under these circumstances, a number of regional cooperation mechanisms actively promoted the development of more effective investment rules, investment liberalization and facilitation, and clarified the capital flow regulatory norms for home and host countries. There were also continuous suggestions from international organizations and experts to establish multilateral investment rules. To guide international investment rule-making, the US and EU jointly issued the "Shared Principles for International Investment" in April 2012, committing to follow seven principles, including open and non-discriminatory investment policies. The OECD investment roundtables also conducted extensive in-depth discussions on investment issues, and became an important platform for exploring international investment rules. At the same time, as overseas direct investment from developing countries such as China increases, these countries are more enthusiastic about the establishment of a more effective investment protection system and reducing discriminatory barriers to investment. China has already accepted the "pre-establishment national treatment and a negative list" rule and sped up investment agreement negotiations with the US and EU. On the whole, international investment rules are moving towards broader content and higher standards. Some new rule templates are expected to be rolled out first in regional cooperation, but because there are still differing opinions on issues such as state-owned enterprises, labor, environmental protection, security review, investment dispute settlement *etc.*, it may still be a long time before unified multilateral investment rules are really formed.

2.4 *New issues brought about by economic and social development will continue to be incorporated in the reconstruction of international economic and trade rules*

The adjustment of rules must always reflect new economic and social developments; new issues must thus inevitably be incorporated into the reconstruction of international economic and trade rules. As early as during the first Ministerial Conference held in Singapore shortly after the WTO was formed, some developed countries had proposed new topics such as investment policy, competition policy, transparency in government procurement, and trade facilitation, known as the "Singapore issues", yet apart from trade facilitation, the other three issues were not included in the DDA. However, in recent years, in various regional economic cooperation forums, besides trade and investment, trade and competition policy and government procurement, more new issues cropped up, including the Internet, climate and environmental issues, labor, human rights, anti-corruption measures *etc.* Some foreign researchers referred to them collectively as "21st century issues", or simply, "new issues".

Some of these new issues reflected the new requirements brought about by development and progress in science and technology. For example, the first decade of the new century was the golden age of the Internet, and rules with regard to Internet for e-commerce, cross-border flow of data, information and communication technology services *etc.* gradually became the focus of attention. In the negotiation on trade in services rules, to prevent some countries from encouraging commercial presence and suppressing more convenient cross-border services, the authorities proposed the principle of neutrality model. Some new issues attempt to respond to the increasingly urgent international problems. For example, on the issue of how countries should deal with the serious climate change situation, discussions on relevant rules such as carbon tariffs, carbon reduction labels, carbon certification *etc.* aimed at reducing carbon emissions, are active. Some new issues broadened the scope of economic and trade issues, including even traditional social policies such as labor, human rights and anti-corruption *etc.* in the scope of regulation.

Overall, the US and EU seem determined to gain the upper hand in promoting new issues. Both entities have developed similar policies, requiring issues such as environment, labor, and others to be included in new FTA negotiations. There are two ways to look at the emergence of new issues in rule negotiations. It must be noted that the developed countries have an advantage with regard to these topics. The reason these new topics have been included is to strengthen their positions. It must also be noted that the emergence of these new issues are a response to needs in economic and social development and should not be simply ignored or opposed. It is important to pay attention to the establishment of fair rules for these new topics that would take into account the difference in levels of development among the countries. At that time, some developing countries resisted including the "Singapore issues" into the Doha Round negotiations mainly because they were worried it would dilute the development issues in the Doha Round. However, from a long-term perspective, if the multilateral trading system is unable to effectively respond to new issues, its dominant position in rule reconstruction is weakened to a certain extent.

3 China and the Reconstruction of Global Economic Rules

The first contact that China had with international rules in the modern sense can be symbolized by the 1840 Opium War. Powerful Western gunboats tore down the walls put up by the Chinese closed-door policy and forced China to accept a series of unequal international rules that they did not even understand. In the 20th century, as China gradually awakened, it began to make efforts to change the various unequal conditions and treaties imposed previously and protect its interests. After the founding of the PRC, the various unequal treaties China had been bound by for nearly a century were finally abolished. Yet, because of its unique history, China's attitude towards the Western dominated international economic and trade rules system was critical and disapproving, and thus was alienated from the mainstream international economic system for a long time. This situation lasted till the early 1970s when China joined the UN. The late 1970s was a historic turning point as China began reform and opening up. Since then, China began seeking full inclusion and participation in the existing system of international economic and trade rules. The restoration of GATT and participation in WTO talks beginning from 1986 were among the most significant events. After 30 years of hard work, China has gradually become an important political and economic world power. Compared to the past 170 years of history, China undoubtedly has greater voice to participate in the reconstruction of global economic rules. In the new round of rule reconstruction, what role can China play? How should it respond? The world is paying great attention to this topic that China needs to seriously consider.

3.1 *China must actively participate in the reconstruction of global economic rules*

After 30 years of hard work, China has become an important member of the global economic system. Actively participating in international economic reconstruction is an inevitable choice for development and an objective requirement circumstances.

First, the existing rules of the international economic system have generally maintained a good environment for development. In the past 30 years, an important reason for China's rapid economic development has been China's insistence on opening up, the introduction of international capital, advanced technology, development of external markets, participation in international division of labor, and integration into the global economic system. Realistically, although the existing international economic and trade rules were set under the guidance of Western developed countries and there is a certain degree of unfairness, the rules do reflect the basic principle of the market economy and, in general, maintain the basic order needed for international economic and trade exchanges, providing a stable and predictable environment for countries to make use of external resources and markets. This system of rules has actively promoted trade and investment liberalization, pushed for the opening of the global market, created greater external space for countries to exploit their comparative advantages and accelerate their own development. This system of rules has also managed the trade and economic disputes in the world more effectively, thereby preventing vicious trade wars and even direct political and military conflict caused by trade problems. In a sense, the opening up of China was also a process of accepting and adapting to international economic and trade rules. It is difficult to explain how China could achieve sustained and rapid development as it opened up and why China is internationally recognized as one of the largest beneficiaries of economic globalization without giving due credit to the existing system of international economic and trade rules.

Secondly, active participation in international economic and trade rule reconstruction is necessary for safeguarding China's sovereignty and interests. On the one hand, after 30 years of reform and opening up, China has become the world's second largest economy, biggest exporter, second largest importer, the world's most important multinational investment destination and an increasingly important exporter of capital, possessing more extensive international economic and trade interests. Active participation in the reconstruction of international rules and the promotion of global trade and investment liberalization are beneficial to China in further expanding the international market and developing overseas investment. On the other hand, as the subject of existing international economic and trade rules, China still needs to participate in negotiations to improve on the rules as there are still some aspects that are not favorable to China. In the new rule reconstruction proposed by the US and EU, there is no lack of highly-targeted and directed content. If China does not participate actively in the discussion and join in shaping new rules, the price to pay would be higher once the new rules are formed and forced on China again.

Thirdly, active participation in international economic rule reconstruction is a positive driving force for China's reform. The opening up of China is not only a process of accepting international economic and trade rules, it is also China's process of promoting economic reform in accordance with international rules. China is currently undergoing a challenging phase in reform. Through active participation in rule reconstruction and by following international rules, China can get useful reference and direction for comprehensive deepening of reform, and by promoting reform, China can find an effective way to create a new institutional dividend.

Fourth, active participation in international economic and trade rule reconstruction is an obligation China should fulfil as a responsible power. China has now become one of the world's major economies. Without China's constructive engagement, it is difficult to accomplish globally significant adjustments in international economic and trade rules. As China grows stronger, it is unrealistic to take the "free-rider" approach in the provision of global public goods. China has to proactively seek to play its role and constructively participate in the establishment of international economic and trade rules in order to safeguard its own interests. It is also an obligation that China, as a responsible power, needs to fulfil.

As China gains more national strength and a more powerful voice in the international arena, it has achieved some success in its participation in international economic and trade rulemaking. Former Chinese Ambassador to the WTO Sun Zhenyu once vividly concluded that in the process of China's participation in multilateral economic and trade rule-making, it has grown from not understanding to understanding contents of discussion, and transformed from struggling to speak about negotiation subjects to having a strong voice. In July 2008, at the time when the Doha Round was closest to the conclusion, China began to rise up to join the ranks of the core G7 countries in the WTO. From then on, China joined the inner circle of decision-making for all negotiations, became one of the members of G11, one of the five core members discussing IP issues, one of the members of the drafting group, and one of the members in the small consultations group for trade and environmental issues *etc.* China has submitted more than 100 proposals covering areas of agriculture, non-agriculture, services, trade and environment, IPR and rules *etc.* to the WTO. For example, in June 2008, China, Brazil, India, and other members submitted the W52 proposal for the simultaneous expansion of high-level protection for geographical indications, a multilateral register of geographical indications and protection of genetic resources. Currently, it has garnered the support of 108 members of WTO.

We must clearly recognize that China is still in the infant stages of participating in international economic and trade rule-making, and it is urgent to improve its capabilities in the task. Take international standards as an example. According to incomplete statistics, the International Standards Organization (ISO) and International Electrotechnical Commission (IEC) have issued nearly 20,000 international standards but Chinese enterprises were only involved in slightly more than 20 of them; there are more than 900 organizations around the world responsible for developing these standards but China is a participant in fewer than 10 of them.[5]

3.2 *The role of China in the reconstruction of international economic and trade rules*

There are three significant changes in the international economic and trade negotiation environment that China is facing: First, China has better conditions for engaging in rule reconstruction. With the rapid development of the Chinese economy, China has a major "chip" to play in the game, *i.e.* its growing domestic market. Thus, it has more bargaining power in international negotiations as well as greater room for maneuver domestically. Second, China has become the focus of conflict in rule reconstruction. As China's position in the world has significantly improved, both developed and developing countries hope that China will make greater contributions. This places China in a position of facing unfavorable disputes over conflicts of interests and being the focus of rule reconstruction. Third, China's own interests are becoming complex. There are many levels, multiple fields and various angles of offense and defense to take care of. It must both protect certain vulnerable industries and at the same time open up the international market for advantageous industries.

---

[5]Wu Daxin, "How China Obtained International Economic Rule-Making Power," *Shandong Social Science*, Issue 3, 2013.

There is no surefire plan in the balance of interests. China can only consider and weigh the benefits and trade-offs comprehensively.

In the face of new changes to the environment, what role will China play in the new round of international economic and trade rule reconstruction? It can be seen from recent history that China has been a passive subject of international economic and trade rules for some time, and has been forced to accept many unfair treaties against its own economic sovereignty and interests. Under these special circumstances, China was critical of the international economic and trade rules, especially after the founding of the PRC. Before the openning up and reform, China generally distanced itself from the international economic and trade rules system and was critical of the system. Since the openning up and reform, China re-opened its doors to the outside world, and according to its own national conditions and analysis of pros and cons, it selectively and gradually accepted most of the international economic and trade rules, and at the same time, began participating in rule adjustments and rule-making. Clearly, China is neither a passive subject of the rules today, nor will it subvert or revolutionize the existing system of international economic and trade rules. China should follow the path it has gone on since the period of reform to be a constructive participant and actively engage in international economic and trade rule reconstruction.

As a more active and constructive participant, China should fully participate in the discussion of international economic and trade rules, put forward clearer ideas to improve rules, and carry out international rule-making coordination more effectively. In the reconstruction of international economic and trade rules, China needs to firmly protect its own core interests and at the same time, assume international obligations corresponding to its own strength and status as a major power. It must find common ground, pursue a win–win solution with inclusive benefits for all,[6] show greater political will and put in more effort to promote the continuous improvement of international economic and trade rules.

Currently, the international community is split in two regarding China's role in rule reconstruction. One group of people has accused China of benefiting from existing rules yet not following them. They regard China as a rule-breaker, playing the role of a challenger. This view clearly ignores the tremendous achievements China has made in fulfilling its commitments and international obligations, and gives away the hegemonic mentality of interpreting and making rules exclusively,

---

[6] He Fan and Zhang Yuyan *et al.*, "How Should China Participate in International Economic Rule-making?", *China Market*, No. 50, 2010.

using them to oppress other countries. There are also many who call on China to play a greater leadership role in international economic and trade rule-making, and even suggest having a "G2" comprising just the US and China. The implication is that China should concede more interests and undertake more international obligations. In fact, China is still a developing country which needs to maintain sustainable development and address many domestic challenges. National conditions do not allow China to invest substantial resources in international affairs, and to become a leader in international economic and trade rule reconstruction within a short time.

3.3 How China can participate in and respond to the new round of reconstruction of international economic and trade rules

There are two main focuses in China's participation in the reconstruction of international economic and trade rules. On the one hand, it should promote sound international economic order to make it reflect the interests of all countries more equitably, and make it more conducive to sustained global economic development. On the other hand, it must integrate with the overall process of domestic reform and opening up to accurately reflect China's long-term interests and serve the strategic needs of comprehensively deepening reforms and the establishment of an open economic system.

3.3.1 Unswervingly promote opening up and push international economic and trade rules towards facilitating trade and investment liberalization

China is the world's leading trading power and has entered a phase of rapid growth of outbound investment. It is in line with China's interests to improve international economic and trade rules, and maintain a free and open world trade order. Currently, there are still all kinds of international trade and investment protectionism. Many countries use export controls, technical standards, security reviews and abuse of trade remedy measures to put up barriers. A number of countries around the world that have spared no efforts in advocating free trade over the years have done so out of pragmatism, and even more emphasize the theory of fair trade in international rules, hoping that making "fairness" a prerequisite for free trade will protect less competitive sectors. Under such circumstances, China should stick unswervingly to the banner of free trade, actively guide international economic and trade rules to oppose protectionism, and actively promote trade and investment. At present, it must, in particular, actively promote various types of investment and trade facilitation initiatives that are more widely accepted and easily implemented.

Of course, openness and interests are a two-way street. When China asks other countries to open up further, China has to reciprocate and open up in exchange. Sometimes unilateral opening up is good for a country exploring reform and opening up, for example, the China (Shanghai) Pilot Free Trade Zone. It is important to strike a balance between offense and defense in opening up. In fact, as China's economic strength continues to grow, it has gained more by being proactive in foreign economics and trade. If China emphasizes defense or protection only without a competitive bid, then it is difficult to achieve anything in the promotion of international economic and trade rule reconstruction and global investment and trade liberalization. In this respect, global pros and cons need to be weighed. China should not only take care of industries and businesses, but also make contribution to national economy and people's well-being. Current competitive advantages as well as the development trends and long-term interests must be taken into account. The overall negotiation strategy should be changed from a secure defensive approach to one that is both offensive and defensive; negotiation principles much transit from maximizing one's interests to striving to attain more benefits than losses. At the same time, China should explore establishment of a domestic compensation mechanism for those suffering from losses so as to overcome resistance to opening up.

3.3.2 Adhere equally to both multilateral and regional cooperation, and participate comprehensively in the reconstruction of international economic and trade rules

The current complex battle over international economic and trade rules is being launched through multilateral and plurilateral channels as well as through regional economic cooperation. The numerous platforms and wide range of topics is unprecedented. China should closely follow new trends in rule reconstruction, maintain an open attitude, not set its own preconditions, participate fully to achieve breakthroughs in key sectors, and be fully engaged in all types of negotiations and discussions related to rule reconstruction as much as possible.

Whether for its own interests or the common interests of the countries in the world, China should continue to adhere to multilateral cooperation as the main channel of rule reconstruction. The multilateral economic and trade rules built up through decades of efforts cover a wide range of the world's interests and has a more democratic decision-making mechanism reflecting the initial results of efforts to build a fair and equitable new international economic and trade order. Without multilateral channels, a few big powers would dominate international economic and trade rules, the interests of developing countries would be harmed and the legitimacy effectiveness of the multilateral system would also be threatened. Presently, the Doha Round negotiations have walked out of the long-term stagnation and finally ushered in an "Early Harvest". Countries in the world, including China, must show greater political will and flexibility to salvage multilateral trade negotiations. At the same time, China should make early preparations for the launch of multilateral negotiations on investment issues and strive to play a greater role.

China should advocate openness and reject exclusiveness in regional economic cooperation. It should maintain an open mind towards regional economic cooperation in Asia, and also be willing to explore issues regarding international economic and trade rules on regional cooperation platforms rather than avoiding various new issues. However, it should stand against exclusive regional cooperation and oppose the formation of discriminatory rules against external economies. At present, the Asia-Pacific region is the world's hotspot of regional economic cooperation. China has already formed a FTA with ASEAN and played an important role in successfully launching RCEP negotiations. China-Korea and China-Japan-Korea FTA negotiations are also being actively promoted. China should strive for the early completion of China-Korea and China-Japan-Korea FTA negotiations, achieve consensus and provide a more powerful driving force for accelerating RCEP. APEC is the region's oldest regional economic cooperation platform with the most number of members and highest levels of engagement. China should support APEC in integrating regional economic cooperation in the region, and play a greater role in promoting Asia-Pacific economic integration.

3.3.3 *Adhere to the principle of reciprocity of rights and obligations, and promote the improvement of a just and rational new international economic order*

For China to strengthen its voice in international economic and trade rule-making, and constructively participate in international affairs, it should take on moderate amount of responsibilities, provide resources and give up interests, and provide more international public goods. However, as a developing country at the primary stage of socialism for a long time with per capita GDP ranking around 90th in the world, China should not and cannot take on obligations beyond or disproportionate to its stage of development and accept rules that reflect imbalanced rights and obligations. China is still a developing country and should continue to strengthen and expand solidarity and cooperation with other developing countries and put in more efforts to promote the formation of a more just and rational new international economic order.

The outbreak of the crisis people has made pay more attention to the world's economic imbalances. One of the purposes for adjusting international economic and trade rules is to help eliminate imbalances. It must be seen that the inherent weaknesses of the current international monetary system revealed after the disintegration of the Bretton Woods System are behind the trade imbalances, currency imbalances and other problems. At a deeper level, the inequality of North–South development is the root cause of severe world economic imbalances. Therefore, in the reconstruction of international economic and trade rules, development should remain a dominant agenda, supporting the enhancement of self-development capacity by developing countries, and improving their status in the division of labor of global value chains. International rules favorable to developing countries ought to be established in response to food and energy security, environmental degradation, climate change, natural disasters, public health and other issues. At the same time, the existing global governance mechanisms must be reformed to promote the G20 to play an important role in balancing North–South development and supporting the increase in shares and voting power of emerging economies in the IMF and WBG, so as to ensure that developing countries get a more fair and just system of rights in global governance and rule reconstruction. China should continue promoting South–South cooperation and strengthening coordination with developing countries, making good use of the mechanisms such as the BRICS bloc to increase the right to speak of emerging economies and developing countries.

3.3.4 *Unswervingly accelerate domestic reforms, and effectively respond to the changing trends in international economic and trade rules*

An important trend in current international economic and trade rules is the move from border measures such as traditional tariff concessions, market opening *etc.* towards domestic regulation and making more demands in government management practices, state-owned enterprises, IP protection, environmental standards, labor standards *etc.* Developed countries are also moving from promoting free trade theories to advocating fair competition theories, their intention being to make use of international economic and trade rules to strengthen restraints on developing countries and safeguard their own competitive advantage. Naturally, China cannot completely accept this and simply be led by the nose. It should hold its ground and defeat those who interfere in the development model and internal affairs of other countries under the pretext of fair trade. However, it should also acknowledge that many motions in rule reconstruction involve a reasonable understanding of the market economy and social development laws, many of which are also in line with China's direction of reform. Although some of these are not favorable to nor attainable for China, they could still be China's long-term objectives. Therefore, China needs a broader vision based on its own internal development needs, to further accelerate the pace of reform and effectively respond to changing trends in international economic and trade rules to avoid being placed in a passive position in the future.

For example, there is increasing attention to environmental and labor issues in international economic and trade rules. China's own development necessitates enforcing a stricter environment protection standard, enhancing social security and gradually eliminating reliance on low-cost land, resources, environment and labor in international competition so as to make ecological progress and improve living standards. For example, as competitive neutrality has become a hot topic of international concern, competitive neutrality has some principles of valuable reference for China in terms of further improving the market economy system, rationalizing the relationship between government and enterprises, and deepening the reform of state-owned enterprises. Another example would be the active participation in the reconstruction of international IP protection rules and enhancing the standard of IP protection which is also beneficial for China to build a conducive domestic environment that supports research and protects innovation, so as to create new competitive advantages and truly build an innovative country. The active promotion of negotiations to join GPA is conducive to accelerating China's financial reform, building an open and transparent public finance, opposing corruption and local protectionism, and promoting the formation of a unified national market.

In short, we ought to have a dialectical view of the pros and cons of the reconstruction of international economic and trade rules. While participating actively in this process of rule reconstruction, China should draw on useful international experiences, use external help to speed up the pace of reform and achieve the goal of opening up to promote reform and development.

3.3.5 *Strengthen strategic planning and improve the ability to participate in international economic and trade rule-making*

Still new to the fierce battle of international economic and trade rules, China should continue to gain experience, and at the same time, China has to draw lessons from world history, constantly improve China's ability of negotiation and response, and strive to translate increasing national strength into a more powerful voice in rule-making.

First, overall planning for participation in rule reconstruction has to be strengthened. There is no denying that in the new round of rule reconstruction, China is still mainly taking a defensive position. China needs its to strengthen its participation in top-level design of international economic and trade rule reconstruction in order to respond well, and put forward more ideas that reflect China's interests. China should build its own long-term development strategy, accurately determine its own core interest amidst the changing trends, identify major issues such as specific objectives and subjects of focus, as well as consider the choices between various directions for rule-making, and others. It should also study the existing international system of rules and the offensive and defensive interests of all countries more thoroughly, propose effective motions and ideas that will gain greater support and enhance its influence and shaping power over international economic and trade rules.

Second, China's soft power in international rules negotiations must be enhanced. The formation of international economic and trade rules reflects the outcome of the battle over interests, and rules are more than a simple formula of dividing spoils but builds on convincing concepts of values and the appropriate legal basis of international law. To gain a greater voice in rule reconstruction, it is necessary for China to improve its soft power in shaping the rules. In particular, China must be good at uncovering and promoting the value of great Chinese traditional culture and summarizing and elaborating on China's understanding and knowledge of development models, paths and concepts which may be based on China's experiences but will have great universal significance and strong international recognition. To portray itself positively as a responsible power, China should articulate its ideas and garner greater moral support.

Third, China should strengthen the team working on international economic and trade rules. First of all, it must strengthen the international economic and trade rules negotiation team. International economic and trade rules cover a wide range of topics and areas, and are highly technical. Strong professional and legal knowledge is required to participate in international economic and trade rules negotiations. Compared with developed countries, China has a relatively small talent pool as it is a late-comer in negotiations and its experts are mainly concentrated in a few specialized departments. As China's participation in negotiations grows broader in scope, it is increasingly urgent for China to strengthen the number of qualified personnel. Secondly, development of a support system for international economic and trade rule reconstruction should be improved. Currently, the attention Chinese academia give to international economic and trade rules negotiation is limited. Many research institutions do not understand the specific processes and content of the reconstruction of international trade and economic rules; relevant government departments should strengthen collaboration with research institutions to encourage more institutions to participate in the study of international economic and trade rule reconstruction, so as to garner more intellectual support for fighting the battle for international economic and trade rules. Thirdly, China should continue sending talents to international organizations. In recent years, Lin Yifu from China has taken up the position of Senior Vice President and Chief Economist of the WBG, Zhu Min is the Deputy Managing Director of the IMF, Li Yong was elected as the Director-General of the United Nations Industrial Development Organization (UNIDO), Yi Xiaozhun was appointed the WTO Deputy Director-General, Zhang Xiaogang was elected as President of the International Standardization Organization *etc.* This indicates that China has come to have a greater say in global economic governance and at the same time, helps China further understand how international organizations work and enhance its capability of participating in global rule-making. Compared with developed countries and even some developing countries, China's representation in international organizations, particularly mid-level employees and below, is relatively low. China should encourage more qualified people to join international organizations to gain work experience and contribute to the country's internationalized talent pool.

Postscript

When I stepped down from the post of Minister of Commerce in March 2013, colleagues reminded me that I ought to make a systemic record of the work done over the past five years. They even helped me put together all the articles I had published all those years, and I deeply appreciate their concern. However, in my opinion, rather than simply collating the information accumulated in the past, it would be better to build upon that and look to the future, inspiring new thoughts covering a broader range of areas and trends, and provide some references that might prove useful for China's new round of reforms and opening up. I therefore decided to write a book to analyze the evolution of international economic and trade rules since the financial crisis in 2008, as well as China's strategic response.

When I brought up the idea and shared the basic concept and content of the book with my colleagues, the feedback was positive. A group of young cadres who "fought" side by side with me in the front line of international negotiations joined the writing team. Over the past 10 months, we held lively discussions about the focus of each chapter and my colleagues greatly enriched my initial thoughts. Most of the chapters have been repeatedly amended, even drafted and rewritten again and again. Each time I gave suggestions and recommendations, these young authors patiently and frankly exchanged their views, sometimes even contending and debating with me. When the final draft was completed, the first thing I wanted to do was to thank these group of colleagues for their hard work despite their busy work schedules.

The colleagues who helped in penning the first drafts of this book are Li Li (Chapter 1), Yang Zhengwei (Chapter 2), Yu Yongbing (Chapter 3), Chen Zhiyang (Chapters 4 and 14), Zhang Yixiong (Chapter 5[1]), Deng Dexiong (Chapter 6), Xu QingJun (Chapter 7[2]), Han Changtian (Chapter 8), Suo Bicheng (Chapter 9[3]), Chen Fuli (Chapter 10), Jiang Chenghua (Chapter 11), Li Yongjie (Chapter 12), Lu Feng (Chapter 13), Chen Rongkai (Chapter 15), and last but not least, Wu Chuan, Xiong Yan, and Yang Guanggong, who participated in discussions, translation, and publishing matters.

Zhang Xiangchen, Yao Jian, Shen Danyang, Liu Haiquan, Li Chenggang, Yin Zonghua, Chai Xiaolin, Song Heping, Wang Shengwen, Yang Zhengwei, Guo Tingting, and other colleagues helped to review the manuscripts and made pertinent recommendations for the overall structure and content of the book. Many relevant experts and scholars from the Development Research Center of the State Council, Chinese Academy of Social Sciences, WTO Research Center, University of International Business and Economics, Nankai University, Chinese Academy of International Trade and Economic Cooperation and other agencies also provided a lot of insights and added perspectives to the book. In addition, I would also like to express my gratitude to the innumerable leaders and colleagues who have shown concern and supported us in the preparation of the book.

For various subjective and objective reasons, some perspectives expressed in the book might be partially biased and open to questions. A lot of rules are still being debated upon and the results remain inconclusive; some explanations of the legal provisions of international rule reconstruction may be dry for a lot of readers, the subject matters and fields of expertise covered in the book are limited and writing styles may not be consistent. Yet, considering the latest developments in the evolution of rules, only colleagues directly involved in the negotiations would be able to provide the best insights into the situation, and

---

[1] Researcher Gao Haihong and Associate Researcher Huang Wei from the Chinese Academy of Social Sciences Institute of World Economy and Politics, as well as colleagues Yang Zhengwei and Li Jigang from the Ministry of Commerce helped to draft and amend the first and second section of this chapter.

[2] Colleagues Wu Feifei and Zhu Songsong from the Ministry of Commerce provided many excellent suggestions and materials for the improvement of the chapter.

[3] Colleagues Chen Rongkai, Yu Yongbing and Chen Zhiyang gave much valuable input and materials for the improvement of the chapter.

we have the responsibility to sort out this information as quickly as possible to store records of these valuable research data and present them to a wider audience so as to draw greater attention and inspire more research interest.

Lastly, I would like to thank Commercial Press for their great effort in publishing this book. I look forward to feedback, criticism, corrections, and further discussion with readers.

Chen Deming
February 2014

Glossary[1]

International or Regional Organizations

Chinese name	English name	English abbreviation
东南亚国家联盟	Association of Southeast Asian Nations	ASEAN
安第斯共同体	Andean Community	CAN
内地与澳门关于建立更紧密经贸关系的安排	Mainland and Macau Closer Economic Partnership Arrangement	CEPA
发展援助委员会	Development Assistance Committee	DAC
海峡两岸经济合作框架协议	Cross-Straits Economic Cooperation Framework Agreement	ECFA
美洲自贸区	Free Trade Area of the Americas	FTAA
关贸总协定	General Agreement on Tariffs and Trade	GATT
海湾合作委员会	Gulf Cooperation Council	GCC
解决投资争端国际中心	International Centre for Settlement of Investment Disputes	ICSID
国际货币基金组织	International Monetary Fund	IMF
中东自贸区	Middle East Free Trade Area	MEFTA
南方共同市场	Common Market of the South	Mercosur

(Continued)

[1] The terms in the book are generally divided into three categories: Firstly, major international or regional organizations; secondly, main international agreements; and thirdly, specific terminology. In this table, they are arranged in alphabetical order according to their abbreviated names.

(Continued)

Chinese name	English name	English abbreviation
北美自由贸易区	North American Free Trade Area	NAFTA
经济发展与合作组织	Organisation for Economic Co-operation and Development	OECD
太平洋联盟	Pacific Alliance	PA
区域全面经济伙伴关系	Regional Comprehensive Economic Partnership	RCEP
南部非洲关税同盟	South African Customs Union	SACU
跨太平洋伙伴关系	Trans-Pacific Partnership	TPP
跨大西洋贸易投资伙伴关系	Transatlantic Trade and Investment Partnership	TTIP
联合国国际贸易法委员会	United Nations Commission on International Trade Law	UNCITRAL
联合国贸发会议	United Nations Conference on Trade and Development	UNCTAD
世界银行集团	World Bank Group	WBG
世界知识产权组织	World Intellectual Property Organization	WIPO
世界贸易组织	World Trade Organization	WTO

International Economic and Trade Agreements

Chinese name	English name	English abbreviation
阿克拉行动计划	Accra Agenda for Action	AAA
反假冒贸易协议	Anti-Counterfeiting Trade Agreement	ACTA
关于解决国家和他国国民之间投资争端公约	Convention on the Settlement of Investment Disputes between States and Nationals of Other States	—
友好通商航海条约	Friendship, Commerce and Navigation Treaty	FCN Treaty
服务贸易总协定	General Agreement on Trade in Services	GATS
政府采购协定	Agreement on Government Procurement	GPA
国际服务协定	International Services Agreement	ISA
信息技术协定	Information Technology Agreement	ITA
京都议定书	Kyoto Protocol	KP
多边投资协定	Multilateral Agreement on Investment	MAI
多边环境协议	Multilateral Environmental Agreements	MEAs

(Continued)

(*Continued*)

Chinese name	English name	English abbreviation
北美环境合作协定	North American Agreement on Environmental Cooperation	NAAEC
北美劳工合作协议	North American Agreement on Labor Cooperation	NAALC
保护工业产权巴黎公约	Paris Convention for the Protection of Industrial Property	PCPIP
部分降税协定	Partial Scope Agreement	PSA
服务贸易协定	Trade in Services Agreement	TISA
与贸易相关的投资措施协议	Agreement on Trade-Related Investment Measures	TRIMs
与贸易有关的知识产权协定	Agreement on Trade-Related Aspects of Intellectual Property Rights	TRIPS
联合国气候变化框架公约	United Nations Framework Convention on Climate Change	UNFCCC
发展筹资国际会议蒙特雷共识	Monterrey Consensus of the International Conference on Financing for Development	—
援助有效性巴黎宣言	Paris Declaration on Aid Effectiveness	—
有效发展合作伙伴关系釜山宣言	The Busan Partnership for Effective Development Co-operation	—

Other Specific Terminology

Chinese name	English name	English abbreviation
经济大类分类	Broad Economic Categories	BEC
《国际收支手册》	*Balance of Payments and International Investment Position Manual*	BPM6
金砖国家	Brazil, Russia, India, China, and South Africa	BRICS
布雷顿森林体系	Bretton Woods System	BWS
共同但有区别的责任	Common But Differentiated Responsibilities	CBDR
美国外国投资审查委员会	The Committee on Foreign Investment in the United States	CFIUS
竞争中立	Competitive Neutrality	—
多哈发展议程	Doha Development Agenda	DDA
争端解决机构	Dispute Settlement Body	DSB

(*Continued*)

(Continued)

Chinese name	English name	English abbreviation
国内增加值	Domestic Value Added	DVA
二十国集团	Group of Twenty	G20
有效发展合作全球伙伴关系	Global Partnership for Effective Development Co-operation	GPEDC
(美国)政府问责办公室	Government Accountability Office (in America)	GAO
全球贸易分析数据库	Global Trade Analysis Project	GTAP
全球价值链	Global Value Chain	GVC
商品名称和编码协调制度	Harmonized Commodity Description and Coding System	HS
信息与通信技术	Information and Communications Technology	ICT
《国际货物贸易统计: 概念和定义》	*International Merchandise Trade Statistics*	IMTS
《国际服务贸易统计手册》	*Manual on Statistics of International Trade in Services*	MSITS
千年发展目标	Millennium Development Goal	MDG
负面清单	Negative List	—
官方发展援助	Official Development Assistance	ODA
生产过程和生产方法	Process and Production Method	PPM
准入前国民待遇	Pre-establishment National Treatment	—
准入后国民待遇	Post-establishment National Treatment	—
量化宽松	Quantitative Easing	QE
服务挚友	Really Good Friends of Services	RGF
中美战略与经济对话	China-US Strategic and Economic Dialogue	S&ED
特别提款权	Special Drawing Right	SDR
国民核算体系	System of National Accounts	SNA
贸易增加值	Trade in Value Added	TiVA
垂直专门化	Vertical Specialization	—
世界投入产出数据库	World Input–Output Database	WIOD
系统重要性金融机构	Systemically Important Financial institution	SIFI

Printed in the United States
By Bookmasters